International
Financial Markets

Francis A. Lees
Maximo Eng

The Praeger Special Studies program—utilizing the most modern and efficient book production techniques and a selective worldwide distribution network—makes available to the academic, government, and business communities significant, timely research in U.S. and international economic, social, and political development.

International
Financial Markets
Development of the Present
System and Future Prospects

PRAEGER SPECIAL STUDIES IN INTERNATIONAL ECONOMICS AND DEVELOPMENT

Praeger Publishers   New York   Washington   London

Library of Congress Cataloging in Publication Data

Lees, Francis A
    International financial markets.

    (Praeger special studies in international economics
and development)
    Includes bibliographies and index.
    1. International finance. 2. Financial institutions,
International. 3. Capital. I. Eng, Maximo, joint
author. II. Title.
HG3881.L437   332.4'5   73-13345
ISBN 0-275-28789-0
ISBN 0-275-89180-1 pbk.

PRAEGER PUBLISHERS
111 Fourth Avenue, New York, N.Y. 10003, U.S.A.
5, Cromwell Place, London SW7 2JL, England

Published in the United States of America in 1975
by Praeger Publishers, Inc.

© 1975 by Praeger Publishers, Inc.

Printed in the United States of America

PREFACE

The nightmare of the international financial crises during the 1930s, the dormancy of international financial market activities during World War II, and preoccupation with the restructuring of the world economy in the postwar era have left the subject of international financial markets in near oblivion. For three decades prior to 1960, there was little interest in the subject. Except for activities in the two leading financial centers—London and New York—only recently has attention focused on the substance of international financial markets.

The revival of the international financial markets in the past decade and a half represents a response to a growing need for liquidity and financial mobility. Since World War II the world economy has benefited from additional injections of liquidity that have come from a variety of sources. In the period 1948-52, Marshal Plan aid from the United States provided over $20 billion of aid and loan funds to reconstruct the West European economy. In the period 1950-58, the European Payments Union provided a considerable amount of (regional) liquidity via multilateral clearing of current transactions and temporary credit swings for member countries. U.S. private investment flows have grown over the postwar years, as have long-term capital flows directed through the World Bank Group. Growth and development of the Eurocurrency market in the 1960s have provided a substantial reservoir of liquidity to finance foreign trade, direct investment, and government financing requirements. Revival of international banking in the decade of the 1960s led by American banks and soon after joined by the banking institutions of leading industrial countries has generated new sources of international liquidity and loanable funds. The Eurobond market also has provided a needed increment to long-term sources of funds on the international scene. Finally, the creation of special drawing rights (SDRs) beginning in the 1970s provided additional international liquidity at the official settlements level. Without these many sources of international liquidity and financing, the world economy could not have attained the levels of production, investment, income, and affluence presently enjoyed. More important from the point of view of this volume, the international financial markets could not have developed to the extent they have without these many sources of international liquidity and the increasing demand for international liquidity.

The new setting of the international financial markets after World War II differs significantly from the old in three important aspects: scope, structure, and functions. With regard to the scope of financial activities, Europe is a more integrated unit financially and politically under the new concept of a European Common Market. Japan has emerged in the Far East as a financial and economic giant as a result of her enormous economic growth and accumulation of international reserves recently made available to international borrowers on a more liberal basis. Australia, Singapore, and Mexico, to name a few, are newcomers to the international financial market club. Another point of distinction is the structure of the international financial markets. London has developed a new money market or "parallel market" in addition to its traditional discount market. Eurodollar and Eurobond markets have become international financial reservoirs for all sorts of customers, including the governments of poor and rich nations. The increasing number of international financial institutions such as the International Monetary Fund (IMF) the World Bank, and regional development banks, has strengthened the structure of the financial markets. The IMF has contributed to the restoration of confidence in the international monetary system after the abandonment of the gold standard in the 1930s. The World Bank has channeled and loaned funds to the less developed countries for economic development. A most important factor in the postwar years is the substantial power of the United States. The U.S. dollar has been used as a key international currency, and New York has played a vital role as a sophisticated financial center serving a global clientele.

Changing structure and scope have also altered many functional activities in the international money and capital markets. For instance, the increasing participation of governments in financial markets has influenced the behavior and structure of interest rates and at times has forced lenders and borrowers to meet each other's needs by direct trading, via the federal funds market and the intercompany loan market. The noted development of international portfolio management has reflected the growing importance of institutional investors and multinational fund borrowers who have tremendous influence on international financial market operations. In response to these changes, the international financial markets have developed new financing instruments such as certificates of deposit and foreign currency bonds and even reformed their structures to meet the changing circumstances and financial needs of the parties concerned . The change of international liquidity and flow of funds resulting from the energy crisis since October 1973 have had profound effects on the behavior of recent international financial market development. Unquestionably, to write a book on modern international financial markets is a difficult undertaking. It is not simply because of the descriptive nature of developments and operations, but for many other reasons. First, it is difficult to bring a discussion of the international financial markets into the general framework of international economics and finance of which they are a part. Second, lack of comprehensive information and conceptual analytical tools makes the subject vulnerable to theoretical and practical criticism. Third, it is difficult to measure the efficiency and effectiveness of a national market or international markets since they are interrelated and interdependent, and their relative merits and demerits depend on one's point of view. For instance, short-term flows of funds may help provide business working capital but may hurt the lending nation's international balance of payments, or may add to an inflationary trend in the receiving nation that is already on an inflation alert. In the 19th century, the British and French exported long-term capital to their colonies, but allegedly retarded domestic economic development. Finally, uncertainty concerning future trends in the international financial markets is a permanent and paramount factor. We are in the computer age, but market prediction is still subject to international political, economic, and social-psychological forces that tend to defy the analysis of econometric models. Moreover, changes taking place in other markets—commodity or real estate—may shift the course of the international financial markets into different directions, or carry them to different operating levels.

Confronted with these difficulties, the authors attempt only to achieve the following limited objectives:

1. to provide a historical, factual, and conceptual framework within which the national and international financial markets function and operate (Part I of this volume is for this purpose);

2. to describe and analyze the financial markets in those countries that have strategic importance in the international flows of funds (we examine these countries in Parts II, III, IV, V, and VI, where we discuss and analyze 14 countries possessing various financial characteristics, and which are exposed to various degrees of internationalization of their financial markets);

3. to analyze the structure and scope of operations of the international financial markets, including the Eurodollar, Eurobond, and international market for foreign exchange (this analysis is found in Part VII);

4. to compare certain financial markets in the industrial countries, to analyze some financial market problems in less developed countries and to point to the new forces emerging in the international economic scene (in Part VIII we analyze the strengths and weaknesses of the international financial markets and the future prospects for their development).

ACKNOWLEDGMENTS

We wish to express our gratitude to the many individuals who were instrumental in the progress and completion of this book. While there are far too many for us to refer to each individually, several must be mentioned. These include Dr. Nicholas Bruck, economist at the Inter-American Development Bank, and Mr. Al R. Wichtrich, executive vice-president, American Chamber of Commerce of Mexico.

A number of international banks and securities firms generously provided information concerning their international operations and recent data concerning the international role of their domestic capital and money markets. Among these are included the First National City Bank of New York, the Chase Manhattan Bank of New York, the Union Bank of Switzerland, Swiss Credit Bank, Swiss Bank Corporation, Nomura Securities Ltd., Nikko Securities Co., and Rio de Janeiro Stock Exchange.

Library research was most important at all stages of our work. Most especially we wish to acknowledge the helpful assistance of the librarians at St. John's University, the Federal Reserve Bank of New York, the Council on Foreign Relations, the United Nations, Columbia University, the International Monetary Fund, and the World Bank. Over the past three years, a number of our graduate assistants have participated in collecting raw data and digging out statistical information. We are most grateful for this indispensable service.

x

LIST OT TABLES

LIST OF FIGURES

FOUNDATIONS
OF INTERNATIONAL
FINANCIAL MARKETS

1

**DEVELOPMENT
AND SIGNIFICANCE
OF INTERNATIONAL
FINANCIAL MARKETS**

Financial markets arise from the needs of human society. Under the barter system, or static social systems such as the Middle Ages and the Communist societies, financial markets are rarely needed. However, in the mercantilistic and capitalistic societies, financial markets have become necessary for many reasons. Merchants need money to finance their trade, and manufacturers must have short-term and long-term capital to facilitate their production and distribution activities. In the last several decades, the financial aspects of industry and commerce have become more important, and the international financial markets have emerged on the scene as part of the growth in international business. Recently, Communist countries have participated in international financial transactions due to their increasing foreign trade with the Western nations.

Since the financial markets are basically related to money lending and borrowing, the cost of money, and activities of financial intermediaries, the expansion and contraction of the international financial markets have generally been influenced by the following elements:

1. natural and social circumstances;
2. role of participants in the markets whether they are individuals, businesses, financial institutions, governments, or foreign citizens;
3. development of money and credit instruments;
4. the volume and price of transactions.

The following sections briefly review the historical development of the international financial markets in order to show the evolution of these elements and their interaction, analyze the proliferous development of the international financial markets after World War II, and examine the importance of international financial markets to the national markets and the world economy.

A BRIEF HISTORICAL SURVEY

Financial market activities can be traced back to about 1900 B.C. when Babylonian temples, under the Code of Hammurabi, were places for safekeeping funds for the wealthy people and lent funds out to merchants who wanted to finance the transportation of merchandise from surplus markets to areas of scarcity. No interest was charged because the loans were for social purposes rather than for the profit motive. Transactions were recorded in clay tablets and kept by the temples. When Greece became the center of world civilization, commerce and finance were also active. From 500 to 300 B.C., Athens' marketplace (forum) became the center of life somewhat like our shopping centers today. Venturous merchants solicited "joint stock" capital for financing their commercial trips to other Mediterranean areas and shared gains earned on these voyages. When a bank was formed by wealthy persons during this period, it advertised payment of interest for deposits, charged interest for loans, and handled foreign money payments. In ancient Greece the progenitors of today's international financial markets were clearly discernable.

As political and economic power shifted to the Roman Empire, international (or regional) trade was very active, and legal instruments such as bills of exchange were widely used by merchants. Regional "fairs" were established in many European trading centers for stimulating commerce. Soldiers and judges were assigned to the "fairs" to protect the participants and regulate commercial and financial transactions. The Romans were pioneers of financial market regulation within a comprehensive legal framework.

Following the Greco-Roman world was the feudal system in which international or interregional financial markets did not function due to the lack of communication between European towns and rural landlords. The "just price" concept prevailing in the Middle Ages did not encourage free trade, and financial activities in this period were similar to the Babylonian days. European monasteries performed the functions of money safekeeping and lending but in much larger scale since they also acted as government tax collectors. However, usury was considered immoral and probited by the churches.

The revival of European financial market activities after the Magna Carta in England (1215 A.D.) and the Renaissance continued during the period of mercantilism. This revival accelerated after the Industrial Revolution. In the thirteenth century, England came to be considered a safe place for free traders. The Lombard bankers of Italy, the East India Company, the Bank of England, and the Royal Commission in the seventeenth century laid a concrete groundwork

4

for the British financial leadership that followed. Stimulated by overseas trade and finance, Holland established banks and a securities exchange in 1611; the Rothschilds established international banking houses in the eighteenth century; and France and Italy were also active in European financial affairs. On the eve of the Industrial Revolution, Europe had developed the roots of the international financial markets.

The Industrial Revolution in England had a profound effect on the world economy and international finance. At home, the growth of industry encouraged the birth of the joint stock banks and insurance companies, which were used for domestic as well as overseas industrial, commercial, and financial purposes. In the nineteenth century, London became the leading financial center, where bill-brokers and bond issues for foreign investments were concentrated. From 1870 to 1912 London exported over £3,000 million of investment capital to the rest of the world, especially to the United States.

Under the shadow of London's financial markets, Amsterdam, Berlin, Paris, Milan, and New York also served the international financial community. Holland's overseas investment and trade were focused mainly with her Far East colonies, and France's financial relations were concentrated in the African and Far East colonies. The broad basis for international financial activities in this period had two things in common: the universal gold standard and a geographically widening industrial development. But the lack of numerous international financial institutions and the strong free enterprise spirit of the times left the international finance markets subject to the influence of strong individuals instead of free competitive market forces. The Rothschilds in Europe and J. P. Morgan in the United States were cases in point.

The period between World Wars I and II was probably the most exciting as well as depressing experience in the financial history of the world. After 1914 New York became a leading financial center as a result of the outbreak of World War I, the weakening of the pound sterling, the strong export position of the United States, the establishment of the Federal Reserve System, and the enormous capital market facility in the United States. Since the war depleted the belligerent countries' resources and depreciated their currencies, the United States was the only major country whose currency remained convertible into gold and where foreign bond issues could be sold. Regardless of the prosperous money and capital markets during the 1920s, the inexperience of the United States as a world financial leader was reflected in the 1929 stock market crash, which became associated with a series of international financial crises during the 1930s. The failure of the Credit-Anstalt in Austria, the abandonment of the gold standard by all major countries, and the restrictions on international trade and foreign exchange during the 1930s reflected a total collapse of the international financial markets.

5

A serious effort was made by the United States and the United Kingdom (UK), the major political and financial powers after World War II, to restore the functioning of the international financial mechanism. The Bretton Woods Agreement in 1944 triggered the establishment of the International Monetary Fund (IMF) and the World Bank; the advent of the European Common Market in 1958 led to the vigorous revival of the international financial markets in Europe; and the growing desire for economic development in Asia, Africa, and Latin America during the 1960s resulted in an increase in the number of new emerging financial centers in various continents.

GROWTH OF INTERNATIONAL FINANCIAL INSTITUTIONS, TRANSACTIONS, AND MARKETS

The restoration of the international financial markets after World War II was a steady but complex process. First, a comprehensive international financial framework had to be reconstructed. Second, capital and technology were urgently needed for the war-torn countries in Europe and the Far East and also for the new independent nations in Asia and Africa. Third, foreign trade and investment had to be encouraged in order to enhance the efficiency of the world economy. To attain these objectives, workable international financial markets were required.

The international financial institutions which laid a necessary groundwork were the IMF and the International Bank for Reconstruction and Development (the World Bank). The purposes of the former were to establish a stable currency system with gold and the U.S. dollar as cornerstones and to help member nations to equilibrate their international balances of payments. The World Bank was designed to pool, borrow, and channel long-term funds from member nations and the major financial markets to the less developed countries. Other financial institutions, such as the Asian Development Bank and the Inter-American Development Bank and several internationally oriented commercial banks also contributed significantly to the flow of funds in international money and capital markets. For example, these institutions have obtained funds from New York, London, Frankfurt, and Tokyo financial markets to provide loans to the developing countries. Commercial banks with worldwide banking networks have extended short-term credits to finance international trade, have helped multinational corporations to finance their worldwide activities, and recently have formed financial consortia to assist less developed as well as Communist countries for financing their domestic economic projects. These international financial institutions

6

plus the major insurance companies, brokerage firms, and offshore mutual funds have provided confidence and substance in the rebirth of modern financial markets.

Flows of funds and technology have stimulated the growth of national economies, international trade, and investment. Over the two decades 1950-70, international trade as measured by the value of world exports has grown at a rate of 8 to 9 percent (see Table 1.1) per year. The flow of net financial resources from the developed countries to the developing countries totaled $15 billion in 1970 and $18 billion in 1972.

The unprecedented growth of international financial markets since 1960 can be attributed to the intensification of world competition for goods, capital, and technology. To protect local interests and to strengthen local trade positions, several regional associations, such as the European Economic Community (EEC), European Free Trade Association (EFTA), and Latin American Free Trade Association

TABLE 1.1

Selected International Financial Transactions
(billions of dollars)

	1950	1960	1970	1972
World exports in current dollars	56.10	113.20	311.39	407.78
Flow of financial resources to developing countries	4.00	9.29	15.01	18.43
International investment position of the United States				
U.S. assets abroad	54.40	85.60	166.76	199.28
Foreign assets in the United States	17.60	40.90	97.08	148.65
Net foreign asset position of the United States	36.80	44.70	69.68	50.63
Size of Eurocurrency market				
Dollar liabilities	—	1.0	58.70	96.73
Other currency liabilities	—	—	16.59	35.20
Size of Eurobond market	—	—	2.99	6.49

Sources: Bank for International Settlements, Annual Reports; World Bank, Annual Reports; U.S. Department of Commerce, Survey of Current Business.

(LAFTA), were formed shortly prior to 1960. The European Common Market countries and Japan have demonstrated a substantial economic growth rate at home and also have enjoyed increased trade and investment abroad. The United States, after a decade and a half of foreign aid and domestic economic prosperity, began to show internatioanl balance of payments deficits that persisted year by year. The imposition of the Interest Equalization Tax (IET) after 1963 on foreign security purchases by U.S. residents compelled foreign fund raisers to turn to the European financial centers. Higher interest rates in Europe in the 1960s attracted U.S. funds, and the Eurodollar market grew to become a familiar name to the international financial community. Market opportunities and lower labor costs abroad attracted investments by U.S. business firms that established operations in many foreign countries. The multinational corporations demanded far more capital abroad, especially in Europe. The development of the Eurobond market since 1963 was partly in response to the needs of corporations and governments that required financial market facilities on a worldwide basis. The amazing growth of the Eurocurrency and Eurobond markets is reflected in Table 1.1.

As the international financial markets grew in size and depth, market instruments increased in number and complexity; interest differentials in various international financial markets stimulated worldwide arbitrage operations; and business, financial institution, and government participation in international financial market activities not only exerted pressures on national interest rate structures but also on national sovereignty and international payments equilibria.

The growth of the international financial markets in the 1960s was not an unmixed blessing since problems followed in the wake of progress achieved. On the one hand, the integration of international financial markets helped to improve on the global allocation of capital funds and productive resources. Alternatively, the development of the international markets has exposed individual nations to massive international capital flows and balance of payments disturbances. As a result, since 1969 the world has suffered from chronic international monetary crises. The pending negotiation and solution of the international monetary problem in the IMF and the now changing structure of the European Common Market will certainly have important effects on the international financial markets in the decade to come.

IMPORTANCE OF INTERNATIONAL FINANCIAL MARKETS

The international financial markets play an important role for individual nations as well as the overall framework of international economic equilibrium. From the national economic standpoint, less developed countries need the international financial markets in financing import-export business and for facilitating inflows of foreign capital for domestic economic development. Conversely, the industrialized nations also require efficient international financial markets for handling an increasing volume of financial transactions, to provide more sophisticated credit instruments, and to make available a more competitive and complex interest rate structure at home and abroad. Without the well-developed financial markets in London during the nineteenth century, flows of goods and capital between Britain and her colonies and other financial centers would not have been possible. Without the excellent capacity of the New York money and capital markets for conducting global financial transactions after World War II, the economic rehabilitation of Europe and the Far East would not have been so successful. However, weaknesses in the international financial markets may hamper economic development.

The international financial markets make it possible for each nation to more flexibly achieve a balance or equilibrium in its international economic relationships. From the standpoint of international economic equilibrium as interpreted from Figure 1.1, the Heckscher-Ohlin model of international trade provides only a partial view of a nation's adjustment toward international equilibrium. A more general view of the domestic and international relationship should include consideration of how a nation achieves a simultaneous equilibration of at least six types of markets. These include the domestic market for goods and services, the domestic capital market, the local money market, the foreign exchange market, and the international financial system and financial markets, and the markets for settling international balance of payments.

In the primitive or agricultural society where local markets for goods and services are limited, the barter system or commodity money can be used satisfactorily to equilibrate the domestic economy. However, in the industrial society where a country is involved in foreign trade and investment, transactions must be conducted through all of these markets, and the adjustment process of achieving a nation's equilibrium depends on the complex forces of all these six market sectors. Any disruption occurring in any one of these markets would have repercussions in all other market sectors including the national and internationally oriented markets. In the period 1950-74, domestic markets have been influenced by government policy as well as by international trade and financial relationships. Heterogeneous national or regional policies on the part of governments may tend to suppress the normal competitive market forces and also make it difficult for a nation or group of nations to restore balance of payments equilibrium through the market system. If these disruptive forces are not

FIGURE 1.1

Simplified Model of a Nation's International
Economic Position

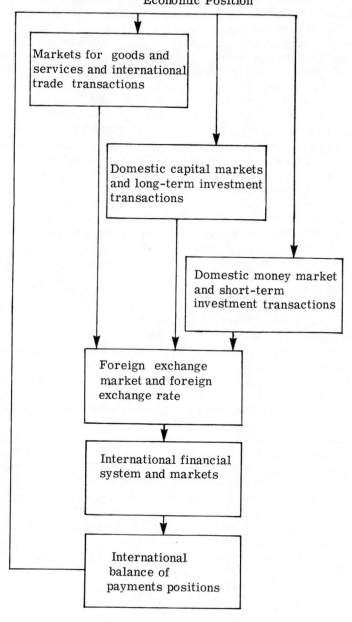

corrected, the entire market system either operates abnormally or eventually breaks down.

During the quarter century 1946-71, more than 100 nations have adhered to the IMF's rules regarding maintenance of fixed exchange rate relationships among their respective currencies. Only in cases of "fundamental disequilibrium" had the IMF sanctioned exchange rate alterations greater than 10 percent of existing parties. Until early 1971 there were only a few significant changes in exchange rate relationships among major internationally traded currencies. With the Smithsonian Agreement on December 18, 1971, the dollar-gold price was officially increased by the United States from $35 per ounce to $38 per ounce. At the same time, the top 10 industrial countries realigned their exchange rate parities. Since then the IMF has endorsed a more flexible exchange rate regime. The devaluation of the U.S. dollar again in February 1973 has raised the gold price from $38 to $42.22 per ounce. This has further encouraged the practices of "floating rates" by many nations in the international financial markets. While the final reform of the IMF system has thus far not been conclusive, the impact of international financial markets on the economics of all nations, whether they are developed or developing, will be enormous in many years to come.

REFERENCES

Madden, John and Nadler, M. The International Money Markets. New York: Prentice-Hall, 1935.

Altman, Oscar. "The Integration of European Capital Market." The Journal of Finance, May 1965.

Eng, Maximo. U.S. Overseas Banking—Its Past, Present and Future. New York: St. John's University Press, 1970.

2

**DEVELOPMENT
NEEDS OF NATIONS:
FINANCIAL SUPERSTRUCTURE
AND FLOWS OF FUNDS**

ECONOMIC GROWTH AND DEVELOPMENT
OBJECTIVES OF INDIVIDUAL NATIONS

In the years since 1950, the attention of economists has shifted toward the problem of economic growth and development. The year 1960 ushered in the United Nations Development Decade of the 1960s. Much energy has been devoted to uncovering the factors that play a key role in the economic development process. It has been well established that financial development is intricately related to economic development and that a nation must facilitate growth of its financial institutions and processes in order to achieve maximum economic development.

Growth of financial institutions and processes is not only required to facilitate a nation's economic development, but also to assist it in achieving broad economic stabilization objectives and a more satisfactory international equilibrium. Moreover, a developed and well-organized financial structure can be conducive to avoiding some of the excesses of inflation and misallocation of resources that have proved so troublesome to many countries in recent years.

Growth and Economic Change

How does economic structure change as economic growth takes place? More important, what effects do these structural changes have on the financial development of nations? In 1970 the United Nations Committee for Development Planning (the Tinbergen Committee) published a blueprint for more effective international development. The report called for growth targets of at least 6 percent (contrasted to 5 percent in the decade of the 1960s) for developing countries and elaborated on the importance of accomplishing structural changes in the economies of these developing nations if they wanted to attain these growth targets.

As shown in Table 2.1, the less developed countries have undoubtedly made progress in their economic development in the two decades from 1950-70, but they must recognize the fact that population growth rates and declining shares of international trade over these same two decades have widened the gap of economic development between these countries and the industrially developed nations.

In 1971 Hollis B. Chenery reported on the changes in economic structure that accompany economic development. His in-depth study included a sample of about 100 countries, in which multiple regressions were used to obtain normal variations in economic structure that accompany different levels of development.

TABLE 2.1

Selected Economic Indicators for Developing and
Industrialized Countries, 1950-70
(in percentages)

	1950-60	1960-70
Developing countries		
Average annual real rate of growth		
Gross domestic product	4.6	5.3
Population	2.3	2.5
Per capita	2.3	2.8
Share of world trade	22.0 (end of 1960)	19.8 (end of 1970)
Industrialized countries		
Average annual real rate of growth		
Gross domestic product	6.9	4.8
Population	1.5	1.1
Per capita	5.4	3.7
Share of world trade	78.0 (end of 1960)	80.2 (end of 1970)

Sources: World Bank, Annual Reports, 1970, 1971, 1972; International Monetary Fund (IMF), Annual Reports, 1970, 1971, 1972.

The range of countries in the Chenery study includes those with per-capita gross national product (GNP)—in 1964 U. S. dollars—as low as $50 and as high as $2,000. The Chenery study distinguishes four major areas of structural change, including (1) accumulation—savings, investment, education, and literacy, (2) composition of output, (3) population and labor force, and (4) trade. In the area of accumulation it was found that

1. gross saving rises from 10 percent of GNP in countries with the lowest per-capita incomes to over 20 percent for developed countries;

2. gross domestic investment exhibits a similar increase relative to GNP as savings, with transfer of capital from abroad providing a small margin (2 to 3 percent of GNP) of investment over savings; and

3. school enrollment and literacy ratios rise from approximately 15 to 90 percent. A transformation inevitably must take place in the composition of output as development proceeds. Chenery finds that three industry sectors increase their contributed share of gross domestic product (GDP) at the expense of a fourth sector. The share of primary production tends to be close to 60 percent of GDP for countries at the low end of the per-capita income scale, falling to 10 percent of GDP or less for advanced countries. The largest increases in sector shares that accompany development accrue to manufacturing and utilities. The service sector also enjoys a significant increase in the share of GDP. The transformation that takes place in the labor force is even more dramatic. According to the findings of Chenery, industrial labor as a percentage of the labor force rises from 4 percent in low-income countries to 40 percent in the more advanced nations. In the fourth area, trade, development tends to be accompanied by an increase in the ratio of imports and exports to GDP.

Growth and Financial Development

The changes in a nation's financial structure that accompany economic growth may be more impressive than the alterations that take place in its economic structure. A small (say 5 percent) shift in the share of GDP produced by the primary (agriculture) sector to the manufacturing sector may be accompanied by fundamental changes in a nation's banking system, financial market structure, and relative dependence on foreign sources of financing domestic enterprises. An increase in the ratio of gross saving and gross domestic investment relative to GNP will have a stimulating effect on the growth of a nation's financial institutions, the volume of financial instruments (stocks, bonds, debentures, bills of exchange, and commercial paper) outstanding, and the opportunities for specialization of functions in the financial services sector. Should foreign trade grow relative to GDP, there will be additional requirements for its financing, and there will exist foreign sector pressures on the domestic money supply, interest rates, and lendable funds.

According to Raymond W. Goldsmith, there is a close interrelation between a nation's financial superstructure, consisting of financial assets outstanding at any particular time, and its real infrastructure (tangible and productive assets). Economic development is accompanied by an accumulation of national wealth, and as this process takes place, financial assets tend to accumulate at a pace that exceeds the growth of national wealth. As a result the ratio of financial assets to national wealth displays an upward trend. This can be observed in Table 2.2, where on average this ratio advanced from 0.81 in 1913 to 1.19 in 1963 for the six countries for which data are shown.

THE PROCESSES OF SAVING AND CAPITAL FORMATION

Economists have attempted to measure the sources of growth in advanced countries and to identify the contributions of technology, capital, and improved skills to the development process. The statistical results are not conclusive, but nevertheless point to the significant role of capital accumulation and technological advance as important sources of economic growth. Since capital accumulation is regarded as one of the key factors in the growth and development process, the financial aspects of the savings and investment functions assume even more importance in any consideration of the ultimate sources of economic advance.

The Role of Savings

What determines the amount of domestic saving? Who saves, and in what form? What motives underlie saving, and does an understanding of these motives improve our ability to explain differences in the level and form of saving, as well as differences in financial structure between nations?

The determinants of saving ultimately influence the major flows of funds that are directed through the financial markets. Some understanding of the motives underlying saving and the form it takes will permit a more accurate assessment of the prospects for improving the gross flows of funds in a particular country and the extent to which these funds are being channeled efficiently to end-users.

15

TABLE 2.2

Ratio of Financial Superstructure to National Wealth, Six Major Countries

	1913	1963
France	0.79	0.65
Germany	0.88	0.75
Great Britain	1.04	1.70
Italy	0.81	1.05
Japan	0.40	1.70
U.S.A.	0.80	1.27
Average	0.81	1.19

Source: Raymond W. Goldsmith, Financial Structure and Development (New Haven, Conn.: Yale University Press, 1969), p. 340.

Chenery has indicated that gross savings tend to represent a greater share of GNP in high-income countries than in low-income countries, with a range of from 10 to over 20 percent of GNP. In his study of saving in the United States, Goldsmith indicates that in the period 1879-1949, national saving has averaged one-eighth of national income, and personal saving has made up three-fourths of national saving. In the period studied by Goldsmith, one-tenth of personal saving was directed into real estate, one-seventh into consumer durables, and the remainder or three-fourths into financial assets (bank deposits, government securities, life insurance reserves, corporate stock, corporate bonds, saving and loan shares, and other). Over the years there has been an increase in the United States in the share of saving directed into consumer durables, life insurance, and pension and retirement funds, as well as a decline in the share going to corporate securities and mortgages.

Goldsmith discerns three motives for saving: (1) acquisition of durable assets, (2) provision for future expenditure needs (retirement, survivors, and education), and (3) provision of an equity fund to establish a business. Objective factors that could influence the amount required to be saved include the length of working life and retirement years, the yields obtainable on saving, the level of income, movements in the cost of living, and the availability of insurance against death and invalidity. Group standards that also influence the saving-to-income ratio include the relation between average real

16

income during retirement and working years that is desired, the role and importance of consumer durables in the standard of living, the value placed on home ownership, and the relative attraction of hired employment versus entrepreneurial status.

Capital Formation and Financing

Capital formation, an economic activity that is intimately related to the economic growth process, is closely dependent upon financial mechanisms and institutions. There is a distinct parallel between saving and capital formation in that both processes are heavily dependent on what economic sectors participate in these types of activity, and what kind of financial patterns of behavior are characteristic of these sectors. The relative importance of the household, business, and government sectors in capital formation will play a determining role in what type of capital goods are accumulated and the financial relationships that are created in the process.

Gross capital formation, which consists of capital replacement (consumption of durable equipment) and net capital formation (increments to the stock of tangible wealth), has accounted for a fairly constant proportion of GNP in the United States. However, there have been significant changes in its composition and methods of financing. According to the exhaustive studies of Simon Kuznets, the proportion of net capital formation has declined, while the share of consumption of durable equipment has increased in gross capital formation. Other changes that have taken place include an increase in the share of producers' durable equipment in total capital formation, a decline in the share of construction, and an increase in the role of the government sector in capital formation.

In the United States, changes in the financing of capital formation reflect an increase in external financing at the expense of internal financing and an increased role of the financial intermediaries in capital formation. While the internal financing of capital formation has given ground somewhat, for nonfinancial corporations the relative importance of internal financing has increased. In total external financing, the share of the federal government has increased, while the share of the private component has declined. In the business sector, corporations account for the largest proportion of external financing.

17

DOMESTIC FINANCIAL INSTITUTIONS AND THE
SAVINGS INVESTMENT PROCESS—THE U. S. CASE

The Growth of Financial Institutions and Assets

As economic growth and development take place, the role of
financial intermediaries in financing capital formation increases.
This is evident in the findings of Kuznets relative to changes that
have taken place in the financing of capital formation in the American
economy in the late nineteenth and twentieth centuries.

According to Kuznets' figures, the share of financial intermediaries in external financing rose from 0.44 in 1900-29 to 0.65 in
1930-49. This increased share of financial intermediaries has been
pervasive, affecting all major users of funds. The household and
government sectors especially help to account for an increased role
of the financial intermediaries in external financing. As the main
source of savings in the United States, households are users of the
services of financial intermediaries. A shift in the United States
from self-employed status to employee status has altered the form
taken by savings, shifting it from savings used to build the business
of the self-owner to saving in financial intermediaries. Urbanization
has provided easier access of the population to financial institutions.
Finally, a reduction in the share of income by upper-income groups
has lowered the proportion of savings seeking venture capital investment and lowered the share of savings channeled directly through
purchase of stocks rather than through financial intermediaries.

While the role of financial institutions has become more significant in the total saving investment process, the relative importance
of individual types of financial intermediaries has also changed. This
is evident from the data found in Table 2.3, which compares the importance of major types of institutions in the United States in 1900
and 1963. These changes are summarized below:

1. Financial institutions now own two-fifths or more of all
financial assets outstanding in the United States and approximately
three-fifths of all financial assets other than claims against financial
institutions.

2. The banking system now accounts for less than two-fifths
of the assets of all financial institutions, compared with over three-
fifths of such assets at the turn of the century.

3. Thrift institutions and insurance organizations together hold
approximately half of financial assets of all financial institutions.
In this respect, insurance organizations play as important a role as
commercial banks.

TABLE 2.3

Financial Institutions in the United States, 1963 and 1900

	Total Assets[a] (billions of dollars)		Distribution of Assets		Relation to National Wealth (percent)		Relation to Total Financial Assets	
	1963	1900	1963	1900	1963	1900	1963	1900
	(1)	(2)	(3)	(4)	(5)	(6)	(7)	(8)
Banking system	374.8	10.0	38.1	62.9	17.4	11.2	14.7	16.6
Federal reserve banks	58.0	–	5.9	–	2.7	–	2.3	–
Commercial banks[b,c]	316.8	10.0	32.2	62.9	14.7	11.2	12.4	16.6
Thrift institutions	165.9[2]	2.9[2]	16.9	18.2	7.7	3.2	6.5	4.8
Mutual savings banks	49.7	2.4	5.1	15.1	2.3	2.7	2.0	4.0
Savings and loan associations	107.6	0.5	10.9	3.1	5.0	0.6	4.2	0.8
Credit unions	8.1	0.0	0.8	0.0	0.4	0.0	0.3	0.0
Postal savings system	0.5	–	0.1	–	0.0	–	0.0	–
Insurance organizations	315.1	2.2	32.0	13.8	14.7	2.5	12.4	3.7
Life insurance companies[d]	145.0	1.7	14.7	10.7	6.7	1.9	5.7	2.8
Private pension funds	53.8	–	5.5	–	2.5	–	2.1	–
Government funds[e]	79.3	0.0	8.1	0.0	3.7	0.0	3.1	0.0
Other insurance companies	37.0	0.5	3.8	3.1	1.7	0.6	1.5	0.8
Miscellaneous financial institutions	127.7	0.8	13.0	5.0	6.0	0.9	5.0	1.3
Finance companies	36.0	–	3.7	–	1.7	–	1.4	–
Investment companies[f]	33.6	–	3.4	–	1.6	–	1.3	–
Mortgage companies	4.5	0.2	0.5	1.3	0.2	0.2	0.2	0.3
Land banks	3.5	–	0.4	–	0.2	–	0.1	–
Security dealers	9.7	0.6	1.0	3.8	0.5	0.7	0.4	1.0
Government lending institutions	40.4	–	4.1	–	1.9	–	1.6	–
All financial institutions	983.5	15.9	100.0	100.0	45.8	17.8	38.6	26.4
Personal trust departments	82.2	3.0	8.4	18.9	3.8	3.3	3.3	5.0

[a] Book value except for investment companies (market value).

[b] Includes agencies of foreign banks (1963: $4 billion).

[c] Individual savings deposits in commercial banks, included in line 3, were $0.9 billion in 1900: R. W. Goldsmith, A Study of Saving, 1, p. 386; and $86.6 billion in 1963: Federal Reserve Board flow-of-funds statistics.

[d] Includes fraternal insurance companies (1963: $3.6 billion; 1900: $0.0 billion) and private insured pension funds (1963: $23.3 billion).

[e] Pension, retirement and social security funds.

[f] Includes small business finance companies (1963: $0.6 billion).

Source: Raymond W. Goldsmith, Financial Structure and Development (New Haven, Conn.: Yale University Press, 1969), pp. 24-25.

Major Components

Every modern economy has a superstructure of financial instruments that exists side by side with the infrastructure of national wealth—the tangible physical assets of the economy. As we have seen in the preceding section, many of these financial instruments are issued or held by financial institutions. As of 1963 approximately two-fifths of financial instruments were held by financial institutions.

The financial superstructure differs from country to country, reflecting differences in the role played by those economic sectors that issue financial instruments (business, government, households, and financial institutions), the level of economic development achieved, the structure of industry, and the role played by the government in assisting economic growth and stabilization.

There is a wide variety of financial instruments, which differ in such characteristics as nature of the contract, marketability, security afforded, duration, and the nature of the owner and issuer. Close to three-fourths of financial instruments outstanding in the United States are in the form of claims, and about one-fourth in the form of corporate stock. Two-fifths of all claims are issued by financial institutions. Money (line 1 in Table 2.4) represents less than 10 percent of all financial instruments outstanding. The financial superstructure in the United States represented by claims and equity securities has a value about 25 percent greater than the real infrastructure (national wealth).

Growth and Change in Composition

Comparisons available in Table 2.4 suggest that the financial superstructure of a nation is not fixed or immutable. A number of important changes have taken place in the financial superstructure of the United States over the years 1900-63.

First, the ratio of the financial superstructure to the real infrastructure increased considerably, rising from two-thirds to one and one-fourth. Second, the share of financial institutions in total financial instruments rose from one-fourth to two-fifths. Third, the share of money in total financial assets declined from one-eighth to one-twelfth. Fourth, in comparison to all financial assets, the claims against nonfinancial domestic sectors in the form of consumer credit, home mortgages, and U.S. government securities have increased considerably. On the other hand, the shares of bank loans to business, security credit, corporate bonds, and trade credit have declined considerably. These trends reflect changes in the character of national wealth (increasing importance of consumer durables and housing)

Financial Instruments Outstanding in the United States, 1963 and 1900

	Amount[a] (billions of dollars)		Distribution (percent)		Relation to National Wealth (percent)		New Issue Ratio[b] 1901-63 (percent)
	1963 (1)	1900 (2)	1963 (3)	1900 (4)	1963 (5)	1900 (6)	(7)
Money[a]	210	7.6	7.8	12.6	9.8	8.5	2.0
Saving deposits[d]	286	3.7	10.7	6.1	13.3	4.1	2.7
Insurance reserves, private	218	1.6	8.2	2.6	10.1	1.8	2.1
Insurance reserves, government	51	0.0	1.9	0.0	2.4	0.0	0.5
Finance company debentures	12	0.0	0.4	0.0	0.6	0.0	0.1
Claims against financial institutions (1 through 5)	777	12.9	29.0	21.3	36.2	14.4	7.4
Consumer credit	70	1.0	2.6	1.7	3.3	1.1	0.7
Security credit	16	1.3	0.6	2.2	0.7	1.4	0.2
Bank loans n.e.c.	79	3.9	3.0	6.5	3.7	4.3	0.7
Mortgages, home	182	2.6	6.8	4.3	8.5	2.9	1.7
Mortgages, other nonfarm	49	1.8	1.8	3.0	2.3	2.0	0.5
Mortgages, farm	17	2.3	0.6	3.8	0.8	2.6	0.1
U.S. government securities	310	1.2	11.6	2.0	14.4	1.3	3.0
State and local government securities	88	2.0	3.3	3.3	4.1	2.2	0.8
Corporate bonds[e]	101	5.2	3.8	8.6	4.7	5.8	0.9
Trade credit	103	5.7	3.8	9.5	4.8	6.3	0.9
Other claims	160	6.5	6.0	10.6	7.9	7.1	1.5
Claims against nonfinancial sectors (7 through 17)	1,175	33.5	44.0	55.6	55.2	37.1	11.0
All claims (6 + 18)	1,952	46.4	73.0	76.9	91.4	51.5	18.4
Corporate stock	720	13.9	27.0	23.1	33.5	15.5	0.9
All financial assets (19 + 20)	2,672	60.3	100.0	100.0	124.9	67.0	19.3

aMarket value for corporate stock; face or book value for claims.
bCol. 1 less col. 2 divided by aggregate gross national product 1901-63, except for col. 20. Stock issues 1901-38 from R. W. Goldsmith, A Study of Saving in the United States (Princeton, N.J.: Princeton University Press, 1955) 1, pp. 482-483; for 1939-63 from Federal Reserve Board flow-of-funds statistics.
cCurrency and demand deposits.
dIncluding time deposits and savings and loan shares.
eIncludes foreign bonds (1963: $7 billion).

Source: Raymond W. Goldsmith, Financial Structure and Development (New Haven, Conn.: Yale University Press, 1969), pp. 10-11.

and shifts in the importance of nonfinancial sectors. Fifth, the share of corporate stock in the market value of all financial instruments was higher in 1963 than in 1900. Finally, in the period 1900-63, the ratio of new issues to GNP has been close to one-fifth. This reflects a new issue ratio of 12 percent for the issues of nonfinancial sectors and 7 percent for the issues of financial institutions.

FLOW OF FUNDS

Domestic Flow of Funds

The flow-of-funds accounts are a relative newcomer to the field of economic and social accounting. The basic principle is that every economic unit in a nation engaging in a transaction can enter that transaction in a double entry. Since there are always two parties to a transaction, there are four entries. For example, if Smith purchases an automobile, he reduces his cash balances and acquires a consumer durable, and the auto dealer increases his cash balances and reduces his inventory of new autos. Therefore, the flow-of-funds accounting calls for quadruple-entry bookkeeping for each such transaction.

Transactions are divided into three major groups, including current nonfinancial, capital nonfinancial, and financial. The great bulk of transactions is represented by current transactions, covering the receipt of income and expenditures for consumption and the payment of taxes. However, the flow-of-funds accounts are not primarily concerned with this area of economic activity, which is described in detail in the national income accounts.

The difference between current receipts and current payments is equal to national saving. The flow-of-funds account concerns itself with this saving and the allocation of funds derived from saving that are channeled into investment in capital goods and inventories.

Detail in the flow-of-funds accounts is focused on capital nonfinancial transactions and financial transactions. Capital transactions represent expenditures for tangible assets that render services over a number of years and include purchases of consumer durables, residential construction, plant and equipment expenditures, and changes in inventories.

Financial transactions receive most of the attention and detail in the flow-of-funds accounts and reflect the increase or decrease in financial assets and liabilities of the various sectors in the economy. Flow-of-funds accounting designates more economic sectors than does national income accounting. The U.S. accounts include the following sectors as transactors in the flow of funds:

22

Households	Monetary authorities
Business	Commercial banks
State and local govern-	Nonbank financial
ments	intermediaries
U.S. government	Rest of the world

Each sector is conceived as enjoying sources of funds that consist of receipts and increases in liabilities and uses of funds that consist of expenses and increases in assets. Sources represent means by which funds are obtained, whereas uses include transactions where funds are dispensed. Conceptually, each sector's total sources and uses of funds are equal, as they are for all sectors taken together.

The flow-of-funds accounts reflect considerable detail regarding the financial flows that take place within a nation. They indicate which sectors account for gross and net saving, and which sectors are responsible for investment in tangible capital assets. Second, the flow-of-funds accounts provide considerable detail concerning the financial sources and uses of funds by sector, and whether specific sectors play a more or less important role as users or lenders of funds (net financial investment). Finally, the flow-of-funds accounts describe the role played by financial institutions in assembling and channeling funds through the financial markets. In the United States, most of the domestic flows of funds are channeled through financial intermediaries in the money and capital markets. In some less developed countries, where domestic saving and investment are insufficient to meet economic development needs, the government and private sectors might use special incentives to attract foreign capital and technology to fill the gap.

International Flows of Funds

Substantial international flows of funds date back to the nineteenth century when the United Kingdom and France invested capital in their colonies and other areas. After World War I, substantial short-term capital movements appeared on the international financial scene as the result of international speculation and increased trade financing. However, the full swing of international flows of funds attracted worldwide attention only after World War II, primarily related to American foreign aid programs, American overseas direct investments, and the emergence of the European Common Market.

Role of International Flows of Funds

In the past quarter century (1949-74) international flows of funds have played an important role for a number of reasons.

TABLE 2.5

Flow of Net Financial Resources from
Developed Countries to Less Developed Countries
(billions of dollars)

	Official	Private	Total
1961	6.16	3.09	9.25
1962	5.99	2.49	8.48
1963	6.18	2.51	8.69
1964	6.01	3.19	9.20
1965	6.35	4.17	10.52
1966	6.67	3.84	10.51
1967	6.99	4.18	11.17
1968	6.90	5.17	12.07
1969	7.21	6.47	13.68
1970	7.95	6.76	14.71
1971	8.98	8.23	17.21
1972	10.14	8.28	18.43

Source: World Bank, Annual Reports, 1970, 1971, 1972.

TABLE 2.6

Changing Shares of Major Creditors
in the International Flows of Funds
to Less Developed Countries
(in percentages)

	1951-55	1956-61	1961-70
United Kingdom	10.5	10.2	6.6
France	2.5	6.2	11.6
Germany	2.2	9.2	13.0
Japan	—	—	8.0
United States	78.4	67.4	44.0
Others	6.4	7.0	16.8
Shares of types of sources			
Official	57	54	54
Private	43	46	46

Sources: United Nations, International Flow of Long-Term Capital and Official Donations, 1951-61; World Bank, Annual Reports, 1971.

1. They facilitate and finance world trade, directly and indirectly.
2. They assist the financial development of many countries.
3. They supplement the flows of funds in the domestic financial markets of individual countries.
4. They facilitate international portfolio management and afford a greater number of alternatives to international investors.
5. They increase the size and scope of financial markets in entrepot centers and furnish a wider base for short-term capital movements.
6. They increase the demand for and scope of activities of internationally oriented financial institutions.
7. They facilitate the international balance of payments at the official levels.

The illustration and substance of these comprehensive reasons will be discussed in various parts of this book, but the immediate focus here concerns international flows of funds as related to the attainment of economic growth and development.

Flows of Funds from Industrially Developed Countries to the Less Developed Countries, and Shares of Creditor and Debtor Nations

According to the United Nations and World Bank Annual Reports, the flow of funds from the developed countries to the developing countries totaled about $5 billion in 1956, $9.25 billion in 1961, and $18.43 billion in 1972. Table 2.5 provides detailed figures on these flows for the period 1961-72. The United States has been the principal contributor among creditor nations. As Table 2.6 indicates, the shares of the United States and United Kingdom have decreased in the 1960s. This is due to difficulties in their international payments positions. Conversely, France, Germany, and Japan have increased their proportion of international assistance due to increasing economic strength. Throughout the past two decades 1950-70, official assistance has exceeded private assistance to the developing countries. This reflects the growing importance of major international financial institutions such as the World Bank and regional development banks. In the long run, the private sector may eventually increase its contribution to these flows of funds as multinational corporations become more important global investors and as the international financial markets further broaden and develop.

Continued flows of funds to the developing areas of the globe have resulted in an increase in the external public debt outstanding of less developed countries as Table 2.7 indicates. The western hemisphere and South Asian countries account for over 50 percent of the total external indebtedness of the less developed countries.

TABLE 2.7

External Public Debt Outstanding and Economic Growth of Less Developed Countries
(billions of dollars)

	Africa	Southern Europe	East Asia	Middle East	South Asia	Western Hemisphere	Total
Debt Outstanding							
1961	3.30	2.26	2.17	1.41	3.60	8.82	21.58
1962	4.04	2.47	2.81	1.66	4.73	10.20	25.94
1963	4.97	2.91	3.23	1.70	5.92	10.96	29.71
1964	5.51	3.43	3.74	1.88	6.88	11.72	33.17
1965	6.61	4.05	3.90	2.44	7.83	12.20	37.06
1966	7.37	4.44	4.39	2.94	9.19	12.89	41.04
1967	8.03	4.90	4.98	3.63	10.11	14.52	46.19
1968	8.80	5.59	6.30	4.35	12.83	16.35	54.25
1969	9.39	6.33	7.76	5.45	13.42	18.52	60.88
1970	10.87	6.97	9.21	7.02	14.95	20.29	69.31
1971	11.92	8.19	11.21	8.89	15.93	23.05	79.21
Population growth rate (1961-70)	2.4%	1.4%	2.7%	2.9%	2.4%	2.9%	
Average economic growth rate (1961-70)	4.0%	7.1%	5.6%	2.9%	4.1%	4.5%	

Source: World Bank _Annual Reports,_ 1970, 1971, 1972.

Unfortunately, their economic growth rates were unsatisfactory over the 1960s.

Capital Flows and Economic Development—
Some Illustrative Cases

In the study cited above, Chenery has classified the high-growth developing countries according to the strategies they employed in supporting growth via international transactions, including capital flows. Two of these classifications are of immediate interest to the present discussion. These are countries with "high capital inflows" and those with "moderate capital inflows."

In the group of seven countries classified with "high capital inflows" (Israel, Taiwan, Jordan, Greece, Puerto Rico, Korea, and Panama), the external finance ratio ranged between 13.4 percent (Taiwan) and 109.1 percent (Jordan), and their respective growth rates were 9.9 percent and 8.3 percent in the period 1960-69. In this same period, four of the seven countries in this group experienced finance ratios in excess of 50 percent and growth rates of about 8 percent.

Seven countries included in the "moderate capital inflows" category experienced external finance ratios ranging from 9.5 percent (Mexico) to 28.6 percent (Costa Rica), and their respective growth rates were 7.1 percent and 6.5 percent in the period 1960-69. Several of these countries have a substantial industrial base to support their economic growth, and at least two of these countries have enjoyed some diversified economies and developed their financial market institutions and instruments. Mexico and Singapore are cases in point.

REFERENCES

Chenery, Hollis B. "Growth and Structural Change." Finance and Development, no. 3 (1971).

Goldsmith, Raymond W. Financial Structure and Development. New Haven, Conn.: Yale University Press, 1969.

——. A Study of Saving in the United States. New York: National Bureau of Economic Research, 1955.

Kuznets, Simon. Capital in the American Economy: Its Formation and Financing. Princeton, N.J.: Princeton University Press, 1961.

3

CONCEPTUAL FRAMEWORK: NATIONAL AND INTERNATIONAL FINANCIAL MARKETS

This chapter examines the relationships between different national financial markets, the role of the national and international financial markets in accommodating the flow of capital funds, and the major reasons that explain the flow of capital between different national markets. By national financial markets we mean the market for loanable funds that has its limits within the geographic confines of one nation and in which debt and equity claims are denominated in one uniform currency of account. This is to be contrasted with the international financial markets, those markets for loanable funds that transcend national status and in which more than one currency may be used to denominate claims. The three major financial market sectors that fall under the title international are the foreign exchange, Eurocurrency, and Eurobond markets.

CHARACTERISTICS OF FINANCIAL MARKETS AND NONFINANCIAL MARKETS

Role of Financial and Nonfinancial Markets

The concept of a market plays a central role in economic analysis and the understanding of how economic-financial processes take place. In Chapter 1 we described in summary fashion how the international equilibrium position of a country, reflected in the balance of payments and foreign exchange rate, is the outcome of what takes place in the markets for goods and services, lendable funds, and investment assets. Competition between demand and supply in these various markets ultimately affects and is affected by the international economic position of the country concerned. The purpose of this and the following sections is to explain in brief how these different types of markets operated, in what ways they mesh together in a given country, and to demonstrate the nature of the various interactions between financial markets on an international level.

The market is a meeting place for buyers and sellers, and when the market is financially oriented, the participants operate as borrowers and lenders. Generally, markets function so as to permit an exchange of the item being traded at a price and quantity that benefits a large number of demanders and suppliers. Markets fulfill an important economic function in that the exchange tends to benefit both parties; the price established reflects an objective valuation; and changes in price brought about by a shift in demand or supply conditions provide incentives for changes in the flow of production or flow of funds. Markets allocate productive resources and lendable funds on the basis of impersonal economic criteria, and where market imperfections are minimal, we expect that the allocation process works optimally.

Financial markets allocate loanable funds that result from saving and bank credit creation. Markets for goods and services allocate productive resources, such as labor, capital, and raw materials. Markets for investment assets perform a liquidity adjustment and portfolio balancing function in that changing preferences for a given type of financial asset results in a higher or lower valuation of that security or asset relative to other financial assets. In turn, these changing valuations tend to bring about a new equilibrium situation wherein investment asset holders hold combinations of assets which satisfy their overall liquidity, income, and risk exposure objectives.

As we can see, all markets perform a valuation and allocation function. Financial markets value and allocate loanable funds. Interactions between these valuation and allocation processes result in a meshing together of financial, goods and services, and investment asset markets both within a national economy as well as between nations.

Money and Capital Markets

The financial markets in a given country may consist of a number of subsectors. These generally are broken down into the money, capital, and other financial market sectors. The money market is an impersonal market for short-term credits and permits participants to adjust their liquidity positions in a relatively flexible manner. The instruments or types of credit that are likely to be exchanged in a country's money market include short-term government securities (often in the form of Treasury bills), commercial paper, banker's acceptances, interbank loans (federal funds in the United States), overnight loans by banks to securities firms, and negotiable certificates of deposit. Major participants in the money market usually include large commercial banks, industrial corporations with liquid funds, financial institutions, the central bank, and government agencies The role of the central bank can be of paramount importance in the operation of a nation's money market since this institution often is in a position to add to or subtract from the cash reserves available to the banking system. This aspect of monetary policy can be of overriding importance at times when the central bank pursues a policy of credit restraint or active support of credit expansion. Central-bank-induced changes in bank reserves can have a magnified effect on the ability of the banking system to make loans and investments.

The capital market allocates long-term credit, which generally takes the form of common stocks, bonds, and mortgage instruments. The capital market generally relies rather heavily on domestic savings as a source of funds. However, in some instances foreign sources of funds play an important role. Banks, insurance companies, building and loan societies, pension funds, and investment trusts represent the most frequently encountered types of capital market institutions that collect funds from individual, business, and other savers and invest in long-term securities. Several of these types of institutions are relatively specialized and concentrate on investing their funds in one or several types of securities. For example, the building and loan societies emphasize real estate mortgage lending almost exclusively. Also, the investment companies tend to specialize in one or a few types of securities. The insurance companies and pension funds, on the other hand, may shift their emphasis from year to year, as between equities, bonds, and mortgages, prompted by relative yield relationships and securities market trends.

Both the money and capital markets include primary and secondary market trading. The primary market refers to new security issues, while the secondary market refers to the trading of existing securities. Performance of the money and capital markets in a nation during a given period of time depends on economic conditions, availability of funds, investors' attitudes, and conditions in the nonfinancial markets. The amount of savings that can flow through the money and capital markets at any time depends on the level of economic activity and the propensity of income recipients and wealth holders to save out of currently received income. Development of Keynesian and post-Keynesian economic theory over the past three decades indicates that total savings flows are inextricably tied to income and production levels.

According to the Keynesian analytical framework, the level of income and employment in a country at any particular time is influenced by aggregate expenditures, which consist of consumption, business investment spending, and government spending. Based on the propensity to consume and the propensity to save, consumers maintain a relatively stable percentage of saving out of current income. As consumer disposable income rises along with economic activity, so also does the flow of household saving generated from this income.

The business sector also can be an important saving sector. This saving assumes two forms: depreciation allowances and retained earnings. This cash flow may be sufficient to finance all or a good portion of fixed investment in plant and equipment undertaken by the business sector in a given year. Within the business sector, some firms will be net lenders of funds and other firms will be net borrowers, even though taken as a unit the business sector will tend to be a net borrower.

Finally, the government sector may be a saver (lender), or a dissaver (borrower), depending upon its overall budgetary position. In a year of budgetary surplus, the government may be an important lender and exert a significant easing influence on the financial markets.

The flow of savings and its allocation among various alternative end-uses influence the portfolio balance of savers and borrowers, business investment and other spending decisions, and ultimately the level of economic activity. In turn, the flow of savings and its allocation are influenced by changing levels of income and employment. The following sections of this chapter further develop these relationships.

Intersectoral Flows of Funds

To understand the operation of the money and capital markets, we must recognize that there are three types of participants: ultimate savers, financial intermediaries, and ultimate borrowers. The sources of funds from ultimate savers include savings of individuals, businesses, governments, and the rest of the world. These funds are channeled directly, or indirectly through financial institutions, to the ultimate users (borrowers) of funds, including individuals, businesses, governments, and the rest of the world.

The financial markets facilitate intersectoral flows of funds in numerous ways:

1. Financial markets establish channels through which funds may flow. These channels consist of financial institutions and competitive markets within which specialized dealers or other intermediaries bring together lender and borrower.

2. Financial markets provide for the valuation and pricing of credit funds, generally within a competitive environment that reflects impersonal and objective market determined forces.

3. Financial markets increase the range of choice available to potential lenders and borrowers by providing alternative loan and credit outlets.

4. Financial institutions or intermediaries stimulate an increased flow of funds by increasing the variety of financial assets that ultimate lenders may hold (deposits, saving and loan shares, pension reserves) and by increasing the variety of financial liabilities that ultimate borrowers may assume (maturity, denomination, and special features). They also act as protectors to fund lenders and as advisors to fund borrowers.

Examples of intersectoral flows of funds that pass through the financial markets include increased corporate deposits in banks the proceeds of which banks may invest in municipal bonds, individual savings flowing into life insurance companies which acquire real estate mortgages, and individuals' deposits in savings banks used to acquire corporate bonds.

How are total funds passing through the financial markets allocated by end-use? The structure of interest rates plays an important role in this connection. Interest rates differ by length of maturity of credit, by type of credit use, and by size of credit granted. Let us examine the connection between maturity and allocation of funds.

The yield curve provides us with a ready analytical framework in considering how differences between short-term and long-term interest rates play a role in the allocation of loanable funds. The yield curve in the United States is derived by plotting maturity and yield of marketable government securities and drawing a smooth curve through the resulting scatter diagram. The yield curve for September 1972 in Figure 3.1 is normal in that it is upward sloping through much of its range. An abnormal yield curve (September 1973) is humpbacked or downward sloping. Normal yield curves are associated with relative ease in the financial markets, whereas abnormal yield curves generally accompany tight money and predominantly high interest rates. The normal situation is for short-term interest rates to be lower than long-term interest rates, except under conditions of tight money when short-term rates rise rapidly and become higher than long-term rates. When conditions of tight money prevail, the allocation of funds in the financial markets is affected in several ways. First, long-term borrowers seek to borrow short-term and/or curtail the overall amount of borrowing. Second, lenders place a greater premium on lending at long term. Third, financial intermediaries reevaluate their position and attempt to maximize

FIGURE 3.1

Yield Curves Based on Marketable U.S. Treasury
Securities, September 1972 and September 1973

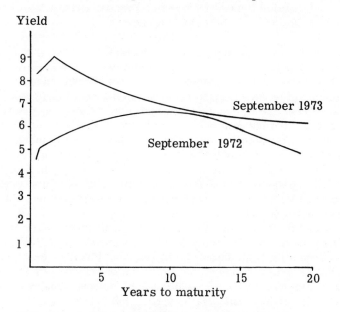

the yields they obtain on new investments. This often results in their
shifting investment commitments in the direction of long-term investments, where yields have behaved more sensitively to rising pressures (corporate bonds). Commercial banks ration funds during
periods of tight money, often giving priority to high-quality borrowers.
Finally, individual investors may stretch out the maturities of securities they hold to take advantage of favorable yields on long-term
securities, including government bonds. Arbitrage between financial
market sectors results from any deviations in interest rate or yield
relationships. Thus, a heavy volume of Treasury borrowing by sale
of U.S. Treasury bills is likely to place upward pressure on Treasury
bill yields, causing investors in related market sectors (commercial
paper, bankers acceptances, and negotiable certificates of deposit)
to sell these instruments and purchase Treasury bills. This interest
arbitrage results in transmitting market pressures and realigning
interest rate relationships.

RELATIONSHIPS BETWEEN DIFFERENT
NATIONAL FINANCIAL MARKETS

Major Types of Financial Transactions
between Nations

During the past quarter century, 1949-74, international financial transactions have grown in amount and complexity. We have singled out five major categories of international flows of funds that are reported among the transactions recorded in national balances of payments. These are (1) changes in bank claims vis-à-vis foreigners, (2) money market transactions of nonresidents, (3) new bond issues by nonresidents, (4) transactions in existing securities (trading in company securities and government issues), and (5) direct investment flows.

The first two categories are essentially short term, whereas the remaining three types of flows are of a long-term nature. In part, these flows may reflect changes in business conditions at home and abroad and the resulting need to obtain financial services on a transnational basis. On the other hand, a substantial part of these flows may remain largely unrelated to changing levels of economic activity, but represent the need for residents of one country to re-establish investment portfolio equilibrium by means of undertaking transactions in offshore financial centers. For example, a U.S. company may purchase (direct investment) a majority ownership in a European company, or individual American investors may purchase foreign equities. Alternately, foreign investors may sell foreign securities and invest the proceeds in the New York money market.

In Table 3.1 we find data reflecting these five types of international flows of funds from the United States. Changes in bank claims reflect increased claims of U.S. banks on nonresidents (outflow of $3.5 billion) and increased deposit liabilities of U.S. banks to foreign commercial banks and nonbank asset holders ($3.1 billion inflow). Changes in holdings of money market assets include a small increase in U.S. resident assets held in offshore money centers and a somewhat larger increase in nonresident holdings in the New York money market. We should remember that changes in official holdings are excluded (central banks and governments) and that in recent years these official institutions have acquired considerable amounts of U.S. money market assets. Line 3 includes new bond issues of nonresidents and transactions in existing securities. Resident outflows consist mainly of new foreign bond issues in the United States, while nonresident inflows consist largely of transactions in existing securities.

TABLE 3.1

Summary of U.S. Capital Transactions on
Private Account (Inflows and Outflows
of Funds) in 1972
(billions of dollars)

		Resident Outflows	Nonresident Inflows
1.	Changes in bank claims	-3.5	3.1
2.	Changes in holdings of money market assets	-0.8	1.4
3.	Portfolio securities (new issues and secondary trading)	-0.6	4.3
4.	Direct investment flows	-3.4	0.2
5.	Total	-7.3	9.0
6.	Errors and omissions	-3.1	—

Source: Federal Reserve Bulletin.

The pattern of U.S. investment flows is particularly interesting from the standpoint of developing an understanding of what factors influence international financial flows. U.S. flows are characterized by (1) substantial short-term flows in both directions, (2) a large volume of direct investment outflows, and (3) a substantial amount of portfolio investment inflows. In a later section we shall subject this pattern to closer scrutiny in connection with developing an analysis of the major factors that influence global flows of investment funds.

In the following sections we describe the problems encountered in measuring international flows of funds and the factors that influence the volume of these international financial flows from an overall point of view as well as with regard to specific conditioning factors.

International Flows of Funds:
Measurement and Analysis

In this section we develop broad estimates of the international flow of long-term capital. Admittedly, these estimates are approximate and only indicate general magnitudes. Numerous problems arise in attempting to develop a measure of the flow of long-term capital. These include conceptual problems, questions of definition, and serious data gaps.

In the conceptual area, we must distinguish between gross and net flows, between resource and financial flows, and the possibility of interplay between portfolio and direct investment flows. International capital flows generally are reported on a partially netted basis. For example, the net change in nonresident holdings of U.S. corporate securities is used as one measure of the portfolio investment flow in the balance of payments statistics. Similarly, the net changes in U.S. bank claims against nonresidents and in U.S. corporate investments overseas are additional inputs used to record the flow of capital. Note there is no netting of resident direct investment outflows against nonresident direct investment inflows.

The addition of resource and financial flows may not net out to a zero balance, due to the large and growing international services component in global business. A major part of international services reflects income earned on foreign investments, and the larger this item the greater the disparity between global resource and financial flows. Finally, we should note that seemingly unrelated portfolio and direct investment flows may be closely linked. For example, U.S. direct investment may be supported by the sale of Eurobonds through an offshore financing affiliate of the U.S. parent company. At the same time, increased demand for funds in the Eurobond market may place upward pressure on bond yields in Western Europe and pull funds from the United States. In short, the direct investment outflow from the United States led to portfolio investment flows relating to supplemental financing of overseas affiliates of U.S. companies and further led to portfolio or short-term capital outflows from the United States related to demand-induced increases in yields in the Eurobond market.

Numerous definitional problems interfere with a neat measurement and analysis of international financial flows. Long-term flows may be reversed within a year, and short-term international bank credits may be renewed several times over and remain outstanding for several years. The distinctions made between direct and portfolio investment are not as sharp as data gatherers imply. In the balances of payments of countries such as Switzerland, Panama, and Luxembourg, it is virtually impossible to make any distinction between portfolio and direct investment flows if only because financial holding companies of expatriate corporations conduct financial transactions that defy classification.

Finally, data gaps in the field of international capital flows are numerous. Many countries fail to distinguish between short-term and long-term portfolio flows. As noted, in some cases there is no separation between direct and portfolio investment flows. In countries that attempt to make careful distinctions such as the United States, gaps in the statistical reporting networks leave substantial errors and omissions which, from year to year, may consist of changing proportions of different types of investment flows.

Despite these difficulties, it is possible to arrive at rough orders of magnitude concerning global flows of long-term investment capital. As indicated in Table 3.2, in 1971-72 the international flow of investment capital was between $35-40 billion, or close to 10 percent of world exports. These figures suggest that portfolio investment flows have become more important in recent years, that flows to developing countries now account for a major part of the global total, and that private capital flows to developing countries now play a more important role than official flows.

The United States continues to play an important role as supplier of long-term investment funds, and as a focal point for portfolio adjustment of securities holdings of foreign investors. In the following section we examine the major factors that influence international flows of funds and the pattern of long-term international investment. Special attention is given to why the United States plays a special role as a long-term investor and recipient of foreign investment funds.

Major Influences on International Flows of Funds

International flows of funds are induced by a variety of factors. In general, such flows are related to international differences in interest rates or investment yields, and these in turn are fundamentally tied to configurations of supply and demand for loanable funds in each country. No doubt, other factors such as political pressures, availability of special international banking deposit and loan facilities, war reparations, and other special factors induce flows as well as affect their pattern and direction.

The neoclassical theory of international trade and investment flows, commonly referred to as the Heckscher-Ohlin theory, offers a generalized explanation on the basis of differential resource endowments, differential returns or incomes on productive resources, and international resource (capital) flows based on the differences in factor incomes or factor returns. A number of assumptions underlie the neoclassical theory of international capital flows, including perfectly competitive (resource and financial) markets, unimpaired mobility of real and financial capital, and an absence of dynamic foreign-exchange-induced pressures on investment flows. Finally, we should note that the neoclassical theory fails to take into account the different forms in which international investment flows are

37

TABLE 3.2

The International Flow of
Long-Term Capital, 1971-72
(billions of dollars)

	1971	1972
Official flows to developing countries via multilateral lending institution[a]	1.3	1.8
Private portfolio flows to developing countries	4.4	4.4
Direct investment in developing countries	3.9	3.9
Direct investment in industrial countries	8.6	5.1
Intergovernmental assistance to developing countries	7.7	8.3
Flight capital flows from developing countries	1.0	1.0
Private portfolio flows to industrial countries	9.0	13.8
Total long-term capital flow, global	35.9	38.3
Long-term flow to developing countries[b]	17.3	18.4
World exports	345.3	407.8
Long-term flow as percent of world exports	10.4	9.4

[a]Includes World Bank Group, Inter-American Development Bank, and Asian Development Bank.
[b]Obtained by adding Lines 1, 2, 3, and 5.

Sources: World Bank and IDA, Annual Reports; Organization for Economic Cooperation and Development (OECD), Financial Statistics; Federal Reserve Bulletin; and authors' estimates. Data for Lines 1, 2, 3, and 5 were obtained from World Bank, Annual Reports. Data for Line 4 were obtained by assuming that direct investment flows to and from the United States represent 40 percent of the global total. Line 6 was obtained by authors' estimates. Line 7 was obtained by combining OECD data on foreign and international bond issues with the portfolio investment inflow to the United States.

embodied, including official flows, private portfolio, and direct investments.

Short-term and long-term international flows play equally important roles. Short-term flows may be speculative, induced by opportunities for interest arbitrage, related to trade financing requirements, or influenced by the need to supplementary finance other internationally oriented business transactions such as plant and equipment
investment or inventory investment of multinational corporations.

Long-term investment flows are influenced by a number of
special forces. These include the existence of opportunities for international portfolio adjustment, differences in financial market structure,
differences in industrial structure, the desire to achieve international
portfolio diversification, and differences in risk preference and assumption.

The international investment position of the United States amply
demonstrates the existence of opportunities for international portfolio
adjustment. U.S. private investors (mainly corporate) tend to acquire
foreign assets in the form of ownership of overseas corporate affiliates, direct investments providing effective control over foreign
subsidiaries and branches. Foreign investors appear to prefer portfolio investments in U.S. corporate securities and more liquid U.S.
Treasury securities. A possible explanation for this international
exchange of claims is national differences in liquidity preference.
In Figure 3.2 we see yield curves reflecting a stronger liquidity preference in Europe with a more steeply sloped yield curve and reflecting

FIGURE 3.2

Yield Curves in Europe and the United States
Reflecting Differences in Liquidity Preference

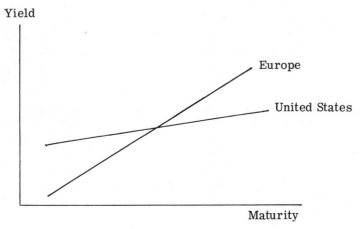

a more moderate liquidity preference in the United States with a flatter yield curve.

The yield-curve comparison explains why Europeans might prefer to purchase short-term securities in the United States and more liquid but lower-yielding long-term securities in the United States. The comparison also provides some insight into why U.S. corporations may find equity-type investments in Europe attractive, that is, the possibility of a higher return. Unfortunately, the above does not fully explain why capital flows to Europe are biased in the form of direct investments. Moreover, we do not have a complete explanation for why the European capital markets have not provided adequate liquidity to European investors.

Some of these unanswered questions are cleared up when we examine the differences in structure between the U.S. and European financial markets. The European capital markets have remained fragmented, relatively small, and inefficient. Flotation and transaction costs tend to remain high, and price volatility is a more critical consideration in Europe than in the U.S. securities markets. As a result, portfolio investment is attracted from Europe to the United States. This portfolio investment outflow tends to place upward pressure on the cost of domestic capital in Europe, discourages direct investment outflows, and tends to narrow the differential between the cost of capital and return on capital in Europe. On the other hand, portfolio outflows from Europe to the United States tend to push up securities prices in the United States, make direct investment take-overs in the United States more expensive, and tend to push up the exchange rate on the U.S. dollar, making direct investment in the United States more costly for European and other corporations. However, these tendencies will encourage U.S. direct investment flows to Europe, since there will be a lower cost on U.S. source financing and a lower foreign exchange cost facing U.S. direct investors.

Differences in industrial structure also assist in explaining the pattern of long-term investment flows. In oligopolistic markets, desire for growth and protection of market shares may exert more influence over corporate investment behavior than the profit motive. This behavior pattern may explain the preference of many companies to attempt overseas expansion rather than intensify competitive pressures at home. At the same time, existence of established oligopolistic market equilibrium in one nation may attract foreign firms. Existence of antitrust legislation in the United States may have been a factor inducing many large U.S. companies to seek growth through acquisitions in other national markets. Finally, we should note that two-way direct investment flows may be explained more easily if we consider imperfections in industrial market structures in host and source countries.

The desire for international portfolio diversification is based upon differential investment opportunities afforded in national securities markets. These differential opportunities stem from yield-risk factors peculiar to each national capital market, which in turn are brought about by differences in liquidity preference, securities market organization, and competitive structure in national capital markets. In a study published in the American Economic Review in 1970, Levy and Sarnat found that in the period 1951-67, the rate of return on common stocks in the United States (average annual percentage change in value) was not too different from that obtained on common stocks in other leading industrial countries. However, the risk measured by the standard deviation in rates of return was much lower in the United States than in most other countries.

While the greater efficiency of the U.S. stock market may attract portfolio investment inflows, it offers no special advantages to direct investors. In fact, U.S. corporate investors may derive an advantage from investing in Europe where stock markets are less efficient at the same time that European investors acquire common stocks in the more efficient U.S. equity market. For example, in Figure 3.3 curves UU and EP represent the investment opportunities available to portfolio investors in the United States and Europe, respectively. The stock market in the United States offers lower risks but equivalent returns (line EP lies to the right of line UU over most of the range

FIGURE 3.3

Comparison of Risk-Return Opportunities Available
in European and U.S. Stock Markets on Control and
Portfolio Stocks

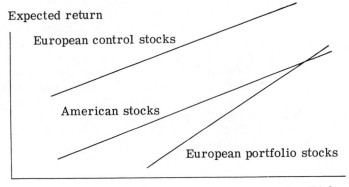

of choices available to investors). Therefore, a large flow of portfolio investment moves from Europe to the United States. The "markets" for European control and portfolio stocks remain separated due to the size of investment that is required to purchase control stocks. However, the U.S. financial market is "efficient," and there is no return or yield advantage in control stocks as compared with portfolio stocks (akin to saying that the market for secondary distributions of control stocks to the investing public blends the control and portfolio segments of the U.S. equity market perfectly).

Direct investment flows from the United States to Europe due to the ability of U.S. corporations to acquire control stocks in Europe. The inefficiency of capital markets outside the United States prevents domestic firms (in Europe) from raising capital, and the supply of risk capital remains limited as it is concentrated in the hands of a few. Under these conditions, U.S. companies can undertake control investments in Europe and offer the only practical alternative to government investment, even for countries that are exporting large amounts of portfolio capital.

Differences in risk preference and assumption have been offered as an explanation for direct investment flows. According to Aliber, when there is a risk of change in the exchange rate, firms in the strong currency area are at an advantage and are likely to invest in the weak currency area. The firm in the source country capitalizes the same income stream of expected earnings (of the host country firm) at a higher rate than the host country firm. When a change in the foreign exchange rate is expected, capitalization rates on equities may be expected to decline in the weak currency area (profit rates are higher). Perfect market adjustment would equate the exchange risk to a capitalization rate in line with the foreign exchange exposure facing equity investors. Aliber argues that this adjustment does not take place, and as a result there is a strong incentive for direct investors to acquire ownership in weak currency area firms.

There are several questions regarding Aliber's thesis that are not easily answered. First, it is not clear why the profitability advantages of weak currency firms (made available by the low capitalization rate on equities) should exceed the expected change in the foreign exchange rate of the weak currency. Second, how can one be certain that the market will capitalize the additional income that accrues to the source country (direct investor) firm without discounting it for the exchange risk? In practice, UK companies have been important direct investors over a period of time in which the pound sterling has been considered weak. Moreover, Germany, with a strong currency, has enjoyed large net inflows of direct investment.

RELATIONSHIPS BETWEEN NATIONAL AND INTERNATIONAL FINANCIAL MARKETS

Distinctive Features of the International Financial Markets

Up to this point in our discussion, major emphasis has been on national financial markets and the mechanisms for effecting flows between markets located in different countries. Now we turn to an analysis of the flows of funds between national and international financial markets. The latter markets operate beyond the confines of national boundaries.

The international financial markets enjoy a number of distinctive features that do not accrue to national financial markets. First, they rely on banks, securities firms, and underwriting groups that transcend national origins and ties. Second, they derive funds on a multinational basis and therefore remain relatively independent from monetary and fiscal policies and credit market conditions in any one country. Third, they lend funds to borrowers who enjoy maximum mobility and flexibility in their ability to seek out and borrow funds under various conditions and credit terms. Finally, the international financial markets play a dual role as complements and competitors to the national financial markets.

Their ability to function both as complement and competitor to national financial markets gives the international financial markets an important role as equilibrator and safety valve. Excessive tightness in one nation's financial markets will result in residents of that nation seeking external sources of financing. Excessive ease in a nation's financial markets is likely to induce nonresidents to withdraw funds and employ them more profitably elsewhere. In either case, the alternatives are to make use of the financial market in another nation, or to use the facilities in the international financial markets. The facilities and services available in the international financial markets are described in Part VII, Chapters 21, 22, and 23.

Major Linkages in International Financial Markets

The growth and development of the international financial markets such as the Eurobond and Eurocurrency markets have been possible due to the many types of linkages that have developed between these markets and the domestic financial markets of many countries. These linkages have developed and grown to support financial transactions between broad market sectors and include institutional linkages and the linkages provided by intermediary securities firms and under-writers.

Three types of institutional linkages may be singled out as important contributors to the integration of national with international financial markets. These include the multinational corporations, the large internationally oriented commercial banks, and the specialized official and private financial institutions and agencies that have been formed to support the internationalization of world finance. In a previous chapter we described the importance and activities of the several hundred multinational corporations that operate production and distribution facilities around the globe. The international financial transactions are responsible for runs into the hundreds of billions of dollars annually. These transactions include long-term debt financing, use of bank credits, sale of goods and services, placing of bank deposits and short-term investments, and remittance of profits and dividends to parent companies. These corporations are major factors in the foreign exchange, Eurobond, and Eurocurrency markets.

The large commercial banks play a vital role in connecting national financial markets, as well as in providing linkages between the international and domestic financial markets. Through their global branch office networks, major banks operate on both sides of the Eurocurrency market, transfer funds from one financial center to another, and function as major money changers and money movers in the foreign exchange market. These major international banks rely on their merchant bank, private bank, and finance company affiliates and ties to participate in new Eurobond issues.

We should note that during the two decades 1950-1970, a number of specialized international agencies have been created to function as financial intermediaries in the global markets for loanable funds. These include the World Bank, the International Finance Corporation, and the regional development banks such as the Inter-American Development Bank and the Asian Development Bank. In addition, a number of private institutions have been organized to undertake investments on an international basis, including Atlantic Community Development Fund for Latin America (ADELA) and the Private Investment Company of Asia (PICA).

Finally, linkages provided by intermediary securities firms and underwriters have become important in such areas as forming Eurobond syndicates, providing specialized information concerning investment in foreign securities, functioning as investment advisers and managers, executing purchase and sale transactions in foreign stocks and bonds, and distributing offshore mutual fund shares to individual investors.

Integration of Financial Markets

Integrative and insulating forces have both been at work in the development of financial markets around the world. However, the preceding discussion suggests that the development of domestic and international financial markets has been accompanied by stronger tendencies toward integration. For example, the spread in yields on long-term bonds between the United States and Western Europe has been narrowed since the emergence of the Eurobond market in the 1960s. These financial markets are developing stronger ties and more numerous linkages year by year.

This integrative process suggests that the financial markets of the world are more capable of servicing the various needs of the world economy, such as the safekeeping of savings and proper allocation of loanable funds to appropriate end-users. Moreover, when inflationary and speculative pressures grow stronger in the international economy, the closer ties established between financial markets present market participants with a greater variety of alternative courses of action.

We should note that the benefits from more closely integrated financial markets are not an unmixed blessing. Development of the national and international financial markets facilitates a smoother and readier international transmission of economic and financial disturbances. For example, a weakness of the pound sterling is reflected almost instantly in the major financial market centers of the world in terms of the tone of the bond market, equity share trading, and money market pressures. Foreign exchange rates quickly reflect changing economic conditions or weakness and strength in a country's balance of payments. In turn, such adjustments in foreign exchange rates influence the volume and pattern of foreign trade taking place between that country and the rest of the world. Closer integration of financial markets permits changes in economic and financial conditions to spread their effects from country to country more quickly. Such influences pose numerous and difficult policy questions for countries whose economies are open to these international pressures.

REFERENCES

Aliber, Robert Z. "A Theory of Direct Foreign Investment." In The International Corporation. Edited by C. P. Kindleberger, Cambridge, Mass.: M.I.T. Press, 1970.

Bain, Joe. S. International Differences in Industrial Structure. New Haven, Conn.: Yale University Press, 1966.

Bank for International Settlements. Annual Reports, 1973.

Basch, Antonin. Capital Markets of the European Economic Community, Problems of Integration, Michigan International Business Studies, No. 3. Ann Arbor, Mich.: University of Michigan Press, 1965.

Cooper, Richard N. The Economics of Interdependence. New York: McGraw-Hill, 1968.

Hogan, John D. The U.S. Balance of Payments and Capital Flows. New York: Praeger Publishers, 1967.

Levy H., and M. Sarnat. "International Diversification of Investment Portfolios." The American Economic Review (September 1970).

Ragazzi, Giorgio. "Theories of the Determinants of Direct Foreign Investment." IMF Staff Papers, July 1973.

World Bank and IDA. Annual Reports, 1973.

THE UNITED
STATES AND CANADIAN
FINANCIAL MARKETS

4

THE UNITED
STATES DOLLAR
AND WORLD FINANCE

THE U.S. TRIPLE THREAT

In the several decades since World War II, the United States has assumed the role of leader in international finance. This has been possible due to the superiority of the United States in three areas, namely, the strength of the U.S. dollar, the efficiency and resources of major financial institutions, and the highly efficient and liquid financial markets.

Role of the Dollar

In the postwar period, the demand for dollars has been an important factor in international finance, as well as in the international market for foreign exchange. This demand has expanded along with the growth in the world economy. The international demand for dollars comes from private as well as official sources and is measurable in terms of the changes in private and officially held dollar balances and in the movements of the price of the dollar on the foreign exchange market.

The reasons for the persistent and growing demand for dollars are not difficult to comprehend. Demand of official agencies including central banks and national treasuries stems from the need to hold liquid international reserves that can be used for supporting the par value of the domestic currency on the foreign exchange market, for financing temporary shifts in that country's balance of payments position, and for maintaining confidence in the viability of that country's international payments position. The private demand for dollars is related to the usefulness of the dollar as a vehicle or denominational currency, the role of the dollar in trade financing, and the important connection between the ability of the U.S. economy to export a large volume of long-term investment capital and the role of the U.S. capital market as a focal point for international investment transactions.

In this connection, the relative stability of the dollar in the foreign exchange market has been of crucial importance. In part the dollar has been demanded because of its stable position in world finance, and this in turn has tended to reinforce the stability of the dollar on the foreign exchanges. Other factors that have tended to enhance the central role of the dollar in international finance include the strong financial institutions in the United States, namely, the banks, large institutional investors, and the multinational corporations, and the efficient financial markets. These are considered in the following sections.

Institutions

Three types of institutions are described briefly in this section in connection with their role in making the United States and the U.S. dollar major factors in world finance. The commercial banks have played an important role in a number of connections. They are major factors in international lending, especially to finance merchandise exports and imports. In the period from December 1968 to June 1973, short-term claims of U.S. banks on nonresidents increased from $8.7 billion to $18.5 billion. Financing U.S. exports has played a significant role in the total amount of U.S. short-term claims on non-residents and has been important to the strength of the U.S. dollar in the foreign exchanges.

American banks have developed substantial foreign branch systems, which service U.S. corporations that have operations outside the United States. These foreign branches engage in Eurocurrency transactions, accept deposits, and make loans denominated in U.S. dollars, local currencies, and other currencies. At year end 1972, over 630 of these foreign branches held assets totaling $80 billion, of which $54 billion was payable in dollars. Operating extensively from a U.S. dollar base, these foreign branches have tended to widen the scope for use of the dollar in world finance.

Institutional investors have contributed to the strength of the dollar in world finance in a less direct manner than commercial banks. Institutional investors in the United States characteristically hold only a small portion of their investments in securities issued by foreign governments and corporations. The contribution of institutional investors to the strength of the dollar is through the role they play in widening and enlarging the scope of operations in the securities markets. Institutional investors of various types tend to add depth, competition, and resiliency to the securities markets in the United States. Therefore, these markets offer better opportunities to foreign investors in terms of number and diversity of investment alternatives, stability of securities prices, and market liquidity. Foreign investors make extensive use of the U.S. financial markets to take advantage of the benefits inherent in a larger, more diversified, and more stable securities market system.

While not classified as financial institutions, the large multinational companies do carry on extensive financial transactions on a large scale. Moreover, their financial transactions cut across national borders. The contributions made by U.S. multinational corporations lie in two important areas. First, their far-flung operations and activities tend to extend the dollar system on a global basis. These corporations engage in deposit, loan, investment, and other transactions around the world, and most often on a dollar basis. Second, their global activities strengthen the role and status of the dollar. In 1972 the net investment income received by U.S. direct investor companies was in excess of $10.4 billion, which compares with $7.9 billion in 1970. This represents 14 percent of total receipts in the U.S. balance of payments and perhaps the most rapidly growing item in the overall balance of payments accounts.

Financial Markets

Financial strength of the dollar in the world foreign exchange market is related to the highly efficient U.S. financial markets. This efficiency in turn is a function of the large size and scale of transactions in the various sectors of the U.S. financial markets and of their ability to attract a substantial volume of short-term and long-term investment funds from outside the United States. The discussion that follows focuses on the ability of three sectors of these markets to attract nonresident funds, namely, the money market, capital market, and the organized stock exchanges.

The U.S. money market is by far the largest in the world and affords nonresidents a wide assortment of short-term investment opportunities with little or no associated credit or interest rate risk. As is indicated in detail in Chapter 6, at mid-1973 U.S. money market credit outstanding was close to $250 billion, against which there was an equivalent 26 percent claim by nonresidents. At mid-1973 nonresidents held over $42 billion in U.S. government securities (mostly U.S. Treasury bills), $14 billion in short-dated bank deposits, and $16 billion in other short-term claims (commercial paper, banker's acceptances, and negotiable certificates of deposit—CDs).

The U.S. capital market also affords foreign investors excellent opportunities to undertake long-term investment commitments on a relatively favorable basis. Foreign investors are active in the U.S. securities markets on both the buying and selling sides. For example, U.S. Treasury data indicate that in 1972 foreign purchases and sales of U.S. stocks were $14.2 billion and $12.0 billion, respectively, resulting in net purchases of $2.2 billion. In the same period, net purchases by foreigners of U.S. corporate bonds approximated $1.7 billion.

The stock exchanges in the United States provide opportunities for nonresident transactions in foreign as well as domestic securities. At year end 1972, the market value of foreign stocks listed on the New York Stock Exchange exceeded $15 billion. At the same time corporate and government bonds listed on the New York Stock Exchange had market values of $0.7 billion and $2.0 billion, respectively. These totals exclude a large volume of Eurobonds that are not classified as foreign, although they are obligations of foreign subsidiaries of American corporations that have been sold abroad.

CHANGES IN U. S. COMPETITIVE POSITION

The United States has been experiencing a gradual change in its competitive position in international finance. This change is related to the growing strength of industry outside the United States, resulting in more intense competition in world markets for goods and services. In addition, many countries are experiencing significant economic development and related changes in their financial structure. This has taken the form of a more balanced growth as between different financial sectors, a more diversified financial intermediary sector, introduction and use of more varied credit instruments, a larger proportion of money transactions, expanded incentives to lend or invest surplus funds in the financial markets, and a higher degree of financial stability and confidence in the domestic currency. This ascendence of the financial markets in countries other than the United States together with the increased productive strength of many emerging export economies has tended to result in a greater independence of the nondollar world from the United States in its international financial relationships. On the other hand, important cohesive forces have operated to maintain the international role and status of the dollar.

Erosive Forces

Over the postwar period, a number of forces have combined to weaken the predominant role and status of the U.S. dollar in world

finance. Paramount in importance in this respect have been the following:
1. increased production and rising productivity in major industries around the world;
2. growth and development of financial institutions outside the United States;
3. emergence of overseas financial markets;
4. the gradual strengthening of nondollar currencies.

The growth of productive efficiency outside the United States has compelled American business firms to reappraise their position in world export markets and to reorganize their strategy toward development of world markets. The American competitive response has been to strive for increased efficiency, to consider production abroad—closer to markets external to the United States, and to diversify output to hedge against adverse competitive pressures. Over the years U.S. exports have grown steadily, but have not maintained their former share of the world total. In addition, U.S. corporations have shifted a substantial portion of their internationally oriented production to regions outside the United States. These pressures have tended to weaken the dollar. This weakening results from any loss of export markets that is attributable to the development of superior productive efficiency overseas and from any similarly induced increase in imports.

In many countries outside the United States, financial institutions have enjoyed an unprecedented expansion. In subsequent chapters we examine these postwar trends in detail. Closely related is the emergence over the 1960s of numerous overseas financial markets. The chapters that follow also describe the development and current status of these financial markets. While the United States once enjoyed an oligopolistic position in connection with the financial market services it could perform for the rest of the world, this condition is fading away at an accelerated pace. The financial markets of countries such as West Germany, Japan, Singapore, Mexico, Brazil, and Australia now can satisfy virtually all of their own domestic financing needs and, in addition, fulfill certain financial services required by neighboring countries.

Many countries have been witnessing a gradual and persistent strengthening of their currencies in world financial markets. This is the outcome of numerous changes taking place in their own economic structure, as well as in the configuration of the world economy. In Chapter 23 we further analyze the forces making for change in the relative strengths and weaknesses of various currencies in the international market for foreign exchange.

Cohesive Forces

The dollar continues to function as a central factor and mainstay in international finance. This pivotal role of the dollar is likely to continue for many years to come. This is because numerous cohesive forces are operating to preserve the strength and stability of the dollar.

One fact of life, which will continue to operate in favor of retaining the dollar as the world's major currency, is the size and strength of the U.S. economy. In 1972 the U.S. gross national product (GNP) was more than double that of the next largest country, the Soviet Union. Moreover, the U.S. national product was nearly four times as large as any other country's national product. The United States continues to be the world's largest exporter of merchandise, largest single source of investment capital, major international banking country, and headquarters country for the largest multinational companies of the world.

A second factor, which is important in explaining the continuing leadership position of the dollar in world financial markets, is the strong financial market mechanism in the United States. The new issues market is by far the largest in the world and offers the lowest flotation costs to corporate and governmental borrowers. The massive size of stock exchanges, money market, over-the-counter market, and other financial sectors provides financial economies and attractive investment alternatives that cannot be duplicated elsewhere.

Another important cohesive force tending to preserve the superiority of the dollar in the international financial markets is the U.S. multinational corporation. With its far-flung operations and tendency to operate and denominate transactions in dollars, the U.S. multinational corporation has extended the geography of the dollar currency area, enhanced the attractiveness of holding and dealing in dollars in the foreign exchange market, and generated substantial foreign exchange earnings that strengthen the U.S. balance of payments as well as the dollar in the exchange markets.

Finally, we must note that the development of international monetary cooperation among major industrial countries has been an important cohesive force, especially since 1970. The West German, Japanese, and Swiss authorities have absorbed substantial amounts of dollars in their own foreign exchange markets, thereby defending the dollar parity and the dollar-oriented international financial system. We might note that the monetary authorities of major countries acted in this manner due to lack of real alternatives. This gets us to the root of the question. In the absence of formal institutional arrangements for managing the world's money, the dollar, like its predecessor the pound sterling, has proved to be a most useful and necessary international currency. The question remains—for how much longer and under what circumstances will the dollar system continue?

A TENTATIVE REAPPRAISAL

At the present time, the international economy operates on the basis of a dollar monetary system. The dollar continues to serve as the predominant vehicle, intervention, and investment currency. The U.S. dollar serves as a major part of official reserve holdings, and central bankers continue to operate on the basis of supporting the parity of the dollar with other currencies. While there are no acceptable alternatives at present to the dollar system, underlying forces are working in the direction of reducing the overall importance of the dollar in world finance. However, these forces have not been able to overcome the political and institutional rigidities that operate on the side of preserving an international monetary system based on the U.S. dollar.

In addition, cohesive forces have been working very powerfully to preserve the role and status of the dollar in international finance. These forces may be expected to assist in maintaining the status of the dollar for a number of years. Therefore, we may expect to see a continuation of the dollar-oriented international monetary system, with mild interruptions based upon market pressures connected with waves of speculative activity. However, political coordination and international monetary agreements will preserve a slightly modified dollar system.

There is no doubt that the future will bring with it a more important role for other currencies, increased importance of non-U.S. financial institutions in international finance, and an expansion in the financial markets of the world that will leave the nondollar world more independent of the supply of dollars and less sensitive to changes in U.S. monetary conditions. As these changes accumulate, there will be increased pressure to more boldly reform the international monetary system and to adopt other institutional practices and operations in place of those dependent on the dollar-oriented system.

However, for the present it is necessary to analyze and describe the operations and practices of the international financial markets in terms of the current situation. Therefore, in the chapters that follow, our approach is focused on the prevailing international monetary system, organized on the basis of the United States providing a supply of dollars that is adequate to the needs and requirements of the international economy.

REFERENCES

Aliber, Robert Z. The International Money Game. New York: Basic Books, 1973.

Officer, L. H., and T. D. Willett, eds. The International Monetary System, Problems and Proposals. Englewood Cliffs, N.J.: Prentice-Hall, 1969.

Yeager, L. B. International Monetary Relations. New York: Harper & Row, 1966.

5

ROLE AND FUNCTION

During the three decades following World War II, the United States has assumed the responsibilities of a world financial center; the dollar has functioned as a keystone in the world payments system; and the financial system of the United States has become more responsive to conditions abroad. Domestically, there has been a very rapid growth in financial institutions. In general, the record achieved by the U.S. financial system in the postwar period has been good. However, numerous questions arise concerning the ability of the large financial mechanism in the United States to adapt to dynamic changes required by international trends and internal developments. Has the nature of the U.S. economy changed so that traditional adjustments and control mechanisms are no longer adequate? Has growth of nonbank financial intermediaries diminished the strength of monetary policy? Has excessive reliance been placed on monetary policy, and not enough on fiscal and debt management policy? Can improved regulation of the private financial institutions more effectively contain inflation?

These and other questions continue to challenge the United States in connection with its past leadership as a financial center and in terms of its ability to retain the present leadership enjoyed by its financial institutions. In this chapter we review the role and operations of the major financial institutions in the United States, assess the extent to which competitive innovation has taken place among these financial institutions, and finally describe the Hunt Commission proposals to strengthen U.S. financial institutions and markets.

Role Played in Financial Markets

Financial institutions play an important role in linking together savers and borrowers and in unifying credit market sectors. This linkage role is crucially important, since it facilitates an economically efficient allocation of lendable funds in the money and capital markets and thereby contributes to the maximization of national product and income.

A second important role of financial institutions lies in the intermediation they provide in the credit and investment markets. There are numerous aspects of this intermediation service. Financial institutions acquire financial assets and simultaneously create liabilities against themselves. The liability claims outstanding against financial institutions add another dimension to the financial markets, in the sense that these claims tend to complete the variety of financial assets that businesses and households may invest in. The alternative financial investments provided by the creation of claims against financial institutions inject an added measure of competition in the financial markets. Finally, we should note that claims against financial institutions provide claim holders with a greater degree of liquidity, diversification, and investment management than could be obtained by acquisition of direct claims against ultimate borrowers.

Financial institutions in the United States are the most highly developed in the world, with the possible exception of financial institutions in the United Kingdom. For this reason, it is generally assumed that the U.S. financial markets tend to be the most efficient in the world. Moreover, the degree of competitiveness of the U.S. financial markets, a direct outcome of the interaction of a large number of differentiated financial institutions, is considered to be unequaled. The high degree of competition among financial institutions in the United States leads to competitive innovation, a topic discussed later in this chapter.

National Balance Sheet

The financial deepening and development of the United States are closely related to previous economic growth and the accumulation of physical and money assets. Financial and economic development of necessity is accompanied by the expansion of an intricate network of financial claims among economic sectors. As this expansion process takes place, the financial institution sector begins to assume a more prominent status in terms of its intermediate position relative to all other sectors.

TABLE 5.1

National Balance Sheet
Financial Assets of Major Sectors
in the United States, 1972
(billions of dollars)

	(1) Total Financial Assets	(2) Percent of Total	(3) Claims on Financial Institutions	(4 = 3÷1) Percent of Total Financial Assets Held
Households	2,413	47.3	1,178	49.1
Business	471	9.2	95	20.4
U.S. government	98	1.9	14	14.3
State and local government	87	1.7	52	59.8
Financial institutions	1,870	36.7	68	3.6
Federal credit agencies	57	1.1	—	—
Monetary authority	96	1.9	—	—
Commercial banks	655	12.8	—	—
Private nonbank finance	1,061	20.8	—	—
Rest of the world	182	3.6	18	9.9
Total	5,121	100.0	1,425	27.9
Total excluding assets of financial institutions	3,251	—	1,357	41.8

Source: Federal Reserve Bulletin, flow-of-funds tables.

It is possible to visualize the prominent position of financial institutions by referring to a national balance sheet consisting of financial assets held by all sectors (Table 5.1). In 1972 financial assets held by all major economic sectors in the United States totaled $5,121 billion, of which financial institutions held $1,870 billion or over 36 percent. Households account for the largest block of financial assets held, with over 47 percent of the total. In the United States assets of financial institutions have been growing more rapidly than real income, money supply, and other key indicators of economic advance, reflecting the relative growth of financial institutions in the credit markets as well as the increase in specialization of financial functions that is exhibited by the growth in claims among financial institutions.

The development of financial institutions in the United States is already a maturing process. This is reflected in the national balance sheet in several ways, including the high ratio of financial assets held by financial institutions and the distribution of these assets among financial institutions. Financial assets held by private nonbank institutions far exceed those held by commercial banks, a reversal of the situation several decades ago when assets held by commercial banks exceeded those held by private nonbank institutions.

The maturity of the financial system in the United States is further reflected in the high proportion of financial assets held by various sectors in the form of claims on financial institutions. At year end 1972, households held nearly half of financial assets in this form, whereas the business sector held one-fifth of financial assets in the form of claims on financial institutions. State and local governments held three-fifths of financial assets as claims on financial institutions.

PRINCIPAL FINANCIAL INSTITUTIONS

The financial system in the United States includes a variety and diversity of types of institutions. In this section we examine the role played by the following types of institution:

Banking Sector	Insurance and Pension Institutions
Commercial Banks	Life Insurance Companies
Federal Reserve Banks	Property and Liability Insurance
Thrift Institutions	Companies
Mutual Savings Banks	Private Pension Funds
Savings and Loan Associations	Investment Companies

These institutions have a number of common characteristics, including the fact that their assets are primarily financial and that they issue claims against themselves that represent a somewhat unique type financial asset for the households, businesses, and governmental units that hold these claims.

Commercial Banks and the Federal Reserve

Measured by assets, commercial banks represent the largest single category of financial institution in the United States. At mid-1973 there were over 14,000 commercial banks in operation in the United States. Commercial banks exert considerable leverage on the U.S. financial markets due to their size, dominant role in the markets for government securities, and flexibility of credit-making activities. At mid-1973 (Table 5.2) assets held by commercial banks exceeded $680 billion.

Loans made by commercial banks serve the financing needs of a broad spectrum of borrowers in the United States. The three largest categories of commercial bank loans, accounting for 75 to 80 percent of total loans outstanding, are commercial and industrial, personal (consumer), and mortgage. Commercial and industrial loans include short-term loans to finance working capital requirements of business firms as well as term loans that extent out in maturity beyond seven to eight years. Term loans represent over one-third of the commercial and industrial loans of large commercial banks and represent a means by which large banks can participate in capital-market lending. Mortgage lending represents another area where commercial banks play an important role in the capital market. In the period 1970-72, commercial bank holdings of home mortgages and other mortgages increased by $14.5 billion and $11.4 billion, respectively. At times bank lending in these areas may be light,

TABLE 5.2

Balance Sheet of All Commercial Banks, June 1973
(billions of dollars)

Assets		Liabilities	
Cash	58.9	Deposits	
Loans and discounts	447.9	Demand	233.8
U.S. government		Time	340.8
securities	56.9	Interbank	32.1
Other securities	118.7	Miscellaneous liabilities	21.4
		Capital accounts	54.3
Total	682.4	Total	682.4

Source: Federal Reserve Bulletin.

due to the availability of more attractive alternative investment and lending areas (business loans and consumer credit).

Commercial bank investments in U.S. government and agency securities and in state and local government securities fulfill an important role in bank portfolio management. Moreover, they bring considerable leverage to bear on these market sectors. In periods of tight money, banks usually shy away from investments in these securities, again due to more attractive alternatives. Such was the case in 1968-69 when commercial banks increased their holdings of state and local government securities by a mere $0.6 billion and reduced U.S. government security holdings by $10.1 billion. These portfolio shifts accommodated a substantial increase in bank lending to households and businesses at a time when Federal Reserve credit policy was extremely restrictive.

Commercial banks rely heavily on a volatile deposit base for over 90 percent of their funds. Moreover, a shift in the direction of time deposits has tended to place upward cost pressures on bank funding operations. As explained in the chapter describing U.S. money market operations, U.S. commercial banks enjoy numerous alternative means of liquidity and reserve adjustment. Nevertheless, they tend to hold a considerable volume of short-term U.S. government securities as a secondary reserve asset. The deposit and lending operations of commercial banks provide important linkages between the money and capital markets in the United States.

Commercial banks represent a major avenue for maintaining international financial links between the United States and the rest of the world. At June 1973 short-term and long-term claims on foreigners reported by U.S. banks exceeded $24.2 billion. At the same time, U.S. bank head offices were indebted to their foreign branches by $2.0 billion. Foreign deposits in U.S. banks exceeded $14.9 billion. Finally, in June 1973 foreign branches of American banks held over $92 billion in assets, representing a 50-percent gain over the year end 1971 amount.

The Federal Reserve is responsible for formulating and implementing monetary policy in the United States. The nearly 6,000-member commercial banks of the Federal Reserve System hold approximately 80 percent of total assets in the U.S. banking system. The major thrust of monetary policy in the United States is by means of Federal Reserve open-market operations in the government securities market. Open-market operations for the Federal Reserve System Account directly influence the monetary base and bank reserves as well as prices and yields in the government bond market. At June 1973 U.S. government and agency securities held in the consolidated Federal Reserve balance sheet exceeded $76.5 billion, suggesting that the Fed can operate in a substantial way in the market in either direction

TABLE 5.3

Consolidated Balance Sheet—
All Federal Reserve Banks, June 1973
(billions of dollars)

Assets		Liabilities	
Gold certificates	10.3	Federal reserve notes	60.8
Federal reserve notes of		Deposits	
other banks	1.0	Member banks	24.8
Advances	1.7	U.S. Treasury	4.0
U.S. government and		Foreign	0.3
agency securities	76.5	Other	0.7
Cash items in process		Deferred availability	
of collection	8.9	cash items	7.0
Other assets	2.1	Other liabilities	0.9
		Capital accounts	2.0
Total	100.5	Total	100.5

Source: Federal Reserve Bulletin.

(Table 5.3). Money market analysts and bond underwriters keep a close watch on the weekly release of factors influencing member bank reserves, to interpret and anticipate shifts in monetary policy emphasis.

Thrift Institutions

Mutual savings banks and savings and loan associations represent the most important types of thrift institutions in the United States. Both institutions offer claims against themselves in the form of low turnover deposit or share accounts. Both invest the greater part of their resources in mortgages. Important differences between the two are that the savings banks have a somewhat more diversified and liquid asset portfolio (Table 5.4) and that the savings and loan associations have enjoyed a more dynamic growth over the two decades, 1950-70.

Savings banks are confined largely to the northeastern corner of the United States. The basic functions of savings banks are to provide a safe depository for individual savings and to invest funds in high-quality investment assets. Nearly all savings bank funds are derived from time deposits, which grow rapidly in times when these institutions can compete favorably for individual savings. During periods of high and rising interest rates, these institutions find it difficult to attract new deposits because of competition with other financial institutions and high yields available on open-market securities. For example, in 1966 and 1969 inflows of new funds to savings banks declined due to the high yields prevalent in those years.

Reduced inflows of funds very much influence the investment strategy of savings banks. Savings banks invest in mortgages, corporate bonds, corporate stocks, U.S. government securities, and other loans and securities. Investments in corporate stocks are limited due to state regulations and concern for preserving the integrity of the portfolio. Eligible securities are generally specified. In periods of rising interest rates and tight money, savings banks cut down on new mortgage lending and sharply curtail purchase of corporate securities. During the period 1968-73, savings banks have been shifting a small part of their U.S. government securities portfolio into federal agency issues, which provide a somewhat higher yield than direct obligations of the U.S. Treasury. Relative yield considerations play an important role in determining the investment activity of savings banks at any particular time.

Savings banks play a significant role in the mortgage market and provide 8 to 10 percent of new funds each year. New regulations in the late 1960s permitting acquisition of out-of-state mortgages have made savings banks important factors in interstate flows of mortgage funds.

Savings and loans associations were developed specifically for mortgage lending. At year end 1972 mortgage loans accounted for over 85 percent of total assets held by these institutions (Table 5.4). Savings and loan associations can obtain either federal or state charters. Associations that obtain federal charters and state associations that meet federal insurance standards are regulated by the Federal Home Loan Bank Board.

Savings and loan associations play a dominant role in the mortgage credit market, providing 55 to 65 percent of new mortgage funds each year. As a result, the flow of funds into mortgage lending in the United States is closely dependent upon the ability of savings and loan associations to attract a steady inflow of savings. Inflows of funds have been interrupted at times when rising interest rates caused individual and other savers to channel funds into open-market securities or other attractive investments. In 1971 and 1972 relatively low interest rates and monetary ease permitted these institutions to achieve substantial inflows of funds for investment, and as a result acquisitions of home mortgages increased rapidly.

TABLE 5.4

Assets of Thrift Institutions, June 1973
(billions of dollars)

	Mutual Savings Banks	Savings and Loan Associations
Mortgages	70.6	222.8
Other loans	3.9	—
U.S. government securities	3.3	20.4
State and local government securities	1.1	—
Corporate bonds and other securities	22.6	—
Cash	1.8	3.0
Other assets	2.3	18.0
Total	105.6	264.2

Source: Federal Reserve Bulletin, flow-of-funds tables.

While savings and loan associations invest heavily in relatively illiquid capital market assets, these institutions are able to derive a considerable measure of liquidity from various sources. Members of the Federal Home Loan Banking system can borrow from their regional Home Loan Bank. Second, balance sheet liquidity is available via holdings of U.S. government securities and amortization of mortgages. Savings and loan associations tend to specialize in amortized conventional loans. Moreover, they are not active in the secondary market for mortgages, as are other institutional lenders.

The operations of savings and loan associations very much influence the mortgage market. In turn, monetary policy affects the liquidity and inflows of funds to these associations. Changes in market rates of interest resulting from Federal Reserve policy influence the ability of savings and loan associations to attract new funds. Changes in interest rates affect only current lending of these institutions. Due to the nature of the mortgage credit market and regulation of practices of savings and loan associations in competing for funds, interest rates paid and received by these institutions tend to lag behind other market interest rates.

Insurance and Pension Institutions

In this section we deal with three types of institutions that invest in a variety of types of capital market securities. Two of these institutions, the life insurance and private pension funds, are referred to as contractual savings institutions due to the long-term contractual relationship that underlies their basic activities. Life insurance companies issue lifetime contracts, and life expectancy tables furnish a basis for pricing life insurance to build up an investment reserve. The investment reserve permits level premium or limited payment policies or accumulation of an annuity for retirement. The private pension funds undertake lifetime contracts, wherein they provide retirement benefits based upon accumulation of a reserve which supports annuity benefits in later years. Property and liability insurance companies do not acquire a large base of assets relative to pension or life insurance reserves. Rather, they hold investment assets that are derived from prepayment of nonlife insurance premiums.

Life insurance companies undertake long-term liabilities in the form of policy reserves that ultimately are payable upon death or longevity of the policyholder. Therefore, their investment policy must emphasize long-term safety of principal and realization of an investment return related to premium payments and compound growth of reserves. Life insurance companies must be kept fully invested. Moreover, the various states specify the categories of investments that may be acquired. The states also specify what percentage of assets may be invested in each category of investments.

While life insurance companies tend to concentrate their assets in two major categories, corporate bonds and mortgages (Table 5.5), they hold a wide assortment of other long-term investments. The greater part of U.S. government securities held is long term. State and local government securities are held to increase diversification and because of the increase in income tax rates on insurance companies.

Corporate bonds provide insurance companies with attractive yields, market liquidity, and diversification. Insurance companies have passed through several phases of priorities in the composition of the corporate bond portfolio. During the 1950s they were shifting from railroad to utility bonds, and in the period since 1960 the industrial bond category has received major emphasis. In recent years life insurance companies have been acquiring over one-fifth of new corporate bonds issued, with many of these new investments obtained by means of direct placements.

Life insurance company interest in mortgage lending has resulted from the high yields—often in excess of corporate bond yields, steady amortization and long maturities, diversity of types of mortgages

TABLE 5.5

Assets of Insurance Companies and Private
Pension Funds, May 1973
(billions of dollars)

	Life Insurance Companies	Property and Liability Companies	Private Pension Funds
Cash	2.0	1.7	2.0
U.S. government securities	4.5	3.8	3.9
State and local government securities	3.4	28.2	—
Foreign securities	3.5	—	—
Corporate bonds	90.3	9.2	29.1
Corporate stock	25.6	23.3	118.9
Mortgages	77.4	0.3	3.4
Real estate	7.5	—	—
Other loans	18.5	—	—
Miscellaneous assets	10.9	5.1	5.2
Total	243.6	71.6	162.5

available, and the special safety features available in government insured mortgages. Life insurance company investment in mortgages follows its own business cycle pattern, based upon relative yields available on alternative capital market assets, growth in assets, and the changing composition of mortgage activity (single family, multifamily, and commercial).

The basic nature of life insurance company operations works against a heavy emphasis on corporate stock investments. By law, life insurance companies are restricted to holding only a small proportion of investments in common stock. Nevertheless, common stock holdings have increased absolutely as well as relatively. Between 1966 and 1972 corporate stock increased from 5 percent to over 10 percent of total assets of life insurance companies. It is likely that their interest in this investment category will continue to grow as insured pension plans expand in scope and as state regulations permit larger proportionate investments in equities.

At midyear 1973 property and liability insurance companies held over $71 billion in assets (Table 5.5). While the bulk of their assets consists of capital market instruments, they acquire those largely in secondary market trading. This is in contrast with the life insurance companies, which acquire a large part of their capital market securities in the new issues or primary market.

Property and liability insurance companies obtain funds from insurance premiums paid in advance, capital stock, surplus, and reserves. In the four-year period 1968-72, new sources of funds exceeded $21 billion, of which 40 percent came from additional capital stock, surplus, and reserves. These funds were invested as follows: $9.4 billion in state and local government securities, $6.8 billion in corporate stocks, and $3.4 billion in corporate bonds.

Unlike life insurance companies, property and liability insurance companies are not able to predict future claims with a high degree of accuracy. This influences their investment policy. Generally, the property and liability insurance companies hold a large proportion of high-quality, readily marketable securities, including U.S. government securities, state and local government securities, and corporate bonds. Concentration of assets in these categories, along with a substantial investment in corporate stocks, permits property and liability companies to carry out the dual functions of underwriting risks and maintaining a diversified portfolio of securities. In a sense, this latter function gives these companies some aspects of mutual funds.

Large holdings of tax exempt state and local government bonds are explained in terms of the taxable status of operating income and the possibility of realizing substantial operating profits in years of low underwriting claim experience. In years of deficit underwriting operations, nontaxable bonds become less attractive. Corporate stocks are important investment outlets, but represent a volatile factor in the portfolios of these companies. Property and casualty insurance companies play an important role in the corporate stock market and more especially in the market for state and local government bonds.

In 1973 private pension funds held over $162 billion in assets. Over $118 billion of this amount was held in the form of corporate stock, and $29 billion in corporate bonds.(Table 5.5). In the period 1950-70, private pension funds have become the fourth most important financial institution in the United States in terms of total assets, ranking behind commercial banks, savings and loan associations, and life insurance companies in that order. In the relatively short period 1968-72, the assets of private pension funds increased by over 50 percent. At year end 1972 it has been estimated that over 32 million persons were covered by private retirement plans.

The expansion of private pension funds reflects acceptance of employers of responsibility for providing for employee retirement, the increase in the number of persons approaching retirement age, the increased use of retirement plans as incentives for improved work and reduced labor turnover, and tax advantages under which contributions become tax exempt to the employer and the employee. In the period 1970-72, the growth in pension funds averaged $9 billion annually. This included total receipts of $16 billion of which $4 billion were in the form of investment income, benefit payments of $7 billion, and $9 billion in asset growth.

The investment policy of private pension funds varies widely from one fund to another. Some funds emphasize purchase of common stock of the employer company. Others emphasize investment in high-grade corporate and government bonds. Nevertheless, broad trends are evident in the persistent shift in emphasis toward corporate stocks, intermittent growth in corporate bonds, and deemphasis of mortgages. Investment policy of individual funds is influenced by whether retirement benefits are fixed or variable, whether funds are essentially company contributed, and whether trust agreements operate as constraints on flexibility of investment management.

Due to the heavy emphasis on common stock investments, the pension funds are a major influence in the market for equities. Slow portfolio turnover, which is characteristic of pension funds, has tended to produce a thinner market for those share issues heavily purchased by pension funds.

While private pension funds have grown rapidly, state and local government retirement funds have enjoyed nearly as strong a growth rate. Total assets held by state and local retirement funds exceeded $71 billion in 1972, consisting mainly of corporate bonds ($43 billion), corporate stocks ($14 billion), and U.S. government securities ($5 billion). Asset growth has been in excess of $6-$7 billion per year since 1969. Since that date these funds have moved rapidly into investments in corporate stocks and corporate bonds and have reduced their holdings of U.S. government securities and state and local government securities.

Investment Companies

This group of financial institutions has achieved impressive growth in the postwar years. In addition to their role as financial intermediaries, the investment companies have influenced investor habits and the entire system of securities trading in the secondary markets. The greatest growth has been in the mutual or open-end investment company, and the following discussion focuses on this type of investment company. Closed-end investment companies have grown slowly, largely due to their fixed capitalizations.

In the decade 1962-72, assets of open-end investment companies increased from $21 billion to nearly $60 billion. This expansion reflects the economic progress of the period, rise in stock market values, increase in number and types of funds, and the general acceptance of these funds by the public. Since 1962 there have been three years in which declines took place in assets of open-end investment companies. This was in 1966, 1969, and 1970, periods when tight money and declining share values induced repurchases of share interests by investors.

Investment companies invest virtually all of their assets in capital market instruments. At year end 1972 the proportion of total assets held in various categories of capital market instruments was as follows: corporate shares (86 percent), corporate bonds (9 percent).

Details on asset holdings for the period 1968-72 can be seen in Table 5.6. The aggregates conceal fairly sharp differences among different types of investment companies. For example, bond funds hold virtually all their assets in corporate bonds, and some balanced funds hold a substantial portion of their assets in bonds.

Investment companies exert their major influence on the capital market in secondary trading of corporate stocks. In the period 1970-72, portfolio purchases averaged $23.3 billion per annum, and portfolio sales averaged $23.3 billion per annum. The bulk of these

TABLE 5.6

Assets of Open-End Investment Companies, 1968-72
(billions of dollars)

	1968	1970	1972
Demand deposits and currency	0.8	0.7	0.9
Corporate shares	46.1	39.7	51.7
U.S. government securities	1.1	0.9	0.7
Corporate bonds	3.4	4.3	5.1
Open-market paper	1.2	2.1	1.4
Total assets	52.7	47.6	59.8

Source: Federal Reserve Bulletin, flow-of-funds tables.

transactions was in corporate stocks. Mutual funds are active traders
of corporate stocks and have the highest activity rate of stock market
trading of all institutional investors. In 1972 the activity rate for
mutual funds on the New York Stock Exchange was 42 percent, meaning these funds traded that proportion of their portfolio holdings during
the year. Whether the high activity rate of mutual funds contributes
to stock price stability or instability remains a question of keen interest.

FINANCIAL INSTITUTIONS AS
COMPETITIVE INNOVATORS

In the United States the early years of the 1970s have witnessed
clearly discernible signs of shifts in the balance of power among the
various types of financial institutions. These shifts are the outcome
of increasing competitive pressures and reflect the need for regulatory reform of the financial institution sector in the United States.
We turn to the question of regulatory reform in the concluding section of this chapter.

Commercial banks have been at the forefront of competitive
innovation in finance. In fact, at the risk of gross oversimplification,
it would be possible to characterize this competitive innovation as a
system in which commercial banks have been rapidly moving into
new areas, or areas formerly reserved for nonbanking institutions.

Bank innovations have been channeled through two major institutional modules, namely, the bank holding company and the international division of the bank. The holding company organizational
format has revolutionized banking and finance in the United States
in at least three important respects. First, bank holding companies
enjoy access to sources of funds that their subsidiary banks could
not as easily tap. These include sale of commercial paper and sale
of capital notes and debentures. Admittedly, commercial banks themselves have sold capital notes and debentures to obtain additional
capital funds. However, they have been carefully monitored and
controlled with respect to the overall amount and proportion of capital funds derived from this source.

A second manner in which the bank holding company has influenced banking and finance is in the many new activities undertaken
by holding companies via their nonbank affiliates. These activities
range from equipment leasing, insurance and underwriting to computer services, investment advisory, and specialized corporate finance. The holding company structure has been important to the
successful initiation and implementation of these new service areas
for several reasons, including the outright prohibition of certain

71

financial activities from commercial banks and the preference of bankers for separate innovative and untested operations from the bank proper.

A third way in which the bank holding company has influenced the development of banking is by facilitating bank activities across state lines. Until the late 1960s there was no exception to the rule that U.S. banks could not operate or transact deposit business across state lines. Beginning in the late 1960s, various activities were extended into states other than that in which the parent bank was domiciled. These include establishment of representative offices, leasing affiliate branches, loan request offices, and insurance affiliates.

Bank innovations also have emanated from the international division. The international divisions of many U.S. banks have taken the lead in establishing out-of-state Edge Act affiliates that could conduct a complete international banking operation. Out-of-state Edge affiliate operations have expanded in scope so that there now are several regional financial subcenters in the United States with several operating Edge Act affiliates of major international banks. The steady growth of foreign banking in the United States in recent years has placed added pressures in the direction of liberalizing the restrictions against interstate bank activities. This is due to competitive advantages available to foreign banks that can operate banking affiliates or agencies in several states, while at the same time U.S. banks are prohibited from similar multistate representation.

THE HUNT COMMISSION REPORT

The United States has undertaken three extensive studies of its monetary and financial system in the past 70 years. The first, the National Monetary Commission (NMC), was an outgrowth of the severe banking and financial crisis of 1907 and the concern for reform. The NMC prepared the way for passage of the Federal Reserve Act of 1913 and the establishment of a full-fledged central banking apparatus.

It was nearly 50 years later that the second study was undertaken. Unlike its predecessor, the Commission on Money and Credit (CMC) was not established by the U.S. government or one of its agencies. The CMC was initiated by the Committee for Economic Development (CED), a private and independent study group supported by leading business and financial representatives in the United States. The Merrill Foundation for the Advancement of Financial Knowledge and the Ford Foundation co-sponsored the work of the CMC. The studies that resulted from the CMC's work were published, and these volumes remain a valuable source of information on the workings of the U.S.

financial system. When the CMC released its summary report in 1961, considerable interest and attention were focused on the prospects for implementing its proposals. Many years passed, and very few of the recommendations of the CMC were embodied in congressional legislation.

Nearly 10 years after publication of the Report of the Commission on Money and Credit, President Nixon established a "Presidential Commission on Financial Structure and Regulation." Establishment of this commission came at the end of a year that contained an extreme money crunch (1969), a Penn Central crisis that temporarily impaired confidence in the liquidity of the U.S. money market, a dismal stock market performance, spiraling inflation and unemployment, and a deteriorating balance of payments. The Hunt Commission, as it was called, submitted its final report, which was published 18 months after it had initiated its study.

The Hunt Commission report contains numerous recommendations in the areas of banking, financial institutions, and financial markets. In the area of banking, the Hunt Commission recommended required Federal Reserve membership for all insured banks, trading area branching for national banks irrespective of state law, removal of Regulation Q interest rate ceilings on time deposits in commercial banks (and removal of similar ceilings on deposits in other institutions), and tax equality between banks and saving and loan associations insofar as the federal corporate income tax is concerned.

The Hunt Commission recommendations in the area of financial institutions are quite complex. In general, the Hunt Commission proposed a broadening of investment opportunities for savings and loan associations, mutual savings banks, and credit unions. According to the report, it would be desirable to permit these institutions to invest in a broad range of construction loans, consumer loans, housing credit, and real estate equity investments. Further, the Hunt Commission recommended that savings institutions be permitted to offer cash transfer services on a demand basis. This is akin to the negotiable order of withdrawal (NOW) deposits initiated by New England savings banks. Finally, the report recommended equality in reserve requirements on deposits between commercial banks and thrift institutions.

The above proposals were intended to inject a more competitive environment in the financial markets and a more stable operational base for financial intermediaries. Numerous questions logically follow concerning the efficacy of the Hunt proposals in these intended directions and the willingness of specialized financial institutions to embark on new and uncharted fields of activity.

The Hunt Commission was very much concerned with financial market performance and stability. Instability in the housing credit market and a near liquidity crisis in the commercial paper market were immediate antecedents of the Hunt Commission. Recommendations of the commission were in part supported by the Board of Governors of the Federal Reserve System. These included removal of interest ceilings on Federal Housing Administration (FHA) insured and Veterans Administration (VA) guaranteed mortgages, removal of state usury limits on mortgage interest rates, and variable mortgage interest rates.

There exists some doubt concerning to what extent the Hunt Commission proposals would serve to stabilize mortgage lending. Flows of funds to thrift institutions and other lenders in the mortgage credit field seem to be a behavioral as well as structural aspect of the highly developed U.S. capital market. Widening the base of investment alternatives open to savings intermediaries, another Hunt Commission proposal, might further expose the mortgage credit market to abrupt shifts in the direction of flows of funds.

A final set of recommendations of the Hunt Commission concerns federal regulation. The recommendations include centralization of the insurance of deposit and savings accounts in a single agency, centralized federal supervisory powers over state banks, removal of the comptroller of the currency from the Treasury Department and extension of additional powers over banks, and a realigned jurisdiction over savings and loan associations.

Clearly, the Hunt Commission recommendations are far too numerous and multifaceted to comment on in detail. However, several broad observations are in order. First, the Hunt Commission report was far more cautious than the 10-year-earlier report of the CMC. The Hunt Commission appears to have been far more concerned with formulating politically acceptable proposals rather than publishing in-depth studies of financial institution performance. The commission published no research papers, only its own lengthy summary report. Whether any significant part of the Hunt Commission proposals will ever be embodied in congressional legislation remains to be seen.

The experience garnered from a review of the Hunt Commission report and the reaction to it in the two years since its publication do make it possible to comment on one important gap in the financial institution and financial market development of the United States, that is, the urgent need for a periodic review of the U.S. financial system. The Canadian government undertakes such a review every decade. The United States apparently does so only in moments of desperation.

REFERENCES

Commission on Money and Credit. Money and Credit: Their Influence on Jobs, Prices and Growth. Englewood Cliffs, N.J.: Prentice-Hall, 1961.

Dougall, E. Herbert. Capital Markets and Institutions. Englewood Cliffs, N.J.: Prentice-Hall, 1970.

Robinson, I. Roland. "The Hunt Commission Report: A Search for Politically Feasible Solutions to the Problems of Financial Structure." The Journal of Finance (September 1972).

The Report of the President's Commission on Financial Structure and Regulation. Washington, D.C.: Superintendent of Documents, December 1971.

6

**THE U.S.
MONEY MARKET**

The money market plays a vital role in the financially oriented and highly competitive U.S. economy. By and large it is an impersonal market for short-term credits in which top-quality borrowers can obtain funds. In addition, it may be regarded as a pool of liquid assets in which ownership claims are exchanged and liquidity positions of participants are readily adjusted. In size comparisons, the U.S. money market dwarfs all other national markets with the exception of the London market, and even there retains a significant edge.

DEVELOPMENT AND STRUCTURE

Development and Major Participants

The money market was slow to develop in the United States and not until after World War I did it begin to assume any significant international status, then largely due to the strength of the dollar in the foreign exchange markets. During the halcyon days of the 1920s, the New York money market specialized heavily in call loans to Wall Street brokerage houses, but this came to a halt in 1929. The banker's acceptance market made fairly good progress in the 1920s, but the series of banking and currency crises that came in the late 1920s adversely affected the New York bill market.

Prior to World War II, the U.S. Treasury bill market was far behind London in its development. However, wartime finance, post-war fiscal policy, and an active open-market role by the Federal Reserve helped to foster the expansion of the Treasury bill market. The market for short-term U.S. Treasury securities became the core of the U.S. money market and assisted materially in unifying yields and prices in widely dispersed regional components of the money market.

During the postwar period, new components of the market made their appearance and developed into integral aspects of money market operations. These include the market in federal funds and the market in negotiable certificates of deposit (CDs).

The development and expansion of the U.S. money market have been associated with growth or relative decline in each of the credit sectors in the market. Similarly, its development can be associated with the changing importance of major participants. At the turn of the century, private bankers played a major role in the market. During the 1920s Wall Street brokerage houses represented a significant part of the demand for money market credit. During World War II, the U.S. government absorbed the bulk of money market credit. More recently major corporations play a dominant role on the demand as well as supply sides of the market. Since the banking reforms of the 1930s, the Federal Reserve has become a dominant factor on the supply side. In the 1960s foreign participants have become a crucial element and, in certain time periods, exert a determining pressure. Given all of these shifting tendencies, the commercial banks sit astride the market and are in a pivotal position to influence the trend as well as transmit pressures throughout the market.

A central conditioning factor is the U.S. money market is the liquidity status of commercial banks. Changes in bank reserves and the various factors that influence commercial bank liquidity are important since the banks occupy a prominent position in all sectors of the money market. Banks increase or diminish their holdings of marketable short-dated U.S. Treasury securities to adjust their reserve and liquidity positions conveniently and at low transactions cost.

Federal Reserve control over the total amount of bank reserves via open-market operations provides the Fed with an effective control over the tone of the market, as well as on the cost and availability of credit. The objective of such control is to stabilize the economy by using the money market and bank reserves as a means of regulating the ability of the banking system to add to the flow of credit in the economic system. Open-market purchases of U.S. government securities tend to add to bank reserves, while open-market sales have the opposite effect.

The amount of bank reserves is affected by a number of factors (Table 6.1). Factors that supply reserves include Reserve Bank Credit, that is, Federal Reserve holdings of government securities, loans (advances) to member banks of the Federal Reserve System, the float related to check-clearing operations, and changes in other Federal Reserve assets. Fed holdings of government securities are

TABLE 6.1

Member Bank Reserves and Federal Reserve Credit, June 1973
(millions of dollars)

Factors Supplying Reserve Funds

Reserve bank credit outstanding		$80,541
U.S. government securities held by Federal Reserve	$75,355	
Loans to member banks	1,788	
Float	2,364	
Other Federal Reserve assets	943	
Gold stock		10,410
Special drawing rights certificate account		400
Treasury currency outstanding		8,518
Total factors supplying reserve funds		99,869

Factors Absorbing Reserve Funds

Currency in circulation		$67,609
Treasury cash holdings		386
Deposits other than member bank reserves with Federal Reserve Banks		3,372
Treasury	$2,408	
Foreign	266	
Other	698	
Other Federal Reserve liabilities and capital		2,732
Member bank reserves on deposit with Federal Reserve Banks		25,770
Total factors absorbing reserve funds		99,869

Note: At this date member bank reserves included an additional $6,085 million in vault cash held by banks. This brought total bank reserves to $32,021 million.

Source: Federal Reserve Bulletin.

affected by open-market operations and the policy considerations that underlie their management. Fed advances to member banks provide an escape valve for banks at times when their reserve positions are becoming tight. Other factors supplying reserve funds include the gold stock, special drawing rights (SDR), and Treasury currency outstanding. At midyear 1973 the factors supplying reserves exceeded $99.8 billion.

Factors absorbing bank reserves include currency in circulation (in the hands of the nonbank public), Treasury cash holdings, deposits at the Fed other than those of member banks, and other liabilities and capital of the Federal Reserve.

Federal Reserve policy must accomplish two objectives insofar as regulation of bank reserves is concerned. First, open-market operations must offset the effects from random fluctuations in the factors that supply and absorb reserve funds. Second, open-market operations must add to or subtract from bank reserves according to the economic stabilization needs of the economy. These two aspects of open-market operations are referred to as the defensive and offensive aims of open-market operations. This means that during inflationary periods, bank reserve growth may be reduced to a zero rate, while during a recession, bank reserves may be permitted to grow at a relatively high rate.

Money Market Credit

In 1973 the amount of credit outstanding in the U.S. money market was approximately $250 billion. This includes a variety of types of credit relationships and uses, ranging from U.S. government securities and CDs to loans to Wall Street investment houses. The dominant segment of the money market is in the form of credit made available to the U.S. Treasury. The volume of U.S. Treasury bills outstanding in 1973 was over $102 billion (Table 6.2). These short-dated government securities constitute the core of the market and effectively permit an instantaneous transmission of money market pressures to all parts of the nation.

U.S. Treasury bills are issued on an auction basis, with three- and six-month bills offered weekly and one-year bills offered at monthly auction. Two kinds of bids may be submitted, namely, competitive and noncompetitive. In the case of competitive bids, large investors tender for substantial amounts (in excess of $200,000) and state the price (discount from face value) they are willing to pay. Awards are made on the basis of the prices bid by prospective buyers up to a cutoff point, and noncompetitive bidders are allotted amounts on the basis of the average price paid under competitive bidding.

TABLE 6.2

Size Comparisons of U.S. Money Market
(billions of dollars)

Money Market Credit	1969	1971	1973[a]
U.S. Treasury bills	$80.6	$97.5	$102.9
Commercial paper	32.6	32.1	35.7
Banker's acceptances	5.5	7.9	6.9
Federal funds purchased[b]	15.8	26.0	36.5
Negotiable certificates of deposit	11.3	33.9	59.7
Bank loans to brokers and dealers	5.6	6.2	6.9
Total	$151.4	$203.6	$248.6
Short-term liabilities to foreigners reported by U.S. banks	$40.2	$55.4	$66.7
Ratio of short-term liabilities to foreigners to total money market credit	26.7%	27.2%	26.9%

[a]Data for early years are at year end. Data for 1973 are as of May.
[b]Includes securities sold under repurchase agreements.

Source: Federal Reserve Bulletin.

Normally tenders are invited on Thursdays and accepted until the following Monday. The Federal Reserve Banks act as agents for the Treasury and accept bids and pass them on to the Treasury.

The secondary market for U.S. government and federal agency securities is the market in which nearly all Federal Reserve open-market operations are carried out. This market includes close to $265 billion in obligations ranging in maturity from Treasury bills at very short maturity to bonds that are repayable at the end of the twentieth century. The volume of transactions in the short-maturity U.S. government securities (less than one year) averages close to $3 billion per day. This is more than four-and-one-half times the average daily dollar volume of trading on the New York Stock Exchange in 1972. Secondary trading is carried on by approximately 10 dealer commercial banks and a dozen nonbank primary dealers. Nonbank dealers carry their inventory by pledging it as collateral for loans. In addition, the Federal Reserve supplies funds by entering into repurchase agreements with nonbank dealers. In undertaking a repurchase agreement on government securities, the Fed purchases short-term securities from a dealer, and the dealer agrees to repurchase the securities at the original price plus interest within a period of 15 days. Repurchase agreements are made at the initiative of the Federal Reserve and have the effect of adding to bank reserves for the length of time the agreement is outstanding.

All dealing in Treasury bills is through a network of private telephone lines which connects the dealers, large banks, and the Federal Reserve Bank of New York. Treasury bills represent a virtually riskless and very liquid investment. They are favored as short-term investments by banks, financial institutions, large corporations, foreign banks and institutions, and individual investors. While commercial banks continue to be important investors in Treasury bills, the expansion of other money market sectors has made these institutions relatively less dependent on Treasury bills and other short-term governments as a means of reserve and liquidity adjustment. For example, in the business expansion from June 1972 to June 1973, large weekly reporting banks derived nearly two-thirds of their liquidity adjustment from sale of additional negotiable CDs, over one-fifth from federal funds and sale of securities under repurchase agreements, and only 6 percent from reduced holdings of short-term and medium-term U.S. government securities (Table 6.3).

The highly organized market in U.S. Treasury obligations, which includes the Treasury bill as its most active and liquid component, makes it possible for the Federal Reserve to carry out its open-market operations in a highly efficient and expeditious manner. It might be said that there is a unique symbiotic relationship between the two in that open-market operations of the Federal Reserve tend to preserve the stability of the money market insofar as erratic pressures are concerned, but that such open-market operations could not be as flexible and sophisticated without this relatively stable and efficiently organized money market sector.

The commercial paper market is the third largest sector in the U.S. money market and the oldest component. The commercial paper market is peculiar to the North American continent, there being no similar money market sector in other countries. Commercial paper is issued directly to investors or to specialist dealers by large corporations whose name and prestige permit borrowing in this form at relatively low interest cost. Since commercial paper is eligible for rediscount by the Federal Reserve, commercial banks have played

81

TABLE 6.3

Reserve and Liquidity Adjustment by Large Weekly Reporting Banks, June 1972 to June 1973

	Billions of Dollars	Percent of Total
Decline in holdings of short-term and medium-term U.S. government securities	$2.2	6.1
Decline in loans to brokers and dealers	1.3	3.6
Increase in large negotiable CDs outstanding	23.7	65.8
Change in level of advances from Federal Reserve Banks	0.7	1.9
Change in federal funds purchased and securities sold under repurchase agreements	8.1	22.4
Change in borrowings from foreign branches	0.1	0.3
Totals	$36.1	100.0

Source: Federal Reserve Bulletin.

an important role as purchasers of these short-term obligations. Three distinguishable types of commercial paper are issued in the United States, namely, finance paper, industrial paper, and paper issued by bank affiliates. The latter type appeared in the tight money period of the 1960s when bank holding companies found it convenient to issue their own commercial paper to obtain funds which could be advanced to their bank affiliates.

Commercial paper is in the form of promissory notes, sold at a discount from redemption value, with maturities that range from several days to six months. Maturities issued directly to lenders can be tailored to satisfy their specific requirements. Discounts depend on the general availability of funds in the market and sensitively respond to changing pressures in all sectors of the money market.

Several factors enter into the use of commercial paper by large corporations as a means of financing their operations. First, commercial paper rates must be compared with prime rates charged by

banks on business loans. In this case, several adjustments must be
made in comparing these interest rates, in connection with compensating deposit balances required by banks of their corporate customers
and in connection with the fact that the discount on commercial paper
is deducted in advance. Also, banks that provide open lines of credit
to business borrowers that have commercial paper outstanding generally charge a small commission, and if the credit line is guaranteed
by the bank, the commission might range between $\frac{1}{4}$ and $\frac{1}{2}$ percent
per annum. During periods of business slack, the differential between
commercial paper rates and prime lending rates at banks widens,
causing a rundown in bank loans to large business firms, increased
bank investments in short-term money market assets (including commercial paper), and further declines in commercial paper rates. Considerations of prestige also tend to enter into decisions by corporations
to make use of commercial paper financing. Certainly, only firms of
very high credit standing can issue their own commercial paper.

While considerably smaller than the commercial paper market,
the market for banker's acceptances is important in terms of the international role of the U.S. money market. The U.S. market in banker's
acceptances is the equivalent to the London bill market. The market
has derived its status from the Federal Reserve Act, which authorizes
national banks to create their own acceptance liabilities. The Federal
Reserve authorities have actively encouraged expansion to this market
to strengthen New York's status as an international financial center.
As of the early 1970s the amount of acceptance credit made available
in the U.S. money market has been more than double the amount available in sterling acceptances. In part, this is the outcome of use of
dollar acceptance credits to finance foreign trade, whereas in Britain
acceptance credit is used in large part to finance domestic trade.

The market in banker's acceptances consists of some 200 U.S.
banks which originate acceptances, a half dozen specialized dealers,
and the Federal Reserve which is empowered to discount acceptances
of member banks. Accepting banks may retain bills in their own
portfolios or swap them through a dealer for bills accepted by other
banks. Swapping adds a third signature, which enhances the status
of the bill for collateral, sale, or discount at the Federal Reserve.
Accepting banks, foreign banks, and central banks constitute the bulk
of demand for acceptances. Their yield is somewhat higher than that
available on Treasury bills and is not subject to withholding tax.
Maturities range from 30 to 180 days. The cost of acceptance credits
may be lower than on bank credits, especially where compensating
balance requirements tie funds up and rates are at relatively high
levels. A firm with a high credit standing generally may expect to
borrow on the commercial paper market at lower cost than through
obtaining acceptance credits.

The market in federal funds is the most important money market sector in the United States insofar as overnight adjustment of bank liquidity is concerned. Federal funds, sight deposits with the Federal Reserve Banks, have the advantage of being available for immediate (same day) settlement as well as instant transfer across the nation via the Federal Reserve wire system.

Originally the market in federal funds developed in connection with the reserve requirements imposed upon bank deposits and the opportunities for member banks of the Federal Reserve to lend their excess reserves to banks with inadequate reserves. During the 1920s the federal funds market took second place to the call money or brokers loan market. In this period large banks adjusted their reserve positions by increasing or reducing their call money loans to Wall Street broker-age houses. The federal funds market began to prosper during World War II in connection with a growing volume of transactions in U.S. government securities. Expansion of the market in the 1960s has made it possible for banks in the western half of the United States to be able to meet their reserve requirements after the New York money market has closed.

As indicated in Table 6.3, over the period June 1972 to June 1973, over one-fifth of bank reserve adjustment took the form of federal funds and related transactions. The importance of federal funds as a means of reserve and liquidity adjustment for commercial banks can be explained in terms of the convenience of interbank transactions within a highly developed system of correspondent banking, the oppor-tunities afforded to large money center banks to arbitrage and deal two ways in the market, the availability to selling banks of high-grade liquid assets which offer attractive yields, and the opportunities for buying banks to expand the amount of credit made available to cus-tomers.

Participants in the market include commercial banks, financial institutions, government agencies, business corporations, foreign banks, and governmental units. Close to three-fourths of transactions are among commercial banks. Brokers dealing in government securi-ties regularly demand federal funds since asquisition of such securi-ties usually is settled in this form of payment. Often repurchase agreements are used to finance inventories of government securities whereby lenders purchase securities from a dealer and sell them to him for a fixed price, delivery taking place one day later.

Federal Reserve Board changes in bank reserve requirements affect the total amount of excess reserves and thereby the volume of federal funds available to enter the market. Member bank borrowing from the Federal Reserve Banks also affects the volume of federal funds. Finally, open-market operations permit the Fed to mop up or increase the volume of federal funds in the market.

While one of the newest sectors in the U.S. money market, the market in negotiable CDs has become the second largest. It is a complex market based upon close competition with alternative sources and uses of funds, regulatory limitations, and structure of the market itself. This market only became important in 1961, largely as a result of the efforts of large American banks to stimulate deposit growth and retain their relative importance in the financial markets. A major factor in the market has been the Regulation Q ceilings on interest rates payable on such deposits, which were removed by the Board of Governors of the Federal Reserve System in 1973.

The primary market in CDs consists mainly of several dozen banks of the highest standing which can issue CDs at the prevailing standard rates. Other banks have to pay somewhat higher rates, depending upon their size and status in the market. All issuing banks must be of a high credit standing. Major investors in CDs include large corporations. At times banks, financial institutions, and central banks also hold substantial amounts of CDs, depending upon their liquidity position and relative yield considerations.

In the primary market, CDs are not issued for maturities of less than 30 days. Maturities of under 30 days are available in secondary trading. Secondary market transactions usually are settled in federal funds. Issuing banks have played an active role in developing a strong secondary market in CDs, thus assuring investors of market liquidity should there be unforeseen changes in their cash position. While the secondary market is largely confined to New York, a network of private telephone lines links other financial centers in the United States. CD dealers are able to borrow against the security of their holdings at rates slightly below prime rates. Usually the rates charged by banks on loans secured by CDs are higher than on loans secured by Treasury bills or other government securities.

Until the 1930s the call money or broker loan market was one of the most important sectors in the U.S money market. However, rapid growth of other market sectors in the past several decades has relegated this market sector to secondary importance. Call loans are based on general agreements among banks and securities dealers and brokers, whereby eligible securities are pledged as collateral. The rates banks charge very from day to day. Beginning in the 1930s the Federal Reserve was authorized to vary margin limits on loans made by banks to finance the purchase or holding of securities. Generally these margin requirements are sufficiently high to discourage large-scale speculative transactions in securities.

At present the call money market plays an important role in financing dealers in government securities. The dealer holding an inventory of government securities transfers them to the call money lender, who holds them until the loan is extinguished. At year end

1972, borrowing by U.S. government securities dealers exceeded $4 billion. Corporations lend to government securities dealers on the basis of call loans, and they hold a significant share of such credits. New York banks also provide a large share of the funds entering the call money market. Close to half of funds going into call loans is derived from banks outside of New York, which lend through New York banks on a commission basis.

An alternative to call financing of dealer positions in U.S. government securities is the repurchase agreement. Here the dealer sells government securities to the lending bank and agrees to repurchase them at an agreed price plus interest. Corporations and banks lend on this basis. The Federal Reserve Bank of New York engages in repurchase agreements with nonbank dealers with a yield cost at or very close to the discount rate. Federal Reserve operations through repurchase agreements tend to influence interest rates to much less extent than open-market operations.

INTERNATIONAL STATUS OF U.S. MONEY MARKET

International Role

The international status of the U.S. money market rests on the wide variety of facilities and services available and on the efficiency at which these facilities and services function for international clientele. The massive size of the U.S. money market is important in this respect.

The international functions performed in the U.S. money market include the following:
1. The money market facilitates short-term deposit and investment of liquid foreign funds.
2. The credit markets provide numerous financing alternatives for borrowers, resident and nonresident.
3. The financial markets in the United States provide clearing and money transfer services for business firms, banks, investors, and financial institutions.
4. The foreign exchange market permits low-cost hedging through spot and forward markets in leading currencies and by means of various other types of future contracts and options.

It is possible to obtain some insight into the scope and importance of the U.S. money market for nonresident users by examining the following data. In the relatively short period from December 1969 to June 1973, short-term liabilities to foreigners reported by U.S. banks increased from $40.2 billion to $66.9 billion. At midyear 1973 foreigners were reported to have held over $14 billion in deposits in U.S. banks, nearly $36 billion in U.S. Treasury bills, and over $16 billion in other short-dated money market assets. In the following section we examine the nature of such asset-holding preferences by category of foreign holder.

Size of Nonresident Holdings

The international orientation of the U.S. money market results in competition with other financial centers and markets. The U.S. market is the largest in the world and holds a major share of international funds. In 1973 U.S. liquid liabilities to foreigners exceeded $92 billion (Table 6.4). The only other international money market that operates at this scale is the Eurocurrency market. However, the Eurocurrency market operates very differently from the U.S. money market in a number of ways. First, the Eurocurrency market is a multicurrency market, whereas the U.S. market operates only in dollars. Second, the U.S. market affords a wide diversity of asset- and liability-type credits, while the Eurocurrency does not. Finally, the Eurocurrency market represents a greater degree of pyramid credit relationships into which funds must come from national money markets. By contrast, the availability of credit in the U.S. money market is very much less dependent on external conditions and more a function of the needs and requirements of the domestic economy.

In 1973 over 77 percent of the liquid liabilities to foreigners were due to official institutions. At the same time, 16 percent of U.S. liquid liabilities to foreigners were due to commercial banks abroad, and 6 percent to other foreigners (including foreign corporations, financial institutions, and individuals). Close to 2 percent of liquid liabilities were due to international organizations. The factors that influence foreign banks, governments, corporations, and central banks to hold various types of liquid dollar assets differ from one group to another.

The largest part of U.S. liquid liabilities to foreigners represents the international reserves of official institutions. It is only since 1969 that dollar holdings of official institutions have come to dominate the structure of U.S. liquid liabilities to foreigners. At year end 1970 and 1969, U.S. liquid liabilities to official institutions represented one-half and one-third, respectively, of total U.S. liquid liabilities. In short, foreign central banks and governments have continued to support the dollar on the foreign exchange markets. Moreover, they have sought to stabilize the international monetary situation at a time when wholesale speculation has been taking place against the dollar and the international monetary system. As a result, foreign

TABLE 6.4

U.S. Liquid and Other Liabilities to Foreign Official
Institutions and Liquid Liabilities to
Foreigners, June 1973
(billions of dollars)

Liabilities to official institutions		$70.8
Deposits in U.S. banks	$ 4.6	
U.S. Treasury bills	35.7	
Money market paper	5.4	
Marketable U.S. Treasury bonds and notes	6.9	
Nonmarketable U.S. Treasury bonds and notes	15.9	
Other marketable liabilities	2.0	
Commercial banks abroad		14.3
Deposits in U.S. banks	5.2	
Money market paper and CDs	8.7	
Other foreigners		5.1
Deposits in U.S. banks	4.0	
U.S. Treasury bills	0.1	
Money market paper and CDs	0.7	
International and regional organizations		1.8
Deposits in U.S. banks	0.3	
U.S. Treasury bills	0.2	
Money market paper and CDs	1.2	
Total liquid and other liabilities to foreigners		$92.0

Source: Federal Reserve Bulletin.

governments and central banks have acquired sizable dollar assets through regular intervention operations on their own foreign exchange markets.

In addition to the substantial expansion in official holdings of dollar assets through intervention operations, foreign central banks require operating balances to sell dollar balances to their own commercial banks, to intervene in the New York foreign exchange market, to provide dollar exchange for repayment of maturing debt obligations, and to service interest and dividend payments on outstanding loans and foreign investments. Central banks often place deposits with U.S. banks in connection with loan agreements made with private banks in the same country. While it is not possible to estimate the volume of liquid dollar holdings that official institutions would need for these regular foreign exchange operations, the amount must be substantial. The extent to which the New York money market is oriented toward servicing international needs can be seen in better perspective if we compare certain figures in Tables 6.3 and 6.4. In 1973 foreign official institutions held over $35 billion in U.S. Treasury bills, representing almost 35 percent of total bills outstanding. In addition, foreign holdings of money market paper and CDs represented over 10 percent of the total amount outstanding.

Foreign commercial banks hold sizable amounts of dollars to service day-to-day operations. This includes foreign exchange trading, compensating balances, cover for letter of credit transactions, and settlement of foreign trade transactions. We should note that the data in Table 6.4 exclude the money market investments of the branches and agencies of foreign banks located in the United States. At year end 1972 close to 80 foreign banks operated agencies, branches, and subsidiaries in the United States, with total assets in excess of $20 billion. A large proportion of these assets is in the form of money market investments. In many cases, commercial banks abroad lack local money market facilities and use the facilities of the U.S. market to employ liquid funds.

Other foreigners include a wide assortment of securities dealers, financial institutions, industrial corporations, and individuals. Part of the liquid liabilities to foreigners represents safe-haven funds held by individuals who wish to keep their assets beyond the reach of exchange control and tax revenue authorities. A significant part of these liquid liabilities accrues to affiliates of multinational corporations that do not wish to repatriate profits to their parent companies. Finally, foreign insurance companies must hold dollar assets that relate to the reserves of policies written in the United States.

Asset Preferences of Foreigners

The asset preferences of foreign holders of liquid dollars vary considerably. For example, official institutions hold approximately half of their dollar assets in the form of U.S. Treasury bills, 30 percent in other marketable and nonmarketable U.S. Treasury obligations, and close to 7 percent in deposits in U.S. banks. By contrast, foreign commercial banks and other foreigners hold practically no U.S. government securities. A high proportion of foreign commercial bank dollar assets is in the form of deposits in U.S. banks (37 percent), money market paper, and CDs (60 percent). Other foreigners hold close to four-fifths of liquid dollars in the form of deposits in U.S. banks. International organizations hold only small amounts of Treasury bills and deposits in U.S. banks. Two-thirds of their liquid dollar holdings are in the form of money market paper and CDs.

Treasury securities have proven to be attractive investments for foreign central banks and governments due to the exemption from the U.S. withholding tax of interest income derived by foreign central banks from this source. In addition, the U.S. Treasury has issued special nonmarketable obligations to foreign governments and monetary authorities at special rates of interest. Also, foreign official institutions have acquired liquid dollars in the form of U.S. Treasury certificates of indebtedness, resulting from reciprocal currency operations between the Federal Reserve and other central banks. Finally, beginning in 1963 the Treasury began issuing foreign-currency-denominated securities.

Foreign commercial banks hold substantial deposits in U.S. banks in connection with their dollar exchange requirements. At midyear 1973, over 90 percent of the $5.1 billion of deposits of foreign commercial banks were in demand deposits, suggesting that the basic motive for such asset holdings is to provide a working supply of foreign exchange to meet day-to-day operating requirements. Foreign banks place "sight deposits" with their U.S. agencies for investment in dollar-denominated assets. In turn, the agencies (Canadian and Japanese banks are important in this respect) invest these funds in call money loans to securities brokers and dealers, commercial paper, banker's acceptances, and negotiable CDs.

Foreign holdings of time deposits in U.S. banks were $5.6 billion at mid-1973. The total amount of time deposits held by residents of foreign countries has been quite stable over the past several years at least. This suggests that a major part of these dollar holdings of nonresidents is held without consideration of yields available on alternative money market investments. Monthly figures since 1969 indicate little fluctuation in the time deposit holdings of official institutions. Possible reasons for this include the desire to maintain open credit lines at U.S. banks and the need to preserve letter of credit financing facilities. Doubtless some foreign commercial banks have maintained time deposit balances in U.S. banks with a view toward retaining and developing reciprocal banking business. Another factor that has been important in permitting U.S. banks to retain the time deposits of foreign official institutions is a 1962 amendment to the Federal Reserve Act, exempting such deposits from the interest rate regulation administered by the Board of Governors under Regulation Q.

EMERGING FORCES IN THE MONEY MARKET

Several important trends, which are likely to influence the functioning and status of the U.S. money market, especially in connection with its international role, are evident. First, we must note that the major participants in the money market are becoming increasingly more internationally oriented. The large industrial corporations are going more and more multinational, and the money market banks as a group have experienced a sharp upward shift in the proportion of their business that is international.

A second factor is the closer integration of New York with international money management functions. U.S. banks with offshore branches operate the so-called Eurodollar desks and Eurocurrency asset portfolios from New York. Moreover, there is a tendency for New York lending institutions to participate in international loan syndicates, whether the credits be of short, intermediate, or long term.

Third, geographic linkages throughout the United States are increasing, so that it is now possible for regional financial subcenters to develop. Closely linked with this is the spread of out-of-state banking offices of U.S. banks. These may assume the form of representative offices or of Edge Act international banking affiliates located in such cities as Boston, Chicago, San Francisco, New Orleans, Miami, and Houston.

Finally, foreign banks have been moving into the United States in significant numbers, further tending to internationalize the money market and banking centers of the U.S. financial markets. In part, the in-migration of foreign banks can be associated with the inward flow of foreign business investment. All of these changes suggest further development and modification in the international role of the U.S. money market.

REFERENCES

Dougall, Herbert E. Capital Markets and Institutions. Englewood Cliffs, N.J.: Prentice-Hall, 1970.

Klopstock, Fred. "Foreing Banks in the United States: Scope and Growth of Operations." Monthly Review, Federal Reserve Bank of New York, June 1973.

Meek, Paul. Open Market Operations, Federal Reserve Bank of New York, May 1973.

Lees, Francis A. "International Banking and Finance" London: Macmillan, Ltd., 1974.

7

CAPITAL MARKETS IN
THE UNITED STATES

ROLE AND FUNCTION

In the strictest sense, capital refers to capital goods used in production of goods and services. Capital formation is the growth in this stock of productive capital and is intimately associated with the process of national income generation. Gross capital formation by the private sector of the economy represents the investment or expenditure for capital goods and additions to business inventories. If we subtract capital consumption allowances (depreciation) from gross investment, we arrive at net private capital formation, which represents the addition to the stock of capital goods (Table 7.1). Gross capital formation must be financed primarily in the capital market. Therefore, we focus our attention on that figure and its relationship to gross national product (GNP) in our evaluation of the performance of the U.S. capital market in facilitating economic expansion.

General Character of the U.S. Capital Market

The capital market is a group of interconnected markets in which dollar instruments, debt or equity, representing claims on productive capital, are traded. While much attention focuses on new issues of securities in the capital market, secondary trading in outstanding securities tends to represent a more important part of the total volume of transactions. This can be seen from data in Table 7.2, where on an overall basis the ratio of new issues to secondary trading in the five major capital market sectors was 32 percent.

A second important characteristic of the U.S. capital market is the relatively high degree of liquidity, in part reflected in the ratio

TABLE 7.1

Gross Private Capital Formation
(billions of dollars)

	1950	1960	1970	1972
Producer's durable equipment	18.7	30.3	64.9	78.2
New construction (nonresident)	9.2	18.1	36.0	42.2
Residential structures	19.4	22.8	31.2	53.9
Change in business inventories	6.8	3.6	4.9	5.8
Gross capital formation	54.1	74.8	137.1	180.2
Capital consumption allow- ances*	8.8	24.9	55.2	67.7
Net capital formation	45.3	49.9	81.9	112.5
Gross national product	284.8	503.7	976.4	1152.1
Ratio of gross capital forma- tion to GNP	15.9%	9.9%	8.5%	9.8%

*Refers to corporate business only.

Sources: Survey of Current Business and Economic Report of the President.

of total volume in the market to total outstandings. Efficient organization of the stock exchanges and securities market trading facilities contributes in no small way to the liquidity and opportunities for high volume of turnover on the capital market.

A third feature of the U.S. capital market is the high proportion of intermediated flows of new funds. This reflects the proportion of private nongovernmental credit market funds advanced by private financial institutions. In the years 1966-72, this proportion fluctuated between a low of 67 percent and a high of 100 percent. The low years (1966 and 1969) reflect conditions of tight money and a tendency toward disintermediation, wherein private investors undertook a larger scale of direct lending in the credit markets as against committing funds to financial intermediaries. The years in which the proportion of credit market funds advanced by financial institutions was high reflect credit market ease, relatively low returns on direct lending in the credit markets, and stronger incentives to pass funds through financial intermediaries.

TABLE 7.2

Comparison of Capital Market Volume in New Issues and Secondary Trading
by Sector, 1972

Type of Issue	New Issues 1	Secondary Trading 2	Total Volume 3	Total Outstanding 4	Ratio of	
					New Issues Secondary Trading 5	Total Volume Total Outstanding 6
U.S. Government (marketable notes and bonds)	8	156	164	166	5%	99%
Corporate bonds and notes	27	30	57	363	90%	16%
Corporate stock	15	220	235	1,090	7	23
Mortgages	65	10	75	565	650	13
State and local government bonds	23	12	35	172	191	21
Total	138	428	561	2,356	32%	23%

Notes: Column 1 refers to gross issues. Column 2 includes authors' estimates of secondary trading due to lack of published data in these areas. Column 3 is obtained from summing Columns 1 and 2. Column 4 on total outstanding securities and debt instruments is calculated from flow-of-funds data published by the Federal Reserve and recent estimates and projections of Bankers Trust Company Annual Investment Outlook. Column 5 refers to the ratio of new issues to secondary trading and is obtained by dividing Column 1 by Column 2. Column 6 is obtained by dividing Column 3 by Column 4.

Sources: Federal Reserve Bulletin; Treasury Bulletin; New York Stock Exchange, Fact Book; Bankers Trust Company, Annual Investment Outlook.

FUNCTIONS

According to Raymond W. Goldsmith in his classic study The Flow of Capital Funds in the Postwar Economy, there are two major functions of capital markets. First, they allocate current saving among alternative users of loanable funds. The allocative efficiency of capital markets is an extremely important topic, and one that is leading development planners in many small nations to seek means for promoting the growth of competitively oriented financial institutions.

The second major function of capital markets is to facilitate the transfer of existing assets, tangible and intangible, among individual economic units. Here, we are more concerned with the operational efficiency of capital markets. We return to both aspects of capital market efficiency in the following sections of this chapter.

SIZE AND EFFICIENCY

Measures of Size

The U.S. capital market dwarfs all others in size. Selected data are presented in Table 7.2, which reflect the size of the market in terms of outstanding instruments. The figures on U.S. government debt exclude short-term Treasury bills and nonmarketable and guaranteed obligations. Corporate bonds and notes exclude debt under one year to maturity and bonds owned outside the United States. Corporate stock figures are approximate, include intercompany held shares, and fail to adequately reflect the stock of small and closely held companies.

In 1972 capital market instruments outstanding in the United States exceeded $2.3 trillion. At that time over 40 percent was comprised of corporate stock and over 20 percent in mortgages. In the period 1960-72, capital market instruments outstanding grew somewhat more rapidly than GNP. The fastest growing types of instruments in this period were corporate stock and mortgages. Much of the growth in corporate stock reflects price appreciation in that period rather than additional share issues.

Efficiency

The capital market brings together net savers and net borrowers permitting an exchange of purchasing power. In this process, resource allocation is influenced. Operation of the capital market widens the choices available to both savers and borrowers and may very well promote a larger volume of saving than would otherwise prevail without the investment alternatives afforded savers.

In the U.S. capital market, there exists substantial breadth, depth, and resiliency, due in part to the large trading volume. This is in sharp contrast with the European capital markets, where new issues volume plays a larger role relative to secondary trading. In short, the European markets are thinner, more susceptible to wider interest rate swings, and subject to greater securities price fluctuation.

These comparisons suggest that the U.S. capital market may enjoy certain advantages in terms of allocative efficiency, or the ability to channel long-term lendable funds to borrowing units that will employ these funds in capital goods investments that are economically more productive. It seems natural to expect that capital markets that are organized on a broader, more flexible basis will be better able to adjust their allocation of funds and resources according to changing final demands and relative productive efficiency.

Operational efficiency can be as important as allocative efficiency where the operation of capital markets is concerned. A useful measure of operational efficiency is the cost of floating debt and equity issues in the capital market. According to the Joint Economic Committee study, published in 1964, A Description and Analysis of Certain European Capital Markets, "the competitive efficiency of the process by which security issues are floated is possibly best indicated by the underwriting spread itself." Available data suggest very strongly that in this respect the U.S. capital market is perhaps the most efficient in the world. Data published jointly by the Investment Dealers Association (IDA) and Investment Bankers Association (IBA) indicate that in the late 1960s flotation costs on straight corporate debt issues averaged around 1.26 percent. On common stock and preferred stock issues, the flotation costs were 7.41 percent and 1.65 percent, respectively.

INVESTMENT BANKING, STOCK EXCHANGES,
AND SECURITIES TRADING

Investment Banking

In the narrow sense, investment banking refers to the underwriting and origination of new securities issues. In the broader meaning, investment banking includes all related aspects of new issues, secondary markets for securities, and investment management.

97

It is this more inclusive definition that we are using in this discussion.

Investment banking embraces four basic functions. The first, securities origination and underwriting, embraces a wide range of methods and techniques for successfully bringing new securities issues to market. These include very close working relationships with corporations, where the underwriter prepares and supports the financing from the exploratory stages to secondary market support, and somewhat looser relationships, whereby the underwriter undertakes only a standby underwriting, or a best-efforts distribution of securities not sold under a rights offering.

A second basic function is to provide facilities for secondary trading in existing securities. Stock exchange listing, over-the-counter trading, dealer organizations, and computer-linked branch systems of broker-dealer houses make up the greater part of these facilities in the United States. A strong dealer organization is as important to the successful operation of an over-the-counter market as a mechanically efficient quote system and clearing facility is to the success of a stock-exchange-type market.

A third function of investment banking is to provide opportunities for security substitution. In this case, a financial institution or securities firm issues claims against an investment portfolio. In the case of a mutual fund, the fund issues equity claims against itself. In the case of a pension fund, the beneficiary (ultimate retiree) receives a claim agsinst the portfolio in the form of an annuity contract.

Finally, investment banking includes the provision of investment management services. These may assume the form of informal advice and information provided by an account representative of a stock exchange member firm, formal account management and supervision services, management of a mutual fund investment portfolio, or some other form. Investment management services are available from the Wall Street community of broker-dealer firms, but also can be obtained from a variety of other sources.

Stock Exchanges and Securities Trading

The securities markets in the United States are regulated with a view toward assuring investors full and complete disclosure of investment information, a relatively competitive market system, and an absence of improper practices such as those that prevailed in the heydey of the 1920s. The Securities Act of 1933, known as the "truth in securities law," requires full disclosure in a required registration statement and prospectus. Moreover, it makes it unlawful to sell or offer securities in a public offering or distribution unless a registration statement has been filed with the Securities and Exchange Commission (SEC).

The Securities Exchange Act of 1934 was designed to assure maintenance of fair and equitable securities markets and to provide for regulation of the nation's securities exchanges. In addition to providing for regulation of brokers and dealers, periodic financial reporting by listed companies, and effective controls over proxy solicitation, the act contains numerous antimanipulative provisions and requires disclosure of insiders' trading in securities.

While effective federal regulation is necessary to assure fair, equitable, and competitive securities markets, such regulation cannot, in and of itself, guarantee a stable and efficient trading market mechanism. Stability and efficiency in the securities markets depend upon the strength of the dealer-broker organization, technical and structural aspects of market organization, level of transactions costs borne by investors, exposure of market to favorable competitive pressures, and many other factors.

Information on dealer-broker organization and its operational performance is provided by the New York Stock Exchange (NYSE). This information is useful in tentatively appraising the strength of dealer organization in the stock and bond markets, as well as in appraising other aspects of competition and performance in the securities markets.

At year end 1972, there were 558 NYSE member firms, representing a decline of 19 from the previous year and the lowest number since 1943. The work force employed by member firms similarly declined between 1971 and 1972. A great deal of consolidation has been imposed upon the exchange community, and the decline in work force and number of member firms reflects a need to rationalize operations and squeeze out unprofitable capital invested in inefficient and noncompetitive securities firms. At year end 1971, member firms had total assets of $22.8 billion and capital funds in excess of $3.6 billion, indicating a capital-to-assets ratio of just under 16 percent. In 1971 over 40 percent of member firm assets consisted of long positions in securities and commodities. We should note that between 1969 and 1971, member organizations of the NYSE had increased their investment in this asset category from $4.9 billion to $9.2 billion.

In the short period 1969-71, member firms' capital positions increased by approximately 10 percent, from $3.3 billion to $3.6 billion. In the same period, total assets and liabilities increased more rapidly, placing downward pressure on the capital-to-assets ratio. Apparently, member firms were caught between two opposing objectives: to support securities market prices via maintaining or increasing specialist positions in securities and inventories of over-the-counter securities and to strengthen the capital-to-assets ratios. The shrinkage in the dealer organization that has taken place in recent years poses real problems for stock exchange member firms and the securities industry.

Analysis of the sources of gross income of stock exchange member firms is important in any analysis of the structure of the dealer organization. In 1971 close to 55 percent of member firms' income came from security commissions, 14 percent from trading on own account, nearly 7 percent from interest on customers' debit balances, 15 percent from underwriting, and the remainder from a variety of other sources. The large share derived from security commissions leaves dealers and brokers sensitive to alterations in trading volume. Trading profits tend to move in the same direction as commissions, and we might conclude that over two-thirds of gross income depends on a rising and active stock market. One of the financial weaknesses of member firms continues to be overreliance on a source of income that itself is overexposed to downward market pressures and declining volume. It is hoped by many that mergers and consolidations in the industry will leave a residue of financially stronger and more income-diversified member firms.

Unresolved Issues

On the basis of international comparisons, the secondary market trading facilities in the United States score among the highest in the world in terms of efficiency, breadth and depth, low cost of transactions, and liquidity. Notwithstanding, in the past five years numerous problems and criticisms have emerged in connection with the efficiency and performance of the U.S. stock exchanges and securities trading facilities. These problems have focused on the growing role of institutional ownership and trading of corporate securities, a tendency for institutions to seek lower-cost off-board trading, a resulting narrowing of the on-board trading of many listed stocks, and increased pressure on the brokerage commission rate structure and specialist function on the NYSE and other exchanges.

Release of the SEC Institutional Investor Study Report in March 1971 focused attention on these and related issues. A basic theme of the SEC report is the need to develop a strong central market system, so that all investors should have ready access to this central market and that dealers and brokers will be free to competitively participate in the market. The report touched off a controversy that escalated with release in August 1971 of the Martin Report, titled The Securities Markets, a Report with Recommendations. The Martin Report had been commissioned by the NYSE and contained two recommendations that ran counter to the SEC report. The Martin proposals called for strengthening the existing specialist system and continuation of fixed minimum commission brokerage rates.

100

Martin proposed that there be an increase in the capital resources of stock exchange specialist firms that would better equip them to provide continuity and stability in the share issues they provide facilities in. Since publication of the Martin Report, controversy has focused on whether a regime of regulated noncompeting specialists can perform their function better than a regime of competitive specialists. Closely related to the controversy over the specialist function is the effective separation of specialists from third market transactions and block trading firms.

The Martin Report also called for maintenance of fixed brokerage commission rates. To accomplish this, the Martin Report urged that the national exchange system be given an exclusive franchise for trading, that stock exchange rules be made uniform, and that institutional membership on exchanges be prohibited. In effect, the Martin proposals would provide a single centralized marketplace. However, there is some question as to the ultimate effects on transactions costs and market efficiency. There exists strong opinion that relatively high fixed commissions and barriers to the NYSE marketplace provide a primary reason for diverting trading in listed stocks to the regional exchanges and the third market. Moreover, high fixed commissions provide a strong inducement for growing institutional interest in stock exchange membership.

A study by Friend and Blume published in the Journal of Finance (September 1973) concluded that flexible and competitive commission rates would not appreciably increase the concentration of economic power in the brokerage industry. Referring to a possible analogy between the market for U.S. government securities and the stock market, these authors point to the high(est) volume handled by the U.S. government bond market at probably the lowest transactions costs. Presumably, free entry of dealers has not impaired operational efficiency.

In 1972 the NYSE adjusted its brokerage commission rate schedule. At the present time, it would appear that lowering commission rates is a move in the right direction. However, it is too early to determine whether the stock exchanges will be able to adjust their commission rates at a pace that will slow down or reverse the shift in trading to the third market and regional exchanges and at the same time permit member firms to operate profitably.

FLOW OF FUNDS

Major Flow-of-Funds Patterns

Analysis of the flow-of-funds data for the United States reveals a number of important characteristics concerning the structure and operation of the capital market. First, there is a high ratio and substantial year-to-year variability in the ratio of funds intermediated through financial institutions. Only in years of extremely tight money (1966 and 1969 most recently) does the ratio of private financial intermediation dip below 80 percent, and in many years it exceeds the 90-percent mark.

Second, the nonbank financial intermediaries have come to play a much more important role than commercial bank intermediaries in the total flow of funds. In recent years nonbank intermediaries have accounted for approximately 60 percent of credit market funds advanced by private financial institutions as compared with the commercial banks, which account for the remaining 40 percent of funds passing through all financial institutions.

Third, the government plays a dual role in the capital market. The federal government exhibits a high degree of variability in the extent to which it absorbs funds in the credit markets on a net basis. This is influenced by alterations in business conditions, which have a significant impact on the overall federal budget position and fiscal policy consciously directed at achieving larger or smaller budgetary deficits with a view toward achieving fiscally induced restraint or stimulus. By contrast, state and local governments are steady borrowers in the capital market.

Fourth, capital consumption allowances have come to represent a large part of capital outlays for the household and business sectors. In recent years, capital consumption in the business and household sectors has represented two-thirds of business capital outlays and three-fourths of household capital outlays. The significance of a high ratio of capital consumption to capital outlays is in connection with opportunities afforded individual economic units in the business sector to self-finance out of depreciation-generated cash flows. Also, a high rate of capital consumption is important in connection with tendencies toward a more stable pattern of (replacement) investment expenditure, which has a feedback effect into the capital market.

Finally, we should note that nonfinancial business tends to exhibit a dominant role as an end-user of funds. In the period 1968-71, the nonfinancial business sector absorbed close to half of funds raised by all sectors excluding the federal government. Inclusion of federal government borrowing lowers the business sector's absorption of funds to approximately 45 percent of the total.

Principal Market Sectors

It is possible to identify six principal capital market borrowing sectors in the data pertaining to flow of funds through the U.S. credit markets. Five of these sectors are analyzed in this section. Discussion of the sixth sector, foreign, is reserved for a later part of this chapter.

Market for U.S. Government Securities and Federal Agencies

The market for U.S. government securities is important for several reasons. It represents an important transmission mechanism through which changes in demand and supply conditions in any one sector of the capital and money markets may be diffused across all other sectors. Changes in ownership of outstanding U.S. government securities represent an important portfolio balance adjustment mechanism. A high degree of organization in the market, through the 20 or more primary dealers in U.S. governments, secondary dealers, and bank and institutional ownership, lends a high measure of liquidity and stability to the market. Yields available on various maturities of marketable U.S. government securities afford a benchmark against which investors, borrowers, and underwriters may base their own activities and investment decisions.

The market for U.S. government securities is closely related to the implementation of monetary policy, and Federal Reserve System open-market operations in U.S. government securities are channeled through this market. Finally, fiscal operations of the federal government and fiscal policy are closely related to changing conditions in the market for U.S. government securities.

At year end 1972, the direct and guaranteed debt of the federal government was over $447 billion (Table 7.3). Over the two decades, 1962-72 the total debt has grown far more slowly than GNP. Compositional changes include a relative decline in nonmarketable debt, no growth in savings bonds outstanding, a substantial relative growth in marketable debt, and a shift toward shorter maturity marketable securities (Treasury bills and shorter maturity notes and bonds). The shifting composition of federal debt can have important effects on yields. Rapid growth in marketable issues can place upward pressure on open-market rates of interest. A shift toward a shorter maturity structure can tend to make the yield curve more downward sloping, or less upward sloping. In turn, these charges can have feedback effects on the maneuverability of the U.S. Treasury in subsequent financing and refunding operations. In this connection, mention should be made of the statutory $4\frac{1}{4}$ percent coupon interest ceiling on marketable U.S. Treasury bonds. This interest ceiling has reduced the flexibility of the Treasury in its debt-refunding operations, which constitute an ever-present operation (close to $160 billion of Treasury securities must be refunded annually). Congress has provided some flexibility in permitting the Treasury to issue up to $10 billion in Treasury bonds with coupons in excess of the statutory limit.

Yields on U.S. government securities are generally the lowest in the capital and money markets, due to the absence of credit risk. In periods of easy money, an upward sloping yield relationship prevails in marketable securities, with the highest yields available on longer-term marketable bonds. During periods of tight money, the yield relationships change, and shorter-term marketable securities offer investors the highest yields.

Treasury offerings of securities are tailored to permit refunding of maturing issues, to cover budgetary deficits, and to provide a satisfactory cash balance. The net changes in outstanding debt are only loosely correlated with Treasury budget surpluses and deficits due to the substantial intragovernmental cash transactions (including trust funds) and fluctuations in Treasury cash balances.

TABLE 7.3

Gross Public Debt, by Type of Security,
1950-72
(billions of dollars)

	1950	1960	1970	1972
Marketable securities				
Bills	13.6	22.3	87.9	103.9
Certificates	5.4	15.7	—	—
Notes	39.3	43.3	101.2	121.5
Bonds	94.2	81.9	58.6	44.1
Subtotal	152.5	163.2	247.7	269.5
Nonmarketable securities				
Savings bonds	58.0	57.9	52.5	58.1
Treasury bonds (savings and investment series)	9.6	12.3	2.4	2.3
Foreign issues	—	—	5.7	21.4
Subtotal	67.6	70.2	60.6	81.8
Special issues*	33.7	43.9	78.1	95.9
Total	253.8	277.3	386.4	447.2

*Held only by U.S. government agencies and trust funds.

Sources: Federal Reserve Bulletin and Treasury Bulletin.

TABLE 7.4

Ownership of U.S. Government Securities, 1972
(billions of dollars)

			Amount	Percent
Private investors			262.5	58.3
Commercial banks	67.0			15.0
Mutual savings banks	2.6			0.5
Insurance companies	6.0			1.3
Other corporations	11.7			2.6
State and local governments	28.3			6.2
Individuals	74.1			16.5
Savings bonds		57.1		12.7
Other securities		17.0		3.8
Foreign and international	55.3			12.3
Other*	17.0			3.8
U.S. government agencies and trust funds			116.9	26.0
Federal Reserve Banks			69.9	15.5
Total			449.3	100.0

*Consists of saving and loan associations, nonprofit institutions, corporate pension trust funds, and dealers and brokers.

The ownership pattern of U.S. government securities reflects the portfolio management requirements of investors together with the alternative opportunities they face in the U.S. financial markets (Table 7.4). Commercial banks and the Federal Reserve Banks each hold 15 percent of outstanding U.S. government securities. In recent years, foreign ownership has increased markedly and in 1972 stood at over 12 percent of the total. U.S. government agencies and trust funds represent the single largest holding, 26 percent. In the relatively short period 1965-72, agency and trust fund holdings nearly doubled.

The operations of the federal credit agencies represent an increasingly more important sector in the capital market. The federal agencies include government-created organizations designed to serve specific purposes in the capital market. Federal credit agencies have an important influence on the capital markets by making loans to member organizations that invest in capital market instruments, by borrowing from the U.S. Treasury, by selling their own obligations to individuals and institutional investors, and by making investments for their own account in government securities and mortgages.

Recent growth in outstanding debt securities of federal agencies is reflected in Table 7.5, which indicates that federal agency securities outstanding exceeded $41 billion in 1972. At times federal agencies place more demand pressures on the capital market than the U.S. Treasury.

Market for Long-Term Corporate Debt

The corporate sector is a major end-user of capital market funds. The financing requirements of the corporate business sector varies from year to year, based on fluctuations in business fixed investment, changes in retained earnings, and the ability of the corporate sector to draw upon existing liquid asset holdings. The financing mix actually utilized each year depends upon the above considerations as well as relative costs of capital funds and short-term funds. As one of the most dynamic elements operating on both sides of the capital and money markets, the corporate business sector can contribute substantially to the ease or tightness of the financial markets.

The sources of funds of nonfinancial corporations for the period 1969-72 are indicated in Table 7.6. The reader should note that these figures are net and, therefore, do not reflect capital market activities resulting from refunding and refinancing operations. Internal sources of funds accounted for close to 60 percent of total corporate funds in the period covered by the table. We should note that availability of

TABLE 7.5

Outstanding Debt Securities of Federal Credit
Agencies, 1967-72
(billions of dollars)

	1967	1972	Increase 1967-72
Banks for cooperatives	1.3	1.9	0.6
Federal home loan banks	4.1	7.0	2.9
Federal intermediate credit banks	3.2	5.8	2.6
Federal land banks	4.9	8.0	3.1
Federal national mortgage association	4.9	19.2	14.3
Total	18.4	41.9	23.5

Source: Federal Reserve Bulletin.

TABLE 7.6

Sources of Funds—Nonfinancial Corporations, 1969-72
(billions of dollars)

	1969	1970	1971	1972
Internal sources				
Undistributed profits	16.0	10.8	14.5	20.0
Corporate inventory valuation adjustment	-5.1	-4.4	-4.7	-6.0
Capital consumption allowances	49.9	52.7	57.3	64.5
Profit tax liability	-3.3	-2.7	4.0	2.5
Total	57.5	56.4	71.1	81.0
Long-term funds				
Net new bond issues	12.1	20.3	18.7	12.9
Net new stock issues	3.4	5.8	12.6	12.4
Total net new issues	15.5	26.1	31.3	25.3
Mortgages	4.8	5.3	11.2	10.5
Term bank loans	5.8	2.0	2.0	3.7
Total	26.1	33.4	44.5	39.5
Short-term funds				
Open-market paper	2.7	2.6	-1.5	1.0
Short-term bank loans	6.3	0.3	1.3	5.3
Finance company loans	4.2	2.3	2.0	1.8
Bank loans held by nonbank investors	0.6	-0.1	-0.1	-0.1
Total	13.8	5.1	1.7	8.0
Other short-term sources				
Payables to U.S. government	0.9	-0.8	-1.7	-0.5
Other liabilities	4.3	3.8	3.9	4.1
Total	5.2	3.0	2.2	3.6
Total sources	102.6	97.9	119.5	132.1

internal funds makes it possible for corporations to engage in a high volume of investment and production without imposing substantial demand pressures on the capital markets.

External sources of funds include long-term and short-term sources. Long-term sources tend to be more important than short-term sources on a three-to-one ratio basis. An exception to this pattern took place in 1969 when tight money conditions led corporations to defer long-term financing to a time when the cost of funds on the capital market was more favorable. In 1969 short-term sources were drawn on far more extensively.

Corporations make use of two methods for selling long-term debt securities in the capital market. The first consists of distribution of public issues of corporate bonds through investment banking (underwriting) syndicates. By influencing the timing, yields, and special features of public corporate bond issues, the investment banker makes an important contribution to the proper functioning of the new issues market. Public issues of corporate bonds may be brought to market as negotiated issues or by competitive bidding. Direct negotiation between two parties, the underwriter and borrowing corporation, is confined to industrial corporation and finance company issues. Federal or state statutes generally require competitive bidding in the case of new issues by public utilities and railroads.

A second method for corporate sale of long-term debt instruments is through private placement (direct sale) with financial institutions, including life insurance companies, banks, and pension funds. Direct placement offers advantages to the borrower, including avoidance of flotation costs, less delay due to exemption of private placements from SEC registration requirements, and possibility of more easily tailoring the loan indenture to the specific requirements of borrower and lender. Smaller companies often find direct placement attractive, since the market for their debt securities may be very thin.

At year end 1972, over 70 percent of corporate bonds were held in the portfolios of banks and financial institutions (Table 7.7). The largest single owner group was the life insurance companies with over 34 percent of corporate bonds, followed at some interval by state and local government retirement funds (15.8 percent) and uninsured corporate pension funds (9.1 percent). In 1969-70 when open-market yields were very high, purchases of corporate bonds by individuals increased sharply, reflecting a tendency toward disintermediation in the financial markets.

Market for Corporate Stock

The market for corporate stock is unique in several respects. First, the market value is influenced by actual and prospective earnings and dividends and a capitalization rate that is applied to these income flows. Expectations play an important role in the valuation of corporate stock. Second, there is no maturity date, no refunding problem, and no distinction between gross and net issues. Third, the major factor influencing growth and size of outstanding issues is price level fluctuation rather than new issues less retirements.

The primary market for new corporate stock includes direct sale of securities (to employees, executives, and others) and sale through investment bankers and dealers. Direct sale of stock often takes place in connection with a rights offering to existing shareholders. When the stock issue already enjoys wide ownership and a

TABLE 7.7

Ownership of Corporate Bonds, 1972
(billions of dollars)

	Amount	Percent
Life insurance companies	86.6	34.5
Commercial banks	3.8	1.5
Mutual savings banks	13.5	5.3
Property and liability insurance companies	8.4	3.2
Uninsured corporate pension funds	23.1	9.1
State and local government retirement funds	39.8	15.8
Mutual investment companies	4.6	1.8
Individuals and others	73.5	28.8
Total	253.3	100.0

developed market, a rights offering may be an easy and relatively inexpensive method of issue. In such cases, the investment banker may participate by entering into a standby agreement, wherein the underwriting syndicate will take up shares not subscribed for by stockholders.

In the period 1965-72, gross new corporate stock issues increased from $3.2 billion to $15.0 billion. In the years 1966 and 1969, corporate borrowers experienced very high interest rates and probably shifted some part of their external financing to sale of equity securities. We should also remember that a large part of new stock issues refinances existing securities. For example, an increasing number of corporate mergers in the late 1960s is reflected in an increase in new issues of corporate stock. Such activities do not generate additional corporate funds, but represent a transfer of ownership and security form. In this connection, closely held companies that go public may initiate a "new issue" that in reality is a secondary distribution.

The secondary market for trading in outstanding securities plays a key role in valuation of corporate stock. This is in sharp contrast with the corporate bond market, where new issues activity tends to influence yields and prices. We should note that a persistent trend in the secondary trading of corporate stocks has been for individuals to be net sellers and financial institutions net purchasers of corporate equities.

The New York Stock Exchange (NYSE) reports institutional ownership of listed corporate stock on a regular basis, and the trends in this dominant sector of the stock market may be regarded as an indicator of trends in stock ownership throughout the equities market. As indicated in Table 7.8, between 1962 and 1972 institutional ownership of corporate stock advanced from 19.9 to 29.6 percent of the market value of listed stocks on the NYSE. In 1972 the largest institutional holdings were those of noninsured pension funds (36.9 percent), investment companies (22.0 percent), and nonprofit institutions (15.1 percent).

Stock price movements in the United States are generally regarded as less extreme than in the stock exchanges of other countries. Nevertheless, in the period 1969-73, a number of unusual pressures have been brought to bear on the U.S. capital market tending to reinforce stock market fluctuations. These pressures include extremely tight money and capital market conditions in 1969-70, at times heavy

TABLE 7.8

Institutional Ownership of NYSE Listed
Stock, 1962-72
(billions of dollars)

Type of Institution	1962		1972	
	Amount	Percent	Amount	Percent
Life insurance companies	4.1	5.9	20.3	7.8
Property and liability insurance companies	7.1	10.3	19.7	7.6
Investment companies	20.7	30.0	57.6	22.0
Noninsured pension funds	18.9	27.4	95.8	36.9
State and local government retirement funds	0.8	1.2	17.4	6.6
Mutual savings banks	0.4	0.6	1.8	0.6
Common trust funds	1.7	2.4	6.4	2.4
Nonprofit institutions (endowments and foundations)	15.2	22.0	39.2	15.1
Total	68.9	100.0	258.3	100.0
Market value of all NYSE listed stock	345.8	—	871.5	—
Percent held by institutions	19.9		29.6	

Source: NYSE, Fact Book.

110

TABLE 7.9

Movement in NYSE Common Stock Index, 1969-73

Direction	Price Movement	Dates		12/31/65=50 Percent Change
Decline	59.32-49.31	5/14/69	7/29/69	-16.9%
Gain	49.31-52.36	7/29/69	1/ 5/70	+ 6.2
Decline	52.36-37.69	1/ 5/70	5/26/70	-28.2
Gain	37.69-57.76	5/26/70	4/28/71	+54.3
Decline	57.76-49.60	4/28/71	11/23/71	-14.3
Gain	49.60-65.14	11/23/71	12/11/72	+31.1
Decline	65.14-54.49	12/11/72	6/30/73	-16.4

purchases of U.S. corporate securities by nonresidents (1972), substantial speculative outflows of funds from the United States (1971) leading to devaluation of the dollar in 1971 and 1973, and persistent inflationary pressures. Movements over the period 1969-73 in the NYSE common stock index are summarized in Table 7.9.

Mortgage Market

As measured by gross new issues and total outstanding credit, the mortgage market is the largest or second largest capital market sector in the United States. Mortgages are attractive to investors since tangible assets are pledged and because yields are higher than on most other debt securities. Mortgage debt outstanding has grown rapidly in the postwar years, from $73 billion in 1950 to $207 billion in 1960 and to $565 billion in 1972. This expansion reflects a pent-up demand for housing that had accumulated over a decade of depression and five years of wartime-postponed housing construction. It also reflects a surge in population, family formation, suburbanization, and rising housing standards.

There are considerable differences in the types of mortgages issued in connection with type of property pledged, type of lien, type of borrower, purpose of loan proceeds, and type of lender. In recent years mortgage loans on multifamily dwellings have become a more important factor in the creation of mortgage debt. Mortgage loans secured by business property (commercial property, office buildings, and bank buildings) are specialized in nature.

111

The volume of mortgage lending tends to follow its own business cycle pattern in terms of timing and amplitude. In part, housing construction and mortgage lending have fluctuated in accordance with the ease of channeling funds into mortgage credit. In turn, this has responded passively to the demand for capital market funds in more dynamic economic sectors such as nonfinancial corporations. Susceptibility of mortgage lending to cyclical variation has been reduced by the activities of the federal credit agencies, which in effect undertake open-market purchases of mortgages, make advances to mortgage-lending financial institutions, and underwrite home mortgages. At year end 1972, federal credit agencies held 8.1 percent of mortgage debt outstanding (Table 7.10). The most important institutional investor in the mortgage credit field is the savings and loan association. In 1972 these institutions held over 37 percent of mortgage debt outstanding. Saving and loan association investments in mortgages fluctuate along with inflows of funds to these institutions. Life insurance companies held nearly 14 percent of outstandings in 1972. Their investments in mortgages vary according to yields available on competing capital market instruments (corporate bonds and stock).

Market for State and Local Government Bonds

State and local governments have been consistent borrowers in the capital market, absorbing between 15 and 20 percent of long-term funds each year. Bonds are generally offered with serial maturities,

TABLE 7.10

Ownership of Mortgage Debt, 1972
(billions of dollars)

	Amount	Percent
Financial institutions		
Life insurance companies	77.3	13.9
Savings and loan associations	206.4	37.3
Commercial banks	99.3	18.0
Mutual savings banks	57.1	10.4
Subtotal	440.1	79.7
U.S. Government agencies	45.8	8.1
Individuals and others	69.0	12.4
Total	554.9	100.0

with each series maturing in successive years over the lifetime of the total issue. This gives states and localities a wide investor demand for their securities. The larger part of such debt is based on the general credit status of the borrower, and these bonds are designated as "full faith and credit" obligations. Counties and school districts generally prefer to sell debt instruments supported by the general credit standing of that local government. State governments have used a mixture of general credit and revenue bonds. The latter are supported by revenue derived from specific sources related to the facility whose construction was financed by the bond issue. The investment status of revenue depends upon the expected ability of the facility to generate sufficient income to service indebtedness. All state and local government securities enjoy exemption of interest from federal income taxation, and this has played an important role in shaping their market demand. Yields, which are lower on state and local government bonds, reflect this interest exemption feature.

The major expenditure purposes for which states and localities borrow include education, highway construction, provision of local utilities, and sewerage construction. While there is no exact correlation between amount and timing of debt issues and actual construction of capital facilities, there is some correspondence between the two. States and localities finance part of capital budget expenses with current revenues rather than borrowing, and sale of debt issues tends to anticipate or lead construction expenditures.

The primary market for bond issues is made up of large investment banking firms and commercial banks, which underwrite new issues in this field. In general, state and local government bond issues must be sold in competitive bidding, wherein buying syndicates submit sealed bids. Bidding is on a yield basis. The winning syndicate may offer all or part of the issue for sale at a markup that tends to be in the 1.0 to 1.5 percent range. This means that a $10,000 denomination bond may be purchased in competitive bidding at par and sold for approximately $10,100 to an investor, yielding a gross profit of $100 to the underwriter. This gross spread must cover such costs as printing, advertising, commissions to salesmen, and other incidentals.

In the past the market for state and local government securities has attracted investors subject to full taxation. At year end 1972, over 90 percent of outstanding issues were owned by commercial banks, property insurance companies, and individuals (Table 7.11). In the five-year period 1968-72, commercial banks absorbed 57 percent of net new issues, property insurance companies 15 percent, and individuals 24 percent.

TABLE 7.11

Ownership of State and Local Government
Bonds, 1972
(billions of dollars)

	Amount	Percent
Commercial banks	89.5	52.0
Mutual savings banks	0.9	0.5
Life insurance companies	3.5	2.0
Property insurance companies	23.9	13.9
State and local government retirement funds	1.5	0.9
State and local governments	2.3	1.3
Business corporations	5.6	3.2
Individuals and others	44.3	25.8
Total	171.5	100.0

Sources: Federal Reserve Bulletin and Bankers Trust Company, Investment Outlook.

INTERNATIONAL ORIENTATION

Foreign demand has played a significant role in the U.S. capital market. The U.S. capital market plays an important role as a source of long-term funds for a narrow range of foreign borrowers. Moreover, it affords excellent facilities for nonresident portfolio adjustment in a wide variety of capital market instruments. The U.S. capital market has never enjoyed a strong international orientation, and foreign pressures have only infrequently had any significant leverage on the tone of the market. However, looking in reverse, the facilities of the U.S. capital market play an important role for the rest of the world.

Foreign New Issues

In the period since World War II, the U.S. capital market is the only such market that has been continuously open to foreign new issues. The only restriction that has been imposed on foreign securities issues is the Interest Equalization Tax (IET), 1964-74. The IET was in the form of an excise tax imposed on U.S. purchases of foreign securities and tended to inject a price effect rather than a quota limit on foreign issues. When originally imposed, it was thought that a significant part of the incidence of the tax would fall on the foreign seller of securities. In this case, there would be little effect on American purchasers, except that they would be offered a smaller volume of foreign new issues. Removal of the IET early in 1974 is expected to increase the role of New York as a new issues market for foreign securities.

The U.S. capital market offers significant advantages to foreign borrowers and to foreign investors wishing to purchase dollar-denominated securities of non-U.S. issuers. Foreign borrowers find the resources of the U.S. capital market virtually limitless. Even the World Bank, which has sold several billions of dollars' worth of its own bonds in the United States, has found a highly elastic supply of credit in the U.S. market. Second, flotation costs are quite low, indicating a highly efficient underwriting mechanism. Finally interest rates in the U.S. financial markets have been quite low over most of the postwar period. The exception to this would be the period since 1969 when a combination of circumstances pushed U.S. interest rates to historic highs.

Foreign investors find the U.S. new issues market attractive. Dollar-denominated bonds and equity securities have been in strong demand outside the United States during most of the period since World War II. Dollar bonds are marketable in the active and liquid U.S. capital market, a condition that is not paralleled in most other countries. Finally, an investment in dollar-denominated securities has represented a useful hedge against currency instabilities in parts of the world where inflation, exchange controls, and political uncertainties prevail.

In the period 1969-72, foreign bond issues in the United States totaled $6.5 billion, an annual average of $1.6 billion (Table 7.12). Issues of the industrialized countries are dominated by Canadian bonds sold by provincial governments and government agencies. The capital and money market ties between the United States and Canada are unusually strong, paralleling the close linkages in foreign trade. The World Bank has also been a heavy user of U.S. capital market facilities and by far leads other international development institutions as a borrower. Finally, we must note that the developing countries have made use of the U.S. capital market only very sparingly. This has continued despite exemption of developing country bond issues from the IET. The two less developed countries that have made the most extensive use of the U.S. capital market are quickly moving toward industrialization and developed country status. These are Israel and Mexico.

115

TABLE 7.12

Foreign Bond Issues Marketed in the
United States, 1969-72
(millions of dollars)

Borrowing Countries	Total Bond Issues 1969-72	Annual Average 1969-72	Percent of Total
Industrialized countries[a]	3,617	904	56
International development institutions[b]	1,920	480	30
Developing countries[c]	923	231	14
Total	6,460	1,615	100

[a]Canada's share of debt issues in this period was over 99 percent of total.

[b]The World Bank's share of debt issues in this period was 93 percent of total.

[c]The share of Israel and Mexico of debt issues in this period was 35 percent and 4 percent of the total, respectively.

Source: World Bank and Investment Dealers Association (IDA), Annual Reports.

Secondary Trading on Foreign Account

Secondary-trading facilities in the United States after exceptional opportunities for foreign investors in terms of variety of securities and investments available; depth, breadth, and stability of the market; and liquidity available due to active trading and relatively high turnover. In part, for these reasons a number of foreign corporations and governments have had their securities listed on the NYSE and other stock exchanges. At year end 1972, the market value of foreign corporate stocks and bonds listed on the NYSE was $15.8 billion and $0.7 billion, respectively. The value of foreign government bonds listed was $1.9 billion.

Foreign investors are active participants in the U.S. capital market in the trading of domestic as well as foreign securities. During 1972 gross transactions by foreign investors in U.S. corporate securities were in excess of $33 billion, whereas gross transactions in foreign bonds and stocks were less than $10 billion (Table 7.13).

TABLE 7.13

Purchases and Sales by Foreigners of
Long-Term Securities, 1972
(millions of dollars)

| | U.S. Corporate | | Marketable U.S. Treasury Notes and Bonds | Foreign | |
	Bonds	Stocks	Bonds	Bonds	Stocks
Purchases	4,679	14,243	—	1,941	2,532
Sales	2,992	11,966	—	2,961	2,123
Net purchases	1,687	2,277	1,613	-1,021	409

Sources: Treasury Bulletin and Federal Reserve Bulletin.

In 1972 foreign investors were net purchasers of U.S. corporate securities by $3.9 billion, net purchasers of U.S. Treasury notes and bonds by $1.6 billion, net sellers of foreign bonds in excess of $1.0 billion, and net purchasers of foreign stocks from U.S. residents of $0.4 billion.

The substantial volume of secondary trading by foreign investors in the U.S. capital market reflects portfolio adjustments by U.S. investors holding foreign securities and foreign investors holding U.S. securities. It has been estimated that at year end 1972, U.S. investors held stocks and bonds of foreign corporations worth $9.0 billion and $15.8 billion, respectively. Further, it has been estimated that at the same time foreign investors held stock and bonds of U.S. corporations worth $27.6 billion and $10.9 billion. Such massive two-way foreign investment holdings may be expected to afford continued opportunities and incentives for a large volume of secondary trading in the U.S. securities markets on foreign account.

REFERENCES

Friend, Longstreet, and Mendelson. Investment Banking and the New Issues Market. Cleveland, Ohio: World Publishing Company, 1967.

Goldsmith, Raymond W. The Flow of Capital Funds in the Postwar
    Economy. New York: National Bureau of Economic Research,
    1965.

Polakoff, M., ed. Financial Institutions and Markets. Boston: Hough-
    ton Mifflin, 1970.

U.S. Congress, Joint Economic Committee. A Description and Analysis
    of Certain European Capital Markets, 1964.

8

INTRODUCTION

Canada, the second largest country in the world, has an area
of 3.8 million square miles. It occupies the northern half of the North
American continent, with the exception of Alaska and Greenland, and
touches on three oceans—the Atlantic, Pacific, and Arctic. In the
south, it borders the United States for a distance of 3,986 miles.
There are five physiographic regions in Canada:

1. Eastern and Central Canada is called the Shield which forms
a vast crescent around Hudson and James bays. This area possesses
a wealth of mineral resources, forests, and water power.

2. The Interior Plains and Lowlands consist of the prairies of
Western Canada and their wooded continuation to the north and the
St. Lawrence-Great Lakes Lowlands. The interior area is the great
grain-growing area. The St. Lawrence-Great Lakes region contains
60 percent of the population and the most industrialized area.

3. The Appalachian region includes the part of Quebec south
of the St. Lawrence River, New Brunswick, Nova Scotia, Prince Edward
Island, and Newfoundland. This area has some agricultural land and
mineral resources.

4. The Cordilleran Region is comprised of Southwest Alberta,
British Columbia, the Yukon Territory, and a part of the Northwest
Territory. This area has extensive and varied mineral wealth. Fine
beef cattle and some crops are raised.

5. The Innuition Region covers the most northerly Arctic
islands.

Canada is very large in size, but it has a relatively small population of 22 million, of which about 44 percent are of British stock
and about 30 percent are of French origin. The size, distance, natural
resources, cultural characteristics, and political history of Canada

have influenced the economic and financial progress of the Canadian people.

The passage of the British North America Act in 1867 by the British Parliament provided Canada with a democratic parliamentary system of government. Parliament consists of the queen, the Senate, and the House of Commons. The governor-general is the representative of the monarch; the Senate is an appointive upper House; the prime minister is normally elected from the majority membership of the House of Commons. The country is broken into 10 self-governing provinces and two territories. The federal Parliament has power over the regulation of trade and communication, defense, shipping, banking, and currency. The provincial governments, on the other hand, have control over education, municipal government, property, and civil rights. While the federal government retains the taxing power on the basis of the government's annual budget, the provincial governments are limited to direct taxation for provincial purposes. For these reasons, there have been some conflicts between the federal government and provinces with respect to the diverse economic setting, the purposes and means of economic development, and financing methods.

The history of Canadian economic and financial development is basically related to its immense natural resources, its substantial international trade, and the inflow of foreign capital and technology first from Britain and later from the United States. Before World War I, the Canadian economy was dominated by farm and fish products. The increasing demand for newsprint and industrial raw materials by the United States in the 1920s stimulated Canada's forest and mining industries. In the meantime, more U.S. capital and technology were employed in Canadian manufacturing industry. After World War II, Canadian manufacturing, construction, mining, utilities, and commercial industries continued to grow, while the agricultural sector became less important. Worldwide demand for raw materials and foods in the 1950s assisted Canadian economic expansion, and the inflow of U.S. capital for this purpose was important. During the 1960s foreign trade accounted for between 20 and 25 percent of Canadian gross national product (GNP), and the United States has accounted for 60 to 70 percent of total trade. According to the "White Paper" issued by the Canadian government in 1969, the United States then held 48 percent of all equity capital in primary and secondary industries in Canada. The Canadian policy since 1971 has been toward less dependence on U.S. trade and capital, increased trade with Japan, China, and Russia, and more federal and provincial government participation in economic development programs.

Table 8.1 illustrates the growth of the Canadian economy, per-capita income, capital formation, and price trends. This growth pattern closely resembles that found for the United States. Canada's

TABLE 8.1

Major Financial and Economic Indicators, 1966-72

Year	GNP in million $	Per-capita GNP	GNP Growth Rate at 1960 price	Consumer Price Index (1960 = 100)	Gross Capital Formation (in millions)
1966	61.83	$3,080	6.9	111.4	15.36
1967	66.40	3,243	3.3	115.4	15.63
1968	72.59	3,500	5.8	120.1	15.75
1969	79.75	3,780	5.3	125.5	17.23
1970	85.45	4,004	2.6	129.7	18.13
1971	93.09	4,310	5.8	133.4	20.13
1972	103.12	4,708	5.8	139.8	22.01

Sources: Bank of Canada, Review, September 1973; International Monetary Fund (IMF), International Financial Statistics, September 1973.

new trade policy has been successful as reflected from her current account surpluses in 1970 and 1971. The main problems confronting Canada in the 1970s seem to be the structural rigidities between primary and manufacturing industries, the regional disparities in income levels, the policy arguments between monetarists and fiscalists, and the serious problems of inflation. The approaches to be taken for solving these problems will undoubtedly influence the development of Canadian financial markets in the decades to come.

THE ROLE OF GOVERNMENT IN NATIONAL ECONOMY AND FINANCE

Changing Role of Federal and Provincial Governments

Like many other Western industrialized nations, Canada emphasizes a free-market economy. The postwar economic expansion stimulated by mining and agricultural industries since 1948 was ended in 1957. The period 1958-68 was particularly interesting and significant to Canada because it reflected not only a changing government

121

philosophy, but also the changing relationship between the federal and provincial governments. These changes bolstered manufacturing expansion, on the one hand, and readjusted the money and capital markets in synchrony with U.S. financial markets conditions. In 1967, when the Expo '67 World Fair in Canada marked centennial independence, the federal government of Canada began to adopt a more active role in the national as well as international economy and finance. The change has resulted in more government spending, more export trade, more housing and consumer expenditures, and higher GNP with inflation.

The changes noted above for the period 1958-68 relate to increased provincial and municipal spending and a leveling off in federal spending. Statistics show that expenditures of the provincial and municipal governments rose as a percentage of GNP from 12.7 percent in 1958 to 19.2 percent in 1968. In the same period, federal government expenditure as a percentage of GNP declined from 17.9 to 16.9 percent. The major sources of funds for both levels of governments were domestic indirect and direct tax revenues as well as borrowing from domestic financial markets and the U.S. capital market. The adoption of the U.S. Interest Equalization Tax (IET) in 1963 and the capital control program in 1968 severely limited Canadian borrowings in the United States even though up to $100 million issues are not applicable to these rules. An additional problem arose through the tying of federal government expenditures for certain programs to provincial expenditures on a cost-sharing basis. In this connection, some federal government expenditures were actually determined by the provincial authorities. Furthermore, the decentralized processes for setting wages and prices in different provinces have made it difficult for the federal government to deal effectively with inflation and unemployment.

In the period 1958-68, there was a policy argument within the federal government. The "baby budget" adopted by the Finance Ministry in 1960 and the tight money policy pursued by the Bank of Canada contributed to a 7-percent unemployment level. The deficit spending and fiscal incentives in terms of favorable depreciation on plant and equipment between 1961-65 indeed stimulated manufacturing industry. The discovery of massive reserves of oil and gas in Yukon and Northwest territories in 1967 generated new waves of exploration activity in those areas. When inflation emerged in 1968, fiscal restraint was strongly suggested by the banking industry, but the Economic Council, which was established in 1963, had an upper hand in the argument.

In order to strengthen fiscal and monetary policy, Canada has taken many important measures since 1967. On the home front, the federal and provincial governments continued to increase spending in order to lessen the regional disparities in personal income. The federal government also developed an incomes policy in 1969 and stressed selective control over the flow of funds, especially in 1970-71 when the Canadian dollar was allowed to float vis-à-vis the U.S. dollar. On the international front, the White Paper on Tax Reform issued in November 1969 was designed to encourage Canadians to invest in Canada and to discourage United States and other foreigners from investing in Canada. Under the new tax system, Canadian-controlled corporations pay a lower rate of tax, while the branches of foreign-owned corporations are singled out for an additional tax on their profits. The new banking legislation passed in 1967 also forced the First National City Bank to give up majority ownership by 1975 of the Mercantile Bank of Canada. International trade policy has also shifted to heavier reliance on countries such as China and Russia and less reliance on traditional trading partners such as the United States and Britain.

Government Finance

The changing role of government requires varied strategies and techniques. While the federal government is more concerned with natural resources development, economic growth, employment, and price levels, the provincial governments carry a heavier financial burden to improve their local economic and social conditions. Total spending by governments of all levels in 1972 was about 24 percent of Canada's GNP. Following is a general picture of the government budgets and the major sources of their financing.

The federal government's policy has been to coordinate the provincial economic programs on a shared-cost basis. Direct outlets were confined to the areas of health, welfare, education, small business loans, and the development of vital industries. According to government and international statistics, in the period 1966-72, federal government expenditures increased from about $10 billion to $19.5 billion; revenues rose from about $9.5 billion to $19 billion; and the average annual deficit was about $500 million. In the same period, federal debt increased from about $20 billion to $29 billion. The increase in government outlays in the period was about 95 percent contrasted to the increase in total federal debt of about 45 percent.

The Canadian federal government has sharpened its debt management techniques since the 1950s when the Treasury bill market was improved. Over the last two decades 1952-72, the Treasury and the Bank of Canada have skillfully marketed government securities in order to influence liquidity without generating inflationary pressures. In 1972 there was about $29 billion in federal debt outstanding, of which Treasury bills shared 15 percent, short-term bonds 50

percent, and savings bonds 35 percent. The holders of federal securities were Bank of Canada 20 percent of outstandings, Chartered
Banks 25 percent, and the public 55 percent. The Chartered Banks
were principal holders of Treasury bills for liquidity purposes,
whereas individuals and nonbank financial institutions absorbed substantial amounts of savings bonds. The Bank of Canada acted as
arbiter in the short-term market and absorbed excessive funds in
accordance with its antiinflation policy.

Budgets of provincial governments have varied depending on the
needs at the time. Most of provincial spending is for local community
welfare, highway construction, and education. In 1972 the provincial
and municipal governments contributed 75 percent of total government spending in Canada.

Table 8.2 indicates the amounts of borrowed funds raised by
the government of Canada from 1970-72. The amounts varied from
$1.5 billion to $3 billion depending on the cyclical nature of the national
economy. The funds demanded by the provincial and municipal

TABLE 8.2

Major Sources of Financing: Federal, Provincial,
and Municipal Governments
(millions of dollars)

	Annual Increase		
	1970	1971	1972
Government of Canada			
Treasury bills	720	189	33?
Canadian dollar bonds	558	277	3?
Canada savings bonds	714	2,519	1,19?
Total	1,992	2,985	1,55?
Provincial and municipal governments			
Canada pension plan funds	863	915	95?
Canadian dollar bonds	1,019	1,695	1,45?
Foreign currency bonds	358	274	91?
Treasury bills and short-term paper	25	29	7?
Loans from Chartered Banks	-36	-37	10?
Loans from government of Canada	243	368	42?
Total	2,477	3,244	3,92?

Source: Bank of Canada, Review, September 1973.

governments steadily increased from $2.4 billion to $3.9 billion in the same period. The major sources of funds for the federal government shifted from Treasury bills to savings bonds. The emphasis of local government financing has been on sale of securities to the general public, pension funds, and foreign currency bonds. Short-term loans from Chartered Banks and the federal government and sale of Treasury bills of the provincial governments have also been employed flexibly, especially by those provinces and municipalities that have close access to the local money markets such as Montreal, Toronto, and Vancouver. Foreign currency bonds were mostly sold in the United States whenever market conditions were favorable to the issuing governments.

FINANCIAL INSTITUTIONS

The financial system in Canada is a blend of that found in England and the United States. While the structure of the financial system is similar to England, the operation of monetary control in closer to the Federal Reserve System in the United States. At the top of the financial pyramid stands the Finance Ministry, which is responsible for both fiscal and monetary policies. The inspector-general of banks and the superintendent of insurance, created by the Bank Act of 1924, have the powers of examining all banks and insurance companies with federal charters. All financial institutions chartered by provinces are supervised and regulated by the respective provincial governments. The Deposit Insurance Corporation was established in 1967, and all Chartered Banks and federal-incorporated loan and trust companies must be members of the corporation. The Bank of Canada, Chartered Banks, insurance companies, trust and mortgage loan companies are under the general supervision of the Finance Ministry. The Canadian financial system and its financial institutions have been re-examined and improved by successive amendments of the Bank Act, which traces back to the original Bank Act of 1871.

Bank of Canada

The Bank of Canada is the central bank and began operation shortly after passage of the Bank of Canada Act of 1934. Its primary function is to execute the Finance Ministry's monetary policy decisions regarding the volume of money and the level of interest rates. It also acts as the fiscal agent of the federal government to sell and buy government securities, gold, and silver, as well as to manage the international reserves. The Bank of Canada is a government-owned central bank, and its functions and powers are comparable to that of the Bank of England. The monetary tools for the central bank to carry out its mission include discounts and advances to the Chartered Banks and Quebec savings banks, reserve requirements for all deposit-receiving financial institutions with federal charters, and repurchases of government securities on an irregular basis. The Bank of Canada directly owns the Industrial Development Bank, which was formed in 1944 to develop certain national enterprises. The policy and operations of the Bank of Canada are reflected from the main items on its balance sheet. While deposits from the Chartered Banks and notes in circulation constitute the major items on the liability side, government securities including short term and long term comprise the largest part of the bank's assets. Securities issued by the United Kingdom and the United States also account for a significant part of asset holdings. The Bank of Canada has played a vital role in the growing national economy and the financial markets. The rate of increase in money supply in the period 1971 to 1973 (annual rate of 12 to 14 percent) has reflected a growing economy and also the increase in price levels (an inflation rate of 8 percent in 1973). The Bank of Canada has exerted tremendous influence on the money market since 1954 when Treasury bills were allowed to be counted as cash reserves for the Chartered Banks. Supplementary measures to assist the government securities dealers, to stimulate the commercial paper market in the 1950s, and to help the banker's acceptance market in the 1960s have contributed to the growth of the Canadian money market. The interest rate has been used as a major weapon to fight inflation in recent years. For example, the central bank increased the bank rate three times between April and September 1973—5 1/4 percent in April, 6 1/4 percent in July, and 7 1/4 percent in September.

Chartered Banks

The commercial banking system in Canada is similar to that of England. In 1973 there were 10 Chartered Banks with over 5,000 branches and agencies at home and abroad. The history, operations, assets, and liabilities of the Chartered Banks have been closely related to Canadian economic development, financial market evolution, and institutional competition.

The first commercial bank, the Bank of Montreal, began business in 1817 and received a charter in 1822. However, the first Chartered Bank was the Bank of Upper Canada in 1821. These early banks were strongly influenced by the "Alexander Hamilton banks" in the United States—the First Bank of the United States and the Bank of New York. The Chartered Banks in the early nineteenth century were to serve local merchants, facilitate trade, advance working capital, and issue notes. When Canada became independent in 1867, the federal government issued Dominion notes as legal tender (1870), which circulated side by side with bank notes which were not legal tender. The acceptance of savings deposits by Chartered Banks in the 1860s, plus demand deposits and note issues, bolstered the Chartered Banks' volume of assets. In 1910 there were 66 Chartered Banks, accounting for 60 percent of total assets of all financial intermediaries. After the waves of bank mergers in the 1920s and 1950s, there were only 10 Chartered Banks in 1973, accounting for 42 percent of the assets of all financial institutions. The relative decline of the asset share of the Chartered Banks has its counterpart in the increased assets of the trusteed pension funds, trust companies, and credit unions. But the growth of Chartered Banks at rates of 19 percent and 15 percent in 1971 and 1972, respectively, was above the average growth rates of all financial institutions in the same period, as indicated in Table 8.3. Increased government, time, and savings deposits and

TABLE 8.3

Assets of Selected Financial Institutions

	Billions of Dollars 1972	Percent Increase from Previous Year		
		1970	1971	1972
Deposit-taking institutions				
Chartered Banks	41.4	9	19	15
Quebec savings banks	0.7	8	13	10
Trust and mortgage loan companies	12.7	14	13	16
Credit unions and caisses populaires	6.7	12	22	27
Subtotal	61.4	11	18	16
Contractual saving institutions				
Life insurance companies	17.2	4	7	10
Pension funds	13.7	11	12	11
Subtotal	30.9	7	9	10
Sales finance and consumer loan companies	5.9	-3	5	13
Total	98.2	8	14	14

Source: Bank of Canada, Review, September 1973.

active participation in consumer and mortgage loan markets have been reported as major factors for the revival of the Chartered Banks. The drawbacks of the Chartered Banks in the three decades 1944-74 were generally attributed to the following events: (1) the note issue privilege being taken over by the Bank of Canada in 1935, (2) restrictive measures on the approval of charters to banks by the Canadian Parliament, and (3) the rise of nonbank financial institutions after World War II.

It should be noted that a substantial portion of the banking assets is controlled by the three or four largest banks that also own overseas branches in many international financial and trading centers, such as New York, London, Paris, Tokyo, and the Carribean area.

Insurance Companies

The life insurance industry is second in importance to the Chartered Banks insofar as asset holdings are concerned. The first life insurance company was founded in Canada in 1847. The industry grew to become an important source of capital for the developing Canadian economy. During the 1970s the growth rates of life insurance companies fell behind other institutions as illustrated in Table 8.3. Their major assets are mortgage bonds, corporate bonds, and municipal bonds. Since 1968 they have been stressing acquisitions of stock and real estate. They might play a more important role in supplying funds should the Canadian capital market become more fully developed. Fire and casualty insurance companies have been established beginning in 1809, but the assets of these companies have been less important as far as the growth of financial markets is concerned.

Trust and Mortgage Loan Companies

Mortgage loan companies began business in 1844, and the first trust company appeared in 1882. Their major asset holding is real estate mortgages. Other assets include short-term investments, government bonds, and a small amount of common and preferred stocks. After World War II, their assets have grown rapidly, reflecting such factors as the great expansion in the construction of buildings (with consequent mortgage debt) and the development of many new financial market instruments, such as investment certificates, debentures, and other term deposits which constitute their major sources of funds.

Other Financial Institutions

All financial institutions are in competition for the public's favor. Some types of financial institutions such as the farm credit companies have been surpassed in growth by institutions such as the pension funds and credit unions. Mutual funds have not been conspicuous in Canada due to the less active capital market. Finance companies and consumer loan companies established before 1930 have not been prosperous until recently when consumer financing became heavily demanded by the public. The growth rate of these companies in 1972 was 13 percent. The growth of credit union and pension funds has reflected increased worker benefits, parallel to the trends in the United States. These institutions are important sources of funds for the long-term credit markets.

FINANCIAL MARKETS

Financial Market Development

Three factors are basically responsible for the development of the Canadian financial markets. Domestic economic conditions determine the needs for financial services. Needs have changed as the national economy shifted its emphasis from agricultural to an industrial economy. Government policy reflected in the revision of the Bank Act every 10 years and the Finance Ministry's efforts in creating an effective monetary mechanism in the 1950s have had decisive effects on the market's development. The third factor is the influence of the United States on the Canadian financial markets. A brief analysis of the market evolution may help in understanding present market conditions and the market trends in the future.

Before 1800 Canada's simple and self-sufficient agricultural economy required very few financial services. Isolated local colonies used a barter system. Some east coast cities such as Montreal and Halifax were trading centers with Europe. Mercantile houses of British and French origin required small banks to handle deposits, credit collections, and make currency exchanges. To facilitate trade and financial transactions, American, French, and Spanish coins were used.

At the turn of the nineteenth century, some merchants formed banks, but these failed. In 1812 the issuance of Canadian Army bills for military supply provided a floating currency medium. The establishment of the Bank of Montreal in 1817 was a landmark in Canadian financial market development, since this was the first bank to issue notes, offer stock, and accept deposits.

Canadian financial market development accelerated after the establishment of the confederation government in 1867. A Board of Brokers was formed in 1866; the confederation issued currency in 1867; the first Bank Act was passed by Parliament in 1870 concerning the size of banks and maximum interest and discount rates that could be charged by banks. There were 35 banks at that time. In 1874 and 1878 the Montreal and Toronto Stock Exchanges were incorporated, respectively, and a formal capital market began to function.

Continued agricultural, commercial, and industrial development in the late nineteenth centruy required far more capital investment and the British-supplied funds to meet needs. World War I was a turning point in Canadian financial market growth. Canada no longer had access to British capital, but turned to the United States for

TABLE 8.4

Major Sources and Uses of Funds on the
Financial Markets
(billions of dollars)

	1970	1971	1972
Funds raised			
Private nonfinancial business	3.2	5.3	4.6
Consumers	0.7	1.4	2.2
Mortgage borrowers	1.5	2.5	4.0
Provinces and municipalities	2.2	2.9	3.5
Government of Canada	2.0	3.0	1.6
Total	9.6	15.1	15.9
Sources of funds			
Bank of Canada	0.2	0.6	0.6
Chartered Banks			
Loans and mortgages	1.0	4.0	4.9
Acquisitions of securities	1.8	1.4	0.1
Other financial institutions			
Loans and mortgages	1.4	2.2	4.0
Acquisitions of securities	1.5	2.9	2.7
Other residents	2.3	3.0	1.7
Nonresidents	1.4	1.1	2.1
Total	9.6	15.1	15.9

Source: Bank of Canada, Review, September 1973.

financing. During the war the Canadian government organized investment dealers and developed a "Victory Loan." A total amount of $600 million in government bonds was sold by 1918. The development of the government bond market further stimulated the growth of finance companies in the 1920s.

In 1935 the formation of the central bank, the Bank of Canada, was a milestone in the evolution of the Canadian financial markets. The Bank of Canada issued currency and Treasury bills. However, the real impetus of the money market was provided by the monetary authorities in the 1950s when several steps were taken by the Bank of Canada. For instance, in 1953 the Bank of Canada began to issue 182-day Treasury bills and three-year bonds; in 1965 a change of cash reserve requirements for the Chartered Banks stimulated their demand for short-term government securities; in the same year the day-to-day loan market was created by the agreements between the Chartered Banks and investment dealers for repurchase or sale of government securities. The purpose of these actions was to increase market efficiency for channeling funds needed for economic growth.

The new Bank Act of 1967 provided more freedom to the domestic market and restricted foreign ownership of Canadian banks to not over 25 percent. Interest ceilings on commercial bank loans and deposits were eliminated. Table 8.4 illustrates the working of the free-market forces in the period 1970-72 when increasing amounts of funds were raised and supplied through financial intermediaries. At present, the financial markets in Canada are well developed and should be able to support the future economic needs of the country.

Money Market

Canadian monetary authorities strengthened the money market after 1953 by creating a better financial mechanism, encouraging the issuance of new financial instruments, and attracting more participants. However, Canadian monetary authorities have been well aware of the profound influence from neighboring financial markets in New York and, to a lesser extent, London.

The Bank of Canada initiated issue of Treasury bills in 1934 and broadened the scope of the market in 1953. The maturities of bills are 91 days and 180 days. Denominations of $25,000, $50,000, $100,000, and $1,000,000 have been used. Only banks and dealers can apply for bills in the primary market on a bidding basis. The Bank of Canada reserves the right to reject bids if the prices submitted are low and unacceptable. The Treasury bills bear no interest, and their yield depends on their discount. Since the primary and the secondary markets are active and well developed, bills have been

TABLE 8.5

Size Comparison of Canadian Money Market
as of End of August, 1973
(millions of dollars)

Treasury bills	5,470
Commercial paper	1,539
Corporate short-term paper	3,872
Day-to-day loans	278
Call loans	783
Banker's acceptances	454
Bank deposit instruments (under one year)	410
Trust-company-guaranteed investment certificates (under one year)	1,096
Foreign currency swap deposits	749
Total	14,651

Source: Bank of Canada, Review, September 1973.

effectively distributed and used by the central bank as vital money market instruments to influence short-term liquidity. The Bank of Canada does not conduct open-market operations regularly as the Federal Reserve does in the United States. A great deal of the transactions in the secondary market is on a buy-back basis, enabling the Bank of Canada to control fluctuations in Treasury bill rates. Among the outstanding Treasury bills of $5,470 million at August 1973, the Chartered Banks held $3,241 million, the central bank held $1 billion, and the remainder was distributed among dealers and the general public. Since Treasury bills are used actively in Canada for arbitrage purposes, their yields are quite sensitive to Treasury bill yields in the United States. In this connection, it is reported that the central bank of Canada intends to discourage inflows of short-term capital and control the liquidity level at home adequate to domestic needs.

Canadian commercial paper was first issued in the 1950s when corporations were caught in a credit squeeze and decided to supplement their short-term credit granted by commercial banks. Recent prosperity has favored development of the commercial paper market in Canada. The amount of outstanding short-term paper was $3,872 million at August 1973, which was second only to the amount of Treasury bills. The tight money policy in the United States forced many U.S. affiliates to issue short-term paper in Canada to achieve lower borrowing costs. Commercial paper issued by sales finance and consumer finance companies appeared in the Canadian market in the 1920s. Increased consumer spending in the last couple of years has stimulated finance company borrowings in the short-term market as well as from Chartered Banks. All commercial paper is sold primarily through investment dealers to corporations, mutual funds, and trust companies. The commercial paper market is highly competitive, and high yields have lured funds away from other short-term credit sectors such as bankers' acceptances.

Day-to-day loans (day loans) started in 1954 when the Bank of Canada encouraged government securities dealers (15 in number) to participate in purchasing Treasury bills and invited the Chartered Banks to accommodate them on a day-to-day basis (day loans) against the pledge of short-dated government securities. The loan is repayable on demand if the lender calls before noon. The interest rate is 3.65 percent per annum (0.01 percent per day). From the banker's standpoint, the sacrifice of yield is offset by an increase in the liquidity of the asset. If liquidity is needed, the bank can call the loan and avoid selling the Treasury bill to the central bank. From the dealer's standpoint, it is profitable to hold bills in inventories at the lower rates of interest without selling the bills or even making a repurchase agreement with the Bank of Canada. The purpose of this arrangement is to maintain a stable but viable money market without disruption by mass selling of Treasury bills to the Bank of Canada. The day-loan market is an impersonal market, with an "exchange broker" acting as a third party between the Bank of Canada and the Chartered Banks for information purposes. The exchange brokers are appointed by the Canadian Bankers Association and located in Toronto, Montreal, and Vancouver. They maintain telephone communications with all parties concerned. Outstanding day loans at the end of August 1973 totaled $278 million.

In the Canadian money market, the Chartered Banks' advance call loans to the investment dealers and brokers to help them finance their inventories comprised of government bonds, corporate bonds, and stocks listed on the stock exchanges. In fact, these loans are seldom called. The market is not large due to the relatively small capital market in Canada.

After several years of investigation and discussion, a market in banker's acceptances was instituted in 1962. Banker's acceptances can be rediscounted by the Bank of Canada. They must be drawn in connection with the manufacture or marketing of merchandise. They are short-term, low risk, and highly liquid. The volume of banker's acceptances has been small, but increased rapidly after 1970 as a result of the growth of Canadian foreign trade and bank financing to traders. At the end of August 1973, the amount of banker's acceptances outstanding was $454 million.

Bank Deposit Instruments and Guaranteed Investment Certificates are instruments equivalent to the American certificates of deposit (CDs). The Bank of Nova Scotia introduced redeemable CDs with maturities ranging from 30 days to one year in 1960. The Chartered Banks have categorized these liabilities as "term note deposits." The outstanding amount of bank deposit instruments at August 1973 was $410 million, which was only a small part of fixed-term deposits in all Chartered Banks. In the same period, trust-companies-guaranteed investment certificates reached $1,096 million. This reflected the different policy on liability management as between commercial banks and trust companies that parallels a different emphasis on asset investments. Commercial banks invest most of their funds in short-term loans, while the trust companies use their resources primarily in the mortgage markets. The competition in this segment of the money market is not generated by the Canadian financial institutions but by the CDs issued by American and British firms with Canadian affiliates.

Swap deposits reflect unique money market activities in Canada developed during the 1960s. Under a swap-deposit agreement, a customer deposits an amount of no less than $100,000 for a period generally ranging from one to six months. During the period, the customer earns a return composed of the interest earned on a deposit of like term in the currency in which the foreign exchange is booked, and plus or minus the premium or discount on the forward exchange. These transactions are mostly related to U.S. dollar funds. The swap deposits represent an outflow of capital due mainly to the existence of an interest differential with one or another foreign money market, usually New York. At August 1973 the amount of such deposits was $749 million in the Chartered Banks.

In August 1973 the total amount of major money market instruments outstanding was $14,651 million, which constituted an important part of the liquidity of the Canadian financial system. The Bank of Canada has carefully watched this figure and its composition, as well as the flow of funds between various sectors of the money market. For example, on November 27, 1972, the Canadian Chartered Banks announced a reduction in their CD rates by 1/8 to 1/4 percentage point. These reductions, though modest in size, had a substantial impact on the domestic as well as foreign exchange markets, since they were unexpected and occurred at a time when interest rates were rising sharply in the United States and Europe. The Bank of Canada quickly intervened to maintain an orderly market and to check the outflow of capital.

Foreign Exchange Market

The foreign exchange market in Canada is closely related to the domestic money market, the U.S. money market, and to a certain extent the UK market. The structure and operations of the Canadian exchange market can be briefly described as follows.

There are four sectors in the Canadian foreign exchange market. First, there is the interbank market in which the banks deal with one another via two foreign exchange brokers in Montreal and Toronto. The brokers are salaried employees of the Canadian Bankers Association and do not operate on their own account or charge the customary brokerage. Their activities are informational but impersonal. When the broker receives an order from a bank, he immediately contacts the banks that he believes are on the other side of the market. When the negotiation is completed, all banks concerned as well as the Bank of Canada are informed of the amount, price, and settlement date. Names are not disclosed to parties not directly involved.

The second sector of the foreign exchange market is the foreign exchange departments at the head offices of the Chartered Banks. They act as wholesalers of foreign exchange for their own branches, especially for their domestic and overseas branches. At the same time, they keep contact with the brokers from whom they receive up-to-date information concerning the foreign currency market. They prepare daily bulletins for dispatch to branches in regard to the buying and selling rates of all major international currencies, especially the U.S. dollar and sterling.

The third sector of the market is the branch banks throughout the country, from which foreign exchange is retailed to individual clients. Every branch bank can conduct foreign exchange business with local customers in accordance with the guidelines laid down by the head office. The special feature of this market is the tremendous communication network involved in the retail market, since the size of the country is so big and most retail transactions are conducted in Montreal and Toronto.

The fourth sector is the direct dealings of Canadian banks with foreign banks. Foreign exchange department trading desks at the head offices correspond with branches overseas. New York, London, and other financial centers are the contact points for international currency transactions.

The Canadian foreign exchange market is usually participated in by the Chartered Banks, insurance companies, and other large financial concerns. Forward exchange through swap transactions (simultaneous spot and forward transaction for the same amount) provide active dealings in the money market. There is active interest arbitrage between New York and Montreal-Toronto when interest differentials exist in the Treasury bill or commercial paper market. U.S. dollar deposits of Canadian banks have been important since 1960 when substantial amounts of U.S. capital moved to Canada. These deposits can buy Canadian short-term credit instruments, can be channeled back to New York agencies of Canadian banks for lending purposes, and can also be relent in their original denomination in the Eurodollar market in London or Paris. At June 1973, U.S. dollar assets and liabilities of the Chartered Banks were about $11 billion, representing a second important market after the Canadian money market of $14.6 billion.

Finally, a word must be said about the exchange rate of the Canadian dollar since it is the key factor in the foreign exchange market. There has been an increase of foreign exchange activities since 1950 when exchange control was abolished by the government. The Canadian dollar was allowed to float in the period 1950-62. In 1962-70, a fixed exchange rate was maintained between the Canadian dollar and U.S. dollar. In June 1970, the Canadian dollar was allowed to float again. The Canadian dollar valuation in the New York foreign exchange market was $0.93 in 1951, $1.07 in 1962, $0.99 in 1972, and $1.00 in August 1973. These fluctuating rates in part reflect the inflow and outflow of capital into and from the Canadian money market, together with changing interest rate differentials between Canada and the United States. Table 8.6 illustrates these differentials between

TABLE 8.6

Comparison of Interest Rates between Canada and
the United States, October 3, 1973

	Central Bank Discount Rate	Day-to-day Money	Treasury Bills (91 day)
Canada	7.25	7.75	6.50
United States	7.50	10.75	7.42
	Commercial Paper	Banker's Acceptances	Certificate of Deposit
Canada	8.85	8.85	8.50
United States	8.00	9.75	9.375

Source: The Chase Manhattan Bank, International Finance, October 8, 1973.

the two countries. It should be noted that the market rates in Canada were generally lower than in the United States except in the case of commercial paper, where there has been a strong increase in paper issued by corporate short-term borrowers (reflected in Table 8.5).

Capital Market

With a high per-capita income, Canada is one of the more affluent industrialized nations of the world. However, its capital market is not developed to the extent warranted by its industrial status. One of the major reasons is that about 50 percent of the Canadian manufacturing industry is owned by U.S. firms, which generally finance their Canadian affiliates through the U.S. capital markets. This trend will continue for some time, but a viable Canadian capital market is developing and will eventually operate side by side with the U.S. market. Two factors underlie this assumption. One is the continuous increase of capital investment in both private and public sectors. Another is the government policy which not only gives incentives to capital spending, but also encourages financial institutions to channel funds to the capital market. The Economic Council of Canada (ECC) has recently launched a major study of Canada's financial markets and the Chairman of the ECC, Dr. Andre Raynauld, noted that the financial intermediary assets in Canada had grown faster than GNP since World War II. In recent years the rate of increase equaled that of the United States. Also, personal savings were channeled through the financial sectors in Canada to a greater extent than in any other Organization for Economic Cooperation and Development (OECD) country except Japan.

Primary Market

The volume and value of securities issued in the Canadian primary capital market have not been large. However, the amount of securities issued is steadily expanding. In 1972 business investment represented 14 percent of Canada's GNP. The distribution of Canada's GNP among industries in 1972 was as follows:

Manufacturing	24%
Mining and petroleum	4
Trade	12
Finance and insurance	11
Utility, transportation, and communication	12
Agriculture and forestry	11
Services	26
Total	100%

137

According to data published by the Ministry of Industry and Commerce, Canada's capital spending has fluctuated widely from year to year. The government has functioned as an anticyclical force to balance the amount of national investment spending. This "compensatory" capital spending has tended to maintain the economy on an even keel.

Tax incentives provided by government for business investment have stimulated housing construction as well as plant and equipment investment. Recently the government has tried to stem inflation by using incentive measures more selectively. Internal funds generated by economic prosperity have been employed for reinvestment purposes. In 1972 internal financing accounted for about 60 percent and external financing 40 percent of the financing of investment by nonfinancial business.

TABLE 8.7

Major Sources of Funds Raised by Private
Nonfinancial Business
(millions of dollars)

	1970	1971	1972	First Quarter 1973
New issues				
Bonds				
Canadian dollars	984	1,376	959	425
Foreign currency	364	96	1	53
Stocks				
Canadian dollars	285	297	385	91
Foreign currency	19	10	12	12
Commercial paper	180	288	-111	440
Banker's acceptances	221	9	-13	87
Subtotal	2,052	2,076	1,233	1,108
Increases in loans				
Chartered Banks	407	2,036	2,297	1,880
Sales finance companies	-174	279	359	280
Industrial development bank	69	54	79	58
Subtotal	302	2,369	2,735	2,218
Direct investment from abroad	835	880	680	325
Total funds raised	3,190	5,325	4,648	3,651

Source: Bank of Canada, Review, September 1973.

Table 8.7 indicates that of the total funds raised by private non-financial business in the period 1970-73, short-term financing has been increasingly stressed. Bond and stock issues accounted for about 50 percent of total funds raised in 1970, but for only one-third of the total in 1971 and 1972. Equity financing has steadily increased, but accounted for only 8 percent of total funds raised.

The bond market is dominated by government securities issued by federal, provincial, and municipal governments. While the federal government emphasizes medium-term bonds (three-year maturity) referred to as "short Canadas," provincial and municipal governments have preferred to use long-term debt. Corporate bonds are comparatively smaller in amount than government bonds, but they have enjoyed a good market. Once the bonds are underwritten, they are distributed in the primary market and will go to the informal market—over the counter—easily. Pension funds and insurance companies are principal bond investors. The market for mortgage bonds is active. Traditionally, trust and mortgage loan companies accounted for over 50 percent of the market, but Chartered Banks have increased their shares in market since the passage of the National Housing Act of 1967 when the Chartered Banks' lending rate was freed from the prior limit of 6 percent. In 1972 Chartered Banks shared 35 percent of the total mortgage market, while trust and mortgage companies shared 40 percent, and other nonbank financial institutions took the rest.

Secondary Market

The secondary market began operation in Canada when the Montreal and Toronto Stock Exchanges were established in the 1870s. Between the two world wars, stocks traded on the exchanges were limited to a few industrial, mining, and oil companies. The government bond market has been active, but debt instruments are transacted on the over-the-counter market. Furthermore, a considerable proportion of Canadian corporations are not publicly owned or are controlled to a considerable degree by foreigners. These corporations do not turn to the capital market for financing. They usually rely on internal financing or on foreign capital. Smaller corporations rely more on short-term financing and, to a lesser extent, on equity financing. In 1964 the Royal Commission on Banking and Finance suggested an improvement of the capital market efficiency by an increased role of financial institutions. However, the basic problem was structural, not institutional. As the Toronto Stock Exchange noted, this Canadian dilemma will continue in the future due to the enormous amounts of capital that will be required to finance the oil and gas pipelines proposed for the coming years. This capital (approximately $2 billion per year) will be raised by the issuing of bonds in New York.

Despite these problems, the Canadian stock market has grown impressively along with the industrial growth of the economy at large. The most active stocks, such as International Nickel Company of Canada, Imperial Oil Ltd., Canadian Pacific Ltd., Iso Mines Ltd., Anglo United Development Corporation, Bank of Montreal, traded over 4 million shares each in 1972. The stock exchanges are prosperous

TABLE 8.8

Comparisons of Common Stock Price Index in
Canada and the United States

	June 1969	June 1970	June 1971	June 1972	June 1973
Toronto Stock Exchange 153 industrials (1965 = 100)	177.0	151.5	180.7	199.7	208.4
Montreal and Canadian Stock Exchanges 65 industrials (1956 = 100)	183.2	150.9	182.5	159.5	230.5
U.S. Dow Jones Industrials 30 stocks	873.2	683.5	891.1	929.0	891.7

Sources: Wall Street Journal: Bank of Canada, Review.

TABLE 8.9

Comparisons of Value of Shares Traded on
Canadian and U.S. Stock Exchanges
(millions of dollars)

	June 1969	June 1970	June 1971	June 1972	June 1973
Toronto, Montreal, and Canadian Stock Exchanges	778.4	300.0	562.8	658.4	468.1
New York Stock Exchange	10,847.0	8,000.0	12,249.0	13,124.0	9,852.0

Source: Bank of Canada, Review, September 1973.

due to the high per-capita income of Canadian citizens. The rapid growth of financial institutions such as pension funds and mutual funds has stimulated the stock markets in Canada. Life insurance companies have also increased their equity holdings to hedge against inflation. The increased demand for stock trading led to the establishment of the Vancouver Stock Exchange in 1968.

The secondary equity market in Canada is influenced by the U.S. stock market but not to the same degree as the primary equity market. Table 8.8 illustrates the same downward price trends in 1970 and upward price movements in 1971 in both countries. The value of shares traded followed the same down-up pattern as indicated in Table 8.9. However, the in period June 1972 to June 1973, the common stock price index went up, but the value of shares traded went down in Canada, reflecting the concentration of trading in "blue chip" industrial securities. The U.S. Dow Jones Industrial Index as well as the value of shares traded on the New York Stock Exchange (which accounts for about 90 percent of all stock trading in the United States in the secondary market) declined. It is not difficult to detect that the Canadian economy has been moving upward on all fronts since 1971, but the U.S. economy suffered a slowdown in 1970-71 as a result of the wage-price control and uncertainty of the value of the U.S. dollar in the international community. After the second devaluation of the U.S. dollar in February 1973 (the first devaluation was in December 1971 after the Smithsonian Agreement), the U.S. economy displayed a real recovery, as did the U.S. stock market.

Another difference between these two countries' stock markets is in stock dividend yields. The stock dividend yield (industrials) as reported by the Toronto Stock Exchange in June 1973 was 3.20 percent. In the same period, Standard and Poor's stock dividend yield (industrials) in the United States was 7.13 percent. This seems to reflect the relatively conservative dividend policy of the Canadian firms, which may have a detrimental effect on the Canadian stock market.

GOVERNMENT POLICY AND
INTERNATIONAL FINANCE

From 1890 onward Canada became increasingly important as a trading nation. In the mid-1960s Canada became the fifth largest foreign trading nation, following the United States, United Kingdom, Japan, and West Germany. Over 20 percent of GNP is related to exports. In statistical terms, the United States accounts for approximately 60 percent of foreign trade, 70 percent of all foreign direct investment in Canada (out of the total $43 billion in 1972), 80 percent

141

of foreign-owned Canadian government bonds, and 65 percent of all foreign portfolio investment in Canada. On the other hand, 65 percent of all Canadian private investment is in the United States. Canadian swap deposits and brokerage loans are closely tied to the U.S. money market. It is said that while Canada is politically close to the United Kingdom, it is economically more dependent on the United States. This presents advantages as well as disadvantages. This explains why the Canadian government wants to maintain healthy relations with the United States and simultaneously develops its trade with Asian, European, and African countries to reduce its dependence on the United States. Major ownership of Canadian manufacturing and mining industries will be gradually transfererd to Canadian citizens. These changes will certainly have enormous effects on the financial markets in both countries.

Balance of Payments

Since 1961 Canada's merchandise trade surplus with the rest of the world has more than offset its traditional deficit with the United States. Although the United States is still Canada's major trading partner, Japan replaced Britain as its number two trading customer. The devaluation of the Canadian dollar in 1962 has contributed to the improvement in its trade balance. Its manufactured goods have been more competitive in the world market, and crop failures in the Soviet bloc and Mainland China raised Canadian wheat sales since 1963. Furthermore, export promotion programs were launched by the government during the 1960s. The establishment of the Export Credit Insurance Corporation and Trade Commission is example of this policy emphasis. Between 1969 and 1972, Canada increased its exports at an annual rate of over 10 percent, while its imports fluctuated down in 1970 and up (by 20 percent) in 1972. From the financial market standpoint, the expansion of Canadian foreign trade requires more capital investment and foreign trade financing. The growing volume of banker's acceptances held by Chartered Banks is probably the best evidence of this.

Canada's general economic prosperity and successes in foreign trade are not without problems. Capital requirements of both industry and public entities can be met only with the help of foreign borrowing, mainly on the New York market. Over a billion dollars a year is required to service interest and dividend payments on foreign loans and investments in Canada. This has been a major factor responsible for the deficit on current account in Canada's balance of payments. 1970 was the first year that the current account showed a surplus since 1952, but the growing debt service account has been a cause for continued concern by the Canadian government.

It is noted that the deficit on current account has been covered by inflows of long-term capital. The overall surplus in most of the postwar years permitted the Canadian central bank to accumulate a substantial amount of international reserves. This strong monetary position has provided a good base for the Canadian dollar in the international currency and foreign exchange markets in recent years.

Other International Financial Activities

Canada has increasingly played an important role in the international financial community after World War II due to its highly developed industrial economy and sound currency. Canadian international financial activities are mainly related to its role in various

TABLE 8.10

Canada's Balance of Payments
(millions of dollars)

Current Account	1960	1969	1970	1971	1972
Merchandise exports	5,392	14,832	16,750	17,929	20,068
Merchandise imports	5,540	14,007	13,833	15,532	18,571
Balance on trade	-148	825	2,917	2,397	1,497
Deficit on services and transfers	-1,095	-1,777	-1,857	-1,996	-2,076
Current account balance	-1,243	-952	1,060	401	-579
Capital account					
Balance on long-term capital	900	2,105	738	394	1,773
Short-term capital movements (net)	304	-1,088	-268	-18	-978
Net capital movements	1,204	1,017	470	376	795
Allocations of special drawing rights	—	—	133	119	117
Net official monetary movements	-39	65	1,663	896	333
Total official international reserves	2,260	3,106	4,679	5,570	6,049

Source: Bank of Canada, Review, December 1970 and September 1973.

143

international organizations and the support of national interests in the world economy.

With regard to its memberships in international organizations, Canada has taken the position of "give and take." As a member of the United Nations, Canada has participated in the International Food Aid Program and the Educational and Technical Assistance Program, in which Canada provided $200 million for aid and $220 million for loans in the period 1971-72 through the Canadian International Development Agency. Canada's association with the United Kingdom and the United States obligated it to aid the Southeast Asian countries under the Columbo Plan, to help the African countries belonging to the Commonwealth, and to contribute funds to the Inter-American Development Bank for the economic development of Latin American countries. However, Canada's membership in the International Monetary Fund (IMF) resulted in many benefits including financial assistance in stabilizing its currency fluctuations in the 1950s.

For its own national interests, Canada has extended short-term credits to many less developed countries as well as Communist countries to finance purchases of Canadian commodities. In order to take advantage of the international financial markets, foreign branches of Canadian banks have been operating on a worldwide basis. Since Canada can provide a financial "bridge" between the United States and the United Kingdom, a substantial amount of unrecorded capital flows back and forth through this "bridge." An agreement was reached between the United States and Canada in 1966 to prevent outflows of portfolio investment funds from the United States through Canada to other countries. In the last several years, the most notable Canadian international activities have been its increased borrowings in the Eurobond market and decreased borrowings in the United States via sale of U.S. dollar bonds. For example, in 1972 Canada issued $273 million of deutsche mark (DM) bonds, $59 million of French franc bonds, and $20 million of U.S. dollar bonds in the international bond market.

REFERENCES

Bank of Canada. Annual Report, 1972.

Bank for International Settlements. Forty-Third Annual Report, June 1973.

Botha, D. J. J. "The Canadian Money Market." South African Journal of Economics (June and December 1972).

Diebold, Jr., William. The U.S. and the Industrial World. New York: Praeger Publishers, 1972.

Dominion Bureau of Statistics. Statistics Canada, various issues, 1973.

Perkins, J. O. N., ed. Macro-Economic Policy. A comparative study: Australia-Canada-New Zealand- South Africa. Toronto: University of Toronto Press, 1973.

Raynauld, Andre. "Financial Market Slated for ECC Scrutiny." The Canadian Banker (November-December 1972).

Report of the Royal Commission on Banking and Finance. Ottawa: Queens Printer, 1964.

Toronto Stock Exchange Review. Toronto: Toronto Stock Exchange, monthly.

9

**FINANCIAL
MARKETS IN
THE UNITED KINGDOM**

STERLING AND LONDON IN WORLD FINANCE

The United Kingdom enjoys a special role and status insofar as the international financial markets are concerned. At various intervals over the nineteenth century, Britain has played the role of major supplier of capital to the rest of the world, as well as that of international banking and financial center. For the century prior to 1914, sterling was the world's major currency, and London financed upward of 60 percent of world trade. The openness of UK financial markets was such in the decade prior to World War I that UK foreign investment was equal to over 7 percent of national product.

Between the two world wars, New York emerged as a leading financial center, competing with London. But the latter was still considered as a major long-term capital exporter, while the former country emphasized providing short-term funds.

The financial expertise of UK financial institutions is barely equaled in other countries at advanced stages of industrial and commercial development. After World War II, the pound sterling has still maintained its popularity in international transactions, and London still retains a commanding role as a financial center for short-term funds, Eurodollars, and gold speculation.

The entry of the United Kingdom into the Common Market in 1973 opened a new chapter in the competitive performance of London and UK banks and financial institutions in an enlarged economic and monetary union. The British already have adopted the decimal system, new monetary controls, and have striven to attain balance of payments equilibrium. All these developments will contribute toward strengthening the financial position of the United Kingdom in the mainstream of international finance in the decade to come.

The Role of Sterling

Since the 18th century, London has carried out the functions and responsibilities of a world financial center. While there have been temporary lapses due to major wars and related financial disturbance, London has adapted to changing conditions and improved its facilities to service international trade, investment, and finance. The financial institutions in the United Kingdom have long been geared to servicing international requirements, an outcome of the openness of the British economy. In the same way, the pound sterling has evolved as an international currency, in which trade financing, temporary and long-term investment, security arbitrage, and various other types of overseas transactions have been effected.

In the decades prior to World War I, sterling reached its zenith as an international currency due to the combination of several forces. These include the importance of Britain in world trade and as a source of investment capital, the trade-financing facilities of the London discount market which offered trade finance on attractive and convenient terms, and the political system that prevailed whereby the trade and investment prerogatives of business firms were well protected by colonial relationships with the United Kingdom. In 1913 British overseas investment in publicly issued securities was £3,763 million, in which the colonies shared 47 percent and the rest of the world shared 53 percent.

World War I swiftly altered these finely balanced relationships, and sterling came into difficulties as foreign markets were encroached upon, colonial ties began to dissolve, and as foreign investments were liquidated or lost part of their value due to changing currency relationships and competitive pressures. During the period between the two world wars, former sterling relationships were rebuilt, but then torn apart again with the world depression of the 1930s. The fixed tie between the pound sterling and gold was cut, and sterling was allowed to depreciate in the exchange markets. An Exchange Equalization Account was established to stabilize the pound in the foreign exchange markets and has since functioned as an important arm of government exchange rate policy. World War II served to compound the problems of the United Kingdom, as sterling balances held by overseas members of the sterling area accumulated in connection with war procurement and related expenses. In 1971 sterling balances held by members of the sterling area and several other countries as foreign exchange reserves totaled over $7 billion.

Sterling continues to play a key role in international finance, even though its relative importance is not nearly as large as it was in 1914. In connection with this, the British have relied on a system of exchange controls to preserve the status and importance of sterling in world finance, while ensuring that the balance of payments pressures that result are minimized.

Exchange Controls

British exchange control is confined mainly to transactions between residents of the United Kingdom and residents of countries outside the sterling area. The latter may use sterling to settle transactions among themselves, and this external account sterling is freely convertible into other currencies. Important restrictions relate to the movement of capital from the United Kingdom to nonsterling area countries.

Due to balance of payments difficulties in the 1960s, exchange control regulations pertaining to investments outside the sterling area have been revised and made more stringent. Exports of goods to destinations outside the sterling area are subject to exchange control and, in general, have to be paid for within six months in foreign currency or external account sterling. Control is exercised over imports to ensure that currency authorized for payment is used for that purpose.

Sterling and UK Overseas Investment

Sterling has long enjoyed a special position and importance in world finance. While the reasons that formerly accounted for sterling's importance seem to be fading, new opportunities and challenges appear to offer promise of extending and revitalizing sterling's role in the future development of global enterprise and finance.

Past foreign investments and the likelihood that Britain's substantial investments overseas will continue to grow in part account for sterling's status as an investment and transactions currency. At year end 1972 United Kingdom private investors held long-term foreign investments of £18,520 million, and the United Kingdom enjoyed a net long-term foreign investment position of £9,015 million (Table 9.1). These long-term foreign investments generate a substantial flow of dividend and interest income for the UK economy. The sizable foreign investments in the United Kingdom by nonresidents also play an important role in strengthening the productivity and competitive efficiency of UK industries, and thereby their export earnings.

During the decade of the 1960s, the pound was repeatedly subjected to bear attacks by speculators, which culminated in the 1967 devaluation. Several plausible reasons have been offered to explain this weakness. First, productivity in British industry has failed to rise appreciably. Second, substantial overseas expenditures by the government in connection with defense and political support of smaller

151

TABLE 9.1

UK External Assets and Liabilities, 1972
(millions of pounds)

External Assets of UK Residents		External Liabilities of UK Residents	
Private sector:		Private sector:	
Direct investment excluding oil, insurance, and banking	8,070	Direct investment	3,980
UK oil companies, net assets abroad	2,150	Portfolio investment	2,700
UK banks and insurance companies direct investment in the United States	500	Oil company investment in United Kingdom	1,700
Portfolio investment	7,800	Other	1,125
Total UK private investment abroad	18,520	Total overseas investment in United Kingdom private sector	9,505
Total banking and commercial claims, of which 23,606 denominated in foreign currency	27,970	Banking and commercial liabilities of which 25,460 denominated in foreign currencies	29,255
Total external assets of the private sector	46,490	Total external liabilities of the private sector	38,760
Public sector:		Public sector:	
Public sector lending	1,605	Public sector borrowing including intergovernmental loans and overseas holdings of public sector debt	5,595
Reserve assets	2,165		
Total external assets of the public sector	3,770		
Total identified external assets	50,260	Total identified external liabilities	44,355

Source: Bank of England, Quarterly Bulletin, June 1973.

countries represented a drain on British foreign exchange reserves. Third, the accumulation of substantial short-term funds in London held by nonresidents left the external status of sterling precarious at times. Withdrawal of funds from London, as a result of rising interest rates in foreign money centers or a shift in the spot-forward relationship that reduced the cost of forward cover for speculators, placed the UK authorities under serious pressure.

International Importance of London

London's role as a major international financial center stems from the involvement of its banks and financial institutions in overseas transactions, from the substantial market for foreign currencies in London, and from the ability of UK authorities to achieve a successful balance between inflows and outflows of short-term funds, which in part are related to the trade finance and international deposit activities of the London institutions.

One of the most far-reaching developments in the international monetary field is the growth in markets for expatriate currencies. The currency most frequently dealt in is the U.S. dollar, and one-half of the volume of this dollar turnover is centered in London. At year end 1972, this market in foreign currencies in London exceeded $100 billion, over three-fourths of which consisted of Eurodollars.

Eurodollars are deposits in U.S. dollars placed with banks outside the United States. In London the overseas branches of large American banks tend to dominate this market. Growth of the Eurodollar market can be attributed to the interest rate structure in the United States, including the ceilings on interest rates that U.S. banks can pay on time deposits. Eurodollar funds frequently command interest rates far in excess of those being paid on time deposits in domestic offices of American banks. Additional factors responsible for growth of this market include the expansion in multinational financing requirements of large corporations that operate on a global basis and the opportunities for forward cover for those who carry on multicurrency financing transactions. In the last connection, the gap between the lower rates at which Eurodollars can be borrowed and the higher rates that prevail on short-term sterling loans has left sufficient room for forward exchange cover. Thus, Eurodollars can be drawn into London to take advantage of high interest rate opportunities, switched into sterling, and the sterling position covered with a forward sale of sterling to ensure no loss on the exchange. For British borrowers and lenders, Eurodollars become the equivalent of foreign-owned sterling with an exchange guarantee.

The London market for expatriate currencies parallels the sterling deposits maintained in the same city by nonresidents. London has served as an international deposit center for many decades. Sterling deposits held by nonresidents in part represent a clearing float that results from the large volume of international payments denominated in sterling and which clear through London banks and other financial institutions. More important, these deposits result from the need of foreign banks, corporations, and official institutions to hold sterling as a reserve for covering swings in liquidity needs. Nonresident individuals and businesses hold sterling in connection with investment transactions, for arbitrage purposes, and at times as speculative balances. In short, sterling is an important investment, arbitrage, commercial financing, and vehicle currency.

Closely associated with London's role as an international deposit center is its efficient trade-financing mechanism. International deposits result in flows of short-term funds into London, while trade-financing activities of UK banks and financial institutions give rise to short-term capital outflows. The balance between these two endeavors plays a significant role in shaping the course of British monetary policy, since an excess of capital outflow implies a drain of exchange reserves and an incentive to speculation against the pound. In addition, the monetary policies that may be pursued, given a drain on UK exchange reserves, will profoundly influence the financial markets in Britain and most probably the pace of economic activity as well.

In short, London serves as the home of the Eurodollar market, the center of short-term trade financing for the pound sterling bloc, and a major insurance underwriter in world business. It not only houses the famous Lombard Street, but also plays host to numerous foreign branch banks and subsidiaries and foreign securities firms. As of 1972 there were well over 100 foreign banks in the city of London, including about 40 American banks and banks of European, Asian, African, and Latin American countries. Communist countries such as the USSR and Mainland China also have branch banks in London for conducting their international trade and gold transactions. During the times of monetary and gold crises in the 1960s, London's gold market, Eurodollar market, and foreign exchange market were the focal point of worldwide interest and activity.

FLOW OF FUNDS

Analysis of the flow of funds through the financial markets in the United Kingdom is important and interesting for several reasons. First, the financial markets in the United Kingdom are highly developed

154

and therefore the financial sector plays an important role as an intermediary between all other sectors. Second, two of the nonfinancial
sectors, the private companies and the public sector, engage in a
heavy mix of transactions with overseas residents. Finally, the overseas sector accounts for close to one-third of all financial sources
and uses of funds.

Nonfinancial Sectors

The three nonfinancial sectors, which include personal, private
company, and public sectors, play distinct roles in the flow-of-funds
picture in the United Kingdom. The personal or household sector is
an important provider of funds to all other sectors. During 1969-70
this sector enjoyed a financial surplus averaging close to £1.1 billion
per annum. In addition, financial sources of funds including bank
borrowing, mortgage debt, and hire purchase finance provided an
additional £1.1 billion per annum. Finally, acquisitions of financial
assets (financial uses) averaged over £2.2 billion per annum, consisting
largely of claims on life insurance and pension funds as well as shares
and deposits in building societies. In addition, smaller amounts of
claims on unit trusts, local authority debt, and bank deposits were
acquired. During the two-year period, sale of company and overseas
securities by the personal sector averaged £0.7 billion per year.

The company sector, consisting of industrial and commercial
companies, incurred financial deficits during the period 1969-70,
averaging £0.7 billion. These deficits measure the excess of capital
expenditures over company saving. Additional transactions requiring
financing by companies include mergers and investment abroad.
Together with the deficit resulting from the excess of investment over
saving, these transactions brought required financing to £1.7 billion
per annum. The major sources of financing in the period 1969-70
were bank borrowing, overseas sources of funds including funds derived from overseas affiliates of UK companies and long-term borrowing abroad and domestic capital issues.

A more detailed analysis of the sources and uses of company
funds is possible based on data for companies whose securities are
quoted on the stock exchange as seen in Table 9.2. In 1969 international sources of funds provided close to 40 percent of total funds.
Short-term funds also furnished close to 40 percent of funds in that
year. Issue of loan and share capital provided the remainder of funds
for these companies. UK facilities for company finance appear to
be somewhat deficient in the area of medium-term credit, although
this gap has been partially filled by the specialized public corporations
such as the Finance Corporation for Industry.

TABLE 9.2

Uses and Sources of Funds of Quoted Companies, 1969

Use	£Million	Percent	Source	£Million	Percent
Expenditure on fixed assets	2,779	60.3	Long-term issue of loan and share capital:		
Increase in inventories	815	18.3	Ordinary shares	641	
Increase in trade credits extended	934	20.0	Preference shares	-3	
Increase in liquid assets	63	1.4	Long-term loans	353	
	1,812			991	21.5
			Short term:		
			Bank credit	492	
			Trade credit	1,064	
				1,556	
			Tax and dividend accruals	224	38.8
			International:		
			International sources, international trading profit, income from investments and other receipts (depreciation provision, 1,117)	1,117	24.4
			(returned profit, 703)	703	15.3
Total uses of funds (Includes data for 1,701 companies)	£4,591	100.0	Total source of funds	£4,591	100.0

Source: Central Statistical Office, Annual Abstract of Statistics. London: Her Majesty's Stationery Office (HMSO), 1971.

The public sector has three major components, including the central government, local authorities, and public corporations (nationalized industries). During the two-year period 1969-70, the public sector enjoyed a small financial surplus. (see Table 9.3).

The central government component includes the National Insurance Funds, the Exchange Equalization Account (EEA), the National Savings Bank Fund, and the Note Issue Department of the Bank of England. Therefore, the financial surplus or deficit position of this component reflects a mixture of types of transactions including changes in the public's holding of currency and coin, receipts and expenditures that influence the cash position of the government, and operations of the EEA. An inflow of foreign funds could result in the EEA requiring additional sterling with which to absorb foreign exchange, compelling the central government to increase its debt issues to obtain the required sterling. This would be reflected in a larger borrowing requirement by the central government.

Overseas Sector

As indicated in Table 9.3 during 1969-70, the overseas sector incurred small deficits, which reflected the UK surplus on external transactions. The UK central government was able to repay overseas borrowing in this period partly through local authority borrowing from overseas and inflows of deposited funds through UK banks. More detailed analysis of the UK external accounts follows in a later section of this chapter.

Financial Sector

There are two dimensions to the importance of the financial sector in the UK money and capital markets. First, the financial institutions bid for funds and in turn allocate them to competing ultimate users. Second, the financial institutions, especially the banks, participate in deposit and loan transactions with the overseas sector, and these transactions affect the domestic financial markets as well as the overall external accounts of the United Kingdom. The detailed activities of financial institutions are analyzed in a subsequent section in connection with discussion of the money and capital markets.

The nonbank institutions that account for the largest flows of funds are the life insurance and pension funds and the building societies. These institutions generally account for 85 to 90 percent of the funds that flow through the nonbank institutions.

TABLE 9.3

United Kingdom: Saving, Investment, and Changes in
Financial Assets and Liabilities
(millions of pounds)

Items	Years	Public Sector	Overseas Sector[a]	Persons	Industrial and Commercial Companies	Banks	Other Financial Institutions
Saving plus net capital transfers	1969	4,107	—	2,058	3,526	218	
	1970	4,971	—	2,443	3,274	271	
	1971	4,209	—	2,664	4,043	303	
Gross domestic capital formation (-)	1969	-3,754	—	-1,165	-3,883	-554	
	1970	-4,109	—	-1,265	-4,261	-596	
	1971	-4,636	—	-1,588	-3,952	-565	
Financial surplus or deficit (-)	1969	353	-443[b]	893	-357	-336	
	1970	862	-611[b]	1,178	-987	-325	
	1971	-427	-952[b]	1,076	91	-262	
Corresponding changes in financial assets and liabilities[c]							
Bank lending	1969	155	-4,859	77	-664	5,271	2
	1970	-402	-2,539	-59	-1,125	4,206	-8
	1971	445	-2,255	-576	-731	3,535	-41
Notes and coin and bank deposits	1969	-130	4,734	381	-130	-5,040	18
	1970	-187	3,328	937	333	-4,683	27
	1971	-205	3,358	1,151	1,096	-5,507	10
Total currency flow[d]	1969	743	-743	—	—	—	—
	1970	1,287	-1,287	—	—	—	—
	1971	3,228	-3,228	—	—	—	—
Overseas loans and investments	1969	30	-214	—	202	—	-1
	1970	297	-144	—	-112	—	-4
	1971	358	33	—	-358	—	-3
Marketable government debt	1969	203	42	78	-12	-592	28
	1970	-280	44	-227	9	140	31
	1971	-3,700	473	454	-1	1,383	1,39
Nonmarketable government debt	1969	-211	59	-235	375	14	-
	1970	326	-32	-50	-231	-21	
	1971	-172	-28	396	-184	-16	
Local-authority debt	1969	-601	29	230	-84	312	11
	1970	-538	-38	-75	-119	483	28
	1971	-657	81	-217	25	772	-
Claims on other financial institutions[e]	1969	—	-2	2,534	56	—	-2,58
	1970	—	51	3,414	-10	—	-3,45
	1971	—	57	4,219	-22	—	-4,25
Shares and securities[f]	1969	13	114	-352	-175	26	37
	1970	6	-108	-753	125	67	66
	1971	85	128	-1,184	-130	180	92
Other domestic loans[g]	1969	146	—	-953	-241	-8	1,05
	1970	154	—	-1,335	-288	39	1,43
	1971	65	—	-1,946	25	91	1,76
Unidentified	1969	5	397	-867	316	259	
	1970	199	114	-674	431	47	
	1971	126	429	-1,221	371	-179	

[a]A negative figure indicates an increase in UK claims (or a decrease in UK liabilities) vis-à-vis the overseas sector.

[b]Balance of goods and services.

[c]A minus sign represents a decrease in assets or an increase in liabilities.

[d]Equals total official financing with overseas sector.

[e]Net inflow to life insurance and pension funds and deposits with other financial institutions.

[f]Including transactions in unit trust units.

[g]Mainly loans for house purchase.

Source: Bank of England.

The major uses of funds of the financial institutions are for company and overseas securities, loans for house purchase (building societies), and acquisition of government securities. In addition, small amounts of funds are used to acquire short-term assets, to make loans to local authorities, and for hire purchase.

BANKS AND THE LONDON MONEY MARKET

Banks and the Discount Market

Four institutions play a prominent role in the London discount market. These include the clearing banks, the discount houses, the Bank of England, and the Accepting Houses.

The London clearing banks play an important role in the London discount market as lenders of funds to the discount market and as investors in Treasury bills and other short-term paper. The clearing banks maintain one-third of their assets in liquid form and the remaining two-thirds in advances and investments. By arrangement with the Bank of England, the clearing banks have maintained a cash reserve of at least 8 percent of gross deposits, consisting of balances with Bank of England and coin and notes in vault. In addition, they maintain other liquid assets, which consist of money at call in the discount market and bills discounted. The latter consists of Treasury bills and other (commercial) bills. Until 1971 a basic understanding between the banks and the Bank of England was that the liquidity ratio would not fall below 28 percent and that the ratio of cash reserves to gross deposits would be maintained at 8 percent. In that year changes, which are described below, were introduced. The clearing banks can resort to sale of Treasury bills to adjust their cash reserve position as well as call advances made to the discount houses.

The Bank of England can influence the volume of liquid assets held by the banks by buying or selling government securities. Purchases of governments increase bank reserves (balances with the Bank of England), and sales have the opposite effect. A leverage attaches to the process since each pound of bank reserves supports several pounds of deposits and advances.

The discount market is peculiar to London, since it functions as a buffer between the commercial banks and the central bank. In other countries, banks rediscount eligible short-term paper directly with the central bank and look to that institution to replenish their liquidity. The Bank of England holds a large part of the cash reserves of the banks, but does not normally allow direct borrowing. When the clearing banks wish to replenish their balances at the central bank,

159

they do so through the discount market. The discount market is a pool of short-term assets and liquid funds, consisting in large part of weekly Treasury bill issues and claims among the various types of banks, discount houses, and other short-term borrowers and lenders. By recalling funds from the discount market, the clearing banks force the discount houses into the Bank of England to obtain short-term accommodation.

By convention, the banks purchase Treasury bills through the discount houses as opposed to submitting tenders for Treasury bills at the weekly auction. In addition to adjusting their liquidity and cash reserve positions by calling money at loan to discount houses, the clearing banks may further adjust their positions by a change in the ownership of Treasury bills and other short-dated assets. Therefore, the discount market provides a ready means by which banks can increase or decrease their liquid asset holdings. In the past, the market has served the purposes of the Treasury, by "covering the weekly tender" of Treasury bills, that is, submitting a bid to take up the balance of bills remaining after outside bidders have received their allocation of Treasury bills. However, this practice was discontinued in 1971.

Since the Bank of England has the function of auctioning off Treasury bills and managing the day-to-day performance of the money market, their exists a complex set of relationships between the bank and the discount market. The bank may support the market when it is short of funds, buying bills and thus alleviating pressures on the discount houses. Alternately, the bank may allow the market to be forced into the bank to borrow at penalty rates which quickly transmits rising rate pressures to all sectors of the money market. When the bank wishes to intervene in the discount market, it does so through its bill-broker (the special buyer). At times the Bank of England may purchase Treasury bills from the clearing banks themselves, or may rely on special deposits to more effectively curb bank credit expansion.

The banks are probably the most important institutions in the city of London. The clearing banks and the Bank of England provide the money supply and short-term credit, and the Bank of England's control over the clearing banks regulates the growth of the money supply and credit base. The merchant banks and discount houses finance the short-term credit needs of business. In addition, the merchant banks play an important role in the new issues and investment management fields. The overseas banks and merchant banks form the nucleus of the foreign exchange market.

In the following sections, we review the structure of the money market and the role of the major institutions in that market. Also, we examine the foreign banking sector in London and the role it plays.

Finally, we examine the new markets in London for short-term funds and the significance they have for the financial structure of the United Kingdom.

Overseas Banks and the Money Market

We turn now to the other banks in London, those that are not included among the clearing banks. These institutions carry on financial activities that are far different from those of the clearing banks and include foreign trade financing, underwriting, international deposits and loan, and foreign exchange transactions.

The Accepting Houses include the 16 members of the Accepting House Committee. These institutions are also referred to as merchant banks, a designation which includes a number of other similar institutions that are located in London and carry on similar activities. Strictly speaking, the Accepting Houses provide lines of credit against which bills can be drawn for purchases of goods. Merchant banks may carry on a mixture of activities including the accepting of bills, organizing and underwriting new issues, and functioning as financial advisors in managing investments and arranging company mergers. Because of their wide overseas connections, the merchant banks have wielded considerable influence in London.* In 1972 over half of the deposits of the Accepting Houses were nonsterling (Table 9.4). There was a fairly close balance between deposits and advances to overseas residents.

London has long been an international banking center and focal point of the Commonwealth banking system. During the late 1960s branches of American banks were attracted to London, due in part to the rapid growth of nonsterling deposit and loan activities. Over 80 percent of the deposits of American banks in London are nonsterling, most denominated in dollars. In addition, London has attracted numerous foreign banks, including banks from European countries, Africa, Japan, and other parts of the globe.

Total deposits of the Accepting Houses and overseas banks in 1972 were in excess of £36 billion, of which £28 billion was nonsterling and £20 billion due to overseas residents. Over £19 billion was allocated in the form of advances to nonresidents and another £1 billion in loans to UK local authorities.

---

*Familiar names long prominent in the ranks of London merchant banks include Baring Brothers, Hambres Bank, Montagu, Rothschild (N.M) and Sons, and Warburg.

TABLE 9.4

Selected Deposits and Assets —Accepting Houses and Overseas
Banks in the United Kingdom, October 1972
(millions of pounds)

| Institution | Deposits | | | | Loans to UK Local Authorities | Assets | |
	Total	Nonsterling	Overseas Residents	Negotiable CDs		Advances to Overseas Residents	Negotiable Sterling CDs Held
Accepting Houses	4,133	2,114	1,389	580	440	1,279	449
British overseas and Commonwealth	8,552	5,788	4,752	1,264	513	3,707	404
American banks	16,353	13,890	9,708	2,153	267	9,773	433
Overseas banks, foreign and affiliates	4,275	3,570	2,659	449	54	2,254	88
Other overseas banks	3,190	2,790	1,839	100	7	2,210	54
Totals	36,503	28,152	20,347	4,546	1,281	19,223	1,428

Source: Bank of England.

162

The connections between the overseas and foreign banking sector and the London discount and money markets are numerous. As a group these institutions held the following discount and money market assets and investments in October 1972:

	(million pounds)		(million pounds)
Money at call to discount market	481	Negotiable sterling certificates of deposit	1,428
Treasury bills	85		
Other United Kingdom bills	250		
Acceptances	1,128	Loans to United Kingdom local authorities	1,281
British government stocks up to five years' maturity	236		
Total	4,889		

The overseas and foreign banking sector provides between one-fourth and one-fifth of the funds employed by the discount houses, plays an important role as investor in Treasury and other UK bills, operates on both sides of the certificate of deposit (CD) market, and provides sizable loans to UK local authorities. In the latter case, the overseas banks may obtain nonsterling (Eurodollar) deposits, which they swap into sterling, and lend to local authorities. Local authority loans represent one of the important new money market sectors in London.

As can be seen, the overseas banking sector plays a prominent role in the London money market. By attracting nonresident deposit funds and investing these in discount market securities and in call loans to the discount houses, these banks provide an added measure of liquidity and growth. Equally important, these banks have played a central role in the development of the new (parallel) money market sectors in London, which include the market for foreign currency loans, local authority loans, CDs, and interbank loans.

New Money Market Sectors

The 1960s witnessed an explosive growth in the money market sectors in London. This growth is closely related to the expansion of various specialist or nonclearing banks, the merchant banks, the foreign banks, and ultimately specialized subsidiaries of the clearing banks. These banking institutions are generally referred to as the money market banks because they find their liquidity in the parallel markets rather than in the discount market. The supply of funds to the parallel markets has been assured because interest rates in these market sectors have been higher than call money rates with the discount houses. The demand for funds comes from the local authorities and hire purchase companies, and an interbank market evens off the positions of individual banks. Since the middle 1960s, even the discount houses have joined in parallel market activities. The discount houses have been trading in new parallel market paper such as local authority bonds and bank-issued CDs, and have bought interests in the brokers that run the parallel markets. As a result, the old discount market and newer parallel markets have merged together.

The sterling CD market represents a way in which the discount houses deal in the parallel market. The sterling CD market has developed as an extension of the interbank market with deposits raised by issuing CDs, in part placed on the local authority market. Sterling CDs were first issued in October 1968. While they do not qualify as reserve assets for banks, they are subtracted from a bank's total deposit liabilities in calculating required reserves against deposits.

The amount of sterling CDs outstanding more than doubled in each of the three years 1969-71, and a substantial acceleration in the 12 months to September 1972 brought the total outstanding to £4.5 billion compared with £1.8 billion a year earlier. As of September 1972, there were 144 issuing banks. Prior to the new arrangements for credit control that were introduced in September 1971, the clearing banks were precluded by the interest rate conventions then in force from issuing CDs in their own names. Since then they have made considerable use of CDs as a means of attracting funds. By September 1972 the clearing banks accounted for 24 percent of the total outstanding.

An active secondary market has developed for sterling CDs, with turnover in any one month approximating 40 percent of all issues outstanding. Holdings by members of the London Discount Market Association form the greater part of the secondary market in sterling CDs. Two forms of forward dealing in sterling CDs have become available in London. The first consists of rollover issues, whereby a one-year maturity CD may be issued with the understanding that at the end of the year it will be extended on a firm rate basis. The second is based on contractual arrangements undertaken by banks, discount houses, and others to buy or sell certificates at some future date based on a foreseeable surplus or shortage of funds. The interest rate is fixed at the time of contract, providing a hedge against the risk of changes in interest rates.

Other sectors of the parallel markets, namely, the local authority market, the interbank market, and the Eurocurrency market, are supported by distinct demand and supply conditions. The local authority market is influenced by the requirements of local authority treasurers for funds. Local authority borrowings via funded debt is strictly controlled. However, this is not the case where direct lending takes place.

The sterling interbank market competes with the sterling CD market as a method of ready adjustment of bank liquidity. Transactions in the interbank market may include Eurodollars swapped into sterling. There is an increasing tendency for banks to become involved in intercompany loans. Some of the large merchant banks are arranging loans for companies through the intercompany market. It is quite possible that a sterling-syndicated loan market, analogous to the Eurocurrency-syndicated loan market, will develop and merge into the intercompany loan market.

CAPITAL MARKET FACILITIES

Major Institutions

The UK capital market is as much influenced by the policies and operations of major financial institutions as any other capital market in the world. The most important institutions in the London market are the insurance companies and pension funds, building societies, investment trusts, and unit trusts.

Insurance Companies

The insurance companies are the largest and embrace companies that carry on both life and nonlife insurance operations domestically and overseas. The life and annuity funds of insurance companies are of major importance to the British capital market. The investment policies of the insurance nonlife funds are distinct from the life funds. A major part of nonlife (fire, accident, and marine insurance) business of British companies is transacted overseas or in London on foreign account, and a substantial part of these asset reserves is invested abroad. Income on these overseas investments and operations represents a sizable part of the invisible earnings in the UK balance of payments.

Measured by their asset holdings, British life insurance companies represent the largest single category of financial institutions in the UK capital market. Only the foreign sector banks in London have combined asset holdings that exceed those of the life companies. As indicated in Table 9.5 during the 10-year period 1958-68, assets of British insurance companies more than doubled, reaching a total

165

of £14,381 million in 1968. A large part of these funds represents life and annuity funds; the remainder represents assets connected with other insurance lines. In 1968 the largest investments of insurance companies were in company shares (one-fourth of total assets), debentures (one-sixth of assets), British government securities (one-seventh of assets), and mortgages (one-seventh of assets). Over the 10-year period, the composition of life insurance company investment portfolios shifted away from British and foreign government securities and toward company shares and debentures. The amount of preferred stocks and shares remained fairly constant through the 10-year period. These changes in portfolio reflect competitive pressures, the desire to use ordinary shares as an inflation hedge, and the pressure on life companies to increase the income and capital value performance of their investments.

The life insurance companies and other savings institutions are now the mainstays of the stock market and new issues market. In recent years the annual increase in life insurance funds to be invested has exceeded £1 billion pounds, which has resulted in substantial acquisitions of company and government securities, as well as mortgages (see Table 9.5).

Taken together, the assets of the building societies, investment trusts, and unit trusts exceed the investments of the insurance and pension funds. However, their portfolio configurations are not at all similar to those of the insurance companies, and their role in the capital market is quite different.

The building societies play a specialized role in the capital market, obtaining relatively small share and deposit amounts from individual savers and investing the bulk of these funds in mortgages. In 1970 the building societies held £10.5 billion in assets, of which £8.8 billion were mortgages and £1.0 billion in government securities. They do not invest in risk (equity) securities on the stock exchange.

The investment trust companies raise capital by selling risk securities on the stock exchange. They use the proceeds to invest in other risk securities. Traditionally investment trusts have allocated a high proportion of their assets in overseas securities. It was reported that in 1953, the 234 investments trusts whose shares were quoted on the London Stock Exchange held £580 million in assets, which were distributed as follows: 15 percent in the Commonwealth, 25 percent in North America, and 9 percent in other overseas countries. As of 1970, investment trusts held assets of £4.5 billion, which included £2.6 billion in company securities, £1.5 billion in overseas investments, and £0.2 billion in government securities. Virtually all of the company and overseas securities are in the form of ordinary shares.

TABLE 9.5

Major Asset Holdings of British Life
Insurance Companies
(million pounds)

	1958		1963		1968	
	£million	Per-cent of Total	£million	Per-cent of Total	£million	Per-cent of Total
Stocks and shares ordinary	1,082	18.0	2,020	22.0	3,603	25.0
Stocks and shares preference and guaranteed	356	5.9	393	4.3	358	2.5
Debentures	822	13.7	1,337	14.5	2,337	16.2
Foreign govern- ment securities	444	7.4	589	6.4	716	5.0
British govern- ment securities	1,232	20.5	1,579	17.1	2,011	13.9
Mortgages	716	11.9	1,229	13.4	1,977	13.7
Land, building, and fixtures	499	8.3	847	9.2	1,369	9.5
Total assets	5,999	100.0	9,211	100.0	14,381	100.0

Source: Central Statistical Office, Annual Abstract of Statistics. London: HMSO, 1971.

The unit trusts differ from the investment trusts in several respects. Unit trusts guarantee that investors can cash in their units on the basis of the market value of the underlying securities, and the price at which the managers of the trust will buy in unit trust certificates is published daily. In 1970 unit trusts held £1.3 billion in assets, of which £1 billion was invested in company (ordinary shares) securities, £135 million in overseas securities (mostly ordinary shares), and £100 million in government securities.

Institutional and Other Demand for Securities

As noted in the previous section, the building societies, investment trusts, and unit trusts are relatively specialized in the types of
investments they make. The latter two categories emphasize risk
securities, with a heavy mixture of shares in overseas companies.
The building societies emphasize mortgages. On the other hand, insurance companies and pension funds hold a broad mixture of investment types, including mortgages, company securities, government
debt instruments, and overseas securities.

An overview of the role of the major financial institutions in
the market for securities can be obtained from Table 9.6, which reflects
the demand and supply for securities. In 1969 some £878 million of
securities passed through the capital market, of which £212 million
represented company shares and £662 million represented bonds.
Company bonds made up the largest part (£416 million) of debt issues.

Acquisitions and sales by various categories of holders reflect
the following:
1. net sales of company shares by persons;
2. net sales of debt issues by monetary institutions;
3. substantial acquisition of shares and bonds by insurance companies
   and pension funds;
4. substantial acquisition of bonds (mainly central government issues)
   by other financial institutions;
5. substantial acquisition of bonds by the rest of the world, including
   central government and company bonds.

It is interesting to note the institutionalization of investment
in capital market issues that is reflected in Table 9.6. Insurance
companies and pension funds and other financial institutions together
added £594 million in bonds to their holdings, representing nearly
all of the net debt issues in 1969. In addition, these financial institutions acquired £376 million in company shares, far more than net
issues of that year. This is explained by the net sales of company
shares by persons.

New Issues

One of the major functions of the new issues market is to bring
together those who require new capital and investors willing to furnish
it.

The new issues market in London consists of a loose but well-
established collection of financial institutions, each with expertise
in the planning, organization, underwriting, and marketing of new
securities issues. While the London market may be dwarfed by the

TABLE 9.6

Supply and Demand for Capital in the Securities Market, 1969
(million pounds)

		Domestic				Foreign		Total	
Holders	Shares	Central Government Bonds	Local Authority Bonds	All Companies Bonds	Total Bonds	Shares	Bonds	Shares	Bonds
Monetary institution	21	-381	24	7	-350	—	19	21	-331
Insurance companies and pension funds	354	102	2	266	370	13	-13	367	357
Other financial institutions	50	176	40	12	228	-41	9	9	237
Rest of the world	28	164	—	200	364	-55	-36	-27	328
Central government	3	—	—	—	—	—	—	3	—
Nonfinancial enterprises	342	—	—	—	—	29	10	371	10
Public	10	—	—	—	—	—	—	10	—
Private	332	—	—	—	—	29	10	361	10
Personal sector	-589	123	7	-69	61	57	—	-532	61
Total	209	184	73	416	673	3	-11	-212	662

Source: Central Statistical Office, Annual Abstract of Statistics. London: HMSO, 1971.

market in New York in terms of volume (probably by a ratio of 10 to 1), London new issue facilities are as efficient as those that can be found anywhere else in the world.

There are several means by which new issues may be made available. New issues of company securities that are quoted on the stock exchange may be made by prospectus, a direct offer by the company to the public; offer for sale, an offer to the public by an intermediary (issuing house); or placing, a private sale to a limited number of investors. Issues to shareholders may be underwritten or not. When such issues are not underwritten, the company saves the underwriting expenses. The company gives shareholders the right to take up a number of new shares proportionate to the number of old shares held, at a price below the current market price. A "rights issue" of this type usually is accompanied by arrangements whereby shareholders who do not wish to take up their quota of new shares can sell the right to do so on the stock exchange.

Another method of issuing new capital is known as "placing" or "introduction on the stock exchange." Generally, it is applicable to small issues of shares or debentures. A stock exchange firm or group of firms agrees to sell the shares or debentures on the stock exchange as it would sell a client's block of quoted securities. The placing method avoids expenses connected with issuing a prospectus. The permission of the Stock Exchange Council must be obtained for placings.

Table 9.7 indicates the volume of capital issues in the United Kingdom in 1971-72. Over 17 percent of the new issues in 1971-72 were by overseas borrowers. Close to 60 percent of the new issues by UK borrowers reflect new long-term financing by quoted public companies. Of the £626 million and £1,117.1 million gross of quoted companies, over £230 million and £475 million, respectively, represented issues to shareholders. The remainder was offered on the basis of public issues via prospectus, offers for sale through underwriter, tenders, and placings. Placing accounted for £253 million or 33 percent of gross company issues in 1971, and £323 million or 28 percent of company issues in 1972. On a gross basis, local authority issues nearly equaled company issues in 1971. However, when allowance is made for redemptions of maturing securities, net issues of companies (£537 million) were more than double the amount of local authority net issues (£247 million).

Costs of new issues in the London market are not an important deterrent to prospective borrowers. It has been established that a medium-size (£2 million) ordinary share issue would cost $2\frac{1}{2}$ percent of the market value of the issue via placing and 4 percent via an offer for sale through an underwriting. A similar comparison in a debenture issue of the same amount indicates a cost of 0.9 percent in a placing and 2.5 percent in an offer for sale.

170

TABLE 9.7

Gross Capital Issues on the UK Market, 1971–72
(million pounds)

	1971	1972
United Kingdom Borrowers		
Local authorities		
Stocks	101.7	93.8
Bonds (all placings)	520.4	498.4
Subtotal	622.1	592.2
Quoted public companies		
Public issues and		
offers for sale	102.3	293.7
Tenders	34.3	24.4
Placings	253.4	323.3
Issues to shareholders		
Ordinary shares	169.9	359.1
Preference and loan		
capital	66.1	116.7
Subtotal	626.0	1,117.1
Total United Kingdom	1,248.1	1,709.3
Overseas Borrowers		
Public authorities		
Public issues	14.4	9.0
Placings	65.4	60.0
Companies		
Public issues	5.3	2.2
Placings	181.5	290.9
Total overseas	266.6	362.1
Grand total	1,514.7	2,071.3

Source: Bank of England.

Official controls do not play a major role in the UK capital market. The share market is well organized and supported by institutional and private resources. However, controls over issues by overseas borrowers are maintained for balance of payments reasons. Official approval is required for such issues. Local authority issues are supervised for the purpose of preserving a healthy and stable bond market. Therefore, a delay of several months may be necessary between the application by local authorities to make an issue and its actual flotation. Issues by companies are completely unrestricted with the exception that brokers are required to consult the Bank of England with regard to the timing of issues. This timing control is maintained to preserve orderly markets and generally does not delay issues for a long period of time.

The Stock Exchange

A rapidly growing part of the UK capital market is the London Stock Exchange, a secondary market in existing issues. In the 10-year period ending in 1971, the market value of quoted securities increased by 140 percent. The London Stock Exchange permits dealings in a longer list of companies than any other stock exchange in the world. London trades in 9,500 different issues, of which 3,300 represent domestic companies and the rest foreign. Many issues of U.S. and Commonwealth companies are represented in London.

In effect, London brokers can deal in any stock quoted on any other exchange in the world. London's secondary market is becoming more internationally oriented year by year. This is reflected in the international clientele as well as by the large proportion of foreign company issues traded on the stock exchange.

Trading on the exchange is specialized with jobbers (dealers) functioning as market makers in those types of securities in which they deal for their own account. Different groups of securities provide markets such as gilt-edged, industrial shares, South African Mining, rubber, oil, foreign railway, and tea shares. Brokers serve as intermediaries between investors and jobbers.

In 1971 the market value of securities quoted on the London Stock Exchange was £120 billion, of which £89 billion was represented by ordinary shares of companies, and £17 billion by British government securities (Table 9.8). The London market is extremely active. During 1971 the monthly average turnover was £5.2 billion, representing an annual volume of over £62 billion. Approximately £12 billion of this was in transactions in ordinary company shares. Ownership of securities on the London Stock Exchange is much more widespread than formerly, with about $2\frac{1}{2}$ million shareholders in the United Kingdom

TABLE 9.8

Securities Quoted on London Stock Exchange, 1971
(million pounds)

	March 1971	1966	1961
Total market value	920,504	78,164	50,951
British government and			
government guaranteed	17,108	15,220	14,900
Bonds of public boards	1,865	1,332	716
Dominion and foreign			
governments and corpora-			
tion bonds	1,889	1,516	886
Company securities			
Total	99,640	60,095	34,450
of which:			
Loan capital	4,407	2,497	1,287
Preference and			
preference capital	566	1,327	1,281
Ordinary	89,652	52,358	30,046
Shares of no par value	5,015	3,914	1,835

Source: Central Statistical Office, Annual Abstract of Statistics,
no. 108. London: HMSO, 1971, p. 347.

However, institutional ownership and trading of quoted securities have
increased steadily over the past decade. Insurance company holdings
of ordinary shares represent 7 to 8 percent of the market value of
securities quoted on the London Stock Exchange. Insurance company
holdings represent an even higher percentage of British government
securities quoted on the stock exchange.

Since World War II, the London Stock Exchange has been affected by a fundamental shift in the sources of investment business.
High taxation, a shift in savings and private investment toward middle-
income recepients, and a gradual replacement of the direct individual
investor by the institutions have been dominant trends affecting the
exchange. Due to the institutionalization of saving and the inter-
institutionalization of dealings, the exchange market has been bypassed
to a large extent. The crux of the market's problem appears to be in
attempting to keep on terms with the institutional growth.

The pattern of trading has altered significantly over the period
1958-73. In earlier times, private investors were buyers and sellers,

but in more recent time periods, dominant institutional traders have been nearly always buyers or sellers. This explains the present tendency to instant boom and instant slump. The institutions tend to act in unison, and jobbers are quick to take evasive action against what appear to be one-way savings. It might be argued that the market is in "too few hands." In this context, the stock market finds itself determining prices and trends, but taking a proportionately smaller reward for its own practitioners.

The Mortgage Market

The mortgage market in the United Kingdom is a limited one. Borrowers have a choice of lenders, and lenders a choice of properties, but the mortgage instruments rarely change hands afterward because there is no effective secondary market in mortgages.

Borrowers are private individuals or companies who charge their houses or commercial and industrial buildings, respectively. Lenders are mainly the building societies, the insurance companies, banks, and pension funds. The amounts of mortgage loan usually range between 66 and 90 percent of the property value, depending on the condition of the properties pledged. The interest rates charged also depend on the status of the borrowers and the nature of the property. Since the interest paid is tax deductible from the borrower's income tax return, the larger the borrower's income, the smaller the effective cost of borrowing.

Statistics covering mortgage of properties and interest rates are very scanty. Undoubtedly, the building societies have the lion's share of the market. Commercial mortgages have been increasingly important as a result of growing real estate business in recent years.

MONETARY POLICY AND THE BALANCE OF PAYMENTS

Monetary Policy Old and New

Monetary policy in the United Kingdom has been under periodic review by the government as witnessed by the famous Macmillan Report in 1931 and the Radcliffe Report in 1959. In the past, monetary policy in the United Kingdom was focused on the long-standing relationships among the Bank of England, the discount houses, and the clearing banks as outlined in the section on "Banks and the London Money Market." Tight monetary policy forced the discount market into the Bank of England at a penalty bank rate, and the banks accomplished liquidity adjustment via calling money at loan to the discount houses. Major credit policy measures used by the Bank of England included bank rate, moral suasion, suggested bank credit ceilings on the part of the central bank, and special deposit requirements. Open-market operations also were used to reinforce or soften developing pressures in the London money market.

Organization of the Treasury bill market was unique in that the clearing banks did not compete for newly issued bills, but bought them from the discount houses. In the past, the discount houses have supported the market for Treasury bills and longer-dated government securities by submitting "collective bids" at the weekly Treasury bill auction. Moreover, the Bank of England has provided important market support at various times.

During the 1960s, a number of developments in the UK financial markets pointed toward inadequacies in the London markets and suggested that the older sectors of the money market were no longer competitive. These included the strong growth of the parallel markets, the eventual entry into these new market sectors of the discount houses and clearing banks, and the obvious inadequacies of the policies during the 1960s that resulted in a stop-go economy and sterling devaluation. Moreover, intellectual fashion had changed, moving toward a new emphasis on controlling the money supply as a target variable. Also, high interest rates experienced during the credit squeeze of 1969-70 had removed inhibitions against high interest rates. Finally, prospective entry of the United Kingdom into the Common Market required a more competitive and flexible money market and monetary policy that would best serve the needs of a wider economic region.

In 1971 Britain's new banking and credit policy was launched. The objectives of the reforms introduced at this time included (1) a shift toward use of changes in money supply as a policy target, (2) a move toward permitting interest rates to play a more significant role in the market allocation of loanable funds, and (3) an increased emphasis in allowing a more competitive environment to develop in the London financial markets.

Implementation of the new monetary policy called for a number of specific measures in each of two areas. In the area of bank operations, three changes are worthy of mention. First, new reserve ratios apply to the banks, replacing the arrangements that are referred to in an earlier section of this chapter. Banks must maintain a $12\frac{1}{2}$ - percent reserve asset ratio relative to sterling deposits, which may consist of Treasury bills, commercial bills, government securities with less than a year to run to maturity, and call money with the London money market. This replaces the previous liquidity ratio. Second, this reserve asset ratio applies to all banks, not simply the large deposit banks. Therefore, the overseas banks and London merchant banks find themselves brought under the scope of reserve asset ratio requirements and of monetary policy pressures as well. Further, the discount houses and finance houses also are subject to reserve ratios that differ from the $12\frac{1}{2}$-percent level. Finally, London and Scottish clearing banks have abandoned their collective agreements on interest rates. Therefore, all conventions that formerly linked bank lending and deposit rates to bank rate no longer exist.

A second area in which the new monetary policy is being implemented is in the money market. First, the collective agreed bid of the discount houses on the weekly Treasury bill auction was abolished, and the authorities have discontinued the practice of agreeing to buy back long-term governments to support bond prices. This measure could have significant repercussions on the sensitivity of interest rates and related ability of the London market to attract internationally mobile funds. Second, agreement was reached with the London Discount Market Association to maintain at least a 50-percent reserve ratio in the form of public sector debt. Third, the net effect of the common reserve ratio for all banks will be that the discount houses can expect to get less funds from the clearing banks, but more from the nonclearing banks (that is, the clearing banks' liquidity requirement is now below the level of money at call formerly maintained with the discount houses, and the nonclearing banks that had no requirements on their liquidity will be strongly encouraged to place funds with the discount market). The discount houses should be well situated to quote attractive rates on call money to the nonclearing banks because a discount house can borrow without incurring reserve requirements on liabilities—the obligation is to maintain 50 percent of funds in public sector debt. By holding public debt securities financed by call money, the discount house is in effect converting a nonreserve asset into a reserve asset.

Balance of Payments

As an outward looking country, the UK economy is influenced by a number of major balance of payments forces. These include merchandise trade, invisible transactions, private long-term capital flows, official long-term capital flows, and monetary and banking transactions of an essentially short-term nature. These transactions have an important bearing on the UK financial markets in connection with overall liquidity, sectoral sources and uses of funds, and the pattern of fund flows and yield relationships.

Generally, the United Kingdom incurs a deficit on merchandise trade transactions. The year 1971 appears to be an exception (Table 9.9). This deficit is often more than offset by other current transaction

TABLE 9.9

Balance of Payments of the United Kingdom, 1971-72
(million pounds)

	1971	1972
Merchandise trade (f.o.b.)		
Exports	8,795	9,135
Imports	8,480	9,830
Trade balance	+315	-695
Services and transfers	+730	+730
Current balance	+1,045	+35
Capital movements		
Official long-term capital	-270	-250
Foreign investment in the		
United Kingdom	+1,180	+755
UK private investment abroad	-855	-1,350
Net foreign currency borrowing		
by UK banks to finance		
UK investment abroad	+ +275	+715
Trade credit	-260	-80
Other nonbank short-term		
capital	+110	-60
Total	+180	-270
Balancing item	+395	-610
Special drawing rights (SDR)		
allocations	+125	+125
Overall balance	+1,745	-720

Source: Bank for International Settlements, Annual Report, 1973, p. 96.

the so-called invisible balance. Invisible transactions include net interest, profits and dividends on private foreign investments (averaging a surplus of £485 million in 1971 and 1972), and government expenditures overseas (yielding a deficit averaging £530 million in 1971-72). Finally invisible transactions include payments and receipts for shipping services, insurance services, and other services which yielded a surplus in 1971-72 averaging over £800 million. The overall surplus on current account in 1971 was equivalent to about $1\frac{1}{2}$ percent of UK gross national product (GNP). In that year export

TABLE 9.10

Flow of Official Long-Term Capital and Private Investment
(millions of pounds)

	Official Long-Term Capital										
	1960	1961	1962	1963	1964	1965	1966	1967	1968	1969	1970
Intergovernment loans											
Loans made by the United Kingdom	61	61	62	66	84	74	94	87	90	82	110
Loans repaid to the United Kingdom	41	109	15	14	19	24	30	26	30	30	27
Intergovernment loans by the United Kingdom (net)	-20	+48	-47	-52	-65	-50	-64	-61	-60	-52	-83
Loans made to the United Kingdom	—	18	—	—	—	—	51	88	98	116	9
Loans repaid by the United Kingdom	72	82	44	45	36	16	48	66	44	112	104
Intergovernment loans to the United Kingdom (net)	-72	-64	-44	-45	-36	-16	+3	+22	+54	+4	-95
Intergovernment loans (net)	-92	-16	-91	-97	-101	-66	-61	-39	-6	-48	-178
Other official long-term capital	-11	-29	-16	-8	-15	-19	-19	-18	+23	-50	-26
Total official long-term capital	-103	-45	-107	-105	-116	-85	-80	-57	+17	-98	-204

Flow of Private Investment[b]

	1960	1961	1962	1963	1964	1965	1966	1967	1968	1969	1970
UK private investment overseas											
All areas											
Direct[b]	-250	-226	-209	-236	-263	-308	-276	-281	-410	-547	-486
Portfolio—London market loans (net new issues)	-6	-15	-2	-21	-6	+14	+18	-18	+10	+7	+16
Other	+43	+43	+41	+16	+3	+80	+65	-41	-246	-41	-95
Other (oil and miscellaneous)	-109	-115	-72	-79	-133	-154	-110	-116	-81	-86	-149
Total	-322	-313	-242	-320	-399	-368	-303	-456	-727	-667	-714
Overseas sterling area											
Direct[b]	160	-124	-122	-135	-161	-186	-119	-142	-177	-311	-209
Portfolio	+13	-11	+5	+8	+25	+50	+39	-41	-157	-20	-15
Other (oil and miscellaneous)	-54	-51	-33	-36	-51	-63	-61	-43	-20	-46	-39
Nonsterling areas											
Direct[b]	-90	-102	-87	-101	-102	-122	-157	-139	-233	-236	-277
Portfolio	+24	+39	+34	-13	-28	+44	+44	-18	-79	-14	-64
Other (oil and miscellaneous)	-55	-64	-39	-43	-82	-91	-49	-73	-81	-40	-110
Overseas investment in UK private sector											
All areas											
Direct[b]	+135	+236	+130	+160	+162	+197	+195	+170	+274	+319	+317
Investment in UK company securities											
Issues abroad (net)	+4	+8	+16	+6	+5	+5	+4	+25	+19	+6	+35
Other securities	+55	+50	+16	-34	-55	-31	-75	-46	+15	+130	+49
Other (oil and miscellaneous)	+55	+75	+57	+97	+31	+67	+140	+211	+259	+218	+326
Total	+249	+369	+219	+229	+143	+238	+264	+360	+567	+673	+727
Overseas sterling area											
Direct[b]	+14	+5	+1	-3	+1	+1	+12	+21	-4	+59	+14
Other	+2	+7	+7	-8	-17	-7	-31	-22	+42	+45	-3
Nonsterling areas											
Direct[b]	+121	+231	+129	+163	+161	+196	+133	+149	+278	+260	+303
Other	+112	+126	+82	+77	-2	+48	+100	+212	+251	+309	+413

[a] Net of disinvestment. Assets: increase-/increase+. Liabilities increase +/decrease-.
[b] Department of Trade and Industry enquiry into overseas direct investment.

Source: Central Statistical Office.

earnings were equivalent to about 15 percent of GNP. Overseas sales and income represent an important part of cash flow to UK companies, as do export receipts to UK exporters.

While the British government has undertaken outward long-term capital transfers of £200 to £250 million per year in 1970-72, long-term private foreign investment flows have been very closely balanced. Investment in the developing countries of the sterling area is, in general, free from control. While the flow to the more developed sterling area countries is subject to prior approval of the Bank of England, this is for balance of payments purposes since the United Kingdom has run consistent deficits on capital account through most of the 1960s. There is a considerable amount of investment each year through retained profits of foreign subsidiaries, and in recent years over half of net direct investment outflow has been financed in this manner. Close to 40 percent of direct investment outflows from the United Kingdom have gone to the sterling area, and much of the remainder to Western Europe and North America. Table 9.10 provides details in these areas. Overseas investors in Britain are free to repatriate the proceeds of the sale of their investments, including capital gains. Earned profit and dividends are transferable irrespective of amount. Approximately three-quarters of direct investments in the United Kingdom have come from North America and one-fifth from Western Europe.

During the late 1960s, British government aid to developing countries averaged £150 million, net of capital and interest repayments. Nearly all of this was directed to Commonwealth countries, much of it in the form of loans.

The UK banking sector accounts for most of the remaining short-term currency flow. For example, in 1970 UK banks borrowed £184 million in foreign currency (Eurocurrency) to finance UK overseas investments and borrowed another £295 million in foreign currency for other purposes. Further, sterling banking and money market liabilities increased by £242 million in the same year. The flow of export and import credit exceeded £200 million net. Finally, exchange reserves denominated in sterling increased by over £180 million. Many of these funds that entered London via short-term flows swelled the reserves of merchant banks, found their way into the local authority market, added to the incentives of overseas banks to provide call money loans to discount houses, and was used to bid up the prices of government and other securities in the London market. Hence, the impact of balance of payments pressures on the UK financial markets is most significant.

REFERENCES

Bank of England. Quarterly Bulletin, various issues.

Bell, Geoffrey. The Eurodollar Market and the International Financial System. New York: Halsted Press, 1973.

Einzig, Paul. Foreign Exchange Crises: An Essay in Economic Pathology. London: Macmillan, 1968.

Fry, Richard. "The Merchant Banking Year." The Banker (December 1973).

Goodhart, Charles A. E. "Monetary Policy in the United Kingdom." In Monetary Policy in Twelve Industrial Countries. Edited by Karel Holbik. Boston: Federal Reserve Bank of Boston, 1973.

HMSO. The United Kingdom Balance of Payments, 1971.

Organization for Economic Cooperation and Development (OECD). Financial Statistics, various issues.

10

FINANCIAL STRUCTURE

The financial markets in France have enjoyed a prestige of long standing based in part upon the early importance of this country in international finance and foreign investment. In the decades prior to World War I, Paris was second only to London as an international financial center. Total loss of investments in Russian bonds, the devastation of the two world wars, and the dirigiste economic policies introduced in the period between the two great wars reduced Paris to a shadow of its former status in international finance. Postwar reconstruction, Marshall Plan aid, a system of well-managed economic planning, and the success of the Common Market have restored France to its former position as a leading financial power on the European continent.

French economic policy in the two decades 1950-70 has emphasized breaking away from the traditional features of capitalism without unduly impairing the functioning of the free-market economy. Economic planning, selective doses of government ownership, a comprehensive system of social welfare, and regulatory and fiscal techniques have been used to dynamize an economy that had been pitifully undynamic in the pre-World War II days. The evidence suggests that French planning has been at least moderately successful. France has enjoyed an economic growth rate higher than the rates achieved in Great Britain and the United States, but not higher than in West Germany or Italy. More important, France achieved a high growth rate with a nearly constant labor force and a relatively low ratio of gross fixed investment to gross national product (GNP). By the middle 1960s France's GNP per capita was on a par with that of the United Kingdom and West Germany.

181

In the half century prior to 1914, France was the second largest exporter of capital in the world. In recent decades the flow of capital has been directed largely into the African countries that retained their ties with the French monetary area. The French balance of payments benefits from a favorable trade balance, a strong attraction for foreign investors based on membership in the Common Market, and a favorable balance on service transactions (travel, shipping, and financial services). In the period 1966-72, the volume of French exports nearly doubled. Official international reserves held by France in 1973 were in excess of $11 billion, ranking that country fourth in amount of international liquidity.

French economic planning has been of the indicative or soft variety, differing from planning of the Soviet type. This type of planning involves persuasion and stimulation, rather than constraint. Collective forecasting by a widely based group of government, industry and financial leaders in an integral aspect of French planning. This system provides the benefits of overall central planning without sacrificing the advantages of decentralization of investment and production decisions. Market mechanisms and competition continue to function, but they are guided by centrally coordinated targets as well as an invisible hand.

The framework of the French economy, most especially the financial side, has not remained unaffected by economic planning. The operation of financial institutions, the incentives for saving, and the character of monetary and credit control all have been shaped and molded by the peculiar nature of French planning. A major objective of economic policy has been to establish public control over the flow of credit so as to assure the financing of investment programs vital to the current phase of the economic plan. In 1945 the Bank of France, the four largest deposit banks, and several insurance companies were nationalized by the government. Moreover, a new body, the National Credit Council was established to determine monetary policy for the government-owned and private banks. The government also owns several other large monetary institutions, as well as narrow sectors of French industry.

Monetary control is primarily concerned with the achievement of national goals that are explicit in the economic plan. In keeping with this, the French system of credit controls assigns a higher priority to the allocation of credit than to control of the total supply of credit. The money supply has been allowed to increase rapidly enough to support a high rate of economic growth, even though at times inflation pressures have threatened the stability of the system. The bias toward inflation carries serious implications for the ability of the French economy to generate voluntary saving adequate to investment requirements. Therefore, French official and private viewpoints reflect concern over inadequate business saving in connection with the low proportion of capital investment programs financed by retained earnings. Doubtless, domestic cost inflation and price controls have played a role in this area. Household saving also has been low in proportion to income. Fifty years of uninterrupted inflation and reliance on indexed bonds (until 1958 when their issue was forbidden) have left householders few attractive saving outlets. Interest paid on savings deposits has been kept low, yielding a negative return in periods of strong price inflation. For these reasons, household savings have remained relatively low and have been invested in short-term liquid assets subject to ready conversion into real estate, precious metals, or consumer durables. An effort has been made to encourage increased saving by households and to allocate a larger share of this saving to the banking system. This has taken the form of permitting deposit banks to compete for savings deposits and providing more equal tax treatment for the various forms of liquid savings.

There is little doubt that the French financial system succeeds in allocating credit according to the general intentions of the economic plan. Moreover, the comprehensive nature of credit controls in France further suggests that there is very little slack between credit allocation and resource allocation.

BANKS AND FINANCIAL INSTITUTIONS

Banking System

The legislation of 1945, which nationalized the Bank of France, provided for the establishment of the National Credit Council, an agency which serves as a focal point for national monetary and credit policy development. The membership of the council encompasses broad representation of diverse economic groups, and its chairman and vice-chairman are the minister of economics and finance and the governor of the Bank of France, respectively. The line of policy implementation passes from the council through the Bank of France and the two major professional associations of bankers. It is the duty of these professional associations to make certain that their membership is informed concerning decisions of the National Credit Council, banking regulations, and agreements concerning banking practices.

The banking system in France includes a wide assortment of bank types. Beginning in 1945, it was decided that banks would be divided into three main categories, namely, deposit banks, business banks (banques d'affaires), and medium- and long-term credit banks. Deposit banks were restricted from accepting deposits of more than two years' duration and could not take up participations in industrial and commercial enterprises of more than 10 percent of the participation or in excess of 75 percent of their capital. The banques d'affaires could undertake participations without limit, but were restricted from taking short-term (under two years) deposits. The medium- and long-term credit banks could carry on an ordinary commercial bank business similar to that of the deposit banks and could raise long-term funds by accepting deposits of long maturity.

The distinction between deposit banks and business banks was largely obliterated in 1966, at which time the French authorities felt it was necessary to stimulate competition between banks. Banks were allowed to undertake all kinds of business, but must continue to register either as deposit or business banks. Moreover, the deposit banks are still prevented from taking up participations of more than 20 percent in industrial or commercial enterprises and from having total participations in excess of 100 percent of capital. In addition, higher capital requirements were continued vis-à-vis business banks. In the two-year period 1966-68, nearly half of the business banks changed over to deposit bank status. Moreover, there has been an increase in the number of mergers between deposit banks and business banks.

At present the deposit banks accept sight and time deposits, make short- and medium-term loans, engage in securities dealing and underwriting, and conduct a general banking business. The banks for medium- and long-term credit make loans and investments with maturities over two years.

Regulatory authority of the National Credit Council, Bank of France, and the Banking Control Commission is funneled to the banks through the Professional Association of Banks. Authority over the nationalized banks takes place through government ownership of their shares and appointment of their boards of directors. The minister of economics and finance must approve the selection of the members of the board, as well as the chairman and financial manager of each nationalized bank.

The Bank of France possesses the key position in the regulatory framework over money and short-term credit. The governor of the Bank of France is also acting chairman of the National Credit Council and permanent chairman of the Banking Control Commission. There is no ready means for direct intervention by the state in the management of the bank, and daily administration remains the responsibility of the governor.

The National Credit Council encompasses a broad representation from its 46 members, including the banks, the public, and semipublic institutions. Its activities focus on setting requirements that the banking system must follow and establishing limits within which the Bank of France may operate. The council is responsible for the organization of the banking system and requires banks operating in France to register with it. While the council wields considerable influence, in practice major policy decisions are made by the Bank of France and the minister of finance. The authority of the council extends to firms whose financial business is in areas such as brokerage, short- or medium-term credit, exchange transactions, discounting and accepting bills, or cashing money market paper.

Special-Purpose Public Institutions

A number of public and semipublic institutions engage in banking and credit activities along lines parallel to those of the registered banks. These include the popular banks that specialize in banking for individuals and small enterprises, institutions for agricultural credit, and the French Bank for Foreign Commerce. These institutions are under the direct control of the government and generally must follow the regulations that apply to the registered banks.

Founded in 1816, the Caisse des Depots et Consignations is the major financial intermediary in the French economy and the most important channel through which private savings reach the money and capital markets. The function of this governmental institution is to sit as receiver and trustee of funds, which in turn are invested in the financial markets. The Caisse des Depots obtains its resources primarily from the public and mutual savings banks, which are legally required to deposit their funds with it. It also holds the funds of the social security system, and until 1967 insurance company and pension funds also were required to be deposited with the Caisse. The institutions that place their liquid funds with the Caisse des Depots receive interest on their funds, the rate being regulated by the Caisse. The Caisse is free to invest funds for its own account or deposit them with the Treasury or Bank of France. The Caisse des Depots intervenes on the bond market when the banks have guaranteed an issue that does not sell well. The concentration of funds in the Caisse makes it an extremely important factor in the money market, although its major effects are focused on the capital market sector.

MONEY MARKET

The money market in France functions quite differently from its counterparts in other major countries such as the United Kingdom,

Canada, and the United States. These differences hinge on the special relationships between the central bank and commercial banks, the tendency toward administrative allocation of short-term as well as long-term funds, and the absence of a competitive interbank market in commercial bills.

A number of special factors in France have prevented progress toward development of a money market with elastic supply and demand components. This is unfortunate in light of the rapid progress made by the French economy in other areas. As recently as in 1968, the Wormser Report commented on the fact that inadequate development of the money market represented a handicap for the French economy. One factor that has tended to retard development of the money market is the deeply ingrained hoarding preference of the French populace. This is evidenced in the relatively high ratio of currency to money supply (42 percent in 1972) and the low ratio of quasi-money (60 percent in 1972). The latter figure compares with ratios of 250 percent in West Germany, 130 percent in Switzerland, 95 percent in Canada, and 180 percent in Spain. The unwillingness of individuals to hold liquid funds in the form of bank deposits dampens the growth of bank sources of funds and prevents the banks from being able to meet credit demand without drawing heavily on central bank credit facilities. Other factors that have tended to inhibit development of the French money market include a fiscal system that levies relatively high taxes on income derived from loans, the desire for privacy in business transactions, the lack of development of foreign trade financing and banker's acceptance market, the desire of borrowers for a personalized interest rate structure, and lack of an effective structure for open-market issue and trading of short-term government securities including Treasury bills. In the past banks have been required to purchase bills issued on tap. Specialized public institutions have been ready to finance the Treasury, including the Caisse des Depots and the savings banks, thereby discouraging competitive market financing. In the period 1968-70, about 39 percent of the increase in assets of the Caisse and savings banks was in claims on the government sector.

The Paris money market may be best discussed in connection with the operation of three distinguishable components, namely, the official market, the unofficial market, and the Eurocurrency market. In the official market, the Bank of France plays a key role as lender to the banks by means of rediscounts with the central bank within established ceilings, by lending to the banks beyond these limits at penalty rates, and by open-market operations. The unofficial or private market ecncompasses interbank dealings in unsecured short-term credits and placement of time deposits of various maturities. The Eurocurrency market in Paris deals largely in dollars and sterling and, to a somewhat lesser extent, in deutsche marks (DMs) and Swiss francs.

French banks have access to rediscount facilities with the central bank up to preestablished ceiling amounts. Until 1971, when several changes were effected in the relative advantage of using rediscount versus open-market credit facilities, the banks made extensive use of their rediscount facilities. These facilities were used for rediscounting bill holdings or for borrowing on the security of Treasury bills or commercial bills through the intermediary of one of the discount houses. Rates on such credits are fixed by the Bank of France, on the basis of the demand for rediscount credit by the banks. French banks generally made use of their credit ceilings with the central bank in preference to borrowing elsewhere at higher cost. When the banks exhausted their credit facilities at the Bank of France, they could turn to the private sector of the money market for additional liquidity. This is because the Bank of France usually applied high (penalty) rates on borrowings in excess of the rediscount ceiling. To be able to borrow from the Bank of France through the discount houses, the banks must own eligible bills. Should the banks be short of eligible bills or not want to reduce bill portfolios, they have the option of obtaining funds in the private or unofficial market. They also have the option to make use of open-market facilities, which recently (1971) were liberalized to make open-market borrowing from the Bank of France more attractive than rediscounts.

It was the Wormser Report in 1968 that criticized the French system of multiple discount rates and proposed substitution of a flexible open-market rate as a key factor affecting bank liquidity. In 1971 the new system was brought into operation; the open-market rate was permitted to fall below the discount rate, which became a penalty rate. From 1971 the banks have found it cheaper to borrow on the open market against mobilizable bills pledged with the Bank of France. The central bank in turn indicated the type of open-market paper acceptable by it, including Treasury bills, bank acceptances, and export and medium-term bills. As a result of these changes, the lowest-cost funds for bank liquidity adjustment are borrowing from the Bank of France via open-market operations, borrowing interbank (described below), and rediscount, in that order.

The unofficial money market in France is an interbank market in which banks provide overnight and day-to-day loans, as well as place time deposits. A large proportion of the business in this market is transacted through brokers or dealers operating for their own account. Nonbank financial institutions participate in this market through bankers, dealers, or brokers. The market in time deposits has expanded, in part due to the increased access of nonbank institutions. Time deposit maturities are for 2 and 7 days, 1 to 12 months, and broken date maturities. French provincial banks, regional banks, and large city banks all play a role in this market. The market permits long-term depositors to borrow in the short-term deposit market, and there is considerable time arbitrage.

The Paris Eurocurrency market is important in its own right, since this center is the second largest market in Eurodollars and the largest market in Eurosterling. The large share of Eurocurrency business focused in Paris affords banks in this center with additional opportunities for money-market-related activities. Occasional speculative pressures on the pound sterling have shunted a substantial amount of Eurosterling and foreign exchange business through Paris-based banking institutions. Similarly, expected revaluation of the DM generally results in a considerable volume of Eurodollar and DM transactions through Paris banking institutions. For example, during the third quarter of 1971, a combination of Eurodollar and foreign exchange transactions resulted in a net inflow of $1.2 billion through French banks and a conversion of acquired Eurocurrencies into French francs. The French authorities have attempted to cope with these capital inflows in a variety of ways, including modification of the regulations concerning net foreign currency positions that may be held by French banks, imposition of higher reserve requirements on nonresident deposits in French banks, and requirement that foreign currency loans to exporters be sold in the financial franc market.

CAPITAL MARKET

State Intervention

The allocation and control of medium-term and long-term credit are subject to governmental authority through the Ministry of Economics and Finance and, to a lesser degree, by the public and quasi-public financial intermediaries that play a role in credit allocation. Due to the overriding need for coordination between credit and resource allocation, general policy affecting medium- and long-term credit is subject to strong influence by the Commissariat General du Plan. Government control over the allocation of credit is facilitated by the tax-subsidy-lending aspects of the central government budget, required redeposit of liquid resources of local government with the Treasury, centralized investment allocation of savings bank funds through the Caisse de Depots et Consignations, and controlled access to the capital market. Public funds are channeled through the Economic and Development Fund and are made available in the form of grants or loans.

The tax structure in France is an important instrument of selective direction, tending to support exports and capital investment, while at the same time retarding the growth of consumption. Postwar tax reform has minimized reliance on income taxes, and the most important tax is that on value added. Sales and value-added taxes together account for over 40 percent of revenues. Corporate profits taxes have rate schedules slightly above those in the United States, but high depreciation rates combined with deductions for incentives substantially depress taxable profits. Social security taxes on households account for in excess of 35 percent of revenues. Extensive recourse to special exemptions (special depreciation writeoffs for exports and capital investment in less developed areas) helps to stimulate business investment spending as well as exports. Moreover, within the business sector, the larger and better organized corporations are favored, since they are in the best position to benefit from accelerated depreciation treatment.

Public Institutions

State influence over the allocation of investment funds operates through several financial institutions of a public and quasi-public character. These include the Credit Foncier, the Credit National, and the Caisse de Depots et Consignations. The Credit National and Credit Foncier operate by granting loans or by approving loans granted by banks, which then become eligible for rediscount at the Bank of France. These two institutions obtain funds by sale of their own bonds in the capital market and by rediscounting with the Caisse de Depots. The Caisse is the major channel through which private saving reaches the capital and money markets. The resources of the Caisse come mainly from the large network of savings banks, which are required to redeposit their funds with it. In addition, the Caisse holds the liquid funds of the social security system. Major lending commitments of the Caisse include finance of housing construction and capital spending of local governments. The Caisse lends to public and mixed ownership industrial firms and invests in their long-term security issues (see Table 10.1). This institution plays an important role in providing financing sources outside the regular budget of the central government, thereby increasing the flexibility possible in carrying out long-term investment plans.

In France the Treasury does not maintain deposits in the commercial banks. Rather, it maintains deposits with the Bank of France. This gives rise to a "Treasury circuit" effect, since transactions among the Treasury, the central bank, and major financial intermediaries can result in an impairment of liquidity in the banking system. This can occur as a result of payment of taxes, purchase of new government securities, placement of savings in savings banks,

TABLE 10.1

Changes in Assets and Liabilities of the Deposit and
Consignment Office (Caisse des Depots et Consignations)
and Savings Banks, 1970
(million francs)

Claims on other	18,784
Other financial institutions	5,251
General government	6,259
Other domestic sectors	4,331
Rest of the world	6
Not allocable	2,937
In the form of	
Monetary gold and foreign exchange	1
Cash and deposits	1,509
Short-term securities	535
Short-term loans	2,003
Bonds	2,028
Shares	909
Long-term loans	11,758
Other financial institutions	5,298
General government	4,240
Other domestic sectors	2,215
Other claims	41
Liabilities of Caisse and Savings Banks	18,467
in the form of deposits by	
Other financial institutions	50
General government	2,594
Other domestic sectors	15,850
Rest of the world	-27

Source: Organization for Economic Cooperation and Development (OECD), Financial Statistics, vol. 1, 1972, p. 152.

or deposit of funds into accounts in the postal giro system. The banking system can on balance lose liquidity due to time lags or permanent shift in the distribution of assets held by the public. There are serious implications for monetary policy and credit availability. Any net drain on bank liquidity that enters the Treasury circuit must be settled in central bank funds. Provision for the rediscounting of medium-term loans by banks at the Caisse, Credit Foncier, Credit

National, and the Bank of France represents a gap in the central
bank's control over money supply and credit.

Credit is offered borrowers through this Treasury circuit at
interest rates well below those prevailing in the banking sector. The
government's control over savings flows in France tends to guarantee
the supply of funds passing through the Treasury circuit.

New Issues and Secondary Trading

The new issues market reflects the role of government planning
in the economic life of France and the pronounced bias in favor of
"channeled capital." In recent years, new issues of securities have
represented 3 percent of GNP (Table 10.2), compared with ratios
of 4.5 percent for West Germany, 22 percent for Belgium, and 10 percent for Spain.

The institutional fabric of the capital market in France is made
up by the business banks, public institutions, and private financial
institutions. The public institutions have been discussed in a preceding
section. The business banks play a key role in the private sector
of the capital market. When a new company is being formed or an
existing firm requires additional capital, the securities that may be
issued are bought by the business banks, which in turn distribute
them to the public. At times these investment banks hold such issues
until conditions in the capital market are favorable for distribution.

While not as large as the public institutions operating in the
capital markets, the life insurance companies play an important
role. In 1970 their acquisitions of shares and bonds represented 21
percent and 25 percent, respectively, of new issues in the capital
market. Moreover, in the same year, life insurance companies
increased their portfolio of long-term loans by 1.2 billion francs,
mainly to business establishments. In 1970 the growth in life insurance
company assets represented approximately 4 percent of gross fixed
capital formation in France.

Problems encountered in France in the new issue of fixed
interest securities focus on the relatively high flotation costs, the
preferential status of "tap" issues of government securities—which
escape the discipline of the market queue, and the limited resources
at the disposal of private institutional investors.

The equity market in France is sizable, reflecting the substantial accumulation of wealth, the long-established status of the Paris
Stock Exchange, and the impressive growth in the French economy.
It has been estimated that in 1970 changes in ownership of shares
were approximately 16.9 billion francs, which compares with new
share issues of 8.7 billion francs. As can be seen in Table 10.3, the

191

TABLE 10.2

Gross New Issues of Securities
(billion francs)

	1970	1971
Shares	8.68	8.03
Bonds	15.68	21.78
Central government	—	—
State and local government	1.53	1.79
Public enterprises	2.67	3.83
Private enterprises	4.96	8.72
Financial institutions	6.52	7.19
Rest of the world	—	0.25
Shares and bonds, total	24.36	29.81
Gross national product	820.00	904.00
Shares and bonds as percent of GNP	2.97	3.96
Gross fixed capital formation	208.00	231.00
Shares and bonds as percent of capital formation	11.2	12.8

Source: OECD, Financial Statistics, vol. 1, 1972, pp. 148–149.

major demand components in the share market have been the Treasury, rest of the world, and other financial intermediaries. The Treasury subscribes to shares of nationalized companies (including the electricity, coal, and railroad sectors) and provides equity funds to enterprises whose financial needs are considered a priority item. Substantial foreign demand for equities is a relatively recent phenomenon and in part reflects the growing internationalization of security investment and portfolio management that has been sweeping across Europe. The Paris Bourse is well recognized as an important channel through which internationally recognized shares may be traded, and this also explains the substantial volume of foreign shares exchanged in Paris.

In the past, the share market has been considered largely the preserve of private investors. This view is no longer valid, especially in the case of France. Nationalized ownership of shares and the growing role of financial intermediaries as channels through which investment funds flow have both worked against an effective functioning of the equity market. Moreover, inflation pressures and profit squeezes have proved detrimental to the performance of the share market in France.

TABLE 10.3

Demand for Shares in the French Capital Market, 1970
(million francs)

Monetary institutions	1,337
Central bank	12
Others	1,325
Caisse des Depots and savings banks	909
Other financial intermediaries	3,557
Treasury	4,134
Rest of the world	3,899
Overseas countries	50
State and local government	-12
Social security and other administrations	119
Nonfinancial enterprises and households	2,954
Total	16,947
Foreign shares included in above figures	1,052

Source: OECD, Financial Statistics, vol. 1, 1972, pp. 144-145.

The financial institutions in France play an important role as intermediate demanders of shares. Based on the data in Table 10.3, the Caisse des Depots and savings banks, other financial intermediaries, and the banks (other monetary institutions) purchased over one-third of the total supply of shares placed on the market in 1970. The closed-end investment company is still an important factor in the share market in France. In 1963 the societe d'investissement a capital variable (SICAV), an open-end investment company, was introduced. In the recent past, French investment companies have played a greater role in the domestic securities markets than their counterparts in West Germany and Belgium. However, the French companies have been restricted in their investments in foreign securities. For example, the SICAVs operate under a rule requiring that they hold 30 percent of their assets in franc-denominated bonds. French life insurance companies' investments in shares have been limited by required percentage allocations as between "first category" and lesser securities. Foreign shares can be purchased by insurance companies only if they are quoted on a French stock exchange. In France the Caisse des Depots et Consignations enjoys relative freedom to purchase shares. In 1966 the Caisse sponsored establishment of a SICAV whose certificates are distributed through the savings banks.

MONETARY POLICY AND BALANCE OF PAYMENTS

Monetary Policy

In France the reserves of the banking system include claims against the central bank and currency. The central bank regulates the terms of access by the banking system to claims against itself, thereby regulating bank loan activity and the money supply. The claims against the central bank available to the banking system are the resultant of monetary policy action, the public's demand for currency, the government budget, and the balance of payments. As in other countries, the traditional general instruments of control, including rediscounting, open-market operations, and changes in reserve requirements, are used by the French to influence total credit. However, there are numerous special features of the French system of monetary and credit controls that must be defined. For example, the general credit control instruments have also been adapted to selective ends. The French have given a higher priority to allocation of credit, rather than control over the growth of the money supply. Moreover, interest rates have been kept low to stimulate exports and business capital investment. In this connection, the discount rate has been kept at artificially low rates, thereby permitting the development of inflationary pressures.

Unable to use the interest rate as a rationing device in controlling the supply of money, the Bank of France has had to fall back on a variety of expedients including rediscount ceilings, asset reserves, a changed definition of paper eligible for rediscount, and imposition of general credit ceilings on bank loans and investments.

Until recently rediscounting was the principal means of regulating bank liquidity. Recent reforms have increased the relative importance of open-market transactions in the adjustment of bank liquidity. Beginning in 1971, the open-market rate, established on a flexible basis by the Bank of France, became the key money market rate. The open-market rate is fixed at a meeting, which takes place each morning between the governor of the Bank of France and the officers of the bank. Factors considered at these meetings include changes in the Eurodollar rate, interest rates in major industrial countries, and the incentives for hot money inflows to France. The banks are left uncertain of what the daily rate will be. However, they can be certain that the open-market rate will not rise above the discount rate without a fundamental change in monetary policy. In 1970 two-thirds of bank credits from the Bank of France were obtained from rediscount. By year end 1971, the rediscount component of central bank funds available to banks had fallen to 20 percent, while the open-market component represented 80 percent of the total. The recent decline in the importance of the discount rate should not lead one to conclude that it has no value. The discount rate is still used by major banks as a reference for establishing the prime lending rate to business borrowers. Moreover, there is a strong announcement effect. The discount rate still has a psychological impact on the financial markets, and a change may point to a new direction taken by monetary policy.

In 1967 the French introduced a system of required reserves, to be held as noninterest-bearing deposits at the Bank of France. Banks may comply with the reserve requirements on the basis of a monthly average of cash reserves relative to deposit liabilities. As at mid-1972, the percentage reserve requirements were 10 percent and 5 percent for resident demand and time deposits, and 12 percent and 6 percent for nonresident accounts. The system of reserve requirements has become the most effective weapon available to the monetary authorities for placing pressure on bank liquidity as well as raising the cost of funds. Reserve requirements are effective restraints on bank credit expansion as long as the banks are prevented on basis of cost considerations or administrative enforcement from offsetting an increase in reserve requirements by recourse to rediscounting of eligible paper.

Liquidity and required portfolio ratios represent an important means of tightening up on the overall effectiveness of the general monetary policy instruments. One such ratio, the "coefficient of retention" specifies a minimum portfolio of rediscountable bills representing medium-term credit. The purpose of this ratio has been to freeze a portion of existing bills in bank portfolios, limiting rediscounting above the ceilings specified for banks. A liquidity ratio has been in operation in France since 1948 and requires banks to maintain a ratio of 60 percent between their short-term assets and liabilities. Beginning in 1971, the French banks have been required to hold minimum cash reserves as a percentage of their assets as well as their deposits. This requirement will give the authorities more direct influence on credit expansion through the banks.

Direct and selective monetary policy instruments employed by the authorities in France include control over deposit and lending rates by banks, regulation of interest rates on government securities, control over the pace of expansion in bank credit, administrative review of loans made by banks, control over securities issues, regulation of installment credit terms, and controls on international capital movements. The Bank of France exercises considerable influence over loan type and quality by means of its power to determine the eligibility of such loans for rediscount. Moreover, this eligibility is determined at the time the loan is being reviewed for possible approval.

Balance of Payments and Foreign Exchange

The French balance of payments performed on a satisfactory basis in the early years of the 1970s, recording a substantial trade surplus and a surplus on long-term capital movements. Private capital inflows were $1.5 and $1.3 billion in 1970-71, respectively. Moreover, France has continued to honor its commitments as a member of the World Bank Group in transferring at least 1 percent of national product to the developing countries in the form of loans and grants.

The French authorities' attention to balance of payments trends is motivated by a desire to prevent inward capital flows from affecting money creation and bank liquidity, as well as the need to consider the influence of shifts in the balance of payments on the position of the franc in the foreign exchange market. French economic planning has focused on investment growth and export expansion as strategic factors in the overall blueprint for success. An excessive up-valuation of the French franc on the exchange markets would be harmful to the competitive position of French export industries. In connection with this, the French authorities have used a system of exchange controls to effectively balance their international payments. These controls have affected capital transactions by residents covering real estate, securities, and direct investment, both with respect to their financing and currency of denomination.

In August 1971 the French introduced a dual exchange market, comprising an official (commercial franc) market to accommodate import and export transactions, trade-related invisibles, and current official transactions, and a financial franc market which would fluctuate in response to supply and demand, and would accommodate all other transactions except those channeled through the security currency market. In effect, the two-tier foreign exchange market gives monetary policy additional flexibility, since there is less need for support intervention by the central bank. Moreover, it is possible to limit capital inflows through the device of changes in market rates, which adjust sensitively to increased pressures from inward or outward directed capital flows. However, operation of the two-tier market does require that the Bank of France consider the effect on short-term capital flows when setting open-market rates. An excessively high rate will draw short-term capital into France via the financial franc market, raising the rate and possibly encouraging fraudulent transfers between the commercial and financial franc markets.

In September 1971, the financing requirements for inward and outward directed investment were eased. Prior to this, French companies had to borrow from overseas sources amounts needed for foreign direct investment in excess of 5 million francs a year.

The September 1971 change permits French business firms to transfer abroad all funds necessary for approved projects. Also, the foreign financing requirements for nonresidents making direct investments in France were relaxed for transactions "deemed useful for the expansion of the economy." Prior to this change, the requirement was that foreign funds should constitute at least one-half of the funds required for the total financing of each branch or subsidiary in France.

Shortly after the liberalization of direct investment transfers, the French authorities merged the security currency market into the financial franc market. The security currency market had functioned as a special conduit for transactions by French residents in foreign securities or French securities held abroad. Purchases of such securities could not be financed with foreign currency acquired on the foreign exchange market. However, they could be purchased with foreign currency received by a resident from the sale of French or foreign securities held abroad. The foreign exchange involved was unofficially referred to as security currency. The 1971 change permits residents to purchase securities on stock exchanges abroad freely and without limit, provided settlement takes place through the financial franc market.

Foreign issues on the French capital market are subject to prior authorization by the minister of economics and finance. Exempt from the authorization requirement are loans backed by a guaranty from the French government and shares similar to securities that already are officially quoted on a French stock exchange.

Since 1970 two distinct trends are visible in the French foreign exchange system. First, establishment of a dual market represents a serious departure from the general move toward market convertibility of the French franc. Secondly, with the dual rate structure, the authorities have been able to liberalize specific types of capital transactions, representing a move toward market convertibility of the franc for specified-type transactions.

REFERENCES

Bank of International Settlements. Annual Report, 1972.

Brunsden, Peter. "Controls over Banking in France." The Banker (September 1972).

European Economic Community. The Development of a European Capital Market, Brussels, November 1966.

Hodgman, Donald R. "The French System of Monetary and Credit Controls," Banca Naziona le del Lavoro. Quarterly Bulletin (December 1971).

IMF. 23rd Annual Report on Exchange Restrictions, 1972.

Lutz, Vera. Central Planning for the Market Economy: An Analysis of the French Theory and Experience. New York: Longmans, Green & Co., 1969.

OECD. Economic Surveys: France, 1972.

11

FRAMEWORK OF THE FINANCIAL SYSTEM

The German economic miracle of the 1950s placed this country in a dominant position in world finance and business. During the period 1958-73, the German mark has been a favored currency in the international financial markets, and export trade has flourished despite the need to revalue the deutsche mark (DM) upwards on several occasions. As of March 1973, Germany's foreign exchange and gold reserves exceeded $30.9 billion, representing over one-fourth of total officially held international reserves of some 25 industrial countries.

Germany enjoys an open economy, exporting close to 23 percent of gross national product (GNP). Moreover, the economy is relatively free of restrictions on international capital transactions, possessing one of the freest capital markets in the world. The structure of the capital market is influenced by the dominant role of the banking sector and the investment of funds held by the social security agencies, which play an important role because of the emphasis on social welfare.

A number of cities in Germany function as important financial and banking centers. Frankfurt is the major financial center, housing the central bank, the head offices of the largest commercial banks, and the corporate headquarters of many foreign and multinational industrial corporations. Dusseldorf has long functioned as a financing center for heavy industry. Munich possesses a number of powerful banks, including several that combine general and mortgage banking activities. Hamburg leads in foreign trade financing and houses a number of foreign banks with branches and representative offices in Germany.

Germany's role in international finance has grown to challenge the United States and United Kingdom for a larger share of the foreign

lending and financing business. Loans of foreign issuers placed on
the German capital market represent a large part of the foreign issues
placed on the capital markets of major industrial countries. Moreover, the DM is being used increasingly as a trading currency throughout the world. Finally, German banks have been actively extending
their international linkages by means of overseas offices, joint ventures, and cooperative agreements with banks in other countries.

BANKING INSTITUTIONS

Banking in West Germany

Banking in West Germany is characterized by a large number
of banks of different categories and types. The big banks in Germany
are diversified into a number of different activities including deposit
and loan, securities trading and brokerage, underwriting new securities issues, and extensive capital market activities. In the past, the
German banks have enjoyed strong links with industry. However,
these ties are gradually loosening.

There are more than 300 commercial banks in Germany, including the big three, over 130 other general-purpose commercial banks,
35 branches of foreign banks, and over 150 private bankers. These
institutions are engaged in mixed banking, which includes short- and
medium-term lending, providing consumer credit, providing risk
capital to industry, acquiring stocks, and engaging in securities
trading and portfolio management. In addition, there are over 750
savings banks in Germany, with close to 14,000 branches, and their
own clearing organization (Giro-zentralen) in each state. In the past,
these institutions have invested mainly in state and local authority
bonds and mortgages. The resources of the savings banks are nearly
as large as those of the commercial banks, and more recently several
savings banks have entered into general banking and international
finance. In addition, there are over 700 industrial and 8,000 agricultural cooperative banks. Finally, there are a variety of additional
institutions including the mortgage banks, building and loan associations, installment sales financing institutions, and post savings bank
offices.

The commercial banks hold approximately one-fourth of the
resources of all banking groups in Germany, and at year end 1972
their assets were in excess of DM 270 billion. Approximately 10
percent of their assets were in the form of cash reserves with the
Bundesbank, the German central bank. Close to one-fourth of commercial bank assets is in the form of loans to and balances with other

banks, reflecting the importance of the interbank market for short-term funds in the German money market and, to a lesser extent, the importance of bank bonds as a means of interbank allocation of funds. Over 63 percent of bank assets are in loans to nonbanks, with short-term loans (under one-year maturity) slightly smaller in amount than long-term loans. German banks hold large amounts of securities in their own portfolios, including equity securities. These represent approximately 4 percent of total assets.

At one time the big banks held a near monopoly in financing the larger industrial firms. Their equity holdings and directorships provided close working relationships with the giants of German industry. At present, most industrial companies use a number of different banks. Moreover, in cases where the parent company in an industrial group uses its own "house bank," the operating divisions use outside banks to service their loan and financing requirements. During the 1960s, the force of competition has operated powerfully in German banking, given the desire of each specialized type of bank to diversify into other lines (mortgage credit, industrial finance, international banking, and securities trading).

The private banks concentrate on portfolio management for wealthy clients and new issue business for smaller firms. Some of the private banks have contacts with big banks or insurance companies and carry out specialized investment and other services for these larger firms. Some of the private banks have become important in the foreign exchange and Eurocurrency business, and several have undertaken specialized activities such as bill brokerage.

Competition and Growth

As in other countries, banking in Germany is undergoing accelerated change as well as expansion. Banks are becoming specialized conglomerates. Bank services have increased in scope and sophistication in such areas as financial advice, acquisitions, international services, and money market transactions. Diversification and mergers have taken place, and along with this a proliferation of services. As a result, a number of institutions are competing in all sectors of the markets for savings, investment funds, and large credits. German banking has become more competitive due to (1) the freedom of interest rates to find their own level, (2) the absence of control over opening new bank branches, and (3) the free convertibility of the DM.

German banks probably never did specialize to the extent that was practiced in other countries. However, in the past the German commercial banks did think of themselves as bankers to industry.

By contrast, the savings banks emphasized small savers, deposits, mortgage investments, and loans to the public authorities. An in-between route was followed by the cooperative banks that lend mainly to small businesses and farmers. Today all of these institutions regard themselves as universal or all-purpose banks. Each can provide short-term, medium-term, long-term credit, engage in securities trading, and perform a wide variety of other financial services.

MONEY MARKET

Considering the size of the German economy and its banking institutions, the money market is not well developed. Nevertheless, it fulfills an indispensable service and plays an important role insofar as bank liquidity is concerned. For this reason, we discuss the money market largely from the point of view of its operation vis-à-vis the dominant participants—the banks.

Structure of the Market

Money market operations in Germany tend to be dominated by banking institutions, of which over 3,000 report statements of condition to the Bundesbank on a monthly basis. The large number and diversity of types of banks suggest that there is considerable opportunity for extensive interbank money market transactions alone. The Bundesbank participates in money market transactions including rediscount of trade bills for banks, open-market purchase of eligible money market paper including Treasury bills and bonds, prime acceptances, export bills, and medium-term notes. Business corporations in Germany operate in the money market to only a limited extent.

The major sectors and linkages of the money market include (1) the interbank market, (2) open-market transactions, (3) international flows of funds, and (4) the bill market.

The interbank market is a short-hand expression for the call money market in which sight deposits of banks with the Landes-Zentral-Banken (central banks of the states of the Federal Republic of Germany, which are in effect branches of the Bundesbank) are loaned and borrowed without secutity. Participants in the call money are the German banks, the Bundesbank, and the Privatdiskont A.G. The latter institution plays the role of intermediary between the bill, market and the Bundesbank. The Privatdiskont A.G. endorses bills, which then become eligible for rediscount at the Bundesbank. It also operates as an intermediary through which banks place bills in the market.

The German banks are required to keep a certain proportion
of their deposit liabilities in the form of sight deposits with the
Bundesbank. The demand for call money results from the efforts of
individual banks to comply with statutory reserve requirements.
Lenders in this market instruct the central bank to transfer funds from
their accounts to those of the borrowing bank. Repayment of call loans
involves a reverse of this transaction. The existence of an efficient
call money market makes it possible for banks to adjust their cash
balances at the central bank in accordance with changing needs. The
call money rate is influenced by official policy through changes in
the bank rate and Lombard rate (rates charged by the central bank
on discounts and advances on securities) and by official intervention
in the market.

Open-market transactions are conducted in Treasury bills and
notes of the government primarily between the Bundesbank and banks.
Interbank transactions in this market sector are limited. The Bundesbank fixes its own buying and selling rates on Treasury bills and other
short-dated government securities. The banks generally hold only
small amounts of Treasury bills and government securities, presumably due to the existence of more favorable alternative means of
liquidity adjustment.

International flows of funds represent an important money market "annex" for German banks. Capital flows have been fully liberalized
for many years. German banks are important and skillful foreign
exchange traders, and they have developed their Eurocurrency links
extensively. According to data published by the International Monetary
Fund (IMF), deposit banks in Germany held $5.3 billion in foreign
exchange assets at year end 1972. The policy of the Bundesbank
has been to encourage capital outflows by providing favorable swap
rates to banks. This results in spot purchase of foreign exchange
(especially U.S. dollars) by banks and simultaneous execution of a
future sales contract for the same currency. This policy has influenced the pace of development of the domestic money market, where
as a result of the increased attractiveness of external money markets
the supply of funds in Germany has tended to fall.

The bill market plays a key role in influencing changes in bank
reserve positions. Bundesbank lending to domestic banks via discount of eligible bills represents a key factor in the overall liquidity
and reserve adjustment of German banks. In order to become eligible
for rediscount, bills must "pass through the market," this is, must
be endorsed by the Privatdiskont A.G. However, banks may deal
with one another, and thereby avoid dealing with the Privatdiskont
A.G.

Bank Liquidity Adjustment

In the strictest sense, bank liquidity refers to cash (including balances with the central bank) and other short-term assets that can be used to acquire cash reserves, less required reserves and advances from the central bank against securities. Individual banks may fall back on the interbank market, use of rediscount facilities within the rediscount quota limits that apply to that bank, use of short-term funds (foreign exchange) employed abroad, and money market paper (banker's acceptances, Treasury bills, export credit notes, and medium-term notes). Therefore, the free liquidity reserves of the banking system consist of (1) excess balances held with the central bank (2) domestic money market paper in bank portfolios, (3) short-term claims on foreign banks and unused rediscount quotas, and (4) less advances on securities obtained from the Bundesbank, which must be repaid.

Factors that influence bank liquidity may be designated as "market factors" or as "credit policy factors." In the period 1970-72, market factors tended to expand bank liquidity each year by a substantial margin, but were more than offset by credit policy factors operating against liquidity growth in 1971 and 1972 (Table 11.1). In each of the three years 1970-72, increases in foreign exchange reserves of the Bundesbank fully accounted for the expansion of bank liquidity. The increase in foreign exchange holdings reflects speculative capital inflows associated with international currency uncertainties, which were a dominant factor in the world foreign exchange markets in this period. Credit policy factors offset the increase in bank liquidity in 1970 by increased minimum reserve requirements and open-market transactions. In 1971-72, minimum reserve requirements continued to function as the major credit policy factor offsetting expansion in bank liquidity. However, cuts in rediscount quotas replaced open-market transactions as a second line of credit policy defense. Additional discussion of credit policy factors follows in the section on monetary policy.

CAPITAL MARKETS

Internal Structure

A number of basic factors have influenced the role and pattern of growth of the capital markets in Germany. Germany enjoys a relatively high saving ratio out of current income, with close to half of domestic saving generated in the household sector. A large part of this saving flows into the financial institutions, especially the banks.

TABLE 11.1

Changes in Bank Liquidity, 1970-72
(millions of DMs)

	1970	1971	1972
Market factors			
Currency in circulation (increase:-)	-1,923	-3,614	-6,033
Nonbanks net balances with Bundesbank (increase:-)	-3,042	-4,473	+2,486
Public authority money market indebtedness to banks (increase:+)	-785	-1,695	-813
Net foreign exchange holdings (increase:+)	+20,239	+15,676	+17,312
Other factors	+2,429	+252	+2,150
Total	+16,918	+6,146	+15,102
Credit policy factors			
Minimum reserve required of banks (increase:-)	-9,779	-5,645	-13,974
Open-market operations (purchases by Bundesbank:+)	-2,289	-382	+150
Cuts in rediscount quotas	-689	-3,237	-6,457
Total	-12,757	-9,264	-20,281
Bank liquidity (I plus II) =			
change in free liquid reserves	+4,161	-3,118	-5,179
Excess balances	-366	+426	-344
Domestic money market paper	+2,218	-1,444	-2,521
Money market investments abroad	+315	+893	+407
Unused rediscount quotas	+1,700	-2,289	-3,948
Lombard loans—advances on securities (increase:-)	+294	-704	+1,227
Bank's free liquid reserves			
in DM million (end of period)	25,419	24,176	19,873
as percent of total deposits	7.8	6.6	4.8

Source: Deutsche Bundesbank, Monthly Report, March 1973, pp. 6-7.

Flow-of-funds data indicate that in the period 1970-71, banks gained five times as much in new sources of funds as insurance companies and building and loan associations together. Financial institutions including the banks generally acquire over three-fourths of the securities issued in the capital markets, suggesting that the role of indirect investment is a major factor. Direct participation of individual and business investors in the capital markets remains relatively limited in its development.

The commercial banks in Germany are general-purpose banks, operating in both the short-term and long-term credit markets. They play a dominant role in the capital markets for several reasons. They are major factors in the stock exchanges, executing buying and selling orders for customers, and fulfilling the functions of stock brokers and dealers. Only recently in Germany have specialized nonbank (foreign) securities firms begun to compete in this service area. Moreover, the new issue business is almost entirely in the hands of the banks. The banking system as a whole plays a dominant role in the bond market as investor and issuer.

In 1972 bank bonds issued in the form of communal bonds, mortgage bonds, and bonds of specialized banks accounted for three-fourths of the new issues of fixed interest securities. In the same year, close to 20 percent of fixed-interest securities were sold by public authorities (including the Federal Railways and Federal Post Office). Only a small amount (less than 4 percent) of new bond issues was sold by industrial corporations. In the past, German industry has made relatively small use of the capital market. This is due to the ability of companies to obtain long-term bank loans and loans against borrower's notes from financial institutions.

Direct indebtedness of public bodies on the bond market is still relatively low, but is displaying a rising trend. Considering the expensive projects contemplated in infrastructure, including education, health, transport, and pollution control, public authority borrowing may become a more significant factor on the demand side of the capital market in years to come.

The new issue markets in Germany generally are efficient as far as bonds are concerned. Secondary security markets have remained relatively narrow. The German authorities, the banks, and the stock exchanges have been attempting to stimulate greater interest in the share market. Foreign banks and brokerage firms have stimulated competition in the share market, but other measures are needed to improve the mechanics of security trading and the dissemination of information on the stock exchanges. The new issue markets have grown rapidly in Germany, outpacing the expansion in GNP. In the period 1950-55, security issues represented 2 percent of GNP. This has increased to well over 4 percent of GNP in 1970-72 (Table 11.2).

TABLE 11.2

New Security Issues on the German Capital Market
(millions of DMs)

	1970	1971	1972
Shares	3,591	4,736	4,128
Bonds			
Total gross public issues	21,083	31,008	48,708
Central government	1,858	3,045	4,228
State and local government	475	1,626	2,218
Public nonfinancial enterprises	1,994	3,385	3,693
Private nonfinancial enterprises	656	1,880	1,300
Financial institutions	15,408	20,325	36,026
Rest of the world	692	747	1,244
Shares and bonds	24,674	35,744	52,836
GNP*	685.6	758.8	828.5
Shares and bonds as percent GNP	3.6	4.8	6.4
Gross fixed capital formation*	181.1	202.9	214.6
Shares and bonds as percent gross fixed capital formation	13.7	17.6	24.6

*Expressed in billions of DMs.

Source: Organization for Economic Cooperation and Development (OECD), Financial Statistics, 1972-73; International Monetary Fund (IMF), International Financial Statistics, 1973.

The capital markets in Germany are closely linked with the money market, in large part due to the dependence on bank liquidity. Generally a restrictive monetary policy leads to a sharp rise in interest rates and a lag in new issue activity. German banks play an important role as pruchasers of fixed-interest securities, while nonbank financial institutions play only a minor role. Individual savers rely heavily on bank deposits as a form of preferred wealth-holding. The banks react to tight monetary policy by investing less heavily in fixed-interest securities, as well as cutting back on new loans.

The key role of banks in the capital market as underwriters of new securities issues also helps to explain the ready transmission of monetary policy pressures to the capital market sector. The Central Capital Market Committee operates as an instrument of voluntary self-control of the banks and coordinates new issues according to the needs of the market with respect to timing, volume, and conditions. A subcommittee of the Central Capital Market Committee undertakes the same duties with respect to foreign issues.

Foreign Issues

The German capital market is probably the freest in the world. When the DM was made convertible in 1958, foreign investors imported capital to take advantage of the relatively high investment yields available in Germany. The high interest rate structure that persisted in Germany through the mid-1960s gave domestic investors little incentive to invest abroad and raised serious questions concerning the substantial surpluses achieved in the German balance of payments on capital as well as trade account. Germany's position as an importer of long-term capital was reversed beginning in 1968. In 1968-69, Germany assumed a leading role as an exporter of long-term capital, with nearly all of its capital exports in the form of portfolio investment. Since 1968 German investors have been strongly attracted to foreign shares and fixed-income securities. German banks have become leading underwriters in the markets for Eurobonds and foreign DM issues.

German investors had been educated in the advantages of foreign investment for over a decade prior to 1968. As early as 1959, the World Bank placed its first DM bond issue. At midyear 1972, almost one-fourth of World Bank bonds outstanding was denominated in DMs. By 1964-65, foreign DM issues accounted for one-fourth of the international loan issues of that period, and the DM was securely in second position alongside the U.S. dollar as a major currency of denomination for long-term international loans.

One factor that has functioned toward the development of Germany as a market for foreign DM issues is the withholding tax of 25 percent on income from German bonds held by nonresidents. This tax was introduced in 1965 to limit capital inflows for balance of payments reasons. The withholding tax is not levied on the interest income of bonds of foreign issuers denominated in DMs and does not apply to residents, to whom interest income is distributed in full. Enactment of this withholding tax made German bonds less attractive to foreign investors, tending to counteract disequilibrating capital inflows. Foreigners shifted from domestic bonds to foreign DM bonds. In the period 1964-67, Germany became an important turntable for foreign capital, with approximately 70 percent of foreign DM issues sold abroad.

In recent years foreign bond issues placed in the German capital market have accounted for between 9 percent (1970-71) and 30 percent

(1968-69) of foreign bond issues placed in the national capital markets of lending countries. In 1971 the value of foreign DM bonds sold in West Germany was $253 million, placing Germany fourth behind the United States ($1.3 billion), Switzerland ($0.9 billion), and Japan ($0.3 billion). In that year only one developed country (Italy) was represented among the borrowers that tapped the German capital market. The bulk of foreign issues in Germany resulted from World Bank bond issues of $153 million and borrowing of other international organizations based in Europe.

The DM has ranked second consistently as a currency of denomination for international bond issues (Eurobonds). In 1971, close to one-fourth of international bond issues was denominated in DMs. The majority of these DM issues (over 75 percent) was sold by borrowers located in the developed countries, especially Canada, United Kingdom, South Africa, United States, Japan, Denmark, and Spain.

Factors that have influenced the role of Germany as a country of issue and the DM as a currency of issue in foreign and international bond markets include interest rate comparisons between different national and international capital markets, the near and medium-term outlook for foreign exchange rate movements, and the willingness of international borrowers and lenders to assume long-term positions (positive or negative) in various foreign currencies. It should be noted that foreign investors generally can transact business in the German capital market under the same conditions as domestic investors.

MONETARY POLICY AND INTERNATIONAL FINANCE

Monetary Policy

In Germany there is a close intertwining of monetary policy and balance of payments factors. This is due to the relative openness of the German economy, the external pressures on bank liquidity that stem from substantial flows of short-term capital, and the consequent need of the central bank to attempt to neutralize the domestic credit markets from the effects on liquidity of these large-scale capital flows.

The German central bank has, at its disposal, a wide array of traditional policy instruments with which to seek to stabilize the economy. The most influential of these is the power to change the minimum reserve ratios of the banks. Additional important powers include those over open-market operations, discount policy (discount rate, conditions for access to rediscount credits), the distribution of public balances between central bank and bank deposits, and the right to intervene in the foreign exchange markets (swap policy).

Compulsory minimum reserves were first introduced in Germany by legislation enacted in 1948. Under the legislation as amended, the Bundesbank may require banks to maintain with it cash reserves relative to deposit liabilities not exceeding 30 percent for sight deposits, 20 percent for time deposits, and 10 percent for savings deposits. With respect to deposit liabilities to nonresidents, the Bundesbank may fix a minimum reserve ratio of up to 100 percent. Minimum reserve requirements are determined on the basis of monthly averages, which allow banks considerable flexibility to use such funds as working balances. As a result, excess reserves generally are very small. Reserve ratio requirements vary according to the location of the bank, type of deposit liability (sight, time, savings), size of bank, whether resident or nonresident depositor, and as between existing and incremental (marginal) deposit liabilities.

Changes in minimum reserve ratios are used by the Bundesbank as a flexible and regular instrument of policy. For example, during 1970 deserve ratios were increased on two occasions vis-à-vis existing resident deposit liabilities and on two occasions vis-à-vis nonresident deposits. Moreover, marginal reserve ratios were imposed on both resident and nonresident deposits and altered on two occasions during the year on nonresident deposit liabilities. At year end 1970 minimum reserve ratios were as low as 5.9 percent on savings deposits in banks located outside of cities where central bank branches are located, and as high as 13.8 percent on sight deposit liabilities of the largest reserve class banks. Moreover, there was a 30 percent marginal reserve requirement on nonresident deposit liabilities of all categories. As of January 1971, a one-percentage point increase (reduction) in the average minimum reserve ratio would entail a decrease (increase) of bank liquidity amounting to some DM 3 billion. When the Bundesbank increases the minimum reserve ratio, banks as a group can convert their open-market paper, draw on short-term claims on foreign banks, or present bills at the central bank for rediscount. The option used will depend on circunstamces including relative yields and interest rates on the instruments and means of credit available to the bank for liquidity adjustment.

Discount policy of the Bundesbank includes establishment of the discount rate and Lombard rate, control over rediscount quotas, and adminsitrative supervision. Section 19 of the Bundesbank Act authorizes the central bank to buy and sell bills at its fixed discount rate including Treasury bills and other eligible paper. Under Section 15 of the act, the Bundesbank is authorized to fix the rates of interest and discount that apply when banks apply for rediscount credit and advances on securities (Lombard credit). The banks have no general claim on rediscount credit, and the Bundesbank must determine if the situation of the individual borrower calls for granting of such credit. The total volume of rediscount credit at the disposal of each bank is limited by rediscount quotas assigned to the bank. The level of the standard quotas depends on the capital and reserves of the bank and the multiplier applicable at the time. Rediscount quotas are calculated individually and the amounts communicated to the bank.

The Bundesbank may grant Lombard credits to banks upon the pledge of specified securities. The Bundesbank grants advances on securities when it is required to bridge temporary liquidity difficulties. Such advances should not exceed 20 percent of the rediscount quota and must be repaid within 30 days. During the period 1970-72, the Lombard rate exceeded the discount rate by 1 to 2 percent. However, in the final quarter of 1969, there was a 3-percent margin of the Lombard rate over the discount rate.

Fixing the discount and Lombard rates is a central element in the interest rate policy of the Bundesbank. In general, the interest rates that banks change borrowers move with the current level of the discount rate. The rate for advances on securities has significance in the formation of money market rates. In times of substantial bank liquidity, the Lombard rate constitutes a kind of ceiling for the call money rate since a bank will not pay rates that are higher than the rates it must pay for short-term recourse to the central bank. On the other hand, when bank liquidity is tight and banks have taken up a substantial volume of advances on securities, call money rates may rise above the rate for advances on securities. Some banks may not be able to switch to advances on securities because they are short of eligible collateral. In this situation, the rate for advances on securities becomes a floor for the call money rate.

The Bundesbank's open-market policy is geared to the special features of the money and capital markets in Germany. Dealings in money market paper, which includes Treasury bills and bonds, storage agency bills, and prime acceptances, take place mainly between the Bundesbank and the banks. There are practically no dealings in money market paper among banks or between banks and nonbanks. Therefore, interest rates in this market are determined by the Bundesbank, which fixes its buying and selling rates on open-market paper. Volume in the market is determined by other participants in the market who take up the paper offered by the central bank.

Money market paper is a suitable investment for banks that possess liquid funds, since it can be readily exchanged for central bank funds. In this connection, the Bundesbank's open-market transactions with banks must be regarded as relating to interest rate policy rather than liquidity policy. Changes in the central bank's selling and repurchase rates have far-reaching effects on the market for central bank funds. Open-market sales of money market paper by the Bundesbank tend to reduce the supply of central bank funds. This tends to tighten the money market. By altering its buying and selling rates on money market paper, the Bundesbank influences the employment of liquid reserves in money market investments at home and abroad. A further factor influencing the incentives toward money market investment abroad is the cost of forward cover for foreign currency, a matter of central bank swap policy.

International Finance

Over the years, the effects of changes in Bundesbank policy vis-à-vis interest rates and bank liquidity have increased in importance, especially insofar as international movements of short-term capital are concerned. In recent years, the German central bank has become more acutely aware of the problems associated with a strong currency and related capital inflows, especially when the authorities have been attempting to control the expansion of credit to avoid an overheating of the domestic economy.

Several factors make it complicated for the Bundesbank to repel, recycle, or neutralize the effects of currency inflows. These include the desire to maintain a fully liberalized and convertible currency, the openness of the German economy, the substantial foreign exchange resources of the German banks, the entrepôt status of the German capital market—especially where foreign DM bond issues are concerned, the extensive Eurocurrency linkages of the German banks, the large number of multinational companies headquartered or with branches in Germany, and the large number of foreign banks operating in Germany.

The Bundesbank has resorted to the following methods of offsetting the disturbing influence of short-term capital inflows: swap policy, differential minimum reserve ratios, recycling of funds, and the Bardepot. In 1958, the Bundesbank initially offered domestic banks swap facilities for U.S. dollars. Since that time the Bundesbank swap policy has been aimed at encouraging banks to export funds. In turn, this has affected development of the domestic money market, which has been kept relatively short of funds. Differential minimum reserve ratios have involved applying at times higher reserve requirements on nonresident deposits and relatively higher (occasionally 100 percent) marginal reserve requirements on nonresident deposits. The Bundesbank has recycled funds by undertaking money market investments in the United States and, prior to 1971, by placing funds in the Eurocurrency market. The Bardepot or reserve requirements imposed on German firms borrowing funds from nonresident sources

has been aimed at discouraging one particular form of capital inflow.
In part, this reserve requirement injects a measure of equity into the
German credit markets. Prior to this, at times of tight monetary
policy, German banks were restricted from expanding loans to German
borrowers, but these same borrowers could secure funds from offshore sources. In effect, the German banks were being discriminated
against due to domestic monetary policy considerations.

FUTURE PROSPECTS

Recent and current trends suggest that Germany and the DM
are destined to play a key role in international finance for many years
to come. The competitive position of Germany in world export markets has remained favorable, providing a broadly based foreign exchange business for the internationally oriented banks. Official foreign
exchange holdings provide an extremely comfortable liquidity cushion,
as well as a basis for functioning in international investment and lending operations. The favored status of the DM in world currency
markets provides opportunities for German banks to expand their foreign trade financing and foreign loan activities. The DM is becoming
a widely used financing and vehicle currency, as well as a major
currency of denomination for Eurobond issues.

Major question marks regarding the future status of Germany
in global finance hinge on the outcome of European Economic Community
(EEC) developments, possible monetary unification in the Common
Market, expanded trade and investment opportunities with the Eastern
European nations, and the ability of major financial institutions and
banks in Germany to continue to assume a leadership position in the
international financial markets. German banking institutions have
developed important cooperative links with counterpart institutions
in France, Britain, Italy, and other countries. While these links have
been confined largely to flexible and loose association agreements
with banks in other countries, they could in the future provide significant advantages and opportunities to German banks.

REFERENCES

Deutsche Bundesbank. Instruments of Monetary Policy in the Federal
Republic of Germany, 1971.

_____. Monthly Review, 1971-73.

Einzig, Paul. Parallel Money Markets: Volume Two, Overseas Markets. New York: St. Martin, 1972.

OECD. The Capital Market, International Capital Movements, Restrictions on Capital Operations in Germany, 1969.

World Bank and Investment Dealers Association (IDA), Annual Reports 1972, 1973.

12

THE SWISS NATIONAL ECONOMY

The Alpine setting of Switzerland has left its impression on the culture of Swiss society and on the special role played by this small nation in world finance. With a population of only 6 million and a relative paucity of natural resource endowments, the energetic Swiss have developed industrial efficiency and financial expertise that rank their standard of living the highest in Western Europe.

The origins of Switzerland's financial development can be traced back several centuries, to the role of Geneva as a financial center during the Spanish War of Succession, to the formation of private banking firms in the early 1800s such as Dreyfus Sons and Company and Wegelin and Company which continue to prosper, and to the more recent expansion of Swiss bank foreign investment activities prior to World War I. The historical record reflects a long-established interest in capital export, but one that has been interrupted by wars, currency instabilities, and depression.

Switzerland is characterized by its respect for privacy in financial matters, as well as by the private enterprise nature of its business, banking, and central banking institutions. This private aspect of the Swiss lifestyle in general extends over into the political relationships between Switzerland and the rest of the world. It is an anomaly that a posture of independence and neutrality has earned this country a high degree of interdependence and cooperative involvement with other major countries in such areas as central bank cooperation, foreign exchange policy, and international monetary policy.

Emphasis on neutrality and maintenance of a people's army have earned Switzerland a deep abiding respect and an extended era of peace. However, this has not been without cost. The Swiss allocate a high percentage of national income to defense expenditures.

Financially, Switzerland has long been a magnet attracting substantial amounts of foreign funds. The ability to attract foreign funds
stems from a combination of factors that are special to the Swiss
nation, and not to interest rates which are relatively low in Switzerland. The currency has long been regarded as one of the safest and
most stable in the world, due to the high gold cover on the currency
issue, the absence of inflationary pressures for many of the postwar
years, and the conservative fiscal policy of the national government.
The banks, financial institutions, and holding companies render in-
numerable services to nonresidents in areas such as portfolio management, deposit safekeeping, administration of funds, and providing
facilities for securities investments and commodities trading. A
favorable tax status may accrue to funds transferred into holding
companies maintained in Switzerland by foreign business firms.
Moreover, the Swiss banking community strictly enforces secrecy
concerning the identity of depositors. Finally, the Swiss franc has
been one of the freest currencies in the world, and this has encouraged nonresidents to transfer funds into Switzerland.

Switzerland has attracted a substantial number of foreign worker
due to the overfull employment market. In 1972, close to 30 percent
of the labor force consisted of foreign workers. The high percentage
of nonresident workers has generated a number of serious problems
that affect the strength and performance of the Swiss financial markets
especially in connection with their international role. Foreign worker
remittances to families in their country of origin have introduced a
negative factor in the current accounts of Switzerland's balance of
payments. The rapid escalation in the number of foreign workers
in the early 1960s placed severe pressure on the housing market
and produced a substantial boom in housing construction and expenditures for new school construction and other facilities. In short, the
foreign workers contributed to consumption and investment spending
in Switzerland, but did not make an important contribution to capital
formation and saving.

In the period 1966-72, real gross national product (GNP) advanced at an annual rate of 4 percent, and in 1972 per-capita GNP
was close to $4,900. The Swiss economy is relatively open to external
pressures, from the foreign trade and capital flow side of international
transactions. In 1972, merchandise exports represented 23 percent
of GNP. In 1970-71, foreign loans and debt issues on the Swiss capital
market were equivalent to nearly one-fourth of gross bond issues.
Foreign trade is closely geared to the European Economic Community
(EEC) and European Free Trade Association (EFTA). In 1972, close
to 60 percent of imports and 37 percent of exports were with the EEC
countries. Exports to the EFTA countries represented 22 percent
of Switzerland's total, while imports from EFTA countries were

close to 19 percent of the total. Major export commodities include metal and machinery, chemicals and pharmaceuticals, textile products, food products, and books and periodicals.

MONETARY AND BANKING SYSTEMS

Monetary System

A sound currency is a cornerstone for the financial ascendency of any nation. Until the foundation of the Swiss Confederation in the middle of the nineteenth century, the money system was a confused assortment of currency and coinage of the various cantons. In 1907, the Swiss National Bank began operations and assumed responsibility for the bank note circulation. Until that time there were 36 banks of issue.

TABLE 12.1

Money Supply, Monetary Reserves, and Gold Cover
in Switzerland, Yearly Averages
(million francs)

	1968	1970	1972*
Central bank money			
Coins in circulation	765	1,319	1,292
Bank notes in circulation	10,578	11,785	14,108
Giro account balances	3,351	4,189	10,526
Demand deposits			
At banks	12,967	16,158	24,141
On postal checking accounts	4,040	4,696	5,810
Money supply	31,701	38,147	55,877
Gold	11,587	11,615	11,880
Foreign exchange	1,603	3,419	10,155
Monetary reserves	13,190	15,034	22,035
Gold cover as percent of			
bank notes in circulation	109.5	98.5	84.1

*January-September data.

Source: Union Bank of Switzerland, Economic Survey of Switzer-land, 1973, p. 15.

217

The Swiss monetary system is based on the gold standard, with the gold parity of the Swiss franc established by the Federal Currency Law of 1952 as amended. The central bank's obligation to redeem its notes in gold, which had been suspended in 1936 when the franc was devalued, was abolished in 1954. The gold content of the Swiss franc is fixed by law, and its par value can be raised or lowered by act of the legislature. In 1970, due to the extreme unsettlement of the international exchanges, the parliamentary bodies granted the federal government the authority to change the parity of the Swiss franc by its own action.

Legal provisions require that the note issue be covered up to its full amount by gold, Swiss and foreign bills of exchange and cheques, sight claims on foreign countries, and short-dated debt securities of the governmental units in Switzerland. As can be seen in Table 12.1, the gold cover on bank notes was above 100 percent until 1970, when it dipped below that level. The Swiss franc has the highest gold coverage of any currency among the industrial countries. Other measures of monetary and financial strength indicate that Switzerland ranks high, if not highest, among the industrial countries. These include coverage of imports by foreign currency and gold reserves, stability of the exchange rate, and maintenance of internal purchasing power.

Banking System

The Swiss banking system is characterized by a large number of banks and a diversity of banking types. As of year end 1972, there were 72 large banks, cantonal banks, and local and savings banks. In addition, there were several hundred other banking institutions operating in Switzerland, including branches of foreign banks, private banks, and the so-called loan banks. The big banks are by far the most important institutions in Switzerland, accounting for over 60 percent of balance sheet totals, as reflected in Table 12.2 In the two decades ending in 1972, the assets of these banks increased over eightfold. Swiss banks are universal, that is, they are active in all lines of business, including business loans, underwriting new securities issues, mortgage banking, and foreign business.

There are substantial variations in the relative importance of different lines of activities for each category of bank. For example, the financing of foreign trade is almost entirely serviced by the big banks, although the private banks also play an important role. The other categories of banks confine themselves largely to domestic business. The big banks also specialize in international money and foreign exchange market activities. Consequently, bills receivable

218

and due from banks represent between 50 and 60 percent of their assets. Investments in mortgages are relatively unimportant, but account for an impressive share of the assets of other categories of banks. For example, mortgage investments account for over half of the assets of the cantonal banks.

Important differences also appear on the liabilities side of banks' balance sheets. The savings banks and loan banks derive over 60 percent of total liabilities from savings deposits. The cantonal banks obtain a third of their funds from savings deposits. By contrast, in the big banks the proportion of savings deposit funds is less than 10 percent of total funds. The big banks derive the bulk of their funds from demand deposits, balances due to other banks, and time deposits.

The three big banking houses in Switzerland (Swiss Credit Bank, Swiss Banking Corporation, and Union Bank of Switzerland) have enjoyed an accelerating growth in the most recent decade. A large part of this growth is attributable to their foreign business—for example, between 1960 and 1968 the linkage between the Swiss banking system and foreign money markets has increased from 7.0 to 28.8 billion Swiss francs on the liabilities side and from 7.8 to 34.4 billion francs on the assets side. Foreign funds flow into the big banks in the form of checking accounts and other types of deposits, and these funds are reinvested on the Eurocurrency market and other international money markets. Also important is commercial business, which accounts for about one-fourth of foreign assets of the big banks. Further, the big banks are safekeepers for Swiss short-term funds that can find no suitable domestic investment outlet. Close contacts of the banks with foreign money markets provide opportunities for profit on

TABLE 12.2

Balance Sheet Totals of Swiss Banks, September 1972
(million francs)

Bank	Total
5 big banks	120,097
28 cantonal banks	57,059
39 local and savings banks	21,510
Total: 72 banks	198,666

Source: Union Bank of Switzerland, Economic Survey of Switzerland, 1973, p. 26.

interest margins. Additional sources of earnings accrue to the big banks on the basis of their administering foreign funds on a commission fee basis, issuing and confirming letters of credit, making markets in foreign exchange, securities syndicate operations, and transactions in precious metals. Financing of export trade, especially at medium term, is an ever-increasing aspect of their activities.

Securities transactions, stock exchange operations, and new issues are important activities for the three big banks. The banks are in an excellent position to place securities with investment portfolios. In recent years, new issues of foreign securities have expanded, providing these institutions with additional outlets for the foreign funds entering Switzerland for investment management purposes. The big banks generally take the lead in the management and underwriting of such new securities issues. The investments, securities transactions, and foreign trade financing activities generate a sizable volume of foreign exchange operations. Consequently, the big banks have well-organized foreign exchange departments.

The private banks have been halved in number during the postwar period. They engage in a wide range of banking, near banking, and investment activities. An important activity is the administration of property and related securities transactions. The Zurich firm of Julius Baer and Company has established a high reputation, founding the Baer Securities Corporation in New York.

In the period 1960-74, foreign banks have expanded their activities in Switzerland by establishing branches and affiliates. American banks have established offices in Switzerland to service American industrial and holding company affiliates. Banks from the Near East have established banks in Switzerland to administer property under a neutral flag. Other banks have been established by foreign banking institutions because the foreign exchange regulations at home were restrictive and impeded the development of international business.

Switzerland has been an attractive center for the establishment of foreign banks. The Swiss authorities have had mixed reactions to this trend. The Swiss fear that sudden withdrawal of funds deposited with foreign banking offices in Switzerland could have unfavorable effects. Moreover, foreign banks may endanger the reputation of Switzerland as a financial center by engaging in activities that reflect adversely on the Swiss banking community. Swiss monetary and stabilization policy depends on close working relationships between the Swiss banks and the Swiss National Bank. The growing influence of foreign banks in Switzerland could make it more difficult to reach satisfactory, workable agreements on credit restraint on a voluntary basis. For these reasons, the Federal Council considered it necessary to introduce a permit system for the establishment of banks by foreigners.

FINANCIAL INSTITUTIONS AND
HOLDING COMPANIES

Financial Institutions

Nonbank financial intermediaries play an important part in
Switzerland's functioning as a turntable for international capital flows.
Included among these are the financial companies—some of which
resemble banks, the investment trusts, and the insurance companies.

Of the 50 or more financial companies operating in Switzerland,
10 accept deposits. The remaining institutions have no ready access
to funds in the Swiss capital and money markets. Approximately 15
percent of the assets of the financial companies are invested in foreign
securities, reflecting the close ties of these institutions to the financial
markets outside of Switzerland. One of the more specialized financial
companies, Eurofina A.G. in Basle, was founded by the European railroads to finance the purchase of rolling stock.

The investment trusts are relative latecomers to Switzerland;
the first was organized in 1930. In the early years of their development, these investment funds placed heavy emphasis on American
and Canadian investments. It has been reported that at year end 1968,
these trusts held assets of close to 7.0 billion Swiss francs. The
inland trusts have extensive real estate investments, with only a
modest percentage of their assets in the form of security holdings.
The remaining investment trusts hold a mixture of real estate, domestic securities, and foreign securities investments. In 1966 federal
legislation, which established rules regarding the responsibilities
of management and the trustee, on publicity, on investment policy,
and on auditing, was enacted. The assets of the investment trusts
stand close to passbook deposits in banks in aggregate amount.

Development of the investment trusts in Switzerland has depended
in part on the interest of foreign investors in this form of investment.
Foreign participation in Swiss investment trusts is estimated at close
to half of the total assets of these intermediaries.

Somewhat over one-third of the asset holdings of the Swiss investment trusts is in the form of foreign assets. Close to half of
this represents assets located in the United States, 15 percent in
Canada, 11 percent in South Africa, and 23 percent in Europe. Germany is the most important country represented in the European
asset holdings of the investment trusts. Several of the trusts specialize in investing in foreign assets in individual countries. These include South African Investment Trust (SAFIT) in South African assets,
Italian Investment Trust (ITAC) which specializes in Italian shares,
European Investment Trust (EURIT) which emphasizes hard currency

countries in Europe, and Rometac-Invest which emphasizes non-European regions and natural resource and mineral investments.

The Swiss insurance companies are large and play an important role by any standards. In 1970, the insurance companies were administering investment funds in excess of 23 billion francs, with the share of the life insurance companies at close to 60 percent of the total. The accident and liability insurance companies were administering close to 30 percent of these assets, and the reinsurance companies approximately 10 percent of the total. Close to a third of the assets managed by the Swiss insurance companies is foreign investment, reflecting the overseas orientation of their business.

The importance of the Swiss insurance companies lies in their contribution to the balance of payments as much as in their role in the Swiss capital market. Over half of the gross premium income comes from abroad, and their contribution to the service income in the Swiss balance of payments is in the area of 300 million Swiss francs annually. With the possible exception of Great Britain, there is no other country in which the foreign insurance business accounts for so large a part of the total.

Holding Companies and Industrial Enterprises

The international financial role of Switzerland is enhanced by the large number as well as extensive operations of the financial and industrial holding companies headquartered in major centers such as Zurich, Geneva, and Basle. Moreover, several of the big industrial concerns in Switzerland have built up their own networks of subsidiary companies that make up a global organization. These foreign subsidiaries generate substantial foreign currency earnings, which are transferred to their parent companies in Switzerland, adding to the receipt of foreign income in the Swiss balance of payments and further linking the financial system to foreign business developments and overseas financial markets.

A number of holding companies have been organized in Switzerland for the purposes of facilitating corporate control, financing far-flung operations, and administering securities investment activities. At year end 1968, there were over 8,500 such holding companies with a total capital of 9 billion francs. The control and financing companies of which there were 1,086 in 1968, had a capitalization of 7.2 billion francs. A large number of the Swiss holding companies exercise working control over patent utilization. It has been estimated that close to 40 percent of the holding companies are Swiss controlled.

The number of foreign-controlled holding companies is large, with American business concerns well represented. American

companies have established Swiss holding companies for the purpose
of administering their European interests under the roof of one holding company. Because of her neutrality, central location, currency
convertibility, and strong banking system, Switzerland has served
well as a suitable center for holding company activities. Tax advantages have been ranked as of secondary importance in the selection
of Switzerland as a locale for holding company operations. Among
the American companies with the largest holding company operations
are Caterpillar Tractor, DuPont, Westinghouse, Chrysler, Dow
Chemical, Procter and Gamble, Burroughs, and IBM. In addition,
there are extensive Swiss holding company interests of French and
Italian concerns.

The large Swiss industrial concerns enjoy numerous and far-
flung foreign interests. Several leading companies such as Nestle,
F. Hoffmann-La Roche, Ciba, Geigy, and Alusuisse probably account
for 60 percent of Swiss direct investments abroad. Several Swiss
industrial firms (Nestle and Hoffman-La Roche) use parallel holding
companies, where the shares of the holding company are chained to
those of the parent so that the same shareholders are represented
in both. In the case of Nestle, the parallel holding company in Panama
(Unilac Inc.) manages the affairs of the organization in the Western
Hemisphere and the Pacific. The parent firm Hoffmann-La Roche
controls the European and Middle East affiliates, whereas the holding
company in Canada administers the affairs of subsidiaries in North
and Latin America, the Pacific region, the sterling area, and the
Far East.

The revenues of the affiliated foreign companies of the big Swiss
concerns represent invisible earnings that offset the deficit in the
balance of trade. These invisible earnings include licensing fees,
dividends, interest, and contributions to cover overhead expenses.

MONEY AND CAPITAL MARKETS

The Money Market

The single most significant feature of the Swiss money market
is the dominant role of bank-participated international flows of funds.
In comparison with the flows of bank funds relating to foreign markets,
the figures pertaining to the domestic money market are small. Since
the government does not issue short-dated bills equivalent to the
three-month Treasury bills that play a dominant role in the U.S.
money market, the closest equivalent type of money market paper consists of government bonds that are close to maturity. The total volume

of these bonds on the market is small; consequently the market remains relatively thin. The Swiss National Bank has issued "sterilization bonds," which are a liability of the central bank. The aim of the Swiss National Bank in issuing these securities is to absorb excess liquidity in the money market and to have banks adjust their liquidity positions on balance sheet dates by depositing these bonds with the Swiss National Bank for a few days rather than by undertaking foreign exchange market operations.

The Swiss money market is largely concentrated in Zurich, where the market in call money is focused. The call money market enjoys a modest turnover. The large commercial banks lend on a regular basis to local banks. Call money rates tend to fluctuate independently of the bank rate, being susceptible to the influence of inflows of foreign funds. When the big banks in Switzerland are receiving large deposit inflows from foreign sources, they can increase their own loans and investments in Swiss francs, increase loans on call at smaller banks, or place Euro-Swiss franc deposits with banks outside Switzerland.

Since the larger volume of bank-oriented money market operations lies outside the borders of Switzerland, the banking system is more dependent on a stable exchange rate of the local currency than banks in other countries. At year end the banks generally transfer dollars to the National Bank in exchange for domestic (Swiss franc) liquidity. The central bank will purchase dollars from the Swiss banks on a spot basis, as well as engage in swaps for limited time periods. In turn, the central bank invests these dollars in foreign money market investments directly, or via the Bank for International Settlements. The growing operations of the Swiss banks in foreign money markets and the need for liquidity at balance sheet dates result in foreign exchange transactions between the commercial banks and Swiss National Bank in ever-increasing volume each year.

There are extremely close linkages between short-term interest rates in Switzerland and the rates available on the Eurocurrency market. The higher the interest rates on the Eurocurrency market, the more the Swiss banks are likely to invest their own funds in the market. Consequently, this can lead to a tightening of liquidity and increase interest rates on the Swiss money market.

Because of the substantial facilities provided by the Eurocurrency markets, the Swiss banks have not felt compelled to develop a more extensive domestic money market. The Swiss authorities have not encouraged growth and expansion of local money market facilities, presumably because of the nature of central banking controls which do not rely on open-market operations as in the United States, but focus more on moral suasion and informal agreement with the banks. Moreover, fiscal considerations and the desire to achieve balanced federal government budgets have worked against growth of a market in short-term government securities. Finally, business needs apparently have not concentrated on money market services. Apparently, the large business concerns can make ready use of bank and foreign sources of funds to adjust their liquidity positions, including remittance of earnings from overseas affiliates and borrowing on the Eurocurrency market. Moreover, the large Swiss banks receive a persistent inflow of foreign funds, which provide them with the resources to extend credits to the business sector and relieve them of the need to borrow from the central bank.

The Capital Market

The Swiss capital market adequately services the substantial investment needs of the domestic economy and at the same time furnishes a considerable volume of capital funds to foreign borrowers. Share and bond issues have represented 10 to 11 percent of GNP and 35 percent of fixed capital formation (Table 12.3). The high ratio of

TABLE 12.3

New Security Issues on the Swiss Capital Market
(billion francs)

	1971	1972
Shares, gross issues	3.0	3.1
Bonds, gross issues	8.2	8.6
Confederation	1.0	0.6
State and local government	1.3	1.3
Nonfinancial enterprises	2.2	2.0
Financial institutions	0.8	1.0
Rest of the world	2.2	2.9
Shares and bonds, total	11.2	11.7
GNP	100.8	115.3
Shares and bonds as percent GNP	11.1	10.1
Gross fixed investment	29.6	34.8
Shares and bonds as percent gross fixed investment	37.8	33.6

Source: Organization for Economic Cooperation and Development (OECD), Financial Statistics, 1973, pp. 194-195; also, Swiss Bank Corporation, Prospects, May 1973, p. 13.

security issues to GNP can be explained by the underwriting and placement power of the major banks and financial institutions, substantial inflows of foreign funds, and the relatively low borrowing costs that prevail in Switzerland and attract borrowers. Internal financing of the private sector made possible by saving out of current income keeps loan demand on the open market moderate and interest rates low. Finally, the Swiss franc is a strong and well-managed currency, which enhances the turntable status of Switzerland in international finance.

The big Swiss banks play a leading role as underwriters of securities issues and in the ultimate placement of securities in investment portfolios. Moreover, the banking syndicate, in cooperation with the Swiss National Bank, supervises the placement of new securities issues on the Swiss market with a view toward avoiding an excessive new issues calendar and maintaining an appropriate balance between foreign issues (see Table 12.4) that generate capital exports and the remaining components of the Swiss balance of payments.

In recent years, the Swiss economy has been deluged with excessive liquidity in the form of inflows of short-term and long-term capital. Given the small size of the Swiss economy and the consequent inability of the domestic capital market to employ these funds, the Swiss have pursued the following policies:

1. Liberalize policy on capital exports. Until 1971 the Swiss permitted only a limited number of foreign loan issues denominated in Swiss francs and placed in the Swiss capital markets. At the same time, the authorities have regulated the size of such issues to avoid excessive pressures on the capital market. Since that date, the Swiss have permitted a much larger number of foreign loan issues, some in amounts of 100 to 200 million Swiss francs. Moreover, there has also developed a large market for medium-term Swiss franc promissory notes of foreign companies. In the first nine months of 1971, these issues reached a total of 3.8 billion Swiss francs.

2. Encourage outward portfolio investment. Capital export by security purchases is difficult to estimate and subject to substantial year-to-year fluctuation. The stock exchanges in the United States have provided an attractive assortment of investment possibilities. While the Swiss banks have not participated directly in underwriting Eurobond issues, they possess considerable placement capacity. According to the best estimates of specialists in the field, Swiss banks are responsible for the ultimate placement of 30 to 40 percent of Eurobond issues.

3. Temporarily freeze foreign funds deposited in Swiss banks. This has been accomplished by limiting or prohibiting payment of interest on foreign deposits placed with Swiss banks.

TABLE 12.4

Foreign Issues Placed in the Swiss Capital Market
by Country and Type of Borrower
(millions of dollars)

	1971		1972	
	Public Issue	Private Placement	Public Issue	Private Placement
OECD countries				
Austria	22.0	—	82.8	—
Canada	2.2	8.5	98.6	21.2
Denmark	—	—	20.8	—
Finland	2.0	—	35.0	—
France	63.4	—	61.5	—
Germany	45.8	—	73.0	—
Iceland	—	—	6.6	—
Italy	—	12.7	—	—
Netherlands	46.1	58.7	—	—
Norway	19.9	25.6	11.7	6.5
Sweden	6.3	—	54.9	—
United Kingdom	24.2	146.7	41.9	15.7
United States	244.7	—	197.0	12.0
Unallocated	20.2	—	—	—
Subtotal	496.8	252.2	683.8	55.4
Non-OECD countries				
South Africa	—	—	26.4	—
New Zealand	—	24.4	—	—
International organizations based in Europe				
Council of Europe	—	—	10.6	—
European Investment Bank	15.2	—	—	—
Others				
Asian Development Bank	9.3	—	—	—
World Bank	18.3	—	52.1	77.5
Inter-American Development ment Bank	29.1	—	21.1	—
Subtotal	56.7	—	73.2	77.5
International enterprises	21.8	—	57.2	—
Grand total	590.5	276.6	851.2	132.9

Source: OECD, Financial Statistics, 1972, 1973.

The important role of Swiss banks and financial institutions in the export of capital and placement of securities in investment portfolios stems from their role as administrators and investment managers of large amounts of foreign property. Moreover, these assets generate substantial interest and dividend income which must also be invested. The volume of Swiss portfolio investments in foreign (currency-denominated) securities has been estimated at close to 39 billion francs (circa 1970). This includes mainly investments in U.S. securities (26 percent of total), French securities (23 percent of total), British securities (15 percent of total), German securities (12 percent of total), and Dutch securities (11 percent of total). These estimates exclude loans in Swiss francs and direct investments. A large number of foreign securities are quoted on the leading Swiss stock exchanges, including American, Canadian, German, British, Dutch, South African, and South American shares. In Europe the Zurich Stock Exchange is second only to the London exchange in

TABLE 12.5

Foreign Assets and Liabilities of Switzerland, 1971
(billion francs)

Assets	
Short-term assets	122.7
Securities	44.7
Direct investments	38.0
Insurance	9.3
Other	2.0
Total assets	216.7
Liabilities	
Bank liabilities	82.5
Securities	15.6
Direct investments	5.8
Insurance	7.0
Other	8.1
Total liabilities	119.0
Net assets	97.7

Source: Swiss Credit Bank, Swiss Statistical Abstract, 1972, pp. 60-61.

trading volume. In 1971 the turnover on the Zurich Stock Exchange was 54.5 billion Swiss francs, and in the first nine months of 1972 was 56.6 billion francs. This is equivalent to approximately one-half of annual GNP.

It was estimated that at year end 1971, Switzerland enjoyed a net foreign asset position of 97.7 billion Swiss francs (Table 12.5). It should be noted that short-term foreign assets exceeded total foreign liabilities at this time. Long-term assets consisted mainly of securities and direct investments.

FOREIGN EXCHANGE AND BALANCE OF PAYMENTS

Foreign Exchange and Gold Market

The Swiss franc has been one of the most stable currencies in the international economy. The May 1971 revaluation of the Swiss franc was the first change in the parity of the Swiss franc in 35 years. Stability of value and free convertibility of the franc have been important contributing factors in making Switzerland a focal point for transactions in foreign exchange, gold and other precious metals, and international securities. Prior to the return to convertibility of the European currencies in 1958 and termination of the European Payments Union, the Swiss franc was the only currency freely convertible into the U.S. dollar. This gave Switzerland a special status in trade with a number of countries, including those in the then existing Transferable Account Sterling group.

The role of the dollar as an intervention and vehicle currency lends it special importance in the Swiss foreign exchange market. The dominant role of the dollar in Europe and especially on the Swiss foreign exchange market has been reflected in the fact that foreign exchange is not bought and sold against Swiss francs but largely against dollars. Foreign exchange transactions between two European currencies are not frequent. In most cases, the dollar serves as the intermediary currency.

Principal dealers in the foreign exchange market include the big three banks, several smaller banks specialized in international financing, a number of foreign banks with direct offices in Switzerland, the Bank for International Settlements, and the Swiss National Bank. Dealings are carried on interbank without brokers. The dollar rate in Swiss francs has been the key rate in the market. Rates on remaining currencies are established on the basis of the dollar rate prevailing in the major financial centers in Europe. Generally, foreign currencies are traded against the dollar, and only rarely are European currencies traded against Swiss francs.

The Swiss forward market is well organized and very efficient. In 1971, the Swiss National Bank was authorized to intervene on the forward currency markets for transactions of up to three months' maturity. The forward rate reflects the interest differential between the Swiss franc and other currencies. When interest rates in Switzerland are lower than in the United States, the dollar will be quoted at a discount in the forward market. In the three-year period 1971-73, only in the first quarter of 1972 did the forward rate on the U.S. dollar rise to a premium relative to the Swiss franc. This was at a time of extremely low interest rates in the United States, as well as immediately after conclusion of the Smithsonian Agreement, which stabilized the international currency markets for many months.

The Swiss National Bank intervenes in the market and, since June 1971, has been permitted to operate in forward transactions. This permits it to make dollars available to the Swiss banks on a swap basis. The Swiss central bank has adequate foreign exchange and gold reserves with which to intervene. At year end 1972, the gold reserves were equivalent to $3,158 million, and the foreign exchange reserves $4,330 million. The dollar serves as the intervention currency on the Swiss foreign exchange market.

Switzerland developed into a full-fledged gold trading center after World War II. This is explained by the fact that the Swiss banks took up the gold business immediately after the war, whereas the London gold market was not reopened until 1954. Since gold trade is conducted in part on a credit basis, the low interest rates prevailing in Switzerland have furnished a competitive edge. Since ownership of gold is forbidden in Britain, the trade tended to shift toward the international markets. Gold bought in London went to foreign markets via the intermediary of the Swiss banks. Switzerland is one of the few countries whose own banks buy substantial amounts of gold for their own account. Heavy liquidity requirements imposed upon the Swiss banks necessitate this. Approximately one-fourth of the gold purchased by the Swiss banks eventually goes to the Middle East and Far East. Another large portion goes to French customers. Each of the three big Swiss banks engaged in the international gold business controls a gold refinery. Therefore, they can offer gold in small or large units during a speculative wave of demand for gold.

The split of the gold market and the decision of South Africa to sell no more gold on the London market has increased the importance of Zurich as a center of gold trade. At present, much of the gold business is handled on a bookkeeping basis. Banks buy and sell gold without need for shipment, and a large clientele actively trades on both sides of the market. The importance of Zurich as a gold-trading center permits prices in that city to play a determining role in the London fixing.

Balance of Payments

The Swiss balance of payments reflects the special role and importance of this nation in international finance and banking. Capital flows and service transactions tend to dominate the balance of payments accounts, as well as exert leverage on the overall balance. Switzerland regularly incurs a merchandise trade deficit, due to the relatively small natural resource endowments and inability to produce sufficient food for the population. In 1970-71, the merchandise trade deficit averaged $1.4 billion.

The service accounts in the balance of payments are influenced by three types of transactions: tourism, remittances, and income on foreign investments. The Swiss derive substantial foreign exchange earnings from travel and tourism. However, this is offset by remittances of foreign workers employed in Switzerland. Close to 30 percent of the Swiss labor force consists of foreign workers.

Earnings on foreign investments play a significant role in the Swiss external balance. In 1970-71, income on investments represented 3.0 and 3.4 billion francs, respectively. While these earnings are not broken down in sufficient detail in the official balance of payments statistics for purposes of analysis, private estimates, which are useful as well as reliable, have been made. According to estimates made by Dr. Max Ikle, in 1968 Switzerland derived earnings on its foreign investments of 2.4 billion francs. This includes income on portfolio investments in foreign securities of 1.4 billion francs, income on foreign bonds issued in the Swiss capital market and denominated in Swiss francs of 0.4 billion francs, earnings on investments of the federal government of 0.1 billion francs, and income on direct investments by Swiss companies of 0.5 billion francs. Analysis of the geographic sources of income on Swiss foreign investments indicates that the EEC is the most important source of income on portfolio investments, but that North America is a more important source of income on direct investments of Swiss companies. Presumably, EEC and EFTA borrowers have ranked first and second, since the interest income derived from these sources ranks in this order. On an overall basis, the percentages of earnings on foreign investments derived from the various geographic regions are as follows: EEC, 40 percent; North America, 25 percent; EFTA, 17 percent; and Latin America, 5 percent.

The capital accounts in the Swiss balance of payments have an overriding importance. At times Switzerland is subject to massive capital inflows, and in order to preserve domestic economic and financial stability, the Swiss must recycle these funds into foreign investment channels. They have been most successful in this endeavor.

Some insight into the importance of capital flows to the Swiss economy and financial system is to note that in 1970-71, foreign bond issues represented 16 percent of new issues in the capital markets. In 1971, a year of extreme international currency turmoil, capital inflows represented 15 percent of Swiss GNP. Another key relationship would be the accumulation of foreign investments by the Swiss relative to GNP. As of 1971, gross foreign assets held by the Swiss represented 216 percent of GNP.

The importance of international capital flows is manifold, affecting Swiss portfolio management, bank lending policies, and monetary policy of the central bank. Considering the pressures imposed on this small nation in recent years through accelerating capital flows and shifting foreign exchange rate relationships, one must respect the ability and ingenuity of the Swiss banks and monetary authorities.

FINANCIAL AND CREDIT POLICY

The Swiss National Bank

The Swiss National Bank was created by Federal Law in 1905 and began operating two years later. In addition to its head offices in Berne and Zurich, the bank has branches and subbranches in several principal cities. Only Swiss citizens and Swiss companies may be registered as shareholders of the central bank. Aside from the public representation on its governing and controlling bodies, the bank gives the outward impression of a large private commercial bank. The bank council contains a majority of members appointed by the federal government and is responsible for broad supervision of the activities of the Swiss National Bank. The bank committee is responsible for more detailed control over operations, including interest rate policy and recommendations for selection of directorate members and principal officers.

The directorate is the bank's highest executive and managing group. It fixes the official discount rate and interest rates on loans. It is the responsibility of the directorate to observe the state of the capital and money markets and the economic situation and to represent the bank in meetings with other groups. Consisting of three members, the directorate holds its weekly meetings in Zurich. Each member of the directorate heads one of the three departments of the bank. Each of these departments is allotted specific functions, includin

232

rendering expert opinion on financial and economic matters, supervision of head offices and branches, issuing of bank notes, gold operations, directing the Bank's participation in the issuing of loans, discount administration, foreign exchange transactions, giro and clearing operations, and dealings with correspondents at home and abroad.

The Swiss National Bank has recourse to a number of policy instruments in the ordinary conduct of its business. For example, the bank discounts short-term claims and provides advances against the security of Swiss bonds, Federal Debt Register claims, and other eligible assets. However, the private economy has made only limited use of central bank credit, largely because of the high degree of liquidity associated with massive inflows of nonresident funds.

In addition to providing discount and advance facilities, the central bank renders a number of important services including effecting the country's clearing and collection systems, services to the Confederation including the issue of federal loans, circulation of coins, and safe custody of the assets of government agencies. To a limited extent, the central bank provides several services to the public that are also carried out by the commercial banks. These include purchase and sale of securities for account of others, acceptance of money deposits on noninterest-bearing accounts, and the hiring out of safe deposit boxes. Finally, the Swiss National Bank reviews proposals for foreign bond issues in the domestic capital market, in light of currency, interest rate, and general economic conditions.

The commercial banks maintain balances at the central bank that represent part of their liquid resources. They use these balances for transfers to other accounts, for withdrawing bank notes, and for general clearing purposes. The Swiss National Bank is a shareholder of the Bank for International Settlements by Federal Act of 1930.

A major aspect of Swiss monetary and credit policy focuses on its responsibility for keeping the gold value of the Swiss franc stable and safeguarding the internal value of the currency. This task is difficult in light of the strong links between Switzerland and the rest of the world and the exposure to external influences. A basic aim of central bank policy is to keep market liquidity under control.

The Swiss National Bank must operate within relatively narrow limits in the pursuit of its objectives. This is because the bank has relatively weak policy instruments at its disposal. As a result, in the past a major thrust of monetary policy has been through seeking the voluntary cooperation of the commercial banks. The policy instruments available to the central bank include administration of discount credit, open-market policy, foreign exchange policy, control of capital exports, and the conclusion of gentlemen's agreements with the banks regarding credit control and other matters.

An important distinction between central banking and the monetary system in Switzerland as compared with other developed countries such as the United States, United Kingdom, and Germany is the absence of formal cash reserve requirements. However, the central bank has negotiated voluntary agreements with the banks in which the latter have agreed to comply with minimum reserves relative to nonresident deposits. More recently (1969), an agreement was reached whereby minimum reserves and overall credit ceilings could be invoked by the central bank to combat inflationary pressures. On the basis of this agreement, it was ruled in 1969 that additional credits by the banks would be limited to 9 percent over the previous level. This agreement was extended in 1971 with much smaller ceilings on credit expansion. In 1971, a new convention between the central bank and commercial banks stipulates that increases in bank liabilities to nonresidents are to be matched by reserves of 100 percent of these additional deposits. The funds are to be deposited in an interest-free special account with the Swiss National Bank. Shortly prior to the conclusion of this convention, the banks had agreed not to pay interest on nonresident funds.

Discount rate policy plays a psychological role in Swiss banking and finance. The commercial banks make only limited use of the discount facility, and the structure of interest rates in Switzerland prevents changes in the discount rate from effecting leverage on bank borrowers. The discount rate is considerably below market lending rates and generally follows already established trends in the money and credit markets.

The Swiss National Bank is authorized to engage in open-market operations under the revised Banking Law of 1953. Permitted transactions cover purchase and sale of Treasury bills and bonds of the Confederation and Federal Railways, Federal Debt Register claims, and bonds of the cantons, cantonal banks, and central mortgage institution. An important restriction is that the central bank's bank note cover cannot include securities that have more than two years to maturity. Article 39 of the Federal Constitution allows only short-term assets to be included in the note cover in addition to gold. The Swiss National Bank has not even been able to use its limited powers in the area of open-market operations due to the high degree of market liquidity related to inflows of funds. However, the bank has engaged in open-market-type activities through the buying and selling of gold and foreign exchange. Moreover, the central bank has found it possible to sell Treasury bills on the market in order to absorb liquidity. In such cases, most of the bills placed have been on behalf of the Confederation. Also, beginning in the 1960s, the central bank has counteracted increases in domestic liquidity resulting from inflows of foreign money by engaging in monetary operations with

foreign central banks. In this connection, the Swiss National Bank
has participated in the central bank swap network in which foreign
exchange reserves are made available to individual central banks
to assist them in stabilizing foreign exchange rates vis-à-vis their
own currency.

International Financial Relations

As noted in the preceding section, the Swiss National Bank has
attempted to counteract growth in domestic liquidity resulting from
inflows of foreign funds. One such measure has been participation
in the General Agreements to Borrow initiated in 1961 by the Group
of Ten industrial countries. In this connection, a reciprocal swap
network has been developed in which central banks provide one another substantial amounts of their own currency for use in bolstering
foreign exchange reserves and stabilization of exchange rates during
periods of balance of payments difficulties. In the period 1961-68,
the Swiss National Bank provided currency credits totaling 14 billion
francs, of which 1.7 billion was outstanding in 1969. Since 1968 the
facilities of the swap network have been expanded in connection with
the introduction of the two-tier gold system and currency instabilities.
In 1973, the currency swap facilities were further increased. Total
facilities in the 15 country network were increased by $6.25 billion
to $17.98 billion. Of this amount the Swiss National Bank undertook
a total commitment of $1.4 billion, and the Bank for International
Settlements (BIS) $0.6 billion.

In the past, the Swiss National Bank has recycled foreign exchange
funds by acquiring the so-called Roosa bonds, named after R. V.
Roosa, undersecretary of the Treasury during the Kennedy administration. These U.S. Treasury obligations are denominated in foreign
currencies and issued to foreign central banks, in part as settlement
of expiring swap facilities, or to absorb dollar exchange held by
foreign central banks.

The BIS is an important factor in the Swiss financial markets,
especially where international monetary relations are concerned.
The BIS was created in 1930 to function as a trustee in connection
with the German external loans (Dawes and Young loans). Its capital
stock is owned by a number of central banks. In the period after
World War II, the BIS functioned as clearing agent for the European
Payments Union, and as depository under the loan agreements (1954-
61) of the European Coal and Steel Community. With headquarters
in Basle, the BIS has played a key role in furthering the development
of cooperation between central banks and international organizations.
In this connection, it has organized meetings of the governors of the

central banks of the Group of Ten countries, studied and reported on the development of the Eurocurrency market, and exchanged information on other economic and monetary problems of interest to central banks.

Banking operations of the BIS include accepting deposits from central banks or from others in connection with trustee agreements; acting as agent or correspondent for central banks; buying and selling gold for its own account or under earmark for central banks; making advances to or borrowing from central banks against gold, bills of exchange, and other short-term obligations; purchase, sale, or discount of Treasury bills and other short-dated instruments; purchase and sale of foreign exchange for its own account or for the account of central banks. Under its statutes the BIS may not issue bank notes, accept bills of exchange, make loans to governments, or open current deposit accounts for governments.

The BIS operates on the international gold markets as well as on the international money and capital markets. In the conduct of these transactions, it must keep in mind the policies of participating central banks. Location of the BIS in Basle has resulted in a close working cooperation with the Swiss National Bank, as well as with the other Swiss banks. The BIS is active in the transactions of the central bank swap facility. In addition, it plays an important role in the Swiss financial markets by taking deposits from Swiss banks and investing the foreign currency counterpart on the international money markets. At March 31, 1972, assets of the BIS totaled 29.3 billion gold francs, having increased from a level of 12.0 billion gold francs in 1968.* These assets are invested in securities (10.9 billion gold francs), time deposits and advances (13.0 billion gold francs), and Treasury bills (1.1 billion gold francs). Over 90 percent of BIS funds are derived from central bank deposits.

REFERENCES

Bank for International Settlements (BIS). Annual Report, 1972, 1973.

_____. Eight European Central Banks. New York: Praeger Publishers, 1963.

---

*The BIS balance sheet and other accounts are kept in terms of the gold franc, which is the equivalent of 0.29032258 grams of fine gold. This compares with the Swiss franc, which was defined as equivalent to 0.21759 grams of fine gold effective May 1971.

Ikle, Max. *Switzerland: An International Banking and Finance Center.* Stroudsburg, Pa.: Dowden, Hutchinson & Ross, 1972.

Schloss, Henry H. *The Bank for International Settlements.* Amsterdam: North Holland Publishing Co., 1958.

Swiss Credit Bank. *Swiss Statistical Abstract*, 1972.

Union Bank of Switzerland. *Business Facts and Figures*, June 1973.

_____. *Economic Survey of Switzerland*, 1973.

POSTWAR DEVELOPMENT

The Japanese economic miracle of the postwar period continues to arouse the interest and attention of economists and policy makers around the globe. This economic miracle has permitted the government to achieve its goal of income doubling during the decade of the 1960s and has resulted in Japan ranking as the third largest productive economy in the world, after the United States and the Soviet Union. During the last half of the 1960s, gross national product (GNP) expanded at a rate in excess of 10 percent per annum.

How has the Japanese economy achieved this impressive growth? A number of factors have contributed, including a high ratio of saving and investment to national income, substantial penetration of world markets by Japanese export firms, an efficient allocation of funds within the financial markets, a competitive industrial framework, and maintenance of a protected yen area.

The household sector in Japan has maintained a high personal saving ratio of 18 to 19 percent, which has played an important role in financing business capital spending. While the Japanese economy (measured by GNP) is barely one-fourth that of the United States, Japanese business investment is approximately 60 percent as large as U.S. plant and equipment investment.

During the past 15 years, Japan's export industries have led the expansion of the domestic economy. In 1970 Japan exported 11 percent of domestic production. During the period 1963-71, Japan's exports increased from 4.0 to 7.7 percent of the world total.

The structure and framework of industry in Japan have contributed to the achievement of a high rate of economic growth. Business firms are aggressively oriented toward expansion in size and share of the market and relatively less influenced by considerations of

241

profitability. Therefore, there has been a growth orientation within the microsetting of competitive behavior by individual firms. Moreover, government policy has aimed at supporting the development of new technology industries and, through various tax, import quota, and guidance policies, has sought to foster development of high technology industries. Finally, close working relationships among industrial corporations, banks, and major financial institutions have provided an environment favorable to the competitive status, financing, and marketing strength of individual firms. For example, keiretsu groupings of business firms in Japan,* based on interlocking directorates, financial ties, and informal gentlemen's agreements, engender a degree of stability and strength to Japanese business firms that face strong competition in their domestic and international operations. A number of these keiretsu groups have, as their nucleus, a major Japanese bank, and they frequently include other financial companies such as insurance and stock brokerage firms.

Official Japanese policy has been to support economic growth through a variety of measures. One of these includes maintenance of a protected yen area. Protective measures include detailed screening of requests by foreign business firms to establish affiliate operations in Japan, import quotas on a wide range of goods produced by newly established domestic business firms, careful control of foreign exchange transactions, and protection of domestic financial markets from international pressures of a destabilizing nature.

FINANCIAL INSTITUTIONS

The financial institutions in Japan, including the banks, insurance companies, trust banks, and other institutions, provide an impressive picture of the financial development of the economy. However, the financial development of Japan is lacking in depth and variety of financial institutions. By far, the banking sector is the most developed and tends to dominate the operations of financial institutions. But even the strength and importance of the commercial banks in Japan leave much to be desired in such areas as money market development, consumer finance, and alternative sources of medium-term business finance.

---

*The informal keiretsu groups have replaced the zaibatsu holding companies, which are now illegal.

Commercial Banks

Japan enjoys a well-developed banking system, and one that has been extremely effective in supporting economic and industrial expansion of the corporate sector. Over 70 commercial banks operate extensive branch systems. A dozen large city banks include several that rank among the largest in the world. The clientele of the large city banks include large corporations which have been heavy borrowers at the banks. These borrowings have financed capital expenditures as well as working capital requirements.

The relatively undeveloped capital market in Japan affects the operations of the city banks in several ways. A large part of the savings and investment financing in Japan is diverted through the large banks as a result of lack of suitable alternatives for savers and business borrowers. Rapid growth of the Japanese economy associated with a high rate of business capital spending has placed heavy pressure on the Japanese banks to supply funds to finance the requirements of the business sector. Consequently, the large banks are characteristically overloaned, illiquid, and overborrowed at the Bank of Japan. For example, the large Japanese commercial banks generally have loan-deposit ratios in excess of 100 percent.

The major sources of funds for the banking sector in Japan are deposits, sale of bank debentures, and advances from the Bank of Japan. Were it not for the readiness of the Bank of Japan to supply generous amounts of funds to banks via the discount window, the large banks would be left without the means to accommodate the demands of the business sector. In the period 1965-70, the Bank of Japan lending to the commercial banks increased at an annual rate of 15 to 16 percent. In part this is due to the lack of suitable sources of liquidity adjustment other than the provision of funds by the central bank. The money market in Japan is extremely backward in its development, with virtually no market for secondary trading in government Treasury bills. The only important device available for banks and other financial institutions to adjust their liquid reserves is the call money market. The major borrowers in this market are the large city banks, with a large secondary demand coming from security finance companies. The local banks lend funds in this market. Specialized dealers are licensed by the Finance Ministry and act as intermediaries in the call loan market. They also buy and sell commercial bills, short-term government securities, and act as foreign exchange brokers.

The banks have played a strategic role in Japan's industrial growth. This is because indirect financing is more important in Japan than direct financing through the securities markets. Japanese business firms operate on highly leveraged capital structures averaging 20 percent equity and 80 percent debt. Much of this debt is in the hands of Japanese banks in the form of short-term loans which are automatically rolled over. Japanese banks also hold a substantial part of equities in industrial companies. At year end 1970, the banks in Japan held 14 percent of equities then outstanding and 52 percent of company bonds and debentures.

In Japan the demand for funds has almost steadily outpaced the supply, and the efficiency of the banks in allocating credit to the most credit-worthy and competitively efficient firms has been an important factor in Japan's economic success. One might go so far as to suggest that the heavy concentration of loanable funds in Japan in the large banks has permitted a more rational allocation than might have been possible under alternative systems of credit allocation. For example, in countries where a large proportion of credit is allocated to business via the securities markets, smaller and often less knowledgeable investors play a greater role in the allocation process.

In addition to the important role played by the Japanese commercial banks as lenders to business, they purchase a large proportion of the debentures issued by the Long-Term Credit Bank, company bonds, and equities. The poorly developed capital market magnifies the importance of bank purchases of these securities.

The large commercial banks also play a key role in supporting the international financial relationships of the Japanese economy. They are extremely active in financing foreign trade and related business activities of Japanese companies. The city banks operate as foreign exchange banks, maintaining foreign exchange accounts with correspondent banks located in other countries, engaging in spot and forward exchange transactions, and assisting the Bank of Japan in administering the foreign exchange regulations. The Bank of Tokyo has held a special status in this connection as the largest and most important foreign exchange bank in Japan and in managing foreign bond issues and functioning as agent for payment of interest to foreign bondholders. The large commercial banks rank among the world leaders in international banking activities, operating numerous overseas branches and affiliate banks throughout the world.

Nonbank Financial Institutions

We have already indicated that the commercial banks dominate the financial system in Japan. Nevertheless, a number of specialized financial institutions play an important role in Japan in channeling credit from ultimate lenders to ultimate borrowers and in accommodating international capital flows.

Long-Term Credit Banks

The Long-Term Credit Banks were organized to fill a gap in the Japanese capital market. The oldest of these, the Industrial Bank of Japan, was established in the late nineteenth century to channel foreign portfolio investment into those domestic industry sectors most in need of additional capital financing. Establishment of the Industrial Bank of Japan fitted into the official policy regarding inward foreign investment, to attract foreign capital but to avoid excessive foreign control over Japanese industry. Another objective of Japanese policy supported through this institution has been to avoid excessive foreign indebtedness, in order to assure repayment of interest and principal to foreign creditors.

Two other long-term credit institutions, the Long-Term Credit Bank of Japan and the Hypothec Bank of Japan, also issue their own debentures to attract capital funds and make loans and investments to Japanese business firms. They also function as trustees for flotation of company debenture issues and provide several services in that field.

Trust Banks

The trust banks are modeled after the U.S. system, where these institutions conduct a regular commercial banking as well as trust business. Seven trust banks and one city bank conduct all of the trust business in Japan. The trust business consists of a truster passing money or property to a trustee (trust bank) with the instruction that the trustee administer it for the benefit of a designated beneficiary. The trust banks carry on a variety of trust activities including money trusts, loan trusts where the pooling of trust funds is uniform and the company issues negotiable trust certificates, pension trusts, and securities and real estate trusts. The Tax Law of 1962 provided a stimulus to the pension trusts by granting tax concessions to funds set aside for company employee pension trusts, provided the assets are held outside the company by a trust bank or insurance company.

Insurance Companies

Insurance companies play an important role in the Japanese capital market. Their holdings of company securities are approximately three-fourths as large as bank holdings of such securities. Insurance company transactions on the stock exchanges represent an important part of institutional trading. Assets held by the life insurance companies are several times as large as those of the non-life companies. Moreover, the composition of the investment portfolios of both types of insurance companies differs, based upon the nature of the risks they insure.

Life insurance company assets consist largely of long-term loans to business firms and the securities (mainly stocks) of large Japanese companies. The bulk of assets are long-term investments, reflecting the long life of policies written. By contrast, the nonlife companies insure against fire, casualty, and marine risks, whose incidence is unpredictable and which requires a high degree of liquid reserves. Therefore, nonlife companies hold a relatively high percentage of cash assets (15 to 20 percent). In addition, they hold a higher proportion of stocks than the life companies.

The portfolio investments of life insurance companies are subject to legal restrictions, and Japanese life companies may not hold more than 30 percent of their assets in stocks and 20 percent in real estate. Establishment of either a life insurance or nonlife company requires approval of the minister of finance.

FLOW OF FUNDS

Patterns Since 1959

During the period 1959-70, the pattern of flows of funds has altered, reflecting structural and other changes taking place in the Japanese economy. In the period 1959-61, the corporate business sector was the only net borrower of funds. These funds were provided by the personal sector, the public sector, and the rest-of-the-world sector. In 1962-64, the public sector came into financial deficit. However, its deficit position was small, owing to the fact that while the local authorities and public corporations were in deficit, the central government registered a financial surplus. The domestic sectors of the Japanese economy were in a position of excess investment in the years through 1964, with the financial deficit offset by funds provided from abroad.

In the period 1965-67, two changes appeared in the flow of funds. First, the rest of the world sector shifted to a net borrower position. Second, the public sector sharply increased its deficit position, as central government expenditures surged ahead. The first change was associated with a shift in the status of the domestic sectors toward financial surplus (excess saving) contrasted with the prior position of financial deficit (excess investment).

In the subsequent period, 1968-70, the public sector declined in importance as a net borrower of funds. Correspondingly, the corporate business sector increased its financial deficit position.

TABLE 13.1

Flow of Funds through Financial Markets
(billions of yen)

	1966	1967	1968	1969	1970
Financial institutions	8,023	9,614	10,173	13,143	15,306
Banks*	3,607	4,621	4,283	5,570	6,395
Other financial institutions	2,910	3,367	3,849	5,160	5,991
Government	1,506	1,626	2,041	2,413	2,920
Percent	98.4	93.8	91.1	90.1	89.0
Securities market	279	290	596	906	1,390
Corporate business					
and personal	419	408	578	745	1,277
Investment trust	-140	-118	18	161	113
Inflow of foreign capital	-147	350	404	538	507
(Percent)	-1.8	3.4	3.6	3.7	2.9
Total	8,155	10,254	11,173	14,587	17,203
Percent	100.0	100.0	100.0	100.0	100.0
Percent change from					
previous year	14.6	25.7	9.0	30.6	17.9

*Includes the Bank of Japan.

Note: For 1967 and 1968, after adjustment for the change in status of Taiyo Bank (reclassified under the ordinary bank group).

This change resulted from an increase in corporate investment spending after 1967 and the increase in corporate demand for funds. The economic upswing increased tax revenues and reduced the size of the public sector deficit. Another important change that took place in this period was an increase in the deficit position of the rest-of-the-world sector. From a balance of payments context, this can be associated with an increased current account surplus for Japan, which stems from the strengthened competitiveness of Japanese exports.

Flows in 1970

As noted in the previous section, the pattern of flows of funds in Japan has varied with the shifts in financial surplus and deficit position of the four major sectors. In turn, these shifts are related

TABLE 13.2

Financial Transaction Accounts for 1970
(billions of yen)

| | Financial Institutions | | Bank of Japan | | | | Banks and Others | | | |
| | | | | | | | Banks | | Others | |
	A	L	A	L	A	L	A	L	A	L
Currency and demand										
Deposits	33	3,329	—	825	113	2,584	63	1,859	284	959
Currency	33	744	—	744	32	—	—	—	32	—
Current deposits	—	106	—	81	81	106	63	-30	37	156
Short-term deposits	—	2,478	—	—	—	2,478	—	1,889	214	803
Government current deposits	—	-4	—	-4	—	—	—	—	—	—
Time deposits	—	5,899	—	—	—	5,899	—	3,066	-26	2,806
Trust	—	812	—	—	—	812	24	—	10	846
Insurance	—	1,196	—	—	—	1,196	—	—	—	1,196
Securities	[a]1,251	1,190	[b]212	—	[a]1,039	1,190	576	663	[a]463	527
Short-term government securities	-28	—	151	—	-180	—	—	—	-180	—
Government bonds	190	—	408	—	-218	—	-149	—	-68	—
Local government securities	164	—	—	—	164	—	121	—	42	—
Public corporate bonds	-4	—	-223	—	219	—	90	—	128	—
Bank debentures	252	827	-123	—	376	827	208	569	167	258
Industrial bonds	235	—	—	—	235	—	97	—	137	—
Stocks	433	105	—	—	433	105	204	93	229	11
Securities investment trust	8	257	—	—	8	257	2	—	6	257
Bank of Japan loans	411	411	411	—	—	411	—	437	—	-25
Call money borrowed and lent	—	16	—	—	—	16	205	531	477	167
Loans	11,508	—	—	—	11,508	—	5,694	-6	5,860	53
Loans by private financial institutions	11,508	—	—	—	11,508	—	5,694	-6	5,860	53
Loans by government	—	—	—	—	—	—	—	—	—	—
Loans by securities companies	—	—	—	—	—	—	—	—	—	—
Trade credit	—	—	—	—	—	—	—	—	—	—
Equities other than stocks	—	43	—	—	—	43	—	—	—	43
Gold and foreign exchange reserves	—	—	—	—	—	—	—	—	—	—
Foreign claims and debts, short term	592	363	—	—	592	363	592	363	—	—
Foreign claims and debts, long term	14	13	—	—	14	13	4	13	10	—
Others	—	539	—	-196	—	736	—	232	—	504
Financial surplus or deficit (—)	—	—	—	—	—	—	—	—	—	—
Total	13,811	13,811	624	624	13,268	13,268	7,159	7,159	7,078	7,078

Government		Public Corporations and Local Authorities		Corporate Business		Personal		Rest of the World		Total	
A	L	A	L	A	L	A	L	A	L	A	L
31	59	74	—	1,581	—	1,668	—	—	—	3,388	3,388
11	54	—	—	75	—	679	—	—	—	799	799
2	4	—	—	86	—	22	—	—	—	111	111
17	—	73	—	1,420	—	967	—	—	—	2,478	2,478
-4	—	—	—	—	—	—	—	—	—	-4	-4
—	1,370	135	—	2,088	—	5,046	—	—	—	7,270	7,270
—	—	9	—	185	—	617	—	—	—	812	812
—	360	—	—	—	—	1,556	—	—	—	1,556	1,556
974	633	13	831	496	1,267	1,419	—	—	—	4,156	c3,923
193	189	13	—	7	—	3	—	—	—	189	189
107	330	—	—	2	—	27	—	—	—	328	330
10	—	—	183	5	—	3	—	—	—	183	183
475	113	—	648	87	—	204	—	—	—	762	762
183	—	—	—	39	—	352	—	—	—	827	827
-2	—	—	—	17	346	94	—	—	—	346	346
5	—	—	—	329	921	493	—	—	—	1,262	1,027
—	—	—	—	6	—	241	—	—	—	257	257
—	—	—	—	—	—	—	—	—	—	411	411
—	—	—	—	16	—	—	—	—	—	16	16
2,115	—	—	966	—	9,417	—	3,239	—	—	13,624	13,624
—	—	—	125	—	8,546	—	2,837	—	—	11,508	11,508
2,115	—	—	841	—	871	—	402	—	—	2,115	2,115
—	—	—	—	-186	31	—	-217	—	—	-186	-186
—	—	—	—	8,907	7,177	—	1,730	—	—	8,907	8,907
27	—	15	42	18	68	94	—	—	—	154	154
—	—	—	—	—	—	—	—	—	d281	—	d281
—	—	—	—	—	369	—	—	595	535	1,187	1,268
147	-21	—	-13	449	172	1	—	158	733	771	884
162	—	-4	—	450	—	101	—	72	—	782	539
—	1,051	—	-1,582	—	-4,497	—	5,753	—	-725	—	—
3,453	3,453	244	244	14,008	14,008	10,505	10,505	825	825	42,849	42,849

Notes: (a) Including 105 billion yen of the investment trust. (b) Including 883 billion yen of net purchases of securities by the Bank of Japan from private financial institutions. (c) Including 97 billion of government-guaranteed bonds. (d) Excluding 43 billion yen of the allocation of IMF special drawing rights.

TABLE 13.3

Financial Assets and Liabilities, December 31, 1970
(billions of yen)

| | Financial Institutions | | | | | | | | | |
| | | | Bank of Japan | | Banks and Others | | Banks | | Others | |
	A	L	A	L	A	L	A	L	A	L
Currency and demand Deposits	890	24,716	—	5,854	1,189	19,159	887	13,812	1,641	6,686
Currency	890	5,556	—	5,556	890	—	628	—	262	—
Current deposits	—	1,870	—	298	298	1,870	258	1,217	208	821
Short-term deposits	—	17,289	—	—	—	17,289	—	12,595	1,170	5,864
Government current deposits	—	16	—	16	—	—	—	—	—	—
Time deposits	—	39,212	—	—	—	39,212	—	22,971	221	16,462
Trust	—	5,224	—	—	—	5,224	102	—	95	5,421
Insurance	—	6,637	—	—	—	6,637	—	—	—	6,637
Securities	[a]16,106	8,324	2,824	—	[a]13,281	8,324	7,013	5,459	[a]6,268	2,864
Short-term government securities	692	—	692	—	—	—	—	—	—	—
Government bonds	2,348	—	1,689	—	659	—	560	—	99	—
Local government securities	1,392	—	—	—	1,392	—	846	—	545	—
Public corporate bonds	2,502	—	435	—	2,067	—	1,030	—	1,037	—
Bank debentures	2,903	6,175	8	—	2,895	6,175	1,484	4,745	1,410	1,429
Industrial bonds	2,677	—	—	—	2,677	—	1,587	—	1,090	—
Stocks	3,530	842	—	—	3,530	842	1,478	713	2,052	128
Securities investment trust	58	1,306	—	—	58	1,306	26	—	32	1,306
Bank of Japan loans	2,353	2,353	2,353	—	—	2,353	—	2,229	—	123
Call money borrowed and lent	—	58	—	—	—	58	771	2,075	3,204	1,958
Loans	70,130	—	—	—	70,130	—	39,477	586	31,571	332
Loans by private financial institutions	70,130	—	—	—	70,130	—	39,477	586	31,571	332
Loans by government	—	—	—	—	—	—	—	—	—	—
Loans by securities companies	—	—	—	—	—	—	—	—	—	—
Trade credit	—	—	—	—	—	—	—	—	—	—
Equities other than stocks	—	387	—	—	—	387	—	—	—	387
Others	—	2,549	693	—	—	3,243	—	1,116	197	2,324
Difference	—	—	—	—	—	—	—	—	—	—
Total	89,480	89,480	5,871	5,871	84,600	84,600	48,251	48,251	43,200	43,200

	Government		Public Corporations and Local Authorities		Corporate Business		Personal		Total	
	A	L	A	L	A	L	A	L	A	L
	103	379	624	—	10,457	—	13,019	—	25,095	25,095
	38	341	—	—	496	—	4,470	—	5,897	5,897
	6	37	3	—	1,672	—	226	—	1,908	1,908
	58	—	620	—	8,288	—	8,322	—	17,289	17,289
	16	—	—	—	—	—	—	—	16	16
	—	7,405	901	—	13,881	—	31,834	—	46,617	46,617
	—	—	47	—	1,251	—	3,295	—	5,224	5,224
	—	2,410	—	—	—	—	9,048	—	9,048	9,048
	4,421	6,327	20	6,666	3,916	11,972	9,741	—	34,206	d33,291
	1,599	2,359	20	—	33	—	14	—	2,359	2,359
	424	3,191	—	—	19	—	358	—	3,151	3,191
	27	—	—	1,476	24	—	32	—	1,476	1,476
	1,662	776	—	5,190	703	—	1,098	—	5,967	5,967
	527	—	—	—	397	—	2,347	—	6,175	6,175
	68	—	—	—	54	3,043	243	—	3,043	3,043
	112	—	—	—	b2,656	8,929	c4,427	—	10,726	9,772
	—	—	—	—	28	—	1,219	—	1,306	1,306
	—	—	—	—	—	—	—	—	2,353	2,353
	—	—	—	—	58	—	—	—	58	58
	13,557	—	—	5,755	—	60,091	—	17,841	83,687	83,687
	—	—	—	731	—	54,165	—	15,233	70,130	70,130
	13,557	—	—	5,024	—	5,925	—	2,608	13,557	13,557
	—	—	—	—	342	55	—	286	342	342
	—	—	—	—	51,271	40,853	—	10,417	51,271	51,271
	272	—	104	351	179	677	861	—	1,416	1,416
	689	—	24	—	335	—	585	—	1,634	2,549
	—	2,538	—	-11,050	-11,050	-31,958	—	40,471	—	—
	19,060	19,060	1,723	1,723	81,692	81,692	69,016	69,016	260,973	260,973

Notes: a) Including 1,040 billion yen of the investment trust. b) 5,949 billion yen at market price. c) 10,464 billion yen at market price. d) Including 2,003 billion yen of government-guaranteed bonds.

to changes in the rate of capital formation, growth of national income, fiscal policy, and balance of payments. In the five-year period 1966-70, the percentage of funds raised by the nonfinancial sectors to gross domestic capital formation ranged between 55 and 65 percent.

A major portion of the flow of funds through the financial markets is channeled through financial institutions. As can be seen in Table 13.1, in the period 1966-70, the proportion of such funds to total funds ranged between 89 and 98 percent. In 1970 approximately 8 percent of the flow of funds was channeled through the securities markets, reflecting the dominant position of indirect (via financial institutions) financing versus financing through the new issues markets in Japan.

In 1970 the banks provided approximately 40 percent of the funds generated by all financial institutions and over 55 percent of new loan funds raised by the corporate business sector. In the same year, the banks purchased approximately 576 billion yen in securities, including two-thirds of local government issues, one-eighth of public corporate bonds, one-fourth of bank debentures, over one-fourth of company bonds, and one-fifth of stocks (Table 13.2). In the same year, nonbank financial institutions provided funds mainly by loans. Acquisitions of securities by nonbank financial institutions amounted to 463 billion yen, the major categories including company stocks, bank debentures, company bonds, and bonds of public corporations. In 1970 banks and other financial institutions reduced their holdings of government bonds and short-term securities by an amount of 398 billion yen. Financial asset holdings of banks and financial institutions at year end 1970 are reflected in Table 13.3.

CAPITAL MARKETS

Several aspects of the capital markets in Japan have already been discussed in sections dealing with the financial institutions and flow of funds. At this juncture we discuss the new issues market in terms of specialized institutions and new issues facilities, secondary trading, and special features of the capital markets in Japan.

New Issues Market

Specialized Institutions

As in other countries, the new issues market in Japan is supported by specialized institutions whose function is to underwrite new issues, provide trading facilities for securities when issued, and to facilitate the financing of these operations. These institutions include the securities companies, securities finance companies, and securities investment trusts.

The securities companies are stock exchange dealers and brokers who buy and sell and act as agents for customers who purchase and sell bonds and shares. These companies also underwrite and distribute bond and share issues and provide ancillary services. Since the 1968 reform, which imposed a licensing system for securities companies, approximately 270 such companies have been in operation. The four largest of these companies, Nomura, Yanaichi, Nikko, and Daiwa, conduct the bulk of the securities business in Japan. In 1972 Merrill Lynch, the largest U.S. securities firm, was granted a license to conduct a securities business in Japan.

Securities companies deal in the new issue market when underwriting bonds and shares and in the secondary trading market for these types of securities. Under the Securities Transactions Act of 1948, underwriting of company bond and shares is reserved for securities companies. Underwriting of government debt securities can be carried out by banks as well as securities firms.

Securities investment trusts are companies that invest trust funds in specified securities for the benefit of participants who hold beneficiary certificates. These trusts are affiliated with securities companies. Three types of investment trusts are offered in Japan, including unit trusts, open-end trusts, and bond trusts. Operations of securities investment trusts are regulated by the Securities Investment Trust Act of 1951 and controlled by the minister of finance. Securities investment trusts are larger investors than insurance companies and, at July 1971, held net assets valued at nearly $4.1 billion.

Securities finance companies provide loans of cash or shares and bonds to facilitate securities transactions. These credit institutions permit margin transactions on the stock exchanges. Speculative buyers borrow funds from these companies on the security of the stocks to be acquired. These companies also lend shares and bonds to speculative sellers of these securities on the security of the proceeds from the sale. Thus, the security finance company covers only the difference between the value of stocks loaned to sellers and the amount of funds loaned to buyers. Their funds are obtained on call loans and loans from banks.

New Issues

The new issue of company bonds and shares in Japan is reserved to securities companies, which enjoy the sole right of underwriting. Government bonds can be underwritten by banks. Public offerings

of company shares are infrequent because of the relatively underdeveloped stock exchange and strength of banking institutions. Nevertheless, in the period 1960-69, new equity issues represented $2\frac{1}{2}$ percent of GNP (Table 13.4). This impressive figure follows from the
large volume of right offerings made to stockholders in this period.
Until 1970 it had been the practice of Japanese companies to issue
new stock to existing shareholders at face value, hence a certain
"rights" value accrues to shareholders. Due to the infrequent resort to new stock issues via the exchange markets, underwriting
and issuing charges on share issues have remained high. A milestone
was reached in 1968 when a Japanese company issued 6 million shares
for public subscription at the market price. In 1970, several companie
issued shares at near market prices.

New bond issues are sold mainly to financial institutions. Private company bonds are issued through the securities companies. In
1970, of the 346 billion yen of company bonds issued, 97 billion yen
were purchased by banks, 137 billion yen by other financial institution:
and 94 billion yen by individuals. In the same year, close to 70 percen
of local government bonds issued were purchased by banks, and nearly
all the remainder of new issues acquired by nonbank financial institutions. The central government in Japan did not issue any long-term
bonds until 1965. The demand for central government bonds in any
one year reflects changes in monetary policy, shifts in bank liquidity,
and required shifts in the investment portfolios of individuals and
financial institutions. Short-term government bonds are not generally
attractive to the banks since they are always short of liquidity and
since the short-term issues offer low yields. For this reason, short-
term issues are purchased by the Bank of Japan. Bank debentures
are issued directly by the banks; however, the securities companies
help to market them.

The bond side of the new issues market has not been well developed. The public has not been strongly interested in long-term debt
securities, largely due to fear of inflation, controlled interest rates,
and the lack of liquidity where no adequate secondary trading market
exists.

Secondary Trading

The trading market in securities consists of the stock exchanges
and the over-the-counter markets. The stock exchanges deal primaril
in listed securities, which are those listed by the respective exchange
according to the rules of the Securities Transactions Act. There are
nine stock exchanges in Japan, of which the Tokyo Stock Exchange is
the largest, handling 70 percent of exchange trading in Japan.

TABLE 13.4

Comparisons of Equities Outstanding and New Equity
Issues for Five Countries, 1960-69
(billions of pound sterling)

Value of Equities Outstanding, 1971		Market Value as Percent of 1970 GNP	New Equity Issues	
			Total 1960-69	As Percent GNP, 1960-69
United States	300	73	12	1/2
United Kingdom	41	85	3	3/4
Japan	22	28	6	2 1/2
Germany	13	18	3	2/3
France	9	15	3	1

There are five types of transactions on the stock exchanges in Japan, including same-day settlement, ordinary transactions with settlement made on the fourth business day from the day of contract, specified-date transactions, when-issued transactions, and margin transactions. Margin transactions were introduced in 1951 to give depth to the market in securities eligible for margin transactions.

Size comparisons of the Japanese stock exchanges with those in other large industrial countries found in Table 13.4 indicate the following. Japan ranks third globally in market value of equities listed on stock exchanges, only behind the United States and United Kingdom. Second, new equity issues by Japanese companies in the period 1960-69 were valued at £6 billion, second only to the amount of new equity issues of U.S. companies. Finally, as a percent of 1970 GNP, market value of equities in Japan represented 28 percent, ranking Japan third on a global basis.

Early in the postwar period, the Japanese modeled their stock exchanges after the U.S. pattern. Any company could become a dealer or broker on the stock exchanges. Free competition was expected to produce a well-functioning secondary market facility. Under this system, the Japanese stock exchanges displayed remarkable growth, and the number of securities companies operating on the exchanges grew to about 600. In the mid-1960s, stock prices fell drastically, creating a crisis in the securities market. Cooperation among the Bank of Japan, the securities companies, and the other banks resulted in the formation of a share price-support program. Subsequent to this, the government reviewed the structure of the securities market and revised the Securities and Exchange Act in 1968. The new system

introduced at this time contained several main features. First, four
distinct types of securities business were identified, including dealer
operations, brokerage, underwriting and distribution, and servicing
subscription and public sale of securities. Second, government licensing replaced simple registration of securities dealers. Each of the
four types of business activities requires a license. Third, increased
administrative guidance has been given to the securities market.
Fourth, the Investment Trust Act was revised for more effective
regulation of investment trusts. Fifth, transactions were concentrated
on the floor of the stock exchange, eliminating unofficial transactions
of officially quoted stocks (baikai). This helps to develop a more
genuine market price on the trading floor. Finally, reporting and
disclosure of company operating conditions have been made more
complete.

The over-the-counter market in Japan includes the "second
floor" of the Tokyo, Osaka, and Nagoya stock exchanges, as well as
the small parcel trading units in the first market and the informal
markets outside the stock exchanges.

GOVERNMENT POLICY AND THE
BALANCE OF PAYMENTS

The remarkable performance of the Japanese economy over the
decade and a half ending in 1973 suggests that there is more to the
explanation of Japan's economic growth than meets the eye. Government policy plays a far more significant role in the economic performance than is apparent from the near lack of formal controls over
business activity. This is because government policy is more of the
framework variety.

Economic planning is a fact of life in Japan. However, it operates
differently than in other countries. It is true that the national government, and especially the Ministry of Finance and Ministry of International Trade and Investment, plays an important role in formulating
the national economic plan. But the role of government almost ends
at this point. Execution of the plan is left to industry and the marketplace, under whatever competitive pressures prevail. Japanese planning is indicative; plans are guideposts to assist the private sector
along the way; and the price mechanism is permitted to facilitate
attainment of these goals. Government sanctions against business
firms that exceed or fall short of targets are moral or psychological
and are reinforced by the patriotic and disciplined nature of the citi-
zenry. For this reason, the government-supported plan is respected,
and its publication carries an "announcement effect" that is too easily
underestimated by those who do not understand Japanese society and
traditions.

In addition to the formulation of the national economic plan and monetary policy which is discussed below, the government resorts to a number of measures to achieve the overall objectives of economic growth, stabilization, and international balance. These include legislative control of particular industries, provision of easy credit from government financial institutions for selected industries, depreciation allowances, use of elaborate machinery for two-way consultation between representatives of industry and government, quantitative import controls and tariffs, government purchase of shares in infant industries, and various public relations measures to disseminate information on the nature of specific economic targets and plan objectives.

Monetary Policy

The Bank of Japan enjoys a prominent status as controlling agency in the financial structure. Through the minister of finance, the government possesses wide legislative and supervisory powers over the Bank of Japan, but has relied on informal discussion and review in coordinating its policies with those of the bank. The Bank of Japan derives much of its importance from the fact that fiscal policy remained in disuse in the postwar period until 1965, leaving monetary policy to carry the entire burden of control. Moreover, the role of the banking sector in Japan in providing credit is probably far greater than in most other industrial countries, making monetary controls a more significant part of government framework guidance of the economy. In this connection, it should be noted that the role of the central bank in Japan is rather unique in that it provides credit to banks on a regular basis rather than intermittently when bank liquidity requires replenishment.

The Bank of Japan is banker for the government and, in that capacity, holds deposited funds, lends against bills and bonds, and handles the issue and retirement of government debt and the Foreign Exchange Special Account. The bank is the agent for the minister of finance for buying and selling foreign exchange from and to the authorized dealer banks.

The bank is also a banker's bank, accepts deposits from banks and other financial institutions, and lends to most of these institutions.

The instruments of monetary control available to the Bank of Japan include bank rate, administrative supervision of the discount window, open-market operations, and reserve deposit requirements. The first two of these have been the more effective of all the instruments used by the bank, although further development of the securities markets and financial structure could improve the usefulness of the latter two instruments.

Loan terms clearly influence willingness to borrow. The Bank of Japan has used a variety of bank rates and has been in a position to exert differential pressure on borrowers seeking various types of discount accommodation. The Bank of Japan has quoted separate discount rates on commercial bills, export trade bills, import trade bills, government securities, and other collateral. The basic bank rate is the discount rate on commercial bills.

Bank rate in Japan is an extremely effective monetary policy instrument. Only small changes in bank rate are required to produce a considerable change in the financial and business climate. This reflects the sensitivity of Japanese commercial banks to changes in discount rates due to their overloaned condition. Effectiveness of changes in bank rate is reinforced by the behavior of business borrowing from commercial banks. Japanese companies are highly leveraged and illiquid, and a sign of tightening monetary policy evokes a ready response as corporations attempt to increase their liquidity positions in anticipation of a smaller volume of more costly credit. The effectiveness of small changes in bank rate in Japan contrasts sharply with the situation in the United Kingdom, where changes of 1 to 2 percent often yield little or no effect.

Discount window operations of the Bank of Japan have been in the form of guidance and advice on the lending policies of borrowers from the bank. In the past, the central bank has emphasized the "quantitative" nature of such guidance, which aims at limitation of total loans to the public by a bank, but not at the composition of such loans. The term "window guidance" has come into use to reflect that such administrative guidance is associated with the use of the discount window. Seemingly, banks and other institutions that do not make use of the discount window would not be subject to this administrative suasion. Apparently, window guidance is a one-sided instrument of restriction used to support or substitute for an increase in bank rate.

Open-market operations are sales or purchases of securities, generally in the open market, and usually involving government securities. There are several peculiarities that attach to open-market operations in Japan which should be mentioned. First, open-market operations in government securities are of recent vintage, dating back to 1966 when government bonds first appeared on the securities markets (the government operated with budget surpluses prior to this). Second, financial institutions are instructed to sell or buy securities by the Bank of Japan. Hence, there is no open-market aspect to these operations. Third, transactions are effected on the basis of prices prevailing prior to the open-market operations. Therefore, market prices are not directly influenced by the transaction. As can be understood from the foregoing, open-market operations more resemble administrative variation of minimum statutory deposits.

Reserve deposit requirements were introduced into the Japanese banking system in 1959 by implementation of legislation passed two years earlier. At that time there was no excess liquidity in the Japanese banking system, which had been the rationale for introduction of similar provisions in the banking system of the United States in 1935. In Japan then existing measures of central bank control over credit expansion were adequate to the task, and we might conclude that the 1957 legislation was based on the desire to incorporate a feature of monetary control that might prove useful at some later date.

Minimum-deposit requirements are expressed as a percentage of deposit liabilities and apply to commercial banks, trust banks, Japanese branches of foreign banks, and the long-term credit banks. In the early 1970s these reserve deposit requirements were in the range of 1 to 2 percent of deposit liabilities.

To summarize, monetary policy in Japan operates as a strong conditioning force on business activity and the flow of funds through the credit markets. Very small changes in bank rate, reinforced by administrative window guidance, have represented the major avenues through which the force of monetary policy has been effected. In the following sections, we examine the record of the period 1965-71 to obtain a general feel of how monetary policy translated in terms of bank rate changes has been applied to stimulate or retard the pace of economic activity to achieve growth-employment-payments objectives.

Balance of Payments

We analyze the Japanese balance of payments for several inter-connected reasons. First, we should have a general picture of the strengths and weaknesses in the balance of payments and the extent to which Japan is a net lender or borrower. Second, the balance of payments provides basic information on the relation between international capital movements and the credit markets in Japan. Finally, a review of the balance of payments permits a brief analysis of the operation of monetary policy where balance of payments objectives are involved.

In Table 13.5 the balance of payments for 1971 is presented in summary form. Japan's current account surplus is quite large, over $6 billion, in large part accounted for by a favorable balance of trade. On capital account there was a substantial inward flow of investment, although this item appears to reverse direction almost every year. Government transfers make up the largest part of the out payments recorded under transfers and reflect the growing role of foreign aid as a method by which Japan is fostering economic development in Pacific Basin countries.

TABLE 13.5

Balance of Payments—Japan, 1971
(millions of dollars)

		Receipts	Payments
Balance on goods and services		6,152	
Trade	7,900		
Transportation	-875		
Central government	587		
Other services	-1,460		
Transfers			254
Capital		1,832	
Banking sector		2,531	
Monetary authority			10,336
SDR allocation		128	
Errors and omissions			53
Total		10,643	10,643

Source: International Monetary Fund (IMF), International Financial Statistics.

The substantial growth in reserve assets held by the monetary authorities, over $16 billion in April 1973, reflects the underlying strength in Japan's balance of payments, as well as the increased tendency toward nonresident capital inflows in response to currency uncertainties and increased confidence in the yen.

The basic strength in Japan's balance of payments is reflected in a growing creditor status on long-term investment account, as well as a substantial upsurge in holdings of short-term liquid assets. While moderate in amount, private capital inflows have played a strategic role in supporting Japan's postwar economic expansion. The commercial banks borrowed heavily from offshore sources in the early 1960s. Intermittently, the Japan Development Bank and the long-term credit banks have floated dollar bond issues to finance heavy capital expenditures in domestic industry. Finally, direct investment inflows and licensing and technology agreements have provided an additional support to the investment growth of Japanese industry. In all of these types of inward capital flows, domestic credit market flows were supplemented by foreign source funds.

Monetary Policy Shifts, 1965-71

At various times, the Bank of Japan has found it necessary to slow down the economy to combat inflationary pressures or achieve balance of payments equilibrium. Under these conditions, it has raised bank rate and applied administrative guidance to bank use of the discount window facility. Alternately, the bank has attempted to stimulate economic advance by easing the credit situation and reducing bank rate.

During the late 1960s and early 1970s, there were two situations which called for shifts in monetary policy. In 1967 a slowdown in the growth of world trade resulted in a weak export performance by the Japanese economy. At the same time, industrial production advanced 19 percent over the 1966 level, resulting in a sizable advance in imports (23 percent over 1966 levels). The resulting adverse shift in Japan's trade balance and international liquidity (Table 13.6) called for more stringent curbs over bank credit expansion. Consequently, in September 1967, the bank rate was advanced from 5.48 to 5.8 percent. Imports continued to climb above exports, and in January 1968, the bank rate was advanced to 6.21 percent. Improvement in exports and a leveling off of imports in the later months of that year permitted a reduction in bank rate in August 1968 to 5.84 percent.

In 1970-71, the Japanese economy faced a somewhat different problem as worldwide inflation spread to Japan and as the economy entered into a recession phase in 1970-71. Industrial production exhibited no growth in the final two quarters of 1970, and declined by approximately 1 percent in the period 1971 (first quarter) to 1971 (second quarter). Bank rate was reduced once in 1970 (October) and on four separate occasions in 1971 (January, May, July, and December). This recession was accompanied by a substantial leap in the favorable trade balance, as well as by a surge in holdings of foreign exchange reserves.

FUTURE PROSPECTS

The Japanese economy may be expected to play a more prominent role in international finance during and after the decade of the 1970s. This is to be expected for the following reasons.

The Japanese banks along with the American banks have taken the lead in building global networks of branch offices, merchant bank and specialty financing affiliates, and subsidiary banks. This trend should enhance the competitive position of major Japanese banks as mobilizers of lendable funds and purveyors of financial services in all corners of the globe. In addition, the widespread location of

TABLE 13.6

Basic Statistics on Japan's Economy, 1965-71

	Industrial Production (1963 = 100 percent increase)		Manufacturing Employment (1963 = 100)	Consumer Price Index (percent increase)
1965	120.0	—	107.4	—
1966	136.0	21.7	108.1	4.8
1967	162.3	19.3	111.6	4.1
1968	191.1	17.8	116.2	5.6
1969	223.2	16.8	120.3	5.5
1970	259.2	11.7	124.2	7.2
1971	271.9	5.0	124.1	6.3

	Bank Rate	Official Reserve Holdings	Trade Balance (millions of U.S. dollars)
1965	6.57-5.48	2,152	1,901
1966	5.48	2,119	2,275
1967	5.48-5.84	2,030	1,160
1968	5.84-6.21-5.84	2,906	2,529
1969	5.84-6.25	3,654	3,699
1970	6.25-6.00	4,840	3,963
1971	6.00-4.75	15,360	7,900

Source: IMF, International Financial Statistics.

Japanese banks and their affiliates should add to the usefulness and acceptability of the yen as a financing, investment, vehicle, and arbitrage currency.

The international status of the yen is nearly as strong as the German mark or Swiss franc. The yen is backed up by more than adequate international reserves, and the Japanese balance of payments remains in a favorable position. The major obstacles to the yen assuming the role of a major international currency are the poorly developed money market in Japan, which affords practically no suitable outlets for nonresident borrowers or lenders, and the policy of the Japanese government, which remains unfavorable to the development of Japan's money market to accommodate international transactions. The Japanese authorities contend that credit availability and bank liquidity would become unduly subject to international pressures, increasing the complexity of carrying out successful monetary policy. We should remember that very small changes in short-term interest rates in Japan exert substantial leverage over business loan activity and ultimately production income levels.

In the future Japan should become a leading capital exporting nation. As of 1973, the World Bank had marketed $1.8 billion in bonds denominated in yen and, in the period since 1969, had relied heavily on obtaining funds in the Japanese financial markets. In 1971, the Japanese authorities liberalized outward portfolio investment, permitting Japanese residents to purchase foreign securities for the first time.

Japan already is an important direct investor, with Japanese companies having made substantial investments in the less developed countries of the Pacific Basin to provide raw materials needed for the domestic economy and manufacturing and trade investments in North America and Latin America.

How long it will take for Japan to open its capital markets to foreign borrowers cannot be answered readily. Already, several prime borrowers such as the World Bank, Asian Development Bank, and Commonwealth of Australia have been given access to bond placements. The finance minister of Japan recently announced plans to hold yen bond flotations by nonresidents to one issue per month. The Japanese economy has the capacity to generate balance of payments surpluses that would facilitate the export of long-term capital. Japan's merchandise export position becomes stronger each year, and the balance of payments remains in a favorable position. What is lacking apparently is willingness on the part of the authorities to further open Japan's capital market to nonresident borrowers. Doubtless, this willingness will increase as international reserves become a larger "embarrassment of riches."

REFERENCES

Bank of Japan. Monthly Economic Review, 1971-73.

Bieda, K, The Structure and Operation of the Japanese Economy. New York: Wiley, 1970

Einzig, Paul. Parallel Money Markets: Volume Two, Overseas Markets. New York: Macmillan, 1972.

Iwasa, Yoshizane. "Japan Ventures into Southeast Asia." Columbia Journal of World Business (November-December 1967).

Kahn, Herman. The Emerging Japanese Superstate. Englewood Cliffs, N.J.: Prentice-Hall, 1970.

World Bank and IDA, Annual Reports, 1973.

14

FINANCIAL MARKETS
IN HONG KONG

ECONOMIC SETTING

Hong Kong, a British Crown Colony, adjoins the Chinese province of Kwangtung on the southeastern coast of the China mainland. With a total area of $398\frac{1}{2}$ square miles, Hong Kong consists of the island of Hong Kong itself, the city of Kowloon, and the New Territory (363 square miles) obtained from China on a 99-year lease that expires in 1997. The commercial and industrial sections and port facilities are located chiefly on the harbor side of Hong Kong Island, known as Victoria, and across the bay in Kowloon. Residential sections have climbed the rocky hillsides of Hong Kong and spread out from Kowloon penninsula to the southern part of the New Territory. Although situated 100 miles south of the Tropic of Cancer, Hong Kong's average daily temperature is about 60°F in the winter and 80°F in the summer.

In 1973, Hong Kong had a population of 4 million, 98 percent of which were Chinese—mostly Cantonese. Historically, the increase and decrease in population in Hong Kong have been closely related to the political and economic conditions in Mainland China. For example, during the Sino-Japanese War, Hong Kong's population increased to 1.6 million in 1941, but fell to 500,000 in 1945 when many Chinese fled to their home villages to escape the Japanese military occupation. Since 1949, when the Communists took over Mainland China, a continuous flow of people immigrated to Hong Kong. These people include intellectuals, entrepreneurs, and skilled workers who have shaped the backbone of Hong Kong's commercial, industrial, and financial development.

Economically, Hong Kong has very little tillable land and virtually no natural resources. The secret of Hong Kong's progress and prosperity, since it was acquired by the British in 1841 as a trading settlement, has been its crossroads location in the Pacific Basin, its magnificent deep-water harbor, a stable government, and free enterprise system. The strategic location has made Hong Kong one of the major entrepôt centers for trade between China and other nations. Furthermore, its full-service international airport and world wide communications network have enhanced its value as an international business and financial center. Free trade, low taxes, a free foreign exchange market, mobile labor force, multitude of small businesses, and legal framework have made Hong Kong resemble the economic model of Adam Smith's free enterprise system.

The economic prosperity of Hong Kong can be attributed to its government structure and political stability. The governor of Hong Kong, appointed by the queen of England, is head of the colony's government. Under the governor are the Executive Council (an advisory body), the Legislative Council which is presided over by the governor, and the Full Court, including the Supreme Court, District Courts, and Magistrate Courts. Foreign relations and defense are the responsibility if of the British government. Recently improved relations between the People's Republic of China and Britain have brightened Hong Kong's economic and political outlook, since its foreign trade and commerce are strongly influenced by conditions in Mainland China.

Despite lack of statistics, the following reflect the essentially sound economic and financial conditions in Hong Kong. Gross national product (GNP) increased from U.S. $996 million in 1960 to U.S. $4.7 billion in 1972. In the same period, per-capita income grew from U.S. $324 to U.S. $1,125. The increase in each case was approximately fourfold. Before 1971 inflation was at a 3-percent average annual rate, but jumped to 5 percent in 1972, and to 8 percent in 1973. Money supply in 1972 expanded by 44 percent due to increased business demand. Government budgets have been in surplus except for 1950, 1960, and 1965 when the government increased spending on housing, social services, water supply, and road building. The financial secretary of Hong Kong made a 1973 budget speech indicating that capital expenditures over the next decade will total some HK $19.5 billion (U.S. $3.8 billion), most of which will go to housing, public works, and mass transit. The financial experts in Hong Kong anticipate that the government may issue bonds, at least partly, to finance these programs.

BANKING DEVELOPMENT AND FINANCIAL INSTITUTIONS

Banking Development in Hong Kong

After Hong Kong was ceded to Britain in 1841, its principal business was entrepôt trade. This continued until 1950 when industry

266

became a major factor in the Crown Colony's economy. The British encouraged UK banks to establish themselves in Hong Kong to handle foreign trade and foreign exchange business. The Chartered Bank was established there for this purpose, and the Hong Kong and Shanghai Banking Corporation was chartered in 1865. The latter institution also conducted local investment activities and provided currency issue. There was very little banking regulation, although the finance secretary was officially responsible in this area. Foreign banks, including American, French, Dutch and Belgian institutions, formed branches in Hong Kong early in the twentieth century. In the 1920s and 1930s, several Chinese banks were established to service the local Chinese community. During World War II, banking activities almost came to a standstill under the Japanese occupation.

British banks, local banks, and foreign banks reopened in Hong Kong after the war, but they found that the political and economic setting in the Far East had changed as Britain relinquished many of its colonies in that area. The drastic change in Mainland China in 1949 and the Korean War in 1950 altered the Crown Colony's political, economic, and social conditions. The influx of people and money from China and the slowdown of international trade compelled the Hong Kong government to shift the emphasis from foreign trade to industry, especially light industries such as textiles and plastics. The diversity of small industries required business financing, and workers needed banks to serve them. Moreover, the limited land area in Hong Kong provided speculative incentives and mortgage loans stimulated banking activities. Overloan and illiquidity finally led to an unprecedented banking crisis in 1965, and the newly appointed banking commissioner found that it was too late to stop the runs on many banks.

There were two important effects from the 1965 banking crisis. One was the strengthening of banking regulation and supervision. Another was the takeover of banks resulting from their financial weakness. For example, apart from the 100-percent ownership of Mercantile Bank by the Hong Kong and Shanghai Banking Corporation (1959), the latter acquired 51 percent of the common stock of the Hang Seng Bank in 1965; the Daichi Bank of Japan purchased a 30-percent interest in the Checkiang First Bank; in 1969 the First National City Bank acquired 67 percent of Far East Bank; in 1970 the Dao Heng Bank turned over an unknown percentage of its shares to the National and Grindlays Bank.

Banking regulation and supervision are enforced by the Banking Ordinance of 1964, which authorized the creation of a banking commissioner. Since 1965, minimum bank capital has been HK$10 million instead of HK$5 million; establishment of branches requires the commissioner's approval; there are restrictions on maximum loans to a single borrower (also applicable to bank directors and their relatives) of not more than 25 percent of paid-up capital and reserves; bank's financial records are subject to inspection; local incorporated banks in Hong Kong are required to appoint auditors and to publish their annual audited accounts in both English and Chinese daily newspapers. The commissioner can enforce regulations and guidelines and advise banks on operating practices. However, he cannot direct banks.

Political and economic events have continued to influence Hong Kong's banking development in the past several years. Cases in point were the political disturbance caused by the Red Guard movement in 1967 and the establishment of the Asian dollar market in Singapore, both of which caused capital outflows from Hong Kong. In order to strengthen the Crown Colony's banking position, the government has applied liberal economic principles such as maintenance of a free foreign exchange market, a free stock market, and low income tax rates (maximum 15 percent). Furthermore, measures to encourage establishment of finance companies, merchant banks, and multinational corporations were adopted by the government. Table 14.1 reflects the situation at the time of the banking crisis in 1965, as well as after the stock market decline in 1973. Despite the financial storms, deposits in Hong Kong banks continued to grow, expanding fourfold since 1965. In the same period, loans and advances, which account for about 40 percent of banking assets, also grew at about the same rate. The ratio of loans to deposits edged upward

TABLE 14.1

Banking Deposits and Institutions in Hong Kong
(millions of HK dollars)

	March 1965	April 1973
Total deposits	6,377	24,358
Demand	2,791	9,755
Time	1,346	7,398
Savings	6,377	7,205
Loans and advances	4,868	20,828
Loan-deposit ratio	76.3%	86%
Number of banks	73	74
Banking offices	371	492
Representative offices	22	47

Source: Hong Kong Monthly Digest of Statistics, various issues.

from 76 percent in 1965 to 86 percent in 1973. While the number of banking units increased by only one (the Barclays Bank), bank branches and foreign representative offices grew substantially. This reflects the tightening of banking licenses and the increasing importance of Hong Kong as a financial observation post in the Far East.

Looking ahead, banking development in Hong Kong will be related to economic growth and the development of relationships with regional and other major countries such as Mainland China, Britain (after joining the European Economic Community—EEC), the United States, Japan, and Singapore.

Financial Institutions

No Central Bank

Hong Kong is a unique financial center in that it does not possess a central bank. The prime reason is that Hong Kong's government finance relies on a balanced budget, absence of debt, and surplus in the balance of payments. Sterling area ties in the past minimized the need of a central banking mechanism. Furthermore, unemployment and inflation have been negligible. In short, past performance suggests that there is little need for a central bank to help manage the economy.

As for the issuance of currency and the lender-of-last-resort functions, the Hong Kong and Shanghai Banking Corporation has been entrusted to carry out these functions in cooperation with the secretary of finance and the banking commissioner. The Hong Kong and Shanghai Banking Corporation, the Chartered Bank, and the Mercantile Bank have been appointed by the governor to issue notes, but more than 95 percent of the paper currency in Hong Kong now is issued by the Hong Kong Bank. Until July 1972, these banks issued currency against a deposit of sterling with the Exchange Fund in London. This fund earns 5-percent interest annually. Since July 1972, when the British government decided to float the pound against the U.S. dollar, Hong Kong freed its currency from a fixed relationship with sterling and tied it to the U.S. dollar. After the devaluations of the U.S. dollar in 1971 and 1973, the exchange rate was set at HK $1.00 being equal to U.S. $0.199.

Besides its note issue function, the Hong Kong Bank is also authorized to buy or sell foreign exchange on request from authorized banks in Hong Kong and to act as a clearing house for the colony. However, it has no authority to hold reserves from other banks as many central banks do in other countries. The Hong Kong Bank enjoys a near monopoly position in terms of deposits and its dominant branch system throughout the colony.

269

Authorized and Nonauthorized Banks

As of April 1973, there were 74 authorized and nonauthorized banks in Hong Kong, of which 71 were authorized banks and 3 were nonauthorized banks. Authorized banks are incorporated and permitted to act as official dealers in foreign currency, while the nonauthorized banks are unincorporated and permitted to deal in foreign currency only through the facilities of the authorized banks. Practically all banks in Hong Kong compete in every phase of banking business since Hong Kong is a "free market."

Among the 71 authorized banks, there are 33 foreign banks, 25 local Chinese banks, and 13 Mainland China banks. The Hong Kong and Shanghai Banking Corporations, the Chartered Bank, and the Mercantile Bank are classified as foreign banks (British). Many authorized banks have substantial branch networks in Hong Kong. For example, Hong Kong Bank has 70 branches; the Chartered Bank has 30; Far East Bank and Hang Seng Bank have about 15 each; and the American banks operate 19 branches. Most foreign banks are interested primarily in foreign trade financing. Only recently have they participated in local industrial and commercial loans and in regional financial activities, such as the formation of banking consortia for multinational financing. Banks originating in the United Kingdom, United States, Japan, France, Holland, and Belgium are particularly interested in joint ventures. Local Chinese banks, together with the Hong Kong Bank, mostly emphasize local deposits and consumer and property loans, since per-capita income has increased and consumer demand has grown.

The 13 Mainland China banks are headed by the Bank of China. They operate several branches, but their main function is to arrange foreign trade financing and to earn foreign exchange for their government. It is said that Hong Kong makes it possible for the People's Republic of China to earn several hundred million dollars in foreign exchange a year. In turn, China respects Hong Kong's position and provides the colony with foodstuffs, consumer goods, and raw materials.

Finance Companies

The growth of Hong Kong's economy has demanded more financial services. However, banking licenses have been restricted, and there are practically no secondary financial institutions such as discount houses and acceptance firms. Finance companies are a logical development. Up to April 1973, there were 100 finance companies, the financial activities of which have been mainly in the areas of underwriting, consumer financing, and real estate loans. Some of these finance companies are subsidiaries of commercial banks, such as Wayfoong Finance which is a subsidiary of the Hong Kong Bank.

Insurance Companies

A number of insurance companies have operated in Hong Kong for many years. They insure foreign trade risks, property risks, and provide life insurance. The latter has grown recently due to increased industrial activities and the government's social welfare programs. There were 206 insurance companies of various kinds at year end 1972. These institutions have been active in local portfolio investment since the primary capital market has not been significant in Hong Kong. Instead, their funds have been invested primarily in overseas areas, especially in London. Lack of institutional investors is probably one of the main obstacles preventing more rapid development as a financial center.

FINANCIAL MARKETS

Flow of Money

As a free economy, Hong Kong is able to attract substantial "hot" money flows. Financial market activities in Hong Kong depend not only on local money, but also on the inflow of funds. As Table 14.1 has indicated, time and savings deposits constitute about 60 percent, and demand deposits 40 percent of total deposits. Banking institutions have emphasized short-term loans instead of long-term investments. The hoarding of bullion, coins, and currency has inhibited development of a more liquid money market facility in Hong Kong.

Local interest rates play an important part in the inflow and outflow of funds to and from Hong Kong. For instance, when overseas Chinese in Southeast Asia encountered unfavorable political and economic moves against them, they transferred their money to Hong Kong; when local investment opportunities were attractive (such as the Cross Harbor Tunnel), American and Japanese capital became available; during the banking crisis in 1965, political trouble with Mainland China in 1967, and the stock market decline in March 1973, funds moved out of Hong Kong to Singapore, London, Japan, the United States, and other centers. These movements of money affected price levels, money supply, and interest rates in Hong Kong.

Money Market

Before 1960, the Hong Kong money market was fully occupied in financing foreign trade and providing local call loans. With the convertibility of the pound sterling in 1958, the market for interbank deposits with terms of 7 days, 15 days, and one month developed rapidly. Rates for these deposits have been fixed by the Exchange Bank Association, composed of all authorized banks. During the period 1950-65, when building financing and land speculation reached a peak, many commercial banks were competing to borrow funds and paid high interest rates. As a result they were compelled to overloan and charge high interest on risky projects. These imprudent banking practices led to the banking crisis of 1965, and money market volume declined.

The money market became active again in the period 1972-73 when many commercial banks financed customer speculation on the stock market. Call loan and interbank deposit volume grew quickly. The stock market decline in March 1973 was quickly reflected in the money market.

Regardless of the ups and downs in the money market over the past several decades, the variety and volume of financial instruments have increased steadily. Moreover, the direction in which bank credit is used has been changing over the years. Before 1950, foreign trade financing absorbed nearly 80 percent of total banking resources, but only 25 percent in 1972. While industrial loans have been provided mostly by large British and Chinese banks which have local interests and obligations, commercial loans are common to all banks in Hong Kong since the market is large, free, and competitive. The Hong Kong government established a small business loan program in 1972, but only loaned out HK$1 million under this program. This was considered a failure because many business borrowers preferred the flexibility of bank loans, even when they paid higher interest rates.

Other areas of growth include consumer loans and the market for certificates of deposit (CD). In the consumer loan market, foreign banks and local Chinese banks are fund suppliers, and the borrowers are local people who have steady jobs and favorable incomes. Since the unemployment rate has remained low, this has proved to be a good line of business for banks and finance companies. The CD market is still limited, but is growing due to the increased flow of business and individual savings in Hong Kong. The dissolution of the sterling bloc since July 1972 forced a substantial amount of Hong Kong dollars to stay home rather than go to London. The increase in external reserves in Hong Kong was one of the reasons for development of a good CD market and a major reason for the stock market speculation in the first quarter of 1973.

The money market has been volatile since March 1973 due to domestic uncertainty and international financial conditions. For example, some Hong Kong borrowers tapped Eurodollar financing to obtain shipbuilding credits, while many Eurobond distributors sold part of their issues in Hong Kong. Furthermore, the much-talked-about Asian dollar market in Hong Kong (competing with Singapore) has not been enthusiastically received by the Hong Kong government since it wishes to retain the 15-percent tax on earnings of foreign currency deposits.

At the time of writing, there is no Treasury bill, commercial bill, or federal fund market in Hong Kong.

Capital Market

Primary Market

Hong Kong did not develop a strong capital market before the 1960s due to many reasons. First, there was no large industry. Two well-known public utility firms (China Light and Kowloon Ferry) issued limited shares. Small companies, which were mostly family owned, relied either on retained earnings or bank loans. Export-oriented industries such as food processing and textiles could easily obtain funds in advance from foreign banks. Second, no government borrowing was needed since the government enjoyed budget surpluses in most years. There is no development bank in Hong Kong as there is in many less developed countries. Third, wealthy people may invest their money in London or in New York through foreign brokers with representation in Hong Kong. Fourth, property and industrial development after 1950 were mostly financed by commercial and industrial loans and mortgage loans. Equity issues were rare.

In 1969 the primary stock market took an important turn. The possibility of ending the Vietnam War after the American presidential election provided a sense of political security for Hong Kong. Another optimistic sign was the continued economic prosperity, which encouraged local people as well as foreigners to explore potential opportunities. As a result, there were nine new equity issues in the later part of that year, including hotel, construction, electronics, and textile companies. Some of these issues were oversubscribed.

In 1972, more and more companies went public, and one or two new issues were added to the bullish market every month. Underwriters of equity shares included the large financial institutions such as the Hong Kong and Shanghai Banking Corporations, Chartered Bank, Hang Seng Bank, and Far East Bank. One land company with assets of $20 million put about 25 percent of all its shares in a public offering. The issue was oversubscribed more than 20 times. The capital market was further encouraged by the establishment of two investment companies: Jardine Metheson and Robert Flemming, which were established to handle offshore funds. Hong Kong Bank and several American banks also formed investment companies for consulting and underwriting purposes.

Regardless of the misfortunes of the March 1973 stock market decline, the primary capital market will continue to develop as long as stability and prosperity prevail in Hong Kong. The evidence of business confidence is reflected in the growth of registered companies, from about 20,000 units to 26,000 units between 1971 and 1972. These companies are potential securities issuers.

Secondary Market

Hong Kong's secondary market began operating in 1891 when the Hong Kong Stock Exchange was created. Shares of the Hong Kong and Shanghai Banking Corporation, Chartered Bank, Jardine Shipping Company, and Kowloon Ferry were active after the turn of the twentieth century. However, the limited trading of equity shares did not spur the secondary capital market. Between 1962 and 1968, the stock market remained in the doldrums since not many people were interested in equity investments at this time. In this period, only 65 stocks were listed on the exchange, and 20 of them were active. Since 1969, the stock market has become more active. At year end 1969, there were 260 stocks listed on the exchange, and 150 of them were actively traded. Stimulated by market activity, the second stock exchange—the Far East Stock Exchange—came into existence in November 1969. In the last month of that year, the value of stock transactions was about $10 million weekly at the Hong Kong Stock Exchange, and $7 million weekly at the Far East Stock Exchange. In 1970, two new stock exchanges were established: the Kam Ngan (means gold and silver) Stock Exchange and the Kowloon Stock Exchange, which also listed shares of companies located in the Philippines and Southeast Asian countries. Up to April 1973, there were four stock exchanges, 340 quoted stocks of which three-fourths were actively traded, 100 brokers, and a small number of foreign brokerage firms but no quoted foreign issues. There are no institutional investors in the Hong Kong Exchanges since the Exchange Bank Association prohibits its members (71 authorized banks) from dealing with the stock exchanges.

The stock market performance from 1969 to March 1973 was a boom and bust cycle. On December 31, 1969, the 33-stock Hang Seng index stood at 191. In December 1972, it stood at 843. By March 9, 1973, the index had climbed to a peak 1,774. After that date, waves of selling orders rushed to the floors of the four stock exchanges, and prices of stocks including the 33 "blue chips" declined drastically. In August the index was around the 600 level (Table 14.2). There is no definite explanation for the dramatic fluctuation of the Hong Kong stock market, but some basic causes can be pointed to. First, local residents had higher income. Unfortunately, they did not have the sophistication to invest their money in other financial centers. Instead, they put their money in local issues and expected to have capital gains. Second, some brokers advised their customers that shares of many land development companies and industrial firms were undervalued and that there existed real opportunities for purchasing these stocks. Third, there were substantial bank reserves in Hong Kong since the dissolution of the sterling bloc in July 1972. These reserves added to the financial power when banks searched for outlets for investible funds, even though the banks were not permitted to speculate on the stock market directly. Fourth, there was no government supervisory agency to regulate the stock market. In fact, high trading volume based on speculative factors generated larger stamp tax revenues for the government.

When the stock market gained momentum in 1972, speculators poured more money into blue chips, and some factory workers quit their jobs for full-time speculation. At one time, the price-earnings ratio of Hong Kong Land Company stock was 300, and Hutchinson International appreciated by more than 400 percent. After the index passed the 970 mark, the chairmen of the exchanges made a joint statement urging restraint. The Hong Kong government moved in with various regulations, such as the introduction of certain standards to be met by brokerage firms, advising banks to call in loans and disapproving some new issues. The government even suspended all afternoon trading for Friday, February 16, 1973, after the index posted a 182-point gain in the morning session.

TABLE 14.2

Hang Seng Stock Index
(1964 = 100)

December 31, 1969	191
December 31, 1971	341
December 31, 1972	843
March 9, 1973	1774
April 31, 1973	735
August 15, 1973	615

Source: Far Eastern Economic Review, August 20, 1973.

The stock market has been calm since March 1973, awaiting a new set of regulations initiated by the establishment of a supervisory body—the Securities Council.

Foreign Exchange Market

The foreign exchange market in Hong Kong deserves a special section since the currency system, market structure, and trading activities are unique among financial centers.

Before 1938, the Hong Kong dollar was tied to the value of silver, which was the monetary standard of China. Between 1938 and July 1972, Hong Kong was a member of the sterling bloc. The issue of currency depended on the reserves deposited with the British banks in London, and the value of the currency was tied to that of sterling. There were advantages and disadvantages in this connection. The advantages were to hedge the impact of inflation and deflation since Hong Kong had balance of payments surpluses in most years, and the outflow of funds to London provided a safety valve for excessive money supply. Moreover, the overseas reserves and deposits returned to Hong Kong when local money was hoarded or dried up resulting from political and economic pressures such as experienced in the period 1965-67. The disadvantages were that these funds could have been used for local economic development and improved social welfare programs. The devaluation of sterling in 1947 and 1967 hurt the value of the Hong Kong dollar. The 1967 devaluation led to the Basle Agreement, under which Hong Kong banks were guaranteed against sterling devaluations until September 1973. The dissolution of the sterling bloc in July 1972 after the British government allowed sterling to float against the U.S. dollar forced the Hong Kong dollar to shift its tie from sterling to the U.S. dollar.

The structure of the foreign exchange market in Hong Kong is a complex one. First, it is a free market where people and business firms can deposit, exchange, and transfer their foreign currencies in and out of Hong Kong freely. There are money exchangers in every street in the business district, and 71 authorized banks must conduct their exchange activities on the basis of the quoted official rates HK$1.00 equals U.S. $0.199. There is no black market. The Hong Kong and Shanghai Banking Corporation has a large influence on the market because it controls the volume of local currency as well as foreign exchange and interbank dealings. The foreign exchange market may change its characteristics should the Asian dollar market be developed, but the government has to think over the whole financial structure in Hong Kong before a final decision is made.

The most active currencies in the market have been the U.S. dollar, British pound, Chinese Renminbi (yen), Japanese yen, and Singapore dollar. Southeast Asian and European currencies are also actively traded due to the presence of foreign branch banks. The revaluation of the Renminbi by 1.45 percent in June 1973 slightly affected Hong Kong's food price levels. Conversely, the devaluation of the U.S. dollar in February 1973 reduced Hong Kong's foreign exchange earnings. Before mid-1972, oil companies of the Persian Gulf were entitled to sell sterling in Hong Kong for interbank deposits or loans. Sterling holders could transfer sterling into dollars or other currencies. These market activities have changed somewhat since the United Kingdom has designated Hong Kong as an External Account Area. Normal exchange transactions were occasionally disturbed by inflows of "hot" money brought by overseas Chinese from Southeast Asian countries when local political and economic conditions were unfavorable to them. The fever of the Hong Kong stock market before March 1973 also attracted substantial amounts of foreign capital from the United States and Japan for short-term profit. They not only stimulated the exchange market, but also contributed to Hong Kong's overall balance of payments position.

For the above-mentioned reasons, Hong Kong's foreign exchange market has been the most active one in the Far East. It is the market-place for Taiwan, Mainland China, the Philippines, Indochina, Indonesia, and Thailand. Its arbitrage activities involve multicurrencies, especially sterling, dollars, and yen.

GOVERNMENT POLICY AND INTERNATIONAL FINANCE

Government Policy

Hong Kong has had a tradition of a free economy based on the Adam Smith model of free competition. Government policy has emphasized budgetary balance, a free marketplace, free trade, and free capital movements. This policy has been working very well except with some minor shortcomings. As all indications suggested, the Hong Kong government will continue to follow this policy of economic freedom with only minor changes.

Politically, Hong Kong hopes to maintain balanced relationships between Britain and Mainland China. Economically, Hong Kong is more independent of the United Kingdom than before.

One specific objective is to maintain a good economic growth rate, and 10-percent real growth per annum seems to be the objective of the government. This would be comparable with achievements in Singapore, Taiwan, and Japan. To achieve this, the Hong Kong government has announced a long-term public investment program destined to improve the welfare of the local people and the colony's transit system and related infrastructure. This public investment program will certainly have a macroeconomic effect on the Crown Colony's income, employment, and financial markets.

International Trade and Investment

As shown in Table 14.3, Hong Kong's trade has increased about sixfold in the two decades 1952-72. In this period, two important changes have taken place in Hong Kong's trade. One was the changing composition of total exports; another was a change in major trade partners. With regard to total exports, reexports in 1952 were far more important than exports of domestic origin. However, the latter have become more significant in total exports, especially after 1960. This reflects the success of Hong Kong's industrial development program initiated during the 1950s. With respect to trade partners, the United States has become Hong Kong's largest customer since 1958, followed by the United Kingdom and West Germany. These countries absorbed the following shares of total exports: 40, 13, and 35 percent, respectively in 1972. Textiles, electronic components, and toys were key items in Hong Kong's export growth. Hong Kong

TABLE 14.3

Hong Kong's Imports and Exports
(billions of HK dollars)

Year	Imports	Total Exports	Exports (Domestic Origin)	Reexports
1952	3.7	2.9	0.5	2.4
1960	5.8	3.9	3.0	0.9
1965	8.9	6.5	—	—
1970	17.6	15.2	12.3	2.9
1971	20.2	17.1	13.7	3.4
1972	21.7	19.4	15.2	4.2

Source: Hong Kong Trade Statistics, June 1973. Hong Kong: Census and Statistics Department.

imports manufactured goods, foods, electronic machinery, and transport equipment from Japan, China, and the United States. These countries shared Hong Kong's import market to the extent of 24, 16, and 12 percent, respectively in 1972. On balance, Hong Kong has had merchandise trade deficits, but showed an overall balance of payments surplus due to financial income from tourism, shipping, banking, and other services. Lack of official balance of payments statistics prevents any detailed analysis of Hong Kong's international transactions.

Since the Hong Kong government receives no aid from any sources, it has to rely on domestic capital formation and foreign investment. At the end of 1972, there were 515 U.S. firms operating in Hong Kong, 100 of which were engaged in manufacturing. Total U.S. investment in the colony was estimated at U.S. $500 million. There were 250 joint ventures or subsidiary plants of other countries represented, with a value of U.S. $177 million. Over 50 percent of these were U.S. business firms. On the basis of trends in trade and foreign investment, Hong Kong's financial relationship with the United States and Japan will become more important in future years. Furthermore, the innovation-oriented banking industry in Hong Kong has been working to make Hong Kong a world financial center. The increasing activities of merchant banks, finance companies, and consortium financing in Hong Kong indicate the growing importance of the financial markets to serve the needs of both Hong Kong and the international community.

REFERENCES

Far Eastern Economic Review, weekly publication in Hong Kong.

Fry, Richard. "Hong Kong—Aftermath and Prospect." Banker (London), June 1973.

Graham, P. A., and others. "Financial Centers of the World: Hong Kong." Banker (London), July 1970.

Hopkins, Keith. Hong Kong: The Industrial Colony. London: Oxford University Press, 1971.

Jao, Y. C. "Recent Development in Hong Kong Banking." Bankers Magazine (London), December 1970.

Paterson, J. C. "Financial Companies Provide Foothold in Hong Kong Market." American Banker, June 27, 1973. (Note: Mr. Paterson was then the banking commissioner of Hong Kong.)

U.S. Department of Commerce. <u>Economic Trends in Hong Kong</u>, May 8, 1973.

15

INTRODUCTION

Singapore, an island republic of 224.5 square miles, is situated at the southern tip of the Malay Peninsula. This crossroads of the southern Pacific has a population of 2.2 million people, of whom 75 percent are ethnic Chinese, 15 percent are Malay, and 10 percent are Indians and Pakistanis. Singapore has a railroad running northward through the State of Malaya to Bangkok, Thailand. Branch lines serve the port of Singapore and the industrial estate of Jurong. Due to its strategic location between the East and the West, Singapore has been a principal naval base for the British and is a famous entrepôt for regional trade and international commerce. Without endowment of natural resources, the most valuable asset in Singapore is its people, most of whom are industrious, frugal, and adaptable to modern technology.

Economic and financial conditions in Singapore are sound and have developed through a process of gradual evolution. In 1867, Singapore became a British colony. In 1959, it achieved internal self-government with the British retaining responsibility for defense, security, and external affairs. In August 1963, the island joined Malaya, Sabah, and Sarawak to form the Federation of Malaysia, but this political union did not last primarily due to internal disputes and external hostility from Indonesia. In August 1965, Singapore seceded from the federation and established itself as an independent republic, but remained a member of the British Commonwealth.

Singapore's political system is similar to that of many Commonwealth nations such as Canada and Australia. There is a president, a Parliament of 58 members, a prime minister chosen by the majority party in Parliament, and a supreme court. The government is considered efficient and friendly toward foreign investment and foreign trade relationships.

Singapore has achieved political stability as well as economic prosperity. It has successfully transformed its entrepôt economy into an industrial economy and improved social well-being in terms of income, housing, transportation, education, and medical care. Moreover, Singapore has developed a sound currency, achieved substantial economic growth, and moved toward developing as an international financial center.

THE ROLE OF GOVERNMENT IN ECONOMY AND FINANCE

Government Policy and Changing Economy

Since its independence in 1959, government policy has had significant effects on the national economy and finance. These relationships can be analyzed in three periods: the pre-Malaysia period, the Malaysia period, and the post-Malaysia period.

The pre-Malaysia period refers to 1959-62 when this island nation began to chart its own course politically and economically. Singapore launched the first five-year economic development plan, with the assistance of the United Nations' Industrial Development Organization experts. To implement the five-year plan, the government formed the Housing and Development Board in 1960 to provide low-income housing for industrial and other workers. By 1972, one-third of workers in Singapore lived in the government-sponsored housing projects. The Housing Board also encouraged the building of hotel facilities for tourism, which has provided substantial income. In 1961, the government set up the Economic Development Board to formulate and implement Singapore's industrialization policy. The investment of $400 million by the government in industrial infrastructure facilities and in social development programs during these five years laid an important foundation for industrial development as well as for encouraging multinational companies to establish operations in Singapore in the late 1960s.

In the Malaysia period, 1963-65, the GNP growth rate slowed down to 6.5 percent per annum, as contrasted with about 8 percent on average between 1959-62. The basic reason for reduced GNP growth was the confrontation between Malaysia and Indonesia which reduced the entrepôt trade of Singapore. When Singapore pulled out of the Malaysia Federation in August 1965, it was facing many critical problems. For one, the unemployment rate was very high (13 percent). For another, it lost the guaranteed domestic markets for its goods. Moreover, a decision was also announced by the British government that its military forces would be pulled out of Singapore by 1970. At that time Singapore was beset by political and economic uncertainty, and its future was not optimistic.

The post-Malaysia period showed two stages of development. First, Singapore had to readjust itself as an independent nation. Second, it had to formulate long-term economic policies.

Tax incentives have been an important means for the Singapore government to attract foreign investments. The Jurong estate, which was completed in 1962-65, has become the location of some 400 factories—with another 300 being built. Corporations such as Texas Instruments, Inc., of the United States and the Royal Shell Oil Company of the Netherlands have established operations in Singapore. The Economic Expansion Incentive Act of 1967 was designed to provide tax exemption and tax relief lasting from 2 to 5 years, but for certain export industries tax relief may be extended to 15 years. Introduction of high-technology industries was particularly welcome.

The Employment Act of 1968 and the Industrial Relations Act set ground rules for labor unions as well as management in providing a peaceful industrial environment, reducing unnecessary strikes, and increasing productivity. With respect to exports, the government has developed local manufacturing industry to stimulate exports. The Economic Development Board of Singapore has launched many overseas promotional programs for trade and investment. Two free-trade zones were established in the late 1960s to bolster entrepôt trade, even though the government's ultimate purpose is industrialization. In the free-trade zones, dutiable goods are imported, stored, processed, repacked, and reexported without paying duties. At year end 1972, about 60 percent of total trade was attributed to these entrepôt activities.

Singapore's economy was prosperous during the period 1961-72 (Table 15.1). GNP increased at an average annual rate of 6.5 percent from 1959-62, 8 percent from 1963-65, and 12.1 percent from 1966-72. Per-capita income was equivalent to U.S.$410 in 1959, U.S.$805 in 1969, and U.S.$1,451 in 1972, the highest in Asia except Japan. The high per-capita income level attained in Singapore can be attributed in part to the low population growth rate.

Domestic capital formation, which reflects a nation's ability to save and invest in productive resources, increased from Singapore-$475 in 1965 to Singapore$2,154 in 1972. About 80 percent of total annual investment was in the machinery, tools, and construction sectors, associated with the industrialization program. Another significant achievement was the relatively stable price level. On average, consumer prices increased at an annual rate of 2 percent in the period 1961-72. This was a singular achievement in light of price trends in other nations in the same time period.

TABLE 15.1

Selected Economic Indicators, 1961-72

	GNP (millions of Singapore$)	GNP Growth Rate (percent)	Per-Capita GNP Rate (percent)	Gross Capital Formation (millions of Singapore$)	Gross Capital Formation (percent increases)	Consumer Price Index (1960=100)
1961	2,240	8.8	6.4	—	65.5	101.0
1965	3,040	12.5	9.8	475	13.1	105.0
1966	3,365	11.1	8.3	473	-0.4	106.2
1967	3,692	9.1	6.8	518	9.3	106.5
1968	4,257	15.3	13.4	735	42.1	107.8
1969	4,833	14.7	11.7	996	29.6	108.1
1970	5,675	16.9	14.9	1,403	44.1	109.5
1971	6,471	14.5	12.4	1,759	35.8	110.2
1972	7,212	13.0	11.0	2,154	22.5	112.2

Sources: Singapore—Yearbook of Statistics, various issues; Singapore—Monthly Digest of Statistics, various issues; International Monetary Fund (IMF), International Financial Statistics, August 1973.

Singapore's economy has undergone significant industrial changes. Table 15.2 highlights the changing economic structures in the period 1960-68. The industry and commodity-producing sectors gained, at the expense of agriculture and services.

TABLE 15.2

Changing Economic Structure in Singapore
(in percent)

	Commodity Production	Agricul- ture	Industry	Production of Services	Nonagri- culture
1960/62	18.9	6.0	12.9	81.1	94.0
1966/68	22.4	3.8	18.6	77.6	96.2
Change	+3.5	-2.2	+5.7	-3.5	+2.2

Source: United Nations, Asia and Far East Bulletin, June/September 1971, p. 29.

Government Finance

Since the Singapore government has stressed industrialization, public investment in infrastructure has increased in recent years. For example, in 1969 and 1972 there was Singapore$996 million and Singapore$2,154 million in gross fixed investment, and the public sector accounted for 30 percent of the total. The industry shares of total investment were machinery 40 percent, construction 45 percent, transportation equipment (ships) 15 percent.

Within the framework of public economic policy, the prime minister submits a budget to the Parliament every year for approval. In general, the government has followed the concept of a balanced budget. Differences between expenditure and tax revenues have been financed by domestic and foreign borrowings. It is interesting to note that the Singapore government budget doubled in amount between 1967 and 1971 (see Table 15.3). The main reason for the large jump since 1969 was the increase in defense expenditures after the British withdrew its military forces. Other major expenses have been for social services and economic development. The government has issued short-term Treasury bills and long-term bonds. The basic purpose of the former was to mop up excess liquidity in the banking sector or to provide operating cash during the slow tax-collection

TABLE 15.3

Major Components of Government Expenditures
(millions of Singapore dollars)

	Current	Investment	Loans and Advances	Total	Tax Revenues
1967	475.0	124.7	83.7	683.4	630.2
1968	535.8	133.5	126.8	796.1	769.2
1969/70	1,032.6	180.7	141.8	1,355.1	964.2
1970/71	891.5	207.6	244.6	1,343.7	954.3

Source: United Nations, Asia and Far East Bulletin, June/ September 1971.

season. The reason for the bond issue (long-term) financing was to finance long-term economic development. In 1969, the government issued the equivalent of U.S.$209 million of short-term bills and $84.3 million of long-term bonds. The total net public debt in 1969 was $312 million, but was reduced to less than $300 million in 1971.

FINANCIAL INSTITUTIONS

Singapore's financial institutions owe their origins to British influence. After independence in 1959, Singapore's government has controlled basic economic organizations such as the public utilities, shipping lines, the Jurong Town Corporation, and the International Trading Corporation. During the 1960s, the government also created many financial institutions to carry on public economic functions as well as regulatory functions over the private financial institutions. These public and private financial institutions are briefly discussed as follows.

Public Financial Institutions

The Ministry of Finance has usually taken care of both fiscal and monetary matters under the directive of the prime minister. As the country reached full independence after the breakoff with Malaysia in 1965, the Currency Act of 1967 authorized the government to establish the Board of Commissioners of Currency of Singapore (the Currency Board). The board is the sole issuer of legal tender, and its primary functions include exchanging Singapore dollars for other convertible currencies and managing a portion of foreign assets used as backing for the Singapore dollar. Under the Currency Board system, the domestic currency must be 100 percent backed by external reserves such as U.S. dollars, pound sterling, or gold.

Before 1931 Singapore was on the gold standard, but changed to the sterling exchange standard. When the sterling bloc dissolved in 1972, Singapore adopted the U.S. dollar as intervention currency. After the devaluations of the U.S. dollar in 1971 and 1973, the exchange rate on the U.S. dollar was set at U.S.$1.00 = Singapore$2.54.

The Monetary Authority of Singapore (MAS) was founded in 1970. It has all the functions of a central bank except the issuance of currency. It consists of a seven-member board of directors headed by the minister of finance. It functions as fiscal agent for the government, promotes monetary stability and economic growth, administers laws concerning banking licenses, administers exchange controls, supervises the stock exchange, issues Treasury obligations, and manages government overseas assets which totaled about $2.2 billion in 1972. The MAS purchases, sells, discounts, and rediscounts Treasury bills, and buys and sells long-term government bonds. It imposes reserve requirements and exerts "moral suasion" over the interest rate structure of the banking system. Also, it provides clearing facilities for the commercial banks.

The Development Bank of Singapore (DBS) was established in 1968. It took over the development financing of the republic's Economic Development Board. DBS stock is owned 49 percent by the government and 51 percent by the general public and several financial institutions. Technically, it is a privately owned institution, but actually it is closely tied to the government's industrial development programs. Its sources of funds are the issuance of bonds at home and abroad. The uses of funds include long-term financing of manufacturing firms and short-term export credits. For example, DBS provided Singapore$485 million in loans, of which 67 percent was long-term credit, 19 percent equity purchases (DBS will sell these equities when the firms are well established), and 14 percent export credits.

The Central Provident Funds, the counterpart of the U.S. Social Security system, was first proposed by the International Labor Organization, secondly endorsed by the Singapore Trade Union Congress in 1951, and finally approved by the Legislative Council in 1955. Employer and employee must contribute 12 percent of the employee's first Singapore$900 of annual wages to the funds. An employee's account earns 5-percent interest, and under certain conditions he may withdraw a portion of his account to make a down payment on a home. In 1972, total assets were about Singapore$500 million, of which 56 percent was invested in government securities.

The Post Office Savings Banks were formed by the colonial government in 1878 to hold the deposits of small savers. A low inflationary rate encourages savings in these institutions. In 1972, there was about Singapore$40 million of deposits in the Post Office Savings Banks, which was invested in medium- and long-term credits.

Private Financial Institutions

Commercial banking in Singapore has developed since the middle of the nineteenth century when British banks, such as the Chartered Bank and Hong Kong and Shanghai Banking Corporation, were actively financing trade and providing foreign exchange.

After World War II, more domestic and foreign banks have been operating in Singapore due to increasing regional and international trade. The development of manufacturing industry and financial markets since 1968 has attracted more foreign banks. The national origins of the foreign banks include the United States, United Kingdom, Holland, France, Germany, Switzerland, Italy, Japan, China, Russia, and Pakistan. In 1972, there were 44 commercial banks with 194 offices. Eleven banks were locally incorporated, and 33 were foreign owned. In addition, there were 39 foreign representative offices. Foreign banks accounted for 40 percent of total deposits and 60 percent of total loans and advances.

As Table 15.4 illustrates, total deposits and assets almost doubled between 1969 and 1972. Changes in the composition of loans and investments are noticeable. For instance, during the period mentioned, overnight (call) loans increased from 12 to 13 percent of the total; discounts on trade bills decreased from 11 to 8 percent; long-term loans to manufacturing increased from 22 to 26 percent reflecting the growing importance of industrial financing. Increased investments in the same period were attributed to the holding of Treasury bills and bonds. Over 90 percent of the Treasury bills were held by the commercial banking system. The purpose of Treasury bill holdings is to maintain adequate liquidity ratio and to condition domestic liquidity which otherwise may shift to the London market. Commercial banks are required to maintain deposits equivalent to 9 percent of their total liabilities with MAS and to maintain assets equivalent to $23\frac{1}{2}$ percent of their deposit liabilities in the form of cash and government securities. A deficiency of reserves is penalized by MAS at the rate of 1 percent a day.

TABLE 15.4

Comparative Deposits, Loans and Investments
of Singapore's Commercial Banks and Finance Companies
at Year End 1969 and 1972
(millions of dollars)

	Commercial Banks			Finance Companies*		
	1969	1972	Percent Increase	1969	1972	Percent Increase
Deposits						
Demand	320	593	85.3	—	—	—
Fixed (time)	615	1,083	75.0	104	244	138.4
Savings	140	216	54.2	4	7	75.0
Other	6	8	33.3	11	13	18.1
Total deposits	1,081	1,900	75.7	119	264	121.8
Loans and advances	813	1,400	72.2	95	192	102.1
Investments	324	650	100.6	8	11	37.5
Loan-deposit ratio	75%	73.7%	—	80%	72.7%	—
Total assets	1,683	3,207	90.5			

*Demand deposits not permitted.

Source: Singapore, Yearbook of Statistics.

Finance companies have been a product of the postwar era. There were about 36 finance companies in Singapore at the end of 1972. They are permitted to accept time and savings deposits, and their financial activities are primarily in the area of making consumer credits such as financing the purchase of homes, appliances, and automobiles. Increased per-capita income and expenditure in the past few years have made consumer credit more attractive to commercial banks. Some large banks have affiliates for this purpose. Table 15.4 indicates that the loan and deposit ratio in financial companies is more volatile than that of the commercial banks.

Insurance companies were originally formed by the British before World War I for the protection of property investment, life insurance, and to insure risks of foreign trade. Like the commercial banks, the insurance companies were integrated parts of London's life and property insurance companies. In 1971, Singapore had 69 active insurance companies, of which 13 were locally incorporated. It is expected that they will play an increasingly more important role in the financial markets during the 1970s as the national economy and saving-investment activities continue to grow.

FINANCIAL MARKETS

Development of Financial Markets

Singapore's financial markets developed parallel to its political background, economy, and international business relations. Until the 1930s, Singapore's financial markets were dominated by the British banks and insurance companies that were engaged in financing and insuring foreign trade and foreign exchange. Local banks began to participate in financial activities in relation to regional trade and remittances in the 1930s. The needs of capital for domestic economic development and regional trade and investment during the 1960s encouraged many foreign banks and multinational corporations to move into Singapore. As a result, Singapore's financial markets have become well known as focal points for deposit-loan-investment activities in the Pacific Basin.

The most important events that accelerated financial market development are briefly described below:

1960—Stock Exchange of Malaysia and Singapore began operations with trading rooms in Kuala Lumpur and Singapore.

1966—Treasury bills were issued in the short-term money market.

1968—Development Bank of Singapore was established. It has actually participated in the capital market by issuing long-term bonds and buying equity of some firms related to economic development programs.

1969—Gold market was established. Nonresidents can buy and sell gold freely. Government levies $3.00 tax per ounce on such transactions. There were 10 gold dealers at the end of 1972.

1970—Monetary Authority of Singapore (MAS), the forerunner of the central bank, was founded. It was a milestone in the development of Singapore's financial markets. It opened the discount market, participated in foreign exchange market, abolished tax on certificates of deposit. This positive government action further encouraged the formation of the Asian dollar market and merchant banking groups in the same year.

1971—MAS authorized a few merchant banks, discount houses, and international brokers to do business in Singapore. The amendment of the Company Act was also approved by the Parliament. This act compels business firms to furnish sufficient information to investors.

1972—MAS abolished the 20-percent requirement for holding short-term assets against commercial banks' foreign currency deposits. This action stimulated foreign capital inflow.

1973—Security Industrial Council was created for advising the administration of stock exchange. Asian dollar bonds were approved by Singapore's Monetary Authorities.

Money Market

Financial markets in Singapore have emphasized short-term lending, with activity concentrated in trade bills (banker's acceptances). The advent of the MAS stimulated development of other short-term credit instruments such as overnight money, eight-day money, certificates of deposit (CDs), and Treasury bills.

Trade bills are handled by both local and foreign banks. Discounted trade bills (usually 90-day import bills) totaled U.S.$191 million in 1969 and U.S.$244 million in 1972, representing 11 and 8 percent, respectively, of total assets of all commercial banks. MAS offers rediscount facilities to commercial banks, similar to the facility in the U.S. Federal Reserve System. The Federal Reserve opens its rediscount window to member banks. In the future, as other money market instruments become used to an increasing extent, trade bills may become less important.

Treasury bills were issued for the first time in 1966 by the Ministry of Finance as part of the strategy to establish Singapore as a money market center. The government has greatly increased the volume of Treasury bills since then. In 1966, the Treasury sold equivalent to U.S.$26 million of three-month Treasury bills, and by the end of 1969, the amount had risen to U.S.$209 million. In 1972, the yield on short-term government securities ranged from $4\frac{1}{2}$ to $5\frac{1}{4}$ percent. Major ownership of these securities is by commercial banks because they can include them and local currency in their liquid-asset ratio accounting. They may become more important in the future if Singapore's Asian dollar market continues its present pace of expansion since these liquid instruments can be used for arbitrage purposes between international financial centers such as London, New York, and Frankfurt.

The market for overnight and eight-day loans is an interbank market. Overnight money is equivalent to federal funds and used in Singapore for adjusting a bank's clearing balance with MAS. Eight-day money is used for interest rate arbitrage and for maintaining liquidity ratios. Interest rates in this interbank market range between 2 and 3 percent per annum. A deficit bank finds it considerably less costly to borrow overnight funds from a surplus bank to make up for any shortfall in its clearing account.

At present, the most important money market activities in Singapore are industrial loans, which accounted for 22 percent (1969) and 26 percent (1972) of total loans and advances in Singapore commercial banks. Interest rates on these loans clustered in the 7- to $7\frac{1}{2}$-percent range.

CDs have also been issued by large commercial banks. They have been important sources of funds in the commercial banking system for supporting bank loans. The abolition of a 1/10-percent tax on CDs by the MAS in 1970 has bolstered the CD market in Singapore.

The government securities market in Singapore is expected to develop further, especially since the United Kingdom helped set up three discount houses in 1972 with borrowing powers limited to 30 times paid up capital. Under this arrangement, "lender-of-last-resort" facilities will be provided by the MAS.

Capital Market

Many companies in Singapore are closely held and financed internally (through retained earnings). Commercial bank loans usually make up the second most important financial source of funds, and equity financing is least important. Since 1966, the completion of the Jurong Industrial Estate and other industrial development programs as well as increased issue of government securities, has provided an impetus to the growth of Singapore's capital market. Foreign manufacturing and financial firms have been attracted by this favorable economic and financial environment.

In the private sector, companies issue equities rather than bonds when they seek long-term financing. This practice seems to be different from that of many other nations, such as the United States and Mexico, where bond markets are preferred by primary fund seekers. In Asia, corporate pride and investor's confidence influence the primary as well as secondary capital market. At times the limited supply of shares of reputable firms provides opportunities for speculation. The stock market of Singapore in 1970 and that of Hong Kong in 1971-72 are cases in point. That is why many new issues are often over-subscribed in Singapore. Aware of this fact, the Singapore government took the initiative in the bond market. First of all, the Development Bank of Singapore (DBS) issued bonds to finance several public projects and new manufacturing companies vital to the national economy. In 1971 there were 28 of these companies' equities held by the Development Bank. The latter expects to ultimately sell these shares to the public when the companies are well established, so that funds may be made available to other industrial companies.

Secondly, the increasing volume of government securities in the capital market for financing housing and utility development has tremendous social, economic, and financial effects on the long-term market. The government issued Treasury bills and bonds with maturities extending to 15 years. The total amount of these issues was equivalent to U.S.$161 million in 1966, U.S.$321 million in 1969, and U.S.$460 million in 1971. The sources of funds for the government bond market are the Central Provident Fund (CPF), commercial banks, the Post Office Savings Bank, insurance companies, and finance companies. CPF is by far the largest purchaser of these securities, with the banks holding about 10 percent of the outstanding issues and other institutions holding even smaller percentages.

The primary capital market in Singapore is expected to develop further when nine merchant banks, including U.S., UK, French, Dutch, Swiss, and Japanese banks expressed their willingness to assist equity financing for multinational corporations in that region. The same process was adopted in Japan when international banking consortia were formed to stimulate the Japanese financial market during the early 1960s.

The secondary capital market in Singapore began operations when the Stock Exchange of Malaysia and Singapore was established in 1960, with trading rooms in Kuala Lumpur and Singapore. After a decade of development, there are approximately 300 equity issues listed on the stock exchange, of which industry and commerce account for about 50 percent, rubber plantations 30 percent, and tin companies and property companies 20 percent. A third of the 300 stocks represent locally incorporated companies, and they are old-line commercial firms. Shares issued by international firms are particularly active.

They help to build up Singapore's capital market since they attract funds from savers, insurance companies, and commercial banks, especially by their overdraft facilities. Trading of these equity securities is handled by a number of stock brokers and finance companies.

Conditions for listing stocks on the exchange are: A firm must have a paid-up capital of at least Singapore$2 million; there are at least 200 individual stockholders of such equity shares; members of the public are holders of at least 200,000 shares in the company. The principal government regulatory agency of the stock exchange is the MAS, which has been considered restrictive to stock speculation such as in the case of 1970. The MAS was further armed by the Company Act of 1971, which was designed to protect investors by requiring disclosure of all pertinent information in connection with a new issue. The creation of the Security Industrial Council in 1973 should provide more definitive policy and technical advice to the stock exchange in the future.

Foreign Exchange Market

Singapore's foreign exchange market is traditionally an interbank market. Almost all commercial banks are authorized to handle foreign exchange transactions. The banks buy foreign currencies from exporters and sell them to importers, trading with other banks to square their positions. Banks in Singapore normally keep two accounts: the external and resident accounts. Any investor who deposits foreign exchange in an external account is not subject to any reserve ratio and is free to remit his deposits abroad.

The MAS participates in the foreign exchange market and encourages spot and future (forward) trading. It allows foreign currency loans against letter of credit. It also has accelerated the foreign exchange market development by its ruling in July 1972 that transactions of more than U.S.$100,000 can be applied to free exchange rate in the market (official rate: U.S.$1.00 = Singapore$2.54 as of August 1973). Previously, this rate had been fixed by the Association of Banks, which artificially maintained wide spreads between buying and selling rates.

The Currency Board also participates in the foreign exchange market as "the exchange of last resort." By law, the chief function of the board is to exchange Singapore dollars for sterling, U.S. dollars, and other convertible currencies. It operates in the market in both directions. Since it only handles transactions in amounts of U.S.-$40,000 or more, its principal customers are the commercial banks.

Principal currencies traded in the Singapore foreign exchange market are the pound sterling, U.S. dollar, and Hong Kong dollar. Some other currencies such as the Australian dollar, Canadian dollar, Japanese yen, Dutch guilder, deutsche mark (DM), and French franc are also frequently quoted. To expand the capacity of this market, three London-headquartered currency brokers were licensed in 1972 to deal in Asian dollars, foreign exchange, and domestic currency.

Asian Dollar Market

The development of the Asian dollar market in Singapore has paralleled the structure and operation of the Eurodollar market in London except under slightly different circumstances. First, it was the initiative of the Singapore government, which intended to make Singapore an entrepôt for money and capital as it had been an entrepôt for trade financing, that led to the initial development of the market. Second, there was a favorable environment conducive to the creation of such a market. This included economic growth in that region of the globe, the need for capital for trade and investment, the political stability of neighboring countries, the dissolution of the sterling bloc, and confidence in the Singapore government concerning political and economic stability. Given the encouragement of the above factors, the Bank of America took the initiative to establish the Asian dollar market in Singapore in 1968, with other large international banks joining the market.

Third, the Singapore government further encouraged the market's development by taking decisive steps:

1. to abolish the 20-percent reserve requirement on foreign currency deposits;

2. to reduce the income tax rate on profits from banks' foreign currency loans to foreign nonbank customers from 40 to 10 percent;

3. to permit foreign currency loans to locally incorporated companies against export orders or letter of credit;

4. to authorize local insurance companies and approved pension funds to invest up to 10 percent of their funds in Asian dollar deposits and approved Asian dollar bonds; and

5. to authorize certain banks to accept deposits from, and make loans to, nonresidents.

At the end of 1972, there were 25 authorized banks conducting an Asian dollar business; five were local commercial banks, and 20 were affiliates or branches of foreign financial institutions. The volume of the Asian dollar market grew from less than $100 million in 1968 to about $3 billion dollars in 1972 (see Table 15.5). More than 90 percent of the foreign currency deposits are denominated

TABLE 15.5

Singapore Asiadollar Market

Year End	Number of Authorized Banks	Gross Foreign Currency Liabilities (millions of dollars)
1968	1	31
1969	9	123
1970	14	390
1971	19	1,163
1972	25	2,976

Source: Morgan Guaranty Trust Company, World Financial Markets, March 22, 1973, p. 8.

in U.S. dollars with the remainder in sterling, DMs, Swiss francs, and Japanese yen. Approximately 70 percent of the Asian dollar deposits represent interbank deposits, and 30 percent are from nonbank sources, mainly multinational corporations. Asian central banks, commercial corporations, and wealthy individuals are suppliers of funds. Users of these funds include commercial loans to local customers and term loans to business customers throughout Southeast Asia. Most of the Asian dollar banks act as brokers. They accept deposits and lend them to American or European banks. Interest rates in the Asian dollar market generally have been within 1/8 percent of Eurodollar interest rates. The Asian dollar market not only has integrated the Singapore money and capital markets, but also the international financial markets.

It should be noted that up to mid-1973, five Asian dollar bond issues totaling $77.5 million have been syndicated for the Singapore and South Korean governments, for the Private Investment Corporation of Asia, and for Brunei LNG (a Shell Oil consortium).

GOVERNMENT POLICY AND INTERNATIONAL FINANCE

Government Policy and Foreign Investment

Prior to 1965, financing the entrepôt trade in rubber, tin, lumber pepper, and pineapples was emphasized in Singapore. Since then the emphasis in Singapore's economy has been changed from primary product to export-oriented manufacturing. Foreign capital investments have been vital to the success of this changing emphasis. To supplement this policy, the government has worked to develop a viable financial market, manufacturing facilities, and foreign service facilities (such as consulting firms). Tax incentives to investors, especially high-technology multinational corporations in the areas of oil refining, shipping, electronic products, precision instruments, and electrical appliances, have been powerful tools in making this policy workable.

It is noted that before 1966 the United Kingdom was the principal investor in Singapore, but the United States has gradually taken a leading position in recent years (see Table 15.6). At the end of 1972, there were over 100 foreign firms in Singapore, of which U.S. firms accounted for about half. U.S. firms have preferred full management control. Joint venture partners usually include trading firms, which are distributors of foreign manufacturing firms with a region-wide network.

Balance of Payments

From 1967 to 1971, Singapore's current accounts have shown deficits (see Table 15.7), but the overall balance of payments in the same period has been consistently in surplus due to increasing inflows

TABLE 15.6

Foreign Investment in Singapore by Major Countries
(millions of Singapore dollars)

| | Gross Fixed Assets | |
	1970	1971
United States	343.8	500.9
United Kingdom	199.4	294.4
Netherlands	182.7	274.5
Japan	67.9	108.2
Hong Kong	51.9	96.9
West Germany	2.6	20.7
Others	146.4	276.9
Total	994.7	1,572.5

Source: International Monetary Fund (IMF), International Survey, May 28, 1973, p. 152.

TABLE 15.7

Singapore Balance of Payments, 1966-71
(millions of dollars at rate of Singapore $2.54 = U.S.$1)

	1966	1967	1968	1969	1970	1971 (Preliminary)
Exports of goods and services	1,672.8	1,727.3	1,901.6	2,287.2	2,340.6	2,707.2
Merchandise including nonmonetary gold	1,247.1	1,275.4	1,412.8	1,760.0	1,743.4	2,047.2
Freight and insurance	3.6	6.0	6.2	8.3	10.4	9.0
Travel and other transportation	157.1	203.0	248.0	283.2	337.5	379.4
Investment income	39.4	40.6	46.1	67.2	80.0	96.3
Government	220.7	197.2	184.3	163.7	164.0	170.1
Other services	4.7	4.9	4.2	4.6	5.1	5.0
Imports of goods and services	1,653.8	1,801.0	2,073.0	2,547.2	3,081.1	3,744.6
Merchandise including nonmonetary gold	1,505.7	1,633.1	1,873.6	2,308.1	2,774.7	3,362.0
Freight and insurance	91.3	103.7	123.9	148.6	183.6	241.5
Travel and other transportation	20.8	23.6	27.3	35.5	41.3	48.0
Investment income	15.9	16.6	17.9	19.9	32.6	32.4
Government	2.8	6.8	8.5	3.3	4.9	6.0
Other services	17.2	17.0	21.6	31.7	44.3	54.8
Resource balance (- = inflow)	18.9	-73.8	-171.3	-260.0	-741.0	-1,037.4
Transfer payments (net)	-17.7	-15.4	-16.1	-15.4	-9.3	-10.6
Private	-15.4	-16.9	-19.2	-19.7	-25.0	-29.0
Central government	-2.2	1.4	3.1	4.3	15.7	18.4
Current account balance	1.3	-89.2	-186.6	-275.4	-749.9	-1,048.0
Nonmonetary capital (net)	20.1	44.5	106.6	68.2	174.8	182.0
Private long-term (net)	22.0	33.9	37.4	44.9	120.4	133.5
Official (net)	2.0	10.6	69.3	23.2	54.3	48.0
International Bank for Reconstruction and Development loans (net)	14.9	(7.1)	11.0	13.0	24.0	21.3
Drawings	15.0	(7.4)	(11.9)	(14.1)	(26.0)	(23.6)
Repayments	(-0.4)	(-0.8)	(-0.8)	(-1.2)	(-2.0)	(-2.3)
Other official	-2.6	3.5	58.3	10.2	30.3	26.8
Balancing item	52.0	186.0	296.6	391.3	756.7	1,198.9
Currency payments surplus or deficit	73.6	141.3	215.8	184.2	181.6	332.5
Monetary movements (net) (- = increase)	-73.6	-141.3	-215.8	-184.2	-181.6	-332.5
IMF accounts	-9.1	-0-	-0-	-0-	-0-	-2.1
Currency Board's foreign assets	-20.7	-11.6	-19.2	40.8	-53.4	-50.2
Commercial banks' foreign assets	-13.4	-21.6	45.4	89.1	40.7	53.4
Central government assets	-30.4	-108.1	-242.0	74.3	-164.0	-333.7
Monetary Authorities' Reserves	228.1	198.4	215.5	224.2	294.4	592.6

Source: IMF, International Financial Statistics, May 1973.

of capital, private and official. For this reason, the MAS reserves have increased from U.S.$228.1 million in 1966 to U.S.$592.6 million in 1971. This comfortable position not only provides a good basis for the domestic money supply, but also builds confidence in the eyes of the international community.

It is understandable that increased imports have resulted from Singapore's industrialization programs, including machinery, tools, and raw materials. Furthermore, the increasing trend of neighboring countries to trade directly with other nations has reduced reliance on Singapore's entrepôt facilities. However, exports generated by domestic industrial production grew rapidly. According to the Singapore Investment News, April 1973, exports in 1972 increased by 14.3 percent to $2.4 billion, while imports rose more slowly by 10.1 percent to $3.8 billion. The overall trade balance was in deficit. However, the balance of payments position (including trade, services, and capital flows) in total was in surplus by U.S.$223 million.

Singapore's service account was in surplus in 1972 due to increased income from tourism and investment income. It is expected that foreign capital inflows will continue to increase, while imports of machinery and tools will decrease because of ongoing import substitution programs.

International Financial Activities

In addition to strengthening its domestic economic and financial position, Singapore has taken advantage of its relationships with international financial institutions, political association with the Commonwealth, and friendly relations with countries in the region whose continued goodwill is important to Singapore.

In 1969, Singapore borrowed U.S.$223 million from the World Bank and the Asian Development Bank. The purpose of the borrowing from the World Bank was to improve public housing, airport facilities, electric power, highways, and reservoirs for water supply. According to the World Bank 1972 Annual Reports, Singapore's external public debt outstanding was U.S.$128.2 million, and debt service payments were 6 percent of merchandise exports. Debt service was low in comparison to the service payments in other countries. The credit from the Asian Development Bank was used for capital formation in the utility industry and for the development of Singapore's secondary capital market (stock exchange).

Singapore also has received minor aid from the United Kingdom to offset the economic effects of withdrawal of British forces after 1969. A small amount of assistance was provided by Japan, West Germany, and several of the Colombo Plan countries.

A "give-and-take" policy was adopted by the Singapore government in the Pacific region. It has extended goodwill to Malaysia and Indonesia. For instance, the Singapore government gives tax exemption to the earnings of Singapore capital invested in Malaysia and Indonesia on projects approved by the authorities of these countries.

REFERENCES

The Banker (London). "Singapore: A Survey," October 1970.

Agnelli, Bernard F. "Singapore: Boom Town." Columbia Journal of World Business (November-December 1971).

Bureau of Statistics, Singapore. Year Book of Statistics, 1972.

_____. Monthly Digest of Statistics, December 1972.

International Monetary Fund (IMF). International Financial Statistics, June 1973.

Morgan Guaranty Trust Company. World Financial Market, March 22, 1973.

The Straits Times, daily newspaper published by the Straits Times Press, Singapore.

United Nations. Asia and the Far East Economic Bulletin, June/ September 1971.

You, Poh Seng, and Chong Yah, Lim. The Singapore Economy. Singapore: Eastern University Press, 1971.

INTRODUCTION

Set apart as an island continent, Australia has exploited commercial opportunities and resource wealth to build a mature but
vigorous economy. With an area twice as large as India and Pakistan
combined, and a population of only $12\frac{1}{2}$ million, the Commonwealth
has achieved a high level of per-capita income, exceeding that of the
United Kingdom and West Germany. Australia ranks sixth among
the nations of the world in land area, close behind the United States
and Brazil. Australia has a relatively dry continent, enjoying modest
rainfall and lacking extensive inland river systems. The climate is
varied, and the terrain is flat. The country enjoys substantial deposits
of minerals, including bauxite, coal, oil, and natural gas.

Australia enjoys a federal system of government, with a delicate
balance maintained between the powers of the federal and state Parlia-
ments. This division of powers follows the American model. However, the British tradition is evident since the Cabinet is responsible
to Parliament. In its international affairs, Australia has been extremely
cooperative with major powers including the United States and United
Kingdom, is a member of the Southeast Asia Treaty Organization
(SEATO), and an original member of the Colombo Plan. The latter
was established at a meeting of Commonwealth foreign ministers in
Colombo early in 1950. Under the Colombo Plan, a Consultative
Committee was established for cooperative economic development
in South and Southeast Asia. All of the original members were Commonwealth members, and the United States and Japan joined shortly
after. Australia's contribution to the Colombo Plan has been close
to Australian $200 million, largely in the form of economic develop-
ment assistance to less developed members.

Australia is an advanced technology country, whose population is largely urbanized and enjoys a high standard of living. The structure of the Australian economy has undergone rapid change in the past several decades, but the key role of overseas trade and the balance of payments has scarcely diminished. Australia exports approximately 15 percent of total production and depends upon foreign investment inflows to balance the foreign exchange position and finance capital investments. In the short period of two decades, Australia has achieved a balanced economy reflected in the relatively low percentage of domestic product originating in agriculture (10 percent), the importance of diversified manufacturing and service industries, and expansion in the financial sector.

HISTORY AND BACKGROUND OF FINANCIAL MARKETS

Several characteristics of the Australian economy have exerted an influence on the pattern and growth of financial markets in the past. These include

1. the importance of primary production and exports, which are responsible for both seasonal and cyclical swings in financial market conditions;

2. sterling area ties, which inhibited the development of central banking institutions in Australia and related growth in financial markets;

3. the dominance and semimonopolistic position of the trading banks, which has broken down in part given competitive pressures from nonbank financial institutions and overseas;

4. an open economy system, which has provided substantial foreign exchange and foreign trade earnings for the trading banks;

5. reliance on foreign investment inflows to finance a substantial portion of capital formation, tending to result in a lethargic growth of open-market trading and issuance of business securities; and

6. a system of social priorities in Australia, which emphasize low-cost housing and government financing of substantial areas of capital formation, resulting in a low interest rate structure and inflated expansion of the government securities market.

Historically, growth and development of the banking system have reflected British origins and traditions. Commercial banking has tended to be concentrated in a few large institutions with extensive branch systems. The eight major trading banks in Australia are responsible for over 90 percent of the ordinary banking business in Australia.

The two decades ending in 1973 have witnessed numerous changes in the Australian financial system including the following:

1. rapid surge in savings banking, assisted by the establishment of savings bank subsidiaries by several of the major trading banks;

2. banking legislation in 1953 and 1959, which modernized the central bank and divested it of its commercial banking department, which became a separate banking institution;

3. growth of the capital market and the related expansion of financial intermediaries;

4. development of a well-organized money market in the form of recognized dealers in government securities with access to central bank credit;

5. introduction in 1962 of term lending by the trading banks, by agreement with and under close supervision of the central bank.

The Australian stock exchanges have enjoyed a healthy expansion in the past several decades, based upon a prosperous economy, substantial growth in retained earnings by companies, increased demand for and trading in listed securities by the private pension funds, other institutional investors, and individuals, and increased interest in Australian securities by foreign investors.

The oldest stock exchange was founded in Melbourne, dating from 1859. The six large capital city exchanges are located in Melbourne, Sydney, Brisbane, Adelaide, Perth, and Hobart. The several exchanges form a national security market in the sense that the major securities are quoted on several or all of the exchanges. There is active arbitrage among these exchanges. The Australian stock market is extremely active, and the future should see the development of Sydney or Melbourne into one of the major financial centers of the world.

Foreign exchange relationships have played a vital role for the Australian economy and the status of the financial markets. Foreign trade and investment comprise a sizable share of domestic production and capital formation. The Australian trading banks have enjoyed a monopoly of the foreign exchange business, and operations from their London offices have been a key factor in their success. The London foreign exchange market continues to be a focal point for Australia's external financial transactions, although it is not as important as it was 15 years ago. It was estimated that in the 1950s, over 80 percent of the Australian banks' overseas transactions were in sterling. This is not the situation today, even though a sizable (major) part of Australia's foreign exchange reserves is in sterling. The trading banks have been the appointed agents of the central bank in conducting foreign exchange transactions under the prevailing system of exchange controls.

Diminution in the role of the United Kingdom as an investor in Australian enterprises and a reorientation of Australian foreign trade toward the Far East, Canada, the United States, and Western Germany and away from the United Kingdom have further lessened the importance of sterling and sterling-Australian dollar exchange parities to the domestic economy and financial markets. In future we might expect to see closer financial ties between Australia and Japan (which ranks first as a market for Australian exports) and between Australia and Mainland China (which ranks fifth as a market for Australian exports).

FINANCIAL INSTITUTIONS

Overview of Financial Structure

During much of the period since World War II, there have been important developments in the Australian financial sector. Many new institutions have been developed, and new forms of credit have appeared. As a result, Australia now enjoys a much wider range of financial institutions and related services. Lenders and borrowers alike enjoy the benefits of improved facilities to accommodate the flow of savings, and the economic growth of the country has been furthered.

The financial structure of Australia, measured by the assets held in the major financial institutions in the country, is impressive. As indicated in Table 16.1, financial assets held by major institutions in 1969 represented 131 percent of gross national product (GNP). One of the reasons for this high ratio is the institutionalization of Australian savings, capital formation, and flows of financial resources. Another is the relative lack of development of direct patterns of lending and investing, which has been characteristic in other developed countries such as the United States, United Kingdom, and continental Europe. Individuals in Australia channel the bulk of their savings into banks, insurance companies, and pension fund assets. Open-market transactions between ultimate lenders and borrowers is less commonplace. This explains why in 1959 government authorities supported the establishment of the money market dealers, who provide Australia with an important open-market trading mechanism, where none was available previously.

In some respects, the structure of Australian financial institutions resembles that of the United Kingdom. The Reserve Bank holds rein over the trading banks indirectly via the government bond market and the money market dealers, which is analogous to the London bill market. Also, the Reserve Bank distinguishes in its balance sheet between the Note Issue Department and Central Banking Business.

TABLE 16.1

Financial Institutions of Australia 1969
(billions of Australian dollars)

Assets of banking sector	
Reserve Bank	2.8
Trading banks	9.6
Total	12.4
Assets of major financial intermediaries	
Savings banks	7.2
Life insurance companies	5.9
Building societies	1.2
Total	14.3
Assets of other important institutions	
Finance companies	2.8
Dealers in government securities	0.5
Government pension funds	1.4
Private pension funds	1.1
Total	5.8
Grand total	32.5
Gross national product	24.8
Grand total/GNP	131%

Source: Yearbook, Australia, 1970.

  Unlike the United Kingdom, Australia's unit trusts are not nearly as well developed or important as they are in the London capital market.

    The financial structure in Australia is geared to the geography and stage of economic development of the country. A small number of large trading banks and savings banks service a broad geographic area with thousands of branch offices and agencies. There is a delicate balance between those banks that service individual state needs by operating within a single state and those banking institutions that service the length and breadth of the Commonwealth. Finally, the operations of the life insurance companies are geared to stimulate home ownership, perhaps at the expense of a more "efficient" and competitive capital market structure. This reflects the social priorities of the country, which have emphasized home ownership to a greater degree than fluidity of financial resources.

Banking Institutions

In this section we analyze the functions and operations performed by the commercial banking sector in Australia and briefly review the relationships between the commercial banks and central bank. Detailed discussion of the operations and policies of the Reserve Bank is included in a following section describing how monetary policy works.

Virtually all of the commercial banking activities in Australia are concentrated in eight major trading banks. A small number of lesser check-paying institutions operate as commercial banks, but account for only an insignificant proportion of total deposits and loans in the banking sector. Two of the major trading banks maintain head offices in London, and another is owned by the Commonwealth government.

The trading banks represent the largest single institutional group in the financial sector in Australia and play a key role as mobilizers of funds and allocators of credit. Approximately one-third of their deposits comes from individuals, over one-half from businesses, and one-twentieth from public authorities. Over three-fifths of their advances and loans are to the business sector, and over one-sixth to individuals. Slightly in excess of half of deposits in trading banks are current account deposits, payable on demand and transferable by check. Interest-bearing deposits assume a variety of forms and maturities. Maturities generally range between three months and two years. Beginning in 1969, the trading banks were permitted to issue negotiable certificates of deposit (NCDs).

The trading bank's portfolio management is influenced by overall considerations of liquidity, profit, and safety, as well as reserve ratio and liquidity ratio requirements established in their working relationships with the Reserve Bank. Their deposit liabilities are overwhelmingly short term. In the Australian context, assets that may be regarded as highly liquid are Treasury notes, deposits with the short-term money market, and certificates of deposit (CDs) issued by other banks. Long-term government securities also are regarded as possessing a high degree of liquidity. During the 1950s, the central bank persuaded the trading banks to maintain a minimum ratio of liquid assets and government securities to their deposit liabilities. This is the so-called LGS ratio, or liquid assets plus government securities. By agreement with the Reserve Bank, each of the trading banks will not allow its ratio of LGS assets to deposits to fall under 18 percent. To ensure this, the trading banks may borrow from the Reserve Bank.

In addition, the trading banks maintain Statutory Reserve Deposits (SRDs) with the Reserve Bank, which are not regarded as cash but as frozen assets. The central bank has the discretion to increase or reduce the percentage of deposit liabilities that the trading banks must maintain in the form of SRDs, and in turn this requirement governs their ability to extend their asset portfolios by lending. Table 16.2 reflects the position of the trading banks and the average liquidity and reserve ratios for the year ending June 30, 1969.

Financial Intermediaries

In this section we examine the role played by three major groups of financial intermediaries. These are the savings banks, the life insurance companies, and the building societies. The largest of these is the savings banks group.

TABLE 16.2

Assets of All Trading Banks Held within Australia,
Weekly Average Year Ending June 1969
(millions of Australian dollars)

	Amount	Percent of Total
Gold, coin and notes, and cash with Reserve Bank	159	2.2
Treasury notes	53	0.7
Government securities	1,390	19.0
LGS assets	1,602a	22.0
Loans to short-term money market	95	1.3
Statutory reserve deposit	568b	7.7
Loans, advances, and bills discounted	4,384	60.2
Other	635	8.7
Total assets	7,282	100.0

aAverage deposits for this period were $6,706 million; average LGS ratio was 23.9 percent.
bAverage Statutory Reserve Deposits (SRD) ratio was 8.5 percent.

Source: Yearbook, Australia, 1970.

309

Savings Banks

In 1969, the 12 savings banks operating in Australia held combined assets of $7.2 billion, representing deposits in over 14 million
separate deposit accounts. At the same time, these savings banks
operated over 5,400 branches in all states and territories of Australia.
The origins of these institutions trace back to the early nineteenth
century, when British social reformers concerned with the welfare
of the less fortunate provided for the establishment of savings banks.
Control of savings banks in Australia is vested in boards of trustees,
and activities of these institutions are subject to the close scrutiny
of the government.

Official interest in savings bank operations can be traced to
1911 when the Commonwealth government established the Commonwealth Savings Bank, which is the largest such institution in Australia,
in 1969 holding close to 43 percent of total assets of all savings banks.
At the same time, private savings banks held 31 percent of total
assets; the two state savings banks held 24 percent; and two trustee
banks held $1\frac{1}{2}$ percent of assets.

Savings banks provide important connecting links between savers
and borrowers, obtaining their funds from the personal savings of
individuals, societies, and other noncommercial groups. Increases
in savings bank deposits form an important part of the funds flowing
into the capital market each year, and in recent years deposit growth
has ranged between $400 to $500 million. Lending policies of savings
banks are strongly influenced by government policies. Government-
owned banks give relatively less weight to the profit motive, emphasizing social objectives. Private savings banks are subject to the
banking legislation of the Commonwealth and cooperate closely with
the central bank in matters relating to monetary policy.

Banking legislation requires that savings banks hold certain
prescribed asset types, including cash deposits with the central bank,
deposits with money market dealers, obligations of the Australian
governments, and loans based on the security of land and housing.
Banks are required to hold assets in certain proportions to their
deposit liabilities. Each bank must hold at minimum 65 percent of
deposit liabilities in the form of cash, deposits with the Reserve
Bank and short-term money market, deposits and loans with other
banks, obligations of Australian governments, and obligations issued
or guaranteed by government authorities. Within this 65 percent, an
amount equivalent to at least 10 percent of deposit liabilities must
be held as deposits with the Reserve Bank or in short-term obligations
of the Commonwealth government. These requirements limit savings
bank loans in the housing field to no more than 35 percent of deposit
balances. Savings banks are the most important lenders in the housing

finance field and play a major role as purchasers of government obligations.

Life Insurance Companies

Life insurance companies rank third among the financial institutions in Australia. Their major source of funds comes from claims against policies, which result from the accumulation of reserves on policies. A high proportion of their assets consists of long-term government bonds, due to strong tax incentives to hold at a minimum 30 percent of assets in a mixture of Commonwealth and state government securities and 20 percent in Commonwealth securities. These tax incentives were introduced in 1960 at a time when life insurance companies were shifting their asset holdings out of government securities. The tax incentive is subject to serious question since it is not necessarily in the best interests of either policyholders or the Australian economy. It should be noted that there exists a partial offset in that substantial income tax concessions accrue to taxpayers paying life insurance premiums. Life insurance is less expensive when the tax-adjusted cost of premiums is considered, and the life insurance companies are able to attract a greater volume of business. Nevertheless, serious distortions are introduced into the capital markets of Australia.

Life insurance company assets are heavily oriented toward government and municipal securities, with approximately 33 percent of the total falling in this category. Approximately 24 percent of assets are invested in mortgage loans, and another 10 percent in freehold and leasehold property. Life insurance companies also allocate a considerable portion of their assets as loans to policyholders. The large proportion of assets invested in mortgage loans appears to be explained in part by their desire to attract new insurance business by making housing finance available to policyholders.

While life insurance companies have allocated only a small part of their resources in lending to private businesses, there has been a considerable increase in their activities in this direction. Hopefully, this tendency will develop further, since these companies represent one of the most important sources of long-term funds in the Australian economy. As large financial institutions, they possess the resources and ability to allocate their funds on the basis of an intelligent appraisal of the needs and financial strengths of the various business sectors of the economy.

Building Societies

Building societies provide funds to finance the purchase of housing. These institutions obtain the bulk of their funds from two sources: deposits from the public and loans from the government and banks. In 1969, these societies held total assets of $1.2 billion, most of which were in the form of loans to finance purchase of dwellings.

Pension Funds and Other Institutions

In addition to those described above, Australia enjoys the benefits of a variety of financial institutions including government and private pension funds, finance companies, and unit trusts.

Pension Funds

Pension funds hold a sizable block of the financial assets in Australia. In 1969, their combined assets were $2.5 billion, with the government pension funds holding $1.4 billion in assets and the private funds the remainder. Pension funds receive regular contributions from those employed by the firms or other bodies controlling the funds and use these contributions to purchase investment securities. From this accumulation they pay retirement income to those employees covered by the pension program. Like the life insurance companies, they are subject to the tax incentives, which require that a minimum proportion of assets be held in government securities.

Over 60 percent of the assets of government pension funds are invested in local and semigovernmental securities, 11 percent in mortgages and loans to building societies, and 10 percent in Commonwealth government securities. Another 7 percent of assets are invested in company shares and debentures. By comparison, close to 20 percent of the assets of private pension funds are invested in local and semigovernmental securities, 3 percent in mortgages, 16 percent in Commonwealth government securities, and 54 percent in company shares, debentures, and mortgage loans. Obviously, the government and private pension funds follow distinctly different portfolio management policies.

Finance Companies

The operations of finance companies have enjoyed rapid growth in recent years. In 1969, finance companies held $2.8 billion in assets, representing a wide assortment of credit forms. The two most important types of credits provided by these companies include installment credit through retailers and wholesale hire purchase. The demand for finance for hire purchase grew rapidly in the 1950s and to a lesser extent in the 1960s as individuals came to accept the idea of purchasing goods on hire purchase. In 1967, banks were given permission to make personal loans at higher effective rates than was formerly permitted, and since that date they have competed agressively for this type of business. During the 1960s, the monetary authorities permitted controlled interest rates to rise more readily, reducing the large differential between bank and nonbank lending rates that had shunted lending away from the banking institutions. As a result of these developments, the finance companies have expanded their lending activities to business firms.

Several of the major finance companies are owned by the banks. This has permitted the banks to enjoy the profits available on rapidly expanding areas of business which could not have been participated in by banking institutions at times of tight monetary controls.

Limits on the rates of interest banks may charge prevent them from undertaking riskier types of lending. This tends to leave much of the higher-risk business to the finance companies. Finance companies play an important role in the Australian capital market and fill an important void in the area of riskier credits that banks cannot easily undertake.

Unit Trusts

Unit trusts are institutions that hold a wide range of publicly issued and traded securities. These trusts issue their own units to small savers and others who acquire a fractional interest in the underlying securities. They afford the small saver investment management and diversification. They also provide an added measure of liquidity in that units can normally be cashed readily at a price that varies with the market value of the securities held by the trust. There are several land trusts in Australia. However, it is difficult to obtain current or daily quotations on their value since the underlying assets (real estate) lack daily market quotations.

MONEY, CREDIT, AND CAPITAL MARKETS

Saving and Capital Formation

The economic welfare and growth of a nation depend upon generation of adequate saving flows with which to finance capital formation. The composition of saving and the channels through which it is directed influence the pattern of capital expenditures and the efficiency of the investment process in general.

In 1969, total capital funds available for investment in Australia were over $8.0 billion, approximately one-third of the GNP of $24 billion. The major sources of these capital funds were depreciation allowances (29.8 percent), personal saving (21.4 percent), public authority surpluses (20.8 percent), capital inflows (14.6 percent), and undistributed company income (7.6 percent). If we add retained investment income of life insurance funds to personal saving, on the basis that it ultimately accrues to individual policyholder beneficiaries, personal saving comes close to depreciation allowances as the largest single source of capital funds.

Depreciation allowances and undistributed company income are generally associated with sources of financing business fixed investment and actually come close in amount to those two items on the "Uses" side of Table 16.3, which can be most closely related to business plant and equipment spending (private other buildings and all other). Official statistics suggest that personal saving is extremely volatile in Australia, with year-to-year percentage changes of as much as 35 and 70 percent. Capital inflows provide an important source of funds for investment, and well over half of these inflows may be related to direct business investments.

Examining the expenditures side of the national capital accounts, we find that private capital expenditures account for close to 60 percent of gross uses of funds, of which dwellings represent 15.9 percent. Plant and equipment expenditures constitute nearly all of the remainder of private expenditures (38 to 40 percent of the total). Public investment accounts for nearly one-third of capital expenditures. Finally, investment in stocks (inventories) represents over 10 percent of gross uses of funds.

Government Securities Market

It has been the experience of many industrialized nations in recent decades that a well-developed government securities market carries numerous advantages, including a more efficiently functioning financial market mechanism and increased opportunities for monetary policy to operate and transmit pressures on the credit system. Australia is one of the nations that has developed its government securities market to the point where such advantages are apparent.

In 1969, government securities outstanding issued by the Commonwealth and states and denominated in Australian dollars totaled $10,815 million (Australian), equivalent to 43 percent of that year's GNP (see Table 16.4). This represents the largest block of credit instruments in Australia. During the 1960s, there was a tendency for this debt to grow about as rapidly as national income. The Australian Loan Council, which consists of the prime minister and the six state premiers, controls the borrowing of the Commonwealth

TABLE 16.3

National Capital Accounts of Australia, 1968–69
(Sources and Uses Format)

Uses	(millions of Australian dollars)	Per-cent	Sources	(millions of Australian dollars)	Per-cent
Gross fixed capital expenditures			Depreciation allowances	2,390	29.8
Private dwellings	1,272	15.9	Increase in dividend and income tax provided	147	1.8
Private other buildings	1,022	12.8	Undistributed company income	611	7.6
Private all other	2,375	29.7	Retained investment income of life insurance funds	433	5.4
Public enterprises	1,425	17.8	Personal saving	1,712	21.4
Public authorities	1,113	13.9	Public authority grants toward private capital expenditure	46	0.6
Total, gross fixed capital expenditure	7,207	90.1	Public authorities surplus on current account	1,662	20.8
Increase in value of stocks			Overseas balance on current account		
Farm	413	5.1	Withdrawal from overseas monetary reserves	-154	-1.9
Other	447	5.5	Net apparent capital inflow	1,168	14.6
Total uses of funds	8,067	100.1	Total capital funds	8,015	100.1
Statistical discrepancy	-52	-0.6			
Total capital funds	8,015	100.1			

Source: Yearbook, Australia, 1970.

315

and state governments. The Commonwealth Treasury is responsible for organizing implementation of the council's loan program. Most of the government obligations issued in Australia are obligations of the Commonwealth government, although over the past 25 years most of the borrowing has been undertaken on behalf of the state governments.

The banking sector together with the life insurance institutions hold over one-half of all Commonwealth and state government securities outstanding (Table 16.5). In the banking sector, the savings banks account for as much of government securities held as do the Reserve Bank and trading banks taken together. Public authorities hold another 21 percent of government securities. Finally, we should note that the principal market traders, the money market dealers, inventory nearly 5 percent of outstandings.

Maturities of government securities in Australia range from 3 months to 35 years. Those with the shortest maturities, Treasury bills, are held by government departments and the government-owned Reserve Bank. Treasury notes also have maturities as short as 13 weeks and 26 weeks and are issued in $1,000 multiples in amounts of $10,000 and up. Treasury notes are issued at a discount and are redeemed at their face value, the difference representing the return (expressed as a rate of discount). The Reserve Bank may purchase these notes on a rediscount basis, with the rate of discount set at a level that makes it necessary to hold the notes for several days before the original purchase price can be obtained. There is a substantial secondary market, which removes the necessity of selling the notes to the Reserve Bank except in abnormal conditions. Treasury notes are negotiable, marketable, and riskless and consequently are in demand by those investors seeking to acquire liquid assets yielding a moderate return. Other Commonwealth obligations include those with relatively short maturities (2 to 3 years), medium-term maturities (7 to 10 years), and long-term maturities (up to 35 years).

Short-Term Money Market

The term money market generally refers to a group of institutions that specialize in borrowing large sums of money for relatively short periods, relending these funds at somewhat higher rates of interest. In Australia major instruments and forms of credit utilized in the money market include short-term government securities, NCDs Reserve Bank credit, intercompany loan transactions, and funds resulting from settlement of share trading on the stock exchanges. The official money market has achieved a successful development due to the efforts and support of the Reserve Bank. In recent years the unofficial money market has also enjoyed rapid expansion.

316

TABLE 16.4

Government Securities Outstanding
(millions of Australian dollars)

	Debt Denominated in Australian Dollars	Debt Denominated in Foreign Currencies
	Commonwealth and States	
1966	9,134	1,505
1967	9,677	1,532
1968	10,358	1,558
1969	10,815	1,698
	Local and Other Governments	
1966	3,574	23
1967	3,876	16
1968	4,196	9
1969	4,569	5

Source: International Monetary Fund (IMF), International Financial Statistics.

TABLE 16.5

Ownership Distribution of Commonwealth and State Government Securities Outstanding by Major Holders, June 1969
(millions of Australian dollars)

	Amount	Percent of Total
Reserve Bank of Australia	846	7.8
Trading banks	1,367	12.6
Savings banks	2,285	21.1
Life insurance companies	1,150	10.6
Pension and provident funds	192	1.8
Money market dealers	524	4.8
Government insurance and pension funds	332	3.1
Public authorities	2,067	19.1
Companies (excluding finance)	183	1.7
Other	1,869	17.3
Total	10,815	100.0

Source: Yearbook, Australia, 1970.

In Australia the official market consists especially of nine officially backed money market dealers having the right to borrow substantial sums from the Reserve Bank. The Reserve Bank has maintained a close scrutiny over the operations of these dealers since the officially backed money market was first established in 1959. Money market dealers are required to have a minimum paid-up capital of $400,000 and sufficient shareholders' funds to permit placement of adequate margin funds with the Reserve Bank. There are two main types of dealers in the official market: (1) money dealers who borrow funds and purchase securities for short and medium term and (2) traders in securities who regard their portfolio as available for sale, and who are in the market to buy anything offered. All houses have been associated with a stockbroker, and most have been linked with some other financial institution such as an insurance firm or merchant bank. A number of overseas banks have acquired participations in Australian merchant banks and in this way developed links with the Australian money market.

The money market dealers obtain funds from a variety of source including governments and government authorities, banks, insurance companies, installment credit companies, and other financial institutions. One of the largest sources of funds is the trading companies that have temporarily idle funds to invest. When one of these lenders has funds to invest, the "deposit" with the money market dealer is accompanied by the Reserve Bank branch in that center, making available a certificate to indicate that it is holding government obligations as the lender's security for these funds. These loans to money market dealers can be withdrawn upon a given period of notice or on a particular maturity date. The official money market is backed by the Reserve Bank, thus providing investors with absolutely safe, liquid claims upon the money market dealers.

In turn, the market uses the funds that it borrows to purchase earning assets, which consist of government securities. Dealers may discount these assets with the Reserve Bank, which assures the market of liquidity. At present, only government securities are acceptable as security for loans to the dealers from the Reserve Bank. However, in the period 1965-69, dealers could secure loans from the bank based upon discounting short-term promissory notes of business, provided they were accepted by a bank. At present, dealers are permitted to hold a much wider range of claims on the private sector, including single-name bills, bank DCs maturing within five years, and limited amounts of other assets. Government securities are likely to remain the major asset holdings of the money market dealers. In 1968-69, holdings of Treasury notes ranged between $100 to $150 million, and other government securities (longer term) of $350 to $400 million. Dealers' holdings of Treasury notes represent close to 40 percent of outstandings.

The Reserve Bank is in daily contact with the market, frequently buys and sells government securities, and regularly quotes the prices at which it is prepared to deal in these securities. By altering its buying and selling prices and the volume of transactions for its own account, it can affect interest rates and yields in the market. The rates of return that dealers are able to earn on their earning assets have an important influence on the rates of interest the dealers are willing to offer depositors. Since the market must remain liquid and settle its transactions on a day-to-day basis, dealers must change the rates they offer on various types of money market loan funds, relying on funds from the Reserve Bank as a lender of last resort.

The official money market described in the preceding paragraphs consists of the market for short-term government securities and Reserve Bank credit used to support other operations of dealers who serve as indispensable makers of the market. The unofficial money market in Australia includes the intercompany loan market, the market for CDs, and the market for funds resulting from settlement of stock exchange transactions. Permission given the money market dealers in 1969 to trade in shares could result in their becoming important intermediaries in the shares market, as well as place them in a pivotal position in handling funds resulting from settlement of transactions in share trading. The initial (1969) offering of NCDs with three months to two years maturities by the trading banks introduced a new dimension to the market for short-term funds. Permission for banks to issue NCDs in part resulted from the hope that business firms and individuals would hold these instruments in preference to making loans through the intercompany loan market, which lies beyond the direct control of the monetary authorities. Banks are free to determine the rates they offer on NCDs subject to a maximum rate that is varied from time to time by the Reserve Bank. In 1972 the trading banks were authorized to fix their own rates for fixed deposits of $50,000 or more and with maturities of one month to four years (subject to rate maximums set by the Reserve Bank).

Business in the unofficial market is conducted by several types of houses including stockbrokers (some associated with authorized dealers), finance companies which raise funds by selling debentures and unsecured notes, and the merchant banks. The unofficial dealers operate in the intercompany market, which is closed to the official houses.

The intercompany loan market consists of dealings among major companies in an informal market for idle funds. The market exists largely due to the wide spread between bank deposit and overdraft loan rates. This spread leaves a margin, which a firm can take advantage of by lending directly to another company, generally at a rate more favorable to both lender and borrower. This market expanded rapidly in the 1960s. The limits of the market are hard to define, since a loan by one company to another may be secured by a commercial bill and yet be defined as falling within the intercompany market. The exact size of this market is not known to the authorities. Interest hinges on the possible cushioning effects it might have on monetary policy pressures. From time to time, efforts have been made to enable banks to offer deposit types to business firms that will be competitive with the claims that result from intercompany loans. These efforts have not met with more than modest success.

The Australian money market still lacks the flexibility and competitiveness of its counterparts in the United States, United Kingdom, and Canada. For example, there is no weekly tender of Treasury notes. Moreover, the relatively fixed interest rates on Treasury notes lag behind changes in the market. Interest rate flexibility has been an area of controversy in Australia. Nevertheless, continued market development necessitates rate flexibility.

New Issues Market and Other Sources of Capital Funds

In 1969, gross fixed capital formation in Australia totaled $8.0 billion, of which $3.4 billion represented investment in plant and equipment by business firms. In the same year, new issues by Australian companies amounted to $887 million (see Table 16.6). Approximately $370 million of new issues was in the form of shares, and the remainder in debentures, registered notes, and secured loans.

The size of the new issues market in Australia measured by volume of new securities issued by business firms is impressive, especially when we consider that financial intermediaries in that country are not as aggressive buyers of these types of securities as they are in other advanced countries. The major purchasers of corporate securities in the United States and Western European countries have been life insurance companies, savings banks, private pension and retirement funds, and investment trusts. Of these, only the life insurance, savings banks, and private pension funds have grown to a size that permits their undertaking substantial investments in the capital market issues of business firms. We have already discussed the tax incentives that favor life insurance investments in government securities and the extent to which banking legislation has channeled savings bank investments away from acquisition of securities issued by business firms. On the other hand, private pension funds have made significant investments in capital market issues of the business sector (see Table 16.7). Over half of their assets are invested in shares, debentures, and other loans to companies, and these investments have been accumulating at a rate of over $50 million annually.

TABLE 16.6

New Money Raised, Listed and Unlisted Companies,
1967-68 and 1968-69
(millions of Australian dollars)

	1967-68	1968-69
	Companies Listed on Stock Exchanges	
Share Capital	122.6	341.3
Debt Capital	348.7	447.4
Total	471.3	788.7
	Companies Not Listed on Stock Exchanges	
Share Capital	50.8	66.6
Debt Capital	18.1	32.4
Total	68.9	99.0
Grand Total	540.2	887.7

TABLE 16.7

Private Pension Fund Investments in Company
Shares and Debt Instruments
(millions of Australian dollars)

	1964-65	1965-66	1966-67	1967-68	1968-69
Company Debentures, Notes, and Other Loans to Companies	167.4	188.6	209.4	230.0	256.8
Loans on Mortgage to Companies	24.3	30.3	42.1	56.2	70.7
Shares in Companies	177.5	198.1	228.7	258.0	299.7
Total	369.2	417.0	480.2	544.2	627.2
Change over Previous Year	—	47.8	63.2	64.0	83.0

Two additional and important channels through which capital funds finance investments in Australia are the Commonwealth Development Bank and foreign business investments in Australia. The Commonwealth Development Bank was established in 1959 and is authorized to provide term credits to primary and industrial firms where credit would not be available on reasonable terms. While authorized to provide equity as well as debt capital, very little of the former has been made available. At June 1969, outstanding balances on loans granted by the bank amounted to $192.2 million, of which $161.8 million represented rural loans and $30.4 million industrial loans. Balances outstanding under hire purchase loans granted to finance equipment totaled $58.0 million. The facilities made available by the Commonwealth Development Bank contain a large element of subsidy by taxpayers and depositors of the Commonwealth Savings Bank, which has provided over half of the funds available to the Development Bank.

In 1968, the Australian Resources Development Bank commenced business with $3 million share capital subscribed in equal amounts by the trading banks, a loan of $20 million from the Reserve Bank, and smaller loans from state rural banks. Objectives of the bank are to mobilize financial resources in Australia, to borrow overseas funds on favorable terms, to provide loans and equity funds to Australian enterprises, and to give special emphasis to the development of natural resources, particularly mineral ores, oil, and natural gas. The Resources Bank gives preference to enterprises owned by Australian interests and is empowered to make equity investments. However, it does not appear likely that the Resources Bank will develop into an institution equipped to raise risk capital for the purchase of equity in new Australian ventures. It has been suggested that there is a strong need for such an institution, and it has been further asserted that the Resources Bank should not assume these tasks.

In 1970, legislation was introduced into federal Parliament to establish an Australian Industries Development Corporation, which will raise borrowed capital from overseas. This development corporation will finance a wide range of Australian industries, lending to companies that are not large enough to borrow on world capital markets.

Foreign business investments in Australia constitute an important means of financing capital investment. In the six-year period 1963-69, private foreign investment in Australian companies averaged close to $680 million, attaining a high of $974 million in 1968-69. As can be seen from Table 16.8, in 1967-68 U.S. and Canadian investment in Australia made up 40 percent of the total and nearly all of the direct investment inflow.

322

TABLE 16.8

Inflow of Private Overseas Investment in Companies
in Australia by Category of Investment, 1967-68
and 1968-69
(millions of Australian dollars)

	Investment from United States of America and Canada		Total Foreign Investment in Australian Companies	
	1967-68	1968-69	1967-68	1968-69
Direct investment				
Undistributed income	102	134	227	284
Direct investment inflow	265	183	305	317
Portfolio investment and				
institutional loans	59	5	416	373
Total	426	323	948	974

Efficiency of Capital Market

Problems associated with the adequacy and efficiency of the
Australian capital market may be discussed under four headings.
These are as follows:
1. excessive controls over banks and financial intermediaries;
2. Lack of development of institutional demand for long-term securities of business;
3. excessive development of market for government securities at the expense of developing an improved market for long-term securities of the business sector;
4. lack of foreign competition.

We have already discussed the official controls over the rates
that banks may offer on deposits and on bank overdraft rates. As a
result, lenders have been inclined to hold their assets in the form
of claims on nonbank financial intermediaries. The resulting rise
in the velocity of money has compelled the monetary authorities to
curb the expansion of bank deposits, reduced the extent to which business
has been financed by bank credit, and resulted in nonprice
rationing of bank funds to borrowers. Some misallocation of capital
market funds must result from these controls over interest rates.
Further, the banking sector tends to be squeezed, and the nonbank
sector stimulated as a result of the manner in which ceilings on

323

bank overdraft charge and deposit rates have kept these rates below competitive rates prevailing outside the banking system.

Official controls over savings bank lending and borrowing rates tend to have undesirable effects on the flow of funds through the capital market. Like the trading banks, savings banks are not free to offer competitive rates to attract deposits. Savings banks are subject to ceilings on rates they can charge on housing loans, which represents a significant subsidy to young couples buying their own home, at the expense of savings bank depositors. An important obstacle to raising ceilings on rates savings banks may apply to loans and deposits is the reluctance of governments to permit savings banks to compete for funds against the government bond market. Bond rates and savings deposit rates are linked in various ways, since government securities represent an important source of earnings for savings banks. During periods of rising interest rates, savings banks suffer disintermediation effects, as funds shift to building societies and finance companies.

As noted previously, there appears to be a contradiction in the development of financial institutions in Australia. The two largest financial intermediary institutions, the savings banks and life insurance companies, provide virtually no institutional demand for long-term securities of the business sector. The substantial financial development that has taken place in this country has not been accompanied by a parallel expansion in the market for business securities, at least where institutional demand for these securities is concerned. An important related factor is an excessive orientation of these and other financial institutions for government securities issued by the Commonwealth, states, local and special agencies of the government.

Finally, we should note that until 1971 very little competition was allowed to enter Australia in the way of foreign banks and financing companies. Government policy has prevented entry of foreign banks, except by means of nonbank affiliates conducting a nonbanking (factoring, leasing, merchant bank) business. A major argument in favor of permitting foreign banks to enter is that they might introduce new methods and ideas and competitively spur financial development in the direction of better servicing the medium-term and long-term financing needs of the business sector. A reason offered by the Australian banks to continue to prevent foreign bank entry is that overseas banks would skim off the profitable foreign exchange business, leaving low-profit branching operations to the Australian banking institutions.

GOVERNMENT POLICY AND INTERNATIONAL FINANCE

How Monetary Policy Works

The functions of the Reserve Bank of Australia resemble those performed by central banks in many other countries. They include exercising control over the banking system and management of growth in bank reserves and credit. The Reserve Bank works closely with the government in these matters, but retains an element of independence. The bank has the authority to create legal tender, which it makes available to the banks for use of their customers. The trading banks can borrow whatever amount of legal tender their customers require, ensuring an elastic currency. The central bank is banker to the government as well as lender of last resort to the trading banks.

The most significant function of the Reserve Bank is its role in stabilizing the economy, on the domestic expenditure side as well as with regard to international payments. Policies are worked out in close coordination with the Treasury. The bank has a number of monetary weapons at its disposal to influence the domestic economy and international payments.

Operations of the Reserve Bank are reflected in its balance sheet, which is reproduced in Table 16.9. Assets consist of gold and foreign exchange, government securities, and loans, advances and bills discounted. Liabilities consist of deposits of trading and savings banks, note issue outstanding, and capital and reserves representing the government's ownership in the bank. The banks maintain a number of different accounts in the Reserve Bank, including Statutory Reserve Deposits (SRDs), Term Loan Funds, Farm Development Loan Fund, and other deposits. These reserves may be frozen, not available to the banks for acquiring earning assets, or represent funds that the banks may draw upon for specific purposes (term lending and farm credits).

The government securities held by the Reserve Bank represent a collateral relative to the note issue. The Reserve Bank maintains segregated accounts for the Note Issue Department, which are consolidated in the data found in Table 16.9. Three types of assets are held in the Note Issue Department, representing the full amount of note issue, including gold and balances held abroad, overseas securities, and Australian government securities. An increase in notes on issue to banks or in banker's deposits with the Reserve Bank (except Statutory Reserve Deposits) permits the banks to create deposits. They can do this by lending or purchasing securities from the public, up to a multiple of their additional cash reserves. The central bank

325

TABLE 16.9

Reserve Bank of Australia Balance Sheet, June 1969*
(millions of dollars)

Liabilities		Assets	
Capital and reserves	60	Gold and foreign exchange	1,234
Notes on issue held by public	942	Treasury bills and Treasury notes	34
Notes on issue held by banks	161	Other government securities	789
Accounts of trading banks		Loans, advances and bills discounted and other assets	631
Statutory Reserve Deposits	568		
Term Loan Fund	29		
Farm Development Loan Fund	24		
Other deposits	6		
Deposits of savings banks	551		
Other liabilities	347		
Total	2,688	Total	2,688

*Liabilities and assets of the Reserve Bank of Australia central banking business (including Note Issue Department), average of weekly figures, June 1969.

Source: Reserve Bank of Australia, Statistical Bulletin.

may create additional "high-powered" money by purchasing a government security from a bank or the public, or by making a loan or advance to a bank. If the Reserve Bank acquires securities directly from the government, there is an increase in the government's account with the Reserve Bank (other liabilities in Table 16.9). When the government makes an expenditure from this account, there is a reduction in the government's account and a corresponding rise in the deposits of the banks. The central bank maintains a Rural Credits Department, which makes advances to state marketing authorities and cooperatives. This has the effect of increasing the money supply until these loans are repaid.

The Reserve Bank has a wide assortment of monetary weapons at its disposal, which permit it to influence interest rates, the money

supply, expenditures, and income. These include (1) direct controls
over bank liquidity, (2) open-market operations, (3) direct control
over interest rates, (4) discount policy, and (5) moral suasion.

The banks maintain a liquid-asset ratio of notes, banker's
deposits with the Reserve Bank, and government securities to deposits
of at least 18 percent. This is the lever with which the Reserve Bank
maintains quantitative controls over bank liquidity. In the past, the
central bank has influenced bank liquidity by call to and releases from
SRDs. Since the latter are not part of the trading banks' LGS assets,
the Reserve Bank can reduce LGS assets by increasing the SRD ratio
that banks must follow, thus making it necessary for the trading banks
to make transfers from their LGS assets. They could accomplish
this by transfers from their ordinary account with the Reserve Bank.
A reduction of LGS assets would require that banks follow policies
that reduce loans and deposits.

An increase in the SRD ratio from 9 percent to 10 percent would
reduce bank liquidity, while a reduction of this ratio to 8 percent would
increase bank liquidity. If a government surplus or balance of payments deficit should reduce the level of their deposits, banks may
find that they have excess SRDs. The Reserve Bank may wish to freeze
this additional liquidity by increasing the SRD ratio. Changes in the
SRD ratio provide the central bank with an effective means of placing
excess liquidity in a form that banks cannot use to expand credit in
the economy.

Open-market operations represent another major instrument
of central bank control in Australia. If the Reserve Bank purchases
government bonds from the public, this increases the level of bank
cash assets and deposits. Therefore, it increases the LGS ratio in
banks and permits them to expand credit. Open-market purchases
have effects that are similar to reduction in the SRD ratio, but also
enjoy certain advantages. An open-market purchase affects the liquidity of the public directly and without delay, while a reduction in the
SRD ratio does not. Also, open-market operations have a direct effect
on interest rates, which is transmitted readily through the bond and
money markets. Changes in the SRD ratio may not have this effect,
since the Reserve Bank maintains a direct control over the rates of
interest that banks may offer on fixed-interest-bearing deposits and
over the rates of interest banks charge on overdrafts.

As lender of last resort, the Reserve Bank may lend to the
banks when their liquidity falls. If the rate of interest charged by
the Reserve Bank is very high (penalty rate), the banks may be expected to exercise care in preventing their LGS ratio from falling
below the required 18 percent. When the central bank wishes to curb
bank lending, it may let it be known that bank borrowing from the
Reserve Bank will carry high interest rates. The rates at which the

TABLE 16.10

Balance of Payments of Australia
(millions of Australian dollars)

	1967-68	1968-69
Payments		
Imports, f.o.b.	3,159	3,203
Transportation	636	679
Travel	140	150
Government transactions	95	111
Other goods and services	97	104
Total imports of goods and services	4,127	4,247
Interest and dividends paid and profits remitted overseas	371	425
Undistributed income accruing to overseas residents	230	295
Personal remittances overseas	84	90
Public authority grants and contributions	154	159
Total credits to nonresidents	4,966	5,216
Receipts		
Exports, f.o.b.	2,941	3,217
Transportation	359	390
Travel	88	108
Government transactions	76	80
Other goods and services	91	95
Total exports of goods and services	3,555	3,890
Interest and dividends received from overseas	109	127
Undistributed income accruing from overseas residents	20	21
Personal remittances from overseas	154	164
Overseas balance on current account	1,128	1,014
Total debits to nonresidents	4,966	5,216

central bank lends to the trading banks are not published, as they are in most other countries.

Balance of Payments

The open-economy status of Australia suggests that balance of payments developments are of critical importance to national income, the volume of investment, and the state of the financial markets. Exports and foreign investment play a key role where the nation's economic performance is concerned.

The balance of payments for Australia is set out in Table 16.10. Australia incurs a deficit on current transactions of between $400 to $500 million, a deficit on foreign investment income of approximately $500 million, and surpluses on investment flows and remittances which approximately offset the two deficit areas.

Australia's foreign trade balance is moderately weighted in favor of imports. While merchandise imports are fairly diversified exports are heavily concentrated in two areas. Approximately one-third of the value of exports is accounted for by food items (meats and cereals) and another one-third by crude materials (textile fibers and metaliferous ores). In short, meat, wheat, cereals, wool and textile fibers, and metal ores constitute a high proportion of Australia's exports, leaving the country heavily dependent on a narrow commodity base insofar as balance of payments earnings are concerned. Seasonal and cyclical pressures are quite an important aspect of the Australian economy, as are fluctuations in commodity prices of major export items. These changing pressures inject a measure of instability into the financial sector, which the large trading banks and central bank are able to cushion.

During the 1960s, Australia received large amounts of foreign investment capital. Direct investment was by far larger than portfolio investment. In part, this difference may be attributable to government policies, which stimulate direct investment via tariff protection to domestic producers. Also, it may stem from lack of an adequate institutional mechanism through which foreign portfolio investment could flow into the country. This includes the investment banking firms, the depth and scope of the corporate bond and stock markets which, while active, are not of sufficient size to attract significant foreign investor attention.

Australian policy has prevented the establishment of foreign banking offices in the country and has limited foreign ownership of finance companies to not more than 25 percent of capital funds. A number of joint-venture merchant banks and finance companies have been established which include foreign partners. This suggests that in future the capital markets in Australia will benefit from additional institutional machinery with which to attract foreign portfolio investment and further develop open-market mechanisms in the allocation and distribution of capital funds.

REFERENCES

Australian Handbook, 1970.

Brash, Donald. American Investment in Australian Industry. Cambridge, Mass.: Harvard University Press, 1966.

Holder, R. F. "Australia." In W. F. Crick, Commonwealth Banking Systems. Oxford: Clarendon Press, 1965.

Perkins, J. O. N., and J. E. Sullivan. Banks and Capital Market: An Australian Study. Melbourne: Melbourne University Press, 1970.

Wilson, J. S. G. "The Australian Money Market," Banca Nazionale del Lavoro. Quarterly Review (March 1973).

Yearbook, Australia, 1970.

17

FINANCIAL MARKETS
IN SOUTH AFRICA

INTRODUCTION

South Africa is located in the lower southern part of the African continent, between the Atlantic and Indian oceans. In covers an area of 472,000 square miles excluding Southwest Africa (mandated territory). Its size is about one-sixth of the United States (excluding Alaska. The country lies between 22° and 35° south latitude, and the land rises fairly steeply in the east from sea level to a high interior plateau of about 6,000 feet, with mountains reaching to over 10,000 feet. Climate varies from "mediterranean" in the southwest to near tropical in the northeast. The Transvaal in the north is temperate, but the western Cape area has more rainfall. The diversity of climate enables South Africa to produce different crops, but large areas of the country are more suited for cattle and sheep ranches.

The most important natural resources in South Africa are mineral deposits, such as gold, diamonds, iron ore, coal, manganese, and chrome, all of which are found mainly in the Transvaal, the Orange Free State, and Natal. Beginning with the gold-mining industry, a vast industrial complex has been built in the northern area where the national capital, Pretoria, and the largest commercial center, Johannesburg, are located. There is an extensive railroad system in the country centering in Johannesburg, with lines leading to the country's three large seaports: Cape Town, Port Elizabeth, and Durban.

In 1973, South Africa had a population 23 million, of which whites accounted for 17.5 percent, coloreds 9.5 percent, Asians 3 percent, and Africans 70 percent. The most highly populated areas are Johannesburg, Pretoria, Cape Town, Durban, Port Elizabeth, and Pinetown.

At present, South Africa is the most industrialized and richest country in the African continent. Its dynamic economic development is attributed to its natural resources, government policy, and inflow of foreign capital. These factors have not only provided South Africa with national wealth, but also with problems—the racial problem and the inflation problem. A brief review of the political and economic history is necessary to understand the evolution of the financial framework of South Africa.

In 1652, Jan Van Riebeeck, an officer of the Dutch East India Company, sailing his ship from Holland to Batavia via the Cape of Good Hope, stepped ashore with instructions to build a fort and develop a farm in the Cape. The fort was to protect from attack by the British and the French; the farm was to provide a place for midway rest of the ship's crews.

At that time the land was sparsely populated. European immigrants, especially young people, gradually came to the Cape and developed farming and cattle ranches. In 1806, the British took over the Cape from the Dutch after Napolean invaded Holland. The British brought more settlers to the Cape in the 1820s, but many of their settlers still preferred to go to Canada, Australia, and New Zealand due to the lack of transportation in South Africa.

The discoveries of diamonds and gold in the period 1867-84 opened a new chapter in South Africa's history. British capital and labor poured into this rich land, and the railroads and coal mines supplemented the development of gold mines and diamond fields. The Johannesburg Stock Exchange mostly handled gold share transactions after its formation in 1889. The new wealth increased the economic conflicts between the British and the Boers. After the Anglo-Boer War (1899-1902), British power was supreme. The Union of South Africa was formed in 1910 under the British government, and its territory was further consolidated when Southwest Africa was taken from the defeated Germany after World War I.

As confidence in South Africa's economy increased, the South African Reserve Bank was founded in 1920 to regulate the money supply and inflow of foreign capital. South Africa broadened its economic base during the 1920s. The formation of the Iron and Steel Corporation (Iscor) is a case in point. During the 1930s when the world plunged into a whirl of economic depression and currency crisis, South Africa still enjoyed prosperity. This was due to the devaluation of the South African pound, which came close after sterling devaluation. World War II provided opportunity for South Africa's booming industry. Infrastructure was broadened in the 1950s when the Coal, Oil and Gas Corporation was formed. The economy continued to expand as new rich gold fields were discovered in the Orange Free State.

South Africa experienced a major crisis when it decided to withdraw from the British Commonwealth in 1961, due to its apartheid policy at home. When South Africa announced itself as a republic, Commonwealth nations removed their investments from the country. In coping with this national crisis, the South African government imposed restrictions on the outflow of foreign capital, on foreign exchange transactions, and on imports. Moreover, the South African rand replaced the pound as the national currency; government spending was increased to strengthen national industries and financial institutions. The main purpose of all of these measures was to develop economic self-sufficiency. But this trend was reversed in 1965 when foreign investments were returning to South Africa; the gold-mining industry was prosperous due to the international monetary crisis; more vigorous monetary and fiscal policies were implemented for a more balanced economic development on all fronts, including South Africa's financial markets and institutions.

As indicated in Table 17.1, South Africa's gross national product (GNP) advanced at an average rate of about 6 percent in real terms in the period 1963-72. It is noted that the consumer price index and the growth of money supply advanced more rapidly after 1971. Personal saving as a percentage of disposable income was about 9 percent in 1972 compared with an annual average of about 11 percent during the 1960s. Increased consumer demand for household appliances and transportation vehicles was the main factor in the inflationary spurt after 1971. Per-capita-income figures in South Africa do not have the same meaning as in other industrialized countries since wage differentials between white union workers and African workers are extremely wide. The growth of African workers' wages of 20 percent in 1972 has narrowed the gap somewhat. At any rate, South Africa's economy still demonstrates vigorous growth regardless of the racial problem.

THE ROLE OF GOVERNMENT IN NATIONAL
ECONOMY AND FINANCE

Government Participation in the Economy

Like many other nations influenced by the British, South Africa has retained a private enterprise system. Government participates in the national economy when the situation requires. The general policy of the government has been to build infrastructure and to develop natural resources. The government first took an active role in guiding the national economy in 1903 when water supply was developed by a government public utility in the Witwatersrand. In 1912, the Land and Agricultural Bank was formed to extend loans to farmers. Between 1920 and 1940, many basic industries such as iron,

TABLE 17.1

Selected Economic and Financial Indicators
(millions of rands)

Year	GNP	Growth of Real GNP (In percent)	Per-Capita Income (rand)
1963	6,305	8.1	322
1964	6,936	6.7	348
1965	7,576	6.6	372
1966	8,231	4.7	394
1967	9,110	7.6	421
1968	9,758	3.8	438
1969	10,913	7.0	475
1970	11,908	5.2	502
1971	13,260	4.0	530
1972	14,850	3.5	585

	Annual Rate of Increase		Gross Domestic
	Consumer Price Index	Money Supply	Investment as Percent of GNP
1963	1.9%	10%	26.2
1964	2.6	9	25.6
1965	4.1	2	25.2
1966	3.9	9	25.6
1967	3.8	6	27.6
1968	2.3	18	25.2
1969	3.8	11	24.6
1970	4.9	1	22.9
1971	7.1	8	23.4
1972	8.6	14	25.0

Source: South African Reserve Bank, Quarterly Bulletin, September 1973.

steel, and electricity were established. The formation of the Industrial Development Corporation in 1940 reflected the intent of government to broaden its influence on industry. The South African Coal, Oil and Gas Corporation (Sasol) began operation in 1949 to provide liquid fuel for the expanding economy. The establishment of the Fisheries Development Corporation in 1946 and the Phosphate Development Corporation in 1952 demonstrated the increasing role of government in developing basic products that have been significant to national consumption and international trade. The ambitious Orange River Development Project undertaken by the government in the 1960s should have a significant influence on power supply, irrigation, and farm production. As Table 17.2 indicates, the share of the public sector has grown from 17.9 percent of GNP in 1960 to 27.5 percent in 1972. In the 1960s, the central government sector and public corporations have grown faster than the provincial and local sectors. In 1972, GNP was R14,850 million of which consumption accounted for 62 percent, government expenditure 23 percent, and business investment 15 percent. Obviously, the South African governments have increasingly played a more important role in the national economy.

Government Finance

Since the central government and public corporations have significantly influenced the national economy, the amounts of government revenue, expenditure, and financing have had a substantial influence on South African financial markets. As illustrated in Table 17.3, government deficit spending has increased faster than government revenue as a result of increased investment in public corporations and infrastructure. Deficit financing has mostly relied on domestic borrowing, emphasizing private sector sources of funds to reduce "demand pull" inflation. Foreign borrowing has fluctuated from year to year, but total foreign debt has been steady. Use of cash balances has required withdrawal of stabilization funds from the Treasury.

TABLE 17.2

Percentage of Public Sector Expenditure in
Total Gross Domestic Product

	1960	1969	1972
Central government sector	7.5	11.2	23.9
Provincial administration	5.6	6.3	
Local authorities	3.6	3.4	
Public corporations	1.2	2.6	3.2
Total	17.9	23.5	27.5

Sources: The Third Report of the Franzen Commission, 1970, p. 12; South African Reserve Bank, Quarterly Bulletin, September 1973.

TABLE 17.3

Central Government's Revenue, Expenditure, and Financing
(millions of rands)

	1966	1970	1971	1972
Revenue	1371	2302	2586	2983
Expenditure	1649	2702	3438	3751
Deficits	-278	-400	-852	-768
Financing				
Net domestic borrowing	472	173	454	902
From: monetary system	227	-34	71	304
Public Debt Commissioners	94	171	122	49
private sector	151	36	261	549
Net foreign borrowing	-27	128	132	93
Use of cash balances	-167	97	266	-227
Total domestic debt	3631	5144	5598	6505
Total foreign debt	121	167	176	142

Source: International Monetary Fund (IMF), International Financial Statistics, September 1973.

Public Debt Commissioners represented the ownership of public debt by various government agencies such as government pension funds, social security, and postal savings.

The government's borrowing power is limited by the General Loan Act of 1964 as approved by the South African Parliament. This act can be amended when necessary. In 1972, the amount of total central government debt was 6,647 million rands, of which 5,462 million represented long-term borrowing and 1,185 million was in the form of short-term debt. Most long-term government bonds were held by the Public Debt Commissioners and nonbank financial institutions. On the other hand, short-term Treasury bills were held by the National Financial Corporation, commercial banks, and discount houses. The central bank, the South African Reserve Bank, accounted for about 2 percent of the total government securities holding. Open-market operations have not been important as a monetary tool. Instead, discount policy has been emphasized.

As far as fiscal policy is concerned, the Franzen Commission suggested that use should be made of indirect taxes as a main instrument of fiscal policy, because the side effects of indirect taxes are minimal whereas the side effects of direct taxes are far greater, and work at the expense of savings rather than consumption. Any increases in income tax probably would not be sufficiently antiinflationary because strong labor unions tend to demand higher wages to make up for the increased taxes. The commission also noted that 60 percent of the outstanding marketable public debt in 1970 was held by the Public Debt Commissioners. Related to this, manufacturing industry could not expand sufficiently because of high interest rates. The commission recommended that the Reserve Bank Act be amended to permit achieving a better flow of funds between the public and the private sectors.

FINANCIAL INSTITUTIONS

Government Financial Institutions

Since the South African government has intended to develop the national economy and has taken initiatives in certain sectors, various special financial institutions were created to finance this development. Moreover, the central bank has had overall power to regulate all financial institutions under the guidance of the finance minister. There are four major government financial institutions: the Reserve Bank of South Africa, the National Finance Corporation, the Industrial Development Corporation (IDC), and the Land and Agricultural Bank.

The Reserve Bank of South Africa

The Reserve Bank of South Africa is the central bank and is privately owned with its shares listed on the stock exchange. The bank is subject to government guidance. Shareholders elect six of its directors, and the government appoints six, including the governor and three deputy governors. The bank is the government's fiscal agent, foreign exchange administrator and regulator, and sole note issue authority. It is required by law to hold a reserve in gold and foreign assets equal to 25 percent of its notes and liabilities. Before 1965, its liquidity controls were mainly exercised on commercial banks, but subsequently all banking institutions have come under its influence by the Banking Amendment Act of 1964. The bank controls credit by use of the rediscount rate and a system of compulsory cash and liquid asset requirements. Since 1972, all banking institutions other than discount houses must maintain a minimum 8 percent cash reserve balance, which has to be kept at the Reserve Bank, and a supplementary cash reserve of 10 percent, which must be kept at the

National Finance Corporation. All banking institutions must maintain liquid assets in specified proportions to liabilities. The ratio varies according to the term of deposit and other liabilities.

The Reserve Bank intervenes in the money market through the issue of 91-day Treasury bills and medium- and long-term bonds, but the central bank does not conduct open-market operations even though it buys and sells government securities at fixed rates. To supplement the tools mentioned above, in 1965 the Reserve Bank introduced a new monetary technique, ceilings on bank lending. As Table 17.4 reflects, credit expansion did slow down in the period 1970-72, but inflation was not checked due to the continued inflow of foreign capital. The Franzen Commission recommended that the Reserve Bank be given the power to issue credit directives and lay down penalties when its directives are not compiled with.

National Finance Corporation

The establishment of the National Finance Corporation in 1949 signified the beginning of the money market in South Africa. The principal function of the corporation is to mobilize temporarily idle funds of all banks, South African Railway, and local governments for purchasing Treasury bills and government bonds, which constitute about 50 percent of its assets. It also accepts deposits at rates lower than market and buys Land Bank bills. The corporation is very active in the call money market and stands between commercial banks and the Reserve Bank as a cushion for liquidity. The rise of the discount houses has reduced the importance of this semigovernment-owned organization in the growing money market.

TABLE 17.4

Changes in Bank Credit Expansion
(millions of rands)

	To Private Sector	To Government Sector	Total Amount	Percentage Increase
1970	432	182	614	18.3
1971	314	270	584	14.7
1972	243	133	376	8.2

Source: South African Reserve Bank, Annual Report, 1972.

338

Industrial Development Corporation
(IDC)

This corporation was formed by the government in 1940 to promote new industries. It takes equity positions (up to 40 percent), but
normally sells its equity investments to the public after they mature.
IDC has invested heavily in state-owned enterprises, but has also
assisted private ventures in needed areas, such as textile and paper
products. IDC from time to time acts as guarantor to arrange foreign
credit with the United States, United Kingdom, French, Belgium, and
Italian banks for medium-term credit extended to South African companies or infrastructure development in the border areas.

The Land and Agricultural Bank

The bank began operations in 1912 to assist agricultural crop
financing. During the period 1960-64, a series of droughts required
stable financial assistance. The bank also provides short-term
financing. The Land and Agricultural Bank has been a main source
of meeting these needs, and the bank is exempt from the ceiling on
lending. The major source of the bank's funds is the Reserve Bank.

Private Banking Institutions

The commercial banking system in South Africa parallels the
British pattern. Banking development has been closely related to
the gold-mining industry, retaining links with the London financial
market. In 1887, Cecil Rhodes formed a "group system" to finance
gold mining. In 1889, Johannesburg Consolidated Investment Corporation was founded. In 1891, the National Bank of South Africa was
incorporated. After the passage of the Banking and Currency Act in
1910, the Standard Bank and Barclays Bank emerged as strong financial
institutions. Changing financial circumstances during the 1920s and
1930s resulted in many mergers of banks and banking concentration.
Banks in South Africa held gold and silver as a first line of liquidity
and transferred secondary reserves to the London money market.
Interest rate differentials between London and Johannesburg could
cause the transfer of funds between banks in these two cities.
After World War II, especially since the 1960s, South African
financial institutions have become more independent of the London
market. The growth of banking institution assets was more than double
between 1964 and 1972. Merchant banks, hire-purchase savings
banks, and other deposit-receiving institutions such as building societies have had faster growth rates and increased their share of total
banking assets in the same period.

Commercial Banks

There are nine commercial banks with about 1,000 branches operating in South Africa. All are privately owned, and some are owned by foreign banks. The four major banks, Barclays National Bank, Standard Bank of South Africa, Volkskas, and Nedbank, have branches in South Africa and also in Southwest Africa, Botswana, Lesotho, and Swaziland. Of total commercial bank domestic deposits (about 4 million rands) in 1972, 47 percent were demand, 13 percent long term, 18 percent savings, 19 percent medium term, and 3 percent short term. The most important assets of commercial banks were short-term credits to businesses and individuals. Remittance in transit (between South Africa and the United Kingdom), short-term government securities, and call money loans to discount houses are of lesser importance. Overdrafts, Treasury bills, and trade bills are insignificant. The other five commercial banks include the Trust Bank, French Bank of South Africa, First National City Bank of the United States, the South African Bank of Athens, and Bank of Lisbon and South Africa. They conduct a full range of banking business. The Bank of Tokyo, the Union Bank of Switzerland, the Dresdner Bank, and several other foreign banks have representative offices in South Africa.

TABLE 17.5

Size of Various Banking Institutions

	Total Assets (millions of rands)			Share in Total Assets (percent)		
	1964	1970	1972	1964	1970	1972
Commercial banks	2,044	3,827	4,680	62.9	58.7	60.2
Merchant banks	264	542	651	8.1	8.3	8.4
Hire-purchase, savings, and general banks	744	1,792	2,004	22.9	27.5	25.8
Discount houses	200	363	438	6.1	5.5	5.6
Total	3,252	6,524	7,773	100.0	100.0	100.0

Sources: Third Report of the Franzen Commission on Fiscal and Monetary Policy, 1970, p. 178; Reserve Bank of South Africa, Quarterly Bulletin, September 1973.

Merchant Banks

There were eight merchant banks in South Africa in 1972, of which the Central Merchant Bank was the largest. Their major sources of funds are demand, medium- and long-term deposits; their major assets are acceptance credits, call loans to discount houses, and government securities. They have played an ever-increasing role in financing industry.

Hire-Purchase, Savings Bank, and Building Societies

These deposit-taking institutions receive funds from savers, especially long-term deposits. About 60 percent of electrical appliances and furniture sales and the great majority of auto sales are made on hire-purchase credit. About 84 percent of the assets of the building societies go to the private individual mortgage. Trust companies also extend mortgage loans and raise their funds through sale of "participation bonds."

Discount Houses

There were three discount houses in 1972, of which National Discount House was the largest and accounted for about 50 percent of the total assets of all discount houses. They are an important channel for investment of call money by companies, commercial banks, and merchant banks with large liquid resources. Discount houses purchase three-month Treasury bills and thus provide short-term finance for the government. They also discount trade bills related to the purchase of goods and thus render important services to private companies.

Nonbanking Financial Institutions

This group includes long-term and short-term insurance companies, private pension funds, and unit trusts (mutual funds). Insurance companies began operations before World War I, but pension funds and unit trusts were products of World War II. At the end of 1971, the total assets of these institutions were: Long-term insurers had R2,846 million; short-term insurers had R205 million; pension funds has R2.099 million; and unit trusts had R543 million. The investment policies of these institutions have varied, but favor common stocks. In addition, long-term insurers hold mortgage and government bonds; short-term insurers hold substantial liquid assets and

short-term government securities; pension funds give equal emphasis
to bond investments of local and provincial governments and the
central government. These institutions have performed an important
function in the development of the South African capital market in the
1960s.

FINANCIAL MARKETS

Money Market

The development of the South African money market can be
traced through several different stages. Before the establishment
of the Reserve Bank of South Africa in 1920, interest differentials
and the availability of funds in the London market were quickly noted
by South African bankers, and determined whether or not they would
transfer their surplus liquid assets to London. In case of need for
working capital, short-term funds were called from London for the
home market. After 1920, the Reserve Bank was authorized to regulate
the money supply, interest rates, and foreign exchange, but the powerful London market still limited the independence of the Reserve Bank.
The domestic money market was substantially strengthened when the
National Financial Corporation was formed in 1949 to create a viable
short-term financial market as previously explained. The growth
of banking financial institutions and the increased liquid assets of
the railways and gold mines stimulated the call loan, discount, and
Treasury bill market sectors during the 1950s. Like the Canadian
money market, the short-term money market in South Africa was an
official creation and has served the national purpose, especially
after 1960 when South Africa severed relations with the Commonwealth.

From 1960 to 1963, the South African government used all financial resources available at home to counteract the absence of foreign
capital inflow. During this period, the central bank expanded credit
and lowered the bank rate to 3.5 percent, the lowest in the decade.
All financial institutions including commercial banks, merchant banks,
hire-purchase and savings banks, and building societies expanded
credits rapidly until 1965 when the Reserve Bank put a ceiling on
bank lending in order to fight inflation. However, the continued expanding economy forced the private sector and the provincial governments
to use foreign credits. Threat of inflation generated by inflow of
foreign capital and consumer finance led the Reserve Bank to impose
controls on interest rates paid by banking institutions (March 1972).
Commercial banks and building societies could pay a maximum rate

of 6 percent for six-month deposits and $7\frac{1}{2}$ percent for one-year deposits. At the end of the year, the intercompany loan rate was 6 percent; the rate for consumer credit was 10 to 15 percent; three-month certificates of deposit (CDs) could earn 6 percent; the Treasury bill yield was $5\frac{1}{2}$ percent; the 3- to 8-year-term loan rate was 10 percent; and the central bank lending rate was $5\frac{1}{2}$ percent.

The size of the money market in South Africa is difficult to assess because there are no specific statistics for CDs (they are included in the fixed-term deposits category), for overdrafts (included in advances), and for intercompany loans. The best estimate for 1972 is as follows: R120 million of Treasury bills, R270 million of fixed short-term deposits, about R500 million call loans from commercial banks and merchant banks to National Finance Corporation and discount houses, and R2,954 million of advanced nonliquid discounts. The total amount was R3,844 million, or about 26 percent of South Africa's GNP. This is a high ratio in comparison with other industrial nations such as the United States and Canada.

The call money area is the most active among all money market sectors. This is because it involves all banking institutions and large business firms, as well as the National Finance Corporation. It reflects the day-to-day liquidity positions of all these institutions. The volume of call money determines the extent of Treasury bill, trade bill, and banker's acceptance holdings of the discount and acceptance houses. In this respect, the money market in Johannesburg is very much like that in London.

In terms of volume, advances and discount are the largest short-term assets in all deposit-receiving institutions except the discount houses. Commercial banks have the lion's share in the market, especially the overdrafts by businesses and individuals. Fixed short-term deposits, which include negotiable CDs, are less important than fixed medium-term deposits. Short-term government securities also have a good market for banking and nonbanking financial institutions, but the Treasury bill only accounts for about 1/8 of the total amount of short-term government securities. Therefore, CDs and Treasury bills stand somewhere between the most liquid call money and the nonliquid discounts.

It is noted that the small volume of Treasury bills outstanding and the absence of a commercial paper market make open-market operations by the Reserve Bank unnecessary. Treasury bills are auctioned weekly with the participation of commercial banks and discount houses. The Reserve Bank is the lender of last resort, but call money adjusts liquidity positions very well, and the Reserve Bank does not use open-market operations to control liquidity. It has been suggested that the strengthening of open-market operations and the creation of a national exchange market as exists in Canada may help the South African money market to develop further. The counter-argument is that as long as the money market serves the purpose of national economic growth and reflects a satisfactory performance in connection with the London market, the market mechanism should not be disturbed.

Capital Market

The exploration for and discovery of diamonds in 1867 and gold in 1884 were financed by local capital. The inflow of British capital and establishment of the Johannesburg Stock Exchange in 1889 marked the beginning of the capital market in South Africa. Railways and gold mines continued to attract foreign capital before World War II. Gold shares were quoted in both the Johannesburg and London stock exchanges. Increased government participation in the national economy after World War II changed the capital market somewhat as government stocks, especially long term, have absorbed substantial amounts of capital from the Public Debt Commissioners and nonbank financial institutions.

In 1972, total gross domestic investment was R4,101 million (27.6 percent of GNP), while total new issues of marketable securities (Table 17.6) was R1,187 million, representing 25 percent of gross

TABLE 17.6

Net Issues of Marketable Securities
(millions of rands)

| | Central Government | Public Copera-tions | Private Sector | | Sub-total | Total |
			Bonds and Preferred	Common Stocks		
1963	184	69	14.4	74.2	89	342
1966	437	75	36.0	126.5	162	674
1968	511	143	20.1	309.4	329	983
1969	344	114	55.3	409.7	465	923
1970	211	70	80.5	55.2	136	417
1971	325	157	113.8	69.3	183	665
1972	772	243	58.1	113.5	172	1,187

Source: South African Reserve Bank, Quarterly Bulletin, September 1973.

344

domestic investment. Approximately 75 percent of investment was financed by internal sources of funds (depreciation allowances and retained earnings) and short-term funds. In the 1960s, new issues of securities have reflected the ups and downs in the government, public corporation, and private sector. It is noted that new issues by the government in 1972 were mostly absorbed by the Public Debt Commissioners. Public corporations also stepped up borrowing from nonfinancial institutions, mainly the Public Debt Commissioners. The private sector shows a decline in securities issues since 1969 as a result of the tight market and high interest rates. New issues by the private sector in 1968-69 were responding to the inflow of foreign capital to South Africa due to the gold crisis in the international financial markets.

The primary market has been active in the past 10 years for many reasons. First, the continued development of manufacturing and gold-mining activities has stimulated long-term investment. Second, building societies, insurance companies, and pension funds have played important roles in the mortgage and stock markets. Third, investment has responded to capital incentives and tax incentives initiated by the government for decentralizing industries from the Pretoria-Witwatersrand area to the underdeveloped areas such as the Bantu homelands. Finally, the vigorous growth of merchant banks serving as lenders as well as underwriters has facilitated the distribution of private issues.

The distribution of equity issues may take place through rights offerings which are less expensive, or private placements which are popular in South Africa, or public offerings which are more expensive but prestigious. In 1969, when the security market was prosperous, many equity issues were oversubscribed 15 times (the Otis Elevator Company of the United States). Corporate debt financing is not commonly used, but convertible bond issues are enjoying some popularity. However, the bond market is facing some difficulties due to continued inflation.

The secondary capital market in South Africa has been developing since the formation of the Johannesburg Stock Exchange in 1889. This exchange handled mostly gold shares up to World War II. This is the only stock exchange in South Africa that is organized as a voluntary association. There is no government supervisory agency comparable to the U.S. Securities and Exchange Commission, but the exchange exercises disciplinary powers of its own. At June 1973, there were about 900 securities listed on the exchange, 97 percent of which were ordinary shares, and 3 percent preferred stocks and bonds. There are about 100 brokerage firms handling security transactions in the big cities such as Johannesburg, Cape Town, Port Elizabeth, Durban, and Bloemfontein. About 53 percent of the outstanding equities are held by individuals and the rest by institutions. Individuals are encouraged to buy stocks by government tax policy. For instance, personal income not exceeding R2,600 can benefit from a 100-percent dividend income deduction; R4,000 income can obtain a 58-percent dividend income deduction; and income over R4,600 receives no deduction. Institutions such as insurance companies and private pension funds have substantially increased their holdings of ordinary shares to hedge against inflation.

As illustrated in Table 17.7, share prices increased in 1966 and 1969. This is primarily attributed to the heavy purchases by nonbank financial institutions and foreign investors. It is also interesting to observe that since 1961 different industry share prices have displayed a variety of trends. Industrial and commercial shares have advanced more than mining and gold shares. On the contrary, dividend yields have declined from over 10 percent in 1961 to 4.23 percent in April 1973. The most popular of the "blue chips" were traded at prices 50 times earnings in 1969. These trends contrast sharply with the movement in yields on the government's long-term fixed-interest borrowings. Interest rates paid by the Reserve Bank and the Treasury have been raised progressively from 5 percent in 1964 to 8.13 percent in 1972. In this period, yields on municipal bonds increased from 5.61 to 8.5 percent; mortgage bond yields went from 6 to 9 percent. The majority of bond issues are transacted on the over-the-counter market.

TABLE 17.7

Share Prices, Yields, and Stock Exchange Activities

	Prices of All Shares	Dividend Yields (Industrials)	Number of Shares Traded
1963	100 (base period)	4.88	100 (base period)
1966	135	5.06	76
1968	202	4.21	186
1969	247	3.42	270
1970	155	5.02	151
1971	142	5.99	138
1972	190	5.15	250
1973 (April)	228	4.23	188

Source: South African Reserve Bank, Quarterly Bulletin, September 1973.

GOVERNMENT POLICY AND
INTERNATIONAL FINANCE

Foreign Exchange and Investment

From 1910 to 1961, the currency of South Africa was the South African pound, which was kept approximately at par with the pound sterling. In the period 1931-32, the close parity was broken when sterling had been devalued, but South Africa remained on the gold standard. In February 1961, South Africa adopted a decimal currency with the "rand" as the basic monetary unit. As required by law, the Reserve Bank holds a reserve in gold and foreign assets equal to at least 25 percent of its notes and liabilities. In December 1971, the South African government devalued the rand by 12.28 percent in response to the Smithsonian Agreement and parallel with the U.S. dollar devaluation of 7.8 percent. In 1972, the rand was once again devalued by 4.402 percent. This had a favorable effect on the South African balance of payments, but worked against curbing domestic inflation. When the U.S. dollar was devalued in February 1973, the rand appreciated by 11.1 percent vis-à-vis the dollar. At present, 1 rand equals 1.4908 U.S. dollars.

It has long been the South African government's policy to encourage foreign investment capital, especially British capital. The business cycles of the South African economy have been fundamentally affected by gold production (which accounts for 80 percent of world gold production excluding USSR production) and the inflow of foreign capital. The inflow of foreign capital generally has favored South Africa's balance of payments, but has tended to raise domestic price levels. The government has taken measures to offset these influences. In 1960, investments of Commonwealth countries in South Africa accounted for over 80 percent of total foreign investment in that country. In 1961, when South Africa left the Commonwealth because of its apartheid policies, foreign investments were withdrawn for several years (1961-64). To deal with this critical situation, the South African government established the "blocked" rand and used tax subsidies to stimulate domestic capital formation and investment. Under the "blocked account," investors who sold their securities had to buy and hold government bonds for a period of five years prior to capital repatriation. However, interest earned from bonds could be remitted freely to any foreign country. As of September 1973, the Reserve Bank restricted local borrowings by foreign-controlled companies. A technical formula is used for computation of the percentage of foreign ownership and the percentage of borrowings allowed. The

TABLE 17.8

Balance of Payments
(millions of rands)

	1960	1968	1971	1972
Merchandise exports, f.o.b.	879	1,513	1,538	2,197
Net gold output	530	769	922	1,161
Service receipts	168	486	640	730
Merchandise imports, f.o.b.	-1,127	-1,885	-2,890	-2,817
Service payments	-424	-880	-1,224	-1,326
Total goods and services (net)	26	3	-1,014	-55
Transfers (net)	-5	72	40	62
Balance on current account	21	75	-974	7
Capital movements Private sector	-165	389	539	306
Central government and banking	12	70	196	91
Total capital movements (net)	-153	459	735	397
Balance of payments transactions	-132	534	-239	404
Change in gold and foreign exchange reserves	-132	534	-156	437
Special drawing rights allocations	—	—	83	33
Total international reserves	171	1,471	711	1,290

Source: South African Reserve Bank, Quarterly Bulletin.

Franzen Commission recommended that the government bring in local shareholders to the extent of 50 percent within a reasonable period. No time limit has yet been set.

It is noted that the foreign investment patterns in South Africa have changed somewhat during the 1960s. For example, total foreign investment in 1966 was R3,810 million, of which the United Kingdom accounted for 63.5 percent, the United States for 15.5 percent, and Western Europe for 16.5 percent. In 1971, total foreign investment in South Africa was R7,043 million, of which the UK share was

55.2 percent, the U.S. share remained unchanged, and the Western European share increased to 25 percent. Foreign direct (R4,220 million in 1971) and indirect investments have been concentrated in mining, manufacturing, insurance, and finance industry sectors. According to the United States Department of Commerce, the rate of return on U.S. direct investment in South Africa in the period 1960-71 was 17.3 to 20.6 percent, above the average rate of return on all U.S. direct investments overseas (between 10.1 and 11.4 percent in the same period).

Balance of Payments

In the period 1946-72, the current account of the South African balance of payments has shown continued deficits except in the short periods 1959-63 and 1968-72, when South Africa increased exports and gold production. From 1964 to 1972, deficits on current account were covered by inflows of capital and by the movement of gold and foreign exchange reserves. The large surpluses on overall payments in 1968 and 1972 enabled the central bank to accumulate international reserves, which stood at R1,290 million in 1972. The major problems in the South African balance of payments have been the drastic increases in imports of capital goods and consumer goods and service payments such as dividends, interest, and insurance. Fortunately, the rising price of gold has helped the South African government to finance deficits and to build up international reserves. At present, the South African government encourages exports and gold output. On the other hand, it imposes restrictions on imports and foreign exchange. The purpose of these actions is to stimulate domestic economic development and to reduce deficits on its balance of payments.

With regard to other international financial activities, South Africa is a member of the International Monetary Fund (IMF) and the World Bank. It is also a member of a customs union with Botswana, Lesotho, Swaziland, and Namibia since 1910. In this common market agreement, South Africa collects tariff revenues and distributes them to other member nations. In connection with international trade, the United Kingdom, United States, Japan, and West Germany account for over 60 percent of imports and exports. In recent years, the South African government has increased investments in bordering countries, not only to develop goodwill and friendly relations, but also to develop an export market. Nevertheless, a strong financial tie continues with London, New York, and Western European financial centers.

REFERENCES

The Banker (London). "South African Money Market," September 1971.

Houghton, D. Hobart. The South African Economy. 2nd ed. London: Oxford University Press, 1967.

The Johannesburg Stock Exchange. The Stock Exchange Handbook, 1973.

Perkins, J.O.N., ed. Macro-Economic Policy, a comparative study on Australia-Canada-New Zealand-South Africa. Toronto: University of Toronto Press, 1973.

"Report of the (Franzen) Commission of Inquiry into Fiscal and Monetary Policy in South Africa," 1969-70.

South African Journal of Economics, various issues.

United Nations. Foreign Investment in the Republic of South Africa. New York: United Nations, 1970.

18

INTRODUCTION

Mexico, a southern neighbor of the United States, is the third largest republic in Latin America after Brazil and Argentina. It possesses a land area of some 761,000 square miles with a population of approximately 51 million in 1970. Despite her exotic beauty which attracts many tourists, much of the Mexican land is hostile to economic activity. The terrain in the north and the south is steep and rugged, and some areas are deficient in moisture. Climate in Mexico varies from tropical in some coastal areas to cool and even frosty in the upper highlands of the Sierra Madre mountain ranges. Seaports such as Veracruz, Tampico, and Acapulco have not been developed for commercial purposes. However, oil, mineral resources, and some agricultural products such as cotton and livestock have provided a valuable base for Mexican economic development.

Due to the geographical proximity, Mexico's governmental system is similar to that of the United States, with separation of powers among the three major branches of government. With 29 states, 2 federal territories, and the federal district, the powerful executive branch shapes the political, economic, and financial environment. However, the president is restricted by the Mexican Constitution to one six-year term of office. Since there is no vice-president, a provisional president is elected by the Senate in case of death or removal of the president. For this reason, national economic policy depends heavily on the philosophy of the one-term president, especially his attitude toward foreign investment.

Adoption of the Mexican Constitution in 1917 has provided a stable government as well as a sound framework for economic growth. The firm commitment of the Mexican government since adoption of the 1917 constitution has resulted in moving toward this goal. The agrarian reform in the 1920s created the Ejido system, under which about 40 percent of the tillable land is owned and worked by cooperative farmers. The nationalization of foreign enterprises, such as petroleum and railroads in 1938, established a firm policy of government control over essential industries. The employment of foreign aid and the encouragement of foreign investment after World War II had a stimulating effect on Mexican industrial development even though foreign ownership of Mexican companies is still a precarious situation. The striking economic achievements during the 1960s have improved the living standards of the Mexican people and created a good base for continuous growth in future decades. Reflecting this achievement, the London Economist once referred to Mexico as "the Japan of the Western Hemisphere."

The decade of the 1960s witnessed solid achievement for the Mexican economy. The growth of real gross domestic product (GDP) in the period 1960-70 was 7.1 percent per annum (see Table 18.1) and per-capita income rose from $336 to $555. In 1971, the Mexican economic growth rate declined to 3.7 percent, the lowest in over a decade. This resulted from readjustment due to inflationary pressure and growing external debts. In 1972, the growth rate advanced to 7.2 percent. The most advanced sector of the Mexican economy is manufacturing industry, which accounts for about 25 percent of GDP and which employs 20 percent of the labor force. The service and commercial sectors account for 45 percent of GDP. The diversification of manufactured and agricultural products has helped to balance Mexican economic development and increased exports, especially to the Latin American Free Trade Association (LAFTA) countries, of which Mexico is a member. Regardless of the chronic currency crises in the Western world in recent years and the economic stagnation in many less developed countries, Mexico has enjoyed relative price stability, a stable currency, increased international reserves, and, above all, a high economic growth rate.

Undoubtedly, there are many problems confronting the Mexican government. First, the inequality of income distribution is a cause of concern. As mentioned by the Newsletter published by the President's Office (September 1972), 10 percent of the Mexican people receive 50 percent of the GDP, and the 50 percent of the people with lowest incomes receive only 10 percent of GDP. Second, economic development is unbalanced among regions. The northern states close to the United States have benefited from the Northern Border Industrial Program. Also, in the Mexico City Plateau, the economy is better developed, and people enjoy high income. South of the Plateau to the Yucatan Peninsula, the economy has remained underdeveloped. Third, industrial development is concentrated in the Mexico City metropolitan area, which has attracted about one-fifth

TABLE 18.1

Mexico's Gross Domestic Product and Money Supply,
1960–72

	Money supply (billions of pesos, year end)	Growth Rate (in percent)	Current GDP (millions of pesos)	Growth Rate (in percent)	Real GDP 1960 prices (in millions of pesos)	Growth Rate (in percent)
1960	16.89	(9.5)	150.51	(13.2)	150.51	(7.8)
1961	18.01	(6.6)	163.27	(8.5)	157.93	(4.9)
1962	20.27	(12.5)	176.03	(7.8)	165.31	(4.7)
1963	23.68	(16.8)	195.98	(11.3)	178.52	(8.0)
1964	27.64	(16.7)	231.37	(18.1)	199.39	(11.7)
1965	29.52	(6.8)	252.03	(8.9)	212.32	(6.5)
1966	32.75	(10.9)	280.09	(11.1)	227.04	(6.9)
1967	35.39	(8.1)	306.32	(9.4)	241.27	(6.3)
1968	39.99	(13.0)	339.15	(10.8)	260.90	(8.1)
1969	44.34	(10.9)	374.90	(10.5)	277.40	(6.3)
1970	49.01	(10.4)	423.10	(12.9)	298.70	(7.7)
1971	53.06	(8.3)	455.40	(8.8)	307.50	(3.7)
1972	64.30	(21.0)	515.00	(13.1)	329.60	(7.2)

Source: Bank of Mexico.

of the nation's population. This has created problems of jobs, housing, water supply, and public health in that area. Fourth, the high population growth rate, averaging 3.5 percent annually in the 1960s, has offset the gains from increasing output and aggravated the already critical unemployment situation. In the agricultural area where the average annual growth rate in production has been less than 4 percent, the people did not improve their livelihood at all since the rural area accounted for a higher population increase. Fifth, foreign capital in Mexico represents about 10 percent of total investment. A continuous influx of foreign capital may increase the burden of debt service and therefore jeopardize the balance of payments in the long run.

In order to alleviate the problems mentioned above, the present administration has made efforts in every strategic area. The focal points of federal policy are as follows:

1. To maintain a continued viable economic growth and a balanced economy, the federal government plays a key role in the allocation of economic resources and the introduction of foreign capital and technology toward the national goals of "Mexicanization" and "industrialization."

2. Toward a more equal distribution of income, the 1972 Tax Reform emphasized progressive taxes on salaries, wages, and especially on capital.

3. Since more than half of all industries and two-thirds of credits are concentrated in the Valley of Mexico, the federal government has provided an Industrial Development Fund (1971) for regional investment outside the valley. The federal government also gives incentives to private industry up to 100 percent tax exemption and technical and financial assistance for investment in other needed areas.

4. Foreign capital is welcome only if it improves Mexican technology, fosters the development of new, dynamic industries, and produces goods for export.

5. The government policy of Mexicanization initiated by the 1961 Mexicanization Law has a double meaning. When it applies to foreign ownership, it means that no foreigners can own more than 49 percent of any Mexican company. The remaining 51 percent may be shared by federal government, Mexican firms, workers, and the Mexican public. When it applied to a Mexican company, it may mean that 51-percent ownership of the federal government is required. The Mexican Telephone Company (Telefonos de Mexico, S.A.) and the National Financiera are cases in point.

FLOW OF FUNDS: A COMPARATIVE ANALYSIS

As previously described, Mexican economic growth in the period 1960-70 was indeed impressive. There are three basic reasons for this. The most important is that the Mexican federal government has played a key role in the process of national capitalism. The second is the financial institutions, which have successfully channeled private savings to the use of both public and private sectors. The last, but not the least, is government policy encouraging foreign capital and technology to assist Mexican industrial development.

The model of economic development and growth in Mexico is a special one, and the flow of funds for this purpose differs from other Latin American countries as well as some industrialized nations. Tables 18.2 and 18.3 reflect some of the highlights of saving and investment flows in the Mexican economy, which should be of interest to financial planners, businessmen, and students of international economics and finance.

1. Mexico's high economic growth rate has permitted a growth in per-capita income, which is above the average achieved in other Latin American countries, but still below that prevailing in industrialized nations such as Ireland ($1,040) and the United States ($4,800).

2. The domestic savings ratio in Mexico is 20 percent of GDP, whereas it is 17 percent in other Latin American countries and 22 percent in the industrialized countries.

3. Mexican gross domestic investment is 20 percent of GDP, compared with 19 percent in Latin American countries and 19.5 percent in industrialized countries.

4. Approximately 90 percent of Mexican gross investment is financed by domestic sources and 10 percent by external sources. The external financing in Mexico is the highest among nations compared by the authors.

5. The share of the private sector in gross investment declined from 1960-64, but regained ground by 1970. The public sector increased its share of gross investment from 37.8 to 45 percent in the period 1960-64, but moved back to 38 percent in 1970.

On the basis of the above comparative analysis, Mexico has achieved a higher growth rate than other Latin American countries. Moreover, the performance of per-capita income, savings and investment out of GDP, external financing, and population growth have also been superior. On the other hand, Mexico remains behind the industrial nations with regard to income, savings and investment, and external financing.

In the course of continued and balanced economic development, it is expected that per-capita income in Mexico will continue to grow,

TABLE 18.2

Income, Savings, Investment, Growth, and Financing
in Mexico, Latin America, and Industrialized
Countries, 1960-70

	Mexico	Latin America	Industrialized Countries
Per-capita Income			
1970	$555	$374	$1040-4800
Savings	20%	17%	22%
	(of GDP)		(of GNP)
Gross Investment	21%	19%	22%
	(of GDP)		(of GNP)
Economic Growth	7.1%	4.9%	4.8%
	(average)		
Population Growth	3.5%	2.9%	1.2%
Internal Financing	90%	93%	99.5%
External Financing	10%	7%	0.5%

Sources: World Bank, Annual Reports, various issues; International Monetary Fund (IMF), Annual Reports; IDB, Statistics; and Bank of Mexico, Annual Reports.

TABLE 18.3

National Gross Investment
(million of pesos)

Investment	1960	1964	1967	1970
Total	23,226	36,652	52,943	77,670
percentage	100.0	100.0	100.0	100.0
Private	14,458	19,184	28,788	48,465
percentage	62.2	52.3	54.4	62.3
Public	8,768	17,468	24,155	29,205
percentage	37.8	47.7	45.6	37.7

Source: Department of Industry and Commerce, General Statistics, 1969 and 1970.

and the accumulation of domestic capital will reduce reliance on external credit. Growing domestic savings will require even more efficient financial institutions and markets. It is also predicted that once the federal government's role in infrastructure industries reaches the saturation point, the private sector is bound to expand. To meet the future needs of an expanding economy, strengthening of money and capital markets is a matter of necessity.

ROLE OF THE FEDERAL GOVERNMENT AND PUBLIC FINANCIAL INSTITUTIONS

The Mexican federal government and the public financial institutions have played a more important role in the Mexican economy than in many nations operating under the private enterprise system. The federal budget absorbs about a quarter of Mexican GDP, and public investment shares about 40 percent of the total national investment. The direct participation of the federal government in the ownership of industry through stock holdings by the National Financiera has provided a financial model for many Latin American countries. This participation definitely affects production, employment, and resource allocation. To supplement this direct fiscal weapon, the federal government also has a strong monetary arm through which the Ministry of Finance and Public Credit exercises influence. Under the minister there is the National Banking and Insurance Commission, the Bank of Mexico (central bank), and a host of public and private financial institutions, which provide a financial framework and which facilitate the economic policy set by the president.

Federal Government: The Arbiter of Financial Resources Allocation

In the four decades ending in 1973, the Mexican government has continuously used its power to influence the national economy. This tendency was accelerated in the period 1960-73 when the federal government took a direct hand in every facet of national economic activity. The economic progress achieved in Mexico did not cover the shortcomings indicated in previous discussion. Specific measures introduced by the Echeverria administration to remedy these weaknesses are as follows:

1. Increase legislation on banking reform in order to meet the needs associated with rising per-capita income and to service decentralized industries in different regions to achieve a more balanced economy.

2. The 1972 Tax Reform was intended to increase capital tax and sales tax revenues (on luxury items increased from 3 to 19 percent). The increased government revenues will be used to finance investment. Further, the capital tax will have a redistribution effect on national income.

3. Improve industrial and agricultural technology in order to increase exports, reduce imports, and minimize the inflow of foreign capital.

4. Streamline the federal budget in order to demonstrate fiscal responsibility and to bring into the Mexican budget an accounting of the amount and destination of funds received from domestic and foreign loans.

5. Automatic reinvestment of retained earnings in public industries and foreign firms is required by the government's new law. Up to 15 to 20 percent of taxable income must be plowed back for this purpose. In connection with this depreciation, law has also been amended.

To achieve the above objectives, the federal government has used its most powerful tools: the federal budget and federal public investment. The 1972 federal budget, totaling 123,381 million pesos (see Table 18.4) not only reflects record-breaking expenditures in the budget history of the government, but also includes expenditures financed by credits that account for 19 percent of total funds. The largest item in the 1972 budget is economic development, which shares 48.6 percent of the total. The next largest is social welfare, which accounts for 26.67 percent. Economic development spending is designed to develop the regional economies through government agencies and enterprises. Social welfare spending is concentrated in the Mexico City area, where the pressure of social needs is the heaviest. The budget increases are substantial. The total budget amount was 79,656 million pesos in 1971 and 123,381 million pesos in 1972.

The main sources of revenue are income from government agencies and enterprises and social security which account for 45.5 percent of total revenues. Revenue from government loans and financing reflects the activities of the government financial institutions in the money and capital markets. With the new reforms, the income tax contributes 14.8 percent of total revenue, and taxes on industry and commerce contribute 9.5 percent of revenues. In short, taxes contribute only about one-third of government revenues, contrasted with the United States where the federal government receives about 70 percent of total revenue from personal, corporate profits and sales and excise taxes. The revenue structure reflects the dominant role of government enterprises and agencies in the savings-investment process in Mexico.

TABLE 18.4

The Federal Budget for 1972
(millions of pesos)

Activity	Amount	Percent of Total
Expenditures		
Economic development	59,967	48.60
Social welfare	32,912	26.67
Defense	3,257	2.65
General administration	3,689	2.99
Public Debt	23,556	19.09
Domestic	13,875	11.25
Foreign	9,668	7.84
Total	123,381	100.00
Revenue		
Income from government agencies and enterprises and social security	56,100	45.5
Income from loans and financing financing	27,671	22.4
Income tax	18,220	14.8
Taxes on industry and commerce	11,705	9.5
Other taxes	9,685	7.9
Total	123,381	100.0

Source: Luis Alvarez Echeverria, Proposal for the 1972 Federal Budget, Mexico, 1972.

Federal public investment, which shares about one-third of the budget, is the key instrument through which the pattern of national investment is set. As Table 18.5 shows, investment in 1972 rose by 67 percent over 1971 levels, and 1971 was 20 percent less than in 1970. The reduction in 1971 resulted from the administration intent to restrain the gradual inflation and rising foreign debt. The stress of federal public investment suggests that the social, transport, and agricultural sectors took two-thirds of the funds at the expense of the industrial sector, which had enjoyed a high priority in previous

TABLE 18.5

Federal Public Investment by Purpose, 1970-72

	Actual 1970		Actual 1971		Budgeted for 1972	
	Million Pesos	Percent of Total Invest- ment	Million Pesos	Percent of Total Invest- ment	Million Pesos	Percent of Total Invest- ment
Industrial	11,096	38.0	9,328	41.3	12,688	33.6
Social welfare	7,719	27.1	5,070	22.5	10,181	27.0
Transport and communi- cation	5,802	19.9	4,589	20.3	8,764	23.2
Agricultural, livestock, and fishing	3,921	13.4	3,265	14.5	5,344	14.4
Administration and defense	465	1.6	307	1.4	799	1.8
Total	29,205	100.0	22,559	100.0	37,777	100.0

Source: Luis Alvarez Echeverria, Informe Presidencial, Mexico, 1971 and 1972.

years. Increasing foreign debt has posed a danger to the federal government, and approximately 75 percent of this debt was used to finance capital spending in the public sector. For this reason a decision must be made by the government regarding how to coordinate major problem areas in the budget and investment fields: economic growth, foreign debt limits, and tax revenues.

Bank of Mexico

Over the past 50 years, Mexico has developed a progressive and comprehensive banking system capable of dealing with domestic monetary affairs. The Bank of Mexico (Banco de México) was created in 1925 to replace the old Monetary Commission to issue paper money. It has functioned as a full-fledged central bank only after passage of the Organization Law (Ley Organica) of 1931. Based on the General Law of Credit Institutions and Auxiliary Organizations in 1941, the

Ministry of Finance and Public Credit created the National Banking and Insurance Commission as well as the National Securities Commission for strengthening the supervision of private financial institutions and the stock market. These three governmental financial arms, which regulate and control the sources and uses of funds in the short and long-term markets, are discussed in the following sections.

The principal objectives of Mexican monetary policy are (1) to promote balanced economic development, (2) to maintain price stability, and (3) to regulate the foreign exchange market and maintain an equilibrium in the international balance of payments. Banco de México is a strong central bank and an important instrument for attaining government objectives in the financial sphere. Its major functions are currency issue as well as the control and regulation of credit for public and private investments. Through the purchase of securities from the federal government, financieras, other national banks, and private investment companies, Banco de México directly and indirectly influences the distribution of funds and interest rates. In the international aspect, it serves as fiscal agent for the federal government in international dealings. It has played an active part in Mexico's relationships with the International Monetary Fund (IMF) and the World Bank.

The major policy weapons used by the central bank include (1) reserve requirements for banks, finance companies, mortgage banks, and credit unions, (2) discounts for commercial documents and regulation of deposits in commercial banks. Open-market operations are not used by the Bank of Mexico since there is no Treasury bill market.

As reflected in Table 18.6, the Bank of Mexico has achieved the objectives of economic growth with price stability reasonably well. Before 1968, price levels were relatively stable regardless of an increasing money supply. Since 1969, demand-pull inflation has forced the government to gradually reduce the growth in money supply from 11.6 percent in 1970 to 8.3 percent in 1971. However, a sluggish economy in 1972 required drastic government action to accelerate the growth of money supply (to 21 percent). The total money supply in 1972 was 85,070 million pesos, of which currency and coin was 53,326 million pesos and demand deposits 31,744 million pesos. It is interesting to note that the major portion of money supply is currency and coin contrasted with the United States where demand deposits are far more important. About 50 percent of the currency and coin was held by banks, and the remaining 50 percent is actually in circulation.

With respect to the attraction of resources and financing of credit by the banking system, the Bank of Mexico uses its policy tools

TABLE 18.6

Changes in Prices and Money Supply, 1965-71

	1965	1966	1967	1968	1969	1970	1971	1972
Annual Rate of Consumer Price Increase	3.8	4.6	2.6	2.6	3.5	4.8	5.5	5.0
Annual Rate of Wholesale Price Increase	1.9	1.3	2.9	1.9	2.6	6.0	3.4	2.2
Money Supply (Percentage Increase During Year) Demand Deposits	8.2	12.4	7.9	12.9	11.9	10.5	8.2	22.2
Currency and Coin	4.9	9.8	8.2	13.0	11.3	10.4	8.3	18.9
Money Supply	6.8	10.9	8.1	12.9	11.6	10.5	8.3	21.0

Source: Banco de México, Informe 1971-72.

flexibily. As reflected in Table 18.7, the growth of its resources in 1972 was 22.7 percent as compared with a growth of 9 percent in 1971. In 1972, its financing increased by 130.5 percent as compared with -11.9 percent in 1971. The reason for increased securities financing and decreased credit financing in 1972 was the government policy emphasized checking inflation pressures in an overheated economy.

National Financiera

National Financiera (Financiera Nacional) was established in 1934 to promote the development of the domestic capital market as well as industrial development. The federal government owns at least 51 percent of the capital stock (class "A" stock), and the rest (class "B" stock) is subscribed by private banking institutions and the public. The National Financiera is managed by seven directors, of which four are appointed by the government including the governor

TABLE 18.7

Attraction of Resources and Financing of Credit by the Banking System,
as of December 31 of Each Year
(millions of pesos)

	1970	1971	1972	Variation percent		
				1970/69	1971/70	1972/71
Total attraction	206,998.1	237,816.1	275,748.5	15.3	14.9	16.0
Banco de México	22,550.3	24,589.9	30,182.1	9.5	9.0	22.7
Government credit institutions	56,014.0	66,396.1	73,808.7	11.1	18.5	11.2
Private credit institutions	128,433.8	146,830.1	171,757.7	18.3	14.3	17.0
Total financing	194,522.3	220,723.3	255,577.7	16.3	13.5	15.8
Banco de México	19,956.9	17,587.1	40,530.2	6.1	-11.9	130.5
Credits	2,147.4	2,832.5	2,001.1	11.2	31.9	-29.4
Securities	17,809.5	14,754.6	38,529.1	5.5	-17.2	161.1
Other government institutions	57,419.0	68,095.0	76,216.5	10.6	18.6	11.9
Credits	51,322.3	60,802.1	67,678.5	9.8	18.5	11.3
Securities	6,096.7	7,292.9	8,538.0	17.7	19.6	17.1
Private institutions	117,146.4	135,041.2	138,831.0	21.4	15.3	2.8
Credits	83,683.2	93,858.2	105,780.5	24.1	12.2	2.7
Securities	33,463.2	41,183.0	33,050.5	15.0	23.1	-19.8

Source: Banco de México.

of the Bank of Mexico. The minister of finance is the board chairman. It is a government-controlled and profit-making organization.

This powerful government institution has grown rapidly since its inception. From 1934 to 1940, it acted as broker and agent to develop the government securities market. During and after World War II, it helped to finance imports and acquired funds from abroad. In the two decades, 1950-70 it has concentrated on short- and long-term financing to industries, commercial enterprises, and development of infrastructure. Over the period 1940-71, its assets have grown from about 18 million pesos to about 34 billion pesos. As indicated in Table 18.8, in 1971 loans and discounts constitute 80 percent and investments 15 percent.

The financial activities of the National Financiera are generally divided into five categories. First, it helps the government to develop the infrastructure, such as highways, airports, and irrigation system. Second, it acts on behalf of the government to buy controlling shares of common stocks of certain basic industries, such as utilities, communications, steel, fertilizer, railroad cars and buses, sugar, and textiles. Third, it extends loans to industries and rediscounts paper from the private financieras (private finance companies) in order to release them from liquidity pressures. Fourth, it provides guarantees of mortgage bonds issued by the mortgage banks for improving industrial and residential construction. Finally, it invests capital and creates conditions conducive to private investment. When the enterprise becomes mature and profitable, National Financiera sells its shares to the public and mobilizes its funds in other needed areas. The diversified roles of the National Financiera exert wide influence upon the development process in Mexico.

Because of its good record, this institution has gained confidence at home and abroad. Domestically it issues bonds (Titulos Financieros) and short-term certificates (Certificados de Participacion), which are all backed by the Bank of Mexico. The credit status is excellent because these short- and long-term credit instruments can be converted into cash freely from the central bank. Internationally, the institution has been notably successful in utilizing external funds for domestic development purposes. In the period 1965-67, it placed four issues of government bonds (amounting to 77.5 million dollars) in the U.S. capital market, in addition to the placement of $25 million of securities in the European financial markets. The sound reputation of the National Financiera has made it a model for emulation in other less developed nations.

TABLE 18.8

Main Items in the Balance Sheet of National
Financiera, 1971
(millions of pesos)

Total assets	34,797
Loans and discounts	28,881
Investment in securities	5,234
Major sources of funds	
Bonds outstanding	11,966
Foreign loans	18,067
Capital, reserves, and profit	1,837

Source: Nacional Financiera, Informe Anual, 1971.

Other National Financial Institutions

The Mexican government has developed a set of financial institutions designed to deal with specific segments of the national economy. The following are the more important of these institutions. Banco Nacional de Obros y Servicio Publicos concentrates its activities in the area of state and municipal public works and low-cost housing development. Banco Nacional de Comercio Exterior deals mainly with short-term credit designed to stimulate exports, especially agricultural exports. Two other financial institutions, Banco Nacional de Credito Agricola and Banco Nacional de Credito Ejidal, were originated at the same time, 1926, but have distinct and different programs. The former (The Agricultural Bank) extends credit to private landowners and sometimes to credit societies formed by cooperative farmers (ejidatarios). The latter's sole purpose is to concentrate its resources on the problems of the Ejidal sector. Both banks are authorized to make short-, medium- and long- term loans.

Undoubtedly, the above-mentioned financial institutions have contributed to national economic development. But many problems remain unsolved due to the fact that the priority of allocating funds between industry and agriculture and determining how to channel private savings to needed areas are tough decisions for the government.

ROLE OF PRIVATE FINANCIAL INSTITUTIONS

The role of private financial institutions has become increasingly more important in Mexico. First, it was necessary to replace foreign capital after the nationalization of some foreign enterprises during the 1930s. Second, it was partly implemented to finance government deficits in the postwar era. Third, these institutions were encouraged to finance national economic development in the 1960s. At the end of 1971, total resources of the Mexican public and private financial system were 237 billion pesos, or 51.1 percent of the GNP. As shown in Table 18.7, the public banking sector share 37.2 percent of this, of which the Bank of Mexico accounted for 10 percent and government credit institutions 28 percent. The private banking sector shared 62.0 percent. Commercial banks accounted for 17.5 percent, private development banks 35 percent, mortgage banks 8 percent, and others 1.5 percent. In 1972, the revival of national economic activities demanded more funds from the private sector, especially the commercial banks. In the 1970s, keen competition among financial institutions can be expected.

Commercial Banks (bancos de deposito y ahorro)

The structure, operations, and branches of commercial banks are governed by the Ley General de Instituciones de credito de 1897 which also limits the bank note issue. By virtue of Ley Monetaria de 1931, the Bank of Mexico is empowered to regulate all commercial banks. This power was strengthened by the Law of 1936, which stipulated that all commercial banks must be members of the central bank, the Bank of Mexico. At the present time, commercial banks must comply with certain investment requirements. They must invest part (10 to 20 percent) of their demand deposit funds in government bonds, 5 percent in livestock bonds, 10 percent in financial bonds of the National Sugar Development Bank, 15 percent in Bank of Mexico reserves, and 15 percent in medium-term loans. Mexican commercial banks obtain 75 percent of their funds from businesses and individuals and 25 percent from the banks' own capital accounts. At the end of 1971, there were 115 commercial banks with about 1,100 branches. The National Bank of Mexico, with assets of over 4 billion pesos and 200 branches, is the largest commercial bank. Two facts explain the growing importance of the commercial banks. One is that Mexican commercial banks, like many European banks, are associated with industrial groups for their underwriting activities. Another is government policy to encourage commercial banks to play diversified roles in different industries and regions, to achieve a balanced economic development program. The tendency of banking concentration is evidenced by the fact that 1 percent of the banks controls 10 percent of banking assets.

Private Development Banks (financieras privadas)

Private development banks came into existence in 1946 for the purpose of channeling funds from savers to public as well as private investments. At year end 1971, there were 97 financieras in Mexico, and their growth rates and financial resources surpass other financial institutions in the private sector. They are authorized to deal in a broad range of business: to keep stocks and bonds of other companies; to make loans up to five years for fixed assets; to provide credits to agriculture, industry, and livestock industry; to provide credits for installment plan sales; to promote and manage all types of business; to underwrite private industrial shares and bonds and to place such securities in the market. From the functional standpoint, the financieras are similar to the investment companies in the United States. Financieras tend to hold securities instead of selling them. They also have the backing of the National Financiera. In case of need, they can submit their loans to the National Financiera for rediscount. The sources of funds of the financieras are time and saving deposits (paying 11-percent interest). The financieras are not permitted to accept demand (checkbook) deposits. They also issue bonds and certificates. Regardless of their financial maneuverability, many financieras are not independent institutions, but are subsidiaries of the larger commercial banks. As directed by the government, these development banks tend to be specialized along either regional or functional lines. About two-thirds of these organizations are located in Mexico City. The government has indicated a preference for decentralization of their operations.

Mortgage Banks (hipotecarios)

As of 1971, there were 30 mortgage banks in operation with assets totaling 19 billion pesos. The primary functions of these banks are to issue and guarantee private individual mortgage bonds and loans. Most of the business is in mortgage bonds with 10-year maturities, with real property as collateral and at an inerest cost of over 8 percent to the borrowers. The issuers of bonds generally pay the banks 2- to 4- percent commission for their services. In order to prevent overissue of these bonds, the Bank of Mexico imposes a 12-percent ceiling on their annual increase. Regardless of this

this restriction, the mortgage banks are still considered to have a high growth rate, second only to the private financieras.

Other Institutions

The capitalization banks are designed by government legislation and direction to directly hold government securities and invest in low-cost housing projects. Funds are obtained through a lottery feature. There were 13 of these banks in Mexico in 1971. Other financial institutions, such as home savings and loan banks, trust companies, insurance companies, mutual funds, and credit unions, play a minor role in the Mexican financial markets. These institutions emerged in the 1950s, except for some insurance companies whose activities date back to the 1930s.

National Banking and Insurance Commission
(Comision Nacional de Bancaria y Seguros)

This institution is one of the financial arms of the Ministry of Finance and Public Credit created in 1941 and designed to supervise the private financial institutions. The commission has broad authority to approve the establishment of financial institutions and to supervise their activities. In the case of banks, it must coordinate with the Bank of Mexico for effective supervision and control. The Bank of Mexico has much more influence on the financial policies of banks, since the central bank has the power to control the money supply and regulate their credits. The commission supervises the technical aspects of bank operations, such as proper composition of assets and liabilities as well as reserve requirements. The commission publishes a monthly bulletin concerning the detailed statistics of financial institutions operating in different regions.

Private Financial Institutions: Their Resources and Distribution of Financing

In the period 1965-71, the growth of the private financial sector (Table 18.9) indicates a rapid development of the financieras and mortgage banks. That was why the Bank of Mexico had to give special support to the commercial banks in order that they could sustain a rate of growth no less than 6 percent annually in loans for productive purposes. On the other hand, the Bank of Mexico increased the legal reserves requirements on deposits obtained by financieras beginning

TABLE 18.9

Resources of Private Financial Institutions, 1965-71
(billions of pesos, end of year)

	1965	1966	1967	1968	1969	1970	1971
Total, private institutions	61.60	74.43	86.21	101.28	122.83	144.96	167.13
Deposit and savings banks	30.46	34.08	37.10	42.75	49.26	54.03	59.43
Financieras	32.81	31.04	38.18	45.87	58.76	73.43	86.43
Mortgage institutions	5.99	7.86	9.42	11.07	13.07	15.55	19.19
Others	1.34	1.45	1.51	1.57	1.74	1.85	1.96

Percentage Increase During Year

Total, private institutions	14.3	20.8	15.8	17.5	21.3	18.0	15.29
Deposit and savings banks	9.5	11.9	8.9	15.2	15.3	9.7	9.99
Financieras	15.2	30.4	23.0	20.1	28.1	25.0	17.70
Mortgage institutions	41.3	31.1	21.1	17.5	18.1	19.0	23.40

Source: Banco de México, Informe Anual,1971.

TABLE 18.10

Distribution of Bank Financing,[a] 1966-71
(billion pesos, end of year)

	1966	1967	1968	1969	1970	1971	Percent Increase 1971/70
Total financing	104.63	121.11	138.77	167.23	194.52	220.72	13.5
Companies and individuals[b]	77.24	91.04	103.58	124.75	147.38	168.96	14.6
Securities	6.75	7.86	8.74	9.77	11.03	12.57	13.9
Credits	70.49	83.18	94.84	115.15	135.34	156.38	14.8
To commerce	17.12	20.70	24.58	31.80	36.73	42.50	15.7
To production	53.37	62.48	70.27	83.35	99.61	113.89	14.3
Industry	40.20	47.44	53.73	65.44	78.81	90.71	14.6
Agriculture	12.55	14.03	15.36	16.19	17.69	20.44	15.5
Mining	0.63	1.01	1.19	1.72	3.10	2.74	-11.6
Federal government[c]	27.39	30.07	35.18	42.31	47.15	51.76	9.8

[a]Including Nacional Financiera credits and securities set aside to cover its participation certificates.
[b]Including companies in the public sector.
[c]Securities represent over 97 percent of credits to the federal government.

Source: Banco de México, Informes Anuales (table on page 42 of Informe Anual 1971).

January 1971 and required at least 5 percent of such deposits to be channeled to business producing for export or operating tourist hotels. The central bank required that mortgage banks channel 15 percent of additional resources into the financing of low-cost housing at interest rates of 6 percent, and for 15-year maturities. They are allowed to pay interest rates of 10 to 12 percent on time deposits of not less than one-year maturity in accordance with market conditions, domestically and internationally.

In 1971, bank financing increased by 13.5 percent in the national economy as a whole. As Table 18.10 indicates, the commerce and agriculture sectors obtained larger shares of bank financing than mining and industry. This trend was manipulated by government policy in order to keep national economic development on a more balanced basis. The amount loaned to the government declined relatively, but remained over 20 percent of total financing.

MONEY AND CAPITAL MARKETS

The Market Development

The development of the Mexican financial markets has been related to Mexican economic conditions, government policy, and relative success of the various financial institutions. Before 1910, the mining and utility industries were largely owned by foreigners. No capital market was needed since foreign capital was transferred to Mexico through foreign branch banks. Local commercial banks took care of short-term loans to local business. During the 1920s, the Mexican government gradually developed its own financial institutions, with the Bank of Mexico as a nucleus supplemented by the National Financiera in the 1930s. Financial markets in this period were primarily tailored to the needs of public enterprises. After World War II, government policy stressed industrial development. To achieve this, a National Securities Commission was established (Comision Nacional de Valores), and a host of financial institutions, such as private financieras and mortgage banks, came into existence under the encouragement of the government. The allocation of funds in the money and capital markets has been strongly influenced by the central bank, but financial institutions are permitted to compete among themselves. At the present time, the Mexican capital market is the largest in Latin America, regardless of its relative underdevelopment from the standpoint of modern financial markets in industrial countries.

372

There are several special characteristics of the Mexican financial markets worth mentioning.

1. The demarcation between money and capital markets is not clear because many short-term loans are automatically renewable and long-term bonds can be redeemed at demand.

2. While the government financial institutions influence capital formation and the securities market, private institutions affect liquidity.

3. Since many large enterprises are owned by the government, government bonds or bonds issued by its agencies have priority over private issues.

4. Most medium- and small-size corporations prefer internal financing and short-term bank loans since security issues involve high cost and control problems.

5. The middle-income group in Mexico has not been developed as in many industrialized nations. Most savings are transferred to financial institutions, and they become dominant forces in the financial markets. Wealthy individuals may be interested more in the real estate and commodities markets than the securities markets since they still remember the nightmare of inflation before the 1960s.

6. The stock exchanges are dominated by fixed-income securities. Variable income securities are not actively traded. Furthermore, brokerage firms and specialists are not important in Mexico since they do not perform the same sophisticated functions as in the United States.

Money Market

As stated above, there is no clear-cut demarcation between money and capital markets. Nevertheless, short-term credit is significant to both private as well as public institutions. Table 18.7 shows that total financing was 255 billion pesos in 1972, of which about 60 percent was short-term credit and 40 percent long-term credit. Among the short-term credits, private institutions accounted for 105 billion pesos; government institutions shared 76 billion; and the Bank of Mexico absorbed only 2.8 billion.

Credits Extended by Private Institutions

Commercial banks have the lion's share of the money market since they are active in business loans, commercial paper, banker's acceptances, and savings and time deposits. No detailed statistics are given by government agencies, but the bulk of this credit is given to business organizations which, in general, rely 70 percent on internal financing and 30 percent on external financing. Since most medium- and small-size corporations are owned by family groups, preference to corporate savings and depreciation is understandable. Moreover, external financing is costly and less flexible. Corporate borrowings from commercial banks are regarded as a last resort due to the fact that the bank lending rate is usually above 10 percent, and borrowers are normally required to leave a 20- to 30-percent compensatory balance. The real cost is over 13 percent. As the needs for liquidity grow, the influence of commercial banks on corporate policy will increase. In this regard, the position of Mexican commercial banks is similar to that of the Japanese.

Another influential private financial institution in the money market is the private financiera, which is allowed to extend consumer credits and business loans. These short-term credits constitute four-fifths of their total uses of funds. In case of needs, these institutions have the privilege to rediscount at the National Financiera.

Credits Extended by Public Institutions

Public institutions also give short-term credits to public as well as private firms. National Financiera is the principal public institution extending short-term credits not only to government-owned enterprises, but also to private companies, especially the private financieras in the form of rediscount. The National Mortgage Bank, the counterpart of the Government National Mortgage Association in the United States, provides liquidity to the mortgage banks should the need arise. Credits granted by the Bank of Mexico represent advances and discounts to commercial banks. It is obvious that the central bank emphasizes direct control over the long-term security market and influences the short-term market through its monetary tools and the National Financiera. That is why the credits granted by the Bank of Mexico in 1972 were only about 5 percent of the total.

The Capital Market

At the present time, the capital market in Mexico is essentially an institutional market dominated by fixed-income bonds mostly issued by National Financiera and mortgage banks. According to the National Securities Commission report, 97.5 percent of transactions in the Mexico City Stock Exchange in 1971 involved fixed-income securities, and only 2.5 percent were in variable-income shares. Another distinctive feature of the market is the specialization of borrowers. For instance, mortgage banks issue mortgage bonds and provide mortgage loans on houses. National Financiera issues financial bonds and certificates and provides short- and long-term capital to industry and commerce. The federal government issues bonds to finance its deficits through the central bank. Following is a brief description of the primary market, the secondary market, and their relative strengths and weaknesses.

The Primary Market

As stated previously, the issuing of long-term securities is limited to certain large corporations that need funds for financing plant and equipment spending. They have the alternative to borrow short-term funds from commercial banks or private financieras. In 1971, total corporate obligations issued were only 655 million pesos, or 5 percent of the total fixed-income securities issued in the private sector (see Table 18.11). This compares with financial bonds issued by private financieras and mortgage bonds issued by mortgage banks, which were 9,260 million pesos, or 65 percent of the total, and 4,580 million pesos, or 30 percent of the total, respectively. The bonds issued by financial institutions are denominated at 100.00 pesos each and pay 8- to 10- percent interest. In turn, these institutions lend money out at rates of 12 to 16 percent, depending on market conditions.

Public issues of fixed-income bonds totaled 15,750 million pesos in 1971, of which federal and state governments accounted for 80 percent, financial bonds and certificates issued by National Financiera 15 percent, and others 5 percent (see Table 18.12). Competition between the public and private sectors is keen, but the former usually have an advantage. For example, Titulos Financieros series "SSS" of National Financiera are guaranteed by the Bank of Mexico and sold to the public to yield 9-percent gross or 8.75-percent net after taxes. National Financiera will repurchase these bonds at any time at 99 1/2 percent free of commissions. In the meantime, the debenture bonds of Altos Hornos, Mexico's largest steel manufacturer, offer 9.5-percent gross rate on face value equal to 9.1 percent after withholding taxes. These corporate bonds are not guaranteed by the government and rarely trade in the market. Most investors would rather receive 8.75-percent net on government-backed securities than earn slightly more on higher-risk corporate obligations.

Funds obtained from fixed-income securities are channeled to different sectors of the national economy. These funds totaled 30,279 million pesos in 1971, of which industry and finance used about 41 percent, governments about 40 percent, private construction 15 percent, public service and works 4 percent. Table 18.13 reflects the sixfold growth of these funds in the period 1960-61. In the same period, the average real growth rate of Mexico's GDP was 6.5 percent.

TABLE 18.11

Fixed-Income Securities Issued by the Private Sector
(millions of pesos)

Year	Total	Financial Bonds	Mortgage Certificates	Corporate Obligations	Mortgage Bonds
1960	1,610	722	479	374	35
1966	11,060	7,259	715	515	2,570
1971	14,529	9,260	33	655	4,580

Source: National Securities Commission, Monthly Bulletin, March 1973, Mexico, D.F.

TABLE 18.12

Fixed-Income Securities Issued by the Public Sector
(millions of pesos)

Year	Total	Federal and States Government	Participation Certificates	Financial Certificates	Mortgage Bonds	Financial Bonds	Corporate Obligations
1960	3,663	2,370	—	700	300	198	950
1966	4,150	600	300	1,800	600	400	450
1971	15,750	12,000	700	1,500	500	1,050	—

Source: National Securities Commission, Monthly Bulletin, March 1973, Mexico, D.F.

TABLE 18.13

Destination of Funds Obtained from Fixed-Income Securities
(millions of pesos)

Year	Total	Public Works and Services	Industry and Finance	Private Construction	Government Sector
1960	5,273	300	2,089	514	2,370
1966	15,210	900	10,424	3,285	600
1971	30,279	1,200	12,465	4,613	12,000

Source: National Securities Commission, Monthly Bulletin, March 1973, Mexico, D.F.

TABLE 18.14

Investments of Banking Institutions in Securities
(million of pesos)

Year	Total	Bank of Mexico	Other National Institutions	Private Institutions
1960	12,132	2,775	1,634	7,721
1966	42,355	11,210	3,111	28,034
1970	81,606	18,519	3,818	59,268
1971	80,523	15,415	5,852	58,617

Source: National Securities Commission, Monthly Bulletin, March 1973, Mexico, D.F.

Investments of the banking system in fixed-income securities also grew sixfold. Among the total investment of 80 billion pesos in 1971 (see Table 18.14), private institutions took 73 percent, representing a large part of the savings transferred from the household sector. The Bank of Mexico absorbed 20 percent, reflecting the important role of the central bank to support the long-term securities market, especially government securities. The distribution of these investments among institutions showed slight charges from year to year due to the shifting emphasis between public and private investments.

The Secondary Market

There are three stock exchanges in Mexico—Mexico City, Monterrey, and Guadalajara.

The Bolsa de Valores in Mexico City was founded in 1898 for trading mining shares. It was reorganized in 1933. The Monterrey Stock Exchange was established in 1950, and the Guadalajara Stock Exchange in 1960. All stock exchanges are supervised by the National Securities Commission. Any issues listed on the exchanges must be approved by the commission, the National Financiera, and the exchange themselves.

In 1971, transactions on the Mexico City Stock Exchange were 38 billion pesos compared to 5 billion pesos in 1960. As indicated in Table 18.15, fixed-income securities represented 97.5 percent of transactions, and variable-income securities represented only 2.5 percent. Among fixed-income bonds, private issues accounted for three-fourths of transactions, and public issues only one-fourth. In fact, many private mortgage bond transactions were directly handled by private institutions, which report formally to the stock exchange for record purposes. At present, the Mexico City Stock Exchange handles over 80 percent of total securities transactions in Mexico. There are about 400 companies listed on this exchange, but only 40 to 60 stocks are actively traded. The popular stocks for trading are National Financiera (finance), Telefonos de Mexico (utility), Aluminio (industry), and El Puerto de Liverpool (commerce). Stock yields average 5 to 7 percent, and high-grade bonds generally yield about 9 percent.

Since there has been very little inflation in the past eight years (4 percent on average), bond investments are favorable in terms of yield, safety, and liquidity. However, variable-income stocks are subject to national economic conditions as well as corporate earnings. For example, the official 30 stock index of the Mexico City Stock Exchange (1959 = 100) was down from 152 in January 1971 to 128 in October 1971, due to the sluggish economy. The increased government

TABLE 18.15

Transactions in the Mexico City Stock Exchange
(millions of pesos)

Year	Total	Variable Income	Fixed-Income Securities		
			Subtotal	Public	Private
1960	5,103	159	4,944	2,292	2,652
1966	23,062	1,411	21,651	3,126	18,524
1971	38,864	830	38,034	9,482	28,553

Source: National Securities Commission, Monthly Bulletin, March 1973.

expenditures and public investment announced in December pushed the stock index up during 1972, and the index was 199.5 in February 1973. Average daily volume of shares traded in the Mexico City Stock Exchange was between 44,000 and 65,000 as of the date mentioned.

The Monterrey Stock Exchange deals primarily with industrial issues since it is located in the iron- and steel-producing center. It has developed rapidly in the 1960s. Total transactions in the exchange were 175 million pesos in 1960, 1,348 million in 1966, and 5,599 million in 1971. The growth of this exchange is attributed to the intensive industrialization of the northern region and the development of the border industries between the United States and Mexico. Like the Mexico City Stock Exchange, the Monterrey Stock Exchange handles more securities with fixed income and less securities with variable income. But unlike Mexico City, Monterrey is almost dominated by the private sector.

The Guadalajara Stock Exchange is relatively new to investors. In 1960, the year of its inception, transactions were 6 million pesos. But the value jumped to 72 million pesos in 1966 and 3,569 million in 1971. The pattern of this new stock exchange is very much like that of Mexico City due to the geographically short distance between these two cities. The major factor accounting for growth of this exchange is that Guadalajara has a lot of foreign capital generated by retired people from the United States. There are direct flight connections from New York to this exotic city.

A Bird's-Eye View of the Mexican Financial Markets

Regardless of the increasing importance of the Mexico City Stock Exchange amid the impressive economic growth in Mexico, it handles only about 15 percent of the transactions in the over-the-counter market. Foreign issues are rarely traded in Mexico except occasionally World Bank bonds. Some criticism has been expressed that the dominant role of government is the obstacle to the proper functioning of the Mexican financial markets. The central bank has encouraged issuing of medium-term bonds by financial institutions designed to minimize interest rate differentials. Increasing industrialization will require more capital, and the present 50-percent debt-equity structure in many important industries is dangerous. Over-specialization of institutions involves special risks due to inadequate portfolio diversification.

Many people argue that the Mexican government's monetary policy has been very successful, first in creating strong public institutions which have filled the gap left by foreign capital. Second, the fixed-income securities supported by the government give confidence to the public and permit channeling of private funds to high-level capital formation, especially in infrastructure industries. In the period 1963-73, the increasing strengths of the private financial institutions and middle-income group have increased demand for variable-income securities. To follow this reasoning, it is suggested that the provision of tax incentives for business corporations to issue common and preferred stocks would be advisable. At any rate, these two views must be studied carefully in light of the current stage of Mexican economic development and the philosophy of the strong executive branch of the government.

GOVERNMENT POLICY AND INTERNATIONAL FINANCE

The Policy of "National Capitalists"

Government policy has played a key role not only in the domestic economy, but also in international finance. Between 1950 and 1970, Mexican government policy has strongly encouraged domestic savings as the main financial source of its industrialization program. In the meantime, foreign capital was given incentives in certain selected industries, such as automobiles, chemicals, food processing, and electronics to ensure adequate domestic investment. In 1970, total long-term foreign capital in Mexico was about $7 billion, of

379

which $3.5 billion was direct investment. American direct investment in Mexico was about $2.5 billion, representing about 10 percent of all American direct investment in Latin America. Total foreign capital accounted for approximately 10 percent of Mexican private investment and about 5 percent of its total domestic investment.

Since 1971, the Mexican government changed its policy somewhat in light of increasing domestic inflation and foreign debt service payments. The year 1971 was called "the year of adjustment" when President Echeverria, reflecting his confidence in capitalism with a national purpose, referred to Mexico as a country of "national capitalists." This policy does not fundamentally differ from the Mexicanization program in the 1960s. Nevertheless, the government has made it known that foreign debt must be limited; foreign ownership of Mexican firms must be restricted to not more than 49 percent even though capital and interest can be remitted to the sending country. The uncertainty of this policy caused a decline in foreign investment in Mexico in 1971 and 1972 and forced the government to increase its external borrowings in the international financial markets. According to the World Bank's 1972 Annual Report, Mexico's external public debt outstanding in 1970 was $3,252 million, the second largest international debtor after India. Its service payments on this debt represent 22.7 percent of its export earnings.

To balance the foreign competition in Mexico with respect to capital and technology, the government has encouraged European and Japanese firms to establish operations in Mexico. Nevertheless, U.S. firms still share about 80 percent of the foreign direct investment, and the United States absorbs about 70 percent of Mexico's exports. American investments are mostly in the manufacturing field, and some American branch banks in Mexico City are handling the flow of short- and long-term credits including trade financing, but they are facing more competition from their European and Japanese counterparts.

Balance of Payments

The Mexican balance of payments has had continuous current account deficits in the 10 year period 1962-72. This is due to the increase in imports for industrial development and the outflow of capital for debt service and earnings on direct investment. These deficits have been covered by the inflow of capital. Regardless of problems in the balance of payments, the Bank of Mexico has managed to accumulate reserves of $6 million in 1966 and $264 million in 1972. The Mexican pesos, equal to U.S.$0.08, is one of the most stable currencies in the foreign exchange market.

In 1972 (Table 18.16), imports increased 22 percent above the 1971 levels. This contrasts with a reduction of imports in 1971 of 2.2 percent. Import growth has been mostly in machines and raw materials for industrial development. Exports advanced only 7.4 percent in 1971, but jumped 22.9 percent in 1972 as a result of increased manufacturing products sold to the LAFTA countries. Despite increasing exports, the deficit in the merchandise trade account rose 20.5 percent, and the current account registered a 19.5-percent increase over 1971. Since direct foreign investment fell by $17 million, the deficit in 1972 was largely financed by short-term foreign credits worth $496 million. At the same time, $60 million in securities was sold in foreign financial markets.

The Mexican government has tried to improve its balance of payments through various means, including increased exports of manufactured and agricultural goods as suggested by the newly created Mexican Institute for Foreign Trade, increased revenue from tourism, increased income from the Border Industrialization Program, additional import substitution, use of government regulation to force domestic and foreign enterprises to reinvest a certain percentage of their annual profits, and rescheduled debt service payments.

Refining International Financial Techniques

Aware of the increasing debt service payments and the leverage of foreign capital in Mexican economic development, the Mexican government has prudently managed foreign borrowings and tactfully managed its foreign exchange market. Domestically, Mexico maintains a free exchange market and free convertibility of its currency. Gold coins can be purchased in Mexican commercial banks; silver coins are plentiful; and foreign firms increase their establishments for manufacturing, commerce, and financing. During the period 1966-72, when currency crises occurred in many financial centers, the influx of speculative funds from abroad was noticeable, and Mexican pesos were frequently used for hedging currency risks by multinational corporations. Undoubtedly, the Mexican peso is one of the stable currencies in the IMF system.

Internationally, Mexico has been an important borrower. Before 1966, the United States was the principal source of funds, but was gradually replaced by European financial centers, in part as a result of the U.S. capital control programs. In 1971, the major sources of Mexican foreign credits were international agencies including the World Bank and the Inter-American Development Bank, Great Britain, the United States, France, and West Germany. The major uses of foreign funds were investments in electric power,

TABLE 18.16

Mexican Balance of Payments
(millions of dollars)

	1971	1972
Balance of goods and services	-714.7	-854
Exports of goods and services	3,389.9	3,973.0
Exports of goods	1,479.7	1,821.4
Silver production	47.1	48.1
Tourism	620.2	730.4
Border transactions	968.6	1,062.5
Other	274.3	310.6
Imports of goods and services	4,104.6	4,827.0
Imports of goods	2,419.9	2,952.1
Tourism	182.8	232.7
Border transactions	615.0	672.6
Transfers abroad from direct foreign investment	389.7	425.0
Interest on foreign debt	238.6	266.1
Other	257.7	278.5
Errors and omissions and short-term capital	375.1	377.8
Long-term capital	500.0	691.0
Direct foreign investment	196.0	179.0
Purchase of foreign companies	—	- 10.0
Securities operations	52.0	60.0
Foreign credits	281.0	496.0
i. New loans	758.0	996.0
ii. Amortization	-447.0	-500.0
Net changes in government external debt*	- 29.0	- 34.0
Special drawing rights	39.6	49.9
Change in reserves of Banco de México	200.0	264.7

*By subtraction.

Source: Banco de México; provisional figures based on the preliminary report of the Banco de México, 1972.

transportation, petroleum, agriculture, and livestock. These funds were mostly obtained or guaranteed by the National Financiera, the powerful Mexican development bank, and supervised by the Special Commission on Foreign Financing. As of the end of 1971, the outstanding foreign debt registered by the Special Commission was $3.2 billion with costs between 4 and 8 percent per annum. It should be noted that the commission is presided over by the minister of finance and public credit. The commission has the authority to decide, supervise, and evaluate foreign borrowings as to purpose, amount, cost, repayment, and the impact on the national economy and domestic financial resources as well as on the international balance of payments.

Optimism has been expressed in recent years that the internal improvement on foreign debt management plus continued efforts of the Inter-American Development Bank to create a better interregional financial market for facilitating the flow of funds and financial information will elevate the status of the Mexican financial markets parallel to other international financial centers.

REFERENCES

Banco de México. Informe Anual, 1965-71.

Basch, Antonin, and Milic Kybal. Capital Markets in Latin America. New York: Praeger Publishers, 1970.

Diego G. Lopez Rosada. Problemas Economicos de Mexico. 3rd ed. Mexico City: University of Mexico, 1970.

Goldsmith, Raymond W. The Financial Development of Mexico. Paris: Organization for Economic Cooperation and Development (OECD), 1966.

Joint Economic Committee, Congress of the United States. Thrift Institution Development in Latin America. A staff study. Washington, D.C.: U.S. Printing Office, 1970.

Nacional Financiera, S.A. Informe Anual, 1971.

Office of the President. Newsletter. Monthly publication, Mexico City.

Shelton, David H. The Banking System: Public and Private in Mexico. Cambridge, Mass.: Harvard University Press, 1967.

INTRODUCTION

Geographically, Brazil is the fifth largest nation in the world behind the USSR, China, Canada, and the United States. Its 3.3-million-square-mile territory accounts for nearly one-half of the South American continent. It has 4,600 miles of Atlantic coastline and 10,000 miles of land frontier bordering every nation of South America except Chile and Ecuador. The main feature of Brazil is its rough terrain consisting of mountains and hillsides. The mountain ranges are modest, and only 3 percent of the country is at an altitude in excess of 3,000 feet above sea level. Most of Brazil is between the equator and the tropic of Capricorn, and the climate varies from tropical to temperate. Temperatures range from a high of 83° F in the Northeast to 60° F in the South.

Brazil has the most extensive river system in the world, dividing the country into four basins. The largest forests in the North are drained by the Amazon River. The grasslands of the South are drained by the Parana, Uruguay, and Francisco rivers. Central Brazil is a vast plateau noted for its dry and healthful climate. The capital of Brazil, Brasilia, is located in this region. In the east central region, there is a triangular area where Rio de Janeiro (Brazil's main port), Sao Paulo (the main industrial center), and Belo Horizonte (the mining area) are located.

Brazil is rich in natural resources. Its iron ore deposit is second only to Russia's. Its tin, recently discovered, is considered the largest in the world. Its hydroelectric power potential, generated by an extensive waterway system, would be important to Brazil's future economic development. However, with all these natural resources, Brazil is not one of the major industrial nations of the world. This is due to basic factors related to its historical, political, and economic background.

Brazil was discovered by Portugal in 1500. It is the only Portuguese-speaking country in Latin America. It became independent in 1822, but the republic was proclaimed in 1889. Brazil adopted a three-branch system of government similar to that of the United States. An important exception is that the president and vice-president are elected by the National Congress. For this reason, the presidents elected in Brazil generally follow the policy views of the National Congress rather than that of the people and the military leaders. When conflicts occurred in the past between these two sides and the major issues could not be resolved, the government was overthrown. This happened in 1930, 1945, and 1964. The instability of government and sometimes ineffective leadership have prevented consistent policy and hampered economic development. However, the dynamic force of the federal government since 1965 has been responsible for an impressive economic performance in Brazil.

Brazil has a favorable endowment of natural wealth. With a population of only 100 million in 1973, there has been less environmental pressure. On the other hand, the traditional tie with Portugal has weakened the industrial drive of Brazil, since Portugal does not have the industrial orientation of Britain. Portugal has emphasized agriculture, and Brazil had tended to emulate Portugal in this respect. The favorable conditions for agricultural products such as sugar, cotton, coffee, and soybeans have made Brazil a land-and-labor-intensive country. The lack of industrial technology, managerial know-how, skilled labor, and capital has also been responsible for the delay of Brazilian industrialization.

The following sections are designed, firstly, to analyze the role of Brazilian government in the economic and financial development process. Secondly, financial institutions that have been modernized are described concerning their allocation of funds in both the private and the public sectors. Thirdly, the development of the Brazilian financial markets is analyzed, especially since 1965. Finally, government policy and international finance are scrutinized, especially attempts at import substitution, the export drive for better foreign exchange earnings, and incentives for foreign capital investment since these are vital to the Brazilian government's ambitious economic development program: industrialization by the year 2000.

THE ROLE OF GOVERNMENT IN ECONOMY AND FINANCE

The changing role of the Brazilian government in the national economy and finance can be divided into three periods: the period prior to 1945 when the boom and bust nature of the economy was evident, the period 1945-64 when Brazil tried to transform its economy to a limited extent but achieved only partly successful results, and the period since 1964 when a new start has proved that Brazil can become a modern country with developing financial markets.

Prior to 1945: The Cycles of a Single-Product Economy

Natural endowment and political relations have determined the shape of the Brazilian economy. In the sixteenth century, Brasilwood, known as dyewood, was the first important product that dominated Brazilian commerce with Europe. It was soon replaced by sugar, which encountered stiff competition from the Dutch, French, and English in the seventeenth century. Brazil shifted to tobacco in the eighteenth century, but this crop declined after independence in 1889, due to the abolition of slavery. Coffee was the main commodity item in the Brazilian economy prior to 1950. Brazil contributed more than half of the world supply of coffee, and coffee exports earned more than half of Brazil's foreign exchange. The boom and bust coffee economy was at the mercy of weather; production volume, and world prices, and the government of Brazil made efforts to reduce the dependence of the economy on this single product. The government commissioned Sir Otto Niemayer of Britain in 1931 and Cooke of the United States in 1945 to study the Brazilian economy and finance. While the Niemayer Report indicated that the principal weakness of Brazil was its reliance on the export of one or two crops, the Cooke mission looked into a number of other factors that were obstacles to rapid industrialization. These factors included an inadequate transportation system, inadequate energy-producing facilities, low levels of technical training, the lack of funds for industrial investment and the financial intermediaries to channel funds in this direction, and restrictions on foreign capital flows. The following analysis reflects the far-reaching effects of the latter report.

Between 1945-64: A Transitional Period

Based on the Cooke Report, Brazil launched its major industrial drive: the import substitution program. The principal tools implemented by the Brazilian government for this purpose were deficit spending, tax incentives, and foreign exchange control. As a result, in the period 1947-61, Brazil achieved an average annual growth rate of 6 percent, per-capita income of 3 percent, and population growth of 3 percent. In this period, industrial production advanced by 262 percent, and gross fixed investment rose by over 150 percent. However, weaknesses of the economy began to appear in the period 1962-64 when inflation soared to 50 percent in 1962, 70 percent in 1963, and 80 percent in 1964. At the same time, economic growth rates plummeted to 1.5 percent in 1963 and 2.9 percent in 1964. Capital flight became a critical problem. Confronting the economic disaster, Brazil's military leaders led a bloodless revolution in March 1964. In this well-balanced study, Financial Structure and Development, Raymond Goldsmith pointed out that the assets of Brazilian financial institutions, which represented 70 percent of the GNP in 1948, had declined to 55 percent of GNP by 1963. In addition, the annual rate of real growth during the period 1948-63 was 3.8 percent, which was lower than in the period 1937-48 when financial institutions experienced a growth rate of 5% per year. Under these conditions, the gap between savings and investment was filled by inflation and foreign debt.

1965-72: Progress, Prosperity, and Problems

The year 1964 was a major turning point in Brazil's economic and financial evolution. The new government, stressing a strong commitment to private enterprise, set about restoring sound fiscal and monetary affairs and bringing inflation under control. Government spending was cut sharply. The profit remittance law was modified to rekindle interest of foreign investors. The Capital Market Law of 1965 began to change the shape of the financial markets and institutions, which are discussed later at great depth. The theme of the government was "Plan for Economic Action," which meant tight money and wage controls. The inflationary rate did decline to 27 percent in 1967, and the real GDP growth rate was up to 5 percent (see Table 19.1). However, the tight money policy of the central bank created a working capital shortage, which caused a liquidity crisis in 1966. In order to improve the situation further, Brazil's government made efforts to deal with the national economic problems on all fronts. The Strategic Development Program for this period included a substantial increase in infrastructure investment, price controls, a new cruzeiro replaced the old cruzeiro at the rate of 1 for 1,000, and a "minidevaluation" of the new cruzeiro vis-à-vis the U.S. dollar. The creation of the fiscal funds system was intended to stimulate the stock exchange market. In 1969, President Medici announced the "Social Integration Program," which was designed to end the disparity between the North and the South, to lower the illiteracy rate (as high as 70 percent in the North and 13 percent in the South), to build two major highways cutting through the jungles of the Amazon to obtain timber and mineral wealth, and to restructure the import and export program.

TABLE 19.1

Selected Economic and Financial Indicators,
1960-72

Year	Real GDP Growth Rate	Rate of Money Supply	Wholesale Price Index (Annual Percent Change)	Gross Investment as Percentage of GDP
1960	9.7%	38.2%	23.8	18.4
1961	10.3	50.5	43.2	19.4
1962	5.3	63.4	50.2	20.3
1963	1.5	64.0	76.0	18.7
1964	2.9	85.8	81.3	18.6
1965	2.7	74.9	53.6	18.9
1966	5.1	16.0	41.1	12.5
1967	4.8	41.9	26.7	14.4
1968	8.4	43.0	22.7	15.0
1969	9.0	32.8	19.1	16.0
1970	9.5	25.0	19.0	17.5
1971	11.3	22.0	21.4	18.0
1972	11.0	22.0	13.9	18.5

Source: Monthly Bulletin, Central Bank of Brazil, various
issues.

To finance these ambitious and profound programs, the federal
government did not rely on inflationary use of the printing machine,
nor on deficit borrowing from the central bank. Instead, it tapped
domestic financial resources by issuing long-term Treasury bonds
(ORTN) and short-term Treasury bills (LTN). To coordinate this
new financing method, an open-market operation was introduced into
Brazil's fiscal and monetary policy in 1970. To restore the confidence
of financial institutions and individuals, the government adopted the
"readjustment plan," which meant that the value of government securities would be guaranteed by an inflation escalation clause. As Table
19.2 indicates, the Brazilian national Treasury debt has increased
substantially since 1969, mostly financed by the placement of bonds
and bills as well as foreign borrowing. Nevertheless, the national
debt to GDP ratio in 1971 was only 6.7 percent, compared with 35
percent in the United States.

TABLE 19.2

Gross Domestic Product and Public Finance
(millions of cruzeiros)

Year	Brazilian National Treasury Debt (A)*	Net Placements (ORTN+LTN) (B)	Federal Budget Deficit (C)
1964	41	40	728
1965	430	337	593
1966	1,401	629	587
1967	2,482	448	1,225
1968	3,491	93	1,227
1969	5,881	797	756
1970	10,112	2,282	738
1971	15,445	2,987	672

Year	Gross Domestic Product (D)	National Debt Divided by GDP (in percents) (A/D)	Net Placements Divided by Federal Deficit (B/C)
1964	28,055	0.2	5.5
1965	36,818	1.2	56.8
1966	53,724	2.6	107.2
1967	71,485	3.5	36.6
1968	99,880	3.5	7.6
1969	133,117	4.4	105.4
1970	174,624	5.8	309.2
1971	230,702	6.7	444.5

*Year end corrected.

Source: Central Bank of Brazil, Monthly Bulletin, various issues.

As a result of this reform, Brazil's inflation rate was reduced to 15 percent in 1972; the real GDP growth rate increased from 5.1 percent in 1966 to 9.5 percent in 1970 and 11 percent in 1972; per-capita income grew from U.S. $280 in 1966 to about $500 in 1972; gross investment as a percent of GNP has been about 18 percent from 1966 to 1972; federal deficits have been reduced since 1969. Despite the political stability, economic progress, and financial soundness in the past few years, Brazil still has many problems. Income disparity, the danger of demand-pull inflation, population concentration in Sao Paulo, and the needs of skilled labor and capital for developing the northern states are tough problems confronting the government.

Looking ahead, the government announced the First National Economic Development Plan for 1972-74 aiming at (1) bringing economic, social, racial, and political democracy into accordance with Brazilian character, (2) to achieve an annual increase in real GDP of 8 to 10 percent with a reduced inflation rate of 10 percent, and (3) to double per-capita income by 1980 (compared with 1969). Strategically, the government would like to maintain at least a 10-percent growth rate in the industrial sector, especially in steel, motor vehicles, cement, and other exportable manufactured goods. The agricultural sector, which accounts for about 60 percent of GDP, has accounted for 80 percent of foreign exchange earnings and 50 percent of employment. The government intends to maintain its 8 percent growth rate as in the 1960s. In order to achieve these goals, the government probably will have to mobilize all its natural, human, and financial resources, especially the private sector which accounts for 75 percent of gross investment.

FINANCIAL INSTITUTIONS

An Overview of the Financial System

In the period 1946-60, there was very little development in Brazilian financial institutions. In the public sector, which accounts for 25 percent of gross investment, the government has used (1) the National Bank for economic Development to finance operations through the government-controlled savings banks, (2) the printing of paper money, and (3) international borrowing. In the private sector, which accounted for 75 percent of gross investment, Banco do Brasil and other commercial banks take care of short-term financing, and finance companies (financieras) take care of medium-term loans. Between 1960-64, competition for funds by the finance companies pared away the dominance of the commercial banks, while public financial institutions such as the government savings banks remained stagnant. Long-term financing facilities in the private sector were lacking.

In 1964, a complete reorganization of the financial system was undertaken. The government improved the monetary decision-making body, and many new financial institutions were established under the government's new laws. The strengthening of the Brazilian financial system was aimed at better coordinating the new government economic development programs and at facilitating government efforts to achieve industrialization.

At the top of the financial pyramid stands the National Monetary Council (NMC), which was created in 1964 to replace the Superintendency of Money and Credit. The NMC has overall authority to coordinate the monetary, credit, budgeting, fiscal, and public debt policies consistent with national goals of economic development and social needs. The principal functions of the NMC are to formulate and control the nation's monetary policy through the supervision of the central bank and the Bank of Brazil, Inc. It determines the currency issue, reserve requirements, discount rate, and open-market operation. In this respect, it is somewhat like the Board of Governors of the Federal Reserve System in the United States.

Next to the NMC is the Central Bank of Brazil, which was founded in 1965. The Central Bank has the authority to implement the monetary and credit policy formulated by the NMC by supervising all public and private financial institutions, regulating foreign exchange and capital, bank credits, and capital markets.

Bank of Brazil, Inc. (Banco do Brasil) is a semiofficial institution organized as a corporation. About 56 percent of its share capital belongs to the federal government, and the remainder is held by the public. It is under the supervision of the NMC and acts as the financial agent of the Treasury, but has to coordinate with the Central Bank. In fact, before the founding of the Central Bank, the Bank of Brazil was an instrument of government monetary policy. At present, the Bank of Brazil receives sight and time deposits (over 60 percent are government funds) and makes loans to industry and agriculture as well as issues export credits. It has been responsible for more than a third of total bank lending to the private sector. It maintains about 800 branches all over the country and in many international financial centers such as New York, London, Tokyo, Hamburg, and throughout Latin America.

Public Financial Institutions

The public financial institutions are auxiliary agencies in the execution of the credit policy of the federal government under the guidance of the NMC and the Central Bank.

The National Economic Development Bank (BNDE) was organized in 1952 as a government agency to stimulate national economic development by means of financing, or sometimes administering development programs. Its primary objective is to build up basic industries, such as electricity, transportation, iron, and steel. Its financial resources are from government financial institutions as well as from international financial institutions such as the World Bank, Agency for International Development (AID), and Inter-American Development Bank (IDB).

The National Housing Bank was established in 1964 to stimulate the mortgage market, which had lagged behind the economy due to prolonged inflation. It is the principal instrument of the federal government's housing policy, and coordinates the real estate credit companies in the private sector. It was capitalized from a special 1-percent tax on wages and salaries. It guarantees bonds issued by the real estate credit companies for financing construction and mortgages. It is somewhat like the Government National Mortgage Association in the United States, but its financial activity is less extensive.

Federal and State Savings Banks are old government financial institutions dating back to the Portuguese era. They have been operated by the federal and state governments. Since the government revamped these institutions in 1964 and 1969, they are an important mechanism for absorbing small savings and extending loans to local communities. These institutions have been active in the mortgage market in making consumer loans. They are exempt from reserve requirements imposed by the Central Bank and, therefore, can afford to lend money at lower interest rates than other banking institutions.

Other government financial institutions, such as the Bank of the Northeast of Brazil and Bank of Regional Development, are designed to provide long-term credit for developing certain backward areas. The National Bank for Cooperative Credit and the Amazon Credit Bank extend short-term credits to rural areas.

Private Financial Institutions

Brazil has been a private-enterprise-oriented country for a long time. However, its financial institutions did not develop fully due to the nature of its economy. Commercial banks came into being following the promulgation of Decree Law No. 4182 in 1920. Under the present law, Brazilian commercial banks are prohibited from receiving savings, issuing bonds and debentures, and acquiring real property except for their own use. About 90 percent of their deposits are sight deposits, and 10 percent are time deposits. A large part of their loans is in the form of discounting receivables, similar to

what is called factoring in the United States. During the 1950s and the
early 1960s when inflation rates were high, commercial banks were
very active in the short-term market to meet the heavy demand for
working capital. As a result, banks expanded rapidly in terms of
assets, personnel, and branches. Since 1965, the number of commercial banks declined from 331 to 158 at year end 1971. This resulted
from inefficient operations, poor earnings, and a tendency for mergers.

Finance companies (financieras) existed before 1960, but they
expanded their activities rapidly between 1960-66 owing to innovations
under special circumstances. For instance, during the early 1960s,
the government limited the interest rate to 12 percent in order to fight
inflation. In order to circumvent the government regulation, letra
de cambio was created as a substitute for bank credit. A letra de
cambio is a bill of exchange issued by a company and normally guaranteed by its account receivables. The letra is accepted by a finance
company which, in turn, sells the paper to the public. While the borrower purports to pay only the legal interest rate, the letra is sold
at a substantial discount; thus the cost to borrower and the return for
the investor substantially exceed the 12 percent fixed by law. As a
result, finance companies grew from 70 in 1960 to 272 in 1966, but
declined to 168 in 1971 due to the emergence of the investment banks
encouraged by the government for long-term financing.

Investment banks were created in 1966 for the purpose of extending loans from six months to two years. The number grew year
by year, reaching 40 at the end of 1971. By 1975, these banks will
be required by law to finance only medium- and long-term borrowings.
They can underwrite security issues, sell certificates of deposit
(CDs), accept letras, purchase shares, and collaborate with foreign
banks such as the First National City Bank of New York, Fuji Bank
of Japan, or Credit Lyonnais of France.

Other private financial institutions include mutual fund companies (since 1957), real estate credit companies (since 1964), savings
and loan associations (since 1966), and fiscal funds (since 1971).
Insurance companies are important in the capital market since they
are required to put 50 percent of their assets in real estate and
under 30 percent in the securities markets.

Financial Institutions—Sources and
Uses of Funds

As Table 19.3 illustrates, sources of funds in financial institutions during the period 1960-72 grew rapidly. Between 1960-64, when
inflation reached its peak, the Central Bank was the most important
source of funds. It doubled the funds supplied (in constant cruzeiros

TABLE 19.3

Financial Institutions—Liabilities
(millions of constant cruzeiros of 1960)

	1960	1964	1968	1970	1971	1972 June
Funds received from the personal and productive sectors	887	1.014	1.602	2.207	2.840	2.913
Debt	819	927	1.447	1.979	2.433	2.599
Equity capital	68	87	155	228	307	314
Funds received from the rest of the world	155	296	272	228	247	309
Central Bank	140	284	216	132	115	116
Other financial institutions	15	12	56	96	132	193
Funds received from the government sectors	146	177	291	461	517	541
Deposits	42	59	48	47	53	60
Government funds	57	65	67	117	108	97
Equity on the net worth of financial institutions	47	53	176	297	356	384
Total	1.188	1.487	2.165	2.896	3.604	3.763

Source: Central Bank of Brazil.

of 1960) from 140 to 284 millions, while total sources of funds increased by only 25 percent. After 1964, the picture changed quantitatively and qualitatively. Between 1964 and 1972, total sources of funds increased by 140 percent, funds received from the personal and productive sectors increased by 180 percent, from the government sector by 200 percent, with virtually no change in the rest-of-the-world sector. In other words, the sources of funds in this period came from all major economic sectors, including international institutions. The declining supply of funds from the Central Bank reflected the consistent antiinflation policy of the government. One hidden problem must be noted. The increased borrowings abroad, which increased from 12 million cruzeiros in 1964 to 193 millions in June 1972, signifies the heavy burden of foreign debt service which may have an adverse effect on Brazil's international balance of payments in future.

The assets or uses of funds of financial institutions also showed drastic changes during the period 1964-72. Table 19.4 shows the evolution of the uses of funds in real terms. The characteristics of this evolution can be described as follows:

1. Financial institutions increased their claims on government mostly in terms of indexed bonds and Treasury bills. This signifies an increase in liquidity holdings and also confidence in government debt.

2. The amount of credit the financial institutions are able to provide to the personal and productive sectors after 1964 has been rising in real terms by 25 percent per year. These were in the form of business and consumer loans, which are the main forces in generating growth in domestic product.

3. The rebuilding of Brazil's international reserves since 1970 has resulted in almost a doubling, which certainly strengthened Brazil's international credit position.

MONEY AND CAPITAL MARKETS

Financial Market Development

The Brazilian money market began to operate in the eighteenth century when gold and diamonds were discovered in the central region. Brazil was the chief source of gold in Europe before the California gold rush in the mid-nineteenth century. Prior to World War II, short-term bank loans and mining and industrial shares trading in the Rio de Janeiro and Sao Paulo Stock Exchanges were the major financial market activities in Brazil. During the 1950s, inflation impaired financial market development because it taxed

TABLE 19.4

Financial Institutions—Assets
(millions of constant cruzeiros of 1960)

	1960	1964	1968	1970	1971	1972 June
Claims on Government	63	11	102	185	245	328
Claims on state and municipal government	33	6	23	32	37	33
Indexable bonds	—	2	79	149	159	212
compulsory	—	2	42	96	102	107
voluntary	—	—	37	53	57	105
Other federal securities	30	3	—	—	—	—
compulsory	21	2	—	—	—	—
voluntary	9	1	—	—	—	—
Treasury bills	—	—	—	4	49	83
Claims on the rest of the world (monetary authorities—assets in foreign currencies)	78	105	67	192	252	360
Claims in the personal and productive sectors	617	530	1.186	1.823	2.274	2.571
Net balance of others counts	430	841	810	696	733	504
Total	1.188	1.487	2.165	2.896	3.504	3.763

Source: Central Bank of Brazil.

investors, shrank the real stock of financial assets, redistributed income among workers and industrialists, and caused misallocation of funds (people preferred putting money in real estate and commodities rather than corporate securities). Nevertheless, inflation helped Brazil's economic development to some extent due to the fact that during the 1950s, wages fell behind prices and industrial owners plowed back their excessive profit. Inflation also created a new money market instrument—the letra de cambio, as previously described.

The Capital Market Law of 1965 was an omnibus bill aimed at replacing inflationary government credit with a functioning capital market. The law has had far-reaching consequences for Brazil's development planning as well as financial institutions and instruments. Five major features of the law are described.

1. To eliminate specific barriers to market development: For example, money correction was authorized to protect lenders against inflation. Obstacles to issue of convertible debentures were also removed by the law.

2. To introduce new institutions: Investment banks were established and became a new dynamic force in the financial markets since they were allowed to deal with almost every kind of financial activity ranging from accepting letra to brokerage business. The mortgage market was also stimulated by the founding of the National Housing Bank, real estate credit companies, and savings and loan associations.

3. To modernize existing institutions: The government revamped the government and state savings banks so they could be more active in the allocation of funds in the local communities. The law broke the monopoly of stock brokers by allowing financieras and investment banks to do brokerage and mutual fund business. This strengthened the secondary markets.

4. To create new regulations on the securities market: Prior to 1965, there was no government regulation on the securities markets. The new law stipulated that securities issues must be registered at the Central Bank. Firms listed on stock exchanges must submit data on balance sheets, financial structure, and insider stock holdings certified by independent accountant.

5. To modernize corporate management: Since most corporations in Brazil at that time were family owned, they were more interested in retaining control over companies, less interested in promoting efficiency and profit, and consequently leaned toward vertical combinations in agriculture, commerce, and industry. In order to open these closed corporations and educate investors, the law introduced a new concept: the "open capital company." For example, taxpayers in Brazil may deduct from gross income a percentage of sums spent acquiring certain securities. Tax incentives were also given to

companies that sold 20 to 49 percent of their voting shares to the public or allowed representation of minority groups on the board of directors.

The law was partly successful. On the positive side, the continued growth of GDP and increased financial activities in the markets were very encouraging to the government's economic planners. On the negative side, tight money led to capital shortage in 1966 and affected the purchase of securities in both primary and secondary markets. Furthermore, continued inflation forced companies to pay lower dividends, to accumulate more retained earnings, and to issue fewer stocks. Investors preferred putting their money in real estate and commodities to hedge against inflation. For these reasons, the law did not achieve the purpose of strengthening the financial markets and democratizing business corporations as originally expected.

The Decree Law No. 157 in February 1967 was issued to improve several provisions of the Capital Market Law of 1965. The key feature of the D.L. 157 system is a special "fiscal fund." The law authorized financial institutions, such as financieras, brokers, and investment banks, to create special mutual investment funds (157 funds). At the same time, it also gave a tax credit from 12 to 14 percent to all tax-payers for sums applied in purchasing shares of these mutual funds. Fiscal funds are required to have a minimum of 25 percent or maximum of 50 percent of their portfolio invested in new issues of small- and medium-size firms approved by the government. The fiscal funds may also be used to invest in national "open capital companies" up to 25 percent within the 50-percent maximum limit. The first was designed to stimulate the primary market, and the second was intended to stimulate the secondary market since all open capital companies have their shares traded on at least one of the exchanges. D.L. 157 played a crucial part in the rapid development of Brazil's capital market between 1968-71, but the redemption of fiscal mutual funds during the second half of 1972 depressed the secondary market somewhat. However, the market revived again in 1973, and the technical aspects of the law are being improved.

Money and Credit Markets

Money and credit markets have existed for more than a century in Brazil, but they have only become prominent after the 1950s. A number of new credit instruments have been created in the 1960s. At present, the most active credit markets in Brazil are the following: Treasury obligations (bonds and bills), acceptance bills (acceptance exchanges), term deposits, mortgage bills (letra imobiliarias), and savings deposits. The following briefly describes these market sectors.

398

Treasury Obligations

Federal securities suffered a drawback during the 1950s and 1960s due to inflation. The issuance of indexable bonds since 1964 restored investors' confidence, but the most important development was the advent of the Treasury bill and open-market operations in 1970. These have had a significant influence on the national credit markets. Even in 1967, the Central Bank of Brazil established a Public Department for the purpose of coordinating all federal, state, and municipal debt issues in order to improve the techniques of debt management. There are two kinds of Treasury obligations: Treasury bonds and bills both are handled by the Central Bank through institutional dealers and sold in the over-the-counter market. Bonds are issued for one- , two- , and five-year maturities, and interest is paid in accordance with rates of indexation based on a coefficient established by the Ministry of Planning and Coordination. They are called indexable bonds and are flexible under inflationary conditions. At the end of 1971, 53 percent of these bonds were held by the Central Bank, and 26 percent were held by the commercial banking system. This is understandable since the Central Bank and commercial banks are major participants in the open-market operation. Treasury bills are issued at a discount rate of 15 to 18 percent per annum for 91- and 180-day maturities. They carry a nominal minimum value of 1,000 cruzeiros. Investment banks are principal holders of Treasury bills (about 60 percent of outstandings), and the commercial banks hold substantial amounts for liquidity purposes. As Table 19.5 shows, Treasury obligations were the fastest-growing credit instrument between 1970-72. They are a major tool of the government's monetary/policy.

Acceptance Bills or Letra de Cambio

Letra de Cambio was instituted in Brazil under specific legislation in 1908. This paper, as discussed previously, was important during the inflationary period. They are issued by firms for working capital purposes, or by financieras and investment banks for consumer finance. Since the advent of the indexable bonds, Treasury bills, and CDs, the relative importance of the acceptance bills in the credit market has been declining.

Term Deposits

Term deposits include CDs at commercial banks and fixed-term deposits with monetary correction at the commercial banks and investment banks. Despite the increasing importance of the CDs since

TABLE 19.5

Credit Market Instruments Outstanding
(millions of cruzeiros)

	1972[b]	1971	1970
Treasury obligations (LTNs and ORTNs)[a]	22,686	15,445	6,031
Acceptance bills	17,909	14,390	9,756
Term deposits	11,284	8,606	4,024
Letras imobiliárias (Mortgage bills)	3,580	2,907	1,862
Savings deposits	5,434	3,784	2,106
Total	Cr$ 60,893	Cr$ 45,132	Cr$ 23,779

[a]Estimated.

[b]At June 30, 1972. The totals at June 30, 1971 and 1970 were, respectively, Cr$33.4 and Cr$18.7 billion.

Source: Central Bank of Brazil.

their creation in 1965, fixed-term deposits in investment banks accounted for over 60 percent of the total or Cr$11,286 million as of June 1972. The growth rate of these credit instruments between 1970 and 1973 has been impressive, owing to the negotiable nature of CDs and monetary correction of fixed-interest rates which protects holders. From the investor's standpoint, these instruments provide protection as well as flexibility.

Mortgage Bills

Mortgage bills were created in 1966 to provide for financing residential construction. These bills are issued by housing finance companies and are guaranteed by the National Housing Bank. The outstanding sales of these bills have been impressive. The total amount of bills outstanding was Cr$12 million in 1966, but grew to Cr$3,580 million in June 1972. Investors like to purchase them because interest received by an individual up to Cr$550 per year is tax exempt.

Savings Deposits

Savings deposits are important sources of funds for both long-
and short-term credits. Government and state savings banks, which
accounted for about 80 percent of the total (Cr$5,434 million), can
use the funds for mortgage loans and consumer loans to local communities. Other institutions, such as housing finance companies and
savings and loan associations, employ the funds mostly for long-term
mortgage credit in the housing sector.

Capital Market

The capital market is a relative latecomer in Brazil. The predominantly agricultural economy did not require a capital market,
and deficit financing result in inflation impaired capital market
development. Furthermore, family-controlled industries relied exclusively on internal financing and bank loans. Investors channeled
their funds to real estate and commodities, or even to foreign financial centers for investment. Shares were issued by several popular
mining firms and Banco do Brasil, but there was no bond issue except
for government bonds.

The year 1958 marked the commencement of securities offers
made directly to the general public. After 1961, as a consequence of
the lack of liquidity, some firms issued shares and bonds but distributed the securities through private placement. Under these circumstances, the primary market remained insignificant. Between
1962-64, hyperinflation and political instability discouraged development of the capital market. Until 1965, the capital market was only
in an emerging stage. As explained previously, the Capital Market
Law of 1965 changed the capital market completely. New financial
institutions and instruments, "open capital companies" and "fiscal
funds," government incentives to issuers and investors, tougher regulations and market control have all made Brazil a classic example
of vigorous capital market development for industrial development
among less developed countries.

As a result of this unprecedented drive, the number of open
capital corporations increased from 289 in 1968 to 526 at June 1972;
issues of shares for public offering in the Central Bank grew from a
value of Cr$263 million in 1968 to Cr$2,306 million in 1971; financial
institutions such as investment banks became pillars of the capital
market; the general public and business firms increased their participation in the market; the number of stock exchanges increased from
10 in 1967 to 16 in 1971; and securities sales agencies grew from
556 in 1968 (the year of their inception) to 572 in 1971.

As regards the primary market, the impressive volume of new issues for public offering was Cr$2,306, which was only about 1 percent of Brazil's GDP in 1971 (Table 19.6). New Issues declined in the first half of 1972 due to the depressed stock market. Table 19.7 illustrates one of the positive results observed in the primary market during the period under consideration. This was the growth of financial institutions which advise, promote, and distribute new issues of shares and bonds to investors. Table 19.8 reflects the use of funds in the primary capital market. Manufacturing industry accounted

TABLE 19.6

New Issues of Shares for Public Offering
(millions of cruzeiros)

1968	263
1969	141
1970	321
1971	2,306
1972 (up to November)	517

Source: Central Bank of Brazil.

TABLE 19.7

Stocks and Debentures for Public Offering
through Financial Institutions

Financial Institutions	1970		1971	
	Cr$ millions	No. of Offerings	Cr$ millions	No. of Offerings
Investment banks	94.1	15	1,149.1	106
Development banks	15.0	1	189.2	5
Finance companies	5.2	4	19.7	2
Brokerage firms	91.9	37	455.4	80
Securities sales agencies	115.6	26	492.1	60
Miscellaneous	—	—	0.7	1
Total	321.8	83	2,306.2	254

Source: Central Bank of Brazil.

TABLE 19.8

Register of Stock and Debenture Issues at Central
Bank for Public Offering, Distribution by Sectors
of Activity
(millions of cruzeiros)

Sectors	1970	1971
Manufacturing industries	238	1,217
Finance institutions	61	344
Public utilities	—	397
Mining industries	—	24
Building trade	—	84
Transportation enterprises	1	50
Communication (TV, radio, and so on)	2	21
Retail trade	12	96
Business administration and trust funds	8	37
Agriculture and livestock	—	3
Total	322	2,306

Source: Central Bank of Brazil.

for about 50 percent of the total Cr$2,306 of new issues in 1971, followed by financial institutions which shared 13 percent, public utilities which took 15 percent, and other industry sectors which made up the remaining 22 percent of new issues. The greatest concentration of fund users is along the Rio-Sao Paulo axis, where most industries, financial institutions, open capital companies, and higher-income groups are located.

As regards the secondary market, the stock exchanges of Rio de Janeiro and Sao Paulo are the largest among the 16 stock exchanges in Brazil. Their transactions account for 90 percent of all stock exchange business in Brazil. It is interesting to note (Table 19.9 and 19.10) that the Sao Paulo exchange surpassed the Rio exchange in 1972 in trading volume, due to the decrease in fiscal funds in the Rio area. The stock market performed excellently in the period 1968-71. But during the first seven months of 1972, pessimism overruled and prices fell to undervalued levels. The stock market indices in Rio were down from 3,720 in December 1971 to 1,850 at year end 1972. In the same period, the Sao Paulo market indices went down from 1,816 to 1,004. The decline was mainly attributable to investors who had purchased mutual funds for the first time in the market peak of 1971, became disenchanted, and sold their participations. As the trend continued, some funds were forced to sell stocks to reach safe liquidity levels, and this put downward pressure on many stocks.

Despite the changing market behavior, the two largest stock exchanges (Rio and Sao Paulo) were gradually transformed from specific markets engaging primarily in trading of shares already in circulation into integrated markets operating in all market phases, including issuance of shares and support of their prices and promotion of genuine liquidity for the securities traded in the market. Use of trading posts was adopted in these two exchanges in 1967, and they now handle round and odd lot transactions. As of 1971, there were 355 firms listed on the Rio de Janeiro Stock Exchange, while only 168 of them had national registration. The exchange initiated a number of innovations since 1969, including a future market in shares, with a maximum term for settlement of 180 days. A system of electronic computation and teleprocessing of data for regular investors was established in 1971. A number of securities studies and weekly publications which are made available to the general public have been used by the Rio de Janeiro Stock Exchange.

TABLE 19.9

Volume of Trading
(millions of cruzeiros)

Stock Exchange	1968	1969	1970	1971	1972
Rio de Janeiro	252.1	1,568.9	2,967.4	14,394.2	7,707.9
Sao Paulo	163.3	1,000.0	1,591.7	11,195.3	10,370.5
Total	415.4	2,568.9	4,559.1	25,589.5	18,088.4
Average dollar rate	3.54	4.09	4.61	5.29	6.095

TABLE 19.10

Volume of Trading
(millions of shares)

Stock Exchange	1968	1969	1970	1971	1972
Rio de Janeiro	203.9	568.9	919.3	2,653.4	2,087.1
Sao Paulo	89.0	311.1	637.6	2,377.6	3,512.0
Total	292.9	880.0	1,556.9	5,031.0	5,599.1

Source: Central Bank of Brazil.

In conclusion, barring unforeseeable developments, Brazil's capital market should provide more substantial support to the growth and development process than in the past. Brazil's government has tried hard to complete the task of rapid industrialization. The outlook is bright. However, development of capital market institutions will require additional time, since they are relatively young and lacking in experience and grass-roots contact with the widespread population of the country.

GOVERNMENT POLICY AND INTERNATIONAL FINANCE

Government Policy toward Foreign Capital and Exchange

Brazil's international finance policy has varied after World War II. It became a member and participated in the activities of the IMF and the World Bank. Between 1947 and 1953, the Brazilian government policy was to maintain a fixed exchange rate with the U.S. dollar regardless of its domestic inflation. As a result, exports decreased due to higher export prices, and foreign investment inflows were only about $27 million. In the period 1954-61, multiple exchange rates were adopted by the Brazilian government in order to protect domestic products and improve exports. Foreign investment increased to $137 million in 1960, but decreased in the period 1962-64 because of hyperinflation and the financial difficulty of the government in meeting external debt repayment schedules. In 1964, the government adopted a free exchange rate and promised to rearrange the payment schedule. This prompt action was well received by international financial institutions and private investors. As indicated in Table 19.11, in the period 1965-72 the annual variation in the dollar/cruzeiro exchange rate was moderate with the exception of one year (1968). International economic assistance to Brazil from 1964 to 1970 amounted to $3,559 million, of which AID accounted for approximately 50 percent, and the rest came from the World Bank, the IDB, Export-Import Bank, IMF, UN Development Program, and Ford Foundation. Total external debt, as illustrated in Table 19.12, was $7,237 million in March 1972, of which one-half was in currency loans. Approximately one-half of the foreign debt was designed to finance economic development projects such as steel, aluminum, highway construction, and hydroelectric power. The remainder was in currency loans partly to provide short-term financing in the domestic money market and partly for the repayment of principal and interest on foreign debt.

405

TABLE 19.11

Official Dollar/Cruzeiro Exchange Rate

December 31	Purchase	Sale	Annual Variation (in percent)
1965	2.20	2.22	—
1966	2.20	2.22	0.0
1967	2.70	2.715	22.30
1968	3.805	3.83	41.07
1969	4.325	4.350	13.58
1970	4.95	4.95	13.79
1971	5.60	5.635	13.84
1972*	6.18	6.215	10.30

*As of December 15.

Source: Central Bank of Brazil.

TABLE 19.12

Brazil's Foreign Debt
(millions of dollars)

End of	Total Debt	Currency Loans	Currency Loans as a Percent of Total
December 1969	4,403.3	1,604.7	36.4
March 1970	4,714.6	1,846.5	39.2
June 1970	4,907.4	1,959.9	39.9
September 1970	5,084.4	2,128.5	41.9
December 1970	5,295.2	2,284.6	43.1
March 1971	5,526.0	2,455.3	44.4
June 1971	5,772.8	2,650.7	45.9
September 1971	6,125.3	2,901.6	47.4
December 1971	6,621.1	3,193.0	48.2
March 1972	7,237.4	3,607.5	49.8
Change from December 1969 to March 1972	2,834.1	2,002.6	70.7

Source: Central Bank of Brazil.

The growth in foreign debt has placed Brazil in third rank as an international debtor, according to the analysis used by the World Bank in its 1971 Annual Reports. The rapid inflow of foreign currency loans has caused concern for Brazil's monetary authority, which intended to lengthen the minimum term on foreign loans to six years and to stretch out the debt repayment schedule over a longer period.

As regards the foreign exchange rate, the Brazilian government adopted a "minidevaluation" system vis-à-vis the U.S. dollar. The gradual devaluation of the cruzeiro has realistically reflected not only domestic inflation, but also international transactions. Brazil still retains exchange control. Foreign remittance and Brazilian tourists abroad have to follow limits set by the Central Bank. Exchange transactions are performed by the Central Bank and the Bank of Brazil which follow the policy formulated by the NMC.

As the needs for foreign capital continue and Brazil faces the problem of inflation, the government and financial institutions will have to become even more active in the international financial markets. The following exemplify past practices in this area. In order to achieve the general investment goal for the 1972-74 period, Brazil's government has appealed to the international financial institutions (World Bank, IDB, and others) to extend loans to support its infrastructure projects. The Bank of Brasil, as the government fiscal agent, issued $30 million in Eurobonds in the first half of 1972 in order to take advantage of the lower interest rate prevailing at that time. Using its worldwide banking network, the Bank of Brasil, together with several investment banks and foreign banks, has formed a "consortium" to provide long-term investment in Brazil and short-term import financing. U.S. banks, UK banks, Japanese banks, and even a Russian bank with a London branch representation participated in these projects. To hedge currency depreciation and high local interest rates, the Bank of Brazil has made available swap loans for multinational corporations doing business in Brazil. All inflows of foreign capital must be registered at the Central Bank, which closely scrutinizes such lending and foreign exchange activities.

Balance of Payments

Prior to 1960, Brazil has experienced deficits on trade account. Between 1960 and 1970, trade surpluses showed in most years, but sizable deficits were incurred on freight and insurance. Capital inflows were an important means of financing total transactions.

Brazil's foreign trade account reflects many changes taking place in the national economy. Agricultural products provide two-thirds of exports, but manufactured goods have gradually become

TABLE 19.13

Balance of Payments
(millions of dollars)

	1967	1968	1969	1970	1971
Current Account:					
Exports (f.o.b.)	$ 1,654	$ 1,881	$ 2,311	$ 2,739	$ 2,90
Imports (f.o.b.)	-1,441	-1,855	-1,993	-2,507	-3,25
Services (net)	-527	-556	-630	-815	-97
Transfers abroad (net)	77	22	31	21	1
Balance on current account	-237	-508	-281	-562	-1,31
Capital account (net):					
Direct investments (net)	76	61	124	108	12
Long-term loans and financing	512	551	1,030	1,440	2,04
Repayment of principal	-444	-484	-533	-673	-87
Short-term loans and other	-117	413	229	140	54
Balance on capital account	27	541	850	1,015	1,83
Errors and omissions	-35	-1	-20	92	3
Surplus or deficit	$-245	$ 32	$ 549	$ 545	$ 55

Source: IMF, International Financial Statistics, April 1973.

important items on the export list. In 1962, manufactured goods only
accounted for 3.8 percent of total exports at a time when coffee shared
53 percent. Conversely, in 1972, while coffee decreased its portion
of export receipts to 24.3 percent of the total, manufactured goods
rose to 25.6 percent. Brazil's imports are mainly machines and
raw materials for industrial development. Brazil's major trading
partners are the United States and Western Europe, each of which
accounted for about a quarter of total trade. The programs for
export diversification and import substitution have been operating
well. The export and import sectors have, in recent years, shown
an annual growth rate of 14 percent, which is above the average of
less developed nations.

While the balance on current account continues to show deficits
(Table 19.13), this has been offset in the capital accounts, especially

long-term loans and financing. Nevertheless, total international reserves have increased from $655 million in 1969 to $3.5 billion in 1972.

At present, the basic philosophy of the Brazilian government concerning its international balance of payments is a sophisticated one. The trade policy is to increase exports of manufactured goods to the Latin American Free Trade Association (LAFTA) countries. Brazil is a member of this group and exports 10 percent of total merchandise exports to LAFTA member countries. At the same time, it wants to cut down imports by producing more at home. However, increasing internal prices have forced imports up. The intangible service items are inflexible components on the deficit side of Brazil's balance of payments. While Brazil intends to encourage foreign direct investment, which was about $6 million at the end of 1972 (the United States shared about one-third of the total), loans have increased at a rapid pace. Brazil's government has had a flexible attitude toward foreign investment and has applied subtle techniques to control loans and financing. Foreign investing countries, including the Organization for Economic Corporation and Development (OECD) countries, and the international financial institutions will have confidence in this fast-growing nation as long as the ratio of capital inflow and international reserves to foreign debt continues to improve. Moreover, continued control of inflation will further add to the confidence of private foreign investors.

REFERENCES

Banco do Brasil, S.A. Prospectus on External Bonds, December 14, 1972.

Bank of London and South America. Bolsa Review, August 1972.

Central Bank of Brasil. Boletim, December 1972.

Basch and Others. Capital Markets in Latin America. New York: Praeger Publishers, 1970.

The Economist. "A Survey of Brasil," September 2-8, 1972.

Ellis, Howard, ed. The Economy of Brazil. Berkeley: University of California Press, 1969.

Four papers presented by the Rio de Janeiro Stock Exchange at the seminar on "Brazilian Capital Markets" in New York at the Securities Industry Association, February 1973.

Goldsmith, Raymond W. Financial Structure and Development. New
    Haven, Conn.: Yale University Press, 1969.

Inter-American Development Bank. The Mobilization of Internal
    Financial Resources in Latin America, 1971.

Trubeck, David M. Law Planning and the Development of the Brazilian
    Capital Market. New York: Institute of Finance, New York
    University, 1971.

20

INTRODUCTION

Argentina covers almost the entire southeastern part of South America. It occupies an area of about 1 million square miles, approximately one-third of the size of the United States, and is bordered by Chile on the west, by Bolivia and Paraguay on the north, by Brazil and Uruguay on the northeast, and by the Atlantic Ocean on the east. Since Argentina has over 2,000 miles of coastline, climate ranges from semitropical in the north to frigid in the south. Temperature readings range from 120°F in the north to 3°F in the south. Buenos Aires, the largest seaport and the nation's capital, has an average annual temperature of about 62°F. The Pampa, Argentina's economic, political, and cultural center, spreads out in a 350-mile arc from Buenos Aires.

As measured by per-capita income in 1973, Argentina is a developed country. It is the most industrialized nation in Latin America. Its farm products such as beef and wheat and its industrial products such as automobiles are closely related to its natural resources, good climate, and immigration policy.

After years of colonization under Spain, Argentina became an independent nation in 1810, but the Constitution of 1853 provided a system of government similar to that of the United States with three branches of government. The term of office of the president in Argentina is six years. During the second half of the nineteenth century, the nation's rulers were landowning aristocracy and intellectuals who developed the country according to the values and needs of the ruling elite. Around 1857, the government began to develop the grasslands and railroads, to improve the Buenos Aires seaport, to explore Chaco State, and to establish meat-packing and flour-milling plants. In this period, Argentina resembled the United States which

411

had a plentiful supply of land, but needed capital and skilled labor. To fill this gap, British investment poured into Argentina in the areas of commerce, railroads, and farming. During this period, immigrants from England, Ireland, Germany, Italy, Hungary, and Austria flowed into Argentina. By 1914, about 30 percent of the population was foreign born, and over 40 percent of total investment was foreign capital. Most immigrants of European origin did provide the skills and entre- preneurial ability needed for economic development.

World War I gave Argentina's development a strong impetus, due to the global scarcity of manufactured goods. This change in economic direction resulted in a shift toward a liberal government, which was elected in 1916. A change in foreign economic relations also took place during the depression of the 1930s when England signed the Ottawa Agreement with Canada in 1932, which extended British preferential trade treatment to Canada over Argentina. Argentina's exports, production, income, and employment were adversely affected. During World War II, Argentina's economy recovered as a result of the increased demand for her industrial and agricultural products. The year 1943 was the first time Argentina's industrial output ex- ceeded agricultural production. According to a report of the United Nations Economic Commission for Latin America, in the period 1930-45, Argentina expanded its population by 40 percent, its gross national product (GNP) by 40 percent, and industrial production by 65 percent.

When General Perón governed the country from 1945-55, the industrial sector had priority over the agricultural sector. During this period, industrial production, workers' wages, and the cost of living increased, but exports were retarded.

The new military government, which ruled from 1960 to 1973, launched a series of antiinflation measures, improved tax collection, cut down public payrolls and government financing, and put equal emphasis on industry and agriculture. However, two major problems persisted: unstable government and inflation. In the period 1960-71 (Table 20.1), the real GNP increased at a 3.7-percent average annual rate, and the cost of living rose at an annual rate of 25 percent. Gross investment as a percentage of gross domestic product (GDP) fluctuated between 16 and 23 percent. Per-capita income was about $526 in 1960, $871 in 1970, and $1,269 in 1972. In fact, 1972 was a year of inflation and social unrest. The election of General Juan Perón as the President of the Republic in September 1973 raised the hope of bringing the country back to normalcy but his death in mid-1974 has left the country's mounting economic and social problems unsolved.

TABLE 20.1

Selected Economic Indicators for Argentina, 1960–72

	GNP (undeflated in billion pesos)	Percent Change in Real GNP	Consumer Prices 1963 = 100	Money Supply (billion pesos)	Cost of Living Index* (percentage) (Based on Construction)	Total Gross Investment as Percent of GDP
1960	956	—	55	218	27.0	22.8
1961	1,140	7.0	63	243	13.7	23.0
1962	1,403	1.9	80	250	28.0	22.3
1963	1,725	3.5	100	322	24.1	17.0
1964	2,360	8.0	122	459	22.1	17.8
1965	3,604	8.6	157	592	28.6	19.0
1966	4,490	—	207	787	31.9	17.8
1967	5,871	1.9	268	1,092	23.2	18.3
1968	6,832	4.8	311	1,364	16.2	19.1
1969	7,982	6.9	335	1,508	6.7	15.7
1970	15,127	4.8	380	1,796	21.7	—
1971	—	3.7	512	2,361	39.1	—
1972	—	4.1	898	—	58.5	—

*Annual percentage change in index.

Sources: International Monetary Fund (IMF), International Financial Statistics; Central Bank of Argentina, Statistical Bulletin; Antonin Basch, Capital Markets in Latin America (New York: Praeger Publishers, 1970), p. 11.

THE ROLE OF GOVERNMENT IN ECONOMY
AND FINANCE

As indicated earlier, the federal government of Argentina has played a key role in the national economy. At the present time, the government's role in the economy can be classified into two parts. One is the government's direct ownership of several key industries, such as utilities, transportation, communication, and firms exploring natural resources. Another is active supervision in areas such as minimum wages, price controls, subsidies and incentive programs, exchange controls, and trade regulations. Within this framework, the government exercises its influence over the national economy mostly through the government budget and the national investment plan.

As illustrated in Table 20.2, the National Investment Plan in 1971-72 emphasized state enterprises and public corporations including railroads, gas and petrochemicals, and steel. In other words, the government still placed great efforts in the areas of manufacturing and public utilities which, together with the private sector, shared 36 percent (contrasted to 13 percent in agriculture and 51 percent in trade and services) of the GNP and accounted for 35 percent of national employment. General budget refers to the amount used for general economic development, such as the improvement of agricultural products for export purposes and the exploration of natural resources in the northern provinces. In view of the recent rising prices of agricultural products in the international commodity markets many arguments have been heard as to whether it would be a good idea for the Argentine government to place more emphasis on beef and wheat exports rather than continuing its import substitution program. In fact, regardless of the government's industrialization and stabilization programs in the past several years, the private sector still accounts for 70 percent of production in the national economy.

The government investment plan and budget have a tremendous impact on the financial markets in Argentine. For instance, Table 20.3 reflects deficits of more than 2 billion pesos in 1971 and 1972, of which the Central Bank of Argentina financed 897 million pesos in 1971 and 1,687 million in 1972. The remainder was financed by obtaining foreign short-term loans and floating foreign bonds. According to Central Bank of Argentina statistics, there was 14 billion pesos of internal debt and $628 million dollars of external debt in 1972. On average, about 10 percent of the government debt has been financed by foreign credits. As a corollary of the government deficits there have been three unfavorable developments in the national economy: The Central Bank financing has generated inflation; the issuance of government bonds has affected people's confidence as well as

414

TABLE 20.2

National Investment Plan
(millions of Argentine dollars)

	1971	1972	Difference
General budget	3,262.8	3,655.0	+12%
State enterprises	3,458.9	5,910.0	+71
Public corporations	1,564.4	2,430.3	+55
Provincial and municipal administration	2,695.9	3,422.8	+27
	10,981.1	15,418.1	+40%

Source: Central Bank of Argentina.

TABLE 20.3

General Budget of the National Administration
(millions of Argentine dollars)

	1971	1972	Difference
Expenditures	16,956.1	21,667.3	+27.8%
Revenues	13,966.9	18,882.6	+34.6
Deficit	2,989.2	2,784.7	- 6.8

Source: Central Bank of Argentina.

investor confidence; and increasing external debt has hurt the balance of payments.

FINANCIAL INSTITUTIONS

Public Financial Institutions

The Central Bank of Argentina (Banco Central de la Republica Argentina) was founded in 1935. It is an autonomous public entity responsible for regulating the volume of bank credit and money circulation, holding and managing international reserves, acting as the government financial agent, and supervising the security markets. Since 1965, it has been authorized to regulate and control nonbank financial institutions. It sets the maximum legal bank interest rate, minimum capital of banks, and loan-capital ratios. In the case of long-term economic development, the Central Bank uses its regulatory power to channel long-term funds according to national priorities. In the area of international finance, it fixes the currency rate, negotiates foreign credits, and issues bonds on behalf of the government. In executing its domestic monetary policy, the Central Bank has three tools to use: open-market operations, discounts, and reserve requirements. The Central Bank has faced tremendous difficulty in the decade ending in 1972 due to the heavy burden of government deficit financing, on the one hand, and the continued inflation, on the other. Improved tax collections since 1967 have helped the monetary authority but the sharp credit expansion in 1971 of 40 percent generated another inflation, which required a tight money policy and price controls in 1972. It is observed that the inconsistent monetary actions will not be ended as long as the high level of inflation continues.

Another powerful public financial institution is the Bank of the Argentine Nation (Banco de la Nacion Argentina), which was founded in 1891. It operates as a commercial bank and accounts for 20 percent of all bank deposits and 30 percent of all bank loans. In 1972, about 80 percent of its resources (deposits of Argentine $6,705 million) were in short-term loans.

There are several specialized public financial institutions in Argentina. The National Development Bank is designed to channel medium- and long-term credits for specified purposes, but it is not as powerful as counterpart institutions in Mexico. Another specialized bank is the National Mortgage Bank, which regulates mortgage funds flowing from the mortgage departments of commercial banks and the savings and loan associations to the construction industry. National Postal Saving Funds are available to make loans to persons of professional and low-income brackets. In addition, these institutions play an active role as institutional investors in the securities market. Also, there are about 20 provincial and municipal banks in different states, of which the Bank of the Province of Buenos Aires is the largest.

Private Financial Institutions

Private banking has a long history in Argentina. In 1822, the Banking Company of Buenos Aires (Compania de Banco de Buenos Aires) was established. In 1854, its name was changed to Banco de

416

la Provincia de Buenos Aires. Before the establishment of the Central
Bank, it was the official bank for government funds. It even issued
30 million pesos of paper currency for the government. In 1887, a
liberal banking law, which imitated the U.S. National Banking System
of 1864, was adopted to stimulate banking development and foreign
banking activities. Some British branch banks were established in
Argentina during this period. The famous government-owned commercial bank, Bank of the Argentine Nation, was formed in 1891.
Between the two world wars, the liberal governments placed more
emphasis on social reforms rather than banking reform, until the
conservative government regained its power in the 1930s when the
Central Bank was established. Another important wave of banking
development in Argentina was in the 1950s when nonbanking financial
institutions such as financieras and mutual funds emerged on the
financial scene and forced the Central Bank to take a new look into
the whole banking structure and control. Unfortunately, political uncertainty and continued inflation have hurt the sound development
of many financial institutions.

The most important private financial institutions are commercial banks, which accept sight, savings, and time deposits. In
Argentina there were 121 commercial banks in 1971, of which 33
were owned by the government, 70 were owned by private citizens,
and 18 were owned by foreigners. They shared 55 percent of the resources of the banking system, while the Central Bank shared 35 percent, and other institutions the remaining 10 percent. All commercial
banks make short-term loans strictly to national enterprises as instructed by the Central Bank. Many commercial banks have mortgage departments and issue 8-percent interest rate mortgage bonds
for financing housing construction. An innovation called "fixed-term"
deposits (minimum one year) has been approved by the Central Bank
since 1971 to attract more deposits to the commercial banking system.
The interest rates are negotiable between the banks and their creditors. The only condition that the commercial banks must comply with
is that at least 50 percent of these funds must be invested in national
production. This measure was adopted to alleviate the inflationary
problem.

Nonbank financial institutions are regulated by the Central Bank
and allowed to pay 19-percent interest for one-year deposits, 23- to
25-percent for 18-month deposits, and 28-percent for deposits of
over 18 months. These institutions include credit unions, private
development banks (financieras), savings and loan associations, and
mutual funds. Credit unions are very popular and powerful financial
institutions in Argentina, especially after the establishment of the
Institute of Cooperative Funds (Instituto Movilizador de Fondos Co-
operativos) in 1958. There were 465 credit unions in 1971, the

members of which included professional people, small manufacturers, and ordinary workers. The credit unions accept time deposits and invest funds in commercial and industrial projects.

Another nonbanking institution is the financieras, which collect savings and issue short-term notes (pagares). They concentrate on financing durable consumer goods, such as automobiles. There were 102 institutions of this kind in 1971. Savings and loan associations recently suffered a setback due to inflation, even though their interest payments and charges are subject to "monetary correction" linked to the cost of construction index. Their deposits represented more than 50 percent of mortgage banking in 1970. Mutual funds began operations in 1960 when the securities market was rising, but the fund units decreased in value when the market declined recently. Insurance companies are relatively unimportant in the Argentine capital market because of their limited amount of resources and their limited investment in real estate and mortgage loans.

Sources and Uses of Funds

Traditionally, Argentina has had a strong sense of self-reliance and mobilizes her financial resources for industrial, commercial, and agricultural development. Exploitation of foreign financial resources is regarded as a last resort. Financial institutions are regulated by the Central Bank. As Table 20.4 indicates, within the period 1968-72, there were substantial increases in sight, savings, and time deposits. However, official deposits did not increase much as a result of inflation. Central Bank obligations represented short-term credits to the public sector. It is worth noting that the Bank of the Argentine Nation, a government-owned enterprise, had 6,705 million pesos in deposits in August 1972, which accounted for one-fifth of total deposits in all commercial banks (32,568 million pesos). This represented 30 percent of all banking loans to the agricultural sector. Savings collected by commercial banks, Development Bank (formerly Industrial Bank), and Postal Saving Funds accounted for over 90 percent of all savings. Growth of time deposits was especially impressive since adoption of the fixed-term deposits in the commercial banks. The growth rates would be lower if they were adjusted by the cost-of-living index.

The sources of funds reflect the lion's share supplied by the private sector. The difference between total sources and uses represents foreign sources of funds that the public sector generally relies upon. In the private sector, industry utilized 35 percent of the total amount. Geographically, the Buenos Aires area absorbed 54.4 percent of the total. The concentration of funds use has tended to be

TABLE 20.4

Sources and Uses of Funds in the Banking System,
1968-72
(millions of pesos)

	1968	1971	August 1972
Sources of funds			
Sight deposits	5,135	10,100	12,977
Savings deposits	3,668	7,500	9,939
Time deposits	611	1,713	3,117
Official deposits	2,786	3,831	4,927
Central Bank obligations	1,130	2,283	2,686
Total sources of funds	13,330	25,427	33,646
Uses of funds			
Public sector	2,288	2,978	5,033
Private sector	11,236	25,010	32,032
Total uses of funds	13,524	27,988	37,065

Source: Central Bank Statistical Bulletin, September 1972.

located in the national capital (Buenos Aires) area, where most industry is located.

Since February 1972, commercial banks have been permitted to pay 18 percent for savings deposits, 22 percent for deposits between 12 and 18 months, and 24 percent for deposits over 18 months in maturity.

MONEY AND CAPITAL MARKETS

Money Market

The money market has been export oriented since the later part of the nineteenth century. From 1880 to 1913, when England exerted economic and financial influence on this developing nation, the London money market was the main source of short-term funds for Argentine commerce, especially imports and exports. Banco de Londres y America de Sur was the principal foreign bank linking financial activities between London and Buenos Aires. The nationalistic tendency since the 1930s has reduced Argentina's reliance on the United Kingdom. Instead, Argentina has built her own financial system headed by the Central Bank and supported by various specialized institutions. After World War II, the advance of Argentine industry has accelerated the demands for short-term funds in all economic sectors, noticeably in industrial and consumer loans.

The most important source of short-term credits is the Central Bank. Its credit policy is carried out by means of rediscounts and advances to commercial banks and the government. It also influences the sources and uses of funds in the entire financial system by imposing ceilings on interest rates that commercial banks and nonbank financial institutions can pay to their depositors.

Short-term commercial bank loans are popular in Argentina due to the reluctance of business corporations to issue securities. Loans can be arranged for three- to six-month maturities and are generally renewable. The maximum interest rate on short-term loans is presently 22 percent, but the effective rate may run to 28 or 32 percent. Overdraft arrangements are also permitted on the same basis. The financieras are active in the money market on two fronts. On the one hand, they issue short-term notes (pagares) for obtaining investors' funds, and they also discount commercial paper and finance consumer durable goods purchases. The maximum rate for these credits is 28 percent.

Savings and loan associations and the mortgage departments of commercial banks extend personal loans to individuals and families for housing purchases. The Federal Savings and Loan Association founded in 1965 is a federal agency similar to the Government National Mortgage Association in the United States. It grants advance loans and discounts loans to savings and loan associations in order to help their liquidity in case of need.

Short- , medium- , and long-term credits are also granted by government-owned financial institutions. The Bank of Argentina Nation offers short-term loans, mostly to the agricultural sector. The National Development Bank provides medium- and long-term credits for specified firms that are considered important to the national economy. In such cases, the interest rate can be as low as 12 percent.

Since Argentina has developed her financial markets to a pretty good extent, Argentine financial institutions and individuals are knowledgeable investors. They can use their funds flexibly in the money and capital markets, or the real estate and commodity markets. The comparative yields on various short-term and long-term investments in 1972 were as follows:

Acceptances	28.63%
Bank deposits	22.84
Foreign bonds	31.34
Public bonds	21.45
Investment and development bonds	20-30
Stocks	39.18

Capital Market

The capital market has developed in Argentina since 1884 when the Commercial Exchange was created to handle diversified stocks in the developing economy. British financial expertise was of assistance in establishing the Commercial Exchange. Railroad securities were the most popular form of investment at that time. The capital market has undergone major changes, especially after 1937 when the National Security and Exchange Commission was established. Before 1960, only government bonds and mortgage bonds were popular investments. In the 1960s, the government revamped the capital market through the following actions:

1. The creation of Common Funds for Investment by Law 15885 of 1961, which was designed to encourage the public to participate in the capital market. Under this law, funds are deposited in banks for periods of three years. About 50 percent of these funds must be invested in certain securities. The intention of this measure was good, but when the market declined, the sale of securities became disruptive in the market.

2. The Stock Exchange Law of 1968 consolidates the whole security industry since it regulates the issue and trading of securities, the organization and operation of stock exchanges, and brokerage firms. The National Security and Exchange Commission implements this law.

3. The Law 19061 of 1971 created the concept of "open capital companies." This law provides many incentives to companies, which receive a 10-percent tax deduction if they issue new common stocks available to the general public. In the meantime, the public investors who put their money in banks under the common funds for investment agreements also obtain a tax deduction. This law is similar to the one adopted in Brazil. As a result of the government's continued efforts, the equity and public bond markets have become increasingly more active, but the mortgage market has remained relatively backward.

The Primary Market

 The industrial background, financial structure, and legal framework have set the limits of capital financing. In Argentina the public
and private sectors raise their long-term funds for investment in
different ways. Firms in the private sector are mostly owned by
wealthy families and foreigners. As in many other Latin American
countries, family-owned companies in Argentina usually relied on
internal financing (depreciation allowances and retained earnings)
and short-term credits from commercial banks and other financial
institutions. Loans are convenient and renewable. These companies
seldom issue equity and bonds for two basic reasons. One is to keep
the firm under family control. Another is the problem of selling
bonds in a period of inflation. Many medium- and small-size companies prefer low-cost financing from the National Development Bank.
This further discourages capital market development. The law of
"open capital companies" in 1971 did not produce the desired result
because investors were afraid of minority participation. High cash
dividends is the only attractive feature for equity investors. Aside
from this, equities lack mobility and liquidity. Since most industries
concentrate in the Buenos Aires area, where short-term funds are
plentiful and interest rates are fixed by the government, there is
very little incentive to business organizations to issue long-term
securities. Moreover, only 30 stocks are considered generally popular on all stock exchanges in Argentina. The purchase of less popular
stocks may tie up the investors' funds in securities lacking liquidity.
For these reasons, many wealthy individuals prefer speculation in
foreign exchange, real estate, short-term gains, or even attempt
to transfer their capital out of the country.
 The public sector, which has dominated both the primary and
secondary markets, also encounters difficulty in raising funds primarily due to fear of inflation. For example, the government issues
fixed-income certificates and bonds with an interest rate of 12 to 14
percent, but annual inflation has been running at rates up to 25 percent. In order to overcome this formidable obstacle, since 1971 the
government issued development and investment bonds with a six-year
maturity and 7-percent interest per annum, further providing that the
value and interest payments will be adjusted in accordance with actual
inflationary rates during the period. These bonds were successful
in the sense that the value of the issue increased from 112 percent
in October to 183 percent in December 1971. The government,
authorized by Congress, issued Adjustable National Securities for
the first time in 1972 in the amount of 400 million pesos, of which
300 millions were sold to the public and 100 millions were absorbed
by the Central Bank. These bonds will be traded over all security

exchanges. They bear a five-year maturity and 7-percent interest rate per annum subject to "monetary correction" on the basis of the wholesale price index as well as external currency depreciation. Obviously, these bonds provide protection against domestic inflation and currency devaluation. The success of these bonds has encouraged the government to issue another 150 million pesos' worth with the same terms. This issue appeared in March 1973.

The Secondary Market

Stock exchanges have been highly organized in Argentina since the nineteenth century. The changing political situation since 1930, inconsistent economic policies of various governments in power after World War II, and continued inflation and instability have definitely been detrimental to further development of the stock market. Government laws, which were designed to bolster the security market, have had limited success due to structural problems. The lack of comprehensive information concerning the Argentine capital market and its operations makes any in-depth analysis impossible.

There are eight stock exchanges in Argentina. They are located in Buenos Aires, Cordoba, Rosario, Mendoza, Tucuman, Mar del Plata, La Plata, San Juan, and Santa Fe. About 98 percent of all business is conducted on the Buenos Aires Stock Exchange. As Table 20.5 shows, transactions in public issues have been increasingly more important, while transactions in private issues have shown little growth. The public issues consisted of Treasury obligations, mortgage bonds, and development bonds, all of which were for the purpose of financing government-owned enterprises, industrial development, and construction. The major participants in public issues are the Central Bank, commercial banks and their mortgage departments,

TABLE 20.5

Transactions on the Buenos Aires Stock Exchange
(millions of Argentine dollars)

	Public Issues	Private Issues	Total
1970	407	227	634
1971	671	318	989
1972	935	313	1,248

Source: Central Bank of Argentina, Statistical Bulletin, March 1973.

pension funds, and mutual funds. With respect to private issues, there are over 500 stocks listed on the Buenos Aires Stock Exchange, but only 30 of these are actively traded and 10 are most popular. Many stocks have a low price value due to future uncertainty. The more active stocks are traded at low price-earnings ratios ranging from 5 to 10. Regardless of government laws, which were intended to bolster the stock market, private issues have been dominated by institutional investors rather than individual investors. The National Development Bank and National Postal Saving Funds, both government enterprises, controlled 15 percent of corporate stocks listed on the Buenos Aires Stock Exchange and accounted for 30 to 35 percent of transactions in private issues. It is obvious that the government dominates the capital market, while individuals and private financial institutions are more active in the money market.

A large volume of securities is traded outside the stock exchanges. We may refer to this as the over-the-counter market. Individuals and institutions like to come to this market because it is "free," which means that the registered and nonregistered securities can be sold and bought without official records and control. The participants are willing to take the risk on the basis of day-to-day economic and financial information since the government policy and law are sometimes confusing.

The key government supervisory agency over the securities industry is the National Security and Exchange Commission, but many problems are beyond the effective control of this law-enforcement body. The Inter-American Development Bank has suggested that issue of convertible debentures may help the development of the Argentine capital market from the standpoint of the private sector, but the basic problems are more complex than this.

GOVERNMENT POLICY AND INTERNATIONAL FINANCE

Policy toward Foreign Capital and Exchange

Before World War II, the development of Argentina's economy was mostly financed by British capital. For many years the British controlled most of the wealth-producing cattle ranches, utilities, meat-packing plants, and grain elevators. The French, Dutch, and the Americans played minor roles in the Argentine economy. A change occurred in 1937 when the Argentine government nationalized the state railroads from the British without compensation and obtained a $250,000 short-term loan from the Export-Import Bank of the United States in 1939 for modernizing the railroad equipment. During World War II, Argentina developed her domestic industries and enjoyed favorable export growth. In 1946, Argentina had $1.6 billion of foreign exchange reserves, which accounted for one-third of all foreign exchange holdings in the Latin American countries. This favorable position permitted Argentina to extend credits to Chile, Bolivia, and Spain in the amount of $300 million. The foreign exchange reserve was rapidly depleted during the 1950s because industrial products, which had been emphasized by the government, were mainly consumed at home. Exports of agricultural goods declined. As a result, the Argentine government encouraged foreign investment during the later 1950s, and the United States quickly became the major source of foreign investment capital. The low GNP growth rate (averaging 3.7 percent) plus inflation and capital outflows in the 1960s forced the government to revamp the Foreign Investment Law in 1971. In spite of the trend toward nationalist preference (for example, 51 percent of capital and voting power of any firm must be controlled by resident Argentine nationals), the law provides favorable treatment for foreign investments, especially of the type that would result in greater exports and technological improvements. No prior government authorization is needed to invest foreign capital in stocks, bonds, mortgages, or other similar property. Under inflationary conditions, foreign firms finance their operations in Argentina either from their retained earnings or from foreign sources. At the end of 1972, total foreign investment in Argentina was about $2.5 billion, one-half of which originated in the United States, one-tenth in the United Kingdom, and the rest in Germany, France, and the Netherlands.

Government policy toward foreign exchange has had a great impact on Argentina's domestic financial markets since many people shifted their capital from normal investment in credit instruments to speculative foreign exchange. This has presented problems in Argentina during the 1960s and early 1970s. Furthermore, the exchange rate between the Argentine peso and U.S. dollar not only influenced the inflow and outflow of capital, but also imports and exports. There have been 10 devaluations of the Argentine peso vis-à-vis the U.S. dollar. The more important devaluations were as follows: by 40 percent in 1967, 12.5 percent in 1970, and 25 percent in 1971 when the two-tier exchange system was announced by the government. At that time a commercial rate was applied to imports and exports subject to some modifications by the Central Bank depending on the products imported or exported. A financial rate was used for all types of transactions except imports and exports; in other words, it is a market rate entirely based on the forces of supply and demand.

As a consequence of inflation and devaluation, the Argentine government announced a new monetary unit, $a or A$P in January 1970 to replace the old monetary unit, m$n (peso moneda nacional). The new unit was exchanged for the old in the ratio of one Argentine peso ($a1.00) equal to 100 national monetary pesos (m$n100.00). It is important to note that since 1970, all Argentine statistics including the GNP have been shown in $a instead of m$n. Exchange rates prevailing in the period 1970-72 between the U.S. dollar and the Argentine peso are summarized below.

Date	U.S.$	Rate ($a)
January 1970	1	4.00
June 1971	1	4.40
September 1971	1	5.00 (official rate)
	1	9.95 (financial rate)
December 1972	1	5.00 (official rate)
	1	9.98 (financial rate)

Balance of Payments

During the period 1961-67, Argentina's current account showed surpluses. Deficits appeared and became more extreme from 1968 through 1971. Unilateral transfers have been running at about $4 billion a year. Balance of payments deficits have been met by the inflow of private or public capital or by Central Bank reserves. Argentina's reserves increased in 1967, but gradually decreased through 1971. According to the Central Bank's report for 1972, both the merchandise trade account and the overall balance of payments showed a reduction in deficits. Total reserves increased by $167 million up to a total amount of $457 million.

As Table 20.6 indicates, the current account deteriorated in the period 1968-71 due to an increase in imports over exports and the high rate of service payments such as dividends and interest on external loans. Argentina has made efforts to improve exports of grain and meat to European countries and, in return, has purchased their capital goods needed for industrial production. A high level of machinery, raw material, and fuel imports was responsible for the increased deficit on trade account, while beef rationing and bad weather were unfavorable factors that decreased exports in 1971. High rates of remittance since 1966 resulting from domestic inflation accelerated the balance of payments deficits. The year 1971 was a bad one for Argentina from the financial standpoint. There was a serious inflation (40 percent annual rate); the national government

TABLE 20.6

Argentine Balance of Payments, 1967-71
(millions of dollars)

	1967	1968	1969	1970	1971
Current account	135	-44.6	-222	-155.7	-386.7
Trade balance	369	198	36	79	-129
Exports	1464	1367	1612	1773	1740
Imports	1095	1169	1576	1694	1869
Services	-188	-217	-259	-234	-265
Unilateral transfers	-3.0	-4.0	-4.3	-3.2	-3.4
Capital and monetary sold	-131.9	54.8	227.9	153.8	370.9
Private long term	42	27.3	57.0	143.6	66.1
Private short term	268.1	150.4	-57.5	158.2	-397.6
Local government	-1.5	-0.5	-0.7	5.3	3.1
National government	0.3	65.2	105.3	77.5	125.3
Monetary authorities	-430.9	175.4	24.8	-230.4	594.9
Various banking institutions	-27.9	12.2	-37.6	-27.4	-20.9
Errors and omissions	-0.2	-6.2	-1.6	-5.1	19.2
Total reserves	727	760	538	673	290
Gold	84	109	135	140	98
Foreign exchange	625	554	285	343	70
Special drawing rights (SDR)	—	—	—	59	3
Reserve—IMF	18	97	118	130	119

Source: Central Bank of Argentina, Supplement of Statistical Bulletin, June 1972.

and the Central Bank increased their liabilities abroad in the amounts of $125 million and $594 million, respectively. At the same time, private short-term capital outflows amounted to $397 million. That was why so many extraordinary monetary actions were taken by the Argentine government in 1971 and 1972.

International Financial Activities

As early as 1824, Buenos Aires Province borrowed 1 million pounds in the London capital market at the interest rate of 6 percent to develop transportation facilities. In 1914, total borrowings of Argentina from the United Kingdom were £320 million, most of which had gone into port improvements and commerce. The first official borrowing from the United States was a $250,000 loan from the U.S. Eximbank in 1939 after the nationalization of the railroads. After 1956, U.S. capital gradually moved into Argentina, mostly in the form of direct investments in manufacturing. In 1963, Argentina had $3 billion of foreign debt, equivalent to approximately 7 percent of GNP. According to the World Bank 1972 Annual Reports, Argentina's public foreign debt outstanding was $2,108 million in 1970, ranking Argentina number five as international borrower after India, Pakistan, Mexico, and Brazil. The debt service to exports earning ratio was 20.9 percent (amortization and interest payments absorbed one-fifth of annual export earnings). In order to alleviate the repayment problem, the Argentine government requested that international financial organizations arrange to reschedule debt payments.

Confronted with domestic financial needs and balance of payments deficits, the Central Bank of Argentina has negotiated short- and long-term credits in various international financial centers. Some $308.9 million in loans was obtained by banking consortia in the United States ($145 million), United Kingdom ($40 million), Japan ($31 million), France ($20 million), and other European countries ($72.9 million). The Central Bank also issued $60 million in bonds, with the World Bank's guarantee, at an interest rate of $1\frac{1}{2}$ percent over the 180 days Eurodollar rate in London and sold these securities in the New York, London, and Zurich financial markets. In addition, a credit in the amount of $100 million was successfully negotiated with the Eximbank during 1972.

Finally, it must be mentioned that Argentina is a member of many international organizations, such as the World Bank, the International Monetary Fund (IMF), the General Agreement on Tariffs and Trade (GATT), the Inter-American Development Bank (IDB), and the Latin American Free Trade Association (LAFTA). Its economic and financial conduct is bound by the agreements of these organizations and influenced by their policies. Argentina attempted to bolster the status of the peso when it accepted Article VIII status in the IMF in 1968. Under this agreement, the government permitted the peso to be freely convertible into gold or reserve currencies. Unfortunately a combination of factors, especially the domestic inflation and political uncertainty in 1971, forced the government to depart from Article VIII status temporarily.

REFERENCES

Basch, Antonin. Capital Markets in Latin America. New York:
Praeger Publishers, 1970.

Central Bank of Argentina. Statistical Bulletin, various issues.

DELTEC. El Mercado de Capitales en Argentina. Mexico City:
CEMLA, 1968.

Ernesto Tornquist and Co. Ltd. Business Conditions in Argentina,
monthly publication.

Maynard, G., and W. Van Rijckeghem. "Argentina 1967-70: A Stabilization Attempt That Failed." Banca Nazionale del Lavoro,
Quarterly Review (December 1972).

Smithies, Arthur. "Economic Growth: International Comparisions,
Argentina and Australia." American Economic Review (May
1964).

United Nations, Economic Commission for Latin America. Economic
Development and Income Distribution in Argentina, 1969.

429

21

INTRODUCTION

The Eurodollar market has developed as a fashionable model
of the international financial markets. This chapter provides an essential but comprehensive and up-to-date picture of this continually
growing international financial force, which already has had far-
reaching effects on international finance in the 1970s. To achieve
this end, this chapter briefly describes the definition, significance,
and overall development of the market and analyzes its origins,
mechanism, sources and uses of funds, and impact on national monetary policy and financial markets.

Eurodollar refers to a U.S. dollar deposited in a bank in Europe
whether it is a European bank, a foreign bank, or a foreign branch
of a U.S. bank established in some European country. A U.S. dollar
deposited in other parts of the world such as Singapore is referred
to as an "Asian dollar," in the Bahamas it is called a "Bahamas
dollar," and in Brazil it is called a "Rio dollar." The amount of
dollar deposits in centers outside of Europe is far less than the a-
mount of Eurodollars. A broader and more encompassing term is
the Eurocurrency market, which comprises foreign currency deposits
in banks outside the country of origin. For example, British sterling
deposited in Paris is called Eurosterling; German deutsche mark
(DM) deposited in Zurich is called Euromark; and Swiss francs deposited in Frankfurt are called EuroSwiss francs. Since the Eurodollar
market accounts for 80 percent of Eurocurrency, it has attracted
worldwide attention.

The significance of the Eurodollar market can be viewed from
several perspectives. On the one hand, it affects international capital
movements, levels of interest rates, international trade and corporate
financing, national economic development, and financial policy. On

the other hand, the changing national and international environment
has influenced the direction and magnitude of the Eurodollar market.
Higher interest rates offered by London bankers attracted more U.S.
dollar deposits from other areas. As a result, monetary authorities
have had to raise their domestic interest rates to cope with the outflow of capital going to Eurodollar centers. Multinational corporations
and international traders can place their surplus funds in the market
in order to obtain short-term gains, or borrow from the market when
they need funds for working capital and other purposes. Less developed nations may find cheaper sources of capital in the Eurodollar
market for financing their important development projects. Governments that have no exchange controls may be forced to impose regulations on the inflow of Eurodollars if inflation is already a problem.
With regard to the international financial environment, the currency
crisis in 1971 was a case in point. From May to August 1971, speculators borrowed Eurodollars as a vehicle currency for converting their
assets into a strong currency (such as the DM) when the upward
valuation of the strong currency was expected. The three-month
Eurodollar rate was pushed up to 9.5 percent in August 1971. However, after the Smithsonian Agreement approved by the International
Monetary Fund (IMF) on December 18, 1971, the speculative pressures
stopped, and the interest rate level receded to 5 percent in May 1972.

The phenomenal development of the Eurodollar market in the
last 12 to 14 years can also be reviewed in terms of growth, breadth,
and resiliency of the market. During the period 1960-72, the size
of the Eurodollar market has grown from about $2 billion to $98 billion. The momentum of the market's development was quickened
after 1968 when the international gold and currency problem developed
into recurring crises every year, and the U.S. balance of payments
deficits supplied additional fuel to the market. More and more participants were drawn into the market due to its economic efficiency and
competitiveness. Besides central banks and financial intermediaries,
multinational corporations, Middle Eastern oil firms, less developed
countries, and Communist countries came to join the parade. The
center of Eurodollar activities has spread from London and Western
European financial districts to other more scattered and strategic
areas such as the Bahamas, Lebanon, Singapore, and Toronto. The
depth of the market is reflected from the longer terms of loans and
the increased channels for obtaining funds. In fact, the Eurodollar
market is the freest and most competitive financial market in the
world. The length of maturities ranges from 1-day call to 2- to 7-
day notice; 1-, 3-, 6-, and 12-month short-term loans to 5- or 10-
year intermediate term loans. As to the ways of obtaining funds,
30-day, 1-month, 3-month, and 6-month negotiable time certificates
of deposit (CDs) have been issued by Eurobanks to depositors. Since

the market is large, efficient, and competitive, interest rates have
fluctuated depending on supply and demand factors internationally.
There were three critical events which have tested the resiliency
of the market. One was in 1969 when U.S. banks drastically increased
their Eurodollar borrowings from their foreign branches in the amount
of $16.5 billion, and the three-month Eurodollar rate in London was
bid up to 12 percent. The market came back to a normal level when
U.S. monetary authorities imposed reserve requirements on such
borrowings and raised the interest ceiling on domestic CDs. The
second case was in 1971 when an international currency crisis occurred.
The third case was in September 1973 when U.S. banks, large corporations, and governmental units increased their borrowings to bid up
the Eurodollar rate to 11.5 percent. We should note that the surplus
in the U.S. balance of payments resulting from the twofold U.S. dollar
devaluations (December 18, 1971, and February 13, 1973) had a negative effect on Eurodollar supply but a positive effect on the interest
rate.

MECHANICS OF THE MARKET

Origin of the Eurodollar Market

The origin of the Eurodollar market can be traced back to the
1920s when U.S. dollars were deposited in Berlin and Vienna and
converted into local currencies for lending purposes. These practices
did influence the local money markets. After World War II, the U.S.
dollar was designated by the IMF as an intervention currency in the
foreign exchange market. This established the common acceptability
of the U.S. dollar as a key currency for international trade, investment, exchange arbitrage, and balance of payments settlements. The
continuous balance of payments deficits of the United States resulted
in a growth of official reserve assets in Western European countries,
and their central banks looked for investment opportunities for short-
term gains. In the 1950s, Russian banks in Western Europe preferred
to place their holdings of U.S. dollars with British and French banks
against the risk of possible seizure by U.S. authorities in case of
crisis. Under these circumstances, Eurobanks simply practiced
the principles of free economy by establishing competitive spreads
between creditor and debtor rates of interest. Some French banks
extended U.S. dollar loans to Italian banks during the 1950s as typical
operations in small amounts.
The real impetus for the development of the Eurodollar market
was provided by three crucial events. First, the UK government

announced in 1957 that British banks were not permitted to finance trade for nonresidents. The UK banks were happy to take advantage of the availability of the U.S. dollar to finance their international customers. The British authorities could have prevented development of dollar financing through UK banks, but realized the advantages of developing London into a leading market in dollar financing. Second, the return to currency convertibility in major Western European countries in 1958 and the formation of the Common Market encouraged European Economic Community (EEC) residents to place their dollar holdings with commercial banks for interest return instead of surrendering them to their central banks. Third, Regulation Q ceilings imposed by the U.S. Federal Reserve on interest payments on time deposits in domestic commercial banks played a highly significant role. Under this restriction, a substantial amount of funds owned by foreigners and U.S. residents was transferred to Eurobanks for higher yields. Since London has enjoyed its long-standing position of dominance in the international money market, international financial lenders and borrowers flocked to the city during the Eurodollar rush of the 1960s and 1970s.

As the size of the Eurodollar market continued to expand, the market mechanism evolved into a more complex structure for facilitating viable but volatile short-term international money movements.

The Market Mechanism

The Eurodollar market is a new financial market rooted in London and spreading out to major financial centers on different continents. It supplements or even supplants some national financial markets. It has competed with national money and capital markets, the foreign exchange market, and even the gold markets for international loan, deposit, and arbitrage activities. Its nature is different, and its mechanism is unique.

Geographically, there are four major focal areas in the Eurodollar market—the United Kingdom, United States, Western Europe, and Canada—processing Eurodollar transactions. Other minor or peripheral areas are illustrated in Figure 21.1, and include Japan and other Asian countries, Bahamas and Latin America, Eastern Europe and the Middle East, and Africa. Statistically, London is the major intermediary in the system. It has an excellent banking system with connections to all financial markets in the world. The Bank of England effectively controls the money market and banking center. With a good financial system, plus over 100 foreign banks represented in London, there is ample scope of interbank activities in that center. Western Europe is the second major intermediary due to the increasing

436

FIGURE 21.1

Geographical Setting of the Eurodollar Market

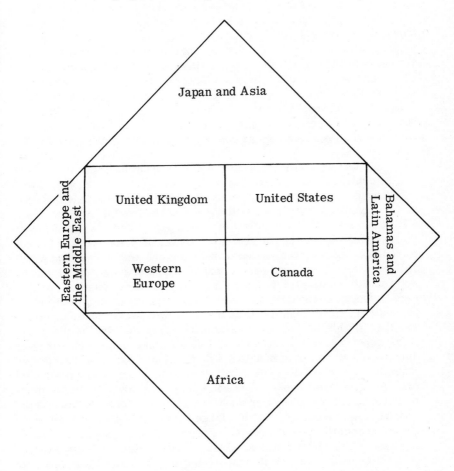

strength of many Eurocurrencies such as the DM and Swiss franc.
While London mostly handles interbank transactions, European banks
handle both interback and relending activities. Canada is another
major intermediary, but is primarily concerned with U.S. dollar
relending activities in Europe or in New York (the so-called street
loans). The United States, home of the dollar, has tended to be a net
borrower and strongly influences the direction and interest rates of
the market. It has been said that Europe lends to all blocs, but the
United States borrows from all blocs.

There are over 800 international financial intermediaries in the market, including banks, finance companies, foreign exchange brokers, and other specialized institutions, dealing in transactions all over the world through telephone and telex with written confirmation after agreements are reached. No collateral is pledged for these borrowings, and only the reputation of the borrower is taken into consideration. Since the core of the market is the interbank transaction, commercial banks in major financial centers are not so much concerned with the safety between them but are extremely keen on interest rate margins. The margins are narrow for prime name banks, ranging from 1/32 to $\frac{1}{4}$ percent, while prime industrial firms borrow at a $\frac{1}{2}$-percent margin. Rates range upward from these margins to $2\frac{1}{2}$ percent beyond deposit costs, depending on the risk involved.

Lenders of funds to the Eurodollar market have been commercial banks, central banks, international monetary institutions, nonfinancial institutions, and individual investors. Commercial banks receiving dollar deposits in countries without well-organized money markets utilize the market as an outlet for short-term funds. Those in countries having functioning money markets are still attracted to the Eurodollar market when rates of return there are higher than available on domestic investments. Central banks usually place their U.S. dollars with commercial banks for periods of three months. At the same time, commercial banks sell them back to the central banks for delivery three months ahead and lend to customers for three months. In this way, central banks still carry the risk of changes in currency value into the future. International monetary institutions such as the Bank for International Settlements (BIS) and the European Investment Bank (EIB) make short-term dollar deposits with participating commercial banks. The BIS sometimes operates in the market on behalf of its member central banks. Multinational corporations and insurance companies with a large volume of American dollars find it financially advantageous to keep their dollar reserves in the higher-yielding Eurodollar market. Wealthy individuals including those with bank accounts in Switzerland may transfer their funds for speculative purposes.

Borrowers of funds in the market include commercial banks, securities brokers and dealers, governmental agencies, international corporations, exporters, and importers. Commercial banks borrow to satisfy reserve requirements or for relending. Securities dealers employ Eurodollars for their customers' purchases of stocks and bonds. Governmental agencies obtain loans for budget spending or fixed investment. Their tax revenues and cash flows eventually repay the loans. International corporations, such as firms in the Norwegian shipping industry and Middle East petroleum companies, may shop around in the Eurodollar centers for cheaper sources of funds. Exporters and importers may borrow Eurodollars to cover their trade transactions, especially when they have to pay U.S. dollars to their customers. To meet different borrowers of funds in the various money markets, merchant banks with extensive international connections and operations have been formed to mobilize funds at the lowest cost to their customers. Development of these specialized institutions constitutes an important improvement in the market.

Instruments for receiving funds include demand deposits and time deposits, or swap arrangements. Negotiable time certificates of deposit have become popular in the Eurodollar market since 1966, and they can be sold in the secondary market if the holder needs liquidity. A typical Eurodollar loan is in the amount of $500,000 with competitive interest rates. Transactions as large as $10 million and as low as $25,000 are not unusual. In any event, interest paid by the borrower (nonbank) will include all costs of intermediation. For this reason, many international corporations like to arrange large dollar amount lines of credit with reputable international banks to obtain low-cost borrowings.

An important aspect of the Eurodollar market mechanism is the much-talked-about Eurodollar credit creation multiplier. This credit creation process is illustrated from several different points of view in the following.

Illustration 1

Mr. X of the Middle East has deposited U.S. dollars with a London bank, which has relent them to a bank in Paris, which in turn has lent them to a nonbank customer, Mr. Y in Mexico, who has used them to buy Eurobonds. The chain of relending will have left its trace in the statistics of dollar assets and liabilities in two banks as financial intermediaries in the market. The spread between the interest rate paid by Y and the rate received by X was divided between two banks. The creation of Eurodollar deposits as a result of the multiple intermediation is obvious.

Illustration 2

A Dutch multinational corporation places a $100,000 deposit with a New York bank, but decides to transfer this deposit to a London bank for reason of higher yield. The $100,000 liability of the London bank is matched by the bank's $100,000 claim on a demand deposit in New York. Suppose that the London bank retains $10,000 of the deposit as a liquid reserve and loans $90,000 to a French bank. There is no change in the balance sheet of the New York bank except the change in name of depositor from the Dutch International Corporation to a London bank. However, an expansion has occurred in the Eurodollar market. The Dutch corporation owns $100,000 of Eurodollars, which is deposited in the London bank, and the French bank owns an additional $90,000 of Eurodollars, which it has borrowed from the London bank. Total Eurodollars are $190,000. If the owner, the Dutch corporation, decides to withdraw the $100,000 dollar deposit from the London bank and exchange this for Dutch guilders, the Eurodollars are destroyed by reversing the procedure.

Illustration 3

A European central bank places some of its New York dollars with the BIS in order to increase the interest yield of its reserves. The BIS credits the European central bank and places its New York dollars with a London bank in the form of a time deposit with a higher interest rate. In turn, the London bank sells the same amount of Eurodollars to a European commercial bank, which sells them to the same central bank for domestic currency. Thus, the New York dollars are back with the central bank, which now has two dollars for each dollar that it placed in the Eurodollar market.

The creation process can be unlimited if there is no reserve requirement and no "leakage" in the 100-percent deposit-loan process. In reality, there are leakages due to various reserve requirements among nations, and the borrowers may use the proceeds for conversion into other currencies (sterling, lira, rupee, yen, or other currencies). That is why it is difficult to calculate the "multiplier" effect from Eurodollar pyramiding. Geoffrey L. Bell estimates the multiplier to be well in excess of 1.0. Boyden E. Lee finds the multiplier was 1.2663 in March 1963 and grew to 1.9213 by December 1969. Fred H. Klopstock puts the multiplier in the 0.50 to 0.90 range. That means the transfer of $1 million to the Eurodollar market from a U.S. bank might eventually result in approximately $1.5 to $1.9 million in Eurodollar deposits. In the illustrations provided above, it can be seen that credit creation in the Eurodollar market is quite different from that in the U.S. domestic banking system, where the reserve requirements for various deposits are fixed by the Federal Reserve, and the creditors can convert their deposits into money, as contrasted to the pure credit transactions in the Eurodollar market.

Sources and Uses of Funds

The Eurodollar market functions as a real international financial market, and its commodity (the U.S. dollar) is a stock in trade for

financial intermediaries, lenders, and borrowers who play an important role in the international financial markets. In order to understand the market behavior and performance, it seems necessary to
analyze the sources and uses of funds as to (1) trends in the flow of
funds and (2) factors that have influenced the flow of funds in the
period 1960 to 1972 (see Table 21.1).

The Eurodollar market maintained a high growth rate in the
period 1968 to 1972. The supply of funds expanded from about $2
billion in 1960 to $26.8 billion in 1968, and to $96.8 billion in 1972.
The annual growth rate was about 50 percent before 1968 and 40 percent thereafter. The major fund suppliers before 1967 were central
banks (they accounted for two-thirds of the total before 1962 and for
one-third of the total by 1967 as estimated by Oscar L. Altman's
article "Eurodollars" in Finance and Development (March 1967),
commercial banks and individuals, insurance firms and multinational
corporations, in that order. It is understandable that the U.S. balance
of payments deficits provided considerable ammunition to the European central banks. The lack of short-term investment opportunities
in their domestic money markets forced many commercial banks
and wealthy individuals to place their funds in the Eurodollar market
to take advantage of interest differentials. The growing internationalization of business has increasingly played an important role in
the development of the market. Multinational corporations not only
place their surplus funds in the market for interest gain, but also
use the Eurodollar as a vehicle currency during international monetary crises to preserve the value of their corporate assets. The
increased issue of dollar CDs since 1966, of Eurobonds since 1968,
and of Eurocommercial paper since 1970 has revolutionized the means
by which international borrowers can accommodate their demand
for funds. From the geographical standpoint, the inside areas, especially the United Kingdom and Switzerland, have contributed about
60 percent of the total sources of funds; the outside areas shared
about 30 percent; and the United States accounted for about 10 percent.

On the demand side, it was estimated that before 1967 about
one-fourth of total funds was used for trade financing. Since 1968,
multinational corporations have tapped funds in the market for worldwide investment under term loan agreements. U.S. commercial banks
have borrowed Eurodollars from their overseas branches to comply
with domestic reserve requirements and to maintain high loan volume.
International arbitragers and speculators, less developed countries,
and Communist nations have increased their borrowings in the Eurodollar market to hedge against currency fluctuations, to finance
domestic development projects, and to facilitate international trade
financing. It is interesting to know that the patterns in the uses of
funds, geographically speaking, differ from that of the sources. The

TABLE 21.1

Estimated Size of the Eurodollar Market
(billions of dollars)

	1960	1964	1966	1968	1969	1970	1971	1972
Sources •								
Outside areas	—	3.1	4.4	8.7	15.3	20.8	24.2	35.5
United States	—	1.5	1.7	3.9	4.5	5.0	6.5	7.1
Total	—	4.6	6.1	12.6	19.8	25.8	30.7	42.6
Total outside areas	—	4.4	8.4	14.2	26.2	32.9	40.0	54.1
Grand totals	2.0	9.0	14.5	26.8	46.0	58.7	70.7	96.7
Uses								
Outside areas	—	1.8	5.0	7.8	9.5	16.0	23.1	35.9
United States	—	2.2	3.2	10.7	17.7	14.0	9.2	10.4
Totals	—	4.0	8.2	18.5	27.2	30.0	32.4	46.3
Total inside areas	—	5.0	6.3	11.9	20.3	30.4	39.1	51.7
Grand totals	2.0	9.0	14.5	30.4	47.5	60.4	71.5	98.0

Note: Sources and uses of funds in the table do not add up to the same totals because: (1) The figures only cover the dollar positions vis-à-vis nonresidents in the reporting eight European countries in the inside areas (Belgium, France, Germany, Italy, Netherlands, Sweden, Switzerland, and United Kingdom), excluding the dollar positions vis-à-vis residents in these countries. (2) Funds are obtained by the banks in domestic or third currencies but relent in the form of dollars or vice versa.

Sources: 1960 figures are estimated by Oscar Altman, "Foreign Markets for Dollars, Sterling and Other Currencies," International Monetary Fund Staff Papers, December 1961; Bank for International Settlements, 39th through 43rd Annual Reports, 1968-72.

United States has used more funds than it has contributed, while the inside and outside areas have used less funds than they have put into the market. For this reason, an increase or decrease of U.S. demand for Eurodollars has significant effects on interest rates in the market and has had further repurcussions on the U.S. domestic interest rate structure.

In the period 1964-68, major factors responsible for growth of the market were the U.S. balance of payments deficits and the capital control programs of the U.S. government. The Interest Equalization Tax (IET) of 1964 discouraged foreign borrowing in the U.S. financial market, but encouraged nonresidents to look for alternative sources of finance. The Eurodollar market has served as a flexible alternative. The voluntary foreign lending and investment controls in 1965 and the mandatory controls in 1968 imposed on U.S. overseas capital investments forced many U.S. multinational corporations to borrow abroad. As a result, interest rates in the market were pushed upward, and more funds were attracted to the Eurodollar market. During the gold crisis in London in 1968, many speculators borrowed Eurodollars to use as margin, bought gold and later sold the gold for quick profit.

The year 1969 was another important year for the Eurodollar market. On the supply side, higher yields attracted more funds from different parts of the world. U.S. residents transferred funds to Eurobanks to take advantage of interest differentials (see Table 21.2); Canadian residents have favored "swapped" U.S. dollar deposits because Canadian monetary authorities have limited the rise in interest rates on domestic Canadian dollar deposits; the Middle East, Latin America, Eastern Europe, and Japan placed more dollars with Eurobanks. On the demand side, American commercial bank borrowings were the single overwhelming factor (they borrowed $16.5 billion out of $46 billion total sources). American banks borrowed funds from their foreign branches to obtain lower cost and more liquidity due to the credit crunch in the United States. During that year, many U.S. banks also established branches in London, Western Europe, and the Bahamas to compete for Eurodollars. As a consequence, U.S. monetary authorities imposed reserve requirements on domestic banks borrowing funds from their foreign branches. These borrowings by U.S. parent banks from foreign branches declined after September 1969.

Financial activity in the Eurodollar market eased off in 1970 due to the drastic decrease in U.S. bank borrowing in the market and the partial suspension of the Regulation Q ceiling in June 1970, which gave U.S. banks greater access to domestic money market funds. In 1970, there was a $4 billion reflux of funds from the United States to the Eurodollar market. With low interest rates prevailing in the market, Japan and Eastern Europe became active users of funds.

443

TABLE 21.2

Interest Rates on Dollar Deposits in London and
New York
(in percentage)

	Three-month Eurodollar (London)	U.S. negotiable time certificates of deposit (three-month market rate)
December 1968	7.50	6.50
December 1969	11.63	9.00
December 1970	6.50	6.00
March 1971	9.25	5.50
December 1972	6.00	5.50
September 1973	11.50	10.00

Sources: Bank for International Settlements and the U.S. Federal
Reserve Bulletin.

From March to August 15, 1971, the American dollar was under
speculative attack mainly as a result of balance of payments deficits
brought about by a deterioration in the U.S. merchandise trade balance
While the U.S. domestic economy slowed down because of the antiinflation policy of the Nixon administration, Eurodollars were heavily
employed by speculators and currency hedgers anticipating eventual
dollar devaluation. In that year, the entire Eurocurrency market was
extremely active. This led to the realignment of exchange parties
among major currencies after the Smithsonian Agreement on December 18, 1971.

In 1972, the Eurodollar market was in the doldrums due to the
lack of borrowers and tight money policies adopted by most industrial
nations. On the supply side, European central banks refrained from
putting funds in the market by general agreement. Most funds were
supplied by non-European, especially Japanese sources. On the demand side, British local governments and hire-purchase companies,
Italian government-owned utility firms, Communist countries, and
less developed nations took advantage of the low interest rates in the
market and became major fund takers. Two important effects followed from the stagnant Eurodollar market. One was the difficulties
of the financial intermediaries, which desperately looked for outlets
for funds. The London-based merchant banks increased their activities in the intermediate-term loan market. Another was the shrinking

share of the dollar in the Eurocurrency market, from 80 percent to 71 percent. Conversely, Euromarks and EuroSwiss francs increased their share in the market. Furthermore, the American banks' share in the London market fell from 30 percent as recently as 1969 to 22 percent in late 1972.

After the second U.S. dollar devaluation on February 13, 1973, confidence in the U.S. dollar increased. Borrowing in the market was still slow until mid-1973 when U.S. domestic borrowers demanded a larger amount of external funds for the prosperous U.S. economy. The Federal Reserve reduced the reserve requirement on U.S. bank borrowing from overseas branches from 20 to 5 percent in late 1973. It is expected that the Eurodollar market will become more active in future.

EFFECTS OF THE EURODOLLAR MARKET ON NATIONAL MONETARY POLICY AND FINANCIAL MARKETS

The Eurodollar market was a natural consequence of national monetary controls and substantial differences in interest rate levels on various national money markets. Many governments have encountered problems in their domestic financial markets as a result of the existence of the Eurodollar market. Some have talked about invoking individual national controls on the market; some have strongly urged that the government should leave the market alone; some have suggested international cooperation or collective action among the major industrialized nations to stabilize the market or prevent it from transmitting instability. The following describes past experience of major nations and their financial markets in connection with the operation of the Eurodollar market.

The United States

The monetary policies of the United States in the 1960s have influenced the growth of the Eurodollar market. In turn, the expansion of the Eurodollar market has reached a point where U.S. monetary policy cannot ignore the role of the market as a transmission mechanism that can generate feedback effects when monetary policy is adjusted.

In the beginning of the 1960s, U.S. balance of payments deficits and the interest ceilings imposed by Regulation Q on time deposits were major factors responsible for the growth of the Eurodollar market. The market did have some favorable effects on the U.S.

balance of payments when the market attracted funds from European central banks that otherwise would have become claims on U.S. monetary gold. Moreover, the Eurodollar market provided funds for U.S. corporations operating abroad that otherwise might have come from the U.S. domestic market and further aggravated U.S. balance of payments deficits.

The major monetary policies developed in the United States in response to the growing importance of the Eurodollar market can be briefly outlined as follows. The partial suspension of Regulation Q vis-à-vis foreign official holdings of dollar deposits in 1962 was intended to encourage foreign short-term funds to remain in U.S. banks. The removal of Regulation Q ceilings in 1970 on short-dated CDs also was associated with the need for restoring bank and corporate liquidity at a time that followed an international money crunch. "Operation twist" in the early 1960s was designed by the Federal Reserve to raise short-term interest rates in relation to long-term yields. The purpose was to reduce the outflow of liquid funds and simultaneously encourage investment at home. The IET of 1964, the voluntary foreign credit restraint in 1965, and the mandatory controls in 1968 also were for the purpose of reducing the outflow of capital. The imposition of reserve requirements of 10 percent and subsequently 20 percent on U.S. bank Eurodollar borrowing from foreign branches (May 1969) was regarded as a strong action taken by the Federal Reserve to reinforce its antiinflation policy. After the suspension of convertibility of the dollar announced by President Nixon on August 15, 1971, the U.S. Treasury conducted a monetary operation in Europe in late 1971 to mop up excessive dollars. The Treasury sold U.S. government securities to Eurobanks for dollars, which absorbed funds that could have been used for speculation during the international currency crisis.

The impact of the Eurodollar on the U.S. money, capital, and foreign exchange market has been considerable. As to the money market, the relationship between Eurodollar rates and domestic interest rates on federal funds, CDs, and Treasury bills has become closer year by year. Arbitrage transactions among U.S. bills, Canadian bills, and UK bills passing through the Eurodollar market have become normal operations. One might go so far as to suggest that the three major money markets (United States, United Kingdom, and Canadian) and the Eurodollar market are gradually merging together to form one unified Atlantic money market.

The relationships between the U.S. capital market and the Eurodollar market were highlighted by two important events. One was the IET of 1964, which discouraged foreigners from issuing securities in the United States, but unintentionally encouraged them to borrow in the Eurodollar market. Another event was in 1968 when mandatory

446

controls on U.S. outflows of direct investment capital were put into effect. Eurobonds issued by U.S. corporations abroad increased from $2 billion in 1967 to $3.5 billion in 1968. Many corporations placed the unused portions of the proceeds with Eurobanks for short-term investment. To a lesser extent, Eurodollars have been borrowed by U.S. brokerage firms and dealers for financing their customers' purchases of stocks and bonds in the U.S. primary as well as secondary capital markets.

United Kingdom and Western Europe

London has been the hub of the Eurodollar market. It has attracted funds from different parts of the world, especially from the United States, Switzerland, the Middle East, and Japan. There has been a considerable impact on the UK domestic financial markets due to the diversified investment opportunities ranging from short-, intermediate-, and long-term lending and borrowing with very little monetary controls from the British authorities. The Eurodollar market has benefited the United Kingdom financially. Local governments in the United Kingdom can take advantage of low interest rates on Eurodollars for financing capital projects.

Germany has been an important lender and borrower. In 1970, under tight monetary conditions, the German enterprise sector turned abroad for credits totaling some DM 20 billion (Monthly Report of the Deutsche Bundesbank, May 1971). After the float of the DM in May 1971, there was an inflow of funds to Germany, and the monetary authorities established the so-called Bardepot scheme including a variety of reserve requirements on resident borrowings abroad. In order to check inflation, the German, Italian, Swiss, and Dutch governments have frequently used dollar swaps for reducing domestic liquidity.

Since 1960, Italian public utilities, the Belgian central bank, and French and Dutch firms have frequently been borrowers in the Eurodollar market, but have imposed restrictions on the inflow of Eurodollars when their domestic economies were affected. Switzerland, which has been a major fund contributor to the London segment of the market, imposed a negative tax on dollar deposits in its domestic banks in 1971 due to the heavy inflow of funds to that country.

Other Countries

Besides the major areas mentioned previously, Canada and Japan have been important participants in the Eurodollar market.

Canada primarily plays a role as financial intermediary recycling funds between the United States and United Kingdom. Japan has been a net borrower in the Eurodollar market during the 1960s. Only after 1972 has Japan contributed funds to the market. Eastern and other European countries as well as the Latin American countries have put more funds into the market than they have obtained from it. Governments in these countries have not formulated specific policies relating to Eurodollar transactions of their residents since they have not had effective money markets at home and the Eurodollar market has served them very well. In fact, it can be said that development of the Eurodollar market has retarded the development of many nations' domestic money markets.

INTERNATIONAL MONETARY COOPERATION

At times, national monetary policy has been ineffective as a result of the flexibility afforded banks in the Eurodollar market. As a result, specialists in international finance have suggested collective action such as stipulated reserve requirements on Eurodollar deposits, to be enforced by the major nations, or international open-market operations to be conducted by an international organization such as the BIS. Alternatively, some have suggested that no international control will be effective.

International agreement on supervision of the Eurodollar market may be difficult to attain. There are different national interests in the Eurodollar market. In cases of extreme difficulty, temporary cooperation may be necessary, such as in 1967 during the British sterling crisis and in 1971 when the U.S. dollar was under speculative attack.

CONCLUSION

After World War II, the IMF and the U.S. dollar became main pillars of the international financial system. A dismantling of exchange controls in Western Europe in the 1950s and eventual convertibility in 1958 encouraged the growth of international flows of funds among nations. In this period, foreign central banks and governments came to prefer to use the dollar as a vehicle currency.

Efficient and flexible British and Western European financial intermediaries made the Eurodollar market mechanism operational by applying the principle of a free-market economy. They accepted dollar deposits and lent them to borrowers in the competitive financial markets with narrow spreads to cover the costs and risks involved.

Regardless of the "dollar surplus" in the 1960s, the Eurodollar market has attracted more lenders and borrowers and found it possible to employ larger amounts of funds with increasing efficiency. In the 1960s, the Eurodollar market has broadened in scope and significance. It performs the following economic functions: (1) efficient allocation of funds and productive economic resources and (2) integration of the international financial markets, as evidenced by the narrowing of interest rate structure in major financial centers.

There have been complaints concerning the Eurodollar market because it has affected national monetary policies and money markets. In fact, the Eurodollar market has substituted for many national markets; it has made it difficult for central banks to restrict the increase in money supply by facilitating inflows of capital when some nations pursued tight money policies at home; it also has affected the conditions of the foreign exchange markets when speculation increased. Furthermore, the Eurodollar may help or hurt balance of payments conditions in some countries. For these reasons, the opinion has been expressed that some sort of international control may be desirable, such as open-market operations in Eurodollars to be conducted by the BIS, or international agreement on reserve requirements on Eurodollar deposits. Some counterarguments have also been heard that it is impossible to control the market internationally since it may harm one country while it benefits another. At best, selective control may be preferable conducted by the central banks of major nations.

With respect to the future of the Eurodollar market, the market is extremely sensitive to national and international pressures. Certain general patterns are likely to persist: The Eurodollar market will continue to grow as long as the U.S. dollar is accepted as a key currency in international financial transactions, as long as nations permit the free flow of funds among major financial markets, and as long as interest differentials continue among nations.

Based on recent developments in the Eurodollar market, some changes have become discernible. Countries outside the industrialized nations have increased their borrowings in the market on an intermediate-term basis. Specialized financial intermediaries have been organized to operate in the market, including medium-term consortium lending banks.

As long as international business operations continue to grow and as long as government agencies find it to their advantage to borrow in the market, the Eurodollar market will continue to expand and find new structural and organizational patterns to service the international demand and supply of loanable funds.

449

REFERENCES

Bank of England. Quarterly Bulletin, various issues.

Bank for International Settlements. 39th through 43rd Annual Reports, 1968-72.

Bell, Geoffrey L. "Credit Creation through Eurodollars?" The Banker (August 1964).

Coombs, Charles A. "Treasury and Federal Reserve Foreign Exchange Operations." Monthly Review, Federal Reserve Bank of New York, September 1972, September and December 1973.

Klopstock, Fred H. "The Eurodollar Market: Some Unresolved Issues." Essays in International Finance, Princeton University, March 1968.

Lee, Boyden E. "The Eurodollar Multiplier." The Journal of Finance (September 1973).

Little, Jane Sneddon. "The Eurodollar Market: Its Nature and Impact." New England Economic Review, Federal Reserve Bank of Boston, May/June 1969.

McClam, Warren D. "Credit Substitutions and the Eurocurrency." Quarterly Review, Banca Nazionale del Lavoro (December 1972).

Scott, Ira O. "The Eurodollar Market and Its Public Policy Implications." Materials prepared for the Joint Economic Committee, Congress of the United States, February 25, 1970.

22

The past decade, 1960s, has witnessed a rebirth of the markets for foreign and international bonds. Prior to 1964, the United States provided nearly all of the capital funds entering the foreign bond markets, with the United Kingdom, West Germany, and Switzerland also contributing nominal amounts each year. Emergence of the international bond market after 1964 as a major source of long-term capital funds reduced the former dependence of the rest of the world on the United States. Further, in the relatively short period 1964-72, it permitted a fourfold expansion in the international flow of capital via the new issue of international bonds.

The international bond market has earned the appellation Euro-bond market, in part due to its concentration in Europe, its being distinct and separated from the New York bond market, and its supra-national status. However, this market extends its influence well beyond Europe, since it draws funds from North America, the Middle East oil countries, and numerous developing countries. Moreover, to an increasing extent, the Eurobond market services borrowers located outside Europe, including Canada, the developing countries, Australia, and the multilateral lending institutions affiliated with the World Bank Group.

ORIGIN OF THE MARKET

Foreign and International Bonds

A prospective borrower may be able to obtain long-term debt capital from three alternative sources. First, he may be able to sell a bond issue in his domestic capital market. The majority of

451

debt capital is obtained in this way. However, a variety of considerations including cost of funds, availability of capital market resources, balance of payments developments, and foreign exchange considerations may prompt a borrower to raise funds in a capital market other than his own domestic market. The traditional source of external funds is by the issue of securities in a foreign capital market, which operates as a counterpart of the domestic bond market. In the first decade and a half after World War II, the New York foreign bond market and Switzerland's market for foreign issues were the major placement markets for foreign issues of this type. In addition, London served as a market for foreign issues, but access was restricted mainly to sterling area issuers. In the 1960s, the capital markets of Germany, the Netherlands, and Japan have absorbed a growing amount of foreign issues.

The international bond market offers a third alternative to borrowers. This market can be distinguished from the national markets for foreign bonds in several respects. First, debt issues are sold through underwriting and selling groups made up of banks and financial institutions from a number of different countries. Second, securities are placed with investors from a number of different countries. In this sense, the international bond market is foreign to borrowers and investors alike. Finally, bond issues can be denominated in any of several basic currencies of issue, or contracted for in terms of a currency option. This flexibility in choice of currency of denomination is a unique feature of the international bond market.

Capital Imperfections in Europe

The international or Eurobond market could not exist in a world in which capital was perfectly mobile and free to flow from one country to another. Its functions would be absorbed into the national markets for foreign bonds. Further, and perhaps even more significant, interest rate differentials among the capital markets of individual countries would tend to disappear. The major reasons for differences in interest rates in national capital markets would then be related to currency premium as between strong and weak currencies and anticipated changes in parity relationships.

Over the two decades 1950-70, a number of economic forces and institutional patterns have tended to perpetuate the imperfections that separate the European capital markets. These include the desire of each country to pursue an independent monetary policy, fear of exchange blockage and foreign exchange rate changes, differing institutional structures in banking and in the nonbanking financial intermediaries, strong liquidity preference and a related weakness in the secondary markets for long-term securities, the special status accorded public or quasi-public borrowers in several countries, the desire to channel capital according to a national economic plan, the regulation of capital issues by a banking committee to avoid undue exposure of the capital market to external pressures, and the need to regulate access of nonresidents to the domestic capital market for balance of payments reasons.

In the Netherlands and Switzerland, access to the domestic capital market has been controlled, due to the small size of these countries and the inability of their financial markets to absorb any significant amounts of foreign issues. Switzerland has been an exception in this respect to the extent that inflows of funds have provided a generous supplement to the small flow of domestic savings that enters the capital market. French authorities have controlled the capital market tightly to achieve economic planning objectives. With the exception of a bond issue by the European Coal and Steel Community (1964), foreign issues were not authorized until 1966.

Germany has been an important exception to the European pattern of tight control over foreign issues. Since 1958, when the deutsche mark (DM) and other European currencies became convertible, there has been no official control of foreign issues in Germany. Moreover, a strong balance of payments position has motivated the German authorities to attempt to promote capital exports in order to offset foreign exchange surpluses.

Until 1963, there were four main sources of long-term capital for borrowers outside of their own national capital market. These included the New York market for foreign bonds, the German capital market, the Swiss market, and the emerging Eurobond market. Numerous factors made borrowers reluctant to use the German capital market, including high interest rates, high flotation costs, and constant pressure in the direction of upward revaluation of the DM. While interest costs were low, the market in Switzerland had only limited capacity, and it was difficult for foreign borrowers to obtain access on favorable conditions (timing and size of issue). Compared to New York, the Eurobond market was an inferior source of capital funds. Low interest costs and underwriting margins as well as a favorable secondary market operated like a magnet and drew new foreign bond issues into New York on a rising scale. The dynamic growth in foreign-bond-issuing activity in New York was dramatically curtailed by announcement of the Interest Equalization Tax (IET) in 1963.

U.S. Capital Restraint

For purposes of our discussion, we might trace the development of the Eurobond market over three distinct phases. The first, from 1958 until 1963, can be noted for the small volume of issues each year, a by-product of the dominance of New York as an international new issues market. In 1963, the volume of Eurobond issues was only $150 million, including $55 million in government issues, $15 million in issues of international institutions, and $80 million in issues of publicly owned enterprises, development banks, and other not easily classified borrowers. The second phase lasted from 1964 to 1969 and is notable for a sharp expansion in new issues ($557 million in 1964 and $2,872 million in 1969), the dominant status of dollar- and DM-denominated issues, and a near monopoly of borrowing by the developed countries and international organizations. The third phase began in 1970 and reflects a resurgence in growth of new issues, a wider base of currencies in which Eurobonds are denominated, the introduction of new currency option arrangements, and a broadening of borrower representation among the developing countries.

Announcement of the proposed IET in 1963 radically altered the institutional arrangements for the international transfer of long-term capital. The purpose of the tax was twofold. Its immediate objective was to increase the cost of debt capital to foreign borrowers from developed countries making use of the U.S. capital market. This was to be accomplished by levying an excise tax on U.S. resident purchases of foreign stocks and bonds. Shifting of the tax would raise the cost of capital funds, tending to equalize the cost of U.S. source and non-U.S. source funds. A longer-run objective of the tax was to accelerate the development and growth of capital market facilities outside the United States.

The IET was successful in shifting the demand for debt capital to the new issues markets outside the United States. In this way, the IET fostered development of the Eurobond market as a parallel to the New York new issues market. Additional measures by the United States after 1964 brought about more permanent changes in the international underwriting of debt issues.

In February 1965, President Johnson initiated a "Voluntary Restraint Program," which applied to 600 major business corporations and U.S. commercial banks engaged in foreign lending activities. The program urged U.S. industrial corporations to improve the balance of payments effects from their activities by expanding exports from the United States, increasing repatriation of income earned abroad, reducing short-term assets held overseas, and postponing direct investment outflows. U.S. corporations were urged to make greater use of foreign source funds to finance their direct investment operations outside the United States. This last-mentioned area of balance of payments improvement was particularly important for the development of the Eurobond market.

Simultaneously, commercial banks and nonbank financial institutions were asked to restrict the amount of credits made to nonresidents, including the overseas affiliates of U.S. corporations. This measure closed off a major part of U.S. source financing for the foreign affiliates of U.S. direct investment corporations as well as other nonresident borrowers, tending to further shift the offshore demand for loanable funds toward non-U.S. sources.

The devaluation of the British pound in November 1967 and related pressures on the U.S. balance of payments led to President Johnson's Executive Order of January 1968, wherein mandatory controls were imposed on U.S. direct investment capital outflows. The mandatory controls restricted direct investment capital transfers of U.S. corporations to developing countries to 110 percent of the amounts invested in the 1965-66 base period, permitted outflows to the United Kingdom, Japan, Australia, and the oil-producing countries up to 65 percent of the base year level, and restricted direct investment outflows to all other countries (continental Western Europe) including reinvested earnings to 35 percent of the 1965-66 average.

The controls program was directed at the balance of payments outflows from the United States, and not at the overseas operations of U.S. companies which, it is recognized, contribute favorably to the U.S. balance of payments over the long run. In effect, the U.S. government was encouraging U.S. corporate investors operating abroad to raise long-term capital funds overseas. The statistical series, which can be used to measure the expansion of U.S. corporate direct investment activities, does not indicate a slowing down of overseas investments, production, and sales. By contrast, the figures indicate that U.S. firms increased their operations abroad after 1965 in spite of the higher cost of offshore sources of funds.

The growing interest of U.S. corporations in investing in overseas areas, especially in Western Europe, made it necessary for them to issue long-term securities abroad. The Eurobond market was the only source in which adequate amounts of capital could be raised.

International Financing Affiliates of U.S. Companies

The success of U.S. corporations in adapting to the new offshore financing requirements associated with the capital restraint program of the Johnson administration attests to the pliability of capital market institutions and international flows of long-term capital funds.

U.S. corporations have established three types of international or overseas financing affiliates to satisfy the requirements imposed on them by both U.S. regulatory agencies and international investors seeking to maximize after-tax returns. These include the Delaware subsidiary, the Luxembourg financial holding company, and the finance subsidiary incorporated in the Netherlands Antilles.

These specialized international financing subsidiaries must satisfy three basic requirements. First, the issuer should be organized so that securities issued by him will be subject to the IET, thus preventing purchase by U.S. residents and ensuring full balance of payments improvement. Second, the issuer should be organized so that interest on its own debt securities will not be subject to withholding taxes. Finally, the income of the issuer should be exempt from application of corporate profit taxes in the United States.

The Luxembourg financial holding became an important means of international finance for U.S. companies beginning in 1965. The advantages of the Luxembourg subsidiary include freedom in relending the proceeds from debt issues, freedom from income taxes, and close proximity to Western European operations of U.S. companies. Delaware subsidiaries must satisfy the requirement that more than 80 percent of their gross revenue comes from foreign sources if the interest income on their bond issues is to be exempt from U.S. withholding taxes. Foreign bondholders do not have to file a tax declaration with the Internal Revenue Service. The Netherlands Antilles affiliate offers the advantages of a stable tax environment and the possibility of tax-free investment of revenues in the United States as a result of the tax treaty in force between the Netherlands Antilles and the United States.

As a general rule, the U.S. parent company provides its own guarantee for payment of all obligations of the finance subsidiary that result from the issue of debt instruments in the Eurobond market.

DYNAMICS OF THE MARKET

Institutional Development

Eurobond issues are usually managed by a syndicate or consortium, consisting of one or two active leaders and up to two dozen other members that subscribe for the issue. A second "selling" group of bankers, securities brokers, and dealers agrees to place the issue. Members of the selling group are selected on the basis of their ability to place the securities in their clients or their own investment portfolios. The selling group is assembled on the basis of obtaining as

456

large a geographical distribution of securities as possible, and a hundred or more individual banks and financial institutions may be represented.

The Eurobond market has been referred to as a placement market, meaning that bonds are not sold on an open competitive basis to the general public. Rather, securities are distributed by means of close and well-established working relationships between members of the selling group and investment managers representing diverse portfolio interests scattered around the globe.

Members of Eurobond consortia generally represent the largest and most respected financial institutions in the national capital markets. American investment bankers and London issuing houses have played a prominent role in managing Eurobond issues as well as participating in selling groups. Nevertheless, various continental bankers have taken the lead as managers or co-managers of numerous issues, including the Belgian, Luxembourg, German, and Italian banking institutions. German banks have managed or co-managed virtually all DM-denominated issues.

Growth in Issues Volume

The growth trend displayed in the Eurobond market since 1964 is impressive. Starting at a base of $557 million, the market reached a sevenfold expansion by 1968 and an elevenfold increase by 1972 (Table 22.1). This growth has been possible because of the strong international demand for funds that has been directed toward the Eurobond market, as well as the ability of the market to attract increased inflows of funds from a widening circle of sources of supply.

Underlying the demand side have been increased opportunities for fixed investment projects by multinational corporations, inflation, and real economic growth, which have contributed to a higher dollar value of fixed investment projects, growing pressures on national and local governments to finance a larger volume of public services, and the lack of adequate capital market facilities in small developed countries and the less developed countries. A wide variety of borrowers makes use of the Eurobond market, and the share of new issues of each group varies considerably from one year to the next, indicating strong competition for loanable funds.

In the period 1967-72, the largest category of borrowers in the market was industrial and financial corporations, with U.S. multinational corporations generally accounting for two-thirds of this borrowing. All multinational corporate borrowing accounted for between 50 and 65 percent of the market total. In some years (1969 and 1972), convertible debentures represented at least half of corporate

TABLE 22.1

International and Foreign Bond Issues, 1964–73
(millions of dollars)

		International Bond Issues			Foreign Bond Issues	Total International and Foreign
	Developed Countries	Developing Countries	International Organizations	Total All Areas		
1964	492	5	61	557	1,754	2,311
1965	746	—	28	773	2,302	3,075
1966	993	58	166	1,217	2,201	3,418
1967	1,602	132	175	1,909	2,606	4,515
1968	3,303	217	25	3,545	3,488	7,033
1969	2,730	103	40	2,872	2,823	5,695
1970	2,730	111	153	2,994	2,290	5,284
1971	3,490	80	186	3,756	3,352	7,108
1972	5,462	542	487	6,491	3,906	10,397

Source: Organization for Economic Cooperation and Development (OECD), Financial Statistics, various issues.

Eurobond issues. The second largest group of borrowers has been municipalities and agencies (government guaranteed) of governments, generally accounting for 20 to 25 percent of the total. Prominent among these issues have been those of major Scandinavian cities, in which countries capital market facilities are most inadequate if not nearly nonexistent. Central governments of small developed countries rank third as borrowers, accounting for 8 to 10 percent of Eurobond issues. International and regional institutions (European Investment Bank and World Bank) account for 5 to 8 percent of issues. Finally, the less developed countries have accounted for only a very small part of Eurobond issues. In the period 1969-71, issues of less developed countries averaged close to 3 percent of the total. In 1972, issues of less developed countries expanded to 9 percent of total issues with a larger number of borrowing countries represented.

Borrowers of good standing have found that they can obtain funds in the Eurobond market at the going rates. Interest rates have been competitive and have adjusted upward at times when this became necessary to accommodate an increased volume of new issues. Demand has remained strong since the efficiency of the market in terms of flotation costs has been favorable, and because the borrower that raises funds has the opportunity to obtain foreign exchange upon the sale of debt securities. This second factor is an important consideration in a world of currency restrictions and exchange rate uncertainties.

On the supply side, growth of the Eurobond market has benefited from a gradual enlargement of the international sources of funds. Rising income levels in the developed countries and a rapid growth in oil revenues in the petroleum-exporting countries have provided a persistent expansion in lendable funds. Second, the efficiency of Eurobond selling syndicates has grown over the years. Selling groups now include 120 or more major banks and financial institutions representing dozens of countries. The strong placement capacity of these syndicates should not be ignored in accounting for the growth of the market. Third, flight capital from less developed countries and developed countries has at times provided a generous portion of the inflow of funds to the market. This can be reinforced with balance of payments statistics, which indicate considerable "error and omission" balancing entries ($10.8 billion for the United States in 1971). Fourth, the international banking systems of major countries have been more fully developed in the 1960s, providing increased opportunities for affiliate placement of Eurobonds in outlying centers, credit facilities for interim financing of securities purchases, and communications linkages concerning availability of new and outstanding securities issues. Fifth, the Eurocurrency market provides an important source of liquidity for banks that "take down" a large block of Eurobonds for their own account. Sixth, international securities arbitrage has become a more important factor in the developing financial entrepôt centers such as Switzerland, Luxembourg, London, Tokyo, Beirut, Hong Kong, and Singapore. In connection with this, gold/securities arbitrage opportunities are available in most of these entrepôt centers, adding to the opportunities for drawing lendable funds into the Eurobond market. Finally, secondary trading facilities have improved considerably. Stock exchange listing and the growth of specialized Eurobond traders (White Weld, Bondtrade, Merrill Lynch, Strauss Turnbull, Peabody, Western American Bank, Krediet-bank, Samuel Montagu, S. G. Warburg, and Deutsche Bank) have been important. Also, development of securities clearing systems (Cedel and Euroclear) has improved the mechanical efficiency of purchasing and selling Eurobonds. In 1972, the annual turnover of Eurobonds was reported at $14 to $20 billion, placing the market second only to the London Stock Exchange in the context of European securities trading.

Currencies of Issue

One aspect of the Eurobond market distinguishes it from all other capital markets. That is the possibility of denominating debt issues in any of a number of currencies or currency options. The U.S. dollar has played a major role as currency of issue in the market, followed at some distance by the DM (Table 22.2). Since 1972, the Dutch guilder and French franc have come to play an important role as currencies of issue. After 1970, a number of new currencies of issue appeared, including the Australian dollar, Canadian dollar, Danish krone, and Luxembourg franc. Currency options have played a minor but technically interesting and significant role since 1961. The wide variety of currencies employed has afforded the Eurobond market a high degree of flexibility in responding to the needs of borrowers and investors alike.

Postwar experience has tended to bear out the claims of economists who have insisted that it is impossible to maintain fixed exchange rates among major currencies over an extended period of time. Therefore, debt securities having 10 to 15 years or longer to maturity must be expressed in a currency that affords maximum stability in real purchasing power and exposes borrower and lender to minimum risk. While a number of currencies potentially satisfy the requirement of stability of value, in practice many factors mitigate against all but a very few currencies of issue. These include the long-term prospects for the currency (which has worked against use of the British pound), opposition to excessive international use of

TABLE 22.2

Currencies of Issue in the Eurobond Market
(millions of dollars)

	1964	1966	1968	1970	1971	1972	1972 as Percent
Australian dollar	—	—	—	—	—	37	0.5
DM	75	146	738	601	860	1,232	19.0
Canadian dollar	—	—	—	—	—	15	0.2
Danish krone	—	—	—	—	—	32	0.5
European Monetary Unit (EMU)	—	—	—	61	95	30	0.5
French franc	—	—	20	—	49	489	7.6
Luxembourg franc	—	—	—	—	16	154	2.4
Netherland's guilder	—	—	—	310	268	473	7.6
Pound sterling	14	20	29	—	61	164	2.5
Swiss franc	—	—	—	8	—	—	—
Unit of account	10	76	57	54	167	—	—
U.S. dollar	458	975	2,701	1,961	2,240	3,864	59.5
Total	557	1,216	3,545	2,994	3,756	6,491	100.0

the currency by monetary authorities and the central government (Swiss franc), fear that domestic interest rates may be unduly affected (Netherlands' guilder), and internal political disturbances (French franc).

The level of long-term interest rates in the national capital market of the currency of issue is likely to play an important role in the choice of currencies. For example, in 1972 U.S. corporations were encouraged to make use of the market by selling dollar issues as the yield spread narrowed between corporate bond rates in the United States and in the international bond market. Similarly, a

461

sharply widening gap in 1972 between yields on German domestic bonds and foreign DM bonds caused German residents to shift funds out of foreign DM bonds and into domestic bonds, thereby pushing down the share of DM issues in the Eurobond market from 23 percent in 1971 to 19 percent in 1972.

Dollar-denominated issues have been a major factor in the Eurobond market, in 1965-67 accounting for 80 to 89 percent of new issues. More recently (1969-72), dollar issues have represented 60 to 65 percent of Eurobond placements. The declining relative trend in dollar issues may be expected, inasmuch as the dominant status of the dollar in the early and middle 1960s and its role as vehicle, intervention, and reserve currency gave it a highly respected status as an international investment currency. More recently, the role of the dollar as a currency of denomination has fluctuated according to the status of the dollar in the foreign exchange markets, the interest premium on dollar as compared with DM and other currency issues, and the inclusion of special features in dollar-denominated issues such as warrants and conversion into equity shares of the issuing company.

The DM has ranked second as a currency of denomination. While not an international reserve currency, persistent balance of payments surpluses and absence of foreign exchange restrictions in Germany have made the DM an attractive currency for investors. On the other hand, prospects of upward revaluation of the DM have made borrowers without a ready source of DM revenues reluctant to issue debt securities denominated in that currency. Other considerations influencing the extent of use of DM issues include the high interest rate structure in Germany, which tends to dampen prospects for secondary trading via sale to German residents, the willingness of investors to accept a lower interest yield in light of DM appreciation possibilities, and the effective separation of the domestic and international DM issue markets via the withholding tax on nonresident purchases of domestic DM issues.

Measured in terms of share of new issues, currency options have not played a major role in the Eurobond market. Nevertheless, their existence and varying degree of use offer a clear indication of the importance of currency aspects in the international bond market. The year 1971 represents the high water mark in usage of currency options in the Eurobond market, which can be explained in terms of the widespread uncertainties concerning exchange rate adjustments that prevailed throughout the year. In 1971, Unit of Account issues totaled $167 million, and European Monetary Unit (EMU) issues totaled $95 million. Currency option issues represented 7 percent of total issues in 1971.

Borrowers and lenders undertake special risks on the international bond market. The lender and the borrower can profit or lose from exchange parity adjustments. Currency options generally employ a currency of account, which is an artificially created monetary unit based on a combination of several national currencies. The oldest, the European Unit of Account, originally was devised for use in settlements effected under the European Payments Union—EPU (1950-58). The Unit of Account is linked to the currencies of the 17 former EPU member countries in terms of par values established with the International Monetary Fund (IMF). The Unit of Account affords investors and borrowers a certain amount of protection from changes in currency parities. A fundamental rule is that the investor selects the currency in which the debtor must discharge the obligation, while the exchange rate applied is made on the basis of the least changed parity relative to those that originally applied when the debt was created. Investors cannot benefit from revaluation unless all 17 currencies have been revalued, and then only to the extent of the smallest percentage revaluation. The Unit of Account has been criticized on the basis of the complicated indenture agreements that are required, the expense of servicing such loans, and the implication that the 17 currencies included have an international status.

Several additional currency options have been employed, including the EMU, which is based on the Common Market currencies, and the European Composite Unit (EURCO), which carries a weighted value relative to the nine reference currencies. A 10-percent revaluation of a currency, which makes up 20 percent of the EURCO, would reduce the worth of the EURCO as expressed in a devalued currency by only 2 percent. A third type of option is the two-currency option, usually expressed in DM and pound sterling. The two-currency option permits the investor to choose the currency in which he wants principal and interest paid, and has the advantage of simplicity. However, it exposes the borrower to the risk of alterations in exchange rates.

Yield Relationships

In the international markets for loanable funds, it is difficult to isolate yield or interest rate considerations from currency premium and currency discount. It is well known that there is a close tie between the opportunity for short-term interest arbitrage between two financial centers in different countries and the spot-forward rate relationship between their respective currencies. In a parallel fashion, there is a tie between the long-term lending rate relationships on major currencies in the international bond market and the imputed currency premium or discount. We refer to imputed or expected changes in parity relationships, since they cannot be reflected in the forward market due to the fact that debt contracts may be written for 10 to 20 years, extending well beyond the possible scope of meaningful forward market capabilities.

We can refer to four major series of data on bond yields that reflect the changing relationships referred to in the preceding paragraph. These include the yields on international dollar bonds, U.S. domestic corporate bonds, international DM bonds, and German domestic bonds. There will be a natural pairing of yields in the two dollar-denominated bond markets, and in the two DM-denominated markets. This reflects the options available to borrowers and lenders to transact either in the domestic or international bond market. Yields in both dollar (or DM) markets may be expected to move in parallel fashion, with two basic factors causing yield spreads to narrow or widen at different times. First, some lenders or borrowers may not be perfectly free to opt as between the domestic versus the international bond market (perhaps due to the U.S. IET and the U.S. mandatory controls on direct investment flows). Second, currency premium and currency discount will be reflected in widening or narrowing yield differentials as between the domestic and international dollar bond market. For example, in 1971 there was a widening yield premium on the Eurobond market for dollar bonds as compared with the yields on U.S. domestic corporate bonds. This yield premium reflected the implicit currency discount that the dollar was exposed to in the currency markets during mid-1971. The same phenomenum developed early in 1973, with a rapidly rising yield premium on international dollar bonds relative to U.S. domestic corporate bonds. In most of this period (1971-73), yields on U.S. domestic corporate issues were relatively stable, whereas yields on international dollar bonds fluctuated widely (between 8.0 and 9.6 percent in 1971 and between 7.6 and 8.9 percent in 1973). It should be noted that in 1972-73, an opposite trend was evident in the yield relationships between domestic and international DM issues. At year end 1971, these yields were very close together. Throughout most of 1972-73, yields on international DM bonds declined, whereas yields on German domestic bonds rose. By the third quarter of 1973, the differential was 2.1 percent (6.8 percent on international and 8.9 percent on domestic DM bonds). In the third quarter of 1973, the yield differential on international dollar and DM bonds was in excess of 2 percent per annum, reflecting a very strong currency premium on the DM versus the dollar.

RELATIONS WITH OTHER MARKETS

There are several practical reasons why we discuss the relationship of the Eurobond market with other markets. Finding linkages with other markets may shed light on the sources of funds of the Eurobond market. Further knowledge concerning the sources of funds can establish a better understanding of the types of investors, their motives, and how their behavior may influence the growth potential and dynamics of the market in the future. Banks and financial institutions that carry on a large part of their business outside their headquarters countries conduct a large portion of the Eurobond business. Investors in Eurobonds include wealthy individuals from countries where future economic and political stability is questionable, sophisticated investors from all parts of the globe, and professional people. Several mutual funds invest in Eurobonds, one specializing in convertible issues. Therefore, investors of relatively modest means can gain access to the market.

The options open to international investors are numerous and have been growing at an accelerating rate year by year. One option is the Eurocurrency market, which must be viewed as an alternative to the Eurobond market. Investors may switch from one market to the other when interest differentials and expectations of future interest rate changes warrant. Borrowers operating on the other side of the market may raise funds in the Eurobond market to consolidate floating debt. Finally, Eurobond syndicate members may obtain very short-term Eurocurrency accommodation to interim finance their position in Eurobonds. Links between the Eurocurrency and Eurobond markets have strengthened with the introduction of Eurodollar CDs, Eurocurrency note issues of medium term, and the development of specialized medium-term Eurocurrency consortium banks.

Relations with Capital Markets in North America

Comparison of trends in interest rates in the U.S. corporate bond market and Eurobond (dollar-denominated issues) market suggests that there are strong linkages between the two capital markets. Given the larger size of the U.S. market (8 to 10 times as large), we might expect that the Eurobond market tends to play the role of passive recipient of U.S.-induced pressures. Since the IET tends to insulate the U.S. market from the Eurobond market, we might inquire as to the mechanism(s) by which pressures initiated in the United States can influence Eurobond yield movements.

At least six avenues are available for inducing parallel movements between dollar-denominated Eurobond and domestic U.S.

corporate bond yields. First, opportunities for international portfolio diversification by nonresidents of the United States have increased. As we have noted in our discussion of the U.S. capital market, the volume of nonresident transactions in U.S. corporate securities has reached a very high level. Second, there is a strong correlation between U.S. domestic plant and equipment investment and the plant and equipment investment of U.S. corporate affiliates in Western Europe. This strong correlation would tend to place upward pressures on yields in both markets with similar timing patterns. Third, unrecorded capital flows from the United States to Western Europe may represent a partial explanation. Fourth, the pace of foreign direct investment in the United States may be influenced by yield (cost of capital) differentials, thereby bringing about closer yield conformity between the U.S. and European (Eurobond) capital markets. Fifth, the Eurodollar market affords close links between U.S. and European financial markets. It is well recognized that the foreign branch offices of U.S. banks provided liquidity backup to their head offices in the tight money periods of 1966 and 1969. Sixth, the "Canadian gap" affords opportunities for indirect interest arbitrage between the United States and Europe via Canada. U.S. and Canadian officials have endeavored to close this gap. However, the relatively free foreign exchange markets in both countries make it impossible to make Canada a watertight compartment.

Relations with the Swiss Market

In a study undertaken seven years ago, David Williams found that Switzerland is the most important country in the placement of Eurobonds with ultimate investors. Subsequent analysis reinforces Williams' conclusion that 40 to 50 percent of Eurobonds are placed in investment portfolios by Swiss banks and financial institutions. In the discussion of Switzerland's role as an international financial and investment center (Chapter 12), we referred to the reasons that make Switzerland a magnet for foreign funds. We also referred to the problems these inflows of funds pose for the Swiss monetary authorities.

Under a gentlemen's agreement, the Swiss banks do not promote the sale of foreign bonds to Swiss investors. This tends to insulate domestic elements of the Swiss capital market from foreign pressures. In addition, the Swiss banks carefully regulate foreign security placements including Eurobonds with a view toward matching inflows of funds with outflows. In this way, Switzerland functions as an entrepôt for capital funds. The Swiss probably have less effective control over inflows than outflows of funds since the volume of inflows is related more to general political and financial conditions outside Switzerland. In this connection, we might expect that the Swiss banking system possesses some discretion in placing nonresident funds into Eurobonds, Eurocurrency deposits, domestic securities in the U.S. or other national securities markets, and increasing the volume of Swiss-franc-denominated foreign bonds for purchase by nonresidents. Naturally, there are foreign exchange considerations involved in these portfolio management decisions, not least of which is protection of the status of the Swiss franc in the exchange markets.

Relations with Other European Capital Markets

The Eurobond market affords an attractive alternative to European investors who otherwise would place their funds in securities offered on their own national capital markets. In cases where the Eurobond currency-yield package offers advantages over securities issued on the domestic market, investors in Europe will endeavor to shift their resources in that direction. In some cases, there will be a strong inducement to acquire Eurobonds denominated in dollars or DMs due to the presumed advantage of these currencies over the domestic currency of the investor. In the past, UK investors have been attracted to Eurobonds due to the recurrent weakness of the pound sterling. Even relatively high interest rates available in the United Kingdom have not completely offset this currency premium relationship. While in the past UK residents have faced restrictions in undertaking foreign portfolio investments, British business interests in outlying Eurobond centers such as the Bahamas, Hong Kong, South Africa, and elsewhere have provided opportunities for Eurobond investments.

A large segment of the funds entering the Eurobond market comes from the Common Market countries. The national capital markets in these countries continue to be largely separated, although effective operation of the Eurobond and Eurocurrency markets has tended to more closely align these markets. Belgium has maintained a relatively liberal policy with respect to resident purchases of foreign securities, and we might conclude that the Eurobond market has received a representative share of Belgian funds invested in offshore markets. However, Belgium is a relatively small country, and its role as a supplier of funds for Eurobond purchases is necessarily limited. Secondly, Belgian financial institutions are subject to strict regulations concerning the amount of foreign securities they may purchase.

The Netherlands has long been an outward looking country, and Dutch businessmen and financial institutions are governed by relatively

467

liberal foreign security investment policies. Relative interest rates in the Netherlands and overseas play an important role in the alternating waves of capital outflows and inflows. In the period 1970-72, Eurobond issues denominated in Dutch guilders ranged between $268 million and $473 million, in 1972 accounting for 7.6 percent of the Eurobond total. Doubtless, the shift toward denominating Eurobond issues in Dutch guilder reflects an increased willingness of the Dutch authorities to permit capital outflows to the international bond market, an improved competitive position for Dutch financial institutions on both sides of the market, and a reduction of currency risk considerations for Dutch investors participating in the market. Nevertheless, we should remember that the Netherlands is a relatively small country and cannot generate substantial internal funds for investment in the international bond market.

France has permitted its residents to trade in foreign securities listed on a recognized stock exchange. However, balance of payments difficulties have at times prompted French officials to impose restrictions on capital transactions by residents. At present, capital transactions are channeled through the financial franc market, which has been in operation for over three years. In the past, wealthy Frenchmen have maintained banking relations in Switzerland (Geneva) and Luxembourg and, no doubt, have used these avenues for a substantial part of their foreign investments including acquisitions of Eurobonds.

During the 1960s, changing interest rate relationships between the Italian financial market and the Eurobond market have brought about successive waves of Italian funds flowing into Eurobond investments. In addition, balance of payments pressures have induced the Italian authorities to adopt a flexible policy toward resident capital transactions. As a result of these developments, Italy has at times proved to be a most important source of capital funds. This is borne out by the important role of Italian banks as managers of Eurobond issues. Italian wealth holders have been noted for their desire to avoid fiscal burdens, and purchases of Eurobonds via Swiss accounts have been important. In the past, Italian investors have become thoroughly familiar with Eurobond investments, and we can expect that when interest rate relationships are favorable, a substantial volume of funds will flow from Italy into the Eurobond market.

The German capital market is one of the freest in the world. German residents are free to purchase foreign securities, and no exchange restrictions have been applied since 1958. However, the German capital market has been characterized by high interest rates, discouraging resident purchases of foreign securities. In addition, the expected trend in currency parities tends to work against outward capital flows. A business recession in 1967 was accompanied by a decline in interest rates, and the yield relationship became more favorable to outward capital flows. In a short interval of time, German investors purchased significant amounts of DM-denominated Eurobonds. Again in late 1969 and throughout 1970, yield relationships favored German resident purchases of DM-denominated Eurobonds as compared with domestic bonds. However, in 1971-73, yields on domestic bonds remained above those available on DM-denominated Eurobonds. As noted earlier, in 1972 the proportion of Eurobonds denominated in DMs declined.

REFERENCES

Aliber, Robert Z. "A Theory of Direct Foreign Investment." In The International Corporation. Edited by Charles Kindleberger. Cambridge, Mass.: M.I.T. Press, 1970.

Bank for International Settlements. Annual Reports, 1972 and 1973.

Dufey, Gunter. The Eurobond Market: Function and Future. International Business Series, Studies in Finance, no. 7. Seattle: University of Washington Press, 1969.

Levy, H., and M. Sarnat. "International Diversification of Investment Portfolios." American Economic Review (September 1970).

Organization for Economic Cooperation and Development (OECD). Financial Statistics, 1972, 1973.

Williams, David. "Foreign Currency Issues on European Capital Markets." IMF Staff Papers, March 1967.

World Bank Annual Reports, 1972 and 1973.

23

THE INTERNATIONAL MARKET FOR FOREIGN EXCHANGE

The market for foreign exchange is probably the single most important financial market and certainly is the largest market in the world. In 1973, the daily volume of transactions averaged close to $20 billion and exceeded that level by a wide margin at intervals where speculative transactions and central bank intervention came into the market.

The foreign exchange market is important because it shapes the opportunities for commercial, investment, and other international payments, and because it is through the foreign exchange market that other types of financial markets are tied together. As we note in the sections that follow, there is a close interplay between the operation of the international foreign exchange market and the structure of the world monetary system. In fact, the international foreign exchange market is a key component of this system, and the international financial policy pursued by each major industrial country will significantly influence the functioning of its own national foreign exchange market as well as the effective working of the world monetary system.

THE WORLD SYSTEM OF FOREIGN EXCHANGE

Structure

In 1946, conclusion of World War II presented the major nations of the world with the task of reconstructing a workable international monetary system. The structure of this system had been shaped earlier at the Bretton Woods Conference, where agreement had been reached to establish an International Monetary Fund (IMF). The basic principles inherent in the fund agreement were that (1) nations should strive to free trade and payments as quickly and as fully as possible, and (2) financial policies should allow for the operation of a relatively stable exchange rate relationship among national currencies. The fund was to consist of gold and convertible currencies that could be made available to member nations should their international payments' positions shift into deficit. Availability of the resources of the fund would permit countries to finance trade and other international payments without the need to impose restrictive policies. Member countries would be permitted to alter the fixed exchange rate (par values) between their own and other currencies only in cases of "fundamental disequilibrium" in their overall international transactions.

Since 1946, the international foreign exchange market has experienced considerable adjustment and change. In the period 1946-50, the foreign exchanges were exposed to postwar inflationary pressures, lingering controls on international transactions, and worldwide shortages of capital and goods. The dollar was in strong demand due to the elastic supply of goods and services available from the United states. From 1950 to 1958, the European currencies gradually moved toward convertibility status, which they achieved in 1958. In this period, major European countries gradually removed quantitative controls on trade and even began to relax restrictions on capital transfers. From 1958 to 1967, the European currencies became considerably stronger and began to play a genuinely international role as financing, denomination, and vehicle currencies. In this period, sterling, deutsche mark (DM), and Swiss franc bond issues became a familiar aspect of the international flow of investment capital. Since 1967, the foreign exchanges have experienced new problems and pressures. Persistent U.S. balance of payments deficits, a growing tendency toward regional trade and payments arrangements, worldwide inflation, and a growing pool of internationally mobile capital funds have resulted in a number of structural as well as policy changes in the area of foreign exchange. These include several devaluations of major currencies, including the U.S. dollar, renewed floating of the Canadian dollar, discontinuance of free gold-dollar convertibility, numerous exchange rate adjustments, and widened bands of permitted fluctuation around currency par values.

In the early years of the 1970s, several currencies attained a competitive position vis-à-vis the U.S. dollar. These include the DM in the area of foreign trade financing and international bond issues, the Japanese yen in Far East trade and payments as well as commercial and business investments, and the Swiss franc in the area of portfolio investment and foreign bond issues. At the same time, a number of the less developed countries have stabilized and strengthened their currencies insofar as international purchasing power is concerned. These include the Brazilian and Mexican currencies. In addition, several currencies of the less developed countries have become considerably more attractive to nonresidents due to the development of manufacturing and commercial opportunities in their respective territories (Singapore-Malaysia and South Africa) and to the growth of local financial markets (Hong Kong and the Philippines).

Official Reserves

The world system of foreign exchange depends heavily on adequate liquid reserves. This reserve liquidity fulfills a number of important functions, including maintenance of existing par value relationships among currencies, financing of short-run swings in a nation's merchandise trade and payments, and provision of needed foreign exchange to the private sector for use in foreign investment and foreign lending activities.

Official reserves held by individual nations are an important part of the world system of foreign exchange. These reserves can be used to supplement or absorb private sector holdings of foreign exchange, thereby operating as a stabilizing element in the foreign exchange markets. Moreover, they function as a necessary liquidity backup to the world network of payments, which embraces transactions covering foreign investment as well as international trade.

While foreign exchange constitutes the largest segment of official reserves held by individual nations, in 1972 three other components accounted for roughly one-third of official reserves (Table 23.1). The importance of the foreign exchange component has increased over the period 1967-72 due to persistent U.S. balance of payments deficits, which have been settled by increases in foreign-held dollar balances, speculative flows of funds across the foreign exchange markets, which have compelled central banks to engage in exchange rate support activities, and to the growth in world trade and payments, which has been accompanied by a substantial escalation in foreign exchange transactions but no equivalent increase in gold production and IMF quotas.

Over two-thirds of the official holdings of foreign exchange is in the form of U.S.-dollar-denominated assets. This suggests that the dollar will continue to play a pivotal position in the official as well as private sectors of the international market for foreign exchange.

TABLE 23.1

Official Reserves Held by National Treasuries
and Central Banks
(billion of dollars)

	1962	1967	1972
Gold	39.3	39.5	35.7
SDRs	—	—	8.7
Reserve position in fund	3.8	5.7	6.3
Foreign exchange	20.1	29.0	93.7
Total	63.2	74.2	144.4

Source: International Monetary Fund (IMF), International
Financial Statistics.

Private Demand for Foreign Exchange

Data provided by the IMF suggest that the private demand for
foreign exchange may be as large as or even more substantial than
the official demand, as reflected in reserve holdings. This should
not be a surprise since the volume of private transactions exceeds
official transactions in the foreign exchange market many times over.

In the relatively short period 1967-70, foreign exchange held
by deposit banks throughout the globe more than doubled, reaching
a total of close to $60 billion in the later year. Banks located in Italy,
Japan, Canada, Belgium, Germany, and the Netherlands hold the
largest amounts of foreign exchange, in that order. As the developing
countries progressively stabilize their currencies, they may be expected to increase their now relatively modest investment in foreign
exchange.

The expansion in privately held foreign exchange can be associated with the rapid upsurge of international banking activities
of major banks that took place in the late 1960s and has continued
into the 1970s. In turn, this has been associated with the larger base
of foreign trade and investment transactions, widened opportunities
to engage in foreign money market activities by means of foreign
exchange transactions, increased scope for participation in international underwriting business, and the increased willingness of large
banks to engage in time, geographic, and currency arbitrage operations.

The increased foreign exchange holdings of deposit banks reflect a growing tendency for the internationalization of financial and creidt markets in all corners of the world. The large deposit banks, which play a central role as holders of foreign exchange, have become thrust more and more to the forefront of international credit market dealings largely due to their initial position as foreign exchange banks. It is likely that in future these major deposit banks will continue to enjoy this important relationship.

NATIONAL FOREIGN EXCHANGE MARKETS

National Currencies and the Foreign Exchange Market

The international market for foreign exchange consists of numerous domestic markets that are closely linked together by arbitrage, telex, and instant computer message systems. These close linkages permit a uniform price of one currency in terms of another currency throughout the global network of foreign exchange markets, and the relative efficiency of competition and arbitrage tends to assure a single price in this global network.

The international market for foreign exchange constitutes the largest single financial market in the world. The market is based on the need for participants to settle international transactions in currencies other than the domestic money. Over three quarters of transactions represent export and import merchandise trade; close to 15 percent represent long-term and short-term capital transactions; and the remainder represent a variety of service transactions including payments and receipts relating to shipping, insurance, and foreign investment income.

The market for foreign exchange renders basic services to the nations of the world, including the provision of international credit, effecting international payments, clearing international transactions, and hedging. The foreign exchange market is influenced by the meshing together of semiautonomous national currency areas, wherein individual nations control the growth and availability of the domestic money supply. The meshing together of these national currency areas is in part accomplished by the working out of demand and supply forces in the foreign exchange market. Exporters, importers, foreign investors, and providers of shipping and other services in one country shape that country's demand and supply for foreign exchange, as well as reciprocally influence the supply and demand of that country's currency on the foreign exchange market. In short, the foreign exchange market may be viewed as a funnel through which demand and supply for each national currency influence the price of that currency expressed in terms of other currencies.

The demand for a particular currency depends on real and financial considerations. Real factors relate to the competitiveness of a country's products in world markets. Financial considerations relate to the usefulness of the currency in the foreign investment, transaction (vehicle), hedging, and short-term financing areas. The strength of these various demand factors for a particular currency is continually changing, and there are numerous cross-relationships wherein an increase in one demand component of a currency may influence other demand components. For example, a downward shift in the investment demand for dollars may enhance the role of the dollar (demand) as a transactions or short-term financing currency. The U.S. dollar is by far the most important national currency, especially in terms of its share of total volume in the foreign exchange market. Next, in order of importance, are the pound sterling, the DM, the Japanese yen, and the Canadian dollar. Several other currencies play an important role in the foreign exchange market, including the Swiss franc, Dutch guilder, French franc, Italian lira, and Belgian franc.

The importance of these national currencies in the international market for foreign exchange is paralleled by the role played by the same national foreign exchange markets. The largest single national foreign exchange market is the market in the United States. The U.S. market is concentrated in New York, and several dozen New-York-based banking institutions constitute the core of the market. Several dozen currencies are regularly traded in the New York foreign exchange market. However, only a half dozen currencies account for the bulk of the trading volume. Approximately half of aggregate volume is in sterling, close to one-fourth in Canadian dollars, and one-tenth in DMs. Other major currencies traded in New York include the Dutch guilder, Swiss franc, Japanese yen, and French franc. Important futures markets exist for the currencies that are most actively traded in New York.

Several dozen large U.S. commercial banks maintain sizable positions in foreign exchange. In addition, the Edge Act affiliates of American banks, foreign bank agencies and branches, and U.S. chartered bank affiliates of large foreign banks deal actively in foreign exchange. In 1972, foreign currency deposits maintained by U.S. banks in banking institutions outside the United States aggregated over $900 million. However, this figure understates the importance of American banking institutions in the international market for foreign exchange. American banks maintain extensive overseas branch networks, and at year end 1972 these banks operated over 630 foreign branches. These foreign branches hold dollar deposits as well as extend dollar loans. Moreover, operating from a dollar currency base, they play a key role in the market for dollar exchange outside the United States.

The foreign exchange inventory maintained by an individual bank is influenced by the size and relative importance of that bank's international operations, the opportunities available to that bank for developing and servicing foreign currency requirements of its customers, and the national origin mix of its internationally oriented clientele. Each bank that maintains a foreign exchange trading position must allocate a given portion of its resources to foreign currency balances held on deposit in overseas banks. This inventory of sterling, Canadian dollars, or DMs may be depleted as customers purchase these currencies for commercial, investment, or other uses. On the other hand, the bank inventory of foreign exchange may be reconstituted as its customers sell their excess accumulations of foreign currency.

The demand and supply pressures that develop in the foreign exchange market relative to a specific currency may be transmitted through three levels of the market. First, the banks operating in the market in that currency can adjust their inventory positions as well as the rate of exchange they quote for purchase and sale of that currency for current (spot) delivery. Second, in the interbank market, individual banks may even off their positions by trades with another bank. Third, banks in one foreign exchange center (New York) may sell excess holdings of a given currency to banks located in another foreign exchange center (Paris).

Banks operate as middlemen dealers in the market, adjusting their inventories of specific currencies to minimize position risks and to earn an attractive return on invested funds. Maximum positions will be specified in each currency that the bank trades, and each bank will attempt to square its position in each currency. This can be accomplished by squaring the books separately for spot and forward transactions and by balancing forward against spot positions overnight.

The extensive foreign exchange operations of major banks throughout the world and the offshore dollar operations of U.S. banks provide considerable opportunities for internationally oriented banks to develop money market activities in several countries simultaneously. Acquisition of excessive foreign currency balances may prompt a bank to invest these funds in short-term money market assets of that foreign currency. Alternately, the foreign currency may be sold and the proceeds invested in another offshore money market or in the domestic money market of the parent bank.

Relations with Other Financial Markets

Growth and development of the international market for foreign exchange have not been in isolation. The foreign exchange market has grown as a result of the expansion of domestic money markets and, at the same time, has supported as well as competed against development of certain national money markets. Moreover, the foreign exchange market has developed along with expansion of the Eurocurrency market.

The mix of competitive and complementary aspects of the foreign exchange and national money markets hinges on the institutional pattern, economic policy, and special factors peculiar to each country. A clearly competitive situation prevails in several European countries, where the foreign exchange market affords domestic banks superior short-term investment outlets outside of the local money market. This is especially the situation in Switzerland where the big banks have found foreign exchange relationships conducive to offshore rather than domestic money market investments.

By contrast, opportunities afforded in the relatively free Hong Kong foreign exchange market have attracted substantial amounts of nonresident funds, increased the liquidity of the Hong Kong banks and financial market, and enhanced the development of the local stock exchanges. Similar complementary relationships have long been a paramount feature of the London foreign exchange market, where that market has furthered development of the traditional and new parallel money markets.

The foreign exchange market similarly enjoys complementary and competitive relationships with the Eurocurrency market. Interest arbitrage on the Eurocurrency market among different maturity deposits is the counterpart of interest arbitrage in the foreign exchange market between spot and forward positions in a given currency. A multinational company operating in Western Europe and holding temporarily excess DMs has the option of placing a short-term DM deposit in a Eurobank or of swapping the DM funds for another currency. The funds can be temporarily invested in the local money market of that currency until the swap is reversed by execution of the futures contract. Therefore, foreign exchange rate relationships spot and future should be considered an important parameter that must be compared with Eurocurrency deposit and lending rates. Close arbitrage between these two international financial channels suggests that there are extremely close linkages operating between the foreign exchange and Eurocurrency markets.

Finally, we should note that at times extremely close ties operate between the foreign exchange market and several of the national and international securities markets. Relative prices and yields of

477

securities in the various capital markets around the globe are an active ingredient in the interplay of shifting foreign exchange rate relationships. Especially important fund flows directed through the foreign exchange markets and into and out of specific securities markets include the following:

1. nonresident purchases of U.S. securities;
2. inflows of funds into Switzerland for eventual investment in U.S. and Western European securities;
3. U.S. purchase of Canadian bonds denominated in U.S. dollars;
4. nonresident purchases of Japanese securities;
5. nonresident purchases of DM-denominated securities.

International portfolio investment and new issues of securities have increased in scope and now represent an important element in shaping pressures on the foreign exchange markets. During the early 1970s, this trend displayed no signs of abating, even with the international crises of 1971 and 1973. In fact, the growing importance of international portfolio investment has reached a point where analysts are endeavoring to determine the most efficient and optimal international portfolio diversification in equity securities.

FOREIGN EXCHANGE AND THE WORLD MONETARY SYSTEM

Functioning of the System

How should the foreign exchange markets function to provide an orderly world monetary system? Doubtless, events in the period 1969-74 have indicated how important an efficient and effective structuring of the international monetary system is to stability and growth of world finance.

To permit a proper functioning of the international monetary system, the foreign exchange markets must provide credit facilities, clearing of foreign-held balances, and facilities for insuring against foreign exchange rate changes that cause losses to business firms and investors. Credit facilities are required to cushion swings in the balance of payments and foreign positions of individual countries until such time as these swings are reversed. These credit facilities take the form of changes in foreign exchange holdings of official and private agencies, short-term loans by international banks and other specialized lenders to nonresidents, and longer-term credits of various types. Credit facilities available via the foreign exchange market vary considerably in form, type lender, maturity, and terms of the credit.

Clearing of foreign-held balances takes place in the foreign exchange market in the private sector as well as in the official sector of the market. In the private sector, commercial banks and other transactors in the market sell excess foreign exchange balances to one another in the same financial center. In addition, transactions take place among participants in different financial centers and currency areas. Finally, official agencies including central banks engage in intervention operations in the foreign exchange market to support the foreign exchange rate of a specific currency when it has reached an outer support limit. Such intervention may add to the credit facilities in the market and at the same time result in additional clearing of funds through the market. Three-cornered arbitrage in the foreign exchange market clears a large volume of transactions and at the same time irons out disorderly cross-rate relationships.

The foreign exchange market also provides facilities for insuring against adverse changes in rates. These facilities include the forward (futures) market and the relationship between the spot and forward rates of exchange. A forward premium or discount on a currency relative to its spot rate results from interest arbitrage opportunities as well as expectations of future changes in the spot rate. In turn, interest arbitrage opportunities relate to the differences that exist in basic interest rate levels in two or more national money markets. Therefore, we can say that one factor that plays a determining role in the cost of obtaining forward cover on forthcoming foreign exchange transactions is the interest rate relationship prevailing in a given country's money market as compared with interest rate levels in other major money markets. In short, we have an important linkage between the insurance or hedging function aspect of the foreign exchange market and the relative interest rates that prevail at a given time in various national money markets.

Central Bank Intervention

Central bank intervention in the foreign exchange market is a relatively new development. Admittedly, important instances of such intervention can be cited going back to the late nineteenth century. However, these were largely isolated situations that came about due to an unusual combination of events. In 1932, the United Kingdom established its Exchange Equalization Account to influence changes in the price of the floating pound in terms of the U.S. dollar and French franc. Two years later the United States established an Exchange Stabilization Fund to prevent undue fluctuation in the dollar price of sterling.

During World War II, revival of exchange controls and termination of convertibility status for major international trading currencies made currency intervention redundant. Blocked accounts and clearing agreements administered by central banks and monetary authorities replaced the free operation of foreign exchange markets supported by central bank intervention. In the years after World War II, major currencies gradually moved toward market convertibility, and the regime of fixed exchange rate relationships came into being. Actively supported by central bank intervention, the foreign exchange market functioned well for a period of over 15 years, during which time there were only sporadic exchange rate adjustments and a progressive trend toward liberalization of international trade and payments. This regime ended in the early 1970s with the exchange crises of 1971 and 1973, devaluation of the dollar, and near demonetization of gold for international settlements purposes.

During the early 1970s, extreme speculation against major currencies including the U.S. resulted in massive support operations by several European central banks, especially the German central bank. Widening of the permitted bands of fluctuation in national currencies since 1971 may well increase the need for as well as complicate the intervention operations of central banks.

Central bank intervention is inherently a difficult process. Aside from domestic and international political considerations, central bankers must make decisions that relate to technical considerations of the market mechanism. These hinge on considerations relating to the desired price level of a particular currency both spot and forward, the optimal pace of change in exchange rates, the spot versus forward rate relationship, the desired proximity of the spot rate to the support limit, in what foreign exchange market to intervene, and whether intervention should be open or concealed. Intervention is becoming a more complex matter due to the swift communications network that has been developing, the large expansion in volume of foreign currency balances held, and the growing role of multinational corporations that are highly sophisticated in matters of money management.

Given the growing importance of international transactions and the present scope of foreign exchange operations, it seems likely that in the future central bank intervention could become a more important factor in the international market for foreign exchange. The question then becomes—how efficient is intervention? What is the optimal intervention strategy? While these questions do not lend themselves to simple answer, some general rules can be set down. First, forward market intervention enjoys certain advantages over spot market intervention. These advantages include the more selective incentives afforded to holders of internationally mobile funds (interest agio), the possibility of accomplishing a given objective with smaller transactions volume in the forward as compared with the spot market (thinner forward market), and the possibility of undertaking transactions that are not included on balance sheets which tends to preserve the secrecy and uncertainty of official transactions. Second, successful intervention is feasible as long as market pressures are of limited dimension and not subject to dynamic alterations. Finally, intervention may be in the process of evolving toward a more unified form of joint action on the part of a large number of central banks. Such unity of action could become an extremely powerful factor in the market for foreign exchange.

Currency Problems of the 1970s

It is not difficult to enumerate the international currency problems of the 1970s. These problems have already manifested themselves. Perhaps the most serious of these include the apparent weakening of the U.S. dollar in the foreign exchange markets, the inability of a regime of fixed foreign exchange rates to operate without repeated substantial exchange rate alterations, the apparent general lack of confidence in the international monetary system as it is presently constituted, and the unpredictable shifts in the rate of growth of international reserves and liquidity.

The international currency problems of the 1970s carry serious implications for the world's financial markets. A weakening of the U.S. dollar relative to other currencies in the foreign exchange markets tends to put pressure on the Eurobond market in terms of yields required on major currencies of issue. Shifts in the growth and holdings of international reserves tend to place political pressure on strong currency countries to liberalize capital outflows as well as current account transactions in the balance of payments. Declining confidence in the international monetary system tends to place upward pressures on interest rates, especially in the financial markets of countries whose currencies are most under suspicion. Finally, repeated exchange rate adjustments tend to induce private capital transfers, which exaggerate foreign exchange rate pressures, weaken the price structure in securities markets in countries with the softer currencies, and tend to compel governments to adopt restrictive measures that are aimed at reducing destabilizing flows of capital funds.

During the 1960s, the dollar has been the principal cohesive factor in the international market for foreign exchange. This role has been possible because of the lack of suitable alternatives, the stability of the dollar/foreign currency price ratio, and the strong private demand for dollars based on transactions, commercial, investment, speculative and precautionary motives for holding dollars.

481

The ability of the dollar to continue to function in this capacity has become questioned, and the very fact that it has been questioned places pressure on the dollar in the world's foreign exchange markets A fundamental question is whether, in the foreseeable future, the architects of international currency reform will design a modified or new system that reduces the international role of the dollar. Such reform, if and when it takes place, will also modify the international market for foreign exchange.

Exchange Markets in the Developing Countries

The foreign exchange markets in the developing countries are characterized by a number of fairly common features. Among these are the following:

1. Central banks establish fixed buying and selling rates centere on a par value.

2. Commercial banks operate at fixed margins from the central-bank-established rates. Banks act as agents and hold only minimal foreign currency balances.

3. Uncertainty in the foreign exchange market is related more to a major change in the exchange rate rather than day-to-day fluctuations in prevailing rates.

4. A key currency is used to effect foreign exchange transaction

5. Surrender requirements generally are imposed on earners of foreign exchange, which reduced flexibility on the supply side.

As a result of these and other conditions, there is generally little scope for development of an interbank market in foreign exchange. Moreover, absence of a domestic money market means that there are only limited uses for the proceeds of converting foreign exchange into local currency.

Alternative employment of funds seems to offer a higher return to commercial banks and other potential participants in the foreign exchange market in developing countries. As a result, banks do not aggressively seek to develop a foreign exchange business. Naturally, there are exceptions to the above, such as Mexico where there is a well-developed export-import business, a strong banking system, and an emerging futures market in foreign exchange.

Attempts by governments of developing countries to foster development of a domestic foreign exchange market have not been very fruitful. In countries with fluctuating rate systems (Argentina, Philippines, Venezuela), inflation and payments crises have made it difficult to stabilize exchange rate relationships. In countries with pegged rates, inappropriate monetary-fiscal policies have required the imposition of foreign exchange and payments controls to balance international payments. In such countries, pegging the foreign exchange rate has provided only the illusion of price and financial stability.

A basic difficulty in attempts to develop a foreign exchange market has been the high return that banks can earn on commercial loans or short-term money market investments. In such countries, there may be an adequate supply of foreign exchange (Korea), but a lack of institutional development in the market.

REFERENCES

Robert Z. Aliber. The International Market for Foreign Exchange. New York: Praeger Publishers, 1969.

_____. The International Money Game. New York: Basic Books, 1973.

Argy V., and M. Porter. "The Forward Exchange Market and the Effects of Domestic and External Disturbances under Alternative Exchange Rate Systems." IMF Staff Papers, November 1972.

Einzig, Paul. A Dynamic Theory of Forward Exchange. New York: St. Martin's Press, 1961.

Hirsch, Fred. "The Exchange Rate Regime: An Analysis and a Possible Scheme." IMF Staff Papers, July 1972.

Holmes, Alan R. The New York Foreign Exchange Market. Federal Reserve Bank of New York, 1964.

International Monetary Fund (IMF). Annual Report on Exchange Restrictions, 1972, 1973.

PART

VIII

COMPARISONS AND
FUTURE PROSPECTS

24

International comparisons of national financial markets must be selective. This is because of lack of comparable data, which presents a real problem in this area. Moreover, the state of knowledge in the area of financial market performance and efficiency is only at an early stage of development. For these and other reasons, we have focused our international comparisons largely in the areas of the capital market sector and new securities issues. Other types of data and information have been brought into the discussion where relevant.

GROWTH, SIZE, AND INTERNATIONAL ORIENTATION

This chapter focuses on several important bases for comparing the financial markets of individual countries. These include the stage of economic growth, the size of the country, and the extent of international influence and international orientation. As a nation's economic growth and development progress, a number of important changes take place in the domestic financial markets. These include changes in savings flows, the volume of gross and net new securities issues, the development and relative importance of financial institutions, and the pattern of operations of these institutions. Economic development generally is accompanied by increased relative and absolute savings flows out of national income, a higher gross and net new securities issue ratio to gross national product (GNP), and a widening differential between gross and net new securities issues as redemption of maturing debt securities becomes a more important aspect of external financing.

The relative importance and pattern of financial institution development are highly significant in the evolution of a nation's financial markets. In his study of "The Development of Financial Institutions during the Post-War Period," published in the Banca Nazionale del Lavoro Quarterly Review, June 1972, Raymond Goldsmith has summarized the main trends that have manifested themselves in the period 1949-67. These include a 12-percent average annual growth in assets of financial institutions for all countries studied, or in real terms 8 percent; a higher growth rate (14 percent) for financial institutions in less developed as compared with developed (10 percent) countries; a greater role of money creation as a source of funds for financial institutions in less developed as compared with developed countries; differential growth rates of the major types of financial institutions during the postwar decades with central banks expanding the least, commercial banks at a moderate pace, and other institutions such as pension funds, mortgage banks, development banks, and insurance organizations growing at the highest rate.

For the period 1949-67 and for the 40 countries for which Goldsmith has assembled data, the growth in assets of financial institutions was 12 percent per annum. The median rate of growth was 10 percent. The average rate of growth was higher for less developed countries (Table 24.1) due to strong inflationary pressures (Argentina and Brazil), the need to pass through a catching-up phase of financial institution development (Philippines and Spain), and a relatively high real growth rate in several of the less developed countries (Venezuela and Mexico). After adjustment for price increases, we can observe that a number of the less developed countries achieved substantial growth in financial institutions. Countries with the highest growth rates in financial institution assets were Japan, Germany, and Italy among the developed countries, and the Philippines, Spain, and Venezuela among the less developed countries.

Size of a national economy can play an important part in financial market development and in the opportunities for financial institution specialization. Moreover, size can determine the kind of international financial market relationships a nation develops. For example, the smallest national economies may not be able to develop their own capital market facilities fully and may depend on international financial markets to provide for new issues and money market investments. In Chapter 22 "The Eurobond Market," we noted that a number of well-developed countries (such as the Scandinavian countries) have made use of the facilities of the international bond market to float new bond issues. Similarly, central banks and private investors in many smaller countries make use of the Eurocurrency, New York, and London money markets to undertake short-term investments. Canada and other smaller countries receive substantial amounts of business investments from larger countries such as the United States, United Kingdom, Germany, and Japan. Presumably, size influences

TABLE 24.1

Growth Rates of Assets of Financial
Institutions, 1948-67
(average annual rate)

	Current Prices	Constant Prices
Developed countries		
Australia	7.21%	2.95%
Canada	8.20	5.45
France	14.92	9.24
Germany	15.32	12.14
Great Britain	6.24	2.80
Italy	15.26	11.79
Japan	21.98	17.15
Netherlands	9.84	5.75
South Africa	8.56	6.06
Switzerland	8.57	5.83
United States	6.80	4.61
Less developed countries		
Argentina	20.46	-4.26
Brazil	35.23	4.65
India	9.98	8.52
Mexico	15.00	8.79
Philippines	13.09	10.48
Spain	16.41	10.36
Trinidad	8.42	5.29
Venezuela	12.50	11.32

Source: Raymond Goldsmith, "The Development of Financial Institutions during the Post-War Period," Banca Nazionale del Lavoro Quarterly Review (June 1972): 141.

the opportunities for financial market specialization and thereby exerts leverage over the kinds of international financial relationships enjoyed by small and large countries. Some large countries enjoy an efficiency advantage in performing numerous financial services and, therefore, can expect to "export" these services to the rest of the world.

The extent of international orientation is most important in our overview of financial center comparisons. We might distinguish among international lenders, borrowers, and financial entrepôts. The United States, United Kingdom, and Switzerland have become important international financial entrepôt centers, while regional financial entrepôts have developed in Nassau, Beirut, Singapore, and Hong Kong. Germany and Japan have tend to become international lenders, while Brazil, Mexico, and Australia have persistently been on the borrowing side of international financial market relationships. Extent of international orientation varies considerably as is indicated below in Table 24.5, where the ratio of foreign bond issues to total debt issues is reflected for 11 developed countries which serve as important markets of issue. The ratio ranges from 0.8 percent in Italy up to a very high figure for Switzerland. Other measures of international orientation might include the ratio of exports to GNP (high for the Netherlands and Venezuela) and the percentage of domestic industry owned by foreign investors (high for Canada and South Africa).

SIZE OF CAPITAL MARKET

The size of a nation's capital market is influenced by a number of factors, including stage of economic growth, past accumulation of productive wealth, ownership pattern of productive resources (capitalist, socialist, mixed or other), extent of development of financial institutions, international use of national capital market facilities, and government policy.

Based on information pertaining to outstanding capital market securities included in Table 24.2, we see that the capital market in the United States surpasses all others. Countries such as Japan and Italy also possess large capital markets. The relatively narrow margin between outstanding securities in the Japanese and U.S. capital markets can be explained in part by the highly intermediated status of Japan's financial markets, where banks and other financial institutions issue capital market securities (bank bonds play an important role in Japan's financial markets), and the highly debt-leveraged capital structure of industrial corporations in Japan. The capital market in Italy has achieved a high level of development in connection with the special role of state enterprise, public enterprises that borrow heavily by issue of long-term debt securities, and the interposition of several specialized quasi-public financial institutions which issue capital market securities to assist the financing of high-priority development projects.

Another measure of capital market size is securities outstanding per capita (Table 24.2). The highest ranking countries are the United States, Denmark, Belgium, and Sweden. The U.S. lead is no surprise. It is explained by high per-capita wealth, a high degree of financial

490

TABLE 24.2

Value of Outstanding Capital Market Securities, Selected Countries
(millions of U.S. dollars)

	Shares of Domestic Issuers	Bonds				Total Bonds	Total Shares and Bonds	Shares and Bonds Per Capita
		Government Issuers	Public Enterprises	Private Enterprises	Financial Institutions			
Austria	1,783	1,123	523	1,120	1,295	3,061	4,844	2,650
Belgium	7,836	12,900	1,308	1,048	4,764	20,020	27,856	2,880
Denmark	4,797	1,721		10,505		12,265a	17,062	3,440
France	11,020	2,175	17,360	4,575		24,110	35,130	685
Finland	2,432	808	53	129	504	1,532d	3,964	860
Italy	20,355	19,150	12,770	1,580	25,290	59,295b	79,650	1,478
Japan	34,260	12,730	26,040	11,965	27,130	77,865	112,125	1,062
Netherlands	9,384	2,909		3,522		6,431	15,815	1,200
Norway	1,112	1,715	482	295	630	3,650c	4,762	1,221
Spain	10,300	5,165	2,249	3,490	931	11,835	22,135	648
Sweden	411	4,929		1,562	9,300	15,791	16,202	2,000
United States	1,030,422	311,165		282,816		593,981	1,624,403	7,846

a Includes $39 million of foreign issues.
b Includes $510 million of foreign issues.
c Includes $529 million of foreign issues.
d Includes $38 million of foreign issues.

Note: Based on 1971 data except for Belgium (1970), Denmark (1970), Norway (1968), Netherlands (1966), Sweden (1970), and Finland (1970).

Source: Organization for Economic Cooperation and Development (OECD), Financial Statistics.

institution development, and government policy that favors deficit-financed expenditure and stabilization policies. In Belgium share issues play a distinctly less important role than in the United States, which suggests something special concerning the U.S. equities market. Moreover, in Belgium government issues account for a significantly larger portion of outstanding securities, suggesting that government policy plays an even more important role than in the United States. In Denmark and Sweden high wealth and income levels provide a necessary ingredient to a substantial level of securities outstanding per capita. However, equally important is the well-developed financial institution sector. For example, in Sweden financial institutions have issued over 60 percent of capital market securities outstanding.

Only 3 of the 12 countries represented in Table 24.2 have a dominant portion of capital market securities outstanding in the form of shares. Nearly two-thirds of U.S. securities represent equities, while 60 percent of the securities of the Netherlands and Finland are in the form of shares. Various reasons explain the high ratio of equity securities to total capital market outstandings in these three countries as contrasted with the low ratios prevailing in the remaining nine countries. We should remember that in the United States and the Netherlands, the notion of private enterprise and highly developed stock exchanges have permitted share issues to expand in amount and value. In many other countries, public enterprise and government ownership of industry have reduced the scope for growth in the share market (France, Italy, and Japan). Finally, government ownership of enterprises and a heavy admixture of fiscal policy have inflated government bond issues and reduced the relative importance of equity securities.

Government issues account for as much as 45 percent (Belgium) and as little as 10 percent (Denmark) of total capital market securities outstanding. If we consider government issues as a percent of debt issues only, the United States, Finland, Italy, and France evidence high ratios (33 percent to 50 percent). High ratios reflect a strong commitment to government intervention in economic affairs (in the form of detailed planning or state enterprise), or an inability to balance central government finances (United States). High ratios further suggest strong competition against private sector borrowers (a problem facing the United States), possible advantages in the form of a large money market-capital market base from which market pressures are easily transmitted, and a constant debt management and refunding problem.

Three countries reflect a high volume of debt issues by financial institutions. These include Italy, Japan, and Sweden. In each case, somewhat different implications can be drawn. In the case of Italy, state enterprises and state intervention in capital investment projects have been the pattern. In Sweden, a high saving propensity and the willingness of banks, insurance, and pension companies to tap these savings flows have resulted in a high volume of issues by financial institutions. Finally, in Japan the commercial banks have tended to dominate the credit markets and have issued their own capital market securities to capture a high proportion of domestic savings.

NEW SECURITIES ISSUES

In this section we analyze the new issues volume relative to gross national product (GNP) in 17 countries and examine the reasons for wide discrepancies in this ratio among the countries included in our sample.

High Overall New Issue Ratio

In Table 24.3 we have ranked 17 countries in descending order according to the overall new issues ratio (new issues of shares and bonds as a percent of GNP). In the period 1969-71, this ratio ranged from 9.42 in the Netherlands down to 2.37 in France.

The six countries with the highest overall ratios of new issues to GNP exhibit wide differences in their capital market development and financial structure. Four patterns are manifested among these six countries. Belgium and the Netherlands reflect highly mature financial market systems characterized by a high percentage of capital market securities held by financial institutions (insurance and pension funds and savings banks), government securities issues accounting for half of new issues, and corporate finance geared toward obtaining direct credits from large financial institutions and banks. Denmark and Sweden, also with high overall new issue ratios, reflect the Scandinavian pattern of capital market development. This includes a high saving rate, a high proportion of financial institution securities in new issues, in Sweden a substantial volume of government issues, and a high proportion of financial sources of funds for business firms as contrasted with internal sources of funds (further discussed in the section on "Nonfinancial Business Sector" in the following). In Italy new issues activity is high, reflecting government efforts to stimulate economic growth via deficit spending, substantial debt financing by state-owned public enterprises, financial institution issues of securities in connection with a growing intermediation role, and frequent use of equity financing by nonfinancial corporations that find it difficult to compete for funds on the bond market. The fourth pattern, in Switzerland, reflects intensively developed financial entrepôt

TABLE 24.3

New Securities as Percent of GNP,
Selected Countries, 1969-71

	Share Issues	Issues of Bonds and Debt Certificates	Total of Shares, Bonds and Debt Certificates
Netherlands	0.16	9.26	9.42
Belgium	1.90	7.26	9.16
Denmark	1.55	7.05	8.60
Italy	1.70	6.43	8.13
Switzerland	2.90	4.78	7.68
Sweden	0.55	6.32	6.87
Spain	2.78	3.63	6.41
Japan	1.36	4.32	5.68
United States	0.99	3.92	4.91
Finland	3.42	1.47	4.89
Germany	0.54	3.16	3.70
United Kingdom	0.35	2.87	3.22
Portugal	2.72	0.40	3.12
Norway	0.72	2.35	3.07
Canada	0.75	2.07	2.82
Austria	0.86	1.59	2.45
France	1.01	1.36	2.37

Source: Organization for Economic Cooperation and Development (OECD), Financial Statistics.

activities in the capital market. This includes a well-developed institutional mechanism for new share and bond issues, substantial capital market liquidity afforded by inflows of foreign funds, and close coordination of a) domestic liquidity; b) capital market issue volume; and c) foreign exchange relationships by active cooperation between the banking syndicate and the central bank.

High Equity Ratio

Two countries in Table 24.3 stand out with a volume of share issues that exceeds the amount of debt issues on the capital market. These are Portugal and Finland. Other countries with relatively high ratios of share issues to GNP are Spain, Japan, Switzerland, and Italy. We have already commented in the preceding section concerning the opportunities for share issues in Italy and Switzerland. One additional comment on Switzerland is in order. A substantial part of public share offerings consists of the equities of financial institutions (banks and insurance companies). In 1970-71, equity issues of these financial institutions represented 24 and 41 percent, respectively, of total public offerings in Switzerland.

Portugal has consistently had a high ratio of share issues to GNP and a low ratio of bond issues to GNP. In the eight-year period 1964-71, share issues were $3\frac{1}{2}$ times the amount of bond issues. In the same period, share issues of nonfinancial corporations represented over 80 percent of the total, with share issues of financial institutions making up the remainder. The bond market has been dominated by the central government (55 percent of gross issues in 1964-71) and nonfinancial corporations (40 percent of gross issues). Government finance in Portugal has been relatively conservative with small deficits incurred by the central government and practically no debt financing by other governmental levels. Public enterprise use of the capital market has been minimal. Financial institutions do not issue any significant amount of capital market securities. A significant amount of Portugese bond issues is placed in overseas capital markets, further dampening the ratio of debt issues to GNP and opening up opportunities for further share financing. To summarize, a heavy dependence of the nonfinancial corporate sector on equity financing, relatively conservative government finance, absence of financial institution activity in the placement of debt securities on the capital market, and substantial use of overseas bond markets have combined to yield an excess of share issues over debt issues and a relatively high ratio of share issues to GNP.

Finland is the second country having a consistently higher new issue ratio of shares relative to bonds. The share market is much less institutionalized in its ownership pattern than in the United States and United Kingdom. At year end 1970, over 75 percent of shares were held by individuals and other nonfinancial holders, 11 percent by financial institutions, 12 percent by the government, and 2 percent by nonresident investors. The share market is not as financially intermediated as in other countries, whereas in the bond market financial intermediaries play a dominant role as holders of securities. In Finland central government bonds make up one-half of outstanding debt securities. However, budget surpluses are a consistent occurrence, and net issues of government bonds are small. Financial institutions sell a major part of new bond issues on the capital market. In Finland bond yields and bank interest rates are considerably higher than share yields. Consequently, corporations make heavier use of share issues as compared with bond issues. Nevertheless, they must rely on long-term direct borrowing from banks and other financial institutions (insurance companies) to obtain the larger part of their financial sources of funds. Foreign banks provided over 35 percent of long-term debt funds to nonfinancial corporations in 1970-71 (equal to 22 percent of external or financial sources of funds).

In Japan share issues represent a high proportion of GNP for the following reasons. Japanese companies do not issue large amounts of long-term bonds. They obtain the bulk of their borrowed funds from bank loans and trade credits. Therefore, share issues of non-financial corporations far exceed corporate debt issues on the capital market. The share market in Japan has been developed to a very large extent due to a number of favorable factors, including government policy, a social attitude favoring share purchases, and inflows of foreign investment funds based upon the dynamic growth of the Japanese economy. Budget surpluses of the central government have limited the volume of new government issues. Major nonbank financial institutions (insurance companies and trust departments) have focused on direct loans to industry rather than purchase of open-market capital market issues. While the outstanding volume of bonds was over twice that of shares in 1971, a large part (one-third) of the bonds outstanding represented issues of financial institutions, a form of financial intermediation that specially characterizes the financial markets in Japan.

Share issues in Spain have represented a high percentage of GNP for several reasons. First, the demand for shares has been quite strong. In Spain financial institutions have absorbed 20 to 25 percent of share issues in recent years, while households and non-financial enterprises have absorbed over 65 percent of share issues. Second, the capital market has not been heavily burdened by securities issues of the government and public enterprises. In 1970-71, government bond issues represented only 18 percent of gross bond issues, and issues of public enterprises only 12 percent of total debt issues. Third, financial institutions have not competed for funds on the capital market to the same extent as in other countries. In the period 1970-71, financial institutions sold 18 percent of the new share issues offered as compared with nonfinancial corporations selling 82 percent of the total. Financial institutions sold 13 percent of new bond issues on the capital market in this period.

Low Equity Ratio

Three countries included in Table 24.3 reflect low ratios of share issues to GNP. These are the United States, United Kingdom, and the Netherlands. In the Netherlands, major financial institutions such as the insurance companies and pension funds have represented one of the two major demand factors in the share market, the other being foreign investors. However, in 1971 their equity holdings represented only 5 percent of their total assets in the case of pension funds and 6 percent of total assets in the case of life insurance companies. These two groups held 88 percent of equities held by all financial institutions in the Netherlands, but less than 20 percent of all domestic equities outstanding in the Netherlands capital market. In the period 1966-68, nonfinancial corporations in the Netherlands obtained 32 percent of long-term financing via sale of equity securities. However, this represented only 10 percent of total sources of funds of nonfinancial corporations.

In the United Kingdom, share issues represent a small part of the total sources of funds of nonfinancial corporations. Share issues of financial institutions are nearly as important as those of nonfinancial corporations. More important, nonfinancial corporations have access to a wide variety of financing alternatives in the complex and sophisticated UK financial markets. Generally, internal funds including retained earnings provide close to half of funds required for expansion of operations. Financial sources of funds generally provide slightly in excess of half of expansion funds, and in 1969-70 consisted of the following: short-term funds 65 percent and long-term funds 35 percent of financial sources. Bank borrowing, other borrowed funds, and trade credit, in that order, are the main sources of short-term funds. Long-term funds consist of bonds (40 percent of long-term funds) and shares (60 percent of long-term funds). Over two-thirds of share issues are in exchange for shares of acquired companies, meaning that net increases in share issues are quite small in amount as well as in relation to total financing. For example, in 1969-70, net increases in share issues (after adjusting for shares issued in connection with acquisitions) represented £180 million, or approximately 2 percent of total sources of funds of quoted UK industrial companies.

In general, the financial market patterns in the United States are similar to those found in the United Kingdom. The same factors tend to work against a large volume of share issues in the capital market relative to GNP, or relative to total capital market financing. First, the corporate sector enjoys numerous alternative sources of external financing. Second, the demand pattern for share issues is one where the household sector is a net seller of equities, while financial institutions have been net buyers. Third, in both countries the corporate sector must compete against government and government agency borrowers for long-term funds. Finally, debt sources of funds tend to be less expensive partly for the reason that interest expenses are tax deductible, whereas dividend payments to shareholders are not.

497

TABLE 24.4

Sources of Funds of Nonfinancial Corporations, 1971
(percent of total)

	Nonfinancial Sources	Financial Sources										
		Total	Short-term debt					Long-term debt				
			Bank Loans	Other Loans	Trade Credit	Other	Total	Bonds	Shares	Bank Loans	Other	Total
United States	53	47	2	2	6	1	11	15	10	1	10	36
United Kingdom[a]	41	59	11	6	2	18	37	9	13	–	–	22
Netherlands[b]	58	42	4	–	12	–	16	11	11	–	4	26
Denmark[a]	32	68	10	–	–	38	48	11	9	–	–	20
Italy[a]	27	73	25	27			52	–	8	–	13	21
Sweden[b]	51	49	18				16	11	3	11	8	33
Japan[a]	26	74	18	8	21	12	51	1	4	17	1	23
Finland	28	72	8	8	7	–	23	1	4	43	1	49
Canada	60	40	4	4	9	3	20	13	4	–	3	20

[a]Data refer to 1970.
[b]Data refer to 1968.

Source: OECD, Financial Statistics.

498

NONFINANCIAL BUSINESS SECTOR

The nonfinancial business sector represents an important net user of funds in the national credit markets. The following discussion briefly compares the patterns of sources of funds of the nonfinancial business sector in several developed countries.

We may distinguish several key differences in the flow-of-funds patterns insofar as the nonfinancial business sector is concerned. These relate to the role of short-term funds as compared with long-term funds, the role of bank and trade credit in short-term sources, and the role of open-market (especially capital market) securities in business sector financing.

In three countries, nonfinancial business obtains a high proportion of total funds from short-term sources (Table 24.4), including Denmark, Italy, and Japan. In Denmark the business sector is especially dependent on trade credit as a source of financing (other short-term debt in Table 24.4). In 1970, trade credit represented over 40 percent of total sources of balance sheet funds for the manufacturing

TABLE 24.5

Foreign Issues of Bonds on
National Capital Markets, 1971
(millions of dollars)

	Foreign Issues			Total Debt Issues	Foreign Issues as Percent of Total Issues on Capital Market
	Public Issues	Private Issues	Total		
Austria	12.5	—	12.5	331	3.8
Belgium	67.8	4.0	71.8	2,015	3.6
Canada	24.9	49.9	74.8	3,041	2.5
France	47.4	—	47.4	3,025	1.5
Germany	218.5	34.0	252.5	7,874	3.2
Italy	24.0	40.7	64.7	8,205	0.8
Japan	96.9	237.4	334.3	12,285	2.7
Netherlands	34.2	—	34.2	3,774	1.0
Switzerland	590.5	276.6	867.1	1,553	56.0
United Kingdom	141.9	—	141.9	9,932	1.4
United States	1,102.0	240.7	1,342.7	47,838	2.7

Source: OECD, Financial Statistics.

sector, as well as for all nonfinancial businesses. Inasmuch as financial institutions dominate the bond market, the nonfinancial sector in Denmark obtains long-term borrowed funds from banks and financial institutions. In Italy bank loans play an important role in business finance, followed at some distance by trade credit. Financial institutions, governmental units, and public enterprises compete aggressively for funds in the bond market. This leaves Italian private enterprise with two major sources of external funds, short-term funds, and issue of shares.

In Japan close working relationships and heavy reliance by industry on the big banks in part explain the high ratio of short-term funds. Extensive use of trade credit also is a characteristic of Japanese business finance. Japanese business firms make very little direct use of the capital market. Countries in which the nonfinancial business sector relies heavily on bank credits and trade credit include Canada, Finland, and the Netherlands.

Sale of open-market securities depends upon an efficient capital market and underwriting mechanism. Countries that exhibit a high ratio of direct open-market securities issues include the United States, United Kingdom, and the Netherlands.

REFERENCES

Carlson, Sune. International Financial Decisions. Amsterdam: North-Holland Publishing Co., 1969.

European Economic Community. "The Development of a European Capital Market." Report of a group of experts appointed by the High Commission, Brussels, November 1966.

Goldsmith, Raymond. "The Development of Financial Institutions during the Post-War Period." Banca Nazionale del Lavoro Quarterly Review, June 1972.

25

Previously we have discussed the financial markets in both developed and less developed countries. This chapter is designed to discuss

1. the need for financial markets in the less developed countries;

2. some common problems that have occurred in the financial markets of many less developed countries in connection with their economic, financial, political, and social conditions;

3. some success cases which shed light on the path leading to improvement of financial markets in the less developed countries and the importance of government policy in providing strong incentives for financial institution growth and development.

THE NEED FOR FINANCIAL MARKETS IN THE
LESS DEVELOPED COUNTRIES

Several fundamental questions have been raised in recent years:

1. To what extent do the less developed countries need improved financial markets as a means of achieving economic development?

2. How should these markets be structured?

3. Can a mixture of public and private institutions achieve a workable allocation of loanable funds in a nation's credit markets?

The first question concerns the economic system of a nation, that is, whether it prefers a planned economy, like Russia, or a free-market economy as in the United States, or some combination of planned and market economy as exists in India. The socialist countries in Eastern Europe do not have well-developed financial markets at home, since their governments directly control and allocate national resources. These nations still participate in the international financial markets in Western Europe, including the Eurodollar market.

Moreover, they have gradually been moving toward the Western system of market-determined allocation of resources. The less developed countries can use their limited resources in more effective ways, through a combination of free-market processes and government-supported financial institutions. As is pointed out in later sections of this chapter, without a well-functioning financial market at home, domestic savings may not be channeled to investment on the basis of efficient resource allocation. Many less developed countries have suffered from this unfavorable condition.

The second question related to the economic backgrounds of nations and the means of strengthening market mechanisms for achieving their development goals. The British Commonwealth Development Corporation helped Singapore and the West Indies to develop certain segments of their financial markets, such as hire-purchase companies and building societies. The United States developed its money market after 1914 and strengthened its capital market after the Great Depression of the 1930s. The Mexican government has long been using its complex financial institutions for various development purposes, but it has implemented its monetary policy to develop a special government bond market only in recent years. Since 1965, the Brazilian government has instituted a host of reforms to improve its bond and equity markets. Tax incentives have been given to investors and borrowers; bond price indexes have been used for compensating inflationary losses suffered by investors; minidevaluation of the domestic currency has frequently been applied as a flexible control tool. In general, as long as the market mechanism serves the main objectives of a nation, the choice among a public, mixed, or private financial structure of the money, capital, and foreign exchange markets is a matter of development strategy. Each nation will opt for that strategy that is most useful, in light of the various constraints that exist, both internally and externally.

The third question must be answered in the affirmative. Many of the countries we have studied, some of which are described in detail in preceding chapters, have employed a rich mixture of public and private institutions to achieve their economic development and growth objectives, as well as to hasten the expansion and scope of their financial markets. France and Italy are important examples among the industrialized countries, as are Mexico and Brazil in the less developed category.

BASIC ECONOMIC PROBLEMS

In the two decades 1950-70, many less developed countries have relied on their primary-product sectors—agriculture, mining, plantation, forestry, and fishery. These products have constituted close to

60 percent of national output with the remainder of output in manufacturing and service industries. By contrast, the primary-product sectors have accounted for only 10 percent of GNP in the industrial nations. According to the Pearson Report to the United Nations (Lester B. Pearson, Partners in Development, report of the Commission on International Development, Praeger Publishers, New York, 1969), in the period 1960-68, the manufacturing sector contributed between 15 to 30 percent of total national income in Latin America, between 15 to 20 percent in Asia, and less than 10 percent (except the United Arab Republic—UAR) in Africa. The average annual growth rate of output in the agricultural sectors in the less developed countries in the same period was 3 percent. The low productivity in these sectors resulting from lack of advanced agricultural technology and adverse weather conditions has also affected the physical volume of their commodity output. The weaknesses of their financial market mechanisms, including lack of short-term credit and the unavailability of long-term funds, have compounded such problems.

Another structural problem is government ownership of infrastructure and basic industries. Heavy-handed government ownership and controls over the national economies definitely discourages individual incentives, depresses the saving-investment process, and raises the cost of funds for borrowers in both the public and private sectors. Governments in some less developed countries have financed publicly owned corporations by inflationary means, weakening private savings incentives, and further discouraging private sector investment opportunities.

The less developed countries have had to rely on primary-product exports to obtain needed foreign exchange. In most cases, the experience has been that the demand for primary products is less elastic than that for industrial products. Consequently, exports of less developed countries have grown more slowly than the exports of developed countries. Moreover, the high tariffs and nontariff barriers imposed by some developed countries have further dampened export growth of less developed countries. Unfavorable terms of trade have tended to create a widening income disparity between the developed and less developed countries. Logically, slower growth in income results in slower growth in domestic savings. There is little scope for generating domestic savings and financial market growth in countries such as Kenya with a per-capita income of $160 (1971), India with per-capita income of $110, the Philippines with per-capita income of $240, or in Colombia with per-capita income of $370.

Domestically, the less developed countries have suffered from economic "dualism," a situation wherein people working in the urban industrial areas have higher income and enjoy better organized money markets than those working in the rural areas who have lower income and face poorly organized money markets. Money and credit markets in the more developed sector tend to enjoy lower interest rates because lenders and borrowers have access to liquidity, and competition is sharper.

The data in Table 25.1 reflect several of the problems we have discussed. In the period 1961-71, all regions showed impressive progress. With the exception of Southern Europe, the less developed countries increased their GNP growth rates. Moreover, saving and investment took a larger share of GNP in several areas (Africa and East Asia). In Southern Europe and South Asia, the ratio of saving investment to GNP declined. In the 81 less developed countries represented in this analysis, domestic savings financed about 80 percent of total investment, with the exception of the Middle East (40 percent) and Latin America (90 percent). By comparison, we should note that the GNP growth rates in the developed countries declined during the period 1961-71 from 5.1 to 4.3 percent.

The higher rate of saving in the Latin American and Southern European countries is generally attributed to higher per-capita income. For instance, in 1971 per-capita income in Argentina was $1,230 and in Mexico $700.

FINANCIAL INSTITUTIONS AND FINANCIAL MARKETS

The weaknesses of financial institutions and market mechanisms in the less developed countries vitally affect the functioning of their money, capital, and foreign exchange markets. A number of operational and structural relationships influence the ability of financial institutions and financial markets to contribute materially to the saving-investment process and a nation's economic growth. Ronald I. McKinnon (Money and Capital in Economic Development, The Brookings Institution, Washington, D.C., 1973) illustrates the importance of these relationships for a number of developing and developed countries in the period 1950-70. His study illustrates how financial institutions directly influence saving by providing attractive opportunities to invest in time and saving deposits, how market liquidity adds to financial market efficiency, how flexible interest rates allocate financial resources, and how prudent and effective national monetary policies provide a financial market environment conducive to development of efficient financial institutions operating under a framework of appropriate economic incentives.

Financial institutions and market conditions vary from country to country, as has been indicated in previous chapters. The following

TABLE 25.1

Selected Economic Indicators for Developing and
Industrial Countries, 1961-71

	GNP Growth Rates	Saving as Percent of GNP	Gross Investment as Percent of GNP
		1961-67	
Developing countries			
Africa	3.9	13.8	16.9
Southern Europe	6.9	21.2	24.4
East Asia	6.0	11.7	16.4
Middle East	7.2	14.3	19.5
South Asia	3.7	12.9	16.1
Latin America	5.1	17.8	19.0
Industrial countries	5.1	22.5	21.9
		1968-71	
Developing countries			
Africa	6.0	15.7	19.4
Southern Europe	6.4	20.8	23.9
East Asia	7.9	16.3	20.5
Middle East	9.0	13.3	20.9
South Asia	4.5	12.2	14.4
Latin America	6.3	17.5	19.6
Industrial countries	4.3	23.4	22.8

Source: World Bank, Annual Reports, 1973.

discussion focuses on several of the more significant weaknesses in
the financial markets and financial institutions of the less developed
countries.

Central Banks

In the period after World War II, the central bank has been a
status symbol representing economic independence and financial
sovereignty. Prior to the twentieth century, the concept of a central
bank was not as important as it is today because only a few European
countries had their own central banks. Moreover, a number of countries had only poorly developed commercial banks and relied upon

foreign banks of large industrial countries such as Britain, France, and the Netherlands to service much of their banking needs. In this period of time, many governments maintained balanced budgets, and a central bank was not an absolute necessity. Japan established a central bank in 1882, the United States in 1914, and the Latin American countries in the 1920s and 1930s. Less developed countries in Asia and Africa established central banks in the 1950s. The general purpose of central banks in the less developed countries is to manage the money supply and interest rates, to finance government spending, and to regulate financial institutions and foreign exchange. However, the central banks in the less developed countries usually do not have the power, as do their counterparts in the developed nations, to control the commercial banks through traditional methods such as the discount rate, open-market operations, and reserve requirements. This is because they do not possess effective financial institutions, market mechanisms, and credit instruments. As a result, they are not able to tap domestic financial resources effectively, but rely on foreign funds provided by foreign banks, or borrow on the international financial markets.

In some less developed countries, the central bank controls a large proportion of banking assets and operates as a commercial bank. In this connection, they may operate more directly in the credit markets, partly in competition with commercial banks. In this case, there may be a strong political overtone in their credit-making operations and allocation of loanable funds.

Central banks in the less developed countries have suffered from the inadequacies of their economic structure, commercial banking development, and imperfection of financial markets. If the financial needs for keeping government-supported industries operating outstrip growth of productive resources, central banks can become the engines of inflation. This damages their image both at home and abroad. If the domestic banking structure is inadequate, a few oligopolistic banks controlled by a small number of wealthy families may exert undue influence over the central banks. The functioning of a central bank is also impaired if the equity market is highly volatile and subject to pressure from speculative funds. Under these conditions, tight money policy and a nonexpansionary fiscal policy would effectively work to erode equity prices; on the other hand, an easy money policy would encourage speculation in the stock market.

Development Banks

In the industrial countries, development banks are less important than in the less developed countries. The formation of a development bank may be designed to achieve a number of objectives, including

506

1. stimulation of capital market expansion;
2. permitting government to more effectively allocate capital funds for investment in high-priority industrial sectors; and
3. obtaining funds from abroad and allocating the foreign funds for certain industries that are considered strategically important to national economic development. The Development Bank of Japan, formed in 1892, borrowed money from Europe and loaned these funds to key domestic industries such as shipping and steel. The National Financiera of Mexico, established in the 1920s, has acted as a fund collector, distributor, and guarantor for public as well as private industries in their development programs. Encouraged and assisted by the United Nations during the "development decade," many less developed countries such as Ceylon, Turkey, Thailand, Iran, and Syria established public or private development banks beginning in 1959. In addition to the above functions, development banks also provide technical assistance to domestic corporations, including the temporary purchase of their securities, providing working capital loans, and extending consulting services in relation to national priorities.

Development banks in the developing countries have served their countries well. They have helped to build infrastructure, played multiple roles in assisting private firms in their initial growth stages, and rescued many important but failing industries. Most significant of all, they have represented their countries as reputable agencies to borrow funds abroad at lower costs which otherwise could not be available to their domestic industries.

Aside from their merits, development banks in many less developed countries have been criticized by the assertion that they have been obstacles to capital market development. First of all, they have dominated domestic capital markets by exercising monopolistic financial power and forcing lower borrowing costs. Wealthy citizens of the less developed nations have hesitated to buy low-yielding government securities under inflationary conditions. Rather, they have preferred to place their funds in the most profitable and inflation-protected investments, including land, commercial enterprises, or foreign assets. In other words, development banks may have unintentionally excluded domestic savings from the mainstream of the saving-investment process. By the same token, they also may have discouraged foreign portfolio investors who do not see any gains or opportunities in putting their money in these countries. From the domestic corporate standpoint, market facilities and financing techniques are not available to help in issuing long-term securities for expansion or new ventures. To associate with the development banks means supervision by government agencies. For all these reasons, many development banks in the less developed countries have recently modified their policies and given more incentives to individual savers and corporate borrowers. Brazil has been a case in point.

Commercial Banks

Commercial banks have played an important role in the economic and financial development of the industrial nations. This has not been paralleled by their counterparts in the less developed countries. Many commercial banks in the emerging countries in Asia and Africa were owned by European banks before World War II, or were controlled by a few wealthy families and political figures. Commercial banks in Latin America still remain in the hands of the social elite. Regardless of their increasing cooperation with central banks, the commercial banks in many less developed countries are not yet integrated parts of financial market development.

Commercial banks in the less developed countries engage in mixed banking, accept all types of deposits, and extend all types of loans. They also buy and sell securities, deal in commodities, and trade in real estate. There is no separation of commercial and investment banking functions as in the United States. For these reasons, these banks will shift their funds into the most profitable projects with less uncertainty and inflation risk. According to Raymond W. Goldsmith (The Mobilization of Internal Resources in Latin America, published by the Inter-American Development Bank, 1971), the bank credit to GNP ratio in the less developed countries during the 1960s was less than 15 percent (Mexico 20 percent and Colombia 10 percent), compared with 75 percent for many developed countries.

The lack of a strong central bank and efficient money market reduces effective control over bank liquidity in times of prosperity or recession. The activities of commercial banks in this case may further aggravate economic and financial instability, especially when fluctuations in income of the less developed countries are caused by export booms and slumps, or other sources of instability.

Nonbank Financial Institutions

In many developing countries, savings institutions such as savings banks, savings and loan associations, insurance companies, mutual funds, and pension funds are lacking or poorly developed. This is a result of low per-capita income and lack of government protection. The absence of contractual saving institutions makes saving and efficient channeling of funds more difficult. For example, in Pakistan, considerable losses have been suffered in attempts to extend a savings bank network to rural areas of the country.

Another problem is the lack of specialized credit banks that could stimulate different sectors of the financial markets. The lack of mortgage banks jeopardizes the mortgage market and housing construction. Inefficient agricultural credit institutions tend to depress the farming sector and indirectly influence the prices and incomes of the agricultural sector.

Foreign Banks

Foreign banks have been a main source for transmitting financial technology to the less developed countries. They also have introduced foreign capital for financing industrial, commercial, and agricultural development. They have been major factors in financing and stimulating foreign trade among nations. According to Goldsmith (Financial Structure and Development, Yale University Press, New Haven, Conn., 1969), by 1913 British and other European countries established over 1,500 branch banks in foreign countries. The United States and Canada rapidly expanded their branch banks on other continents, especially in Latin America after World War I. However, the relative share of foreign banks has declined since World War II, except in Africa and the Near East. For instance, assets of foreign banks declined from 22 percent in 1938 to 12 percent in 1960 (India nationalized all domestic commercial banks in 1970); the share of foreign banks to domestic banks in Argentina decreased from 15 percent in 1929 to 7 percent in 1963; but in Nigeria foreign banks still accounted for two-thirds of the total resources of commercial banks as recently as 1966.

It has been argued that foreign banks have been mainly interested in obtaining local deposits, financing the import-export sector for short-term profits, speculating in foreign currencies, and transferring surplus funds to their home territories. But this argument has not been convincing. British banks have assisted Argentina, Australia, and South Africa to develop their natural resources before World War I; a foreign banking consortium helped China to build the Canton-Hankow Railroad in 1912. After World War II, many foreign banks operating in the less developed countries participated in local development projects, introduced foreign manufacturing firms to the host countries, joined local banks to finance local and regional business activities, and loaned to local governments in time of balance of payments difficulties. Recent introduction of the Asian dollar market to Singapore by American banks is another step evidencing cooperation between foreign banks and local banks for mutual benefit. To be sure, in future foreign banks will play an important supplementary role in the local banking markets and will act as an important link to facilitate the flow of capital among nations.

International Financial Institutions

One of the important innovations in international finance after World War II has been the emergence of the international financial institutions, such as the World Bank, International Finance Corporation, International Monetary Fund (IMF), regional development banks (Inter-American Development Bank and Asian Development Bank), and the European Investment Bank. The Agency for International Development (AID) and the Overseas Private Investment Corporation (OPIC) of the United States were formed by the U.S. government to assist the less developed countries. The major purposes of these institutions are to aid the developing countries to develop their natural resources, to train their managerial classes, to educate their investors, and to develop their financial markets. The most important work of these institutions has been in the transfer of technology and capital to increase production. The flow of capital from the advanced countries to the developing countries in 1972 was over $18 billion, of which about 55 percent was contributed by official government aid and loans, and the rest by private sector investors.

The Marshall Plan was successful in Western Europe after World War II because the countries receiving aid had well-organized financial institutions. The absence of efficient financial market mechanisms in less developed host countries may cause cancellation of projects because certain types of foreign aid require local participation which is not available on favorable terms. Without a well-functioning foreign exchange market, foreign currencies received by host countries may go to the black market to benefit from higher exchange rates. This may tend to inflate local price levels. Failure to make use of financial techniques such as the concepts of cash flow and rate of return in the host countries may result in the refusal of international financial institutions to grant loans to applicants. It was reported that the Asian Development Bank disapproved several loan applications from its member nations because of the unsatisfactory financial analysis. From the standpoint of the receiving countries, such conflict with international financial institutions leaves the aid-receiving countries in confusion as to whether they should rely on foreign capital or attempt to raise funds in their domestic funds.

Financial Markets

Defects of financial market mechanisms in the less developed countries have vitally affected the flow and allocation of funds, the mobility of financial assets, and the value of money. Financial dualism between the organized money market in the urban and developed areas and the unorganized money market in the rural areas can result in channeling funds to low-priority and inefficient investment projects. Lack of short-term financial instruments in the developing countries has at times forced lenders to place funds in the call loan market or in speculative loans because they did not have better short-term investment opportunities such as certificates of deposit (CDs) and commercial paper. Banker's acceptances are mostly held by foreign banks. They generally are sold in foreign money markets because no rediscount facilities are offered by local central banks. Since the money market is the natural point of contact between the central bank and the financial sector in a flexible free-market economy, poor functioning of the money market prevents government borrowing from local financial sources and often forces the government to rely solely on central bank financing. This can result in inflationary financing. Furthermore, the absence of a market in short-term government securities leaves a vacuum in which flows of short-term funds and interest rates fluctuate without a true anchor.

The lack of a properly functioning capital market has vitally affected economic development in the less developed countries. In many of these countries, equity shares are mainly held by a few wealthy families and large financial institutions. The majority of the public have very little opportunity to buy stocks or bonds. In some countries local banks exclusively control the capital markets by restricting their inputs (deposits) and outputs (loans). Oligopolist banks take similar action to put an interest ceiling on deposits and set a rate floor on loans. Some governments in the less developed countries have tried to prevent such undesirable market practices by imposing "just" prices on bank deposits and loans, but this policy has made the market condition deteriorate. Government domination of the bond market further discourages the private sector to issue stocks or bonds due to the fact that the government dictates market rates that are usually below equilibrium rates in the international financial markets. Under these circumstances, domestic funds either shift to an unorganized market or leave the country for foreign financial centers. In turn, lack of funds in the domestic market compels borrowers to issue securities abroad with higher yields than is required on domestic counterparts.

Another defect of the capital markets in the less developed countries is the absence of developed stock exchanges that affects the mobility and allocation of domestic capital. Moreover, foreign portfolio investors hesitate to buy local securities because it is hard to sell them in the market. Foreign exchange control works against foreign capital coming to the domestic market; therefore, it hurts development of the domestic capital market in the primary as well as secondary market sectors.

511

PROBLEMS OF GOVERNMENT AND SOCIAL
STRUCTURE

Frequent changes of government in the developing countries have made any application of consistent and stable economic and monetary policies impossible. Political security has always had priority. Even those countries that have enjoyed political stability still face economic dilemmas in connection with emphasizing present consumption over investment in future production and stressing income equality versus economic growth. Governments have had to choose between deficit financing to accelerate economic growth, or less inflationary slower growth and growing public discontent. Moreover, they have been torn between policies that increase income distribution versus those that expand capital formation. More frequently, they have chosen policies of deficit financing and increased income equality As indicated in Table 25.2, the record of less developed countries in reducing inflation has not been completely successful.

Many governments in the less developed countries have adopted short-run and piecemeal approaches in developing their financial markets and have not built a strong and permanent legal structure. As Goldsmith describes, this requires company law; statistical, accounting, and auditing standards; provision for issue of company prospectus; and publication of corporate financial information for investors. Without an adequate groundwork, a financial market cannot function properly. Lack of tax and other incentives to investors and corporate borrowers leaves an unbroken vicious circle of underdeveloped financial markets. A related problem is fear of foreign domination and remembrances of unpleasant colonial relationships. Governments in the developing countries also have made some tactical mistakes. Many governments in the developing countries firmly control the bond markets to achieve deficit financing for the government sector at the expense of developing their equity and money markets. They have used subsidies to domestic borrowers and lenders in order to stimulate some market activities, but this policy is harmful to foreign investors and creates an atmosphere of uncertainty in the financial community.

The social structures in the developing countries are generally more rigid than those in the industrial nations, especially in connection with adaptability to economic and technological change. The traditional social value systems in Africa, Asia, and Latin America generally emphasize personal and family relations, involve a preference for clerical rather than manual work, and tend to emphasize saving for the rainy day but not for investment. The populace has little confidence in government, financial institutions, and the institution of money. Family control of business means less interest in public

Price Increases in Less Developed and Industrial
Countries, 1965-72
(in percent)

	1965-70 (annual average)	1971	1972
All less developed countries	11.8	10.2	14.7
Africa	5.7	5.2	5.0
Asia	10.7	6.6	8.2
Middle East	3.0	6.2	7.2
Latin America	18.8	18.0	29.4
All industrial countries	4.1	5.5	4.5

Source: IMF, Annual Report, 1973.

investment. Lack of entrepreneurial talents means a lag of innovation
in industrial technology and financial expertise. Stock markets are
the domain of security speculators, and not for investors desiring
regular income because most family-owned companies pay very little
dividends but retain most of their earnings for reinvestment. The
upper-income groups often prefer to put their accumulated wealth
in foreign banks and invest in foreign securities for reasons of safety
rather than to achieve high yields.

BALANCE OF PAYMENTS PROBLEMS

One objective relating to the international financial policies of
the less developed countries has been to increase exports and substitute domestic production for imports. In the meantime, they borrowed
foreign capital to finance imports of industrial goods to achieve domestic industrialization. In the long run, they will balance their international payments or even have a surplus. While there is nothing wrong
with the idea of evolving from debtor to creditor status, the problems
many developing countries have faced in the decade of the 1960s have
been more complex than they originally imagined. In general, the
share of less developed countries in world export markets has shrunk
from 30 percent in 1960 to 20 percent in 1970; conversely, their imports have increased faster than their exports. The use of international trade as an instrument of achieving economic development has
been hardly realized by the developing countries.

TABLE 25.3

External Debt Outstanding and Debt Service Payments
of 81 Developing Countries, 1961-71
(millions of dollars)

	1961	1965	1971
Africa	3,309	6,698	11,922
East Asia	2,176	3,891	11,217
Middle East	1,419	2,496	8,899
South Asia	3,600	8,625	15,929
Southern Europe	2,261	4,051	8,196
Latin America	8,822	11,701	23,052
Total	21,587	37,465	97,218
Debt service payments (DSP)	2,314	3,336	6,789
DSP/total debt (in percent)	17	9	6.5

Source: World Bank, Annual Reports, 1971 and 1973.

Many developing countries have tried to overcome their trade problems by regional trade integration, such as the Latin American Free Trade Association (LAFTA), but they produce primary products that are competitive rather than complementary in world markets. Furthermore, the lack of short-term financial markets at home has forced the developing countries to rely on the industrial countries to finance their international trade. In the two decades 1950-70, the terms of trade have been most unfavorable to the less developed countries. At times they have lost international reserves and have been forced to devalue their currencies. Many developing countries have simultaneously suffered inflation and devaluation.

In order to cover deficits on their trade accounts, the developing countries have had to obtain foreign capital. This has created other difficulties. For one thing, lack of domestic money and capital markets drove domestic funds to foreign financial centers. The outflow of capital aggravated the balance of payments problem. For another, the continued borrowing from other financial centers and international financial institutions not only weakened their credit standing, but also increased their debt service burden. As indicated in Table 25.3, external debt outstanding of 81 developing countries was $21 billion in 1961, $37 billion in 1965, and $97 billion in 1971. The total debt increased by only 75 percent in the period 1961-65, but by 160 percent in the period 1965-71. However, the debt service ratio (debt service payments to exports) declined from 17 percent in 1961 to 9 percent in 1965, and to 6.5 percent in 1971. This resulted from rescheduling of debt payments between creditors and debtors to achieve lower net payments to net borrowings ratios. The most important criterion for measuring the ability of a debtor nation to pay back has been the ratio of debt service payment to export earnings. Among the large borrowing nations in 1971, the ratio of India was 23.5 percent, Pakistan 21.6 percent, Brazil 17.6 percent, and Mexico 24.7 percent. However, the UAR was a light borrower, but its service payments to export earnings ratio was 25.5 percent. It has been generally held that a ratio of 25 percent should be regarded as the limit beyond which a nation's international credit standing may be subject to question.

As a result of the deficits on trade account, service accounts (insurance, shipping, interest payments), and continued increases in capital inflows, the less developed countries have not been optimistic about their overall balance of payments. IMF credits are their last resort in case of temporary and fundamental disequilibrium. Without doubt, the less developed countries must more actively promote the development of their financial markets. Success in this direction will provide more powerful incentives to domestic savings, reduce the disincentive system that operates against productive investment at home, and provide attractive domestic financial investment opportunities that will discourage flight and speculative capital outflows.

SOME SUCCESS CASES

Regardless of the many problems that reduce the efficiency of the financial markets in less developed countries, there have been several important success cases. We have selected four countries for illustration. Three are less developed, and one country fits into the developed category. Their market characteristics deserve special attention. These countries include Canada, Singapore, Kenya, and Brazil. The first three countries have inherited the British financial technology, whereas the last has received financial and technical assistance from the United States. While three (Canada, Singapore, and Brazil) of these countries were discussed in Chapters 8, 15, and 19) of this book, the special merits of their financial market development are worth recapitulating.

The Canada Case

Development of the Canadian money market was purposely stimulated by the Canadian Treasury and the Bank of Canada. Short-dated Treasury bills are issued by the Bank of Canada and distributed to the Chartered Banks and government securities dealers on the basis of competitive bidding. The central bank relies on transmitting money market pressures through day-to-day loan market participation by the securities dealers and commercial banks. In contrast with the United States, the central bank's intervention in the Treasury bill market is occasional and a last resort. The simple, flexible, and efficient Treasury bill market is the cornerstone of the entire money market structure, based on which holdings of other short-term credit instruments such as commercial paper, negotiable CDs, and banker's acceptances are adjusted. Externally, the Canadian Treasury bill rate sensitively responds to its counterparts in the New York and London money markets. Government policy aimed at developing the Canadian money market has permitted this financial market to become one of the three or four largest money markets in the world.

The Singapore Case

With a strong sense of self-sufficiency since it seceded from the Federation of Malaysia in 1965, Singapore has aimed at building high-technology industries at home and establishing itself as a key financial market in Southeast Asia. In cooperation with U.S. banks, and encouraged by the government's fiscal and monetary policies, the Asian dollar market emerged in Singapore in 1968 and has continued to grow to the amount of over $3 billion in 1973. The Asian dollar is and will continue to be important for several reasons.

1. It creates a focal point for Singapore's domestic financial markets. In turn, this provides a good financial base for industrialization in Singapore.

2. The Asian dollar market in Singapore has become a financial magnet in that region. It has attracted funds as well as supplied funds to regional borrowers, including governments, businesses, and banks.

3. It has become another focal point for trading in the U.S. dollar and other currencies for multinational banks and cooperations.

4. The Asian dollar market established links between the Euro-dollar market in London and the more localized money markets in the Far East. Therefore, it facilitates the flow of funds between the Far East and Europe, and the United States. Because of its strategic location in world finance, Singapore has earned the designation "Switzerland of the Far East."

The Kenya Case

After achieving independence from Britain in the 1950s, this East African country established the Nairobi Stock Exchange in 1954. There was no stock exchange facility at that time, no building, and no middlemen or stock jobbers. The six registered stock brokers began by conducting transactions from their respective offices. Prices of the 85 originally listed securities were established at daily meetings of the brokers. There was speculative device, such as put and call options. By 1968, the stock exchange inhabited its own building and had 154 listed stocks. The most interesting aspect of this stock exchange is its regional characteristics. Of the 154 listed stocks in 1968, there were 66 public stocks, of which 15 had been issued by the government of Tanzania, 7 by Uganda, and 8 by the East African Community (a regional agency responsible for transport and port facility development). A number of industrial and commercial enterprises of the above countries also had their shares quoted on the Nairobi Exchange. The existence of the Nairobi Stock Exchange has had a great impact on regional financial activities and financial market integration. For example, it provides common facilities for financing long-term loans from regional consortia of banks. To achieve mutual benefits, governments in the region may liberalize internal regulations affecting the investment policies of insurance companies, pension funds, and financial institutions.

The Brazil Case

The economic and financial reforms achieved in Brazil over the 1960s have been of considerable importance. In the capital markets, the Brazilian government has built an appropriate and effective legal infrastructure, first by the Capital Market Law of 1965, and second by the Decree Law of 1970. The former was intended to encourage private companies to go public, whereas the latter was designed to establish the "federal fund" for long-term investments. Funds were contributed by business corporations and individual employees under a broad tax incentive program. These two significant actions taken by the government not only stimulated Brazil's equity market development, but also stabilized its bond market since the yields of bonds would keep pace with the domestic price level and the foreign exchange rate between the Brazilian cruzeiro and U.S. dollar.

The increased utilization of domestic savings has also helped Brazil attract more direct and portfolio investment funds from foreign countries because the rates of return have been reasonably high.

The increased effectiveness of the public sector has reduced Brazil's reliance on international capital and foreign aid. In fact, the Brazilian government has rearranged foreign aid debt repayment schedules with international creditors, such as the World Bank, Inter-American Development Bank, and the United States.

Since Brazil has pursued the reform of its financial markets, there has been success mixed with some difficulties. However, once the concrete framework has been established, the market mechanism should be able to function more effectively, in line with the economic development needs of the country.

REFERENCES

Cameron, Rondo. Banking and Economic Development. New York: Oxford University Press, 1972.

Friedman, Irving S. "Dilemmas of the Developing Countries—the Sword of Damocles." Finance and Development. Published by the IMF and World Bank Group, March 1973.

Goldsmith, Raymond W. Financial Structure and Development. New Haven, Conn.: Yale University Press, 1969.

McKinnon, Ronald I. Money and Capital in Economic Development. Washington, D.C.: The Brookings Institution, 1973.

Mikesell, Raymond F., and James E. Zinser. "The Nature of the Savings Function in Developing Countries: A Survey of the Theoretical and Empirical Literature." Journal of Economic Literature, American Economic Association, March 1973.

Park, Yung Chul. "The Role of Money in Stabilization Policy in Developing Countries." IMF Staff Paper, June 1973.

Shaw, Edward S. Financial Deepening in Economic Development. New York: Oxford University Press, 1973.

CHAPTER

26

NEW FORCES IN
THE INTERNATIONAL
FINANCIAL MARKETS

In previous chapters we have observed how financial forces and
structures have been vital to national and international economic
growth and development. The complexity of financial forces and structures varies from country to country depending on geographical setting,
political and social conditions, and government economic policies.
In the international aspect, financial market processes have become
more dynamic since there are so many elements that are not easily
controllable by any single nation or group of nations. For these reasons, international financial cooperation, or the lack of it, has a far-
reaching effect on the achievement of increasing national wealth and
better living standards.

There have been many important developments in the international financial markets over the two decades 1950-70. First, as a
result of economic progress in many countries, more financial centers
have developed in Europe (Frankfurt and Luxembourg), in Asia (Tokyo,
Hong Kong, and Singapore), and in the Western Hemisphere (Toronto,
Bahamas, Mexico City, and Rio de Janeiro). Second, more governments, business firms, and international financial institutions have
participated in the process of international flows of funds including
the developing countries and socialist nations, as illustrated in the
Eurodollar and Eurobond markets. Third, financial expertise evidenced
by the use of certificates of deposit (CDs), Eurocurrency financing,
foreign currency swaps, and convertible bonds has dramatized the
evolution of financial market methods. Fourth, increasing flows of
funds and competition in world financial markets have exerted strong
pressure on the international exchange markets and led to the narrowing of interest rate differentials among major financial centers.

While in the last 15 to 20 years, the international financial markets have contributed much more toward global economic growth and
development than in the first half of this century. In the 1970s, the

519

world faces a more universal industrial revolution, which will pose tremendous challenges and opportunities. Nations will face the pressures of rising population but limited natural resources, the need to use more capital and technology but also more competition, increased desire for national self-reliance but also more international mutual dependence. All of these will shape a new political, economic, and financial environment in which the international financial markets and their new forces will operate.

FORCES IN THE DEVELOPED COUNTRIES

According to the World Bank statistics, the developed countries in the world economy contributed about 80 percent of international trade in 1972, 100 percent of international direct investment, about 80 percent of the world's gross national product (GNP), and about 90 percent of the international and foreign bond issues. These figures sufficiently reflect the overwhelming financial power with which the developed countries can influence the world economy and international finance in the 1980s. The important forces emerging in this group can be categorized as follows: (1) structural changes in expenditures by industrial nations, (2) trade and investment among the industrial nations, and (3) financial expertise.

Structural Changes in Expenditures by Industrial Nations

A study prepared by the Organization for Economic Cooperation and Development (OECD) in 1972 described the structural changes in expenditures in OECD countries and the influence on their national economies since 1955 and projected trends to 1980. Table 26.1 reflects the share of private consumption in the OECD nations, which declined from 63.0 percent in 1955-57 to 60.2 percent in 1967-69. A further decline in the percentage of private consumption is anticipated to 59.1 percent in 1975 and to 57.7 percent in 1980. In fact, all nations have shown declines in their private consumption over the entire period. These developments may be attributed to the heavier taxation of private households, and, to a lesser degree, to the increase in private savings. The OECD study points out that with the exception of Luxembourg, Sweden, and the United States, the saving rate rose in all OECD countries. On average, the saving rate increased from 11.5 percent to 13.1 percent of disposable income in these nations over the period 1955-69. The highest saving rate of 23.8 percent was recorded in Japan, while the lowest rate of 8.7 percent was registered in Britain.

TABLE 26.1

Total Expenditures of Various Industrial
Nations, 1955-75

	Year	Consumption in Percentage of GNP		Private and Public Capital Spending
		Private	Public	
West Germany	1960-62	56.9	14.1	25.5
	1967-69	56.2	15.8	23.6
	1975	54.9	15.8	25.8
France	1959-61	61.7	13.0	20.7
	1967-69	60.6	12.4	25.2
	1975	58.6	12.1	26.1
United Kingdom	1955-57	66.1	16.9	14.9
	1967-69	62.8	18.0	17.9
	1975	60.1	19.3	18.5
Japan	1955-57	61.6	9.6	23.6
	1967-69	52.1	8.4	33.9
	1975	49.8	7.9	38.9
Sweden	1955-57	61.1	16.8	20.4
	1966-68	55.5	20.8	23.9
	1975	51.2	24.5	22.3
Switzerland	1955-57	65.0	10.6	21.3
	1967-69	58.2	11.7	24.0
	1975	52.8	12.6	25.2
United States	1955-57	63.1	17.3	17.8
	1967-69	61.2	20.9	16.6
	1975	61.6	18.2	18.5
OECD nations	1955-57	63.0	15.2	19.6
	1967-69	60.2	17.4	20.5
	1975	59.1	16.4	22.4

Note: 1975 figures were estimates by OECD.

Source: OECD, The Structural Changes in Expenditures Made by OECD Countries on Their National Economies, Paris, 1972.

Public consumption in all OECD countries rose from 15.2
to 17.4 percent in the period 1955-69, with the exception of France
and Japan where a decline was registered. As to total private and
public capital spending in the selected OECD countries, it is expected
to rise from 19.6 percent in 1955 to 22.4 percent in 1975. The increase
in public expenditures, as explained by the OECD, was due to the expansion of government services in the fields of health, education, and
social welfare.

From the international financial market standpoint, the increase
in public expenditure and private capital accumulation will absorb
the savings accumulated in the private sector. This will have important
effects on money and capital markets in these nations, the nature of
these influences depending on whether the respective governments
and private firms will emphasize short-term or long-term financing.
In any event, the continued expansion in the public and private sectors
in the OECD countries may inevitably stimulate national economic
growth as well as contribute to inflationary tendencies.

Trade and Investment among the Industrial Nations

Among the industrial countries, the European Economic Community (EEC) countries, the United States, and Japan have played a
key role in international trade and investment. The nine members
of the EEC countries (France, Belgium, Luxembourg, Netherlands,
Denmark, Italy, Germany, United Kingdom, and Ireland) represent
the world's largest trading unit. They accounted for about 40 percent
of total world exports in 1972 ($154 billion out of $372 billion), while
the United States shared about 14 percent and Japan shared about
8 percent. According to International Monetary Fund (IMF) statistics,
70 percent of the international trade of these industrial countries was
conducted among themselves, and this tendency is not subsiding.
Furthermore, the EEC has concluded an important trade treaty with
those members of the European Free Trade Association (EFTA) that
are not entering the Community (Sweden, Norway, Finland, Austria,
Switzerland, Iceland, and Portugal). Under the treaty, these countries
and the nine in the EEC will eliminate tariffs on one another's industrial goods by July 1, 1977. The creation of a 16-nation industrial
free trade area in Europe will have significant effects on international
trade and also on the European money markets, especially the Eurocurrency market.

The outlook for trade and investment in the United States has
been more optimistic since 1973 as a result of the surplus on both
the trade and capital accounts. The devaluations of the U.S. dollar
by 8.5 percent in December 1971 and 10 percent in February 1973

522

have had favorable effects on international trade and the foreign exchange market. It is expected that strengthening of the U.S. dollar,
the basic soundness of the U.S. economy, and the recent elimination
of the capital control programs imposed during the 1960s will attract
more foreign funds to the U.S. money and capital markets, especially
long-term funds for direct investment from other industrial countries
such as the United Kingdom, Germany, Netherlands, Switzerland, and
Japan. For example, the accumulation of foreign direct investment in
the United States was $7 billion in 1960, but increased to $15 billion
in 1972. This trend is expected to grow as long as tariff agreements
among the industrial nations remain at an impasse. The Western
European nations and Japan have stepped up their investment in the
United States in the 1960s in the manufacturing field (which accounted
for 39.5 percent in 1965 and 50.3 percent in 1972 of their total direct
investment in the United States), in order to surmount high tariff and
nontariff barriers to their goods. For the same and other reasons
(access to the market), the United States in the 1960s has shifted some
overseas direct investment from the Western Hemisphere to Western
Europe. In 1972, total U.S. direct investment in foreign countries
was $94 billion, of which Western Europe shared 32 percent, Canada
27 percent, Latin America 18 percent, Japan 2.3 percent, and the rest
of the world 22 percent. While the trends in U.S. overseas investment
in the future are not clear, over 61.3 percent of global direct investment in other nations that is controlled by U.S. companies will operate
as a strong force in the international financial markets of the world.

Japan and Canada have emerged as strong financial powers.
They have been important U.S. trade partners, and most of their direct
investments have been in the United States. They may be expected
to shift their trade and investment toward other countries, especially
to the less developed countries and the socialist countries as opportunities for profitable business and financial relationships expand in these
areas of the globe.

Financial Expertise

The entry of the United Kingdom into the European Common
Market in 1973 will add significantly to the financial expertise available in the European financial markets. First, the EEC Commission
has taken various steps to harmonize tax law, trade standards, and
social policy. Among the major items that will affect the financial
markets are

1. the treatment of withholding tax rates on bond interest, which
would encourage a more unified European capital market to compete
with the Eurobond market;

2. less control on capital flows among the EEC countries, which would strengthen their national money markets and compete with the Eurodollar market;

3. the creation of European Monetary Cooperation Funds in April 1973, intended to reduce exchange fluctuation and disturbances of member currencies in the foreign exchange markets as experienced in the past.

Second, there will be some changes in the continental and British banking systems, which will become more alike in the years ahead. For example, the British financial system is oriented around the complex but highly efficient London money market. Different financial institutions and credit instruments service various kinds of customers. The Bank of England exerts influence on credit and interest rates indirectly. However, the continental banks engage in the so-called universal banking, combining commercial and merchant banking under one roof. Continental banks often take an active interest in company management and hold directorships. Due to the elimination of many banking regulations among the EEC countries, commercial banking institutions in Western Europe will increase competition, mergers, and engage in more financial dealings with their growing business demand for funds. As a result, American banks in Europe will encounter stiffer competition than they have in the past.

Third, failure to adequately reform the international monetary agreements and the continued float of many currencies in the world foreign exchange markets have increased financial risks in international transactions. In order to reduce these risks, European bankers have recently invented the European Composite Unit (EURCO), which is a "currency cocktail" of the nine Common Market currencies primarily reflecting the relative size of their GNP. For instance, German marks account for the biggest part of the package (28.77 percent), and Irish pounds the smallest (0.97 percent). A 10-percent revaluation of the German mark, which makes up 28.77 percent of the value of the EURCO, would reduce the worth of the EURCO expressed in the devalued currency by 2.877 percent, whereas the value losses caused by such a parity change would amount to 10 percent in respect to the other currencies. Thus, when individual currencies are devalued or revalued or if they float up and down, the EURCO holder suffers minimal fluctuation compared with the holder concentrated in one or another of the individual currencies. The EURCO was originated by N.M. Rothschild & Sons Ltd. in July 1973 to facilitate long-term financing via bond issues and to avoid the uncertainty associated with U.S.-dollar-denominated Eurobond issues. The first EURCO-denominated Eurobond issue came from the European Investment Bank in September 1973. The value of the EURCO has been quoted daily by the Luxembourg Stock Exchange vis-à-vis the nine reference currencies and the U.S.

dollar. The major criticisms of the EURCO are its multiple calcula-
tion and its changing value which makes the cost of repaying difficult
to anticipate (see Wall Street Journal, January 14, 1974).

INTERDEPENDENCE OF THE DEVELOPED AND
DEVELOPING COUNTRIES

The relationships between the developed and the less developed
countries have changed and will continue to change. Before World
War II, most less developed countries depended on the developed
countries politically and economically. Their political independence
in the last 20 years has encouraged them to seek more complete
economic independence under the United Nations assistance and foreign aid programs. The forces that may influence international financial market operations between these two groups of nations are as
follows:

1. In several of the more advanced of the less developed countries, the financial markets have developed rapidly (Singapore and
Brazil). These countries may become regional financial market
centers functioning as links between the financial markets of the
developed countries and the small local financial markets of the less
developed countries. This assumption is based on the continued
financial strength of these countries as to their growing domestic
savings and their increasing flows of funds with other international
financial centers. According to a survey conducted by The Banker
(London), foreign exchange market activities have increased in many
financial centers in the period 1971-72. Foreign currency liabilities
in the banks of the nine European financial centers plus Canada,
Bahamas, Panama, Japan, and Singapore increased from about $143
billion in 1971 to $185 billion in 1972. U.S. dollar liabilities alone
increased by $35 billion. A noticeable change in this period was the
smaller proportion held in Europe. In 1971 the European financial
centers accounted for 82 percent of total foreign currency liabilities,
but in 1972 their holdings declined to 79 percent of the total, while
the rest of the world increased its share from 18 percent in 1971 to
21 percent in 1972. Despite the volatility of the foreign exchange
markets all over the world, the increasing importance of many new
international financial centers in the more advanced developing countries will attract more capital from the major financial centers in
Europe as well as in the United States.

2. The continued efforts of many less developed countries to
pursue their industrialization programs will need more capital and
technology which only the developed countries can provide, either
through the international development institutions or direct borrowings

in the major international capital markets. Table 26.2 indicates the extent to which the international development institutions have stepped up their borrowings in the period 1966-72 from $584 million to $2,124 million. In this period, the developing countries increased their bond issues from $307 million to $1,053 million. The borrowings of these two categories accounted for 24 percent of the total in 1966, but increased to 28 percent in 1972. About 40 percent of their bond issues were in the United States, and the remainder in Europe and Japan. The less developed countries are expected to increase their borrowings from the major world financial markets in the future.

3. The energy crisis will continue to focus worldwide attention on the economics of the world petroleum industry and related international flows of investment capital. While no one knows how international energy problems will be solved in the long run one thing is certain; the oil-exporting nations will become wealthier and more influential in the international financial markets. Increasing prices of petroleum products will have a tremendous impact not only on the oil-producing and oil-consuming countries but also on the international financial markets. All industrial nations, except the United States and Canada, largely depend on the importation of oil for running their industries. Higher oil import bills will affect their merchandise trade accounts and their willingness to offer financial aid to the less developed countries. It may become necessary for the oil-producing countries to use their oil-export revenues to buy more industrial goods for domestic development purposes. In this connection, the less developed countries that do not produce oil will suffer; the industrial nations

TABLE 26.2

Foreign and International Bond Issues by
Borrowers, 1966-72
(millions of dollars)

	1966	1970	1972
Industrial countries	2,578	4,110	7,124
Multilateral European institutions	285	215	830
International development institutions	584	1,260	2,124
Developing countries	307	380	1,053
Total	3,755	6,021	11,131

Note: Total does not add due to rounding.

Source: World Bank, Annual Reports, 1971 and 1973.

will gain or lose depending on their trade relationships with the oil-producing nations. Further, the increasing oil revenue funds in the hands of the oil-producing nations will be partly recycled back into the economies of the oil-consuming countries. These funds could put a serious strain on the operation of the financial markets in the industrial nations, or even cause severe instability in their balance of payments if these funds are shifted across currency boundaries without adequate financial cooperation among the industrial countries. It has been reported that some countries such as Japan have considered moving capital and technology close to the oil-producing countries for mutual benefits. For example, the United States is negotiating with Egypt, Iran, and Saudi Arabia to build a steel mill, gas liquefying plant, and pipelines.

EAST-WEST TRADE AND FINANCIAL ACTIVITIES

The year 1973 witnessed continued expansion in East-West trade. Regardless of differences in ideology and economic systems, the socialist countries in Eastern Europe have increased their trade and financial contacts with the Western industrial countries. From the Eastern countries' point of view, they need Western capital and technology to boost their lagging industrial and agricultural productivity. These desires have been compatible with the Western nations' goal of expanding their trade and obtaining raw materials, especially after the energy crisis.

Growth of East-West Trade

As Table 26.3 shows, in 1970 the Eastern European countries accounted for 35.5 percent of world population, 38 percent of world industrial output, and 11.3 percent of world trade. Their desire to increase trade with the market economy countries is understandable since their share of world trade is relatively low. Per-capita foreign trade also is low in the Eastern European countries. According to UN statistics, the Eastern European countries exported $7,630 million and imported $8,708 million with developed and less developed countries in 1970. They incurred a $1,078-million deficit on their trade account with the West. It was estimated that the annual growth rate of their trade with the Western countries was 11 percent in the 1960s, and it is expected to be higher in the 1970s since Russia, which accounted for 43.3 percent of the total trade of the Eastern bloc, has stepped up transactions with the West.

527

TABLE 26.3

Indicators of World Population, Industrial Output, and Foreign Trade in 1970

| | Percent of Total | | Foreign Trade Turnover | |
	Population	Industrial Output	Percent Share	Per-capita U.S. Dollars
Developed countries	21.5	55.0	69.3	142
Less developed countries	43.0	7.0	19.1	20
Eastern European countries	35.5	38.0	11.3	14
World	100.0	100.0	100.0	43

Source: United Nations, Monthly Bulletin of Statistics, New York.

According to the Joint Economic Committee of the U.S. Congress (Soviet Economic Prospects for the Seventies, 1973), Russian exports to the West were estimated at less than $1 billion in 1960, $2.3 billion in 1970 (annual growth rate of 8.2 percent), $2.7 billion in 1971 (of which Eastern Europe took about 55 percent; the developed countries accounted for 21 percent, and the less developed countries the remainder). Russian crude oil, petroleum products, wood products, and metals were the major export items, while their imports from the developed countries were mostly machinery and equipment (accounting for an average of 40 percent of their imports) (see Table 26.4). Large grain imports in 1972 and 1973 increased the Russian trade deficits with the West to about $1 billion. Until the mid-1960s, these deficits were primarily financed by gold sales. In the late 1960s, Russia increased the use of Western-government-guaranteed medium-term and long-term credits. As a result, the estimated Soviet debt to the West grew rapidly from an estimated $1,374 million in 1965 to about $3 billion in 1972 (see Table 26.5), and the debt service ratio increased from 12 to 19 percent. Since Russia has substantial gold reserves most Western banks and governments probably would consider a debt service ratio of 25 percent a reasonable level for the USSR. In addition to the above-mentioned medium- and long-term credits, Russia has used short-term credit facilities in the Euro-currency markets extensively in the period 1966 to 1972. Russian banks have been active in the financial markets in London, Paris,

TABLE 26.4

Soviet Orders for Plant and Equipment from the West
(millions of dollars)

	1971	1972
Total	841	1,965
United States	239	465
France	76	391
West Germany	147	358
Italy	66	169
Japan	138	155
United Kingdom	118	78
Other	57	349

Source: Joint Economic Committee of the U.S. Congress.

TABLE 26.5

Debt Burden of the USSR
(millions of dollars)

Year	Hard Currency Debt	Debt Service	Debt Service Ratio (percent)
1960	768	39	5
1965	1,374	166	12
1966	1,517	169	11
1967	1,711	181	11
1968	1,909	253	13
1969	2,125	327	15
1970	2,197	398	18
1971	2,652	483	18
1972*	2,900	563	19

*Preliminary.

Source: Joint Economic Committee of the U.S. Congress.

Frankfurt, and Zurich to help arrange short- and medium-term credits.

Growth of Financial Activities

Following the increase in foreign trade, the Eastern European countries have welcomed capital and technological investment from the Western countries, especially the United States. The most extensive proposal under discussion is the American-Soviet venture for gas pipeline systems from Northern Russia to East Coast United States, and from Eastern Russia to the West Coast United States. Russia also signed a 20-year agreement with an American company, Occidental Petroleum, to build a chemical complex with a total investment of $8 billion. A number of Western companies have also reached an agreement with Russia to construct a truck-manufacturing complex. In the computer field, Russia has negotiated agreements with International Business Machines (IBM) and the Control Data Corporation, but these are subject to Washington's licensing procedures.

There have been numerous agreements signed by the East and the West in 1972 and 1973. For example, Japan has extended about $1.3 billion of credit to Russia for timber projects and port development. The U.S. Eximbank and Commodity Credit Corporation granted credit to Russia for grain purchases. West Germany, the largest trade partner of the Eastern bloc, and France, United Kingdom, and Norway have extended credits to Russia to finance foreign trade. Poland and Rumania have also obtained trade credits from these Western European countries. Even the United Nations, under its development programs, has participated in many important projects in the Eastern European countries: a highway program in Poland, a Computer Education Center in Hungary, a Shipping Design and Research Institute in Bulgaria, and construction of a nuclear power plant in Rumania.

The recent intensity of financial activities between the East and the West has brought about many new banking establishments on both sides, including U.S. banks in Moscow and a Polish bank in Frankfurt. This, in turn, will increase the scope of financial market activities in Europe and the United States.

GLOBAL FORCES

It is hazardous to talk about global forces affecting the international financial markets because they are overly exposed to changing pressures. For example, in the relatively short three-month

530

period November 1973 to January 1974, the strength of the U.S. dollar in the foreign exchange markets has been sufficient to encourage the U.S. government to eliminate the network of capital outflow controls; recently the European and Japanese governments have removed capital inflow controls; the energy crisis threatens to create major balance of payments problems around the world; and the Tokyo Stock Exchange has become a place for handling the world's largest capital stock transactions. Barring any radical changes, four significant elements will likely influence the world economy and its financial markets. These include international monetary agreement and reform of the world monetary system, multinational corporations, multinational banking, and international securities distribution.

International Monetary Agreement

The old international monetary system based on fixed exchange rates with the U.S. dollar and gold as cornerstones in international finance has been upset by U.S. balance of payments deficits and international currency speculation. Chronic gold and currency crises in the last several years have prompted the major currency nations to take action to save the world monetary system from collapse. Many remedial measures have been taken such as enlarging quotas in the IMF, the two-tier gold system (recently abolished), the special drawing rights—SDRs (paper gold), numerous revaluations and devaluations of currencies, and the more popular floating foreign exchange rates. All of these measures have not solved the international currency problems, nor have they satisfied nations dependent on a sound international financial system. There were three basic differences in viewpoint reflected at the IMF meeting in Nairobi, Kenya in 1973. First, the European countries, especially France, stated that they wanted to end the reserve currency role of the U.S. dollar and to move toward a resumption of dollar convertibility into gold. In addition, they wanted to redeem the overhang of $90 billion in liquid dollar claims held outside the United States, either by issue of U.S. government bonds or securities denominated in other acceptable currencies. Second, the less developed countries indicated that they would like the IMF to issue additional SDRs and increase their share so that the less developed countries can command a larger portion of goods produced and purchasable with marks, yen, francs, pounds, and U.S. dollars. They complained that they have lost a substantial amount of their international reserves as a result of the currency crisis and devaluation of the dollar. Besides this basic argument, France endorsed this proposal by the less developed countries. Third, the United States, still a principal force in the IMF, suggested that in the

531

future the SDRs should gradually replace gold, and that a more stable but adjustable monetary system should be developed. It is likely that the final recommendations submitted to the IMF after the mandatory date (July 31, 1974) will include a compromise of some sort among these three major blocs of countries. For example, several other major currencies may be accepted as reserve currencies along with the U.S. dollar. More flexible exchange rates among currencies may be accepted as part of the revised international exchange market mechanism. The role of gold probably will not be the same as before due to the fact that gold production in the world is limited, and frequent changes in the price of gold are neither desirable nor practical. In view of the energy crisis and the new strength of the U.S. dollar, no other single currency will be able to take the dollar's place in the future. SDRs may be issued as supplementary reserves only under the condition that inflationary pressures will not be aggravated. It is also possible that a package of monetary reform, trade agreements, economic assistance, and financial cooperation will be reached with hard bargaining among nations.

Multinational Corporations

The increased importance and growing number of multinational corporations (MNCs) are attributed to the growth and prosperity of the world economy, the emergence of the European Common Market, lower production costs abroad, and the need for access to local markets. The nature of the overseas investments of these corporations has emphasized manufacturing, petroleum, mining, and food-processing activities. Recently, the MNCs have moved into the Eastern European countries under special organizational forms. These corporations are prime movers of capital and technology from the developed countries to other areas. They also contribute to economic development of the host countries and function as most important foreign traders of the world.

According to the United Nations' publication (Multinational Corporations in World Development, New York, 1973), approximately 500 MNCs with total assets of over $500 billion accounted for one-fifth of the world's GNP in 1971. Important also is the fact that for the first time, international trade among their affiliates exceeded world trade as the main vehicle of economic exchange. The figures indicate $330 billion for MNC affiliate trade versus $310 billion of world exports in 1971. This trend is expected to continue. Total 1971 sales of the 25 largest MNCs were about $200 billion. A total of 15 out of the 25 were U.S. corporations, and three-fourths of the total sales were made by these U.S. firms.

The gigantic operations of the MNCs exert a tremendous impact on the international financial markets. The U.S. Tariff Commission study in 1973 revealed that 70 percent of total Eurobond issues in 1971 (the total in 1971 was $3,635 billion) were put out by multinational corporations. The share of Eurobond issues by the U.S. MNCs dropped from 47 percent in 1966 to 25 percent in 1971 as a result of their increased internal financing (32 percent from retained earnings, 26 percent from depreciation allowances, 16 percent from parent companies, and 26 percent from financial markets). Over 50 percent of the funds of U.S. MNCs were for plant and equipment expenditures, about 25 percent for working capital needs, and 16 percent for dividend remittance to home offices in the United States. The Tariff Commission's figures do not mean that all MNCs are relatively independent of the capital market. For one thing, many MNCs have established financing companies, some even banks, owing to the declining level of internal cash flows. For another, according to a study of 21 of the largest multinational companies by the Union Bank of Switzerland, the total long-term debt of these 21 companies in 1972 was more than $23 billion, which had increased about $7 billion in the period 1968-73. The Union Bank of Switzerland noted that this sum was roughly equivalent to the total volume of public issues and private placements on the Swiss capital market over the past five years (Union Bank of Switzerland, Business Facts and Figures, January 1974).

The MNCs have influenced the international money market by their cash management. They are able to transfer their surplus funds from one country to another in order to gain higher interest rates, and they borrow short-term funds around the world at the lowest rates possible. Small corporations generally pay higher rates than the giant corporations since the latter have more financial resources as well as bargaining power on a global basis. Furthermore, capital controls do not fully affect short-term flows of funds. The trends on the Eurodollar market often reflect these practices.

As to the foreign exchange market, the U.S. Tariff Commission pointed out that multinational corporations hold about $268 billion in short-term liquid assets. They disposed of 1 percent of this sum in the 1971 monetary crisis in order to preserve the balanced value of their foreign currency holdings, but this action was strong enough to upset the world currency market. While it is difficult to judge whether the MNCs have affected the foreign exchange market or vice versa, their growing assets and currency holdings will undoubtedly be a considerable force in the international financial markets, especially under a weak international monetary system, and under a system of floating rates.

Multinational Banking

Banks go where international businesses go. British, French, and Dutch banks established their overseas operations since the nineteenth century in all strategic commercial ports. The U.S. and Swiss banks went international after the turn of the twentieth century. Other nations such as Japan and Canada expanded their foreign banking only after World War II. Since the decade of 1960-70, banking business has become more worldwide, and international banking has broadened its scope and activities. The oligopolistic pattern of the international banking industry, represented by a few big banks from a few large countries, has changed since the 1960s into a massive participation in international banking by not only the medium-size banks in the industrialized countries but also the large-size banks in the less developed countries. This change has primarily reflected the growth of international trade and investment, as well as the flows of funds among financial markets.

The environment of international banking in the 1970s will probably change somewhat. First of all, the increase in nationalistic policies toward foreign banking in many developed and less developed countries will force multinational banks to adopt a more flexible form of banking activities. Second, the growing strength of many local banks and increased number of international banks will stiffen overseas competition. In turn, more financial expertise will be required to cope with this increased competition. Third, rising demand for consumer finance in the more advanced of the less developed countries as a result of their rising per-capita income, continued industrialization programs in the less developed countries, sophisticated financing methods of the multinational corporations, and the increasing flows of international capital and currency will require tremendous banking resources, mobility, coordination, and decision.

Under these circumstances, multinational banking will influence the international financial markets at four levels: the major financial centers, the newly emerging financial markets, the less developed countries, and global business finance.

The home bases of the multinational banks are mostly in major financial centers such as New York, London, Zurich, and Tokyo, and these cities enjoy a diversified representation of such banks. In recent years, more and more banks and banking services have been provided in these major centers. For example, the number of foreign branches, agencies, representative offices and affiliates in the United States, especially in New York, increased from 67 in 1963 to 430 in 1972. Total international transactions handled in New York run at about $25 to $30 billion each business day, which accounts for perhaps one-third of the market share (Wall Street Journal, May 10, 1973).

534

Foreign banks participate in the federal funds market, medium-term loans, and multinational corporate financing. The dismantling of U.S. capital outflow controls will encourage foreign bank activities in the United States. In other major financial centers, multinational banks have sharpened their financial expertise, such as the merchant banks which participate in the security underwriting function, investment research and advice, equipment leasing and mortgage lending. At the end of 1972, there were 627 foreign branches of American banks, of which 49 were in the United Kingdom, 27 in West Germany, 17 in France, and 21 in Japan. They are among the foremost financial forces in the leading financial centers.

The newly emerging financial markets such as Hong Kong, Singapore, Brazil, and Mexico have attracted many multinational banks to conduct business individually and collectively. For example, the Bank of America, European banks, and Mexican banks formed a merchant bank to finance economic development in Mexico. On the other side of the world, Bank of America opened a finance firm in Hong Kong to deal with the rising consumer market. This trend is expected to continue in many countries as their national economies continue to gain.

While multinational corporations sometimes hesitate to establish their operations in the less developed countries due to the risk factor, multinational banks often diversity their financial activities in these countries. They establish branches or affiliates there to finance trade and foreign investment. They even make joint ventures with other international banks. American, Japanese, and French banks jointly own a finance corporation in Indonesia for business loans, capital financing, and consulting services. In the future, development finance, joint venture, and consortium financing may increase due to the fact that foreign multinational banks want to avoid being accused of capital market domination. The moderate role played by foreign banks may also eventually help the less developed countries to develop their local money markets.

One of the most dynamic and constructive financial forces in recent years has been the package financing offered to multinational corporations. Centralized cash management, global financing, and currency transfers of the MNCs will require closer working relations with the multinational banks since the latter have the facilities, economic research, and financial information. In this connection, American banks are in a favorable position to serve since these banks hold close to 44 percent of the deposits of the 25 largest international banks. Recently, U.S. banks such as the Chase Manhattan and First National City Bank established representative offices in Moscow.

Multinational Securities Distribution

International securities distribution was a well-developed activity before World War I, when Austria, Russia, the Ottoman Empire, China, and Japan issued bonds in London and Germany. Financial institutions such as Lloyds Bank, Rothschilds & Sons, the Hong Kong and Shanghai Banking Corporation were reputable agents in this process. Most issues were guaranteed by the respective governments since these borrowings represented government financing for building railroads and other infrastructure projects. Between the two world wars, international bond issues were not popular due to the massive defaults of the 1920s. International bond issues became popular once again after the 1950s. The characteristics of the international bond market have changed due to the fact that New York has become a focal point for government as well as private issues. The capital outflow controls imposed by the U.S. government during the 1960s opened the doors for development of the Eurodollar and Eurobond markets in Europe. For instance, London has developed as the home of the Eurodollar market, and Luxembourg has been the center of the secondary market in Eurobonds. After 1970, Tokyo has emerged as an international capital market.

The mushrooming of the international capital market may be primarily attributed to the growth of income and savings in developed countries, capital accumulation and technology, multinational corporations, multinational banking, and multinational securities distribution. They are all parts of the international financial market mechanism. While international securities distribution has only recently emerged, it offers promise of substantial growth. At year end 1972, the New York Stock Exchange had 215 foreign securities listed with a market value of close to $15 billion. These securities represented 34 foreign stocks and 181 government and private bonds and were issued by borrowers from different continents including British Unilever, Royal Dutch Petroleum, Japanese Sony, and Canadian Pacific Railway. On the London Stock Exchange, 400 foreign stocks listed in 1972 included General Motors, General Electric, Ford, IBM, and Sony. On the Tokyo Stock Exchange, several American stocks were listed including Dow Chemical, First National Bank of Chicago, and Citicorp. On the Tokyo exchange, domestic stock transactions have been very active in recent years. Table 26.6 illustrates that the Tokyo Stock Exchange was the largest stock market of the world in terms of share volume (third quarter of 1973). It should be noted that the U.S. stock market is still the largest capital market of the world if all exchanges and over-the-counter markets are included.

In addition to the increasing number of common stocks listed in the major international financial centers, more and more commercial

536

TABLE 26.6

Selected Stock Exchanges of the World, Third
Quarter of 1973
(average daily volume)

	Million Shares
Tokyo	193.2
London	71.2
Paris	28.0
Frankfurt (includes all German markets)	21.0
New York Stock Exchange	14.6
Toronto	14.6
Amsterdam	11.8
Brussels	5.3

Source: Finance Magazine, January 1974.

banks and brokerage firms have been participating in international
underwriting syndicates. Morgan Guaranty Trust and White, Weld
& Co. of the United States, and N.M. Rothschild & Sons of Britain,
Deutsche Bank of West Germany, and Nomura of Japan have become
well known to international bond issuers whether they are governments
or corporations. Since the international demand for capital is likely
to keep increasing, flows of funds across national borders will continue to expand and offer new prospects for international portfolio
investment.

REFERENCES

Cooper, Richard. The Economics of Interdependence: Economic
Policy in the Atlantic Community. New York: McGraw-Hill,
1968.

Eng, Maximo. "U.S. International Banking: Challenge and Opportunity." Bankers Magazine, Boston (Spring 1971).

Gabriel, Peter P. "MNC's in the Third World." Harvard Business
Review (July-August 1972).

Economic Committee of U.S. Congress. Soviet Economy in the 1970s.

Kirschen, Etienne-Sadi, and others. Financial Integration in Western Europe. New York: Columbia University Press. 1969.

Organization for Economic Cooperation and Development (OECD). Structural Changes in Expenditures Made by OECD Countries on Their National Economies, Paris, 1972.

Robbins, Sidney, and Robert Stobaugh. Money in the Multinational Enterprise. New York: Basic Books, 1973.

United Nations Department of Economic and Social Affairs, Multinational Corporations in World Development, New York, 1973.

U.S. Tariff Commission. Implications of Multinational Firms for World Trade and Investment and for U.S. Trade and Labor. Washington, D.C.: Government Printing Office, February 1973.

MAXIMO ENG is Associate Professor of Economics and Finance at the College of Business Administration, St. John's University. He was formerly a member of the Investment Research and International Banking staff at the First National City Bank, and has frequently participated in financial seminars sponsored by the Federal Reserve Bank of New York and the New York Stock Exchange.

Dr. Eng is co-author of the book, The Management of Forecasting, and author of the monograph U.S. Overseas Banking—Its Past, Present, and Future, which has been well received by leading financial and academic institutions at home and abroad. He has published articles on banking and finance in journals such as Bankers Magazine and The Canadian Banker.

Dr. Eng received his M.B.A. and Ph.D. degrees from the Graduate School of Business Administration, New York University.

FRANCIS LEES is Professor of Economics and Finance at the College of Business Administration, St. John's University. His professional experience includes consulting work with the New York State Education Department, affiliation with a leading Wall Street investment firm, and a summer residency with a prominent United States bank.

Dr. Lees' publications include a volume entitled International Banking and Finance, as well as numerous articles in professional journals such as the Economic Journal, Financial Analysts Journal, and the Journal of Regional Science. He is co-author of the monograph Foreign Investment, Capital Controls, and the Balance of Payments.

Dr. Lees holds a Ph.D. in economics from New York University.

RELATED TITLES
Published by
Praeger Special Studies

AMERICAN BANKS ABROAD: Edge Act
Companies and Multinational Banking

>James C. Baker and M. Gerald
Bradford

THE BANKS OF CANADA IN THE COMMON-
WEALTH CARRIBEAN: Economic Nationalism
and Multinational Enterprises of a Medium
Power

>Daniel Jay Baum

THE EURO-BOND MARKET: Function and
Structure

>Yoon S. Park

THE IMPACT OF U.S. INVESTMENT IN
EUROPE: A Case Study of the Automotive and
Computer Industries

>Y. S. Hu

INTERNATIONAL FINANCE AND FOREIGN
EXCHANGE

>Duane Kujawa

INTERNATIONAL CONTROL OF INVESTMENT:
The Dusseldorf Conference on Multinational
Corporations

>edited by Don Wallace, Jr.
assisted by Helga Ruof-Koch

JAPAN: FINANCIAL MARKETS AND THE
WORLD ECONOMY

>Wilbur F. Monroe

JAPANESE INVESTMENT IN THE UNITED
STATES: With a Case Study of the Hawaiian
Experience

> H. Robert Heller and Emily E. Heller
> Emily E. Heller

MANAGING FOREIGN INVESTMENT IN
SOUTHERN ITALY: U.S. Business in
Developing Areas of the EEC

> Douglas F. Lamont
> with the special assistance of
> Robert Purtshert

MONEY AND ECONOMIC DEVELOPMENT:
The Horowitz Lectures of 1972

> Milton Friedman